Edited by
Ganapathy Subramanian

Continuous Processing in Pharmaceutical Manufacturing

Related Titles

Subramanian, G. (ed.)

Biopharmaceutical Production Technology

2012

Print ISBN: 978-3-527-33029-4 (Also available in a variety of electronic formats)

Flickinger, M.C. (ed.)

Downstream Industrial Biotechnology

Recovery and Purification

2013

Print ISBN: 978-1-118-13124-4 (Also available in a variety of electronic formats)

Eibl, R., Eibl, D. (eds.)

Single-Use Technology in Biopharmaceutical Manufacture

2011

Print ISBN: 978-0-470-43351-5 (Also available in a variety of electronic formats)

Flickinger, M.C. (ed.)

Encyclopedia of Industrial Biotechnology

Bioprocess, Bioseparation, and Cell Technology, 7V

2010

Print ISBN: 978-0-471-79930-6 (Also available in a variety of electronic formats)

Carta, G., Jungbauer, A.

Protein Chromatography

Process Development and Scale-Up

2010

Print ISBN: 978-3-527-31819-3 (Also available in a variety of electronic formats)

Edited by Ganapathy Subramanian

Continuous Processing in Pharmaceutical Manufacturing

WILEY-VCH
Verlag GmbH & Co. KGaA

The Editor

Dr. Ganapathy Subramanian
44 Oaken Grove
Maidenhead, Berkshire
SL6 6HH
United Kingdom

Library of Congress Card No.: applied for

British Library Cataloguing-in-Publication Data
A catalogue record for this book is available from the British Library.

Bibliographic information published by the Deutsche Nationalbibliothek
The Deutsche Nationalbibliothek lists this publication in the Deutsche Nationalbibliografie; detailed bibliographic data are available on the Internet at http://dnb.d-nb.de.

Print ISBN: 978-3-527-33595-4
ePDF ISBN: 978-3-527-67371-1
ePub ISBN: 978-3-527-67370-4
Mobi ISBN: 978-3-527-67369-8
oBook ISBN: 978-3-527-67368-1

Cover Design Bluesea Design, McLeese Lake, Canada
Typesetting Thomson Digital, Noida, India
Printing and Binding Markono Print Media Pte Ltd, Singapore

Printed on acid-free paper

Contents

List of Contributors

Marc Bisschops
Tarpon Biosystems, Inc.
Worcester, MA
USA

and

Tarpon Biosystems Europe B.V.
BioScience Park
Archimedesweg 17
2333 CM Leiden
The Netherlands

Mark Brower
Merck & Co., Inc.
Merck Research Labs
BioProcess Development
2000 Galloping Hill Road
Kenilworth, NJ 07033
USA

Leda R. Castilho
Federal University of Rio de Janeiro (UFRJ)
Cell Culture Engineering Laboratory
COPPE, Chemical Engineering Program
21941-972 Rio de Janeiro
Brazil

William Cataldo
EMD Millipore
80 Ashby Rd.
Bedford, MA 01730
USA

Véronique Chotteau
KTH (Royal Institute of Technology)
School of Biotechnology
Cell Technology Group
Roslagstullsbacken 21
106 91 Stockholm
Sweden

Marie-Francoise Clincke
KTH (Royal Institute of Technology)
School of Biotechnology
Cell Technology Group
Roslagstullsbacken 21
106 91 Stockholm
Sweden

and

UCB Pharma S.A.
Allée de la Recherche, 60
1070 Brussels
Belgium

Aloke Das
Supply chain Management
Senior Analyst at Dell Inc.
Ireland

Willem A. de Jongh
ExpreS2ion Biotechnologies
DTU Science Park
Agern Allé 1
2970 Horsholm
Denmark

Alison Dupont
EMD Millipore
80 Ashby Rd.
Bedford, MA 01730
USA

Suzanne S. Farid
University College London
Department of Biochemical
Engineering
The Advanced Centre for
Biochemical Engineering
Torrington Place
London WC1E 7JE
UK

Pedro Ferreira Gomes
University of Porto
Faculty of Engineering
Laboratory of Separation and
Reaction Engineering (LSRE)
Associate Laboratory LSRE/LCM
Department of Chemical
Engineering
Rua Dr. Roberto Frias, s/n
4200-465 Porto
Portugal

Christopher Gillespie
EMD Millipore
80 Ashby Rd.
Bedford, MA 01730
USA

Sanjeev K. Gupta
Ipca Laboratories Ltd.
Department of Biotechnology
(R&D)
Plot #125, Kandivali Industrial
Estate, Kandivali (W)
Mumbai 460007
Maharashtra
India

Sa V. Ho
Pfizer
Biotherapeutics Pharmaceutical
Sciences
1 Burtt Road
Andover, MA 01810
USA

Ying Hou
Merck & Co., Inc.
Merck Research Labs
BioProcess Development
2000 Galloping Hill Road
Kenilworth, NJ 07033
USA

Jad Jaber
EMD Millipore
80 Ashby Rd.
Bedford, MA 01730
USA

Nika Janež
The Centre of Excellence for Biosensors, Instrumentation and Process Control – COBIK
Center for Biotechnology
Tovarniška 26
5270 Ajdovščina
Slovenia

Maik W. Jornitz
G-CON Manufacturing Inc.
6161 Imperial Loop
College Station, TX 77845
USA

Mark-Henry Kamga
University of Massachusetts Lowell
Department of Chemical Engineering
1 University Avenue
Lowell, MA 01854
USA

Namjoon Kim
University of Massachusetts Lowell
Department of Chemical Engineering
1 University Avenue
Lowell, MA 01854
USA

Mikhail Kozlov
EMD Millipore
80 Ashby Rd.
Bedford, MA 01730
USA

Hae Woo Lee
Clinical Manufacturing Center
Daegu-Gyeongbuk Medical Innovation Foundation
Cheombok-ro 80
Dong-gu, Daegu
South Korea

Ping Li
East China University of Science and Technology
State Key Laboratory of Chemical Engineering
College of Chemical Engineering
130 Meilong Road, Xuhui
Shanghai 200237
China

José M. Loureiro
University of Porto
Faculty of Engineering
Laboratory of Separation and Reaction Engineering (LSRE)
Associate Laboratory LSRE/LCM
Department of Chemical Engineering
Rua Dr. Roberto Frias, s/n
4200-465 Porto
Portugal

Sunil Mehta
kSep Systems
1101 Hamlin Road
Durham, NC 27704
USA

Massimo Morbidelli
ETH Zurich
Institute for Chemical and Bioengineering
Vladimir-Prelog-Weg 1
HCI F 129
8093 Zurich
Switzerland

and

Chairman Dept. of Chemistry &
Applied Biosciences
Institute for Chemical and
Bioengineering
ETH Zurich
Vladimir-Prelog-Weg 1/HCI F129
CH-8093 Zurich-Hoenggerberg

Thomas Müller-Späth
ETH Zurich
Institute for Chemical and
Bioengineering
Vladimir-Prelog-Weg 1
HCI F 137
8093 Zurich
Switzerland

Nico M.G. Oosterhuis
Easthouse Biotech Solutions BV
Landschrijverlaan 35
9451KT Rolde
The Netherlands

Sadettin S. Ozturk
MassBiologics of the University of
Massachusetts Medical School
Process and Analytical
Development
460 Walk Hill Street
Mattapan, MA 02126
USA

Matjaž Peterka
The Centre of Excellence for
Biosensors, Instrumentation and
Process Control – COBIK
Center for Biotechnology
Tovarniška 26
5270 Ajdovščina
Slovenia

Michael Phillips
EMD Millipore
80 Ashby Rd.
Bedford, MA 01730
USA

Aleš Podgornik
The Centre of Excellence for
Biosensors, Instrumentation and
Process Control – COBIK
Center for Biotechnology
Tovarniška 26
5270 Ajdovščina
Slovenia

and

Faculty of Chemistry and Chemical
Technology
Ljubljana University
Večna pot 113
1000 Ljubljana
Slovenia

David Pollard
Merck & Co., Inc.
Merck Research Labs
BioProcess Development
2000 Galloping Hill Road
Kenilworth, NJ 07033
USA

James Pollock
University College London
Department of Biochemical
Engineering
The Advanced Centre for
Biochemical Engineering
Torrington Place
London WC1E 7JE
UK

Ajish Potty
EMD Millipore
80 Ashby Rd.
Bedford, MA 01730
USA

Lars Poulsen
ExpreS2ion Biotechnologies
DTU Science Park
Agern Allé 1
2970 Horsholm
Denmark

Thomas C. Ransohoff
BioProcess Technology
Consultants, Inc.
12 Gill Street
Woburn, MA 01801-1728
USA

Alirio E. Rodrigues
University of Porto
Faculty of Engineering
Laboratory of Separation and
Reaction Engineering (LSRE)
Associate Laboratory LSRE/LCM
Department of Chemical
Engineering
Rua Dr. Roberto Frias, s/n
4200-465 Porto
Portugal

Romas Skudas
Merck Millipore
Frankfurter Str. 250
64293 Darmstadt
Germany

Franc Smrekar
Jafral d.o.o.
Koprska ulica 94
1000 Ljubljana
Slovenia

L. Richard Stock
BioProcess Technology
Consultants, Inc.
12 Gill Street
Woburn, MA 01801-1728
USA

Matthew Stone
EMD Millipore
80 Ashby Rd.
Bedford, MA 01730
USA

William G. Whitford
GE Healthcare
HyClone Cell Culture
925 West 1800 South
Logan, UT 84321
USA

Alex Xenopoulos
EMD Millipore
80 Ashby Rd.
Bedford, MA 01730
USA

Seongkyu Yoon
University of Massachusetts Lowell
Department of Chemical
Engineering
1 University Avenue
Lowell, MA 01854
USA

Ye Zhang
KTH (Royal Institute of
Technology)
School of Biotechnology
Cell Technology Group
Roslagstullsbacken 21
106 91 Stockholm
Sweden

Preface

A continuous process requires the ability to think laterally and have a proactive mindset across the entire team from lab development through to production. Continuous manufacturing process is not new. It has been in use by the chemical, food, and beverage industries successfully. The biopharmaceutical industries are reluctant to engage in applying advanced technology on continuous processes, and are still using the batch process, which has been is use since the nineteenth century. The batch process is an archaic process that progresses sequentially step by step, creating a specified and fixed amount of therapeutic product, which in modern times is not state-of-the art. Several reviews and articles have shown that considerable advances have been made by technologist in offering systems for continuous processes. It has been established that continuous processing promises efficiency because it is a well controlled and flexible process, and there is less waste and produces higher quality products. There is considerable economic benefit in applying the continuous process in manufacturing.

Momentum is gathering pace behind the implementation of continuous manufacturing in the pharmaceutical industry. The regulatory bodies are now encouraging companies to move toward continuous manufacturing. Consequently, leading biopharma industries seem to be in the mend of thinking that the time is right for a major effort in the development of continuous processes in their organizations. As more companies look at the practical evidence from pilot and demonstration units, the adoption and commercialization of the new technology is picking up speed and currently several leading global biopharmaceutical industries are moving to implement continuous manufacturing processes in collaboration with technologist and suppliers. It will not be far away that industries will apply the continuous manufacturing process and thus we are setting up a Gold standard for the future, maybe in 10 years or more.

This book presents the most recent scientific and technological advances of continuous processing, as well as methods and applications in the field of biomanufacturing. Each chapter provides introductory material with an overview of the topic of interest; a description of the technology and methods, protocols, instrumentation, and application, and a collection of published data with an extensive list of references for further details.

It is our hope that this book will stimulate a greater appreciation of the usefulness, efficiency, and the potential of single-use systems in continuous processing of biopharmaceuticals, and that it will stimulate further progress and advances in the field of continuous processing to meet the ever-increasing demands and challenges in the manufacturing of therapeutic products.

The completion of this book has been made possible with the help and encouragements of many friends and colleagues. It is a great pleasure for me to acknowledge, with deep gratitude, the contribution of 19 authors of the chapters in this book. Their outstanding work and thoughtful advice throughout the project have been important in achieving the breadth and depth of this book.

I would be most grateful for any suggestions that could serve to improve future editions of this volume.

Finally, my deep appreciation to Dr Frank Weinreich of Wiley-VCH for inviting me to edit the volume and also to Lesley Fenske and her colleagues for their sustained encouragement and help.

Maidenhead, UK *G. Subramanian*
June 2014

1
Proteins Separation and Purification by Expanded Bed Adsorption and Simulated Moving Bed Technology

Ping Li, Pedro Ferreira Gomes, José M. Loureiro, and Alirio E. Rodrigues

1.1
Introduction

Proteins not only play an important role in biology, but also have large potential applications in pharmaceuticals and therapeutics, food processing, textiles and leather goods, detergents, and paper manufacturing. With the development of molecular biology technologies, various kinds of proteins can be prepared from upstream processes and from biological raw materials. However, there exist various proteins and contaminants in these source feedstocks, and the key issue is that proteins can be separated and purified efficiently from the source materials, in order to reduce the production cost of the high-purity protein. The development of techniques and methods for proteins separation and purification has been an essential prerequisite for many of the advancements made in biotechnology.

Most separation and purification protocols require more than one step to achieve the desired level of protein purity. Usually, a three-step separation and purification strategy is presented, which includes capture, intermediate separation and purification, and final polishing during a downstream protein separation and purification process. In the capture step the objectives are to isolate, concentrate, and stabilize the target proteins. During the intermediate separation and purification step the objectives are to remove most of the bulk impurities, such as other proteins and nucleic acids, endotoxins, and viruses. In the polishing step most impurities have already been removed except for trace amounts or closely related substances. The objective is to achieve final purity of protein.

In the capture step, as the primary recovery of proteins, the expanded bed adsorption (EBA) technology has been widely applied to capture proteins directly from crude unclarified source materials, such as, *Escherichia coli* homogenate, yeast, fermentation, mammalian cell culture, milk, and animal tissue extracts [1,2]. The expanded bed is designed in a way that the suspended adsorbent particles capture target protein molecules, while cells, cell debris,

Continuous Processing in Pharmaceutical Manufacturing, First Edition. Edited by Ganapathy Subramanian.

particulate matter, and contaminants pass through the column unhindered. After loading and washing, the bound proteins can be eluted by elution buffer and be concentrated in a small amount of elution solution, apart from the bulk impurities and contaminants in source materials. With specially designed adsorbents and columns, the adsorption behavior in expanded beds is comparable to that in fixed beds. Various applications of EBA technology have been reported from laboratory-scale to pilot-plant and large-scale production [1–9].

During the intermediate purification and final polishing steps, the techniques of the conventional elution chromatography have been applied successfully. A new challenge should be the application of simulated moving bed (SMB) to the separation and purification of proteins. SMB chromatography is a continuous process, which for preparative purposes can replace the discontinuous regime of elution chromatography. Furthermore, the countercurrent contact between fluid and solid phases used in SMB chromatography maximizes the mass transfer driving force, leading to a significant reduction in mobile and stationary phase consumption when compared with elution chromatography [10–14]. Examples of products that are considered for SMB separation and purification are therapeutic proteins, antibodies, nucleosides, and plasmid DNA [15–23].

When the binding capacities of proteins on adsorbent are close to each other, an isocratic SMB mode may be used to separate and purify the proteins, where the adsorbents have the same affinity capacity to proteins in all sections in SMB chromatography. However, usually the binding capacities of proteins are so different that we cannot separate them by the isocratic mode with a reasonable retention time. In conventional elution chromatography, a gradient mode should be used for the separation of proteins. It is most commonly applied in reversed-phase and ion exchange chromatography (IEC), by changing the concentration of the organic solvent and salt in a stepwise gradient or with a linear gradient, respectively. For SMB chromatography, only a stepwise gradient can be formed by introducing a solvent mixture with a lower strength at the feed inlet port compared with the solvent mixture introduced at the desorbent port; then the adsorbents have a lower binding capacity to proteins in sections I and II to improve the desorption, and have a stronger binding capacity in sections III and IV to increase adsorption in SMB chromatography. Some authors state that the solvent consumption by gradient mode can be decreased significantly when compared with isocratic SMB chromatography [17–19,24–29]. Moreover, when a given feed is applied to gradient SMB chromatography, the protein obtained from the extract stream can be enriched if protein has a medium or high solubility in the solution with the stronger solvent strength, while the raffinate protein is not diluted at all [24].

In this chapter, we shall describe the developments made at the Laboratory of Separation and Reaction Engineering (LSRE) for proteins separation and purification by expanded bed chromatography and salt gradient ion exchange simulated moving bed technology.

1.2 Protein Capture by Expanded Bed Technology

1.2.1 Adsorbent Materials

The design of a special adsorbent is a key factor to enhance the efficiency of expanded bed adsorption. The EBA process will be more effective for those adsorbents that have both high-density base matrix and salt-tolerant ligand. The high-density matrix means minimizing dilution arising from biomass or viscosity in feedstock and reducing dilution buffer consumption; the lack of sensitivity of the ligand to ionic strength and salt concentration means there is no need for dilution of feedstock [30–32].

"Homemade" adsorbents are commonly used for research purposes. Agarose and cellulose are the major components utilized on the tailoring of the adsorbents. Table 1.1 shows a list of such adsorbents.

Table 1.1 "Homemade" adsorbents.

Year	Core	Adsorbent	Reference
1994	Crystalline quartz	6% Agarose	[33]
1994	Perfluorocarbon	Polyvinyl alcohol – perfluorodecalin	[34]
1995	Crystalline quartz - Red H-E7B	6% Agarose	[35]
1995	Perfluorocarbon	Polyvinyl alcohol – perfluoropolymer	[36]
1996	Crystalline quartz - Cibacron blue (3GA)	6% Agarose	[37]
1997	Fluoride-modified porous zirconium oxide		[38]
1999	Polyacrylamide gel	Silica	[39]
1999	Glass	Agarose	[40]
2000	Celbeads[a)]	Cellulose	[41]
2000	Stainless steel	Agarose	[30]
2001	Celbeads[a)]	Cellulose	[42]
2001	Nd–Fe–B alloy powder	Agarose	[43]
2002	Stainless steel	6% Agarose	[44]
2002	Stainless steel	6% Agarose	[45]
2002	Crystalline quartz	6% Agarose (Streamline DEAE) modified with a layer of polyacrylic acid (PAA)	[46]
2002	Nd–Fe–B with Cibacron Blue 3GA (CB)	4% Agarose	[47]
2002	Zirconia-silica (ZSA) ZSA - Cibracron Blue (CB)	4% Agarose 4% Agarose	[9]
2003	Zirconia-silica (ZSA)	Agarose	[48]
2003	CB-6AS	Cellulose	[49]
2003	Titanium oxide	Cellulose	[50]

(continued)

Table 1.1 (*Continued*)

Year	Core	Adsorbent	Reference
2004	Glass	4% Agarose	[51]
2005	Titanium oxide	Cellulose	[52]
2005	Stainless steel powder	Cellulose	[53]
2006	Stainless steel powder	Cellulose	[54]
2007	Nickel powder	Cellulose	[55]
2007	Tungsten carbide	Cellulose	[56]
2008	Tungsten carbide	Cellulose	[57]
2008	Stainless steel powder with benzylamine (mixed mode)	Cellulose	[58]
2008	Zirconia-silica	Agarose	[59]
2009	Zirconium dioxide	Polyglycidyl methacrylate β-cyclodextrin	[60]
2009	Tungsten carbide	β-Cyclodextrin polymer	[61]
2010	Tungsten carbide	β-Cyclodextrin polymer	[62]
2010	Tungsten carbide	Agarose	[63]
2011	Tungsten carbide	Cellulose	[64]
2012	Nickel (nanoporous)	Agarose	[31]
2012	Zinc (nanoporous)	Agarose	[32]
2013	Tungsten carbide	3% Agarose	[65]
2013	Titanium dioxide	Polyacrylamide-based Cryogel	[66]

a) Celbeads: Rigid spherical macroporous adsorbent beads with surface hydroxyl groups.

The drawback of agarose/cellulose-based adsorbents is their low density. Therefore, EBA adsorbents were developed by incorporating a dense solid material in the beads. Table 1.2 shows a list of commercial adsorbents.

Adsorbents used in EBA have been developed by some major companies as shown in Table 1.3. The name of the adsorbents are influenced by the ligand used, for example, diethylaminoethyl (DEAE), sulphopropyl (SP), quaternary amine (Q), recombinant protein A (r-Protein A), imino diacetic acid (Chelating), multimodal function (Direct CST I), carboxymethyl (CM), sulfopropyl (S) and polyethyleneimine (PEI) [3,30,71].

The trend is to use a dense solid core material to allow processing of higher flow rates and therefore reach a better productivity [30–32].

Streamline DEAE and Streamline SP (specially designed for an expanded bed), are classical ion exchangers, in which binding proteins are primarily based on interactions between charged amino acids on the protein surface and oppositely charged immobilized ligands. Protein retention on an ionic surface of adsorbent can be simply explained by the pI-value (isoelectric point) of a protein. But in practical applications, it is found that these ion exchangers have a lower binding capacity to proteins in high ionic strength and salt concentration feedstock. Streamline Direct CST I is a cation exchanger with multimodal functional groups, which not only takes advantage of electrostatic interaction, but also takes advantage of hydrogen bond interaction and hydrophobic interaction to tightly bind proteins. In other words, the new type of

Table 1.2 Commercial adsorbents.

Year	Core	Adsorbent	Commercialized series	Reference
1995	Crystalline quartz	6% Cross-linked agarose	Streamline DEAE	[67]
1995	Crystalline quartz	6% Cross-linked agarose	Streamline SP	[68]
1996	Crystalline quartz	6% Cross-linked agarose	Streamline DEAE	[69]
1996	Crystalline quartz	6% Cross-linked agarose	Streamline SP	[70]
1996	Crystalline quartz	4% Cross-linked agarose	Streamline r-Protein A	[3]
1997	Crystalline quartz	6% Cross-linked agarose	Streamline DEAE	[71]
1997	Crystalline quartz	6% Cross-linked agarose	Streamline Phenyl	[72]
1998			DEAE Spherodex LS	[73]
1999	Crystalline quartz	Agarose	Streamline DEAE DEAE Spherodex LS	[74]
1999	Crystalline quartz	Agarose	Streamline DEAE	[75]
1999	Crystalline quartz	6% Cross-linked agarose	Streamline SP	[76]
	Crystalline quartz	6% Cross-linked agarose	Streamline DEAE	
	Crystalline quartz	6% Cross-linked agarose	Streamline Chelating	
1999	Crystalline quartz	6% Cross-linked agarose	Streamline SP	[77]
	Crystalline quartz	6% Cross-linked agarose	Streamline Q XL	
2000	Crystalline quartz	6% Cross-linked agarose	Streamline Phenyl	[78]
2000	Crystalline quartz	6% Cross-linked agarose	Streamline Chelating	[79]
2001	Crystalline quartz	6% Cross-linked agarose	Streamline SP	[80]
	Porous ceramic	Hydrogel	S Ceramic HyperD LS	
2001	Crystalline quartz	6% Cross-linked agarose	Streamline DEAE DEAE Spharose FF	[81]
2001	Crystalline quartz	6% Cross-linked agarose	Streamline DEAE	[42]
	Crystalline quartz	6% Cross-linked agarose	Streamline SP	
2001	Crystalline quartz	6% Cross-linked agarose	Streamline SP	[43]
2001	Crystalline quartz	6% Cross-linked agarose	Streamline Q XL	[82]
2001	Crystalline quartz	6% Cross-linked agarose	Streamline SP	[83]
	Crystalline quartz	6% Cross-linked agarose	Streamline DEAE	
2002	Crystalline quartz	6% Cross-linked agarose	Streamline SP	[84]
	Crystalline quartz	6% Cross-linked agarose	Streamline DEAE	
2002	Crystalline quartz	6% Cross-linked agarose	Streamline Quartz Base Matrix	[45]
2002	Crystalline quartz	6% Cross-linked agarose	Streamline SP	[5]
	Crystalline quartz	6% Cross-linked agarose	Streamline Q XL	
2002	Crystalline quartz	6% Cross-linked agarose	Streamline DEAE	[44]
	Crystalline quartz	6% Cross-linked agarose	Streamline Q XL	
	Glass	6% Cross-linked agarose	UFC DEAE/PEI	
2002	Crystalline quartz	6% Cross-linked agarose	Streamline	[9]
	Kieselguhr particles	4% Cross-linked agarose	Macrosorb K4AX	
2003			DEAE Spherodex M	[85]
2003	Crystalline quartz	6% Cross-linked agarose	Streamline DEAE	[86]
2003			DEAE Spharose FF	[7]
	Crystalline quartz	6% Cross-linked agarose	Streamline DEAE	
2004	Crystalline quartz	6% Cross-linked agarose	Streamline SP	[87]
2004	Crystalline quartz	6% Cross-linked agarose	Streamline SP	[13]

(continued)

Table 1.2 (*Continued*)

Year	Core	Adsorbent	Commercialized series	Reference
2004	Tungsten carbide	Agarose	Rhobust Fastline SP	[88]
2004	Tungsten carbide	Agarose	Rhobust Fastline SP	[89]
2005	Stainless steel	4% Cross-linked agarose	Streamline Direct CST I	[90]
	Crystalline quartz	6% Cross-linked agarose	Streamline DEAE	
2005	Crystalline quartz	6% Cross-linked agarose	Streamline DEAE	[91]
	Crystalline quartz	6% Cross-linked agarose	Streamline SP	
2006	Stainless steel	4% Cross-linked agarose	Streamline Direct CST I	[92]
2006	Crystalline quartz	6% Cross-linked agarose	Streamline DEAE	[93]
2007	Zirconium oxide	Hydrogel-filled	Q/CM HyperZ	[94]
2007	Stainless steel	Agarose	Streamline Direct HST	[95]
2008	Crystalline quartz Nickel (primed)	6% Cross-linked agarose	Streamline Chelating	[96]
2008	Crystalline quartz	6% Cross-linked agarose	Streamline DEAE	[59]
	Zirconium oxide	Hydrogel-filled	CM-HyperZ	
2009	Stainless steel	Agarose	Streamline Direct HST	[97]
2009	Macroporous acrylic polymer		Amberlite XAD7 HP	[98]
2010	Crystalline quartz	6% Cross-linked agarose	Streamline Chelating	[99]
2010	Crystalline quartz	6% Cross-linked agarose	Streamline Phenyl	[100]
2011	Crystalline quartz	6% Cross-linked agarose	Streamline DEAE	[101]
2011	Zirconium oxide	Hydrogel-filled	CM HyperZ	[102]
2012	Crystalline quartz	6% Cross-linked agarose	Streamline DEAE	[103]
	Crystalline quartz	6% Cross-linked agarose cover with polyvinyl pyrrolidone	Streamline DEAE modified	
2013	Tungsten carbide	6% Cross-linked agarose	Fastline HSA	[104]
	Tungsten carbide	Agarose	MabDirect MM	
	Zirconium oxide	Hydrogel-filled	CM HyperZ	
2013	Crystalline quartz	6% Cross-linked agarose	Streamline Q XL	[105]
2013	Tungsten carbide	Agarose	Rhobust Fastline SP	[106]
2013	Tungsten carbide	Agarose	MabDirect ProteinA	[107]
2013	Tungsten carbide	Agarose	MabDirect MM	[108]

multimodal ligand on adsorbent is able to interact with proteins through various intermolecular forces to get a high binding capacity in high ionic strength and salt concentration feedstocks [90,92,109–111].

Figures 1.1a and b shows the effects of salt concentrations in buffer on bovine serum albumin (BSA) adsorption isotherms on Streamline DEAE and on Streamline Direct CST I materials, respectively, where Streamline DEAE and Streamline Direct CST I were purchased from Amersham Pharmacia Biotech (now GE Healthcare). Streamline DEAE is a weak anion exchanger with $-O-CH_2CH_2-N^+(C_2H_5)_2H$ functional group, with the following characteristics: its matrix consists of macroporous cross-linked 6% agarose constraining crystalline quartz core materials, with a particle density of 1200 kg m^{-3}, a particle size distribution of 100–300 μm, and a mean particle size of 200 μm. Streamline Direct CST I is an ion exchanger with multimodal functional group, with the

Table 1.3 Suppliers of commercial adsorbents.

Manufacturers	Adsorbent		Matrix
GE Healthcare	Streamline Series	Q XL XL	6% Cross-linked agarose containing a quartz core with dextran surface extended.
		DEAE SP Phenyl Quartz Base Matrix Heparin Chelating	6% Cross-linked agarose containing a quartz core.
		rProtein A	4% Highly cross-linked agarose containing a quartz core.
		Direct CST I	4% Cross-linked agarose containing stainless steel core material.
		Direct HST	Cross-linked agarose containing small stainless steel particles with multi-modal functional groups.
	Sepharose Fast Flow Series		6% Cross-linked agarose without core. The polysaccharide chains arranged in bundles with different degree of intra-chain cross-linking provide high matrix rigidity.
UpFront Chromatography A/S	UFC		6% Cross-linked agarose containing a glass core.
DSM Biologics	Rhobust Fastline Series MabDirect Protein A/MM		Cross-linked agarose containing a Tungsten Carbide core.
Pall BioSepra Corporation	DEAE – Spherodex LS DEAE – Spherodex M		The porous silica matrix is coated with a continuous layer of ionizable dextran to yield high exchange capacity and improved stability.
	CM/S/Q/DEAE – Ceramic HyperD F		Hydrogel polymer with porous ceramic beads.
	Lysine HyperD		Hydrogel polymer within the large pores of rigid beads.
	Heparin HyperD M		Porous rigid mineral bead containing heparin bound, hydrogel filled pores.
	Q/CM HyperZ		Hydrogel-filled porous with zirconium oxide particles.
The Dow Chemical Company	Amberlite XAD7HP		Macroporous acrylic polymer.
Others	Macrosorb K4AX		4% Cross-linked agarose with Kieselguhr particles.

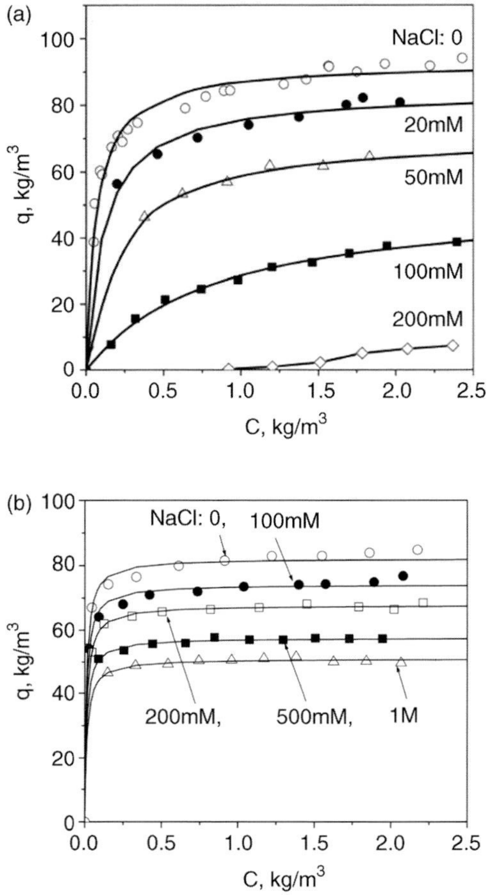

Figure 1.1 Effect of salt concentration in buffer on BSA adsorption isotherms on Streamline DEAE. (a) (20 mM phosphate buffer, pH = 7.5) and on Streamline Direct CST I. (b) (50 mM acetate buffer, pH = 5). Circle points: experimental data. Reprinted from Ref. [90] with permission from John Wiley & Sons.

following characteristics: its matrix consists of macroporous cross-linked 4% agarose constraining stainless steel core materials, with a particle density of 1800 kg m^{-3}, a particle size distribution of 80–165 μm, and a mean particle size of 135 μm.

As shown in Figure 1.1a, the ligand of Streamline DEAE is very sensitive to salt concentration in buffer, so BSA adsorbed on Streamline DEAE can be eluted easily by increasing the salt concentration to 0.5 M in 20 mM phosphate buffer, pH = 7.5. Streamline Direct CST I has a multimodal ligand that is less sensitive to the salt concentration, as shown in Figure 1.1b. Therefore, it is very difficult to elute BSA from Streamline CST I in the column only by increasing the salt

(a) (b)

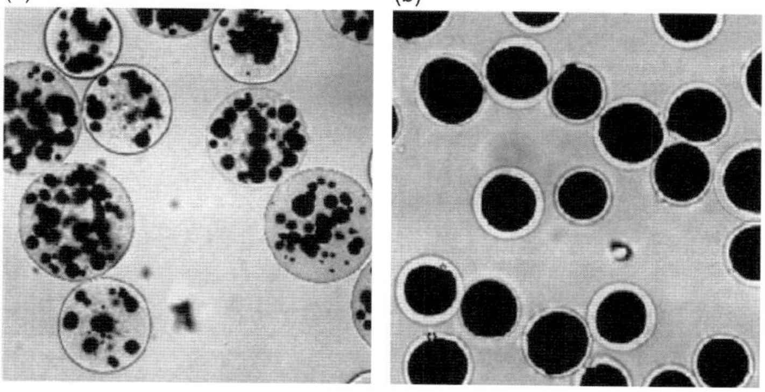

Figure 1.2 Adsorbents with a high-density matrix used in expanded bed. (a) Streamline DEAE/Streamline Direct CST I. (b) Pellicular adsorbent/inert core adsorbent.

concentration in 50 mM acetate buffer, pH = 5. Therefore, to accomplish elution of adsorbed BSA proteins, both salt concentration and pH value in acetate buffer are increased.

In an expanded bed, adsorbents with a high-density matrix are used to form a stable expansion. Recently, some authors have improved the design of the high-density matrix of adsorbent, by including a single heavier inert core material in the macroporous resin matrix, which is called pellicular adsorbent or inert core adsorbent, as shown in Figure 1.2 [30,44]. The inert core adsorbents not only increase the particle density to form stable expansion at high feed flow rate, but also reduce the protein diffusion resistance inside the adsorbent due to shortening of the diffusion path, which made the adsorption behavior in EBA process more efficient.

Usually, the column efficiency is expressed by the theoretical plate number and the height equivalent to a theoretical plate (HETP). HETP is the sum of the independent contributions of liquid axial dispersion, film mass transfer resistance, pore diffusion resistance, and the restricted adsorption–desorption rate. Based on our works [12,49,90,112,113], the theoretical analysis on HETP* is given in Equation 1.1, to demonstrate the potential application of the inert core adsorbents in the fast, high-performance liquid chromatography (HPLC) for the resolution of biological macromolecules as a result of the decrease of the intraparticle diffusion resistance.

$$\mathrm{HETP}^* = \frac{2\upsilon(1-\xi_C^3)}{[1+\upsilon(1-\xi_C^3)(1-\xi_C)]^2}\left(\frac{\varepsilon_S u R^2}{\varepsilon_B L}\right)$$
$$\left[\frac{(1-\xi_C)^2(1-\xi_C)^3}{3}\left(\frac{1}{\Theta}\frac{1}{\varepsilon_S D_P}+\frac{1}{k_f R}\right)+\frac{\xi_m^2}{R^2}\frac{1}{k_{ads}}\right]+\frac{2\varepsilon_B D_L}{uL} \quad (1.1)$$

It is found that the decrease of the intraparticle diffusion resistance by inert core adsorbents is quantitatively estimated by the parameter $1/\Theta$ as

$$\frac{1}{\Theta} = \frac{(1-\xi_C)^2}{(1-\xi_C{}^3)}\left[\xi_C + \frac{(1-\xi_C)^3}{5(1-\xi_C{}^3)}\right] \tag{1.2}$$

For conventional adsorbent ($\xi_C = 0$), $1/\Theta = 0.2$; with the increase of ξ_C, the value of $1/\Theta$ drops quickly.

Based on this discussion, we conclude that the efficiency of a chromatographic column packed with inert core adsorbent can be enhanced, especially for systems where the intraparticle diffusion rate is slow. This is the case of biological macromolecules separation by liquid chromatography where biomacromolecules slowly diffuse in the adsorbent pores, including the case of the expanded bed chromatography.

1.2.2
Expanded Bed Adsorption/Desorption of Protein

Expanded bed adsorption technology has been widely applied to capture proteins directly from crude feedstocks, and various applications have been reported from laboratory-scale to pilot-plant and large-scale production [1–8].

In our laboratory, experiments were carried out for the whole expanded bed BSA protein adsorption process with Streamline Direct CST I (Figure 1.3) and with Streamline DEAE (Figure 1.4), where a Streamline 50 column is packed either with Streamline Direct CST I or Streamline DEAE with the same amount of the adsorbents (300 ml). With the same degree of expansion (twice settled bed height), $2\,\mathrm{kg\,m^{-3}}$ BSA aqueous solution is applied to the expanded beds and BSA protein is adsorbed; after the adsorption stage, the bed is washed and BSA protein recovery processes at the elution stage. With Streamline Direct CST I, the

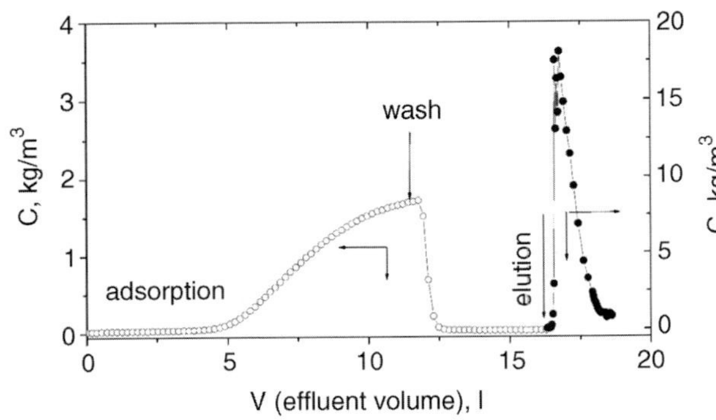

Figure 1.3 Effluent curves of BSA protein during adsorption, washing, and elution stages in expanded bed packed with Streamline Direct CST I. Reprinted from Ref. [90] with permission from John Wiley & Sons, Inc.

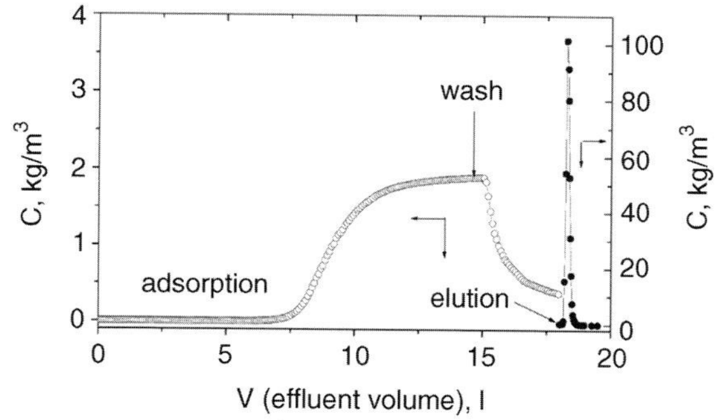

Figure 1.4 Effluent curves of BSA protein during adsorption, washing, and elution stages in expanded bed packed with Streamline DEAE. Reprinted from Ref. [90] with permission from John Wiley & Sons.

operating conditions are as follows: at the adsorption stage, $2\,kg\,m^{-3}$ BSA aqueous solution, prepared with 50 mM acetate buffer, pH = 5, is applied from the bottom of the expanded bed at $181\,ml\,min^{-1}$ flow rate; at the washing stage, 50 mM acetate buffer, pH = 5, is applied from the bottom of the expanded bed; and at the elution stage, 50 mM acetate buffer with 1 M NaCl, pH = 7, is applied from the top of the settled bed at $39\,ml\,min^{-1}$. With Streamline DEAE, the operating conditions are as follows: at adsorption stage, $2\,kg\,m^{-3}$ BSA aqueous solution, prepared with 20 mM phosphate buffer, pH = 7.5, is applied from the bottom of the expanded bed at $83.6\,ml\,min^{-1}$ flow rate; at washing stage, 20 mM phosphate buffer, pH = 7.5, is applied from the bottom of the expanded bed; and at the elution stage, 20 mM phosphate buffer with 0.5 M NaCl, pH = 7.5, is applied from the top of the settled bed at $37\,ml\,min^{-1}$.

Based on the experimental results, the comprehensive evaluation of the hydrodynamics, BSA dynamic adsorption capacity, and BSA recovery in the expanded bed adsorption process with Streamline DEAE and with Streamline Direct CST I are summarized as follows:

1) For the same degree of expansion and the same expanded bed height, the high-density Streamline Direct CST I allows a higher feed flow velocity ($553\,cm\,h^{-1}$) to pass through the expanded bed; in contrast, a low feed flow velocity ($259\,cm\,h^{-1}$) is allowed to pass through the expanded bed packed with low-density Streamline DEAE.
2) At 5% BSA breakthrough point during expanded bed adsorption, BSA dynamic binding capacity on Streamline Direct CST I is 34 mg (BSA) ml^{-1} of settled bed volume (50 mM buffer) and BSA dynamic binding capacity on Streamline DEAE is 50 mg (BSA) ml^{-1} of settled bed volume (20 mM buffer). However, BSA binding capacity on Streamline Direct CST I is not sensitive to ionic strength in feedstock, which means there is no need for dilution of feedstock arising from high ionic strength. In contrast, BSA binding capacity on Streamline DEAE is very sensitive to the ionic strength

in feedstock; when the ionic strength in feedstock is increased to 50 mM, the BSA adsorption capacity decreases by half.

3) At the washing stage, it is found that BSA effluent concentration quickly drops and approaches the baseline for the expanded bed of Streamline Direct CST I, which means almost irreversible adsorption for BSA binding to Streamline CST I. BSA adsorption on Streamline DEAE is reversible; when washing, some BSA can be desorbed from Streamline DEAE so that the effluent concentration approaches a relatively stable value.
4) The ligand of Streamline DEAE is very sensitive to salt concentration in buffer, so BSA adsorbed on Streamline DEAE can be eluted easily by increasing the salt concentration to 0.5 M in 20 mM phosphate buffer, pH = 7.5. BSA recovery in the whole expanded bed adsorption process reaches 91%. Streamline Direct CST I has a multimodal ligand that is less sensitive to the salt concentration, so it is very difficult to elute BSA from Streamline CST I in the column only by increasing the salt concentration in 50 mM acetate buffer, pH = 5. To accomplish elution of adsorbed BSA proteins, both salt concentration and pH value in acetate buffer are increased. Here, when the elution buffer is 50 mM acetate buffer with 1 M NaCl at pH = 7, BSA recovery attains 87%.

In practical applications, various proteins in source materials prepared from an upstream process or prepared from biological raw materials can be present. When the target protein is captured from these crude feedstocks by an EBA process, the other proteins also competitively bind to adsorbents with the target protein. Therefore, it will be more significant to research multicomponent protein competitive adsorption in an EBA process.

An experiment was carried out to capture both BSA and myoglobin from feedstock by an EBA process, where a Streamline 50 column was packed with 300 ml of Streamline Direct CST I. The feedstock with a mixture of 1 kg m^{-3} BSA and 0.2 kg m^{-3} myoglobin was applied to the expanded bed at 517 cm h^{-1} flow velocity. The expansion degree was about twice settled bed height (30.3/15.3 cm). BSA and myoglobin are adsorbed by suspended Streamline Direct CST I adsorbent in an expanded bed. After the adsorption stage, the bed is washed and the bound BSA and myoglobin are desorbed at the elution stage. The detailed operation procedures have been previously described. The experimental results are shown in Figure 1.5, where circle points represent BSA and triangle points represent myoglobin. The operating conditions are as follows: at the adsorption stage, the feedstock with 1 kg m^{-3} BSA and 0.2 kg m^{-3} myoglobin, prepared with 50 mM acetate buffer (pH 5), is applied from the bottom of the expanded bed at 169 ml min^{-1} flow rate; at the wash stage, 50 mM acetate buffer with pH 5, is applied from the bottom of the expanded bed at about 169 ml min^{-1} flow rate; and at the elution stage, 50 mM phosphate buffer with 1 M NaCl, (pH 7) is applied from the top of the settled bed at 44 ml min^{-1}.

At the binding condition with 50 mM acetate buffer (pH 5), Streamline Direct CST I can efficiently capture both BSA and myoglobin from the feedstock in the

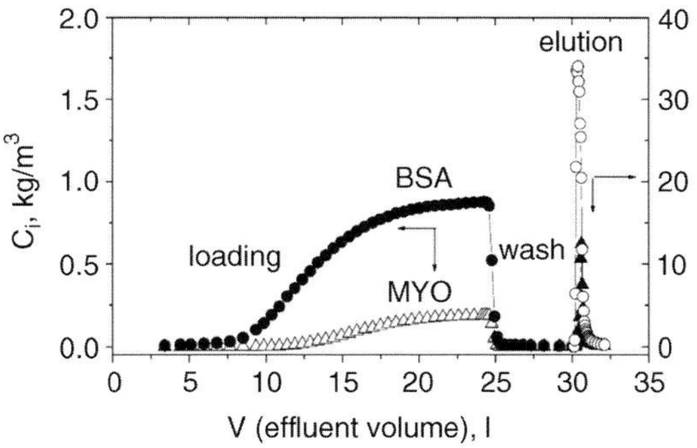

Figure 1.5 Effluent curves of BSA and myoglobin during adsorption, wash and elution stages in expanded bed packed with Streamline Direct CST I. Reprinted from Ref. [92] with permission from John Wiley & Sons, Inc.

expanded bed. At the breakthrough point of 5% BSA feed concentration, BSA dynamic binding capacity is 28.5 mg (BSA) ml^{-1} of settled bed volume, and myoglobin dynamic binding capacity is 5.65 mg (myoglobin) ml^{-1} of settled bed volume. At the washing stage, 50 mM acetate buffer (pH 5) is used to wash the column. It is found that the effluent concentrations both of BSA and myoglobin quickly drop and approach the baseline in an expanded bed of Streamline Direct CST I, which means almost irreversible adsorption of both BSA and myoglobin on Streamline Direct CST I. When the elution buffer, 50 mM phosphate buffer with 1 M NaCl (pH 7), is used in the elution stage, BSA recovery in the whole EBA process can reach 95% and myoglobin recovery reaches 88%, and the consumption amount of the elution buffer is very small, as shown in Figure 1.5.

1.2.3
Modeling of the Expanded Bed

The hydrodynamics and adsorption kinetics in expanded beds are more complex than in fixed beds. The liquid axial dispersion in expanded beds is more significant than in fixed beds; because of the fluidized nature of the expanded bed, adsorbent particle axial dispersion occurs. Moreover, there are variations of particle size axial distribution and bed voidage axial variation in expanded beds for the specially designed adsorbents with wide particle size distribution [78,83,87,114]. Models available for fixed beds may be not adequate to describe the hydrodynamic and adsorption behavior in expanded beds.

Wright and Glasser [80] developed a mathematical model to predict the breakthrough curve for protein adsorption in a fluidized bed, where intraparticle diffusion resistance, film mass transfer resistance, liquid axial dispersion, and adsorbent particle axial dispersion were taken into account. Later, Tong *et al.* [47] and Chen *et al.* [115] used this model to predict the breakthrough curves in the expanded bed adsorption. When capturing proteins in an expanded

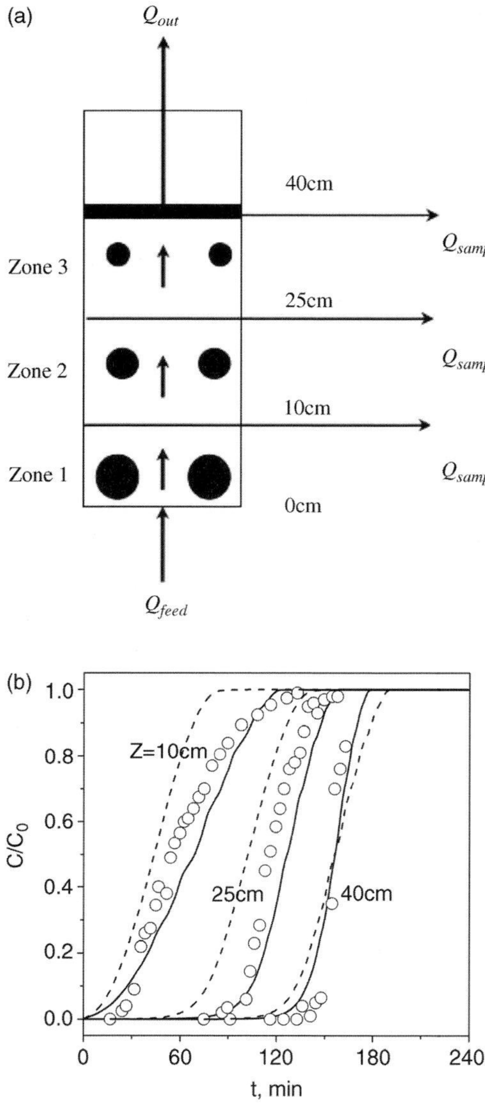

Figure 1.6 (a) Expanded bed with three-zones in Bruce and Chase experimental system (2001) $Q_{feed} = 60.2\ mL \cdot min^{-1}$; $Q_{out} = 58.9\ mL \cdot min^{-1}$, and $Q_{sample} = 1.3/3.0\ mL \cdot min^{-1}$ (b) Comparison among the in-bed experimental breakthrough curves and the simulation results. Circle points: experimental data [83]; solid lines: simulation results with three-zone model; dashed lines: simulation results with uniform model. Reprinted from Ref. [13] with permission from Elsevier.

bed with a high flow velocity, the slow diffusion rate of proteins results in high intraparticle diffusion resistance, significantly affecting the breakthrough curve. It is argued that, in this case, the particle size, characterizing the diffusion path in the adsorbent particles, should have a substantial effect on the breakthrough curves [71]. Therefore, simulation results should be improved when the particle size axial distribution and bed voidage axial variations are taken into account in the model. Tong *et al.* [86] modified the mathematical model by taking into account the particle size axial distribution in expanded beds. Following their experimental research using in-bed monitoring in expanded beds, Bruce and Chase [84] predicted the in-bed breakthrough curves in expanded bed by using zonaly measured parameters. Recently, Kaczmarski and Bellot [116] also made the theoretical investigation about the effects of the axial and local particle size distribution and bed voidage axial variation on the breakthrough curves in expanded beds.

In our laboratory, a three-zone model was developed [13] to predict in-bed breakthrough curves and confirmed the effect of the particle size axial distribution and bed voidage axial variation on the breakthrough curves in expanded beds. In expanded beds, the adsorbent particle size, bed voidage, and liquid axial dispersion coefficient are very different at the bottom zone, the middle zone, and the top zone of the column, and significantly affect the adsorption behavior. The three-zone model, in which the zonal values for these parameters are used, can predict simultaneously in-bed breakthrough curves at the bottom, the middle, and the top of the column. The simulation results by this three-zone model closely fit the experimental data from literature of Bruce and Chase [84], as shown in Figure 1.6. By contrast, the conventional uniform model, in which all the model parameters are estimated by averaged values over the whole column, does not satisfactorily predict in-bed breakthrough curves. When the uniform model is modified by taking into account the bed voidage and the adsorbent particle size axial distribution, the accuracy of the modified uniform model is improved. According to the simulation results, it is found that even for small proteins (i.e., lysozyme), the intraparticle diffusion resistance is also high in expanded bed adsorption. When capturing macromolecular protein at high flow rates in expanded beds, the intraparticle diffusion resistance is expected to be significant. This work supports observations that the use of pellicular and inert core adsorbents can improve the separation performance of proteins in expanded beds due to significant decrease of the intraparticle diffusion resistance by shortening the adsorbent's diffusion path.

1.3 Proteins Separation and Purification by Salt Gradient Ion Exchange SMB

In downstream processing, the frequently used chromatographic methods for separating and purifying proteins take advantage of physical properties that vary from one protein to the other, including size, charge, hydrophobicity, and specially binding capacity. The separation method based on the difference of protein size or shape is called size exclusion (gel filtration) chromatography (SEC). Ion exchange chromatography takes advantage of the charge–charge interaction between protein and ligand, while hydrophobic interaction chromatography

(HIC) or reversed-phase chromatography (RPC) takes advantage of the hydrophobic interaction between protein and ligand, and affinity chromatography (AC) is based on the specific binding between protein and ligand.

Research on the separation and purification of proteins by SMB technology started with size exclusion–simulated moving bed (SE-SMB) chromatography, for its design simplicity in terms of the liquid and solid flow rate ratios (linear distribution coefficients for all proteins on porous stationary phases). In the last decade, it was found that the process performance of the separation and purification of proteins by ion exchange SMB can be improved when a lower salt concentration is formed in sections III and IV to increase the adsorption of proteins and a higher salt concentration is formed in sections I and II to improve the desorption of the bound proteins, called salt gradient ion exchange SMB.

1.3.1
Adsorption Isotherms and Kinetics of BSA and Myoglobin on Ion Exchange Resins

Small molecules, such as small peptides, interact with the ligand on adsorbent by single point attachment, and their migration velocity depends directly on the binding constant of a single bond. Large molecules, such as proteins and nucleic acids, interact with the ligand on adsorbent by multipoint attachment, and their migration velocity depends on the sum of several bonds. Therefore, proteins competitive adsorption on adsorbent is more complex than small molecules. In the published works, Skidmore and Chase [117] investigated the simultaneous adsorption of lysozyme and BSA in a fixed bed packed with the cation exchanger SP-Sepharose-FF; Weinbrenner and Etzel [118] investigated the simultaneous adsorption of BSA and lactalbumin on cation exchange membranes; Martin *et al.* [119] and Lewus and Carta [39] investigated the adsorption of lysozyme/cytochrome C mixtures on the cation exchanger SP-Sepharose-FF and S HyperD-M, respectively; and Hubbuch *et al.* [120] measured the breakthrough curves of an IgG/BSA solution in a fixed bed packed with the cation exchanger SP-Sepharose-FF. These authors reached the same conclusion with regard to the competitive nature of protein binding also leading to a roll up of concentration of the less strongly adsorbed protein in some binding conditions.

In our laboratory [121], ion exchange equilibrium isotherms of BSA and myoglobin on Q-Sepharose FF anion exchanger resin were studied experimentally over a wide protein concentration range, as shown in Figure 1.7. Q-Sepharose FF is a strong anion exchanger with $-CH_2-N^+-(CH_3)_3$ functional group, with the following characteristics: its matrix consists of macroporous cross-linked 6% agarose, a particle size distribution of 45–165 μm, and a mean particle size of 90 μm. From Figure 1.7, BSA has a high ion exchange capacity on Q-Sepharose FF resin at pH 8 Tris buffer (10 mM), with a high favorable nonlinear equilibrium isotherm, as a result of isoelectric point (pI 4.7) of BSA far from buffer pH value (pH 8). The ion exchange equilibrium isotherm of BSA on Q-Sepharose FF resin with the dependence on NaCl concentrations can be represented by the SMA model as follows:

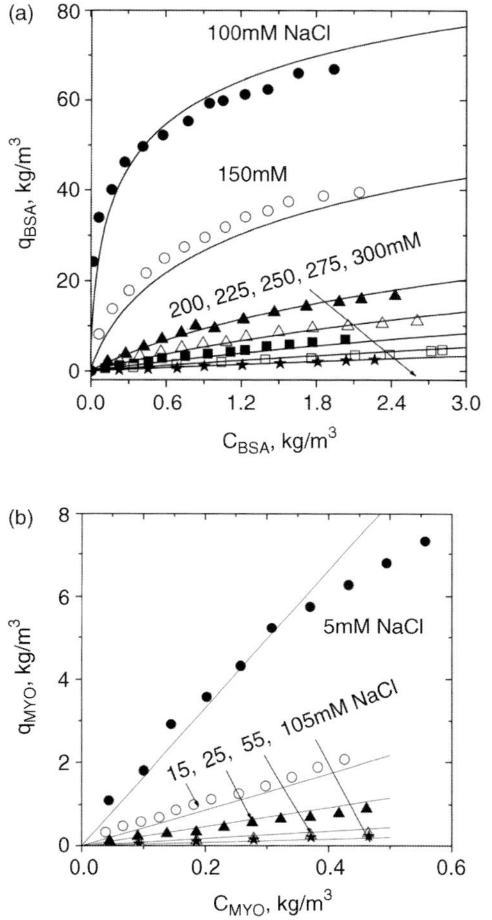

Figure 1.7 Ion exchange equilibrium isotherms of (a) BSA and (b) myoglobin on Q-Sepharose FF resin at room temperature (~25 °C), in 10 mM Tris buffer (pH 8). Points: experimental data; lines: calculated by Equation 1.3 for BSA, by Equation 1.4 for myoglobin. Reprinted from Ref. [121] with permission from John Wiley & Sons, Inc.

$$\begin{aligned} C_{\mathrm{BSA}} &= \frac{q_{\mathrm{BSA}}^{\mathrm{IE}} C_{\mathrm{S}}^{Z_{\mathrm{BSA}}}}{K_{\mathrm{BSA}}[q_0 - (Z_{\mathrm{BSA}} + \sigma_{\mathrm{BSA}}) q_{\mathrm{BSA}}^{\mathrm{IE}} / M_{\mathrm{BSA}}]^{Z_{\mathrm{BSA}}}} \\ &= \frac{q_{\mathrm{BSA}}^{\mathrm{IE}} C_{\mathrm{S}}^{6.03}}{10.83[0.210 - (6.03 + 75) q_{\mathrm{BSA}}^{\mathrm{IE}} / M_{\mathrm{BSA}}]^{6.03}} \end{aligned} \tag{1.3}$$

Since pH value (pH 8) in 10 mM Tris buffer approaches the isoelectric point of myoglobin (pI 7.4), the ion exchange amount of myoglobin on Q-Sepharose FF resin is very small even at lower salt concentrations. Over a wide myoglobin concentration range, linear ion exchange equilibrium isotherms can be found at

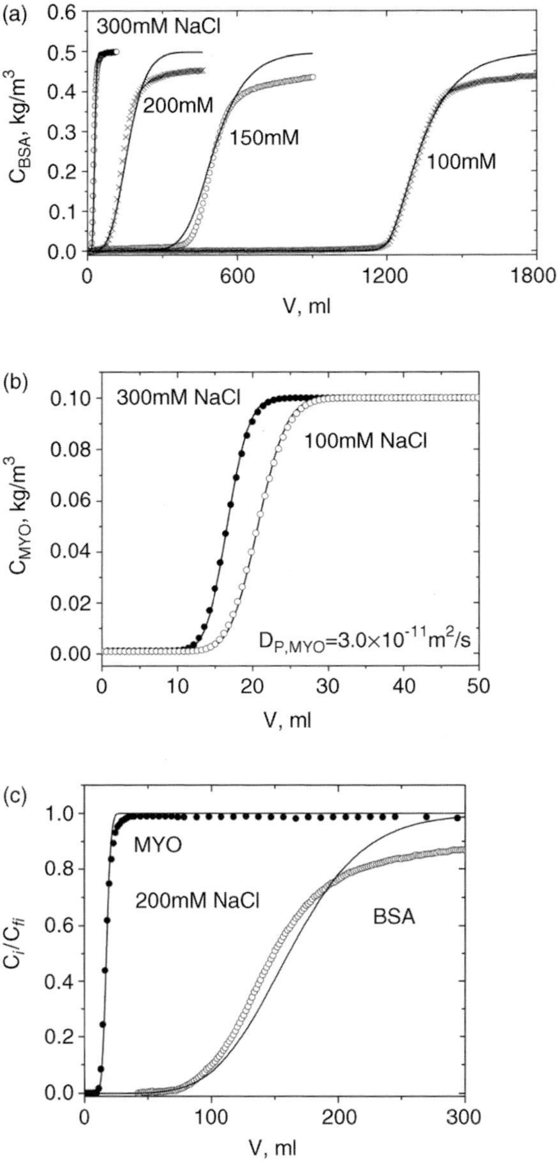

Figure 1.8 BSA and myoglobin breakthrough curves at various NaCl concentrations. Circle points: experimental data; lines: simulation results with LDF model. (a) BSA; (b) myoglobin; (c) BSA and myoglobin competitive adsorption. Reprinted from Ref. [121] with permission from John Wiley & Sons, Inc.

various NaCl concentrations. Based on the experimental results shown in Figure 1.7b, the linear ion exchange equilibrium isotherm of myoglobin on Q-Sepharous FF resin is expressed as follows:

$$q_{\text{MYO}}^{\text{IE}} = \frac{K_{\text{MYO}} q_0^{Z_{\text{MYO}}}}{C_{\text{S}}^{Z_{\text{MYO}}}} C_{\text{MYO}} = 0.02576\, C_{\text{S}}^{-1.22} C_{\text{MYO}} \tag{1.4}$$

Furthermore, breakthrough curves of BSA and myoglobin are measured in a fixed bed, as shown in Figure 1.8a–c, where a XK16/20 column is packed with Q-Sepharous FF anion exchangers, packed height of 100 mm, column diameter of 16 mm, and bed voidage of 0.35. The experimental breakthrough curves are compared with the simulation results, as shown in Figure 1.8, to confirm the accuracy of ion exchange equilibrium isotherm expressions (Equation 1.3 for BSA and Equation 1.4 for myoglobin). The diffusion coefficients of BSA and myoglobin are evaluated by fitting the experimental data of breakthrough curves with LDF model, as $D_{\text{Pe,BSA}} = 1.5 \times 10^{-11} \text{m}^2\,\text{s}^{-1}$ and $D_{\text{Pe,MYO}} = 3.0 \times 10^{-11} \text{m}^2\,\text{s}^{-1}$, respectively.

In ion exchange chromatography, the separation factor of proteins depends evidently on salt concentration. Table 1.4 lists the separation factors of BSA to myoglobin by Q-Sepharose FF anion exchanger at various salt concentrations; here, separation factor is defined as $S_{1,2} = (q_1/C_1)/(q_2/C_2)$.

With a low NaCl concentration in Tris buffer (pH 8), the separation factor of BSA to myoglobin is large; for example, with 200 mM NaCl, $S_{\text{BSA,MYO}}$ goes up to 18.23, BSA and myoglobin can be separated easily by ion exchange chromatography. With the increase of salt concentration, the separation factor decreases. When salt concentration is 400 mM NaCl, the separation factor approaches unity, which means BSA and myoglobin cannot be separated by ion exchange chromatography. This phenomenon is called azeotrope [17–19], like azeotropic

Table 1.4 Separation factor of BSA to myoglobin by Q-Sepharose FF anion exchanger under linear adsorption equilibrium isotherm.

Salt concentration in 10 mM Tris buffer (pH 8)	K_{BSA}	K_{MYO}	$S_{\text{BSA,MYO}}$	Comments
200 mM NaCl	15.02	0.82	18.23	BSA: the more retained Myoglobin: the less retained
250 mM NaCl	4.28	0.78	5.48	BSA: the more retained Myoglobin: the less retained
300 mM NaCl	1.75	0.75	2.33	BSA: the more retained Myoglobin: the less retained
350 mM NaCl	0.99	0.73	1.35	BSA: the more retained Myoglobin: the less retained
400 mM NaCl	0.71	0.72	0.99	Azeotrope
500 mM NaCl	0.55	0.70	0.78	Myoglobin: the more retained BSA: the less retained Similar to size exclusion SMB

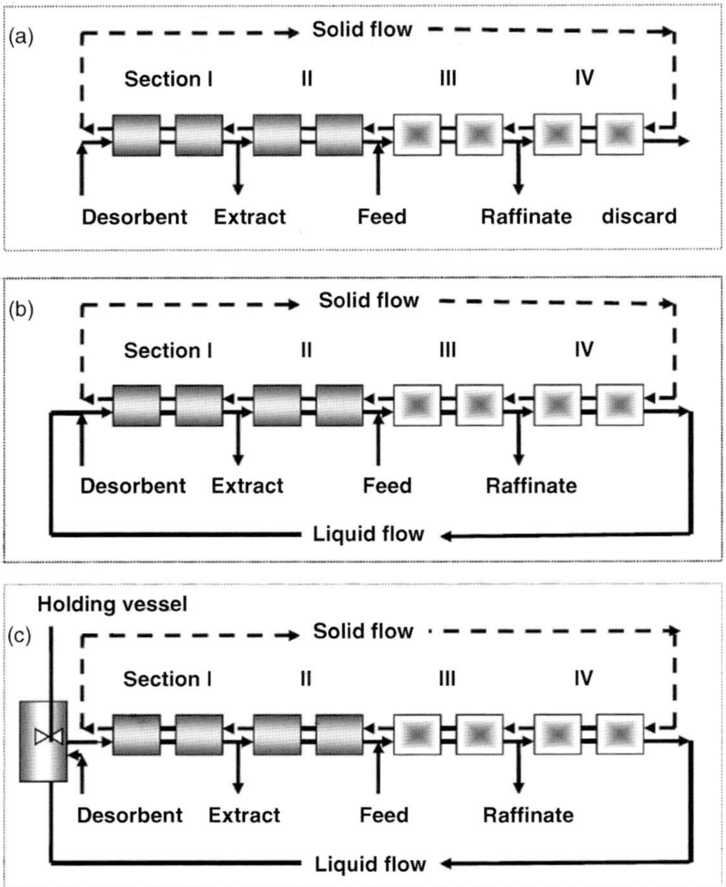

Figure 1.9 Operation modes for gradient IE-SMB: (a) gradient IE-SMB with open loop; (b) gradient IE-SMB with closed loop; (c) gradient IE-SMB with closed loop and a holding vessel. : higher solvent strength; : lower solvent strength. Reprinted from Ref. [121] with permission from John Wiley & Sons, Inc.

distillation. Further increasing salt concentration, it will be found a reversal of separation since myoglobin becomes the more retained component and BSA becomes the less retained component, and the separation behavior of BSA and myoglobin in ion exchange chromatography is more close to that in size exclusion chromatography.

1.3.2 Salt Gradient Formation and Process Design for IE-SMB Chromatography

It is well known that the binding capacity of the classical ion exchanger to proteins is sensitive to salt concentration in the feedstock; the higher the salt concentration is, the lower the binding capacity to the proteins is. Therefore, a stepwise gradient can be formed by introducing a lower salt concentration at the feed port compared to a higher salt concentration introduced at the desorbent port; then the ion exchanger has a lower binding capacity for proteins in sections I and II to improve the desorption and has a stronger binding capacity in sections III and IV to increase adsorption in the IE-SMB chromatography.

In the separation and purification of proteins by SMB chromatography, the open loop configuration was used by many authors in order to avoid the accumulation of contaminants in the columns, as shown in Figure 1.9a, where the liquid stream from section IV is discarded, instead of being recycled to the desorbent stream for further reduction of desorbent consumption. It is well known that one advantage of SMB chromatography compared with fixed bed chromatography is the reduced desorbent consumption. This can be achieved in the closed loop configuration by recycling the liquid stream from section IV to the desorbent inlet of section I, as shown in Figure 1.9b, which is very important for Reverse phase simulated moving bed RP-SMB chromatography. However, in gradient SMB chromatography, the recycling of liquid stream is more complicated. The solvent strength in the eluent is different in sections I and IV, and the effluent composition from section IV varies in a dynamic manner during a switch time interval. This complicates the direct recycling of the eluent [122]. In Figure 1.9c, a holding vessel with a given volume is added to the system to mix the desorbent with the recycled liquid stream from section IV during a switch time interval, in order to reduce the fluctuation of the solvent strength in the columns, as shown in Figure 1.10.

1.3.3 Separation Region of Salt Gradient IE-SMB Chromatography

With a stable stepwise salt gradient IE-SMB chromatography, if one wants to recover the less retained protein (myoglobin) from the raffinate stream and the more retained protein (BSA) from extract stream with a high purity, some constraints have to be met. These constraints are expressed in terms of the net fluxes of proteins in each section: BSA must move upward in section I, myoglobin must move upward while the net flux of BSA must be downward in sections II and III, and the net flux of myoglobin has to be downward in section IV. Table 1.5 summarizes these constraint conditions to the net fluxes for the separation of BSA and myoglobin in salt gradient IE-SMB chromatography.

The operating conditions given in Table 1.5 are only necessary and not sufficient. Usually, a separation region is used for the selection of the optimum flow rate in each section of SMB unit. The separation region is the area in a $\gamma_2 \times \gamma_3$ plot where both extract and raffinate are pure. This plot [123], is an important tool in the choice of the best operating conditions, provided that the constraints in sections I and IV are fulfilled, that is, the flow rate ratios in sections I and IV are far from its constraint values. When resistances to mass transfer are

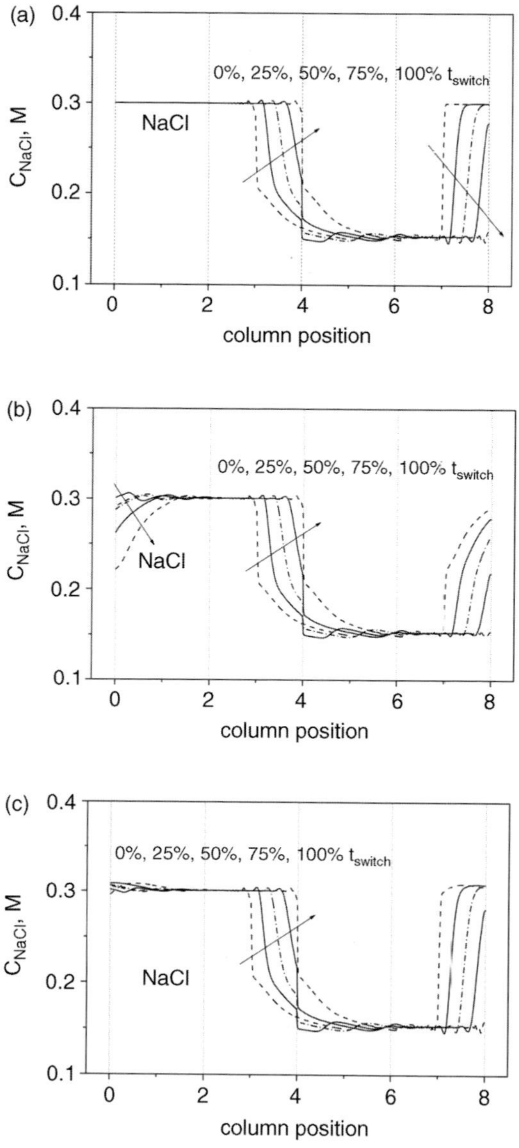

Figure 1.10 Salt gradient formations in IE-SMB chromatography with (a) open loop, (b) closed loop, and (c) closed loop with a holding vessel ($V_s = 10$ ml). Reprinted from Ref. [121] with permission from John Wiley & Sons.

significant, the separation region will shrink, especially for the macromolecular bioseparation where the intraparticle diffusion resistance is more important [124–126]. Here, γ_j are the ratios between the net fluid and solid interstitial velocities, and are related to the m_j ratios used by Morbidelli and coworkers by

Table 1.5 Some constraints to the net fluxes for BSA and myoglobin separation in salt gradient ion exchange SMB.

	Salt	BSA	Myoglobin
Section I	$\frac{Q_I^{TMB}}{Q_S}\frac{C_{SI}}{q_{SI}} > 1$	$\frac{Q_I^{TMB}}{Q_S}\frac{C_{BSAI}}{q_{BSAI}} > 1$	
Section II	$\frac{Q_{II}^{TMB}}{Q_S}\frac{C_{SII}}{q_{SII}} > 1$	$\frac{Q_{II}^{TMB}}{Q_S}\frac{C_{BSAII}}{q_{BSAII}} < 1$	$\frac{Q_{II}^{TMB}}{Q_S}\frac{C_{MYOII}}{q_{MYOII}} > 1$
Section III	$\frac{Q_{III}^{TMB}}{Q_S}\frac{C_{SIII}}{q_{SIII}} > 1$	$\frac{Q_{III}^{TMB}}{Q_S}\frac{C_{BSAIII}}{q_{BSAIII}} < 1$	$\frac{Q_{III}^{TMB}}{Q_S}\frac{C_{MYOIII}}{q_{MYOIII}} > 1$
Section IV	$\frac{Q_{IV}^{TMB}}{Q_S}\frac{C_{SIV}}{q_{SIV}} > 1$		$\frac{Q_{IV}^{TMB}}{Q_S}\frac{C_{MYOIV}}{q_{MYOIV}} < 1$

$$\gamma_j = \frac{\nu_j^{TMB}}{u_S} = \frac{1-\varepsilon_B}{\varepsilon_B} m_j \tag{1.5}$$

And

$$m_j = \frac{Q_j^{TMB}}{Q_S} = \frac{Q_j^{TMB} - Q_S\varepsilon_B/(1-\varepsilon_B)}{Q_S} \tag{1.6}$$

In this work, the separation regions are evaluated by the gradient SMB model where both mass transfer resistance in particles and axial liquid dispersion in columns are taken into account, as shown in Figure 1.11. In this figure, three separation regions are demonstrated for the separation of BSA and myoglobin by salt gradient IE-SMB with open loop configuration under nonlinear adsorption equilibrium isotherm. The configuration of the IE-SMB unit and operating

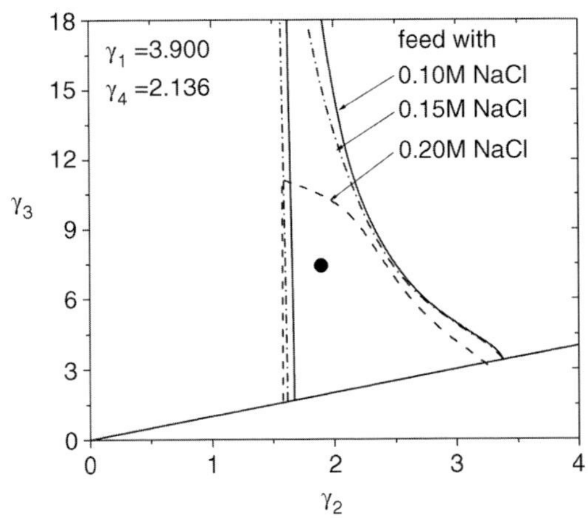

Figure 1.11 Separation regions for BSA and myoglobin separation by salt gradient IE-SMB with open loop at nonlinear adsorption isotherm. Circle point: operating conditions for the calculations in Figure 1.12. Reprinted from Ref. [127] with permission from Taylor & Francis.

conditions for calculations are listed in the published paper by Li *et al.* [121], γ_1 and γ_4 are assigned to be 3.900 and 2.136; and protein purities are imposed to be above 99% for both raffinate and extract streams for the design of the separation region. During the simulations, the NaCl concentration in desorbent is constant and equal to 0.3 M, while the NaCl concentration in the feedstock is assigned to be 0.1, 0.15, and 0.2 M, respectively.

Based on the simulation results shown in Figure 1.11, the effect of the salt concentration in feed on the separation region is significant, and the separation region shrinks with the increase of the salt concentration in feedstock (0.1, 0.15, and 0.2 M NaCl, respectively) if the NaCl concentration in desorbent is constant and equal to 0.3 M. The range of the allowable flow rate in section II (γ_2) is narrower as a result of the higher NaCl concentration formed in sections I and II and resins having a small separation factor to the separation of BSA and myoglobin. The range of the allowable flow rate in section III (γ_3) is broader as a result of the lower NaCl concentration formed in sections III and IV and resins having a big separation factor; moreover, the lower the NaCl concentration formed in sections III and IV, the broader the range of the allowable flow rate in section III, as shown in Figure 1.11 for the cases formed by the feedstock with 0.1, 0.15, and 0.2 M NaCl, respectively. When the feed has a lower NaCl concentration, such as 0.1 or 0.15 M, the BSA adsorption capacity on Q-Sepharous FF resin is very high, the maximum allowable flow rate in section III (γ_3) will probably be restricted either by the pressure drop limitation or by the re-equilibrium (the sufficient retention time) for proteins and salt, instead of being limited by the adsorption equilibrium isotherm of BSA, which is very different from that for the resolution of similar products with a small separation factor. In addition, for our model system (BSA/myoglobin separation by Q-Sepharose FF resin) the minimum flow rate in section II is restricted by the salt upward movement, instead of being limited by the myoglobin adsorption equilibrium isotherm, in order to obtain a stable salt gradient in the IE-SMB unit.

1.3.4 Proteins Separation and Purification in Salt Gradient IE-SMB with Open Loop Configuration

Figure 1.12 shows the typical concentration profiles of BSA, myoglobin, and NaCl in the salt gradient IE-SMB chromatography, where the actual operating condition is selected inside the separation region for the case of the feed with 0.15 M NaCl (represented as a circle point in Figure 1.11). With the setup salt gradient in IE-SMB unit packed with Q-Sepharose FF resins, BSA is recovered completely from the extract stream with 2.76 enrichment of BSA concentration to that of the feed, while myoglobin is eluted both from the raffinate stream and from the section IV exit in the open loop SMB unit. The practical example is that binary separation of proteins with the requirement of complete recovery from extract stream and from raffinate stream in salt gradient SMB chromatography with open loop configuration, for our separation system, which is BSA

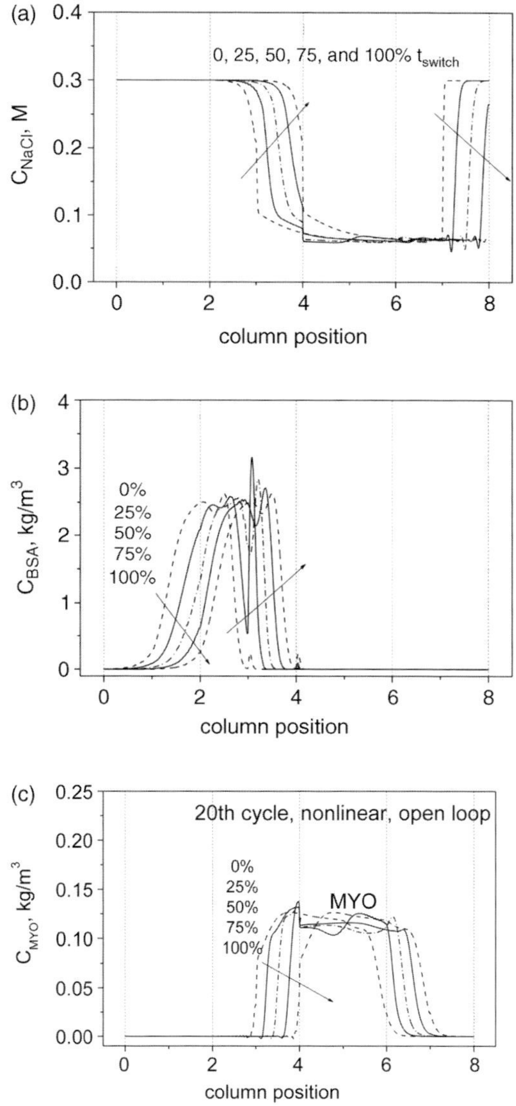

Figure 1.12 Cyclic steady state internal concentration profiles during a switch time interval in salt gradient IE-SMB with open loop when $C_S^F = 0.05$ M NaCl and $C_S^D = 0.3$ M NaCl for BSA and myoglobin separation at nonlinear equilibrium isotherm. Operating conditions as shown by circle point in Figure 1.11. Twentieth cycle, nonlinear, open loop (a) NaCl and (b) BSA (c) MYO. Reprinted from Ref. [127] with permission from Taylor & Francis.

recovered completely from extract stream and myoglobin recovered completely from raffinate stream. For this case, the selection of flow rate in section IV is constrained both by the upward movement of the net flux of salt and the downward movement of the net flux of myoglobin to the raffinate port. As shown in Figure 1.12, a relatively lower salt concentration should be formed in sections III and IV by introducing the feed with 0.05 M NaCl, in order to increase myoglobin ion exchange amount and promote the downward movement of myoglobin in section IV to raffinate port. However, with such a low salt concentration formed in sections III and IV, the other contaminants probably adsorb to the anion exchangers. An alternative method is to adjust the pH value in the buffer to improve the myoglobin ion exchange amount in sections III and IV, such as increasing the pH value in the buffer to 8.5 or 9, in order that a relatively high salt concentration can be used in sections III and IV to prevent the other contaminants from being adsorbed on Q-Sepharose FF resin.

Although an open loop configuration in salt gradient IE-SMB unit is adopted to avoid the accumulation of contaminants in the columns, there exists the possible denaturation or the loss of biological properties of the proteins after a number of cycles of IE-SMB. The buffer compositions, pH value, salt concentration, protein concentration in columns, and flow rate in each section of SMB unit will also affect the bioactivity of the proteins during the actual operation. Therefore, the actual operating conditions for protein separation by salt gradient IE-SMB chromatography should be selected based on the comprehensive considerations of protein purity, recovery, and bioactivity.

1.4 Conclusion

The EBA process will be more effective for those adsorbents that have both high-density base matrix and salt-tolerant ligand. Multimodal functional groups are immobilized on Streamline Direct CST I adsorbents, which not only take advantage of electrostatic interaction, but also take advantage of hydrogen bond interaction and hydrophobic interaction to tightly bind proteins, in order to get a high binding capacity in high ionic strength and salt concentration feedstock. Moreover, the inert core adsorbents not only increase the particle density to form stable expansion at high feed flow rate in the expanded bed, but also reduce the protein diffusion resistance inside the adsorbent due to shortening of the diffusion path. More work is needed when multimodal ligands are immobilized on inert core adsorbents to effectively capture proteins in expanded bed adsorption process.

The process performance of the separation and purification of proteins by ion exchange SMB can be improved when a lower salt concentration is formed in sections III and IV to increase the adsorption of proteins and a higher salt concentration is formed in sections I and II to improve the desorption of the bound proteins, called salt gradient ion exchange SMB. The selection of salt gradient is a key issue and also is flexible in the design of salt gradient ion exchange SMB chromatography. In sections I and II of ion exchange SMB, a high salt concentration will favor the desorption of the bound proteins and reduce the desorbent consumption, but too high salt concentration should be avoided, as a result of the significant decrease of separation factor in section II; in sections III and IV of ion exchange SMB, a lower salt concentration will favor the adsorption of proteins, but for the case of protein purification from a stream with some impurities, the salt concentration should be raised a little to decrease the adsorption of impurities and contaminants on ion exchangers. Moreover, when the gradient SMB is run in closed loop to reduce further desorbent consumption, it is better that a holding vessel with a given volume is added to the system to mix the desorbent with the recycled liquid stream from section IV in order to reduce salt or solvent strength fluctuation in the columns of section I.

References

1 Chase, H.A. (1994) Purification of proteins by adsorption chromatography in expanded beds. *Trends Biotechnol.*, **12**, 296–303.

2 Hjorth, R. (1997) Expanded bed adsorption in industrial bioprocessing: recent developments. *Trends Biotechnol.*, **15**, 230–235.

3 Thömmes, J., Bader, A., Halfar, M., Karau, A., and Kula, M.R. (1996) Isolation of monoclonal antibodies from cell containing hybridoma broth using a protein A coated adsorbent in expanded beds. *J. Chromatogr. A*, **752**, 111–122.

4 Ujam, L.B., Clemmitt, R.H., Clarke, S.A., Brooks, R.A., Rushton, N., and Chase, H.A. (2003) Isolation of monocytes from human peripheral blood using immuno-affinity expanded-bed adsorption. *Biotechnol. Bioeng.*, **83**, 554–566.

5 Clemmitt, R.H. and Chase, H.A. (2002) Direct recovery of glutathione S-transferase by expanded bed adsorption: anion exchange as an alternative to metal affinity fusions. *Biotechnol. Bioeng.*, **77**, 776–785.

6 Smith, M.P., Bulmer, M.A., Hjorth, R., and Titchener-Hooker, N.J. (2002) Hydrophobic interaction ligand selection and scale-up of an expanded bed separation of an intracellular enzyme from *Saccharomyces cerevisiae*. *J. Chromatogr. A*, **968**, 121–128.

7 Bai, Y. and Glatz, C.E. (2003) Capture of a recombinant protein from unclarified canola extract using Streamline expanded bed anion exchange. *Biotechnol. Bioeng.*, **81**, 855–864.

8 Anspach, F.B., Curbelo, D., Hartmann, R., Garke, G., and Deckwer, W.D. (1999) Expanded-bed chromatography in primary protein purification. *J. Chromatogr. A*, **865**, 129–144.

9 Jahanshahi, M., Sun, Y., Santos, E., Pacek, A., Franco, T.T., Nienow, A., and Lyddiatt, A. (2002) Operational intensification by direct product sequestration from cell disruptates: application of a pellicular adsorbent in a mechanically integrated disruption-fluidised bed adsorption process. *Biotechnol. Bioeng.*, **80**, 201–212.

10 Broughton, D.B. and Gerhold, C.G. (1961) Continuous sorption process employing fixed bed of sorbent and moving inlets and outlets. US Patent 2,985,589.

11 Juza, M., Mazzotti, M., and Morbidelli, M. (2000) Simulated moving-bed chromatography and its application to chirotechnology. *Trends Biotechnol.*, **18** (3), 108–118.

12 Li, P., Xiu, G.H., and Rodrigues, A.E. (2004) Modeling breakthrough and elution curves in fixed bed of inert core adsorbents: analytical and approximate solutions. *Chem. Eng. Sci.*, **59** (15), 3091–3103.
13 Li, P., Xiu, G.H., and Rodrigues, A.E. (2004) A 3-zone model for protein adsorption kinetics in expanded beds. *Chem. Eng. Sci.*, **59** (18), 3837–3847.
14 Ruthven, D.M. and Ching, C.B. (1989) Countercurrent and simulated countercurrent adsorption separation processes. *Chem. Eng. Sci.*, **44** (5), 1011–1038.
15 Gottschlich, N. and Kasche, V. (1997) Purification of monoclonal antibodies by simulated moving-bed chromatography. *J. Chromatogr. A*, **765** (2), 201–206.
16 Imamoglu, S. (2002) Simulated moving bed chromatography (SMB) for application in bioseparation. *Adv. Biochem. Eng. Biotechnol.*, **76**, 211–231.
17 Houwing, J., van Hateren, S.H., Billiet, H. A.H., and van der Wielen, L.A.M. (2002) Effect of salt gradients on the separation of dilute mixtures of proteins by ion-exchange in simulated moving beds. *J. Chromatogr. A*, **952** (1–2), 85–98.
18 Houwing, J., Billiet, H.A.H., and van der Wielen, L.A.M. (2002) Optimization of azeotropic protein separations in gradient and isocratic ion-exchange simulated moving bed chromatography. *J. Chromatogr. A*, **944** (1–2), 189–201.
19 Houwing, J., van Hateren, S.H., Billiet, H.A.H., and van der Wielen, L.A.M. (2002) Effect of salt gradients on the separation of dilute mixtures of proteins by ion-exchange in simulated moving beds. *J. Chromatogr. A*, **952** (1–2), 85–98.
20 Xie, Y., Mun, S., Kim, J., and Wang, N.H. L. (2002) Standing wave design and experimental validation of a tandem simulated moving bed process for insulin purification. *Biotechnol. Prog.*, **18** (6), 1332–1344.
21 Paredes, G., Mazzotti, M., Stadler, J., Makart, S., and Morbidelli, M. (2005) SMB operation for three-fraction separations: purification of plasmid DNA. *Adsorption*, **11**, 841–845.
22 Geisser, A., Hendrich, T., and Boehm, G. (2005) Separation of lactose from human milk oligosaccharides with simulated moving bed chromatography. *J. Chromatogr. A*, **1092** (1), 17–23.
23 Andersson, J. and Mattiasson, B. (2006) Simulated moving bed technology with a simplified approach for protein purification: separation of lactoperoxidase and lactoferrin from whey protein concentrate. *J. Chromatogr. A*, **1107** (1–2), 88–95.
24 Jensen, T.B., Reijns, T.G.P., Billiet, H.A.H., and van der Wielen, L.A.M. (2000) Novel simulated moving bed method for reduced solvent consumption. *J. Chromatogr. A*, **873** (2), 149–162.
25 Antos, D. and Seidel-Morgenstern, A. (2001) Application of gradients in the simulated moving bed process. *Chem. Eng. Sci.*, **56** (23), 6667–6682.
26 Antos, D. and Seidel-Morgenstern, A. (2002) Two-step solvent gradients in simulated moving bed chromatography–numerical study for linear equilibria. *J. Chromatogr. A*, **944** (1–2), 77–91.
27 Abel, S., Mazzotti, M., and Morbidelli, M. (2002) Solvent gradient operation of simulated moving beds. I. Linear isotherms. *J. Chromatogr. A*, **944** (1–2), 23–39.
28 Abel, S., Mazzotti, M., and Morbidelli, M. (2004) Solvent gradient operation of simulated moving beds. 2. Langmuir isotherms. *J. Chromatogr. A*, **1026** (1–2), 47–55.
29 Ziomek, G., Kaspereit, M., Jezowski, J.J., Seidel-Morgenstern, A., and Antos, D. (2005) Effect of mobile phase composition on the SMB processes efficiency stochastic optimization of isocratic and gradient operation. *J. Chromatogr. A*, **1070** (1–2), 111–124.
30 Pålsson, E., Gustavsson, P.-E., and Larsson, P.-E. (2000) Pellicular expanded bed matrix suitable for high flow rates. *J. Chromatogr. A*, **878**, 17–25.
31 Asghari, F., Jahanshahi, M., and Ghoreyshi, A.A. (2012) Preparation and characterization of agarose-nickel nanoporous composite particles customized for liquid expanded bed

adsorption. *J. Chromatogr. A*, **1242**, 35–42.

32 Asghari, F. and Jahanshahi, M. (2012) Fabrication and evaluation of low-cost agarose–zinc nanoporous composite matrix: influence of adsorbent density and size distribution on the performance of expanded beds. *J. Chromatogr. A*, **1257**, 89–97.

33 Hansson, M., Ståhl, S., Hjorth, R., Uhlén, M., and Moks, T. (1994) Single-step recovery of a secreted recombinant protein by expanded bed adsorption. *Biotechnology*, **12**, 285.

34 McCreath, G.E., Chase, H.A., and Lowe, C.R. (1994) Novel affinity separation based on perfluorocarbon emulsions: use of a perfluorocarbon affinity emulsion for the direct extraction of glucose-6-phosphate dehydrogenase from homogenized bakers' yeast. *J. Chromatogr. A*, **659**, 275–287.

35 Chang, Y.K., McCreath, G.E., and Chase, H.A. (1995) Development of an expanded bed technique for an affinity purification of G6PDH from unclarified yeast cell homogenates. *Biotechnol. Bioeng.*, **48** (4), 355–366.

36 McCreath, G.E., Chase, H.A., Owen, R.O., and Lowe, C.R. (1995) Expanded bed affinity chromatography of dehydrogenases from Bakers' yeast using dye-ligand perfluoropolymer supports. *Biotechnol. Bioeng.*, **48**, 341–354.

37 Garg, N., Galaev, I., and Mattiasson, B. (1996) Polymer-shielded dye-ligand chromatography of lactate dehydrogenase from porcine muscle in an expanded bed system. *Bioseparation*, **6**, 193–199.

38 Griffith, C.M., Morris, J., Robichaud, M., Annen, M.J., McCormick, A.V., and Flickinger, M.C. (1997) Fluidisation characteristics of and protein adsorption on fluoride-modified porous zirconium oxide particles. *J. Chromatogr. A*, **776**, 179–195.

39 Lewus, R.K. and Carta, G. (1999) Binary protein adsorption on gel-composite ion-exchange media. *AIChE J.*, **45** (3), 512–522.

40 Lihme, A., Zafirakos, E., Hansen, M., and Olander, M. (1999) Simplified and more robust EBA processes by elution in expanded bed mode. *Bioseparation*, **8**, 93–97.

41 Pai, A., Gondkar, S., and Lali, A. (2000) Enhance performance of expanded bed chromatography on rigid superporous adsorbent matrix. *J. Chromatogr. A*, **867**, 113–130.

42 Gondkar, S., Manudhane, K., Amritkar, N., Pai, A., and Lali, A. (2001) Effect of adsorbent porosity on performance of expanded bed chromatography of proteins. *Biotechnol. Prog.*, **17**, 522–529.

43 Tong, X.-D. and Sun, Y. (2001) Nd-Fe-B alloy-densified agarose gel for expanded bed adsorption of proteins. *J. Chromatogr. A*, **943**, 63–75.

44 Theodossiou, I., Elsner, H.D., Thomas, O.R.T., and Hobley, T.J. (2002) Fluidization and dispersion behavior of small high density pellicular expanded bed adsorbents. *J. Chromatogr. A*, **964**, 77–89.

45 Tong, X.-D. and Sun, Y. (2002) Particle size and density distributions of two dense matrices in an expanded bed system. *J. Chromatogr. A*, **977**, 173–183.

46 Dainiak, M.B., Galaev, I.Y., and Mattiasson, B. (2002) Polyelectrolyte-coated ion exchange for cell-resistant expanded bed adsorption. *Biotechnol. Prog.*, **18**, 815–820.

47 Tong, X.-D., Dong, X.-Y., and Sun, Y. (2002) Lysozyme adsorption and purification by expanded bed chromatography with a small-sized dense adsorbent. *Biochem. Eng. J.*, **12**, 117–124.

48 Jahanshahi, M., Pacek, A.W., Niewon, A.W., and Lyddiatt, A. (2003) Fabrication by three-phase emulsification of pellicular adsorbents customized for liquid fluidized bed adsorption of bioproducts. *J. Chem. Technol. Biotechnol.*, **78**, 1111–1120.

49 Li, P., Xiu, G., and Rodrigues, A.E. (2003) Modeling separation of proteins by inert core adsorbent in a batch adsorber. *Chem. Eng. Sci.*, **58**, 3361–3371.

50 Lei, Y.-L., Lin, D.-Q., Yao, S.-J., and Zhu, Z.-Q. (2003) Preparation and characterization of titanium oxide-densified cellulose beads for expanded bed adsorption. *J. Appl. Polym. Sci.*, **90**, 2848–2854.

51 Zhou, X., Shi, Q.-H., Bai, S., and Sun, Y. (2004) Dense pellicular agarose–glass beads for expanded bed application: fabrication and characterization for effective protein adsorption. *Biochem. Eng. J.*, **18**, 81–88.

52 Lei, Y.-L., Lin, D.-Q., Yao, S.-J., and Zhu, Z.-Q. (2005) Preparation of an anion exchanger based on TiO_2-densified cellulose beads for expanded bed adsorption. *React. Funct. Polym.*, **62**, 169–177.

53 Miao, Z.-J., Lin, D.-Q., and Yao, S.-J. (2005) Preparation and characterization of cellulose–stainless steel powder composite particles customized for expanded bed application. *Ind. Eng. Chem. Res.*, **44**, 8218–8224.

54 Lin, D.-Q., Miao, Z.-J., and Yao, S.-J. (2006) Expansion and hydrodynamic properties of cellulose–stainless steel powder composite matrix for expanded bed adsorption. *J. Chromatogr. A*, **1107**, 265–272.

55 Xia, H.-F., Lin, D.-Q., and Yao, S.-J. (2007) Spherical cellulose–nickel powder composite matrix customized for expanded bed application. *J. Appl. Polym. Sci.*, **104**, 740–747.

56 Xia, H.-F., Lin, D.-Q., and Yao, S.-J. (2007) Preparation and characterization of macroporous cellulose–tungsten carbide composite beads for expanded bed applications. *J. Chromatogr. A*, **1175**, 55–62.

57 Xia, H.-F., Lin, D.-Q., and Yao, S.-J. (2008) Chromatographic performance of macroporous cellulose–tungsten carbide composite beads as anion-exchanger for expanded bed adsorption at high fluid velocity. *J. Chromatogr. A*, **1195**, 60–66.

58 Gao, D., Yao, S.-J., and Lin, D.-Q. (2008) Preparation and adsorption behavior of a cellulose-based, mixed-mode adsorbent with a benzylamine ligand for expanded bed applications. *J. Appl. Polym. Sci.*, **107**, 674–682.

59 Jahanshahi, M., Partida-Martinez, L., and Hajizadeh, S. (2008) Preparation and evaluation of polymer-coated adsorbents for the expanded bed recovery of protein products from particulate feedstocks. *J. Chromatogr. A*, **1203**, 13–20.

60 Song, H.-B., Xiao, Z.-F., and Yuan, Q.-P. (2009) Preparation and characterization of poly glycidyl methacrylete-zirconium dioxide-β-cyclodextrin composite matrix for separation of isoflavones through expanded bed adsorption. *J. Chromatogr. A*, **1216**, 5001–5010.

61 Zhao, J., Lin, D.-Q., and Yao, S.-J. (2009) Expansion and hydrodynamic properties of β-cyclodextrin polymer/tungsten carbide composite matrix in an expanded bed. *J. Chromatogr. A*, **1216**, 7840–7845.

62 Zhao, J., Lin, D.-Q., Wang, Y.-C., and Yao, S.-J. (2010) A novel β-cyclodextrin polymer/tungsten carbide composite matrix for expanded bed adsorption: preparation and characterization of physical properties. *Carbohydr. Polym.*, **80**, 1085–1090.

63 Lihme, A., Hansen, M.B., Andersen, I.V., and Burnouf, T. (2010) A novel core fractionation process of human plasma by expanded bed adsorption chromatography. *Anal. Biochem.*, **399**, 102–109.

64 Shi, F., Lin, D.-Q., Phottraithip, W., and Yao, S.-J. (2011) Preparation of cellulose–tungsten carbide composite beads with ionic liquid for expanded bed application. *J. Appl. Polym. Sci.*, **119**, 3453–3461.

65 Lin, D.-Q., Tong, H.-F., van de Sandt, E.J. A.X., den Boer, P., Golubović, M., and Yao, S.-J. (2013) Evaluation and characterization of axial distribution in expanded bed. I. Bead size, bead density and local bed voidage. *J. Chromatogr. A*, **1304**, 78–84.

66 Zhan, X.-Y., Lu, D.-P., Lin, D.-Q., and Yao, S.-J. (2013) Preparation and characterization of supermacroporous polyacrylamide cryogel beads for biotechnological application. *J. Appl. Polym. Sci.*, **130** (5), 3082–3089.

67 Thömmes, J., Weiher, M., Karau, A., and Kula, M.-R. (1995) Hydrodynamics and performance in fluidized bed adsorption. *Biotechnol. Bioeng.*, **48**, 367–374.

68 Thömmes, J., Halfar, M., Lenz, S., and Kula, M.-R. (1995) Purification of monoclonal antibodies from whole hybridoma fermentation broth by fluidized bed adsorption. *Biotechnol. Bioeng.*, **45** (3), 205–211.

69 Chase, H.A. and Chang, Y.K. (1996) Ion exchange purification of G6PDH from unclarified yeast cell homogenates using expanded bed adsorption. *Biotechnol. Bioeng.*, **49**, 204–216.

70 Chase, H.A. and Chang, Y.K. (1996) Development of operating conditions for protein purification using expanded bed techniques: the effect of the degree of bed expansion on adsorption performance. *Biotechnol. Bioeng.*, **49**, 512–526.

71 Karau, A., Benken, C., Thommes, J., and Kula, M.-R. (1997) The influence of particle size distribution and operating conditions on the adsorption performance in fluidized beds. *Biotechnol. Bioeng.*, **55**, 54–64.

72 Smith, M.P. (1997) An evaluation of expanded bed adsorption for the recovery of protein from crude feedstock. PhD thesis. University College London, UK.

73 Finette, G.M.S., Baharin, B., Mao, Q.M., and Hearn, M.T.W. (1998) Optimization considerations for the purification of α1-antitrypsin using silica-based ion-exchange adsorbents in packed and expanded beds. *Biotechnol. Prog.*, **14**, 286–293.

74 Lan, J.C.-W., Hamilton, G.E., and Lyddiatt, A. (1999) Physical and biochemical characterization of a simple intermediate between fluidized and expanded bed contactors. *Bioseparation*, **8**, 43–51.

75 Pai, A., Gondkar, S., Sundaram, S., and Lali, A. (1999) Expanded bed adsorption on supermacroporous cross-linked celulose matrix. *Bioseparation*, **8**, 131–138.

76 Bruce, L.J., Clemmitt, R.H., Nash, D.C., and Chase, H.A. (1999) Monitoring of adsorbate breakthrough curves within an expanded bed adsorption column. *J. Chem. Technol. Biotechnol.*, **74**, 264–269.

77 Thömmes, J. (1999) Investigations on protein adsorption to agarose-dextran composite media. *Biotechnol. Bioeng.*, **62** (3), 358–362.

78 Willoughby, N.A., Hjorth, R., and Titchener-Hooker, N.J. (2000) Experimental measurement of particle size distribution and voidage in an expanded bed adsorption system. *Biotechnol. Bioeng.*, **69** (6), 648–653.

79 Clemmitt, R.H. and Chase, H.A. (2000) Facilitated downstream processing of a histidine-tagged protein from unclarified histidine-tagged protein from unclarified *E. coli* homogenates using immobilized metal expanded-bed adsorption. *Biotechnol. Bioeng.*, **67** (2), 206–216.

80 Wright, P.R. and Glasser, B.J. (2001) Modeling mass transfer and hydrodynamics in fluidized-bed adsorption of proteins. *AIChE J.*, **47** (2), 474–488.

81 Hu, H.-B., Yao, S.J., and Zhu, Z.-Q. (2001) Study on adsorption performance of BSA in Streamline DEAE and DEAE Sepharose FF adsorbents. *Chem. Eng. (China)*, **29**, 37–41.

82 Fernández-Lahore, H.M., Lin, D.-Q., Hubbuch, J.J., Kula, M.-R., and Thömmes, J. (2001) The use of ion-selective electrodes for evaluating residence time distributions in expanded bed adsorption systems. *Biotechnol. Prog.*, **17**, 1128–1136.

83 Bruce, L.J. and Chase, H.A. (2001) Hydrodynamics and adsorption behavior within an expanded bed adsorption column studied using expanded-bed sampling. *Chem. Eng. Sci.*, **56**, 3149–3162.

84 Bruce, L.J. and Chase, H.A. (2002) The combined use of in-bed monitoring and an adsorption model to anticipate breakthrough during expanded bed adsorption. *Chem. Eng. Sci.*, **57**, 3085–3093.

85 Chen, W.-D., Tong, X.-D., Dong, X.-Y., and Sun, Y. (2003) Expanded bed adsorption of protein with DEAE spherodex M. *Biotechnol. Prog.*, **19**, 880–886.

86 Tong, X.-D., Xue, B., and Sun, Y. (2003) Modeling of expanded-bed protein adsorption by taking into account the axial particle size distribution. *Biochem. Eng. J.*, **16**, 265–272.

87 Yun, J., Yao, S.-J., Lin, D.-Q., Lu, M.-H., and Zhao, W.-T. (2004) Modeling axial distributions of adsorbent particle size and local voidage in expanded bed. *Chem. Eng. Sci.*, **59**, 449–457.

88 Yun, J., Lin, D.-Q., and Yao, S.-J. (2004) Variation of the axial dispersion along the bed height for adsorbents with a density difference and a log-normal size distribution in an expanded bed. *Ind. Eng. Chem. Res.*, **43**, 8066–8073.

89 Yun, J., Lin, D.-Q., Lu, M.-H., Zhong, L.-N., and Yao, S.-J. (2004) Measurement and modeling of axial distribution of adsorbent particles in expanded bed: taking into account the particle density difference. *Chem. Eng. Sci.*, **59**, 5873–5881.

90 Li, P., Xiu, G., and Rodrigues, A.E. (2005) Experimental and modeling study of protein adsorption in expanded bed. *AIChE J.*, **51** (11), 2965–2977.

91 Yun, J., Lin, D.-Q., and Yao, S.-J. (2005) Predictive modeling of protein adsorption along the bed height by taking into account the axial nonuniform liquid dispersion and particle classification in expanded beds. *J. Chromatogr. A*, **1095**, 16–26.

92 Li, P., Xiu, G., Mata, V.G., Grande, C.A., and Rodrigues, A.E. (2006) Expanded bed adsorption/desorption of proteins with Streamline Direct CST I adsorbent. *Biotechnol. Bioeng.*, **94** (6), 1155–1163.

93 Chow, Y.M., Tey, B.T., Ibrahim, M.N., Ariff, A., and Ling, T.C. (2006) The performance of anion exchange expanded bed adsorption chromatography on the recovery of G6PDH from unclarified feedstock with high biomass concentration. *Biotechnol. Bioprocess Eng.*, **11**, 466–469.

94 Xia, H.-F., Lin, D.-Q., and Yao, S.-J. (2007) Evaluation of new high density ion exchange adsorbents for expanded bed adsorption chromatography. *J. Chromatogr. A*, **1145**, 58–66.

95 Chang, Y.-K., Chou, S.-Y., Liu, J.-L., and Tasi, J.-C. (2007) Characterization of BSA adsorption on mixed mode adsorbent. I. Equilibrium study in a well-agitated contactor. *Biochem. Eng. J.*, **35**, 56–65.

96 Poulin, F., Jacquemart, R., De Crescenzo, G., Jolicoeur, M., and Legros, R. (2008) A study of the interaction of HEK-293 cells with streamline chelating adsorbent in expanded bed operation. *Biotechnol. Prog.*, **24**, 279–282.

97 Lin, D.-Q., Chen, C.-Q., Wu, Y.-C., and Yao, S.-J. (2009) Separation of lactoferrin from whey by expanded bed adsorption with mixed-mode adsorbent. *J. Zhejiang Univ. (Eng. Sci.)*, **43** (3), 472–476.

98 Li, J. and Chase, H.A. (2009) Use of expanded bed adsorption to purify flavonoids from *Ginkgo biloba* L. *J. Chromatogr. A*, **1216**, 8759–8770.

99 Yap, W.B., Tey, B.T., Alitheen, N.B.M., and Tan, W.S. (2010) Purification of His-tagged hepatitis B core antigen from unclarified bacterial homogenates using immobilized metal affinity-expanded bed adsorption chromatography. *J. Chromatogr. A*, **1217**, 3473–3480.

100 Niu, J.F., Chen, Z.-F., and Wang, G.-C. (2010) Purification of phycoerythrin from *Porphyra yezoensis* Ueda (Bangiales, Rhodophyta) using expanded bed absorption. *J. Appl. Phycol.*, **22**, 25–31.

101 Shahavi, M.H., Jahanshahi, M., Najafpour, G.D., Ebrahimpour, M., and Hosenian, A.H. (2011) Expanded bed adsorption of biomolecules by NBG contactor: experimental and mathematical investigation. *World Appl. Sci. J.*, **13** (2), 181–187.

102 Alibolandi, M. and Mirzahoseini, H. (2011) Purification and refolding of overexpressed human basic fibroblast growth factor in *Escherichia coli. Biotechnol. Res. Int.* doi: 10.4061/2011/973741

103 Boeris, V., Balce, I., Vennapusa, R.R., Rodriguez, M.A., Picó, G., and Lahore, M.F. (2012) Production, recovery and purification of a recombinant β-galactosidase by expanded bed anion exchange adsorption. *J. Chromatogr. A*, **900**, 32–37.

104 Kelly, W., Garcia, P., McDemott, S., Mullen, P., Kamguia, G., Jones, G., Ubiera, A., and Göklen, K. (2013) Experimental characterization of next-generation expanded-bed adsorbents for capture of a recombinant protein expressed in high-cell-density yeast fermentation. *Biotechnol. Appl. Biochem.* doi: 10.0002/bab.1133

105 Moraes, C.C., Mazutti, M.A., Maugeri, F., and Kalil, S.J. (2013) Modeling of ion exchange expanded-bed chromatography for the purification of C-phycocyanin. *J. Chromatogr. A*, **1281**, 73–78.

106 Du, Q.-Y., Lin, D.-Q., Xiong, Z.-S., and Yao, S.-J. (2013) One-step purification of lactoferrin from crude sweet whey using cation-exchange expanded bed adsorption. *Ind. Eng. Chem. Res.*, **52**, 2693–2699.

107 den Boer, P., Doeven, M., van der Merwe, J., Lihme, A., Bendix-Hansen, M., Vaarst, I., Pontoppidan, M., and Linz, F. (2013) Rhobust EBA processing high-cell density mammalian cell cultures: process parameters and performance. DSM Biologics. Available at http://www.dsm.com/content/dam/dsm/pharmaceuticals/en_US/documents/ECCE%20Den%20Haag%20April%202013%20FINAL.pdf (last accessed October 16, 2013).

108 Kelly, W., Kamguia, G., Mullen, P., Ubiera, A., Göklen, K., Huang, Z., and Jones, G. (2013) Using two species competitive binding model to predict expanded bed breakthrough of a recombinant protein expressed in a high cell density fermentation. *Biotechnol. Bioprocess Eng.*, **18**, 546–559.

109 Johansson, B.L., Belew, M., Eriksson, S., Glad, G., Lind, O., Maloisel, L.J., and Norrman, N. (2003) Preparation and characterization of prototypes for multi-modal separation media aimed for capture of negatively charged bimolecular at high salt conditions. *J. Chromatogr. A*, **1016**, 21–33.

110 Johansson, B.L., Belew, M., Eriksson, S., Glad, G., Lind, O., Maloisel, L.J., and Norrman, N. (2003) Preparation and characterization of prototypes for multi-modal separation aimed for capture of positively charged biomolecules at high-salt conditions. *J. Chromatogr. A*, **1016**, 35–49.

111 Li, P., Xiu, G.H., and Rodrigues, A.E. (2003) Analytical breakthrough curves for inert core adsorbent with sorption kinetics. *AIChE J.*, **49** (11), 2974–2979.

112 Li, P., Yu, J.G., Xiu, G.H., and Rodrigues, A.E. (2010) A strategy for tailored design of efficient and low-pressure drop packed column chromatography. *AIChE J.*, **56** (12), 3091–3098.

113 Li, P., Yu, J.G., Xiu, G.H., and Rodrigues, A.E. (2011) Perturbation chromatography with inert core adsorbent: moment solution for two-component nonlinear isotherm adsorption. *Chem. Eng. Sci.*, **66** (20), 4555–4560.

114 Willoughby, N., Habib, G., Hoare, M., Hjorth, R., and Titchener-Hooker, N.J. (2000) The use of rapid on-line monitoring of products and contaminants from within an expanded bed to control separations exhibiting fast breakthrough characteristics and to maximize productivity. *Biotechnol. Bioeng.*, **70**, 254–261.

115 Chen, W.D., Dong, X.Y., and Sun, Y. (2003) Modeling of the whole expanded-bed protein adsorption process with yeast cell suspensions as feedstock. *J. Chromatogr. A*, **1012**, 1–10.

116 Kaczmarski, K. and Bellot, J.C. (2004) Theoretical investigation of axial and local particle size distribution on expanded bed adsorption process. *Biotechnol. Prog.*, **20**, 786–792.

117 Skidmore, G.L. and Chase, H.A. (1990) 2-Component protein adsorption to the cation exchanger S-Sepharose-FF. *J. Chromatogr. A*, **505**, 329–347.

118 Weinbrenner, W.F. and Etzel, M.R. (2004) Competitive adsorption of alpha-lactalbumin and bovine serum-albumin to a sulfopropyl ion-exchange membrane. *J. Chromatogr. A*, **662**, 414–419.

119 Martin, C., Iberer, G., Ubiera, A., and Carta, G. (2005) Two-component protein adsorption kinetics in porous ion exchange media. *J. Chromatogr. A*, **1079**, 105–115.

120 Hubbuch, R., Linden, T., Knieps, E., Thömmes, J., and Kula, M.R. (2003) Mechanism and kinetics of protein transport in chromatographic media studied by confocal laser scanning microscopy – Part II. Impact on chromatographic separations. *J. Chromatogr. A*, **1021**, 105–115.

121 Li, P., Xiu, G.H., and Rodrigues, A.E. (2007) Proteins separation and

purification by salt gradient ion-exchange SMB. *AIChE J.*, **53** (9), 2419–2431.

122 Jensen, T.B. (2003) Gradient SMB chromatography. PhD thesis. Kluyver Laboratory for Biotechnology, Delft University of Technology.

123 Mazzotti, M., Storti, G., and Morbidelli, M. (1997) Optimal operation of simulated moving bed units for nonlinear chromatographic separations. *J. Chromatogr. A*, **769** (1), 3–24.

124 Azevedo, D.C.S. and Rodrigues, A.E. (2001) Fructose–glucose separation in a SMB pilot unit: modeling, simulation, design and operation. *AIChE J.*, **47** (9), 2024–2051.

125 Minceva, M. and Rodrigues, A.E. (2005) Two-level optimization of an existing SMB for *p*-xylene separation. *Comput. Chem. Eng.*, **29** (10), 2215–2228.

126 Rodrigues, A.E. and Pais, L.S. (2004) Design of SMB chiral separations using the concept of separation volume. *Sep. Sci. Technol.*, **39** (2), 245–270.

127 Li, P., Yu, J.G., Xiu, G.H., and Rodrigues, A.E. (2008) Separation region and strategies for proteins separation by salt gradient ion-exchange SMB. *Sep. Sci. Technol.*, **43** (1), 11–28.

2
BioSMB Technology as an Enabler for a Fully Continuous Disposable Biomanufacturing Platform

Marc Bisschops

2.1
Introduction

Many process industries have implemented continuous processing during the twentieth century. One of the best known examples is the manufacturing of cars. Henry Ford installed a belt-driven moveable production line to enable continuous flow production of the famous Model T Ford. The manufacturing process of the car was broken down into 84 areas. The conveyor belt took the intermediate product from station to station where the assembly employees would perform their tasks. By implementing this system, the time to construct a car was reduced from 13 h to 93 min, while using less manpower. The costs went down from USD 850 to below USD 300. Mass production had made cars affordable for common people.

Other notable examples of continuous processing can be found in petrochemicals, pulp and paper, metal, and food industries. In all these areas, continuous manufacturing has enabled mass production, thereby realizing significant cost savings and making the products available to a larger population.

In most process industries, continuous production has also resulted in improved process control and improved safety. Reports indicate that 60–70% of the accidents in chemical industries occur during nonroutine operations such as startup and shut-down. As a result, continuous processes are inherently safer than batch processes, where startup and shut-down operations are required more often. The pharmaceutical industry has already started to gradually implement continuous manufacturing. For some large-scale products, such as over-the-counter (OTC) products, this has been a reality for a few decades now. In most cases, the choice for continuous processing was driven by the economies of scale. This has, for instance, also been driving many antibiotics manufacturers toward (semi-) continuous processes.

The manufacturing process of biopharmaceutical products involves multiples steps, all of which are conducted in batch mode. Although the biopharmaceutical industry utilizes state-of-the-art process chemistries to manufacture their drugs, the technological implementation of these processes lags behind compared to other mature manufacturing industries.

Continuous Processing in Pharmaceutical Manufacturing, First Edition. Edited by Ganapathy Subramanian.

Until recently, the drivers for change were very limited due to a combination of reasons, including lack of competition, relatively small production volumes, and limitations in process understanding and process control. Some of these factors are now rapidly changing. Biosimilars are already a reality in Europe and it is inevitable that the impact of their presence will grow in the next decade. In addition to this, the demand for biopharmaceutical products and monoclonal antibodies in particular, is growing steadily and some products have exceeded ton-scale demands. Meanwhile, technological advancements have improved process understanding and the ability to measure and monitor the manufacturing processes has improved significantly. This transformation coincides with the US Food and Drug Administration (FDA) initiatives on quality by design (QbD) and process analytical technologies (PAT). With these trends in the market, the biopharmaceutical industry has started exploring continuous production strategies for recombinant proteins and monoclonal antibodies.

In this chapter, we will review which of the individual building blocks are needed to assemble an integrated continuous bioprocessing platform. In addition to this, the opportunities to combine continuous processing and disposable bioprocessing solutions will be addressed. The main focus of the chapter is on the downstream processing section of the production process. More in particular, the impact of the recent advancements in multicolumn chromatography processes will be discussed.

2.2 Integrated Continuous Bioprocessing

Today's manufacturing of biopharmaceutical products involves a cascade of batch processes. The cascade can be divided into two sections, being the upstream process (USP) and the downstream process (DSP). During the cascade of batch unit operations, the intermediate product solution is collected after each step. Only after completion of the process step the intermediate product solution is connected to the next process step. This batch-wise manufacturing procedure results in relatively low capacity utilization.

The potential benefits of an integrated continuous biomanufacturing approach include time savings and improved capital utilization. In an industry where the costs of goods are dominated by fixed costs, this represents a significant business driver. A typical scheme for a cascade of batch process steps is displayed in Figure 2.1a and for an integrated continuous biomanufacturing process is displayed in Figure 2.1b.

The schedules in Figure 2.1 show the following features of a continuous process:

a) The overall processing time is determined by the slowest step. All other unit operations are sized to match this flow rate. In most downstream

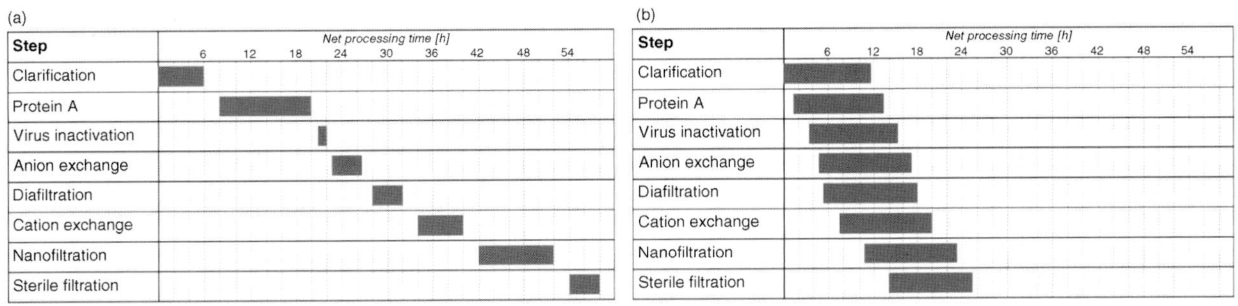

Figure 2.1 Typical DSP manufacturing schedules for (a) a cascade of batch-wise operated unit operations, and (b) an integrated continuous downstream process.

processing cascades, the slowest process step is the capture chromatography step.

b) As a result of the continuous flow from one unit operation into the next, the interstage product hold bags can be eliminated or minimized.
c) Each unit operation is only started as soon as the first product comes off the previous unit operation. As a result, there will be a cascaded startup and shut-down procedure.

In order to implement an integrated continuous biomanufacturing process, all unit operations need to be compatible with continuous flow of the product solution. The compatibility chart with this requirement for unit operations that are normally found in the manufacturing of glycosylated proteins or monoclonal antibodies is indicated in Table 2.1.

Based on existing technologies, one can identify a few unit operations that are not yet fully compatible with an integrated continuous bioprocessing cascade.

Virus inactivation relies on a residence time under certain conditions, most commonly reduced pH in a hold tank. Translating such process into a continuous process may be done in various ways. Brower had presented a strategy based on a continuous flow plug flow reactor [1]. Alternatives that rely on hold times in smaller sublots have been described elsewhere [2]. Thus far, none of these approaches have been validated, but there seems to be no reason to assume that virus inactivation cannot be transformed into a continuous process. The critical process parameters are the pH and the hold time and these can be adequately controlled in a continuous flow process too. Alternative flow-through virus inactivation procedures, such as the UV inactivation, were reported to be less effective for enveloped viruses, which is the main target for the low pH inactivation [3,4].

Table 2.1 Summary of typical DSP unit operations and their compatibility with continuous flow processing.

Step	Compatible with continuous processing	Examples and/or comments
Clarification	Yes	Continuous centrifugation Depth filtration
Capture chromatography	No	Protein A chromatography
Virus inactivation	Yes/no	Requires a cascade of mixers or a tubular contactor
Ultrafiltration	Yes	Single-pass Tangential flow filtration
Trace impurity removal	Yes	Q membrane adsorbers
Aggregate removal	No	Cation exchange chromatography Hydrophobic intereaction chromatography
Virus filtration	Yes	

The concept of multistage, single-pass tangential flow filtration has been used in other process industries, such as the dairy industry. A similar approach has recently been implemented in the Cadence^{TM} single-pass tangential-flow filtration (TFF) technology [5]. Although multistage tangential flow filtration has also been used for diafiltration processes in other industries, the Cadence^{TM} system seems to be mainly tested for continuous concentration processes.

Chromatographic purifications have been the workhorse for biopharmaceutical purification. A typical production process comprises three chromatography steps. Traditionally, chromatographic separations are performed in a single packed column. In traditional process industries, batch chromatographic separations are transformed into continuous processes by adopting the concept of multicolumn chromatography. This is the basis for simulated moving bed technology and all other continuous ion exchange and continuous chromatography processes that have been implemented in a wide range of process industries.

2.3 Multicolumn Chromatography

The principle of multicolumn chromatography is to create a (simulated) movement of the chromatography columns in opposite direction of the process solutions. This results in a countercurrent contact between the liquid and the chromatographic media, which allows overloading the columns beyond their dynamic binding capacity without suffering loss of material. When product breaks through from the first column, it will be captured on a second column in the load zone. With this, countercurrent chromatography processes can offer a significant gain in capacity utilization.

Another benefit of the countercurrent contact approach is that it eliminates idle zones in the process. In a batch chromatography column, the mass transfer zone only covers a small portion of the overall chromatographic media volume. The media above the mass transfer zone is in equilibrium with the feed solution and has no additional capacity to bind more product. The media below the mass transfer zone is in contact with depleted feed solution and hence is waiting for the first product to arrive. In a countercurrent process, these idle zones are eliminated and the load zone can be designed to only cover the length of the mass transfer zone. This generally corresponds to a small part of the batch column volume. These two features are schematically demonstrated in Figure 2.2.

In batch processes, the column size is proportional to the total mass of protein that needs to be purified and hence there is a direct relationship with the feed concentration. In a continuous chromatography process, the load zone is mainly designed around the contact time associated with mass transfer zone. The total volume of chromatographic media in the load zone thus hardly depends on the static binding capacity and the feed concentration. Instead, the process is designed around the volume that needs to be processed, or more precisely, the feed flow rate.

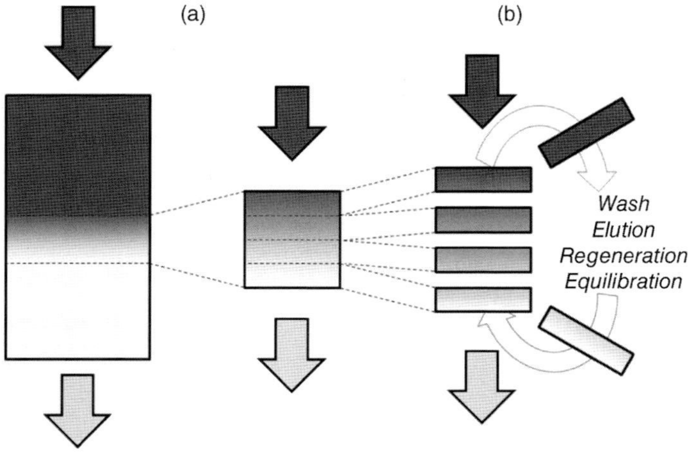

Figure 2.2 Schematic comparison between (a) a batch process and (b) a multicolumn countercurrent chromatography process.

2.4
BioSMB Technology

In order to provide a practical way to implement multicolumn chromatography in the biopharmaceutical industries, Tarpon Biosystems has developed the BioSMB® Technology that relies on a fully disposable flow path. All valves that are required to direct flows to and from all columns are kept within a single disposable cassette that can be mounted to the BioSMB system. The overall layout of the system is schematically shown in Figure 2.3.

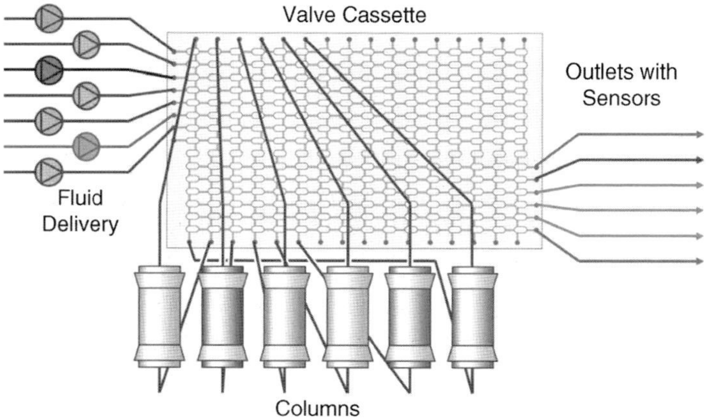

Figure 2.3 Schematic lay-out of the BioSMB® system for continuous multicolumn chromatographic separations.

Table 2.2 Some examples for which BioSMB technology has been successfully tested [6–11].

Case study	Chromatographic mode	Specific productivity
Capture of antibodies	Protein A chromatography	2–6 × batch
Aggregate removal	Hydrophobic interaction (HIC)	2–3 × batch
Aggregate removal	Ion exchange	4–8 × batch
Capture of recombinant proteins	Ion exchange	2–5 × batch
Capture of VLP vaccines	Ion exchange	3–7 × batch
Polishing of a VLP vaccines	Size Exclusion (SEC)	6–14 × batch

When the BioSMB system is combined with prepacked columns, membrane adsorbers or any other chromatographic devices designed for single-use applications, the entire chromatography process can be translated into a viable single-use option. With this, the BioSMB® Technology provides a promising answer for those companies who are developing completely disposable platforms for the entire biomanufacturing process.

For various chromatographic separations, proof of concept has been demonstrated. The majority of applications that have been investigated involve Protein A affinity chromatography for the purification of monoclonal antibodies [6–8]. Other notable examples include aggregate removal using cation exchange [9] or hydrophobic interaction chromatography [10] and vaccine purification using ion exchange and size exclusion chromatography [11]. In all these cases, the specific productivity gain was substantial (Table 2.2).

Continuous multicolumn chromatography processes can be designed to either operate at maximum specific productivity or at maximum capacity utilization. In order to operate at maximum specific productivity, the process should be designed for a minimum residence time in the load zone. This can be achieved by compromising on capacity utilization. This may well represent the most attractive design for clinical manufacturing, where the costs of the chromatographic media are dominated by the actual volume that needs to be installed. During a typical clinical manufacturing campaign, the resin is depreciated well before it has reached its maximum lifetime in terms of process cycles. The costs for chromatography media in clinical manufacturing are therefore governed by the amount of media installed. The lower capacity utilization is compensated by running more cycles per batch on each column.

During commercial or routine manufacturing of biopharmaceuticals, on the other hand, the chromatographic media is generally utilized to its full lifetime. This may involve 100 or 200 cycles, depending on the process and the validation constraints. As a result, the costs for chromatographic media per unit of purified product depends on the amount of product bound (and eluted) in each cycle per liter of chromatographic resin, which corresponds to the capacity utilization. Continuous chromatography for routine manufacturing should probably be optimized around maximum capacity utilization, which requires longer residence times than in the scenario listed earlier. This translates into larger column sizes

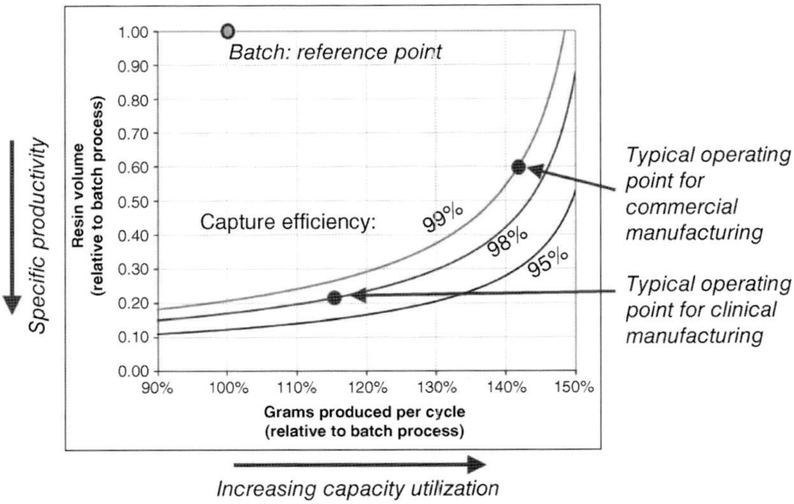

Figure 2.4 Schematic representation of the typical operating points for clinical manufacturing and commercial manufacturing in a Protein A based BioSMB process.

and hence the replacement frequency will be lower, yet still higher than with traditional batch chromatography.

Two typical operating points representing commercial and clinical manufacturing are shown in Figure 2.4. On the vertical axis, the relative volume compared to a typical batch process is shown. The design calculations underlying this graph have been presented elsewhere [7]. On the horizontal axis, the capacity utilization is plotted relative to the reference batch process. On the vertical axis, the amount of chromatographic media that is required for the process is plotted (relative to the reference batch process). The graph shows how one can decide to either operate at more or less the same capacity utilization as the batch process, with only 15–20% of the chromatographic media.

On the other hand, the preferred scenario for commercial manufacturing may lead to approximately 40–50% more protein produced in each cycle per liter of resin, thereby representing 35% cost savings. Even at that operating point, the process still requires significantly less chromatographic media than the batch process. In addition to this, the (smaller) amount of media is distributed over multiple columns, the size of which is significantly smaller than the batch equivalent. This allows a manufacturer to purchase prepacked columns, thus minimizing column packing operations and the associated costs.

A key aspect of continuous chromatography is that the amount of media installed is predominantly governed by the residence time that is required to reach the desired capacity utilization. This is mainly related to the mass transfer resistance (or diffusion) associated with the mass transfer process. Neither the titer nor the static binding capacity has a (huge) impact on the residence time.

The column size therefore mainly depends on the flow rate and therefore on the volume to be processed and the processing time. This gives operational flexibility in handling variations in titer in a facility. In various proof of concept studies, the ability of the BioSMB® technology to handle different feed solutions with the same equipment and column dimensions was already demonstrated [8,9]. In these studies, the antibody concentration in the feed stock was varied from approximately 2 to 10 mg ml^{-1}.

The number of columns that is required to run a continuous process does depend on titer. In order to transform the load step into a continuous countercurrent step, at least two columns are needed. This brings the minimum number of columns for a continuous process to three, provided that one column provides sufficient time to do all wash steps, elution, regeneration and re-equilibration steps. As soon as the load volume becomes relatively low compared to total process time, which is the case for medium and higher titers, the load time becomes proportionally smaller and one column is no longer sufficient. This is schematically displayed in the circular chronograms in Figure 2.5. These chronograms display all steps in the chromatography process, where the inlet for each step is displayed on the outer ring and the outlet of each step is displayed on the inner ring. The columns are represented by the spokes that will travel clockwise over the chronogram. At increasing titer, the volume that can be loaded on the columns will be less and hence the load time will become shorter. Since the mass transfer kinetics is not (or hardly) affected by the increasing titer, the residence time in the load step will remain the same and hence the column volume can remain the same. The consequence of an increasing titer thus is that each column will spend less time in the load zone of the process cycle. The time

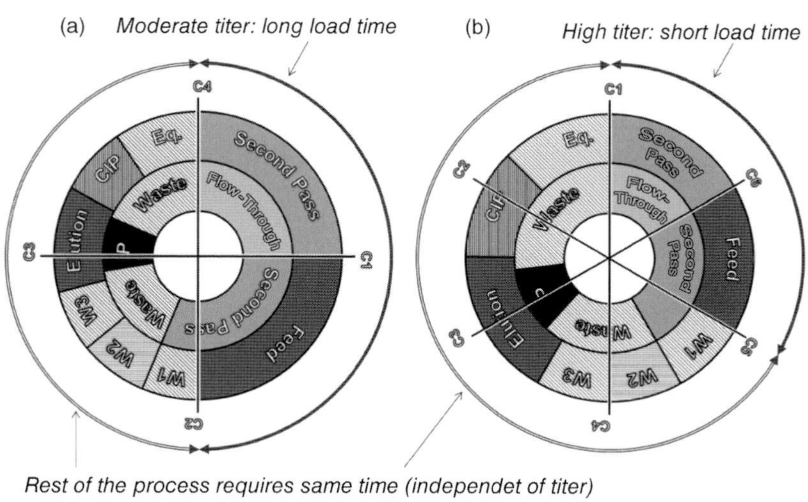

Figure 2.5 Circular chronogram for (a) a low-titer process with minimum number of columns and for (b) a high-titer process with a minimum number of columns.

required for the other steps in the process remains the same. Relative to the load time, however, the rest of the cycle therefore becomes longer. This needs to be compensated by adding extra columns to provide the required time in the rest of the cycle.

One of the key features of BioSMB® Technology is the ability to connect extra columns without adding complexity to the system. This is particularly beneficial in accommodating processes with different titers as discussed earlier. The flexibility in terms of the number of columns may also provide a means to enhance specific productivity by using more, yet smaller columns. This allows one to design a capture process with the same yield but with an overall lower inventory of resin, simply because the media is divided into smaller increments. Additional columns may also allow further optimization of the process in terms of advanced elution schemes to boost product titers without compromising on product yield. Last but not least, in general more complex separations may require more columns.

2.5 Fully Disposable Continuous Processing

Disposable and single-use bioprocessing technologies have been implemented throughout the entire field of biopharmaceutical manufacturing. Most notable examples are buffer containers, product containers, and single-use bioreactors. For downstream processing, filters and membrane adsorbers are most likely the best known examples of disposable technologies.

Table 2.3 lists the most common unit operations for the downstream processing of glycosylated proteins and monoclonal antibodies and their availability in a single-use or disposable format. The agreement between the compatibility tables

Table 2.3 Summary of typical DSP Unit Operations and their availability in a disposable or single-use format.

Step	Available in single-use or disposable format	Examples and/or comments
Clarification	Yes	Disposable centrifugation, depth filtration
Capture chromatography	No	Protein A chromatography
Virus inactivation	Yes	Regular hold bag
Ultrafiltration	Yes	Single-use TFF
Trace impurity removal	Yes	Q membrane adsorbers
Aggregate removal	No	Cation exchange chromatography Hydrophobic intereaction chromatography
Virus filtration	Yes	

shown in Tables 2.1 and 2.3 is striking. The nature of continuous flow unit operations is that the system can be smaller and hence disposable design becomes a viable option. For this reason, continuous chromatography is an enabler for designing a fully disposable downstream processing cascade.

Single-use or disposable multicolumn chromatography fills the main gap in the entire cascade and with that, BioSMB® Technology is an enabler for a fully continuous and fully disposable downstream process.

Such an integrated, fully continuous downstream processing scheme has recently been presented by Merck [12]. The upstream process was based on fed-batch cultivation. The downstream process utilizes two BioSMB® systems: the first system for Protein A chromatography and the second system for cation exchange. Processing an entire batch took approximately 30 h, which was significantly shorter than the traditional batch process. During a single batch, the columns in the Protein A chromatography process were cycled more than 20 times. Longer batch processing times combined with shorter process cycle times could significantly increase the number of column cycles in a batch, thereby promoting disposable bioprocessing.

Continuous manufacturing in combination with a perfusion bioreactor process has also been explored, albeit not in a fully disposable format [5]. Typically, perfusion processes are operated for 20–60 days (160–480 h). Considering the lower titer that comes from perfusion processes, the process cycle times in the chromatography process by nature will be longer and hence, it is realistic to design the process such that the columns reach their maximum lifetime within a single perfusion campaign.

A fully disposable implementation of a multicolumn chromatography technology should also consider the format in which the chromatographic media is provided. Prepacked columns offer significant advantages. In a continuous multicolumn chromatography process, consistency of the column packing is more important than the absolute HETP and asymmetry, since inconsistency in column packing will translate into column-to-column variations in comparing the elution repetitive peaks. It has, however, been demonstrated that multicolumn chromatographic capture processes are quite robust and can handle significant variations in column packing without observing significant effects in performance [13–15]. One of the main advantages of prepacked columns is the ease of use, since it eliminates column packing operations and associated testing.

In this respect, membrane adsorbers also offer an attractive combination with continuous multicolumn chromatography. The main disadvantage of membrane adsorbers for capture chromatography is the relatively low binding capacity. In continuous processes, the impact of binding mainly affects the buffer consumption. The total volume of chromatographic media that is required to run the process is governed by mass transfer kinetics. In this respect, membrane adsorbers are superior to particulate media. The use of membrane adsorbers in combination with BioSMB® Technology for capture processes has been evaluated. These studies confirm the significant gain in specific productivity as well as the impact on buffer consumption [1,16]. The use of membrane adsorbers in combination with a multicolumn chromatography system leads to very short cycle times. This facilitates designing the process in a completely single-use format in a single batch, even in combination with fed batch cultivation processes at moderate expression levels.

2.6 Case Studies

In order to evaluate the impact of continuous bioprocessing and the potential of transforming such process into a fully disposable format, a process design for a 2000 l fed batch bioreactor that produces 4 mg ml^{-1} monoclonal antibody has been considered. With an overall yield of 85%, this would allow a total manufacturing capacity of 136 kg purified drug substance per year in 20 batches (Table 2.4).

Most steps for such process scale are available in disposable format already. The comparison therefore is limited to the two chromatography steps (Protein A and cation exchange). In this comparison, the dynamic binding capacity for the Protein A chromatography media is set at 35 mg ml^{-1} for the batch process. The continuous process was scheduled to run for 12 h on all unit operations. This would result in a total batch processing time of approximately 15 h (assuming approximately 40–45 min average delay time in starting up subsequent unit operations).

A similar process design can be made for a perfusion bioreactor. For a 1000 l bioreactor that has a perfusion rate of 1 bioreactor volume/day and a (steady state) output of 0.85 mg l^{-1}. This compares to an annual manufacturing capacity of approximately 130 kg, assuming six perfusion campaigns per year (30 days each). The results in Table 2.5 are based on the assumption that the downstream processing cascade truly runs fully continuously.

Table 2.4 Key figures for the two chromatography steps in a fed batch cultivation process with a 2000 l bioreactor at 4 mg ml^{-1} expression level.

	Batch	Continuous
Protein A chromatography		
• Cycles per batch	4	15
• Column size	60 cm ID × 20 cm H	14 cm ID × 8 cm H (8 columns)
• Resin volume	57 l	10.2 l (total)
Cation exchange		
• Cycles per batch	4	23
• Column size	40 cm ID × 20 cm H	10 cm ID × 8 cm H (8 columns)
• Resin volume	25 l	4.9 l (total)

Table 2.5 Key figures for the two chromatography steps in a perfusion process with a 1000 l bioreactor at 1.25 mg ml^{-1} expression level.

	Batch	Continuous
Protein A chromatography		
• Cycles per batch	2 per day	8 per day
• Column size	30 cm ID × 20 cm H	10 cm ID × 5.6 cm H (6 columns)
• Resin volume	14 l	2.54 l (total)
Cation exchange		
• Cycles per batch	2 per day	35 per day
• Column size	20 cm ID × 20 cm H	2.5 cm ID × 7 cm H (8 columns)
• Resin volume	6.3 l	315 ml (total)

In both scenarios, the chromatographic media goes through many more cycles in the continuous process than in the batch process. As a result, disposability of the entire fluid path, including columns, becomes an economically viable option much sooner than in the batch process. For the perfusion bioreactor, one should actually consider installing larger columns than shown in Table 2.5 in order to slow the process down and allow for fewer cycles per day. In this way, the process can be designed to meet the maximum lifetime of the columns at the end of the perfusion campaign. If we assume a 30 days perfusion campaign, the Protein A columns would have to be 20% larger and the cation exchange columns would have to be approximately five times larger than shown in Table 2.5 in order to reach 200 cycles during one campaign. Even with this effect taken into account, the continuous process requires significantly less chromatographic media than the batch downstream process.

These two case studies focus only on the impact of continuous processing on the chromatography steps in order to assess the viability of transforming these steps into a disposable process. The impact on other steps is not addressed in detail, but it is clear that the system volume of all other continuous unit operations will also be significantly smaller compared to their batch equivalents.

2.7 Regulatory Aspects

The US FDA has repeatedly confirmed that continuous processes should be a viable option for biopharmaceutical manufacturing (e.g., Ref. [17]). The advantages of continuous processing in terms of process control should also translate into improved product quality control. In spite of the encouraging messages from the authorities, there are a few concerns that need to be taken into account in the development and filing of products manufactured in continuous processes.

First of all, the definition of a lot and/or batch needs to be considered. Regulators have repeatedly stated that the cGMP guidance does not give any restriction that would suggest that the definition of a lot or a batch is not compatible with continuous processing. As a result, any manufacturer can choose to link the definition of a lot or batch to a certain amount of product produced, a certain time frame or to the use of raw materials or consumables. It makes sense to perform a risk analysis for the sizes of the lot and batch as to balance the costs associated with release testing against the chances and the impact of failure and recalls.

Among the most common reasons for batch rejections, one can find contamination, operator error and equipment error [18]. In continuous processing, the systems by nature will be fully automated. This will lower the chance of operator error. Over the past five years, the average number of batch failures decreased by almost 50% [19]. This was mainly attributed to improved process development and the adoption of the principles of Quality by Design and Process Analytical Technologies. These concepts are natural for continuous processing.

The chance of contamination in a continuous process may be lower due to the fact that there will be fewer and shorter hold steps in which the process solution is held stagnant for a certain period. In general, most process solutions are flowing most of the time and hence the chance of a contamination to occur is smaller. This is further supported by the fact that continuous equipment by nature will have a superior segregation of process solutions. This is an automatic consequence of the requirement of continuous flow of the product solution. For chromatography equipment, this is schematically shown in Figure 2.6. This

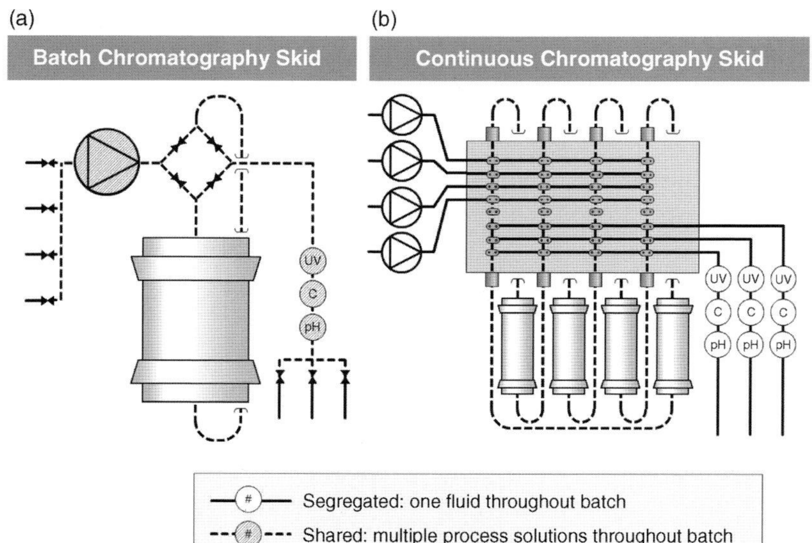

Figure 2.6 Segregation of process solutions in (a) a batch chromatography system and (b) a continuous chromatography system.

Table 2.6 Summary of segregated and shared flow paths in the batch and continuous systems.

Process step	Batch	Continuous
Buffer selection valves	Shared	NA
Pump(s)	Shared	Segregated
Sensors (inlet)	Shared	Segregated
Column bypass valves	Shared	NA
Integrated valve system	NA	Partially shared
Sensors (outlet)	Shared	Segregated
Outlet selection valves	Shared	NA

figure displays a schematic overview of the flow path in a batch chromatography process and in the BioSMB® system. The shared flow paths are shown as dotted lines, whereas all flow paths that are uniquely assigned to a single process solution throughout the entire process cycle are shown as solid lines. The diagrams clearly show how channels and instruments (pumps and sensors) are in contact with all process solutions in the batch process, whereas most channels and all instruments are exclusively in contact with a single process solution in the continuous process. In the continuous system, only the channels to and from the columns – and of course the columns themselves – are in contact with all process solutions, whereas the rest of the entire flow path is dedicated to a single process solution.

The shared and segregated flow paths in the batch and continuous chromatography systems as shown in Figure 2.6 are summarized in Table 2.6.

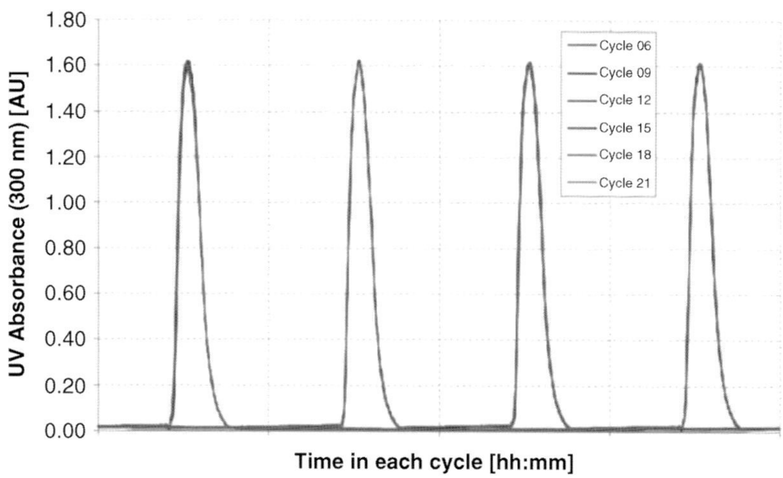

Figure 2.7 Repetitive elution peaks for a four-column chromatography process, showing the elution peaks for six selected cycles overlaid.

Another advantage that continuous processing has to offer is the vast amount of data that is being recorded during the run. In traditional chromatography, the Protein A capture step may only be operated two or three times during a batch. In continuous chromatography, the Protein A capture step can involve hundreds of elution peaks. These repetitive signals provide a very valuable source of information to assess whether or not the system is operating according to its desired (steady) state. An example of such repetitive elution cycles is shown in Figure 2.7 for a four-column chromatography process, displaying the elution peaks of six cycles overlaid.

With a continuous flow of such valuable information, any deviation from the desired (steady) state can be immediately detected. This should favor the risk ranking according to the Failure Mode and Effect Analysis (FMEA) principles.

2.8 Conclusions

The field of biopharmaceutical manufacturing is gradually maturing. As a result, certain manufacturing platforms will gradually evolve into more efficient approaches and as part of this evolution, continuous production is most likely to become a reality in the next decade. Most of the necessary building blocks to implement an integrated continuous biomanufacturing platform are already established and the missing elements are currently being developed. The most important technology to support integrated continuous biomanufacturing is continuous multicolumn chromatography.

One of the key advantages of continuous processing is that the size of most bioprocess systems will be significantly smaller than their batch equivalents. As a result, a disposable format becomes a viable option, even for those steps for which disposable technologies were less attractive in the batch processing platform. Combined with the rapid cycling of media, which is an inherent feature of multicolumn chromatography, the entire fluid path including the columns can be transformed into a viable disposable solution. On the other hand, disposable technologies can mitigate the concerns related to the higher complexity of continuous bioprocessing equipment. The BioSMB® is an example of a technology that can bring this promise.

There is good reason to assume that there will also continue to be batch and hybrid processes. A good example of a viable hybrid process is the combination of a fed batch bioreactor in combination with a (partly) continuous downstream process. The most attractive combination between batch and continuous processing systems depends on an analysis of the risks and benefits of such combination.

From regulatory point of view, there is no objection to continuous processing. Based on a preliminary technical analysis of continuous manufacturing technologies, there seems to be little or no reason to believe that the hurdles will be significantly larger than for batch processes. The same principles of risk-based validation apply and in certain areas the risks associated with continuous biomanufacturing technologies may actually be lower than the batch equivalents.

Many companies in the biopharmaceutical industries have launched lean six sigma initiatives to streamline their operations. The most notable textbook in the field of Lean Six Sigma is "The Toyota Way" [20]. This book, and the principles of lean manufacturing as implemented at the Toyota car company, has been the foundation for the modern Lean Six Sigma philosophies. With this in mind, one would expect that the adoption of continuous flow manufacturing as practiced by modern car manufacturing would be a logical next step in the biopharmaceutical industry.

References

1 Brower, M. (2013) A simple strategy for continuous viral inactivation. Integrated Continuous Biomanufacturing Conference, Castelldefels, Spain, October 2013.

2 Ransohoff, T.C. and Bisschops, M.A.T. (2012) Continuous processing methods for biological products. Patent application WO/2012/078677.

3 Sofer, G. (2003) Virus inactivation in the 1990s – and into the 21st century. Part 4: Culture media, biotechnology products, and vaccines. *BioPharm. Int.*, **16** (1), 50–57.

4 Sofer, G., Lister, D.C., and Boose, J.A. (2003) Virus inactivation in the 1990s – and into the 21st century. Part 6: Inactivation methods grouped by virus. *BioPharm. Int.*, **16** (4), 42–68.

5 Warikoo, V. *et al.* (2012) Integrated continuous production of recombinant therapeutic proteins. *Biotechnol. Bioeng.*, **109**, 3018–3029.

6 Allen, L. (March 2011) Developing purification unit operations for high titre monoclonal antibody processes. IBC Antibody Development and Production Conference, Bellevue, WA.

7 Bisschops, M. and Brower, M. (2013) The impact of continuous multicolumn chromatography on biomanufacturing efficiency. *Pharm. Bioprocess.*, **1** (4), 361–372.

8 Noyes, A., Coffman, J., Godavarti, R., and Bisschops, M. (2010) Development of a protein A SMB step for a mAb with up to 10 g/L titers. Biopharmaceutical Manufacturing and Development Summit, Boston, November.

9 Brower, M. (2011) Working towards an integrated antibody purification process. IBC Biopharmaceutical Manufacturing and Development Conference, San Diego, CA, September 2011.

10 Pieracci, J., Mao, N., Thömmes, J., Pennings, M., Bisschops, M., and Frick, L. (2010) Using simulated moving bed chromatography to enhance hydrophobic interaction chromatography performance. Recovery of Biological Products XIV, Lake Tahoe, August.

11 Jiang, H. (2010) Purification of H5N1 and H1N1 VLP based vaccines. IBC Single-Use Conference, La Jolla, CA, June 15, 2010.

12 Brower, M. (2013) Platform downstream processes in the age of continuous chromatography: a case study. Integrated Continuous Biomanufacturing Conference, Castelldefels, Spain, October 2013.

13 Bisschops, M. and Brower, M. (July 2012) Variations in column packing on the performance of BioSMB® multicolumn chromatography. PREP Conference, Boston.

14 Mihlbachler, K., Fricke, J., Yun, T., Seidel-Morgenstern, A., Schmidt-Traub, H., and Guiochon, G. (2001) Effect of the homogeneity of the column set on the performance of a simulated moving bed unit. I. Theory. *J. Chromatogr. A*, **908**, 49–70.

15 Mihlbachler, K., Jupke, A., Seidel-Morgenstern, A., Schmidt-Traub, H., and Guiochon, G. (2002) Effect of the homogeneity of the column set on the performance of a simulated moving bed unit. II. Experimental study. *J. Chromatogr. A*, **977**, 3–22.

16 Bisschops, M., Schwan, P., and Lobedann, M. (2013) Membrane adsorbers in a multicolumn chromatography configuration as a viable option for capture chromatography. PREP Conference, Boston, July 2013.

17 Chatterjee, S. (2012) FDA perspective on continuous manufacturing. IFPAC Meeting, January 2012.

18 Langer, E. (2008) Biotech facilities average a batch failure every 40.6 weeks. *Bioprocess Int.*, **6** (8), 28–29.

19 Langer, E. (2012) Biomanufacturing shows signs of maturity, PAT adoption. *Pharmaceutical Manufacturing*, June 5, 2012.

20 Liker, J.K. (2004) *The Toyota Way: 14 Management Principles from the World's Greatest Manufacturer*, McGraw-Hill.

3
Impact of Continuous Processing Techniques on Biologics Supply Chains

Aloke Das

3.1
Introduction

3.1.1
The Biologics Industry

The biologics industry has been constantly on the rise. Close to 21% of the total pharmaceutical revenue came from biologic products in 2012. This percentage is expected to rise to 25% by 2018 [1, pp. 3–37]. This growth will be driven by increased development in vaccines and monoclonal antibodies. The monoclonal antibodies market is expected to grow at a compounded annual growth rate (CAGR) of more than 5% to reach a value of USD 58 million in 2016, from a value of USD 44.6 million in 2011 [2]. The monoclonal antibodies market is expected to be driven by the oncology market, which currently accounts for 25% of the total pharmaceutical therapeutics market in 2013 [3]. A significant percentage of all drugs in the US Food and Drug Administration (FDA) pipeline are presently monoclonal antibodies or Mabs. However, the classical monospecific Mabs market is expected to become saturated in the near future, as newer companies enter this industry and biosimilar monoclonal antibodies are developed. Barriers to entry in the Mabs market being low, small-scale biologic manufacturers are flooding the market with more cost-effective means of manufacturing Mabs [4]. As the major blockbuster Mabs in the market are expected to go off patent by 2015–2016, all big biopharma companies would need to look at newer avenues to maintain their profit margin. One such profitable venture that most biopharma companies would be looking at is bispecific antibodies. As bispecific Mabs become more common, they are expected to substitute classical monoclonal antibodies and also drive up the demand for biologic drugs in the near future [5].

Continuous Processing in Pharmaceutical Manufacturing, First Edition. Edited by Ganapathy Subramanian.

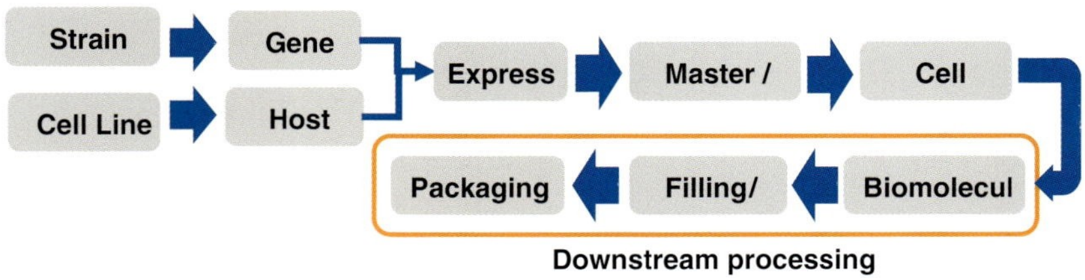

Figure 3.1 General flow chart of a biologic drug manufacturing value chain *Source:* Ref. [6].

3.1.2
The Biologics Value Chain

The biologics value chain is long and complicated as compared to the small-molecule drug manufacturing. Refer to Figure 3.1 for a general overview of the biologic manufacturing value chain.

Each of these steps requires specific time and temperature specifications, due to which the complexities in biologics manufacturing is higher [6]. Due to the complexities involved, the initial costs involved in manufacturing of biologics drugs are generally higher than small-molecule manufacturing. This is also the reason that follow-on biologics or biosimilars are fewer in the market as compared to small-molecule generic drugs [7]. Small-molecule drugs have a specific path of derivation, which can be easily reproduced to give rise to generic drugs. However, in biologics manufacturing, the high amount of complexities and technical challenges make the process of biosimilars less cost efficient. The increased costs in manufacturing are directly reflected in the higher final costs of treatment using biotherapeutics as compared to traditional small-molecule therapies. Moreover, traditionally manufacturing used to happen in batches, which led to a significant time factor in the biologic manufacturing value chain.

Interestingly, biologic manufacturers operate on a significantly higher operating margin as compared to small-molecule manufacturers. Recent studies have shown that the operating margins for biologic products are usually around 32% for branded biologic products as compared to 24% for branded small-molecule drugs. Moreover, follow-on biologics manufacturers operate at margins above 24%, which is equivalent to the operating margins of a traditional blockbuster small-molecule drug [8]. Due to such high operating margins, more and more drug manufacturers have started to move toward biologics as their future revenue generator as compared to their present small-molecule portfolio.

3.1.3
Downstream Purification Costs

One of the key cost factors that manufacturers are looking at to increase their operating margin is the use of more cost-efficient techniques in downstream

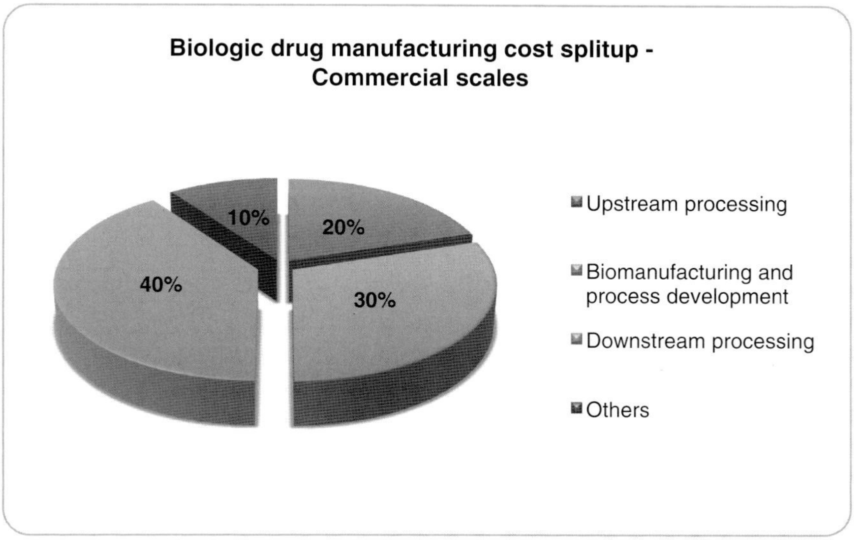

Figure 3.2 Breakup of manufacturing costs in biologic drug manufacturing in commercial scales *Source:* Expert interactions.

purification of biologic drugs. Downstream processing costs account for close to 40% of the manufacturing costs of a biologic drug. This percentage goes up to 60% of the total manufacturing cost in the case of biologics manufacturing at research scales [9]. The downstream stages include the stages of actual purification, lyophilization, and packing of vials. The downstream purification is a very sensitive and time-consuming process, which is directly linked to the high cost of manufacturing of the biologic drug. The downstream process consists of multiple methods such as specialized filters, centrifugation, and chromatography [10]. Recent research has been directed at looking at alternative options in downstream purification to reduce the time and costs involved in the process. Refer to Figures 3.2 and 3.3 for an overview of the manufacturing cost split for biologic drugs.

3.2 Chromatography Techniques Used in Downstream Purification of Biomolecules

There are a variety of chromatography techniques that are used in downstream purification of biomolecules:

- Adsorption chromatography
- Partition chromatography
- Ion-exchange chromatography
- Exclusion chromatography

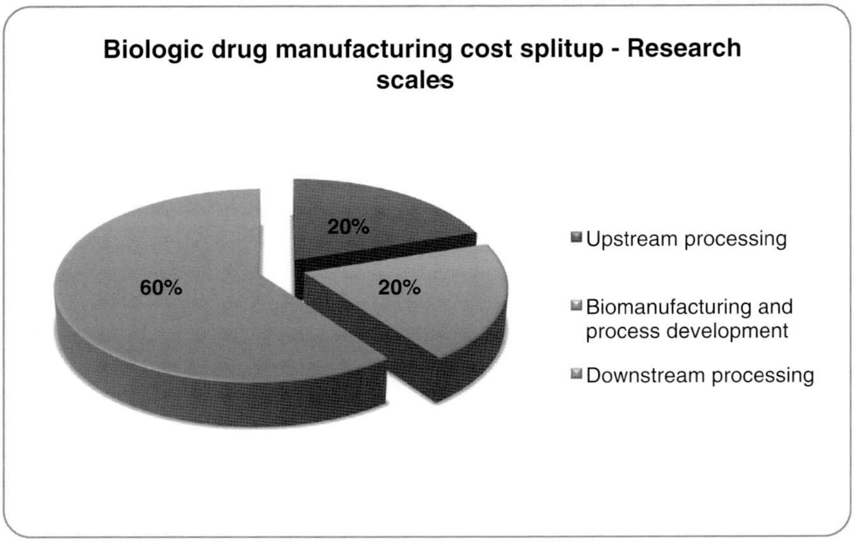

Figure 3.3 Breakup of manufacturing costs in biologic drug manufacturing in research scales *Source:* Expert interactions.

- Affinity chromatography
- Thin-layer chromatography
- Size exclusion chromatography.

The global chromatography market is expected to grow at a CAGR of close to 5% between 2011 and 2017 to reach a value of USD 8.9 billion in 2017 (Refer to Figure 3.4) [11]. The robust market growth is expected to be driven by the significant demand from the biologics industry, which is the major end-use demand for the chromatography industry. These traditional chromatography techniques have limitations in their yield and raw material requirements. Newer advanced techniques in chromatography are being developed, which eliminate these limitations in these traditional techniques.

3.2.1 Need for Continuous Manufacturing in Downstream Purification

With more attention being given by pharma companies to improve efficiency and effectiveness of manufacturing processes, the need to develop continuous manufacturing techniques in downstream processing was felt significantly. Continuous manufacturing techniques have already been adopted in upstream processing, such as the use of disposable bioreactors for cell culture development [10].

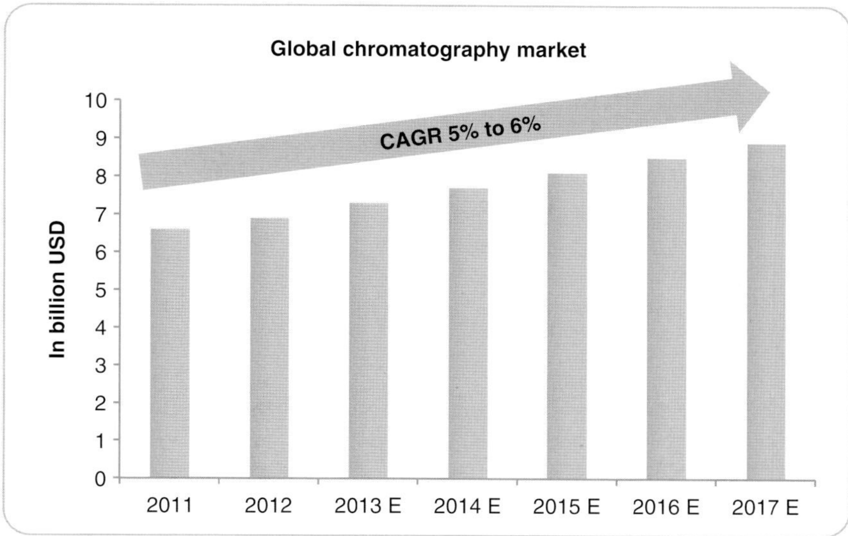

Figure 3.4 Overview of the global chromatography market *Source:* www.prnewswire.co.uk.

Continuous chromatography techniques in downstream processing fall under advanced chromatography techniques. The advanced chromatography market is expected to increase at a CAGR of close to 6% between 2011 and 2017 to reach a value of USD 1.4 billion (refer to Figure 3.5) [11].

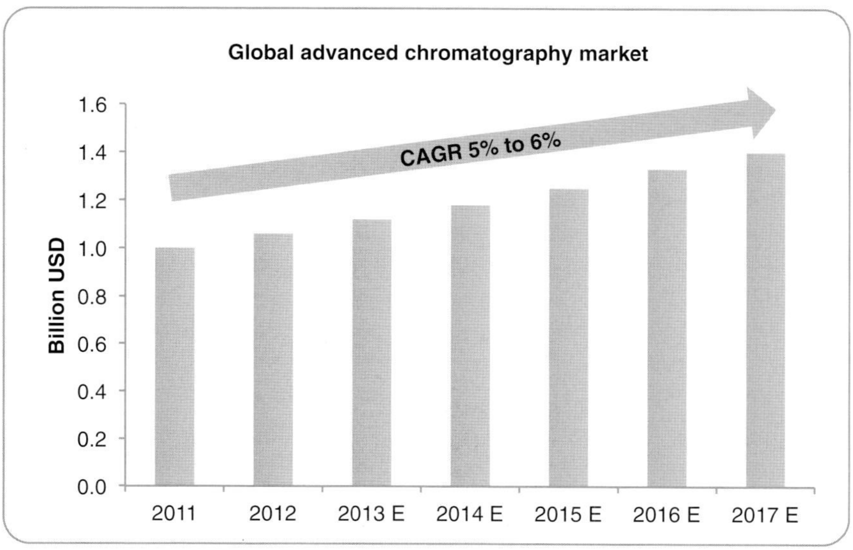

Figure 3.5 Overview of the global advanced chromatography market *Source:* www.prnewswire.co.uk.

New advanced chromatography techniques such as the BioSC process of Novasep and the multicolumn countercurrent solvent gradient purification chromatography system (MCSGP) process of Chromacon AG have shown significantly better results than the traditional batch-based downstream processing methods [10].

There are various distinct advantages that can be observed by continuous chromatography techniques over traditional batch processing methods:

- Better utilization of the chromatography resins as compared to batch processing.
- Lesser requirement of raw materials and consumable.
- Reduced time of manufacturing of biologic product.
- Higher yield of final product and less loss due to wastage.
- Less space requirements with respect to facilities and equipment required.
- Flexibility in manufacturing: New ingredients can be added to the flow at specific points, and components can be swapped in and out to create different drugs.
- Higher cost savings between 15 and 50% as compared to batch processing of biologics [12].
- Continuous monitoring and Quality assurance testing of biologic products throughout the manufacturing of the biologic [13, p. 52].

This article specifically discusses the MCSGP process and its advantage over batch processing in biologics supply chains.

3.2.2
The Multicolumn Countercurrent Solvent Gradient Purification Chromatography System

The multicolumn countercurrent solvent gradient purification system or MCSGP consists of twin chromatographic columns arranged in a specific arrangement such that the continuous feed gets separated and purified into several fractions. The key principle is the recycling of product-containing side fractions inside a contained process achieving significant improvements in yield purity and throughput. The MCSGP efficiently purifies complex mixtures containing early and late eluting impurities that overlap with the target product [14,15]. In batch chromatography, the overlapping sections in the chromatogram are usually lost, leading to a high product loss. The MCSGP chromatography process utilizes ion-exchange chromatography and has been bracketed under advanced chromatography. The MCSGP process has recently been developed and presently Chromacon AG holds the patent for a technology called Contichrom©, which utilizes MCSGP system as one of its core processes [9].

The technology has been recently developed in response to the complexities with respect to biologic product purification, which was hindering most biopharma manufacturers throughout the years. The process utilizes significantly less amount of raw materials and consumables as compared to traditional batch chromatography processes [16]. To understand the impact of MCSGP on the downstream costs of a biologic manufacturer, we tried to look at an example of a biologic molecule, more specifically, a bispecific monoclonal antibody.

3.3 Next-Generation Biologic Products – Bispecific Monoclonal Antibodies

Bispecific monoclonal antibodies or BsMabs are second-generation biologic products and are an upgraded version of normal monoclonal antibodies due to their structure and functionality. Bispecific antibodies are artificial proteins composed of conjugated chains of two different monoclonal antibodies that bind to two different types of antigens or two different epitopes of one antigen target. The manufacturing process of bispecific antibodies is highly complicated, as the two different monospecific antibody chains produced by mammalian cell culture have to dimerize in an effective manner into a bispecific antibody [17, pp. 9785–9792].

The advantage of bispecific antibodies over normal monoclonal antibodies is their ability to attach to two separate antigens in the Fab sections, which gives them better effectiveness and efficiency as compared to normal monoclonal antibodies. Bispecific antibodies are currently being used in cancer immunotherapy, where they are engineered to bind simultaneously to a cytotoxic cell and a target tumor cell, for a more effective treatment.

First-generation bispecific antibodies called trifunctional antibodies have already impacted the drug research market. These antibodies consist of two heavy and two light chains, and can bind two separate antigens through their Fab segments, while the Fc segment makes up for the third binding site [18, pp. 129–136].

Bispecific Mabs are the future of the biologics industry. In the near future, bispecific Mabs are expected to spearhead the biologics market growth. With some of the major biopharmaceutical companies such as Amgen, Fresenius Biotech and so on already being out on the market with new advanced bispecific Mabs, the future biologics market is expected to see a spike in this segment, as more companies realize the potential of this technology.

3.3.1 Major Biopharma Companies and Their Interest in Bispecific Mabs

Major biopharma companies have already started investing on R&D in bispecific antibodies. One such development can be seen in the recent takeover of Micromet by Amgen in January 2012, for a value of USD 1.6 billion [19]. Refer to Table 3.1 for a list of major biopharma companies and their bispecific mabs portfolio.

Table 3.1 Major biopharma companies and their BsMabs portfolio.

Company	Bispecific Mab technology investments
Macrogenics	DART (dual-affinity retargeting) platform [20]
F-star	Modular antibody technology [21]
Amgen/Micromet	BITE (Bispecific T-cell engager) technology [19]
Fresenius Biotech/TRION Pharma	Catumaxomab [22]
Domantis/GSK	Dual targeting domain antibodies (dAbs) [23]

Source: References [19–23].

Some other companies active in the field of bispecific monoclonal antibodies research and development are Roche, Chugai, Novartis, Sanofi, Merrimack, and Genmab.

3.3.2
Challenges in Purification of Bispecific Monoclonal Antibodies

The classic way of purifying BsMabs was by standard batch chromatography processes. Historically, bispecific antibody development has been hampered by the manufacturing challenges posed by the occurrence of homodimeric and heterodimeric isoforms that were difficult to separate resulting in low product yields [9]. Some of the major issues that bispecific antibody manufacturing pose, as compared to monoclonal antibodies are given in Table 3.2.

One of the major hurdles faced by bispecific antibody manufacturers is the stage of downstream processing during the process of manufacturing. During the process of manufacturing, bispecific antibodies are expressed in mammalian cell cultures along with a high amount of impurities. Impurities include monospecific isoforms of the respective bispecific antibodies, proteins, and so on. High purity and high yield of bispecific antibodies is difficult to obtain with traditional batch chromatography methods. The yield of ultrapure (above 90% purity) bispecific antibodies through batch chromatography was as low as 50%, as quoted by experts in the industry [9].

Table 3.2 Challenges in biologic drug manufacturing and their impacts.

Challenges	Impact
Manufacturing complexities and raw material availability	High
Product stability and quality concerns	High
Downstream purification concerns	High
Technology issues	Medium

Source: Reference [24].

3.4 Improving the Downstream Processing of Bispecific Mabs by Introduction of MCSGP in the Value Chain

As mentioned earlier, the use of batch chromatography processes leads to significantly high inefficiencies in the purification of bispecific Mabs. Using the MCSGP process, a high yield can be obtained due to the systemic recycling and polishing of product-related impurities. The MCSGP process impacts the polishing stages of biologic product purification and selectively enriches any impurity in the process, thus enabling better downstream processing of biologic products.

3.4.1 Advantages of Utilizing MCSGP Process in Bispecific Mabs Purification as Compared to Batch Chromatography

The MCSGP system has a distinct impact on the biologic drug manufacturing process as compared to batch chromatography. Some of the distinct impacts are in the volumes of drug processing, savings on consumable usage, increased yield of final product and increased purity. A list of the advantages and their impacts on the biologic manufacturing value chain is given in Table 3.3.

Table 3.3 Advantages of MCSGP in bispecific Mabs purification as compared to batch chromatography.

Advantages	Impact on the product value chain
Large volume processing of BsMabs	Low Medium High
Savings on an average 30% of Capital expenditure	Low Medium High
Savings on an average 50% of Operational expenses	Low Medium High
Increases purity and yield on average by 50%	Low Medium High
Increases on average throughput 10-fold	Low Medium High
Reduces process development time by up to 50%	Low Medium High
Reduction of footprints of units and utilities in the manufacturing process by 70%	Low Medium High
Buffer consumption reduction by 75%	Low Medium High
Low switching costs	Low Medium High

Source: References [9,10,13] and [24, p. 52]

The above estimates have been based on a comparison between batch chromatography and MCSGP process, for batches of bispecific monoclonal antibodies. It should be noted that Chromacon AG has developed an all in one system, Contichrom©, which utilizes multiple techniques in impurity capturing and polishing, and which has shown a distinctive advantage on a company's net present value of a biologic product [10].

3.4.2 Impact of MCSGP System on Biologic Supply Chains

The introduction of the MCSGP process as part of a system, such as Contichrom©, in a supply chain impacts a prime cost area for biologic manufacturers. A 70% less usage of consumable by conversion of batch to MCSGP purification automatically leads to significant reduction in cyclical supply of raw materials and subsequent cost savings [24]. Consequently, it impacts the lead time of the drugs to reach the hospitals. Refer to Figure 3.6 for an overview of the impact of MCSGP on the supply chain of a biopharma manufacturer.

It was observed that a 70% reduction in the usage of consumables for downstream processing led to a 50% reduction in lead time for biologic manufacturers [9]. The system is expected to show similar results for bispecific Mabs, which are going to be launched into the market in the near future. The introduction of the MCSGP technique in the downstream processing supply chain of bispecific Mabs would lead to significant cost savings for any contract biologic manufacturer, service provider for biologics purification, or big biopharma company doing in-house manufacturing.

3.4.3 Impact on Patent Approval Structure of Biologic Drugs

One of the main advantages of introducing the MCSGP chromatography system in biologic drug manufacturing is that a drug manufacturer will not have to modify its patent application process for that drug.

3.4.3.1 For a Manufacturer Who Already has a Biologic Drug in the Market

The manufacturer does not have to reapply an existing patent on a biologic drug due to the introduction of MCSGP in the process flow chart. This saves a large amount of time and revenue that would have been lost, if a manufacturer had to go through the patent reapplication process for its existing drug. This also implies that a manufacturer can better cater to the demand of the drug to the market due to improvement in the manufacturing process and better and faster supplies [13, p. 52].

3.4.3.2 For a Manufacturer Who is Developing a Biologic Drug

The MCSGP system not only optimizes the downstream process for a current manufacturer, but also impacts the manufacturing of a drug presently in its clinical stages. The MCSGP process, if used in small scales for purification of any drug in clinical stages, can highly impact biologic drug manufacturers, who traditionally

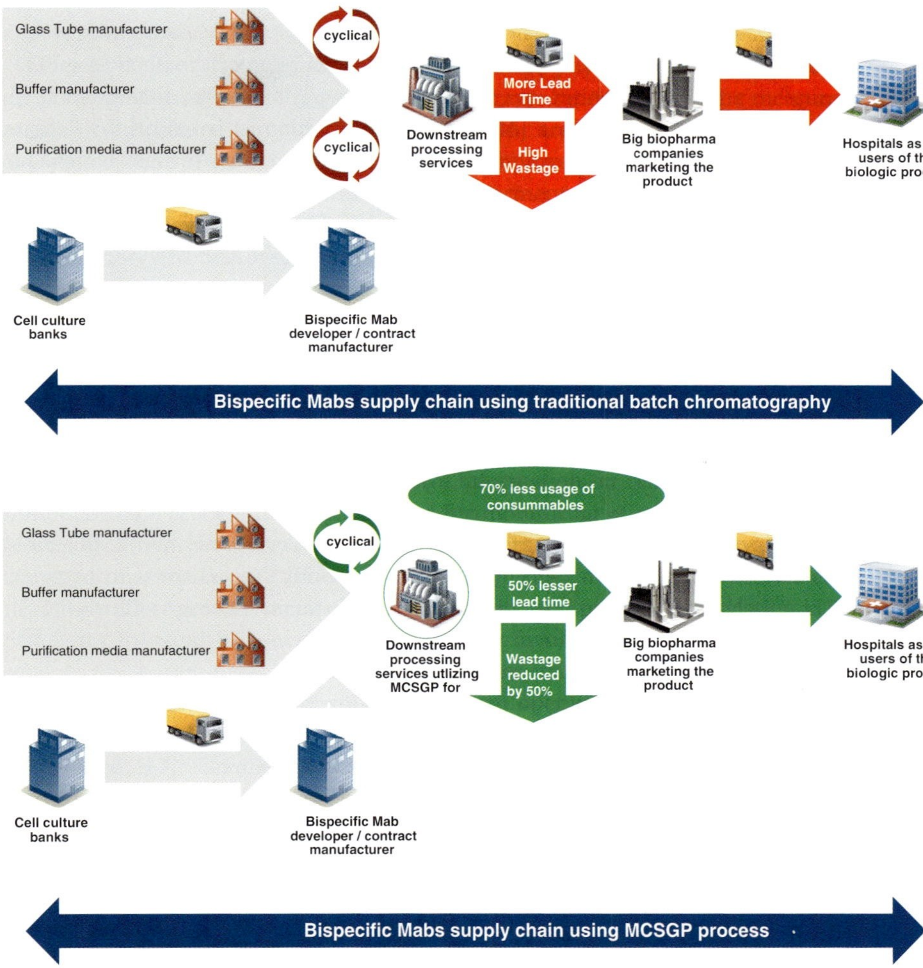

Figure 3.6 General overview of the impact of MCSGP on biologics supply chains *Source:* Beroe Consulting India Pvt. Ltd.

invest close to 15 to 20% of their revenue in R&D of their drugs [1, pp. 3–37]. The drug manufacturer does not have to modify its patent application process due to the introduction of the MCSGP system in its supply chain.

3.4.4
Impact on Big Biopharma Companies

Big biopharma companies such as Amgen, Biogen IDEC, and so on have already shown interest in bispecific monoclonal antibodies as the next big thing in the biologics market. The revenue growth trends of Catumaxomab in the last 2 years have been a major eye-opener for big biopharma companies as they realize the potential of bispecific Mabs in the near future. The impact can be seen in the recent takeover of Micromet by Amgen who is majorly looking into the bispecific Mabs industry [19].

With the introduction of bispecific mabs in the market, big biopharma companies would move toward advanced chromatography technologies, such as MCSGP, to bolster their production of these bispecific Mabs. With the success of MCSGP in the purification of bispecific Mabs in trial stages, biopharma companies would definitely be moving toward MCSGP in the future to support their downstream processing strategies.

3.4.5 Impact on the Chromatography Market

As major pharmaceutical companies are starting to direct their R&D toward bispecific Mabs, the demand for multicolumn countercurrent gradient chromatography is going to increase in the future. Companies offering contract purification and chromatography services are expected to adopt the MCSGP system more readily as compared to batch chromatography in the future. The multicolumn countercurrent solvent gradient purification chromatography market presently holds close to 15% of the overall chromatography market, as quoted by experts [9]. This market share is expected to increase in the future as the demand for MCSGP in the biologics market increases.

3.4.6 Limitations of the MCSGP System

In spite of the MCSGP system having distinct advantages, there are certain limitations to the system too, which need to be considered by a biologic manufacturer while implementing the system in their supply chains. Some of the limitations are as follows:

- High complexities in manufacturing of the system leading to delays in the actual launch of the product in the market. Commercial manufacturing of the system commenced only in late 2011, in spite of the first prototype being developed in 2005 [9].
- Requirement of technical personnel for setting up of the system at the manufacturing facilities.
- Greater time to market.
- Lack of easy availability of the system due to current patent restrictions.

3.5 Conclusion

As the Mabs market gets more saturated and fragmented with multiple competitors and manufacturers, big biopharmaceutical manufacturers would move into innovative biologic drugs such as bispecific Mabs, which have a higher effectiveness and require lower dosage requirements as compared to normal Mabs. With the significant impacts shown by bispecific monoclonal antibodies in the treatment of cancer, bispecific monoclonal antibodies are expected to bring a revolution in the oncology market in the near future. As the demand for innovative antibodies increases, so will the demand for continuous processing used in biologic manufacturing. Traditional purification techniques have shown limitations in their usage in bispecific monoclonal antibody purification. As companies venture into the next-generation biologics market, they would require the usage of more advanced continuous chromatography technologies, such as the multicolumn solvent gradient chromatography process. Demand for continuous processing systems, such as the Contichrom© of Chromacon AG, would be expected to be on the rise in the near future, as more and more biologic manufacturers realize the utility of such systems in their supply chains. With better contract structures being developed in the downstream biologics industry, procurement models are expected to undergo alterations and generate more worth to biologics clients. As lesser known contract manufacturers launch bispecific Mabs in the market using optimized supply chains and process flows, big biopharma companies are bound to adapt and adopt with the changing manufacturing environments in the near future.

3.6 Further Research

This chapter looks into the advantages of continuous processing in a specific area of the biologics industry. The chapter describes the advantages that continuous processing techniques have, such as the multicolumn solvent gradient chromatography, on value chains of next-generation biologics, such as bispecific monoclonal antibodies.

However, the actual impact on a company's bottom line due to the adaptation of continuous processing in bispecific monoclonal antibody value chains is yet to be analyzed. We have a fairly good idea of the expected advantages of the process on a company's turnover. However, we need to look into accurate figures of net present value and return on investments for companies who are already manufacturing bispecific monoclonal antibodies and have adopted MCSGP systems in their value chains.

The other possible research avenues could be to look into the other continuous processing techniques such as the BioSC system of Novasep and their effectiveness in the purification of bispecific monoclonal antibodies. Extensive research has already been conducted to understand the impacts on the supply chains of monoclonal antibody manufacturers due to the introduction of continuous processing techniques in biologic drug manufacturing, but research specific to next-generation bispecific and trispecific Mabs is still required.

Another avenue for research could be to look into existing bispecific Mabs in the market to understand the impact of introducing continuous processing techniques on the manufacturer's future bottom lines. Bispecific Mabs such as Catumaxomab of Fresenius Biotech could give us an insight into the impacts of continuous processing on the company's revenues in the near future [25].

Acknowledgments

I would like to convey my heartfelt gratitude to Dr. Guido Stroehlein, CEO Chromacon AG, and Ms. Patricia Van Arnum, Executive Editor at Pharmaceutical Technology, for their valuable suggestions and key inputs in this chapter. Their observations on the benefits of continuous processing in biologic drug manufacturing were instrumental to the completion of this chapter.

Abbreviations and Symbols

CAGR	Compounded annual growth rate
FDA	Food and Drug Administration
MCSGP	Multicolumn countercurrent solvent gradient purification
BsMabs	Bispecific monoclonal antibodies
EU	European Union
USA	United States of America
SFDA	State Food and Drug Administration
CDSCO	Central Drugs Standard Control Organization
TRIPS	Trade Related Aspects of Intellectual Property Rights
ANVISA	Agência Nacional de Vigilância Sanitária

3.A
Appendix/Additional Information

Table 3.A Patent Details of Top Mabs in the Market

Brand	Company	Global annual sales (billion USD)		Patent approved date	Patent expiry date	CAGR (2009–2016)
		2009	2016 E			
Humira	Abbott/ Eisai	5.6	10.1	December 21, 2002	December 31, 2016	9%
Avastin	Roche	5.7	8.9	February 26, 2004	April 25, 2017	6–7%
Rituxan	Roche/ Biogen	5.6	6.8	December 26, 1997	April 2015	3%
Herceptin	Roche	4.9	6.2	September 25, 1998	April 29, 2015	3–3.5%

Source: Beroe Consulting India Pvt. Ltd.

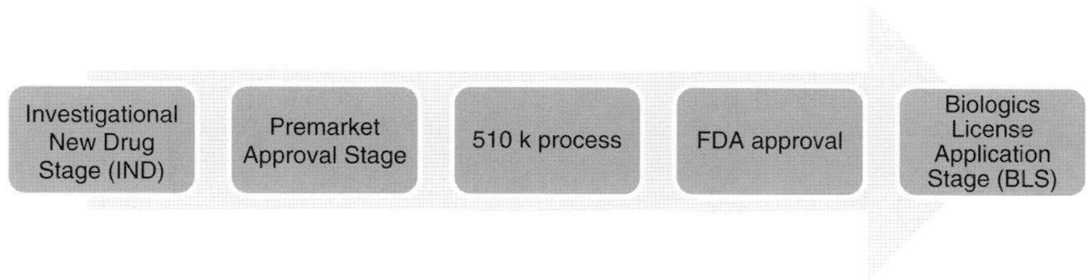

Figure A.1 Regulatory pathway for biologic drug applications *Source:* Beroe Consulting India Pvt. Ltd.

The table shows some of the top monoclonal antibodies in the market presently and their patent details. With an impending patent cliff in the area of monoclonal antibodies, big biopharma companies will be encouraged to move into advanced research into bispecific monoclonal antibodies to sustain their revenues.

3.A.1 Regulatory Structure for Bispecific Monoclonal Antibodies

The BsMabs industry is governed by the same regulatory structure as other biologic products. The approval process for biologic products, such as BsMabs, is a long drawn process and happens primarily in five stages [26]. Refer to Figure A.1 for an overview on the regulatory pathway of biologic drug applications.

3.A.1.1 Regulatory Compliance Comparison between US, EU, and Emerging Economies

USA [26]
Present Regulatory Effectiveness: *High*
Extremely strict regulations. BsMabs have to go through all trial stages, similar to Normal Mabs before being approved by the FDA.
Future Regulatory Effectiveness: Medium
Regulations would get more liberal with time as pharmaceutical companies start manufacturing BsMabs at a more massive scale.

European Union
Present Regulatory Effectiveness: Medium
Strict regulations. However, the regulatory framework is comparatively less strong than the American regulations. The governing body for Biologic drugs in the EU is the EMA.
Future Regulatory Effectiveness: Medium
The regulations in Europe are expected to be less stringent in the future. EMA has shown more tolerance in acceptance of Biologic drugs as compared to FDA.

China

Present Regulatory Effectiveness: Low
Chinese regulatory agencies such as the SFDA are extremely liberal and counterfeiting of drugs remains one of the major issues in China. BsMabs research is still in nascent stages of developments in China due to high quality specifications of the product.
Future Regulatory Effectiveness: Medium–Low
China would have more difficulty in reforming the regulatory system due to the sheer size of the country's economy and extreme inequality between cities and rural areas. Therefore, regulatory reforms would be slower.

India

Present Regulatory Effectiveness: Medium–Low
Liberal regulations. Bispecific Monoclonal Antibodies and other Mabs can be easily introduced into the market. The governing authority for Biologic drugs in India is the Central Drugs Standard Control Organization or CDSCO.
Future Regulatory Effectiveness: Medium
With the development and growth in economy in India, regulations are bound to get stricter and the Mabs markets would get more organized and controlled.

Brazil

Present Regulatory Effectiveness: Medium–Low
Liberal regulatory environment. Brazil has already been facing issues due to their repeated violations of the TRIPS agreement and the government's support to generic manufacturers. Big pharma manufacturers are hesitant to introduce a new product such as BsMabs in the Brazilian pharma market. The governing authority for Biologic drugs in Brazil is the Anvisa.
Future Regulatory Effectiveness: Medium
Brazil has already started implementing reforms in the pharmaceutical sector and strengthening its regulatory mechanism for new drugs. The regulatory situation in the country is expected to improve in the future.

References

1 Evaluate Ltd (2013) *World Preview 2013, Outlook to 2018 Returning to Growth* (Report), Evaluate Ltd, London, pp. 3–37.
2 Bosklopper, E. (2013) Antibody Drugs: Technologies and Global Markets, http://www.bccresearch.com/market-research/biotechnology/antibody-drugs-technologies-markets-bio016h.html (accessed December 25, 2013).
3 Rnrmarketresearch.com (2013) Biosimilars Market Product [Recombinant Non-Glycosylated Proteins (Insulin, Filgrastim, Somatropin), Glycosylated (Monoclonal Antibodies, Erythropoietin), Peptides (Glucagon, Calcitonin)] & Application

(Oncology, Blood Disorders) – Global Forecast to 2018 – RnR Market Research, http://www.rnrmarketresearch.com/biosimilars-market-product-recombinant-non-glycosylated-proteins-insulin-filgrastim-somatropin-glycosylated-monoclonal-antibodies-erythropoietin-peptides-glucagon-calcitonin-applicatio-market-report.html (accessed December 25, 2013).

4 Mintz, C. (2011) Monoclonal Antibodies: The Next Generation – Life Science Leader, http://www.lifescienceleader.com/magazine/past-issues3/item/3451-monoclonal-antibodies-the-next-generation?list=n (accessed December 25, 2013).

5 IMAP (2011) Pharmaceuticals & Biotech Industry Global Report: 2011. IMAP Healthcare Report, pp. 3–41.

6 Ho, K. (2011) Manufacturing process of biologics. International Conference on Harmonisation of Technical Requirements for Registration of Pharmaceuticals for Human Use, http://www.ema.europa.eu/docs/en_GB/document_library/Presentation/2011/06/WC500107832.pdf (accessed December 25, 2013).

7 Datamonitor (2011) Pharmaceutical Key Trends 2011: Biosimilar Market Overview. Datamonitor report, p. 14. www.datamonitor.com.

8 Yang, J. (2011) Pathway to follow-on biologics. *A. Hastings Sci. Technol. L.J.*, **3**, 217.

9 Ströhlein, G. (2012) Interview on continuous chromatography techniques in the biologics industry, Interviewed by Beroe Consulting India Pvt. Ltd [radio] Beroe, Consulting India Pvt. Ltd, Chennai, India, November 5, 2012.

10 Takizawa, B. (2011) Evaluation of the financial impact of continuous chromatography in the production of biologics, Massachusetts Institute of Technology.

11 Prnewswire (2013) Chromatography market is expected to reach USD 8.9 billion. http://www.prnewswire.co.uk/news-releases/chromatography-market-is-expected-to-reach-usd-89-billion-globally-in-2017-transparency-market-research-165106566.html (accessed December 25, 2013).

12 Das, A. (2012) Continuous flow manufacturing: implications on downstream biologics processing. http://www.contractpharma.com/issues/2012-09/view_features/continuous-flow-manufacturing/ (Accessed December 25, 2013).

13 Pellek, A. and Van Arnum, P. (2008) Continuous processing: moving with or against the manufacturing flow. *Pharm. Technol.*, **9** (32), 52.

14 Bavand, M. and Ströhlein, G. (2013) Dr. Michael Bavand and Dr. Guido Ströhlein: Is Continuous Chromatography the Answer? - ChromaTALK. http://www.chromatalk.com/2012/10/25/dr-michael-bavand-and-dr-guido-strohlein-is-continuous-chromatography-the-answer/ (accessed December 25, 2013).

15 Krättli, M., Müller-Späth, T., Ulmer, N., Ströhlein, G., and Morbidelli, M. (2013) Separation of lanthanides by continuous chromatography. *Ind. Eng. Chem. Res.*, **52** (26), 8880–8886.

16 Grossmann, C., Ströhlein, G., Morari, M., and Morbidelli, M. (2010) Optimizing model predictive control of the chromatographic multi-column solvent gradient purification (MCSGP) process. *J. Process Control*, **20** (5), 618–629.

17 Debaene, F., Wagner-Rousset, E., Colas, O., Ayoub, D., Corvaia, N., Van Dorsselaer, A., Beck, A., and Cianferani, S. (2013) Time resolved native ion-mobility mass spectrometry to monitor dynamics of IgG4 Fab arm exchange and “Bispecific” monoclonal antibody formation. *Anal. Chem.*, **85** (20), 9785–9792.

18 Linke, R., Klein, A., and Seimetz, D. (2010) Catumaxomab: clinical development and future directions. *mAbs*, **2** (2), 129–136.

19 Amgen Inc. (2013) Acquisition includes a novel cancer treatment in clinical trials for hematologic malignancies: Micromet's Proprietary BiTE® Platform has potential to improve treatment in multiple tumor types. Press release, January 26, 2012.

20 Macrogenics (2013) DART™ Platform. http://www.macrogenics.com/Platforms-DART.html (accessed December 26, 2013).

21 F-Star (2013) Modular antibody technology. http://www.f-star.com/technology-modular-antibody.php (accessed December 26, 2013).

22 Lifescience (2009) TRION Pharma: trifunctional antibody catumaxomab kills cancer stem cells. http://www.lifescience-online.com/TRION_Pharma__Trifunctional_Antibody_Catumaxomab_K,16211.html?portalPage=Lifescience%20Today.News (accessed December 25, 2013).

23 Tomlonson, I. and Mather, S. (2013) Building an early stage drug candidate pipeline with human Domain Antibodies (dAbs). Scientific Publications and Presentations. www.bioscan.com.

24 Das, A. (2013) *Implementation of Advanced Chromatography Techniques to Mitigate Purification Concerns in Bispecific Monoclonal Antibody Manufacturing*, ChromaCon AG, Zuerich, Switzerland, pp. 3–16.

25 Chelius, D., Ruf, P., Gruber, P., Ploscher, M., Liedtke, R., Gansberger, E., Hess, J., Wasiliu, M., and Lindhofer, H. (2010) Structural and functional characterization of the trifunctional antibody catumaxomab. *mAbs*, **2** (3), 309–319.

26 Schacht, W. and Thomas, J. (2012) Follow-On Biologics: The Law and Intellectual Property Issues. Congressional Research Service, pp. 4–20.

4
Integrating Continuous and Single-Use Methods to Establish a New Downstream Processing Platform for Monoclonal Antibodies

Christopher Gillespie, Mikhail Kozlov, Michael Phillips, Ajish Potty, Romas Skudas, Matthew Stone, Alex Xenopoulos, Alison Dupont, Jad Jaber, and William Cataldo

4.1
Introduction

Monoclonal antibodies (mAbs) are a class of proteins belonging to the immunoglobulin family that function by stimulating the body's immune system to identify and destroy compromised cells, malignant proteins, or pathogens, such as bacteria or viruses. Since the first successful Food and Drug Administration (FDA) approval of a mAb for therapeutic use in 1986 [1,2], the biotechnology industry has directed significant effort to their development and production. This advent of mAb therapies has ushered in a new field of biomedical research targeted at conquering chronic diseases such as cancer. In 2011, sales of mAbs constituted about 36% of all biotherapeutics and the market is projected to exhibit significant future increase [3].

As active pharmaceutical molecules, mAbs are produced on scales that dwarf any other biotherapeutic molecule, with production levels reaching as high as 100 kg year^{-1} [4]. MAbs, consequently, are one of the most expensive biologics to produce. Recognizing the influences of a competitive landscape of biosimilars, the lack of blockbuster molecules, and upcoming patent expirations, the need for process efficiency improvements and innovative technologies is paramount.

Recombinant mAbs are produced by mammalian cells grown in suspension where the cells are genetically engineered to secrete the protein product. The mAb is then harvested and purified to remove impurities using a cascade of separation technologies to achieve the high degree of product purity required by the various regulatory agencies. Examples of impurities include host cell proteins (HCPs), nucleic acids, endotoxins, viruses, and product-related impurities (e.g., aggregates or fragments). MAbs are a unique protein modality in that they share a commonality through the Fc-region that enabled the development of a template or platform downstream processes centered around protein A chromatography. As early as 2000 the primary focus of development was on the upstream production (i.e., cellular production) of mAbs as product concentrations were

Continuous Processing in Pharmaceutical Manufacturing, First Edition. Edited by Ganapathy Subramanian.

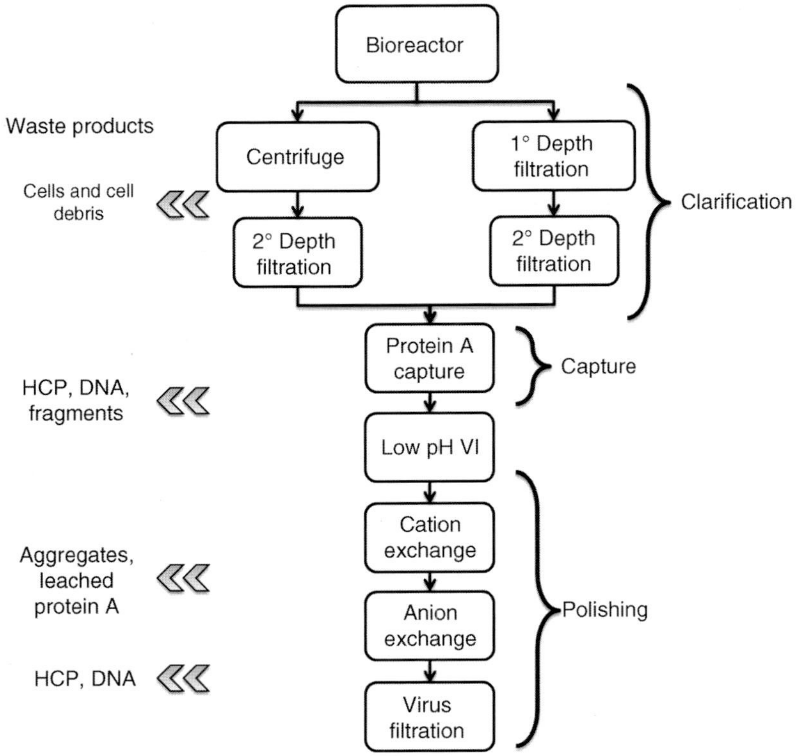

Figure 4.1 Basic mAb production platform process flow diagram. Three basic DSP steps are expected, clarification, capture, and polishing, with the number and identity of the unit operations varying based on process requirements. Within the DSP the types of impurities removed by each step are identified.

rarely exceeding $0.5\,g\,l^{-1}$. Today, however, mAb product titers are routinely capable of reaching $>1\,g\,l^{-1}$, where the so-called bottleneck of the process has shifted to the downstream purification process (DSP) [5].

Regardless of the industry, it is inevitable that economic pressures will be expected to drive innovation. For mAbs, one of the first rounds of innovation came in the form of templated downstream processes centered on the protein A chromatography capture step. A basic mAb production and purification process is shown in Figure 4.1. The template process can be broken down into five areas (of which four are shown in Figure 4.1):

1) Upstream
2) Clarification
3) Capture
4) Polishing
5) Formulation.

Technology selection for each of the process areas is related to the requirements of the product. For example, mAbs require *N*-glycosylation, limiting the types of production environments to mammalian cell lines. Each subsequent downstream step is chosen and optimized based on the final product requirements for purity and yield as well as the identity and amount of the impurities (see Figure 4.1). Typical DSP steps include centrifugation, filtration, protein A chromatography, and a series of ion-exchange chromatography steps, where variations on this template are inevitable. Most of the chromatography steps are performed in bind and elute mode, a method that is inherently discontinuous. Operation of the chromatography steps in bind and elute mode also presents scaling constraints dictated by the product capacity of the media. The exception is the anion exchange chromatography step that is typically operated in a flow-through mode (aka negative chromatography) where only the impurities are expected to bind to the solid phase. Thus, loading is dictated by the impurity capacity.

In spite of the ubiquity of protein A templated purification processes, there are several shortcomings that have been identified in the journal and patent literature and are being addressed. Examples include increasing resin capacity and lifetime, maximizing facility flexibility and productivity, and reducing water consumption and waste, to name a few. Regardless of the step identity or order, process development is regularly focused on optimization of each unit operation independently, where the combined final process is expected to be robust and reliable. These expectations often lead to other inefficiencies such as redundant filtration and poor resin capacity utilization. Because of the high cost of production and stringent regulatory environments, there is also a high aversion to risk. Hence, this has led to the development of quality by design (QbD) methods.

The biopharmaceutical field is frequently identified as conservative [6], due to its highly regulated nature. As with the small molecule pharmaceutical industry, the relationship between the number of failed macromolecules to the number of successful commercial macromolecules is quite large and continues to grow. The result is that innovation is seen as a necessity while adoption of new technologies is sluggish. The focus within the industry tends toward improving efficiency throughout the process with changes occurring incrementally. This evolutionary process has proven successful for the upstream production of mAbs and somewhat for the downstream process as well. Improvements in reactor design, media, and cell line development have diverted the bottleneck to the downstream process steps where significant changes to the purification paradigm has not been able to keep up.

While in the past the production bottleneck was localized to protein expression and upstream processing, it now shifts toward downstream processing. Rising economic pressure as well as increased cell culture titers require improved manufacturing processes, enhanced throughput, and optimized purification yield [7,8]. Within the mAb downstream paradigm, the majority of the bottleneck issues are considered to be within the chromatography steps [5,9]. There are several options to address these criteria including increasing chromatography column capacity, improving process efficiency, as well as increasing column dimensions. Alternatively, chromatographic columns can be operated in a continuous manner, potentially enabling time and cost savings.

The biopharma industry has trended slowly toward technologies that reduce the burden placed on the DSP process. The mAb sector has been especially focused on leveraging new technologies. A clear enabling technology for mAb production is the protein A chromatography capture step due to solution condition robustness (i.e., loading clarified cell culture fluids directly), the bulk purification factors achieved, as well as more recent additions of caustic stable ligands. Although protein A chromatography is robust, it is also quite expensive. As a result, replacing this step has been investigated for some time. Only at manufacturing levels is the resin expected to be used to its full lifetime (typically > 100 cycles) where the cost impact on the product produced would be minimized. During earlier stages of development (i.e., clinical), the protein A resin is expected to be used significantly less often and discarded if the molecule does not move forward. Additionally, companies are finding other areas where improvements are needed, such as with facility limitations and overhead costs.

Following the evolutionary paradigm of the typical biopharmaceutical manufacturer, we describe an approach to transition from the per-unit operation approach to development and manufacturing to more integrated and continuous methods. We seek to provide a strategic approach to developing an integrated and continuous process through the selection of necessary technologies to the methods of process development. In contrast to the canonical methods used during process development, we aim to stress the need to design the process taking a holistic view to seek out a global optimum for the process rather than a combination of local optima.

The organization of this chapter follows the basic DSP steps shown in Figure 4.1. We introduce the basic concepts of each step followed by an identification of many of the different technologies in use or in development. Throughout these sections, a common theme of strategic technology selection provides direction toward a more integrated and continuous mAb downstream process. Where applicable, relevant practical examples in the form of case studies focusing on process development for the entire process as compared to the canonical per-unit operation approach are provided. A brief analysis of the economics of traditional and integrated and continuous processes is also provided.

4.2
Harvest and Clarification

4.2.1
The Challenge and Technology Selection

The basic need for a harvest and clarification step is to separate as much of the solid material from the soluble product as possible before moving on to subsequent purification steps. The required scale and economics of this step has resulted in the development of a number of different technologies ranging from mechanical separation (e.g., centrifugation), to chemical separation (e.g., precipitation), to even more passive methods (e.g., settling).

The selection of clarification methods is dependent on multiple factors that include process characteristics (i.e., cell density, sensitivity to shear, and volume) as well as economic, spatial, and logistical characteristics (i.e., availability of capital equipment, facility utilization, process time, and resources). Ultimately, the final clarification method is expected to be robust to changes in feed properties like cell density and impurity levels and be reproducible. Other attributes also play an important role, such as product quality and scalability [10].

Complicating the separation of solids from the soluble product is the diversity of solids present in a bioreactor at the time of harvest. (Harvest in this context is the act of removing the contents from a bioreactor with clarification being the method of solid–liquid separation.) During production, cells are exposed to different levels of stress throughout the process such as chemical stress from pH excursions or lack of nutrients to mechanical stress from shear forces near mixing zones or sparging zones. Such stresses cause additional cells to break apart [11] or alter their normal expression patterns, further diversifying the impurity population. Because of the batch nature of the cell culture process, the dead cells and their debris remain within the bioreactor until harvest.

Over approximately the last decade, advances in cell culture techniques, improvements in media and cell lines, and improvements in bioreactor design have made it possible for cell densities to increase from $<5 \times 10^6$ to $>20 \times 10^6$ cells ml^{-1} with a concomitant increase in mAb expression levels [11]. Traditionally, clarification employs a combination of unit operations; typically centrifugation followed by secondary depth filtration for large scale and primary depth filtration followed by secondary depth filtration for small scale. The harvest fluid contains the cells and cell debris that are on the order of 0.5–20 μm. Separation difficulties lie in the compressible solids having densities close to water that can become impermeable. As a result alternative methods of clarification have been the focus of research, such as precipitation or flocculation, with the goal to alter the solid characteristics such that the solid–liquid separation can be achieved more easily using traditional methods as well as enabling alternatives.

Through the entirety of the mAb DSP process (i.e., clarification, capture, and polishing), large amounts of biomass and soluble impurities must be removed while maintaining acceptable mAb recovery and quality. This requirement imposes a significant challenge to the traditional harvesting technologies described earlier as well as to downstream chromatography steps typically employed to remove soluble impurities [12,13]. For example, feed streams with typical host cell densities may be harvested using a disk stack centrifuge with high efficiency [14]. However, the centrifuge solid holdup volume is limited and an increase in the amount of the biomass in the feed necessitates more frequent stops for solid discharge, translating into increased operating time. Furthermore, any product entrained in the solid paste is lost [15].

4.2.1.1 Centrifugation

Disk stack centrifuges are more often present in the large stainless steel manufacturing plants of today. Their ability to handle the largest-scale processes coupled with the large capital investment lends to their frequent adoption. Disk stack centrifuges are typically operated at rotational speeds that are less than optimal to remove cellular debris, which may be abundant in high titer feed streams due to decreased cell viability [16] or because of cell disruption from shear forces generated during centrifugation [15,17], resulting in a highly turbid centrate. The consequence is that the submicron-sized residual particulates require secondary normal flow depth filtration steps prior to any column chromatography steps. Hence, depth filtration steps are often plagued with mediocre efficiency (throughput), adding cost and increased complexity to the harvest and clarification step.

There are a few examples of "continuous" centrifuges that are being marketed as alternatives to the discontinuous disk stack centrifuges [18–20]. These continuous centrifuges have been shown to harvest bioreactors at scales similar to depth filtration (~2000 L) with a reduced level of shear, but they are not expected to be able to handle the 10 000 L or larger-scale processes. Similarly, the high cell density processes that are more frequently being encountered require an increase in the number of solid-discharge cycles, reducing the productivity of the clarification step.

4.2.1.2 Filtration

Filtration can occur in two forms, where the flow is normal or tangential to the filtration area. For low- to medium-range biomass loadings, normal flow depth filtration is often employed. Because of the scaling limits of depth filters, centrifugation is sometimes used at the largest scales followed by secondary depth filtration. The implementation of depth filtration is not solely within clarification, it has been shown to improve post-protein A performance [21] as well as enable removal of other soluble contaminating species [22,23]. The single-use nature of depth filtration and the simplicity of implementation have made depth filtration the method of choice for most clarification processes.

Tangential-flow microfiltration (μTFF) has been identified as a promising technology that can handle higher biomass loadings. μTFF for clarification is not without issues, however. For example, poor yield has been observed, probably because of rapid polarization of cells at the membrane surface [24]. Cell lysis at the membrane surface, because of shear forces, further limits the utility of μTFF [12]. Additionally, performed with either flat-sheet membranes or hollow-fibers, μTFF media is typically not treated as a single-use for cost reasons, thereby requiring cleaning and validation. Moreover, compared with depth filtration, μTFF is technically more complicated and possibly more expensive due to the reduced number of reuses possible.

To achieve continuous processing for clarification using either of these filtration methods, different approaches must be taken [25–27]. Depth filtration, by its single-use nature, is not obviously amenable to continuous processing.

Through a combination of scaling and flow rate modifications the depth filtration step can be made to be pseudocontinuous. μTFF, however, may be performed in a "single-pass" mode where the filtration happens across a series of devices such that the fluids are not recycled as is the case for standard tangential-flow filtration (TFF) processing [28–30].

4.2.1.3 **Impurity Precipitation**

Multiple alternatives to centrifugation and normal flow filtration aimed at streamlining development and production while reducing the cost of the mAb harvest step are being investigated. One such strategy that has been used extensively in the wastewater treatment industry [31] is precipitation or flocculation (here precipitation is used interchangeably with flocculation for concision). Precipitation occurs through the addition of an agent, typically an acid, salt, or polymer, where coacervation of cells, cell debris, and some soluble materials with the agent produces solids of increased size and density compared to the unagglomerated materials. Examples of precipitating agents include chitosan [32], acetic acid [33], and polydiallyldimethylammonium chloride (pDADMAC) [34]. The increased particle density enables higher centrifuge efficiency, thus reducing the submicron particulate load on subsequent secondary clarification steps. Additionally, as more efficient depth filters optimized for use with precipitated feed streams are being made available, precipitation may obviate the need for a centrifuge step completely. Another benefit of precipitation is in the reduction of other soluble impurities prior to capture and polishing steps. Lydersen *et al.* treated cell culture suspensions with acid [35] to flocculate whole cells, debris, proteins, DNA, and other impurities [15].

4.2.2
Summary

The product of the clarification step is composed of the soluble product (i.e., mAb) as well as many soluble impurities, such as host cell proteins, DNA, and product-related impurities. Depending on the initial titer of the cell culture and the efficiency of the clarification step, the purity can range from 50 to 80%. Although this is quite good for a starting point, the required mAb purity is >99.999%. Additionally, the clarification step provides minimal product pool volume reductions, thus requiring the use of large intermediate holding tanks and long processing times for all subsequent steps.

The decision regarding what method(s) of clarification to use in a process requires consideration of process impacts, cost, and robustness. The combination of precipitating technologies with the next-generation single-use depth filters should span the biomass bandwidth enabling single-use methods that are scale independent. Similar to filtration methods, combinations of precipitation and filtration have not been developed for continuous operation. Because of the condensing of the particle size distributions provided by different precipitation technologies it may be possible to apply combinations of filtration modes in such a way as to simulate a continuous process.

4.3 Capture

4.3.1 Background

Primary capture of mAb from the clarified cell culture is expected to significantly increase the purity with high yields and, ideally, product concentration. This can be achieved using many different techniques, such as chromatography, crystallization, or precipitation.

Affinity chromatography as an initial capture step offers a number of performance attributes that can streamline the process development for new molecules, such as robustness to solution conditions for loading and washing. For mAbs, protein A chromatography using recombinant *Staphylococcus aureus* protein A [36] has been broadly employed. The consistency of the Fc-portion across mAbs, the targeted binding region for protein A, has led to protein A chromatography becoming the keystone of the downstream purification train for capture.

Alternately, precipitation or crystallization of the desired protein out of the fermentation broth is capable of meeting all of the production requirements. However, with either precipitation or crystallization, an added step of solid–liquid separation is required. As discussed earlier, such separation methods are still being investigated and have been applied primarily in a batch format. There are few technologies outside of chromatography that are capable of enabling continuous capture.

4.3.1.1 Protein A Chromatography

The use of the protein A ligand for chromatography was reported as early as the 1970s [37], a time in which clinical efficacy of mAbs as a therapeutic molecule was not commercially realized. Protein A is a staphylococcal cell wall protein that is known to interact with the Fc-portion of most antibodies [38]. Because of the robust performance of the protein A chromatography step, it has formed the basis of the mAb downstream process. Although there are significant benefits to using protein A chromatography as the capture step, it is still considered expensive with costs ranging from $6000 to $17 000 per liter [39]. The perceptions of low capacities compared to ion exchange media, the potential for ligand leaching and immunogenicity and harsh elution conditions all lend toward investigating alternatives [40–42]. As upstream titers increase, the concentration factors once enjoyed with protein A chromatography may in fact result in product pool dilution in addition to purification.

4.3.2 Chromatographic Methods

4.3.2.1 Slurried Bed Methods

The use of chromatographic media packed in a column has been the traditional method to perform separations for over 100 years. Although this method has been scaled to astounding levels, the use of the media in the packed bed format is not a necessity. There are many different strategies that have been employed using the resin material where the resin is used in the slurry form at least part of the time.

Within the context of continuous processing, one such approach uses a combination of resin slurries and TFF (via hollow fibers) to affect a separation. Proof of concept has been shown with multiple modes of interaction with recoveries of >90% [43,44]. Benefits to this method include the ability to reduce media consumption through increased reuse as well as the elimination of column packing. The method is also flexible as to the level of purification and recovery that are desired by varying the number of stages (hollow-fiber filtration) steps. Drawbacks to the use of resin slurries for capture or polishing are related to the resins and methods used for solid–liquid separation, that is, filtration. For example, current preparative scale chromatography media is often mass transfer limited during loading and elution with fast binding kinetics. To reduce buffer volumes and processing times, new media with reduced or no mass transfer limitation is necessary (e.g., pellicular media). Although increasing the number of stages can improve recovery and resolution, it also increases the overall complexity through the use of multiple hollow-fiber filtration processes occurring simultaneously with multiple sets of relevant hardware (e.g., pumps, static mixers, and detectors).

4.3.2.2 Continuous Chromatography

Continuous chromatography first originated in the mid-twentieth century in the oil and sugar industries [45] and since then has become accepted in a number of industries including small molecule pharmaceuticals. More recently, biopharmaceutical manufacturers have begun to adopt the technology for the production of macromolecules [46], a trend that should intensify as the industry continues to strive for more productive, cost-effective processes.

The main gain of implementing continuous chromatography is an improved utilization of the chromatography resin, thereby increasing the step's productivity. Additionally, this may lead to reductions in buffer volumes [47]. Because of the increased level of operational complexity and the tacit need for more complex process development than for a batch process [48], slow adoption rates of this technology have been observed in the biopharmaceutical environment.

Continuous chromatography has been identified as a way to improve process efficiency in terms of speed and cost. Questions remain about whether continuous chromatography could deliver shorter production times and enable the use of smaller devices, thus reducing the cost of goods. Indeed, for manufacturing flexibility, single-use devices may be appropriate. The widespread implementation of continuous chromatography will require robust media and processes as well as hardware to reduce risk and costs.

The potential of continuous chromatography can best be shown by a comparison of the same capture methods used in a batch mode, that is, an affinity-based separation, but the basic ideas can be applicable to any chromatography mode. There have been a number of reports on the use of continuous protein A chromatographic steps using equipment from different sources, where the number of columns used varies from as low as two [49] to as high as 20 [50]. Regardless of the number of columns used in the process, a basic scheme is followed where one or more columns are in the loading phase while the remaining columns are dispersed among the different other steps of the process such as washing, elution, cleaning, and equilibration.

The true benefits of continuous chromatography are based on the increased media utilization achieved through the use of multiple columns being loaded in series. Numerous examples exist describing how this works [51,52], but a brief introduction is provided here. When a column is loaded with protein under binding conditions, there is a gradient of protein concentration along the length of the column such that the top of the column is more concentrated than the bottom. As the loading proceeds, a point is reached at which the product starts to exit the column without being retained. This so-called breakthrough is what is measured to determine the practical loading level of the column, also known as the dynamic binding capacity (DBC). Typically, the DBC experiment is run until a breakthrough concentration reaches a defined threshold value that ranges from 1 to 10% of the feed concentration. Commercially, product breakthrough equates to yield losses, thus the effective capacity of the column is usually set as 80–95% of the measured DBC. Figure 4.2a provides a basic breakthrough curve where the 10% breakthrough and the commercially relevant effective capacity are shown. In continuous capture, a second column is in series with the first in order to capture the product breakthrough from the first. Figure 4.2b shows the potential capacity increase when two columns are loaded in series with the first column loading farther into the breakthrough curve. This increased effective capacity of the media translates to an improvement in productivity (i.e., mass of product produced per unit of media per unit of time, g L^{-1} h^{-1}).

The benefits of multicolumn loading are dependent on the specific properties of the media, including the mass transfer characteristics. The rates of mass transfer translate into the ultimate shape of the breakthrough curve. The sharper the curve, the more flexibility that is possible for the column switch timing, that is, for a media with a shallow breakthrough curve, the amount of material being captured on the secondary column will increase, leading to shorter subsequent loading volumes possible when the secondary column moves to the primary position. This also requires that the column necessary for secondary loading is ready in enough time. The loading titer, number of

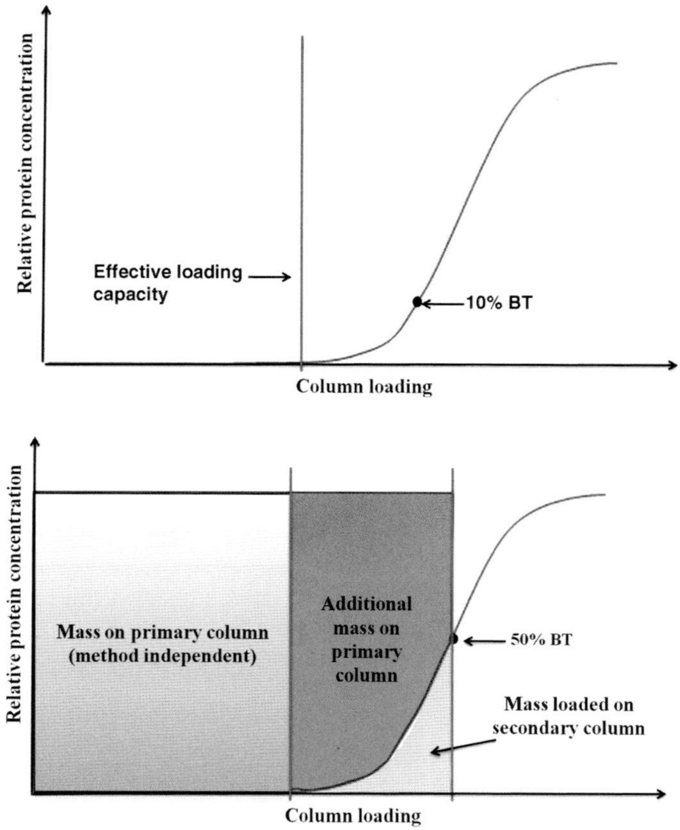

Figure 4.2 Example of a chromatographic breakthrough curve with the % breakthrough and the effective capacity identified for a batch (single) column with loading to 10% breakthrough (a) and for two columns in series with the first column loaded to 50% breakthrough (b).

intermediate steps (i.e., nonloading steps), and flow rates all need to be considered when designing the process. The use of more columns provides added flexibility with an added level of complexity and increased resin consumption. Therefore, selection of the appropriate media requires consideration of not just the capacity but also the shape of the breakthrough curve coupled with flow restrictions that are specific for each media.

In addition to the capacity and productivity benefits realized with multicolumn loading, increased resin utilization offers the potential to use smaller columns that are cycled more frequently. During clinical-phase manufacturing campaigns a protein A column may be used as few as four times before being discarded. By shrinking the column volumes to as much as a tenth of the original size, columns can be cycled more often to process the same mass of product in a continuous chromatography process. However, the number of cycles can approach the expected lifetime of the media. This moves the clinical scale media costs to an order of magnitude that was previously only seen in the latest manufacturing stages. Combining these benefits one could envision the use of smaller columns for more cycles thus enabling disposable chromatography columns in production.

4.3.3 Capture Case Studies

4.3.3.1 Continuous Protein A Chromatography Capture Case Study

Provided is an example comparison of a single-column batch protein A capture chromatography process to a three-column continuous protein A capture process for a clinical-scale operation. Table 4.1 defines the assumptions for the different media being used, including the effective dynamic capacity at the residence times being used to process a 1000 L batch of mAb at 1 g L^{-1}, that is, a 1 kg batch at an average titer.

When comparing a single-column batch process to a three-column continuous process there are a number of realizable benefits. With highly efficient and mechanically stable media, reduced residence times can be used while maintaining the loading capacity achieved at the slower flow rates, utilizing a multicolumn approach (Table 4.1). The increased flow rates, however, require media and systems that can handle the increased pressure drops, which can be partially addressed through reductions in bed heights. The volume of media consumed is also expected to be significantly decreased (by as much as 90% in some cases). Table 4.1 also demonstrates how the combination of the reduced media consumption and increased flow rates results in an increased productivity rate. Ultimately, through prodigious adjustment of the variables (residence time, media volumes, and production times) users can design a process to achieve their desired combination of benefits. What has not been discussed here, but could also be treated as an adjustable parameter, are the levels of buffer consumption, which are directly related to the media volumes and process cycle numbers.

Table 4.1 Example performance data for a Protein A chromatography step processing 1000 L of a 1 g L^{-1} mAb producing cell culture comparing a single column batch process run for multiple cycles sequentially to a continuously loaded three-column process.

Method of operation	Residence time (min)	Effective dynamic capacity (g L^{-1})	Consumed resin volume (bed height in cm)	Number of cycles	Total process time (h)	Productivity (g L^{-1} h^{-1})
Batch	4	38.7	21.2 (20)	5	11.5	4.1
Three-column continuous	0.5	45	2.8 (5)	29 (total)	9.6	37.2

Table 4.2 Summary of performance characteristics (i.e., mAb yield and HCP removal) as a function of the method of precipitation technology used.

Treatment	mAb Yield (%)	HCP removal
Traditional depth filtration[a)]	95	63%
Acid precipitation	98	50%
Cationic flocculent	99	50%
Mixed-mode polymer	98	61%

a) No precipitant was used prior to depth filtration.

4.3.3.2 Effect of Clarification Method on Protein A Performance

In addition to the improvements in throughput that precipitation/flocculation can bring to the clarification step, it also offers the potential for removal of soluble impurities, such as HCPs, which can impact the efficiency of downstream purification steps. Table 4.2 provides a summary of the performance of the different clarification methods for a CHO-based mAb process stream, where all clarification methods included some kind of depth filtration to achieve the necessary solid–liquid separation in a batch mode. Clearly, selecting the method of clarification based on yield or HCP removal alone is not obvious, other aspects are necessary for selection such as ease of use and cost.

As clarification is the operation poised to have the most significant impact on the entirety of the downstream process, it only makes sense to treat the process development holistically, that is, to select the ideal clarification method based on the combined performance of different clarification methods and the nearest adjacent step, which in this case is protein A chromatography. Table 4.3 provides that next level of comparison to more clearly illuminate the point. As shown, the impact of different clarification methods stands out. While the use of the cationic flocculent reduced the mAb yield from the protein A step below reasonable expectation, the mixed-mode polymer was also able to reduce the HCP concentration by an order of magnitude while maintaining high product yield.

To further support the notion of combined process development of multiple unit operations, an example of a challenging feed is provided. High levels of HCP in the protein A elution pool have been related to the increased propensity

Table 4.3 Protein A chromatography yield and HCP concentration following four different clarification methods.

Treatment	Yield (%)	HCP (ppm)
Traditional depth filtration	100	301
Acid precipitation	99	541
Cationic flocculent	86	512
Mixed-mode polymer	97	64

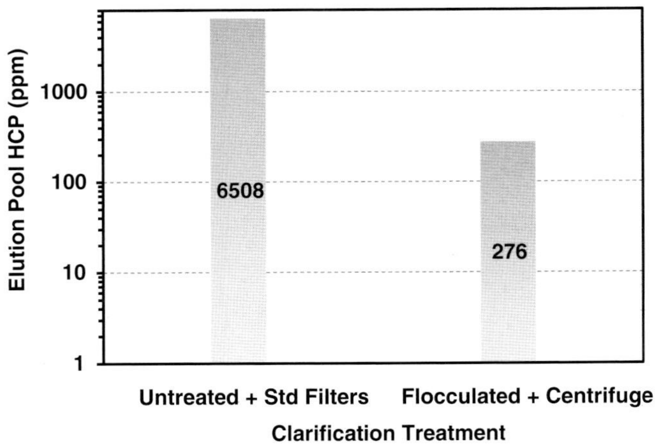

Figure 4.3 Protein A elution pool HCP levels as a function of the treatment method used prior to depth filtration, that is, depth filtration of feeds from two different clarification methods.

for turbidity generation upon pH neutralization. The mixed-mode polymer treated cell culture resulted in similar yield and purification as the traditional depth filtered cell culture within the clarification step. However, the protein A elution pools showed significant differences in purification. Figure 4.3 shows the resulting host cell protein after protein A purification. The polymer-treated cell culture results in similar protein A yield as depth-filtered only (untreated) cell culture while providing a >25-fold reduction in HCP, thus reducing the burden on the polishing steps further compressing the overall purification process.

The importance of taking a holistic approach when evaluating new technologies is made clear by these examples. Through this combined method an ideal combination of clarification and protein A methods can be identified. Without investigating the impact on the subsequent downstream purification process the clear advantages of one precipitant over another may be lost to the researcher.

4.4 Polishing

4.4.1 Background

The polishing steps in a mAb process reduce the impurities present in the post-protein A product pool to levels that are clinically acceptable. Figure 4.4 provides a more detailed version of the traditional DSP steps, focusing on the polishing steps, as well as an alternative integrated set of technologies that have been more recently described [53]. For a traditional process template, following

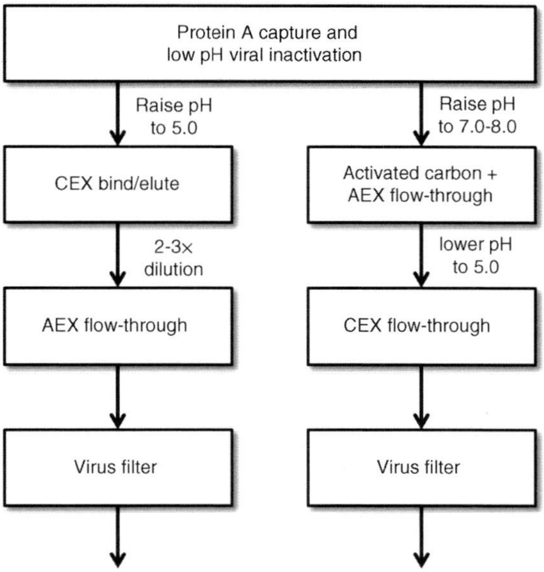

Figure 4.4 A comparison of traditional mAb downstream processes (left) and a flow-through based approach (right). Examples of intermediate solution conditioning steps are identified for each train.

primary capture, several polishing steps are often employed, usually with one step being operated in the bind/elute mode. Depending on the specific impurity populations present, polishing consists of combinations of ion exchange, hydrophobic interaction, and mixed-mode chromatography.

One of the most common downstream templates employs bind/elute CEX chromatography, wherein elution from the CEX medium occurs via increased salt concentrations with or without pH changes. Further polishing may require conditioning of the CEX elution to enable different modes of interaction. Replacing the bind/elute CEX step with flow-through alternatives is becoming increasingly advantageous. Implementation, however, has been limited by the lack of available chromatographic media designed specifically for flow-through impurity removal.

The implementation of integrated and continuous processing for polishing applications will ideally reduce the complexity of the multistep process with requisite gains in flexibility and productivity. Obviously, multiple bind/elute steps and numerous solution changes are contrary to this idea. Therefore, technologies that reduce or eliminate product capture while maintaining separation performance will be required. Moreover, the reduction or elimination of solution changes would be expected to simplify the process and reduce intermediate tank volumes. Furthermore, the use of flow-through devices for trace contaminant removal should reduce the cost of manufacturing through a reduction of media volumes concomitant with reduced buffer consumption.

Toward this end, the development of a new downstream polishing template for mAbs composed entirely of flow-through chromatography steps is ideal. Application of flow-through technologies should streamline process development while reducing the cost and complexity of the downstream polishing steps. Scaling media volumes based on trace impurity loadings can reduce media volumes, buffer consumption, and tank sizes while also facilitating the economical use of single use chromatography devices that eliminate the costs and complexities of packing, cleaning, storage, and tracking.

4.4.2 Technology Selection Strategy

Developing a downstream polishing process composed entirely of flow-through chromatography steps requires a cascade of media that are able to selectively remove a wide variety of impurities that persist after the protein A affinity capture step. Figure 4.5 pictorially shows a rational method to analyze the different types of process related impurities by considering their molecular weight and isoelectric point. Using these two characteristics, identification of flow-through adsorption media to address these specific populations of impurities can be achieved.

Figure 4.5 illustrates that there are three broad categories of impurities where differences in physicochemical properties can be leveraged to enable their extraction from the product containing stream. The first is composed of lower molecular weight impurities including low molecular weight HCP, mAb fragments, and residual small molecules (e.g., cell culture components). The

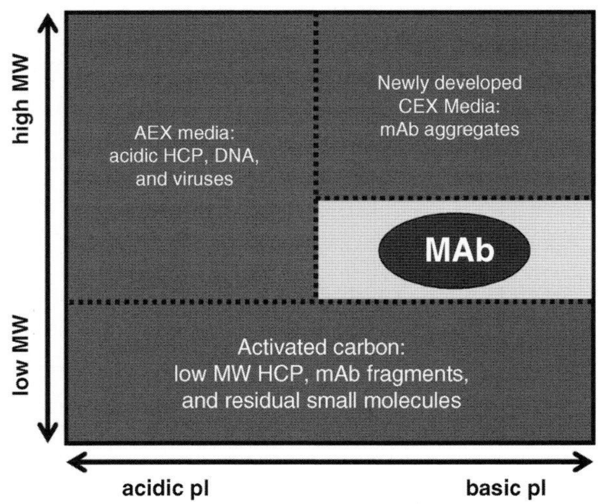

Figure 4.5 A schematic analysis of the various mAb process impurities based on their molecular weight and isoelectric point with examples of media types that can be employed for their selective removal.

selective removal of many of these impurities can be achieved through a variety of hydrophobic interactions [54] using activated carbon. Activated carbon is a low-cost, porous, and high-surface area material [55] that is not commonly employed for the purification of therapeutic biomolecules [56], but has been employed for the removal of small molecules from proteins [57–59]. Size exclusion chromatography (SEC) may also be used as an alternative to activated carbon, but this media is notoriously slow and difficult to scale up.

The second group is composed of negatively charged impurities including acidic HCP, nucleic acids, and viruses. These impurities are readily removed with commercially available AEX media [60,61] or salt-tolerant AEX adsorbers [62–65], which have been shown to have excellent performance at higher conductivities.

The final collection is composed of larger basic species including product-related impurities, such as mAb aggregates that are particularly difficult to remove since they share many of the same characteristics as the mAb product [66,67]. CEX is most often employed in bind/elute mode where resolution between the product and impurities is critical. There have been different approaches to transition the CEX step from a capacity-limited bind/elute step to a more flow-through step including overloading and weak partitioning [68–71]. To facilitate the flow-through removal of aggregates, a new CEX media has been developed that discriminates between mAb monomers, dimers, and higher-order aggregates [72]. Capitalizing on avidity, this newly developed CEX media has a reduced affinity for the mAb monomer while maintaining sufficient strength to bind mAb aggregates.

4.4.3
Complete Flow-Through Polishing Case Study

We provide an example of a continuous flow-through polishing process recently described that integrates these two newly identified flow-through media [53]. As shown in Figure 4.6 three flow-through chromatographic media (i.e., activated carbon, AEX media, and CEX media) were employed followed by a viral filtration step. The performance was evaluated with two different mAb protein A eluates. The order of the three components was based on a number of considerations including economic advantage, simplicity, and performance. Activated carbon

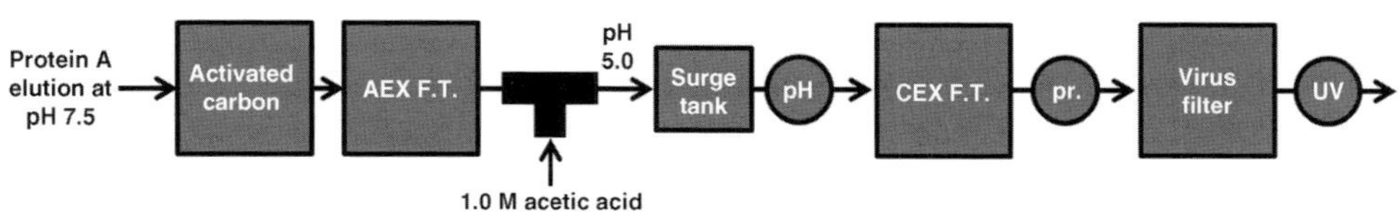

Figure 4.6 A schematic of a connected flow-through purification process. Process monitoring devices integrated into the system are included where process conditions might fluctuate (e.g., pH is measured after adjustment and pressure is measured prior to virus filtration).

was employed first in the sequence of polishers because it is the least expensive and it reduces the concentration of impurities that would otherwise be capacity limiting to the more expensive AEX and CEX media. The AEX media was placed directly after the activated carbon since it could be effectively operated under the same solution conditions. Therefore, the two components could be linked into a single flow-through step. The CEX media was employed prior to the viral filtration step to reduce the mAb aggregates levels that have been associated with plugging of viral filters, thereby reducing the effective filtration area of the virus filtration step. Effective use of the CEX media requires the solution pH to be lowered to about 5.0 for effective aggregate removal.

The system can be assembled as described in the schematic in Figure 4.6 where different solution conditioning steps are identified. First, the pH of the protein A eluate is raised to 7.5 with the addition of an effective base solution. The addition of a base can be accomplished either as a batch or a continuous in-line process. The effluent from the AEX media is next contacted with an acidic solution (preferably in-line with mixing) to reduce the pH. The inclusion of a surge tank would be expected to average the impacts of any upstream process variations (e.g., varied pump flow rates, and pH excursions) as well as provide an opportunity for an intermediate hold and sampling. Options for various in-line sensors are shown as well (e.g., pressure monitoring is included to monitor the performance of the virus filter).

This proof of concept flow-through polishing system was found to reduce impurity levels below the target levels for both mAb feeds tested as shown in Table 4.4. In both cases the mAb recoveries exceeded 90% with HCP reductions to below 1 ppm. Virus filter capacity adequately met loading expectations and aggregate reductions were significant without the need for a large dilution of the process feeds. The minimal dilution of the process feed is notable since in the traditional template a dilution after the bind/elute CEX step could be as high as 10-fold. These more concentrated polished mAb solutions are advantageous since they decrease the membrane area requirements and process times for the UF/DF steps. Additionally, the lower volumes of chromatography media used in the all flow-through system also increase the economic feasibility of single-use chromatography devices.

Table 4.4 Performance summary of a connected flow-through purification (FTP) process for two mAbs after protein A capture. HCP is shown in ppm with the starting and final levels given. The mAb aggregates are provided as a percentage of the total aggregate concentration and viral filtration (VF) capacity is shown in kg of mAb per m^2 of membrane area. The overall dilution factor is also provided.

mAb	Monomer recovery	HCP (ppm)	mAb aggregates	VF capacity (kg/m^2)	Dilution factor
mAb05	92.0%	591 → <1	5.0% → 1.1%	3.7	1.25
mAb07	91.4%	82 → <1	1.4% → 0%	3.7	1.15

4.5 Cost of Goods Analysis

Most of the tangible parameters described in the previous sections can be used as inputs to perform a detailed cost of goods (CoGs) analysis. We are thus provided with objective numbers that can be unambiguously compared across process options.

4.5.1 Methodology

Multiple software packages are commercially available [73]. *Biosolve,* an Excel-based software package provided by Biopharm Services, Ltd (UK) (www.biopharmservices.com/) for process modeling and economic analysis, was used. The program allows for a comprehensive analysis of CoGs based on detailed user inputs [74].

Different scales are presented spanning a range of 1 to 25 kg. This range covers the vast majority of processes with clinical represented by the low end and commercial by the higher end. The examples here used both stainless steel and disposable equipment, as appropriate (i.e., above 2000 L stainless steel was used and disposable was used below that).

All consumables (filters, chromatographic resins, bags) and process equipment (chromatography and filtration skids) were priced at list prices available from vendors.

4.5.2 Clarification

Three processes for the clarification unit operation are compared, centrifugation followed by secondary depth filtration (Hybrid), two-stage depth filtration (Depth), and flocculation-assisted depth filtration using polymers and novel filters (Flocculation). The costs per gram of mAb for the unit operation are shown in Table 4.5.

Clearly, at smaller scales, depth filtration is economically preferred. As the scale increases, a centrifuge-based process is less expensive, as the number of

Table 4.5 Cost per gram of mAb processed for the clarification unit operation based on scale and clarification method. See text for a description of the methods used.

Method	Hybrid	Depth	Flocculation
1000 L @ 1 g L^{-1}	38	31	46
3000 L @ 5 g L^{-1}	4.9	6.1	7.0

depth filters and corresponding clarification skids increases exceeds practical limits. This scale dependence is well reflected by actual practice.

Even though the assumptions used for our modeling show no concrete economic advantages for the flocculation-assisted process, several intangible advantages might make its selection beneficial or even necessary, especially when considering the holistic process (impurity reduction leading to small DSP devices for example).

Two practical case studies where the benefits of flocculation-assisted clarification were clearly shown are cited by Felo and coworkers [34,75]. Improved yield and impurity clearance provided economic advantages mostly related to higher filter throughput and process and implementation time savings.

4.5.3
Capture

Table 4.6 shows the economic impacts of changing the protein A capture step from single batch operation to a three-column continuous alternative. The processing time was fixed for the two cases to about 13 h by varying the number of cycles for CMC. Multiple product scales were considered by varying bioreactor volumes and mAb titer.

Table 4.6 clearly shows how the impact of a change to a single unit operation can look appealing, while the broader implications reduce the overall cost differences. Contributions from facility costs are significant for CMC because of the smaller columns required.

The advantages of CMC are more pronounced at clinical scales. During clinical phases, reaching the resin lifetime is unlikely when batch chromatography is used. CMC allows for reduced column size and resin volumes by increasing the number of cycles. Assuming the processing of three batches, the media from the batch case would be cycled only 12 times, whereas three CMC runs at 50 cycles per column per run would push the cycles to 150. Table 4.7 shows the relative cost difference for the process described as a function of the starting mAb titer. Only the CMC operation is used under the conditions described for clinical operation, in order to highlight the effect on this particular unit operation. As expected, the cost benefits are very significant and even the effect on the total process cost cannot be ignored.

Table 4.6 Relative percent cost difference for CMC to batch operations at different scales for commercial operation. Relative cost differences are provided for both the single unit operation and the impact to the overall process cost (including upstream).

Scale	1 kL @ 1 g L^{-1}	1 kL @ 5 g L^{-1}	5 kL @ 1 g L^{-1}	5 kL @ 5 g L^{-1}
Unit operation cost ($/g)	+5.4%	−3.7%	−16%	−21%
Total process cost ($/g)	−0.6%	−0.8%	−3.4%	−4.1%

Table 4.7 Relative percent cost difference for CMC to batch operations at different scales for clinical operation. Relative cost differences are provided for both the single unit operation and the impact to the overall process cost (including upstream).

Scale	1 kL @ 1 g L^{-1}	1 kL @ 2 g L^{-1}
Unit operation cost ($/g)	−51%	−66%
Total process cost ($/g)	−13%	−19%

4.5.4 Polishing

Table 4.8 shows the equivalent economic impacts of changing the polishing steps from bind/elute CEX followed by flow-through AEX to an all flow-through process (see Section 4.4) as a function of scale. In both cases virus filtration was included. Across all scales, savings of 15 to 30% for the FTP process could be realized, with a smaller benefit that persists for the overall process costs. The savings come from facility (elimination of columns), less dilution, and higher loading capacities.

4.5.5 Overall

Globally, the integrated template aggregates the savings from the individual unit operations. The combined effects on process economics are provided in Table 4.9. The proposed technologies are provided in both batch and continuous cases.

The most significant savings for the proposed new template are connected to the facility. Fewer pool tanks, less stainless steel, smaller and fewer process skids are all contributing factors. Increased costs of consumables apply for the new template, as can be expected from the use of single-use, filters and chromatography devices throughout. Finally, the labor cost is lower, given the shorter processing times and fewer interventions.

Table 4.8 Relative percent cost difference for the flow through polishing process relative to the traditional batch operation template as a function of scale. Relative cost differences are provided for both the single unit operation and the impact to the overall process cost.

Scale	1 kL @ 1 g L^{-1}	1 kL @ 5 g L^{-1}	5 kL @ 1 g L^{-1}	5 kL @ 5 g L^{-1}
FTP unit operations cost ($/g)	−15%	−19%	−27%	−14%
Total process cost ($/g)	−6%	−15%	−9%	−6%

Table 4.9 Relative percent cost difference of the proposed template to the traditional template at different scales. Two modes of operation are provided, batch, where the proposed technologies are used sequentially (i.e., batch) and in a continuous mode. In all cases, only the DSP components are included in the cost and the savings.

Scale	1000 L @ $1\,g\,L^{-1}$	1000 L @ $5\,g\,L^{-1}$	5000 L @ $1\,g\,L^{-1}$	5000 L @ $5\,g\,L^{-1}$
Proposed process in batch mode	−6%	−12%	−11%	−18%
Proposed process in continuous mode	−16%	−21%	−23%	−24%

There is roughly a 10% additional cost savings switching from batch to continuous. Although there is only a 10% realized cost savings suitable from batch to continuous, there are a lot of "intangible" benefits. These include minimal solution condition adjustments, reduced process development, smaller footprint, reduced buffer consumption, and the increased use of single use devices. With respect to scale, the proposed template exhibits the most benefit in a clinical setting. The result is that the combined process advantages exceed those provided by each operation separately. As such, the use of economic modeling must be used in the context of the process in its entirety. Without that appreciation, benefits and repercussions of process changes could be overlooked.

4.6 Summary

The evolutionary nature of biopharmaceutical process development and manufacturing is likely directed toward integrated and continuous processing. As the industry begins to adopt new technologies and methods, considerations of holistic process development will be a key requirement. Technology selection based on the batch unit operation approach will no longer be preferred as cost, robustness, and process efficiency are all going to be intimately related to the choices of technologies and their methods of implementation and integration.

Scaling these new processes will require further process engineering. Strategies must be developed to address operational challenges, such as pressure regulation. Regulatory concerns also exist and methods must be developed to address monitoring, sampling, analytical control, batch definition, validation studies, and documentation. Finally, various advantages of connectivity must be understood and evaluated in comparison to "highly connected" system where only the most advantageous linkages are employed and prohibitively complex linkages are avoided.

We have attempted to provide a framework for future process development of mAb processes in an increasingly cost-conscious business climate. From technology screening to cost modeling, it is expected that the reader will be able to more deftly work through the maze of technologies available now and in the future to streamline the future development of mAb processes. Although this framework is focused on the downstream aspects of mAb production, it has not escaped our attention that future developments will be expected to couple upstream information and process development methods to the downstream to better design and control the production facilities of tomorrow. Indeed, the connection of perfusion reactors to continuous chromatography is a logical extension of the individual technologies.

References

1 Leavy, O. (2010) Therapeutic antibodies: past, present and future. *Nat. Rev. Immunol.*, **10** (5), 297–297.

2 Shukla, A.A. and Thömmes, J. (2010) Recent advances in large-scale production of monoclonal antibodies and related proteins. *Trends Biotechnol.*, **28** (5), 253–261

3 Aggarwal, S. (2011) What's fueling the biotech engine: 2010 to 2011. *Nat. Biotechnol.*, **29** (12), 1083–1089.

4 Jain, E. and Kumar, A. (2008) Upstream processes in antibody production: evaluation of critical parameters. *Biotechnol. Adv.*, **26** (1), 46–72.

5 De Palma, A. (2013) Downstream process bottlenecks. *GEN*, **33** (13), 1, 36. doi:10.1089/gen.33.13.17.

6 Langer, E. (2013) Keeping new technologies coming. *BioPharm. Int.*, **11** (6), 12–15.

7 Sommerfeld, S. and Strube, J. (2005) Challenges in biotechnology production: generic processes and process optimization for monoclonal antibodies. *Chem. Eng. Process: Process Intensification*, **44** (10), 1123–1137.

8 Wurm, F.M. (2004) Production of recombinant protein therapeutics in cultivated mammalian cells. *Nat. Biotechnol.*, **22** (11), 1393–1398.

9 DePalma, A. (2011) Getting around downstream bottlenecks. *GEN*, **31** (11), 1–36.

10 Zaman, F., Allan, C.M., and Ho, S.V. (2009) Ultra scale-down approaches for clarification of mammalian cell culture broths in disc-stack centrifuges. *Biotechnol. Prog.*, **25** (6), 1709–1716.

11 Westoby, M., Rogers, J.K., Haverstock, R., Romero, J., and Pieracci, J. (2011) Modeling industrial centrifugation of mammalian cell culture using a capillary based scale-down system. *Biotechnol. Bioeng.*, **108** (5), 989–998.

12 Liu, H.F., Ma, J., Winter, C., and Bayer, R. (2010) Recovery and purification process development for monoclonal antibody production. *mAbs*, **2** (5), 480–499.

13 Lutz, H., Blanchard, M., Abbott, I., Parampalli, A., Setiabudi, G., Chiruvolu, V., and Noguchi, M. (2009) Considerations for scaling-up depth filtration of harvested cell culture fluid. *BioPharm. Int.*, **22** (3), 58–66.

14 Belter, P.A., Cussler, E.L., and Hu, W.S. (1988) *Bioseparations: Downstream Processing for Biotechnology*, John Wiley & Sons, Inc., Hoboken.

15 Shukla, A.A. and Kandula, J.R. (2008) Harvest and recovery of monoclonal antibodies from large-scale mammalian cell culture. *BioPharm. Int.*, **21** (5), 34–45.

16 Shpritzer, R., Vicik, S., Orlando, S., Acharya, H., and Coffman, J.L. (2006) Calcium phosphate flocculation of antibody-producing mammalian cells at pilot scale. The 232nd ACS National Meeting, September 10–14, 2006, San Francisco, CA, p. BIOT-80.

17 Roush, D.J. and Lu, Y. (2008) Advances in primary recovery: centrifugation and membrane technology. *Biotechnol. Prog.*, **24** (3), 488–495.
18 Filipowicz, M. and Filipowicz, P. (1980) Continuous filtering-settling centrifuge. US Pat. 4199459A (April 22, 1980).
19 Tokashiki, M., Arai, T., Hamamoto, K., and Ishimaru, K. (1990) High density culture of hybridoma cells using a perfusion culture vessel with an external centrifuge. *Cytotechnology*, **3** (3), 239–244.
20 Pattasseril, J., Varadaraju, H., Lock, L., and Rowley, J. (2013) Downstream technology landscape for large-scale therapeutic cell processing. *Bioprocess Int.*, **11**, 46–52.
21 Yigzaw, Y., Piper, R., Tran, M., and Shukla, A.A. (2006) Exploitation of the adsorptive properties of depth filters for host cell protein removal during monoclonal antibody purification. *Biotechnol. Prog.*, **22** (1), 288–296.
22 Eschrich, J., Cyr, G., and Dorsey, N. (1997) The role of charge in the retention of DNA by charged cellulose-based depth filters. *BioPharm. Technol. Bus.*, **10** (1), 46–49.
23 Hou, K., Gerba, C., Goyal, S., and Zerda, K. (1980) Capture of latex beads, bacteria, endotoxin, and viruses by charge-modified filters. *Appl. Environ. Microbiol.*, **40** (5), 892–896.
24 van Reis, R. and Zydney, A. (2001) Membrane separations in biotechnology. *Curr. Opin. Biotechnol.*, **12** (2), 208–211.
25 Rossignol, N., Vandanjon, L., Jaouen, P., and Quemeneur, F. (1999) Membrane technology for the continuous separation microalgae/culture medium: compared performances of cross-flow microfiltration and ultrafiltration. *Aquacult. Eng.*, **20** (3), 191–208.
26 Crespo, J., Xavier, A., Barreto, M., Goncalves, L., Almeida, J., and Carrondo, M. (1992) Tangential flow filtration for continuous cell recycle culture of acidogenic bacteria. *Chem. Eng. Sci.*, **47** (1), 205–214.
27 Vaks, B., Mory, Y., Pederson, J., and Horovitz, O. (1984) A semi-continuous process for the production of human interferon-αc from *E. coli* using tangential-flow microfiltration and immuno-affinity chromatography. *Biotechnol. Lett.*, **6** (10), 621–626.
28 Jungbauer, A. (2013) Continuous downstream processing of biopharmaceuticals. *Trends Biotechnol.*, **31** (8), 479–492.
29 Dizon-Maspat, J., Bourret, J., D'Agostini, A., and Li, F. (2012) Single pass tangential flow filtration to debottleneck downstream processing for therapeutic antibody production. *Biotechnol. Bioeng.*, **109** (4), 962–970.
30 Teske, C.A., Lebreton, B., and Reis, R.V. (2010) Inline ultrafiltration. *Biotechnol. Prog.*, **26** (4), 1068–1072.
31 Bolto, B. and Gregory, J. (2007) Organic polyelectrolytes in water treatment. *Water Res.*, **41** (11), 2301–2324.
32 Riske, F., Schroeder, J., Belliveau, J., Kang, X., Kutzko, J., and Menon, M.K. (2007) The use of chitosan as a flocculant in mammalian cell culture dramatically improves clarification throughput without adversely impacting monoclonal antibody recovery. *J. Biotechnol.*, **128** (4), 813–823.
33 Romero, J., Chrostowski, J., De Vilmorin, P.G., and Case, J.Y. (2007) Method of isolating biomacromolecules using low pH and divalent cations. US Pat. 20100145022 A1 (November 1, 2007).
34 Kang, Y.K., Hamzik, J., Felo, M., Qi, B., Lee, J., Ng, S., Liebisch, G., Shanehsaz, B., Singh, N., and Persaud, K. (2013) Development of a novel and efficient cell culture flocculation process using a stimulus responsive polymer to streamline antibody purification processes. *Biotechnol. Bioeng.*, **110** (11), 2928–2937.
35 Lydersen, B.K., Brehm-Gibson, T., and Murel, A. (1994) Acid precipitation of mammalian cell fermentation broth. *Ann. N. Y. Acad. Sci.*, **745** (1), 222–231.
36 Sjöquist, J., Movitz, J., Johansson, I.-B., and Hjelm, H. (1972) Localization of protein A in the bacteria. *Eur. J. Biochem.*, **30** (1), 190–194.
37 Hjelm, H. (1975) Isolation of IgG3 from normal human sera and from a patient with multiple myeloma by using protein

A-Sepharose 4B. *Scand. J. Immunol.*, **4** (6), 633–640.

38 Kronvall, G., Quie, P.G., and Williams, R.C. (1970) Quantitation of staphylococcal protein A: determination of equilibrium constant and number of protein A residues on bacteria. *J. Immunol.*, **104** (2), 273–278.

39 Lain, B. (2013) Protein A: the life of a disruptive technology. *Bioprocess Int.*, **11**, 8.

40 Arunakumari, A., Wang, J.M., and Ferreira, G. (2007) Alternatives to protein A: improved downstream process design for human monoclonal antibody production. Biopharm International.

41 Thommes, J. and Etzel, M. (2007) Alternatives to chromatographic separations. *Biotechnol. Prog.*, **23** (1), 42–45.

42 Ghose, S., Hubbard, B., and Cramer, S.M. (2006) Evaluation and comparison of alternatives to protein A chromatography mimetic and hydrophobic charge induction chromatographic stationary phases. *J. Chromatogr. A*, **1122** (1–2), 144–152.

43 Shinkazh, O., Kanani, D., Barth, M., Long, M., Hussain, D., and Zydney, A.L. (2011) Countercurrent tangential chromatography for large-scale protein purification. *Biotechnol. Bioeng.*, **108** (3), 582–591.

44 Napadensky, B., Shinkazh, O., Teella, A., and Zydney, A.L. (2013) Continuous countercurrent tangential chromatography for monoclonal antibody purification. *Sep. Sci. Technol.*, **48** (9), 1289–1297.

45 Broughton, C.B. and Gerhold, C.G. (1961) US Pat. 2,985,589.

46 Sá Gomes, P. and Rodrigues, A.E. (2012) Simulated moving bed chromatography: from concept to proof-of-concept. *Chem. Eng. Technol.*, **35** (1), 17–34.

47 Strube, J., Altenhöner, U., Meurer, M., and Schmidt-Traub, H. (1997) Optimierung kontinuierlicher simulated-moving-bed-chromatographie-prozesse durch dynamische simulation. *Chem. Ing. Tech.*, **69** (3), 328–331.

48 Seidel-Morgenstern, A., Keßler, L.C., and Kaspereit, M. (2008) Neue entwicklungen auf dem gebiet der simulierten gegenstromchromatographie. *Chem. Ing. Tech.*, **80** (6), 725–740.

49 Mueller-Spaeth, T., Angarita, M., Baur, D., Lievrouw, R., Lissens, G., Stroehlein, G., Bavand, M., and Morbidelli, M. (2013) Increasing capacity utilization in protein A chromatography. *BioPharm. Int.*, **26** (10), 33–38.

50 Andersson, J. and Mattiasson, B. (2006) Simulated moving bed technology with a simplified approach for protein purification: separation of lactoperoxidase and lactoferrin from whey protein concentrate. *J. Chromatogr. A*, **1107** (1–2), 88–95.

51 Pollock, J., Bolton, G., Coffman, J., Ho, S.V., Bracewell, D.G., and Farid, S.S. (2013) Optimising the design and operation of semi-continuous affinity chromatography for clinical and commercial manufacture. *J. Chromatogr. A*, **1284**, 17–27.

52 Mahajan, E., George, A., and Wolk, B. (2012) Improving affinity chromatography resin efficiency using semi-continuous chromatography. *J. Chromatogr. A*, **1227**, 154–162.

53 Gillespie, C., Phillips, M., Mann, F., and Andrecht, S. (2013) Next-generation downstream template for continuous mAb processing. Continuous Processing in Biopharmaceutical Manufacturing, July 1–2, 2013, Cambridge, UK.

54 Nanying Bian, C.G., Stone, M., Kozlov, M., Chen, J., and Siwak, M. (2013) Methods of reducing level of one of more impurities in a sample during protein purification. EMD Millipore Corporation. Patent WO2013028330.

55 Marsh, H. and Rodríguez-Reinoso, F. (2006) *Activated Carbon*, Elsevier Science Ltd, Oxford.

56 Kopper, R.A., Kim, A., Van, T., and Helm, R.M. (2008) Adsorption of peanut (*Arachis hypogaea*, Leguminosae) proteins by activated charcoal. *J. Agric. Food Chem.*, **56** (22), 10619–10624.

57 Chen, R.F. (1967) Removal of fatty acids from serum albumin by charcoal treatment. *J. Biol. Chem.*, **242** (2), 173–181.

58 Nakano, N.I., Shimamori, Y., and Nakano, M. (1983) Activated carbon beads for the

removal of highly albumin-bound species. *Anal. Biochem.*, **129** (1), 64–71.

59 Nikolaev, V.G., Sarnatskaya, V.V., Sigal, U.L., Klevtsov, V.N., Makhorin, K.E., and Yushko, L.A. (1991) High porosity activated carbons for bilirubin removal. *Int. J. Artif. Organs*, **14**, 179–185.

60 Weaver, J., Husson, S.M., Murphy, L., and Wickramasinghe, S.R. (2013) Anion exchange membrane adsorbers for flow-through polishing steps: Part I. Clearance of minute virus of mice. *Biotechnol. Bioeng.*, **110** (2), 491–499.

61 Weaver, J., Husson, S.M., Murphy, L., and Wickramasinghe, S.R. (2013) Anion exchange membrane adsorbers for flow-through polishing steps: Part II. Virus, host cell protein, DNA clearance, and antibody recovery. *Biotechnol. Bioeng.*, **110** (2), 500–510.

62 Riordan, W.T., Heilmann, S.M., Brorson, K., Seshadri, K., and Etzel, M.R. (2009) Salt tolerant membrane adsorbers for robust impurity clearance. *Biotechnol. Prog.*, **25** (6), 1695–1702.

63 Riordan, W., Heilmann, S., Brorson, K., Seshadri, K., He, Y., and Etzel, M. (2009) Design of salt-tolerant membrane adsorbers for viral clearance. *Biotechnol. Bioeng.*, **103** (5), 920–929.

64 Faber, R., Yujing, Y., and Gottschalk, U. (2009) Salt tolerant interaction chromatography for large-scale polishing with convective media. *BioPharm. Int. Suppl.*, October, S11–S14.

65 Woo, M., Khan, N.Z., Royce, J., Mehta, U., Gagnon, B., Ramaswamy, S., Soice, N., Morelli, M., and Cheng, K.S. (2011) A novel primary amine-based anion exchange membrane adsorber. *J. Chromatogr. A*, **1218** (32), 5386–5392.

66 Joubert, M.K., Luo, Q., Nashed-Samuel, Y., Wypych, J., and Narhi, L.O. (2011) Classification and characterization of therapeutic antibody aggregates. *J. Biol. Chem.*, **286** (28), 25118–25133.

67 Philo, J.S. (2009) A critical review of methods for size characterization of non-particulate protein aggregates. *Curr. Pharm. Biotechnol.*, **10** (4), 359–372.

68 Yigzaw, Y., Hinckley, P., Hewig, A., and Vedantham, G. (2009) Ion exchange chromatography of proteins and clearance of aggregates. *Curr. Pharm. Biotechnol.*, **10** (4), 421–426.

69 Kelley, B.D., Booth, J.E., Brown, P., Coffman, J., Godavarti, R., Iskra, T., Sun, S., Switzer, M.B., Vunnum, S., and Yu, T. (2011) Method of weak partitioning chromatography. US Pat. US8067182 B2 (November 29, 2011).

70 Liu, H.F., McCooey, B., Duarte, T., Myers, D.E., Hudson, T., Amanullah, A., van Reis, R., and Kelley, B.D. (2011) Exploration of overloaded cation exchange chromatography for monoclonal antibody purification. *J. Chromatogr. A*, **1218** (39), 6943–6952.

71 Brown, A., Bill, J., Tully, T., Radhamohan, A., and Dowd, C. (2010) Overloading ion-exchange membranes as a purification step for monoclonal antibodies. *Biotechnol. Appl. Biochem.*, **56** (2), 59–70.

72 Mikhail Kozlov, W.C., Potty, A., Galipeau, K., Hamzik, J., Umana, J., and Peeck, L. (2013) Removal of protein aggregates from biopharmaceutical preparations in a flow-through mode. EMD Millipore Corporation. Patent WO2013138098A1.

73 Rathore, A.S., Latham, P., Levine, H., Curling, J., and Kaltenbrunner, O. (2004) Costing issues in the production of biopharmaceuticals. *BioPharm. Int.*, **17**, 46–146.

74 Sinclair, A. and Monge, M. (2010) Measuring manufacturing cost and its impact on organizations. *BioProcess International*, **8** (6), 10–15.

75 Felo, M., Christensen, B., and Higgins, J. (2013) Process cost and facility considerations in the selection of primary cell culture clarification technology. *Biotechnol. Prog.*, **29** (5), 1239–1245.

5
Modeling of Protein Monomer/Aggregate Purification by Hydrophobic Interaction Chromatography: Application to Column Design and Process Optimization

Mark-Henry Kamga, Hae Woo Lee, Namjoon Kim, and Seongkyu Yoon

5.1
Introduction

Hydrophobic interaction chromatography (HIC), such as ion exchange (IEX) and gel filtration (GF), is a widely used purification technique for protein purification [1]. HIC operates by exploiting the differences in hydrophobicity of target proteins [2]. However, despite its wide use, its mechanism is still not fully understood [3]. Multiple attempts have been made to develop comprehensive models describing the separation mechanism. Studies have shown that all process parameters, such as adsorbent density, adsorbent hydrophobicity, protein properties, operating temperature and pH, salt identity, and concentration can affect the effectiveness of the process [4]. However, none of these models proposed this far leverage all of this knowledge in order to improve process and column design.

The earliest model advanced enough to explain protein solubility and retention in HIC is the solvophobic theory [5]. The theory proposed that the salt-promoted adsorption of protein on the surface of the ligand occurs in two steps: (i) A cavity is formed in the solvent above the adsorption site in the solvation process and (ii) the protein molecule fills the cavity causing protein aggregation and precipitation on the surface of the resin. Hydrophobic interactions between the proteins and surface lead to adsorption [5]. Using the change of total free energy for the entire process, an expression was developed for the capacity (or retention) factor of different solutes at a fixed temperature and flow rate. The salt molality and the molal surface increment of the salt determine the effect of salt on the retention in HIC [4]. However, the model does not indicate the optimum amount of resin and flow rate required to carry out a specific purification resulting in significant time and effort requirements during process development.

Continuous Processing in Pharmaceutical Manufacturing, First Edition. Edited by Ganapathy Subramanian.

The preferential interaction analysis, which focuses on the interaction of solutes with proteins, was investigated as an alternative to the solvophobic theory [6]. This theory has not been widely applied to adsorptive chromatography; however, it was extended by Perkins *et al.* [7] to HIC. The preferential interaction theory has been used to explain the effect of solutes on a variety of assembly processes, including protein stabilization, precipitation, aggregation, ligand binding, and adsorption. This theory proposed a hydration model in which the proteins are preferentially hydrated due to the effect of the salt [8]. In a mixture of solvent, protein, and solute, the solution is divided into a bulk and local region. The bulk solution is unaffected by the presence of protein, while in the local region, preferential accumulation or exclusion of solutes occurs. Using this approach, an expression for the preferential interaction coefficient is derived. This expression is used to obtain the capacity factor of the column as a function of the moles of ions in solution, molal concentrations of solute and solvent, number of ions in solution and molal concentration–activity gradients. This model does not take into account the adsorption process and thus does not predict the amount of resin required for purification.

A modified competitive Langmuir binary isotherm [9], and homogenous diffusion model, was proposed by McCue *et al.* [3] to describe protein adsorption/desorption, and mass transfer, respectively. They found that a fraction of aggregates bind irreversibly to the resin. Inclusion of this irreversible term improved the model predictions over a wide range of conditions. They also showed that the separation was improved at lower elution velocity and shorter volume. However, their model did not estimate the amount of resin required to carry out purification. By using the static capacity in the presence of a binary mixture, q_{m} (units $\mathrm{mg\,ml^{-1}}$), McCue *et al.* [3] assumed that the monomer and aggregates are of similar dimensions. This is not entirely accurate, as the sizes of the aggregates can be two to five times larger than the native protein in most cases. This means that a gram of native protein will contain significantly more particles than a gram of aggregates. Our approach extends their work by considering the unsteady state kinetics of adsorption/desorption and by modifying the units of static capacity to account for the differences in mass of the monomer and aggregate species. With these modifications, the optimum amount of resin and ideal flow rate necessary for a target purification level can be predicted. This additional information could result in significant savings within the biopharmaceutical industry by minimizing excessive use of resin in chromatography column packing and also by reducing the time needed for purification process development.

The remaining sections are arranged as follows: in Section 5.2, the rate-limiting steps in hydrophobic interaction chromatography and the mathematical aspects of the proposed model are described. The corresponding flow schemes within the column are explained. In Section 5.3, the experimentation, which supports the proposed model, is explained. In Section 5.4, key aspects of the proposed model and potential applications are addressed.

5.2 Mathematical Model

5.2.1 The Rate-Limiting Step in the HIC Process

Substantial amounts of research efforts have been made to understand the HIC adsorption mechanism to the stationary phase through hydrophobic interaction. HIC is an entropy driven process, mediated by the rearrangement of water molecules during protein absorption to the stationary phase. A reversible interaction between a protein and the hydrophobic ligand of the matrix results in separation. However, questions are still open for the steps that control the separation process of a protein mixture consisting of both monomers and aggregates. The Langmuir adsorption isotherm can be applied to account for this process. A limitation of the proposed model could be when there is more than two distinct species in the system. A future study will address this limitation. The effect of protein concentration on the equilibrium binding capacity can be evaluated with various model proteins using different HIC stationary phases. The maximum binding capacity under a static condition can be predicted, along with information about the resin affinity constant, from the isotherm approach [10]. Several studies proposed that characteristics of the aggregates, and a conformational change upon adsorption, contribute to the overall mass transfer rate; the kinetics of the conformational change is the rate-limiting step [3,11,12]. The equilibrium and kinetic parameters for the adsorption of protein onto the stationary phase of HIC also have been intensively studied by various groups. The research results strongly support that adsorption is the rate-limiting step in chromatographic systems [13–17]. Bankston and Carta [13] found that for the adsorption of apolipoprotein A-IMilano (apoA-IM) and bovine serum albumin (BSA) on Q-Sepharose-HP and Macro-Prep-HQ anion exchangers, there was a transition from a pore- to a surface-dominated kinetics. Ferreira *et al.* [14] also found that for the adsorption of supercoiled plasmid onto quaternary ammonium anion-exchangers, there exists an initial stage with low amounts of adsorbent that was controlled by mass transfer and a later stage with high amount of adsorbent that was controlled by adsorption kinetics. Low plasmid concentrations and high solid-phase volumes also cause surface kinetics to control the overall process. Hage *et al.* [15] found that taking adsorption as the rate-limiting step in the binding of human serum albumin (HSA) to an immobilized anti-HSA antibody column, they could successfully predict what fraction of the protein would elute from the column. Kasche *et al.* [16] studied the adsorption of different proteins on single biospecific and hydrophobic adsorbents using scanning microscopy. They found that over 70% of adsorption occurs on the outer 25% of the resin particle where an almost constant bulk concentration of the molecule of interest leads to an overall surface-dominated process.

5.2.2 Dimensional Considerations

Wang and Carbonell [18] published an interesting study on the separation of staphylococcal enterotoxin B (SEB), a major toxin that causes food poisoning, using column affinity chromatography with an immobilized stationary phase. By modeling the transport and kinetic properties of the peptide affinity chromatography, they discovered that both the intraparticle mass transfer and the intrinsic adsorption were rate-limiting in the adsorption of molecules onto resin particles. In most cases, chromatography column performance is dictated by the mass transfer and adsorption inside of the chromatography particles. Both the mass transfer and adsorption occur at the same rates if the process is occurring in a microtiter plate well or in a packed column [19]. This means that a model using either mass transfer, or adsorption, as the rate-limiting step should hypothetically give identical results. Important factors controlling the rate-limiting step(s) in a chromatographic operation include the concentration of ions, pH, temperature, column geometry, and the type of buffer system. It would be difficult to draw a single conclusion as to which stage is rate-limiting in the process. In this study we consider the evidence proposed for the use of adsorption as the rate-limiting step, and develop a model based on an adsorption-driven process. To simulate mixture of monomers and aggregates, and to develop the mathematical model that can be extended to the separation of mixture of different kind of proteins, we selected the well-defined proteins BLG and BSA.

5.2.2.1 Adsorption Capacity vs. Concentration of Vacant Sites (q_{mi} vs. C_{vi})

McCue *et al.* [3] defined $q_{\mathrm{m}i}$ as the adsorption capacity, and evaluated it in units of mg ml^{-1}. This approach might prove problematic when developing comprehensive mechanistic models. The milligram numerator represents both the monomers and aggregates. This is valid only when the monomers and aggregates are approximately the same size. However, aggregates are known to have molar weights two to five times larger than that of the monomers. Thus, for the same mass of monomers and aggregates, there will be two to five times as many molecules in the monomer than in the aggregate sample. The current mechanistic model resolves this conflict by estimating the number of vacant sites (moles) in a gram of resin, which would give a more realistic approximation of the number of molecules being adsorbed on the resin's surface (number of moles). It is logical then to change the units of $q_{\mathrm{m}i}$ from mg ml^{-1} to units of mol g^{-1} of resin to match the units of $C_{\mathrm{v}i}$.

5.2.2.2 Concentration of Protein Adsorbed on Resin (q_i vs. C_{ia})

Measuring resin amounts in volume unit (ml) is very convenient and commonly used. However, this might result in problems associated with reproducibility, since the actual ratio of resin to solvent constantly varies. Therefore, we suggest the use of grams of resin, weighed after rinsing through a vacuum filtration system. Although there is still a residual amount of solvent in the resin at this stage,

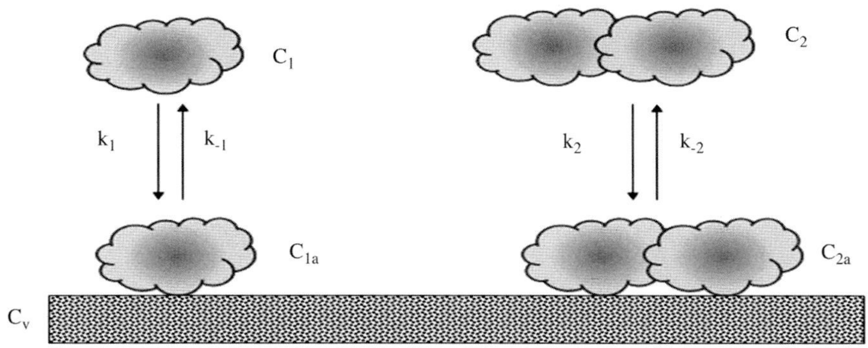

Figure 5.1 Adsorption of protein monomer/aggregate on resin surface with no irreversible adsorption. Liquid phase material balance in chromatographic column.

it offers more consistent measurements when compared to measurements in the volume of slurry. Moreover, using this unit offers dimensional synchrony between the concentration of protein adsorbed on resin (C_{ia}) and the concentration of vacant sites (C_{vi}).

5.2.3
Mathematical Model

Consider a Langmuir-type adsorption mechanism for protein and aggregates onto a resin surface, with no irreversible adsorption of aggregates, as shown in Figure 5.1. Usually, the aggregate mixture contains dimer and multimer species. These species that are adsorbed onto the resin ligands are specific chromophores. This implies that the aggregates undergo similar kinetics. Adsorption of monomer/aggregates can only occur on specific sites in the resin (where ligands occur). Since a unit mass of resin has a specified ligand density, there exist a finite number of elementary spaces capable of holding these molecules [9]. These spaces might be single ligand molecules, or a combination of ligand molecules, on the surface of the resin. Whatever mechanism takes place, there will only be a limited number of spaces/sites available for adsorption. Thus, for a given resin, the concentration of vacant sites will be given by

$$C_{\mathrm{v}} = \frac{N_{\mathrm{v}}}{N_{\mathrm{A}}}, \tag{5.1}$$

where N_{v} is the number of vacant sites per gram of resin, N_{A} is Avogadro's number, and C_{v} is the moles of vacant sites per gram of resin. If irreversible adsorption [3] is ignored, the rate of adsorption of monomer and aggregate species in a binary mixture will be given by

$$\begin{aligned}\text{Rate of adsorption of monomer} &= \frac{\mathrm{d}C_{1\mathrm{a}}}{\mathrm{d}t} \\ &= k_1 C_1 \left(C_{\mathrm{v}} - C_{1\mathrm{a}} - C_{2\mathrm{a}}\right) - k_{-1} C_{1\mathrm{a}} \end{aligned} \tag{5.2}$$

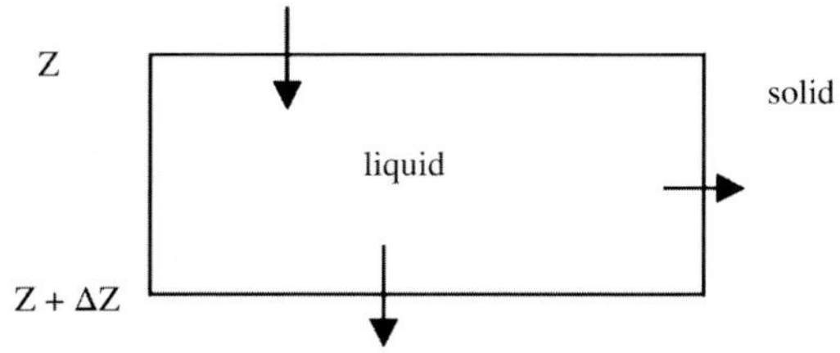

Figure 5.2 Conventional Langmuir-type kinetic experiment.

$$\text{Rate of adsorption of aggregate} = \frac{\mathrm{d}\,C_{2a}}{\mathrm{d}\,t} = k_2 C_2 \left(C_v - C_{1a} - C_{2a}\right) - k_{-2} C_{2a}, \tag{5.3}$$

where C_{1a} is the concentration of monomer adsorbed (mol g^{-1}), k_1 is the monomer adsorption constant (ml mg^{-1}·s), C_1 is the liquid phase concentration of the monomer (mol l^{-1}), C_v is the maximum adsorption capacity in the presence of a binary mixture (mol g^{-1}), C_{2a} is the concentration of the aggregate adsorbed (mol g^{-1}), k_{-1} is the monomer desorption kinetic constant (s^{-1}), k_2 is the aggregate adsorption kinetic constant (ml mg^{-1}·s), C_2 is the liquid phase concentration of the aggregate, and k_{-2} is the aggregate desorption kinetic constant.

There are only two phases present in the system: (i) a mobile liquid phase and (ii) a stationary solid phase. The rate at which the protein molecules are leaving the liquid phase is equal to the rate at which they are being adsorbed on the resin. Consider an infinitesimally small region, Δz, in the liquid phase, shown in Figure 5.2. Assume that there is no radial variation in the concentration of the monomer/aggregate species. A material balance of the region shown in Figure 5.2 gives

$$\varepsilon A \Delta z \frac{\partial C}{\partial t} = V_s A \varepsilon C|_z - V_s A \varepsilon C|_{z+\Delta z} + r_{ad} \Delta M. \tag{5.4}$$

Simplifying and taking the $\lim_{\Delta z \to 0}(4)$ gives

$$\varepsilon A \frac{\partial C}{\partial t} = -V_s A \varepsilon \frac{\partial C}{\partial z} + r_{ad} \frac{\Delta M}{\Delta z}. \tag{5.5}$$

If $\Delta M = \Delta V \xi$ and $\Delta V = A \Delta z$ then (5) simplifies to

$$\varepsilon \frac{\partial C}{\partial t} = -\vartheta \xi \frac{\partial C}{\partial M} + \xi r_{ad}. \tag{5.6}$$

Equation 5.6 was written for the monomer and aggregate species. Equations 5.2 and 5.3, and the two equations generated for monomer and aggregates from Equation 5.6, were solved simultaneously using the finite difference numerical method. Here, 48 internal finite difference points were used in the axial direction together with the entry and exit boundary conditions, which were approximated by the forward and backward finite difference approximations. This resulted in 50 × 4 ordinary differential and algebraic equations, which were solved using the "ode15s" solver in MATLAB (Mathworks, Inc., Waltham, MA).

The differences in the binding and elution phases would be from the change in the adsorption and desorption kinetic constants under the binding and elution conditions. The changes in the output are modeled from changes in the feed volumetric flow rate. This treatment assumes laminar flow within the chromatographic column. The Reynolds number for flow in a packed bed is given by

$$\mathrm{Re_p} = \frac{\rho V_s D_p}{\mu(1-\varepsilon)}, \tag{5.7}$$

where ρ is the density of the fluid ($\mathrm{g\,l^{-1}}$), V_s is the superficial velocity ($V_s = \vartheta/A$ where ϑ is the volumetric flow rate ($\mathrm{l\,s^{-1}}$) and A is cross-sectional area ($\mathrm{m^2}$)), D_p is the equivalent spherical diameter of the resin particles in the bed ($D_p = 6\,(\text{Particle volume}\,(\mathrm{m^3})/\text{particle surface area}\,(\mathrm{m^2}))$), μ is dynamic viscosity (Pa·s) and ε is the porosity. This condition is in line with the operating conditions for our column and system in the experimental section. For example, the highest expected Reynolds number, based on our experimental conditions, should occur for the highest superficial velocity, since density, particle diameter, and viscosity remain constant for the different conditions.

$$\mathrm{Re_p} = \frac{2\rho QR}{\mu A(1-\varepsilon)} = \frac{2\times 1\,\mathrm{kg\,l^{-1}} \times 1.67\times 10^{-4}\,\mathrm{l\,s^{-1}} \times 45\times 10^{-6}\,\mathrm{m}}{1\times 10^{-3}\,\mathrm{kg\,m^{-1}\cdot s} \times \pi \times (16\times 10^{-3}\,\mathrm{m})^2(1-0.3)}$$
$$= 0.03.$$

5.3 Experimentation

Absorbance data were recorded on a Perkin-Elmer Lambda 25 UV–VIS Spectrometer (PerkinElmer, Waltham, MA, USA) and were reported in absorbance units. All commercial grade reagents were used without further purification, except as otherwise stated in the procedure.

5.3.1 Protein Solutions

Purified and crystallized proteins were used as feed. Bovine serum albumin (Sigma-Aldrich, St. Louise, MO, USA) (BSA, $M_r \sim 66.7$ kD) and β-lactoglobulin (Sigma-Aldrich) (BLG, $M_r \sim 18.4$ kD) were used in the experimental studies due to their differences in mass; BSA was modeled as the aggregate and BLG as the protein monomer.

5.3.2
Determination of Adsorption and Desorption Kinetic Constants

Equilibrated Octyl Sepharose (GE Healthcare Lifesciences, Piscataway, NJ, USA) (0.6–1.0 g) was placed in a 100 ml beaker. Two milliliters of a 1–3 mg ml^{-1} solution of protein in phosphate buffered solution containing ammonium sulfate (0.05 M sodium phosphate + 1.0 M ammonium sulfate) at a pH of 7 was poured instantaneously into the beaker containing the resin. The resulting mixture was swirled, and a 200 μl solution was pulled out of the mixture every 15 s. Care was taken not to pull in any resin. Once the solution was removed, the semi-dry resin was transferred onto a Buchner funnel with filter paper using a spatula. The resin was rinsed using distilled water (2 × 5 ml). Then, the rinsed resin was carefully transferred into a 100 ml beaker, and 2 ml of phosphate buffered solution containing ammonium sulfate (0.05 M sodium phosphate + 0.25 M ammonium sulfate) at a pH of 7 was added to simulate elution conditions. The mixture was swirled continuously while samples were extracted every 15 s. The rinsing step was repeated using distilled water, and the batch contact was repeated to verify any irreversibly bound protein using 1.0 N NaOH. The absorbance of the solution was read at 280 nm and the concentration was calculated using Beer's law. The amount of protein adsorbed by the adsorbent was obtained from a material balance. The adsorption and desorption kinetic constants were determined using a geometric approach [20]. Detailed discussion on the method is provided in Section 5.4.

5.3.3
Column Chromatography

Octyl Sepharose was packed into an XK 16/20 I.D. glass column (GE Healthcare Lifesciences, Piscataway, NJ, USA). Bed heights ranged from 2 to 20 cm. A QuantaSep® 100 chromatography system (Sepragen, Hayward, CA, USA) was used in all of the chromatography experiments. After equilibration of the resin, a slurry containing ~ 70% resin in a packing solution (20 mM sodium phosphate, pH 7.0) was degassed under vacuum while swirling. The column was mounted vertically and flushed with packing solution. The column outlet was sealed, and about 2 ml of packing solution was left at the bottom of the column. A slurry containing known weights of the resin were prepared by mixing with the adsorption buffer (0.05 M sodium phosphate + 1.0 M ammonium sulfate) at a pH of 7. The slurry was degassed by exposure to ultrasonic waves for 20 min using a VWR B2500 A – MT tabletop ultrasonic cleaner set to high. The degassed slurry was poured into the column in one motion while avoiding the introduction of air bubbles. The resin was allowed to settle for 30 min and the inlet was connected to a reservoir of packing solution. The pump was set to a 10 ml min^{-1} flow rate, and the packing solution (0.05 M sodium phosphate + 1.0 M ammonium sulfate) at a pH of 7 was passed through the column until a steady height was reached.

The column was loaded with a known mixture of the monomer/aggregate and flushed using the adsorption buffer. The column was then eluted with a phosphate buffer (0.05 M sodium phosphate + 0.25 M ammonium sulfate) at a pH of 7. About 1.5 ml fractions were collected while monitoring the UV absorbance at 280 nm both during adsorption and elution. The fractions were analyzed for the concentration of the individual components.

5.4 Results and Discussion

5.4.1 Kinetic Constants

The adsorption and desorption kinetic constants were the most important parameters required for input into the model. Previous modeling work by McCue *et al.* [3] considered a steady state model to explain adsorption, and considered the binding strength constant as the equilibrium constant. However, the mechanistic model here considers unsteady state conditions, and thus it becomes important to decouple the binding strength constant into the adsorption and desorption kinetic constants. In order to achieve this, a modification of the Kuan approach [20] is used.

For a Langmuir-type adsorption process where species S is adsorbed on ligand molecule L, such that S + L⇔SL, then the typical surface coverage versus time diagram is shown in Figure 5.3, where θ_e is the equilibrium coverage, k_0 is the initial slope, and t_e is the time required to reach equilibrium. Figure 5.3 shows an initial phase with fast kinetics and a latter phase with slower kinetics.

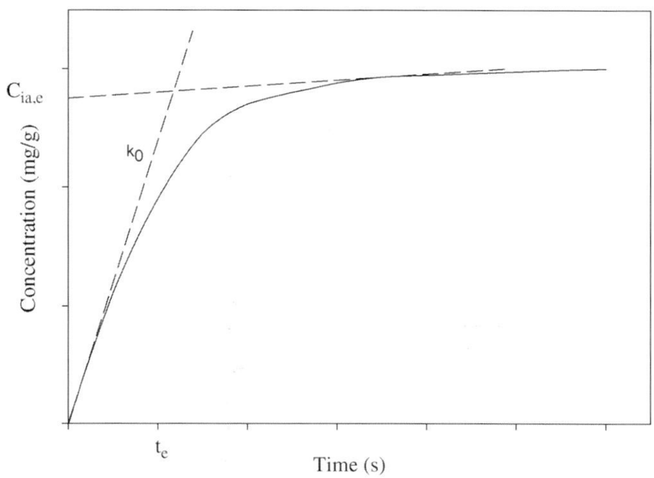

Figure 5.3 Reaction rate as a function of concentration adsorbed.

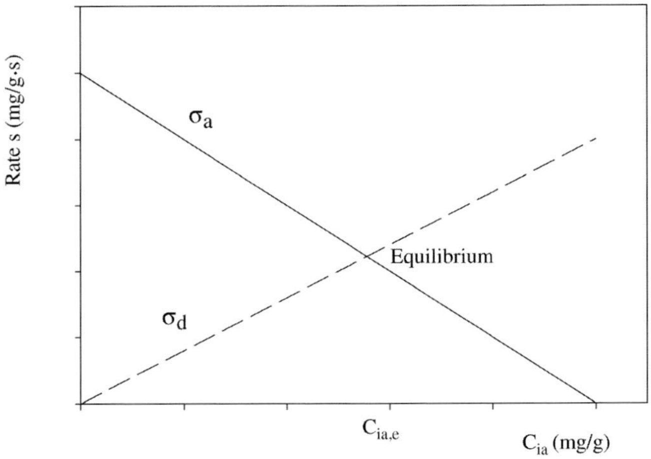

Figure 5.4 Breakthrough profile for β-lactoglobulin (8 g of resin with total bed height: 4.5 cm).

Figure 5.4 shows the rate curve as a function of concentration of the monomer/aggregate adsorbed.

The rate of adsorption σ_a and desorption σ_d is given by

$$\sigma_a = k_i C_i (C_v - C_{ia}) \tag{5.8}$$

$$\sigma_d = k_{-i} C_{ia}. \tag{5.9}$$

At equilibrium, the rate of adsorption and desorption are equal and the concentration of protein on the surface of the resin is given by $C_{ia,e}$. From Figure 5.3, the concentration of protein adsorbed per gram of resin is given by Equations (5.10) and (5.11) for the early and late stages, respectively:

$$C_{ia} = k_0 t \tag{5.10}$$

$$C_{ia} = C_{ia,e}. \tag{5.11}$$

The time required for the system to achieve equilibrium, t_e, is therefore given by Equation 5.12

$$t_e = \frac{C_{ia,e}}{k_0}. \tag{5.12}$$

Substituting Equation 5.12 into Equations 5.8 and 5.9, and noting that at equilibrium the rate of adsorption is equal to the rate of desorption, yields Equation 5.13 for equilibrium situations.

$$k_i C_i (C_v - k_0 t) = k_{-i} k_0 t. \tag{5.13}$$

At any point in the process, the overall rate is given by the rate of adsorption minus the rate of desorption. Thus, the rate times the time elapsed should give the amount of protein adsorbed. Therefore, the concentration of protein

Table 5.1 Batch contact vs. equilibrium experiment data.

	Protein	k_i (ml mg^{-1}·s)	k_{-i} (s^{-1})	K (ml mg^{-1})	$K_{\text{batch contact}}$ (ml mg^{-1})
Adsorption conditions	BSA	4.33×10^{-2}	1.19×10^{-1}	3.6×10^{-1}	4.55×10^{-1}
	β-Lactoglobulin	9.65×10^{-2}	2.40×10^{-2}	4.02	4.61
Desorption conditions	BSA	2.31×10^{-2}	1.30×10^{-1}	1.77×10^{-1}	1.9×10^{-1}
	β-Lactoglobulin	1.73×10^{-1}	1.05×10^{-1}	1.65	1.89

adsorbed at equilibrium is given by Equation 5.14.

$$C_{ia,s} = \int_0^t (\sigma_a - \sigma_d)\mathrm{d}t. \tag{5.14}$$

Substituting Equation 5.13 into 5.14, then integrating and rearranging, yields an expression for the adsorption and desorption kinetic constants:

$$k_i = \frac{2k_0}{C_i C_v} \tag{5.15}$$

$$k_{-i} = \frac{2(C_v - k_0 t_e)}{C_v t_e}. \tag{5.16}$$

The results obtained from the geometric approach are compared with results from the batch contact experiments and are given in Table 5.1.

5.4.2 Protein Denaturation

An important aspect worth mentioning is the observed unfolding of proteins on hydrophobic resins [21–23]. This phenomenon is applicable to our model's proteins and the Sepharose resins used in this study, and was analyzed well by Jungbauer *et al.* [24]. Protein unfolding was not directly accounted for by our model, but we believe the results still offer valuable insight into HIC modeling: First, Jungbauer *et al.* [24] showed that at low buffer ionic strengths (< 0.3 M $(NH_4)_2SO_4$), there is virtually little to no unfolding of bovine serum albumin on phenyl, butyl, and methyl Sepharose hydrophobic resins; for up to 1 M $(NH_4)_2SO_4$ there was less than 10% unfolding. Second, our method used for estimating the desorption kinetic constants generated values that take into account any surface modifications that may have occurred since we measured the changes in concentration of the protein in solution under desorption conditions over time. This current approach gives initial insight into understanding the mechanism of separation within the column, and in order to build a more comprehensive model, surface modification of the proteins would be incorporated into the model in future work.

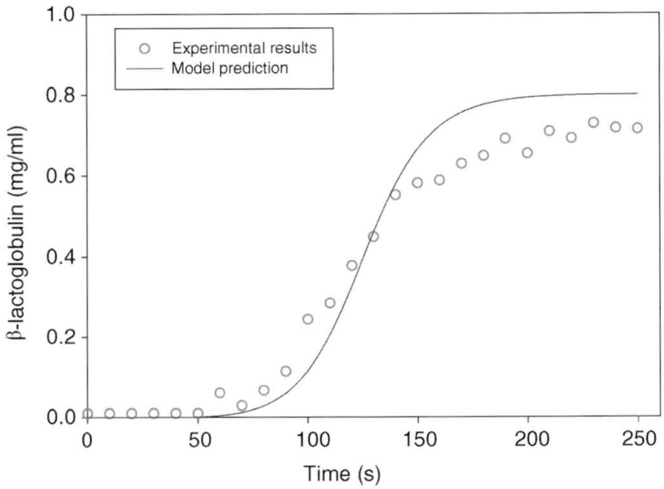

Figure 5.5 Elution profile for β-lactoglobulin.

5.4.3
Model vs. Experimental Results

Experimental and mechanistic models that fit breakthrough and elution curves for the protein (BLG) are shown on Figures 5.5 and 5.6, where one set of experiments was selected for visualization. The experimental results were obtained by estimating the concentration of the individual components of the fractions collected from the column chromatography. Similar plots were obtained from BSA

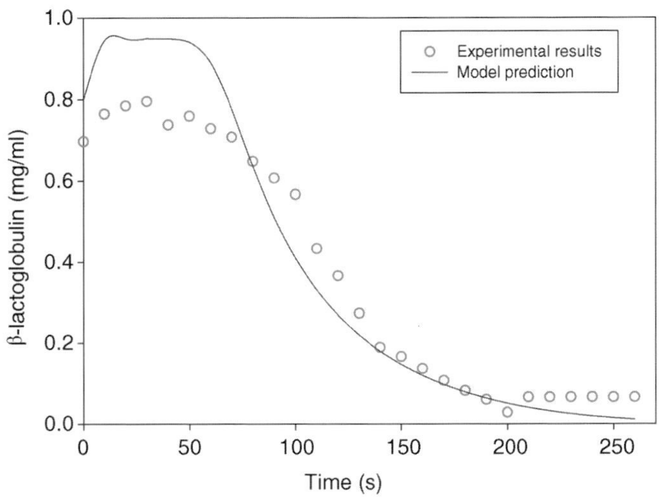

Figure 5.6 BLG distribution in column during binding.

Table 5.2 Experimental versus fitted results for C_v.

Experimental C_{v1} (mol g^{-1})	Experimental C_{v2} (mol g^{-1})	C_v from curve fitting (mol g^{-1})
1.09×10^{-7}	2.7×10^{-7}	7.36×10^{-8}

(not shown). The elution model was obtained by changing the adsorption and desorption kinetic constants from binding to elution mode (Table 5.1), and by setting the final column conditions from the breakthrough stage as the initial conditions for elution. Similar experiments were conducted for a column packed with 17.55 g of resin, and the obtained results were fit equally well. From the experimental results, the value of C_v could not be independently verified; thus, starting with the initial guess of the value, obtained from Table 5.1, the model was fit with experimental results in order to obtain a more accurate value of C_v. The results obtained are shown in Table 5.2. These values are the actual estimation of the number of moles of vacant sites, from which the actual number of vacant sites can be estimated; agreement between the results show that this technique can be useful in applications such as evaluating lot to lot variability of ligand density in resin production.

5.4.4 Applications

After correctly fitting the model with the experimental results, the distribution of protein and aggregate species within the column during binding and elution was examined to obtain a clearer picture of the concentration changes as a function of time and space. The amount of resin required for purification can be calculated based on the new mathematical term that is different from the previous modeling of other groups. It is well described in Section 5.2.2.1 (q_{mi} vs. C_{vi}) and Section 5.2.2.2 (q_i vs. C_{ia}). The modified units for static capacity used in our calculation allow us to optimize the amount of resin necessary to produce the target purification level and the ideal flow rate. This information, plotted in Figures 5.7 and 5.8, is useful when designing efficient separation processes. For instance, current practices in process development for the purification of proteins involve screening multiple factors and optimizing them. This model can offer more flexibility by offering the process developers the ability to observe the expected outcomes under different buffer/flow/resin schemes rapidly, and without the added costs associated with buffers, resin, and time. Then, the results obtained from this model screening phase can be used to reduce the design space, keeping the experimental requirements minimal.

Figures 5.7 and 5.8 are used to evaluate the ideal point to stop adsorption and begin elution in order to ensure optimum separation between the monomer and the aggregates. From these figures, the best separation between the monomer and aggregate species occurs between time units 10 and 15. Beyond these points,

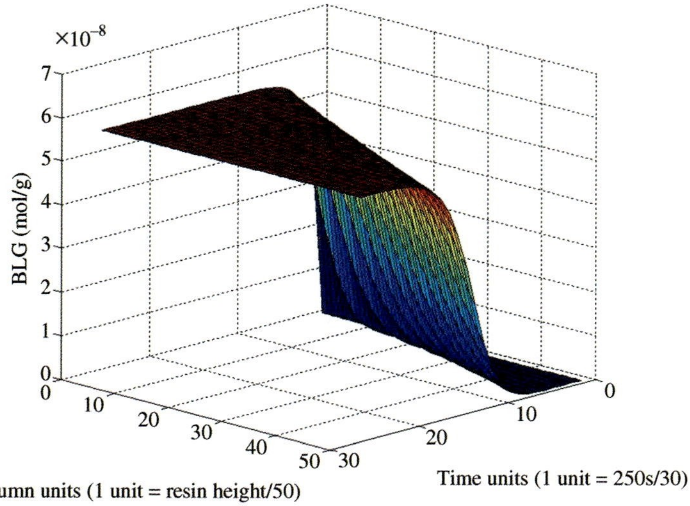

Figure 5.7 BLG distribution in column during binding.

fraction purity is reduced. This is shown clearly in Figure 5.9. At 12 time units, there is good separation between the monomer and the aggregate making it an ideal point to stop binding and begin elution. This approach is further confirmed by the concentration distribution of unbound monomer and aggregate in the liquid phase at time unit 12, which will be "washed-out" with buffer during elution as shown in Figure 5.10.

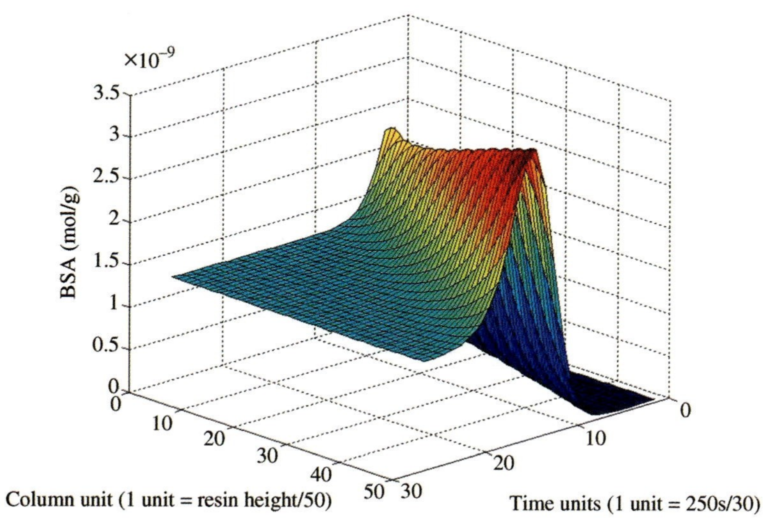

Figure 5.8 BSA distribution in column during binding.

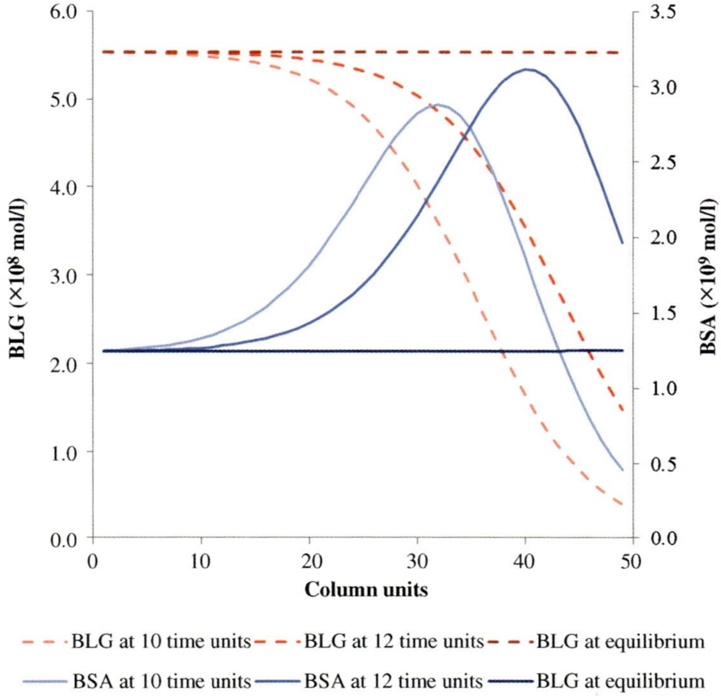

Figure 5.9 BLG and BSA distribution at (a) 10, (b) 12, and (c) 30 time units.

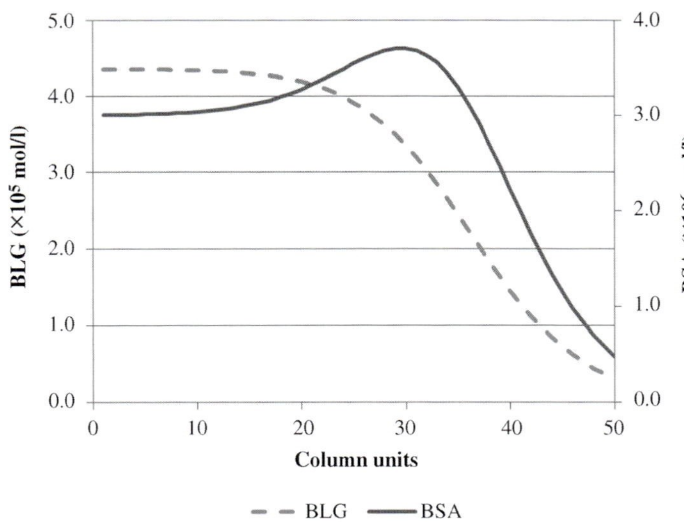

Figure 5.10 Liquid phase concentration of BLG and BSA at time unit 12.

Current practices recommend stopping adsorption at 5% breakthrough to minimize waste [25]. However, based on the model predictions, elution at different breakthrough levels might be beneficial when striking a balance between yield and purity. For instance, for this mixture, elution at 10% breakthrough gives increased purity due to better separation between the monomer and aggregate species.

5.5 Conclusion

This research confirms that protein adsorption and desorption can be used as the rate-limiting step in the modeling of a separation of a protein aggregate mixture by HIC. By using a competitive binary Langmuir isotherm and performing a material balance on the liquid phase in the column, the binding profiles for BSA and BLG were predicted.

The mechanistic model is also useful for understanding the variation of the distribution of protein and aggregate components in the column as a function of time and distance traveled in the resin. This is useful for choosing the optimum conditions for interrupting binding and starting elution. The model developed can be used for predicting purification performance when using different column sizes and amounts of resin. This is useful in a scale up study. Incorporation of this model into a user interface can be useful for assessing the efficiency of different flow rates, packing density, and resin amount combinations in order to improve product yield and purity.

Acknowledgments

The authors would like to thank financial support provided by Massachusetts Life Science Center and the University of Massachusetts (New faculty start-up grant, and the President Office Science and Technology funding).

The authors would like to thank the Massachusetts Life Science Center and the University of Massachusetts (New Faculty start-up grant and the President's Office of Science and Technology Funding) for the financial support in this project.

List of Symbols

A	Cross-sectional area of column (dm^2)
C_1	Monomer concentration in solution ($mol\,l^{-1}$)
C_{1a}	Concentration of monomer adsorbed ($mol\,g^{-1}$)
C_{2a}	Concentration of aggregate adsorbed ($mol\,g^{-1}$)
$C_{ia,e}$	Concentration of species i adsorbed at equilibrium ($mol\,g^{-1}$)

C_v	Concentration of vacant sites (mol g^{-1} of resin)
D_p	Equivalent spherical diameter of the resin particles in the bed (m)
k_0	Initial slope of Langmuir-type kinetic experiment (mol $g^{-1}\cdot s$)
k_1	Monomer adsorption constant (ml $mg^{-1}\cdot s$)
k_{-1}	Monomer desorption constant (s^{-1})
k_2	Aggregate adsorption constant (ml $mg^{-1}\cdot s$)
k_{-2}	Aggregate desorption constant (s^{-1})
M	Mass of resin (g)
N_A	Avogadro's number (6.02×10^{23} sites/mol)
N_v	Number of vacant sites per gram of resin (sites/g)
r_{ad}	Net rate of adsorption (mol $g^{-1}\cdot s$)
Re_p	Reynolds number for a packed bed
t_e	time required to reach equilibrium (s)
V_s	Superficial velocity (m s^{-1})
z	Column length (dm)

Greek Symbols

ε	Porosity
μ	Dynamic viscosity (Pa·s)
ξ	Packing density (g l^{-1})
ρ	Fluid density (g l^{-1})
σ_a	Adsorption rate (mol $g^{-1}\cdot s$)
σ_d	Desorption rate (mol $g^{-1}\cdot s$)
υ	Volumetric flow rate (l s^{-1})

References

1 Harris, S.A.E. (1995) *Protein Purification Methods: A Practical Approach*, IRL Press, Oxford, UK.

2 Sivasankar, B. (2006) *Bioseperations: Principles and Techniques*, PHI Learning Pvt. Ltd, New Delhi, India.

3 McCue, J.T., Engel, P., Ng, A., Macniven, R., and Thommes, J. (2008) *Bioprocess Biosyst. Eng.*, **31**, 261–275.

4 Queiroz, J.A., Tomaz, C.T., and Cabral, J.M.S. (2001) *J. Biotechnol.*, **87**, 143–159.

5 Horváth, C., Melander, W., and Molnár, I. (1976) *J. Chromatogr. A*, **125**, 129–156.

6 Arakawa, T. and Timasheff, S.N. (1982) *Biochemistry*, **21**, 6545–6552.

7 Perkins, T.W., Mak, D.S., Root, T.W., and Lightfoot, E.N. (1997) *J. Chromatogr. A*, **766**, 1–14.

8 Arakawa, T. and Timasheff, S.N. (1984) *Biochemistry*, **23**, 5912–5923.

9 Langmuir, I. (1918) *J. Am. Chem. Soc.*, **40**, 1361–1403.

10 Pakiman, N., Isa, N.H., Abol Hassan, M.A., Walter, J.K., and Abdullah, N. (2012) *J. Appl. Sci.*, **12**, 1136–1141.

11 Hahn, R., Deinhofer, K., Machold, C., and Jungbauer, A. (2003) *J. Chromatogr. B*, **790**, 99–114.

12 Weaver, L.E. and Carta, G. (1996) *Biotechnol. Prog.*, **12**, 342–355.

13 Bankston, T.E. and Carta, G. (2010) *Biotechnol. J.*, **5**, 1040–1049.

14 Ferreira, G.N., Cabral, J.M., and Prazeres, D.M. (2000) *Biotechnol. Prog.*, **16**, 416–424.

15 Hage, D.S., Thomas, D.H., and Beck, M.S. (1993) *Anal. Chem.*, **65**, 1622–1630.

16 Kasche, V., Boer, M.de., Lazo, C., and Gad, M. (2003) *J. Chromatogr. B*, **790**, 115–129.

17 Nilsson, M., Hakanson, H., and Mattiasson, B. (1992) *J. Chromatogr. A*, **597**, 383–389.

18 Wang, G. and Carbonell, R.G. (2005) *J. Chromatogr. A*, **1078**, 98–112.

19 GE-Healthcare (2009) http://www.gelifesciences.com/aptrix/upp00919.nsf/Content/E08E8523054FCEECC1257628001D5795/$file/28940362AA.pdf.

20 Kuan, W.H., Lo, S.L., Chang, C.M., and Wang, M.K. (2000) *Chemosphere*, **41**, 1741–1747.

21 Benedek, K. (1988) *J. Chromatogr. A*, **458**, 93–104.

22 Goheen, S.C. and Engelhorn, S.C. (1984) *J. Chromatogr. A*, **317**, 55–65.

23 Wu, S.-L., Benedek, K., and Karger, B.L. (1986) *J. Chromatogr. A*, **359**, 3–17.

24 Jungbauer, A., Machold, C., and Hahn, R. (2005) *J. Chromatogr. A*, **1079**, 221–228.

25 Willoughby, N.A., Kirschner, T., Smith, M.P., Hjorth, R., and Titchener-Hooker, N.J. (1999) *J. Chromatogr. A*, **840**, 195–204.

6
Continuous Animal Cell Perfusion Processes: The First Step Toward Integrated Continuous Biomanufacturing

Leda R. Castilho

6.1
Introduction

Recombinant biopharmaceuticals were first approved for human use in 1982, when commercialization of recombinant human insulin produced by *Escherichia coli* was authorized by regulatory agencies. Four years later, two products derived from mammalian cells were approved: (i) OKT-3, a monoclonal antibody secreted by hybridoma cells, and (ii) tissue plasminogen activator (t-PA) produced by Chinese hamster ovary (CHO) cells [1].

However, in spite of over 30 years of industrial reality, the biopharmaceutical industry remained highly conservative in terms of the introduction of new production technologies, with only incremental process improvements being implemented over time [2]. Because in the beginning the products were unique and protected by patents, the technologies adopted by the companies in the sector focused on the concept of time-to-market rather than on process efficiency and cost [3]. Thus, to shorten process development times and keep process complexity as low as possible, batch and fed-batch processes became prevalent in the biopharmaceutical industry, despite the higher volumetric productivities that can be achieved by perfusion processes. While many other sectors, such as the petrochemical, chemical, food, and pharmaceutical industries, have invested over time in process intensification through transition from batch to continuous manufacturing, as of 2012 approximately 90% of the biopharmaceutical products were still manufactured at industrial scale through batch or fed-batch processes [4]. Traditionally, industrial continuous perfusion processes remained restricted to the production of unstable products, such as enzymes and coagulation factors, due to their need to be quickly removed from the bioreactor environment to avoid degradation.

However, the current business context – characterized by hundreds of biopharmaceutical products in development, multiple product pipelines, rapidly changing market demands, and rising competition from off-patent biopharmaceuticals – is increasingly challenging industry conservatism [2,3]. Thus, the biopharmaceutical industry interest in continuous bioprocessing has been growing

Continuous Processing in Pharmaceutical Manufacturing, First Edition. Edited by Ganapathy Subramanian.

in the last few years, aiming not only to implement efficient perfusion cell culture processes, but also to integrate them with continuous downstream operations, aiming at higher throughput, lower costs, and product/scale flexibility. The current business scenario is strengthening a trend to disruptive innovations and to the establishment of a new paradigm in biopharmaceutical manufacturing.

Several companies, such as Amgen, Baxter, Bayer, Biomarin, Boehringer Ingelheim, Janssen, DSM, EMD Serono, Genzyme/Sanofi, Novartis, Pfizer, and Shire, already have perfusion cell culture facilities, and several of them (e.g., Amgen, Bayer, Genzyme/Sanofi, and Pfizer) are investigating continuous downstream operations [5].

The focus of this chapter is on perfusion cell culture processes for the production of recombinant therapeutic proteins. Since the development of an efficient continuous high-cell-density cultivation platform is strongly linked to developments in correlated areas, after a section on basic aspects of perfusion processes, issues such as cell banking, seed train development, culture media, cultivation conditions, cell retention devices, and integration with downstream operations will be discussed.

6.2
The Basics of Perfusion Processes

Among cell culturists, continuous cultivation processes with cell recycle have primarily been known as perfusion processes. Because of the continuous cell retention in the bioreactor, associated to the continuous supply of nutrients and continuous removal of metabolites, perfusion cultures allow overcoming two drawbacks of animal cells: (i) their low specific growth rate (in the order of $0.03\,h^{-1}$) and (ii) their sensitivity to accumulated metabolites (e.g., ammonia).

The continuous medium exchange allows cells to keep growing exponentially until a desired threshold concentration is reached, which is usually determined according to the maximum oxygen transfer capacity of the bioreactor system or by other conditions that could turn the process unstable if cell density further increased. When the desired threshold concentration is achieved, either cell growth can be arrested (e.g., by temperature shifts) or controlled cell bleed can be started, keeping cells in a growing state. Optimal process strategy will depend on cell characteristics, on product stability, and on whether product formation is growth-associated or not.

Cell viabilities in perfusion processes are typically high, which is beneficial for downstream processing. Moreover, at high cell densities, perfusion rates increase and the residence time of the product inside the bioreactor decreases, which is good for product quality, specially in the case of unstable products. Quick harvesting of the product to store under refrigerated conditions and in the absence of cells or to rapidly start purification can be crucial for proteins that are easily degraded due to process conditions or due to the action of proteases in the culture broth, such as some therapeutic enzymes and coagulation factors.

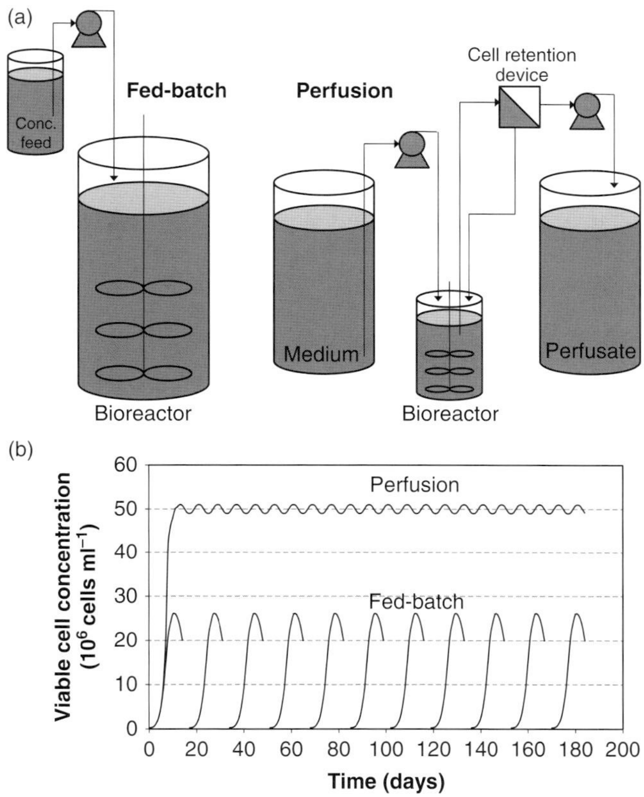

Figure 6.1 (a) Overview of bioreactor and tanks (medium and/or harvest) in fed-batch and perfusion process. (b) Comparison of frequency of perfusion and fed-batch runs over a given time period.

Achieving higher cell densities usually translates into reaching relatively high product concentrations. This, combined with the continuous harvesting of the perfusate, translates into high volumetric productivities and allows achieving a given annual production capacity using bioreactors that are much smaller than in batch or fedbatch processes, but with higher medium consumption (Figure 6.1a).

Perfusion runs are usually designed to run for very long periods (usually a couple of months), and this decreases frequency of cleaning-in-place (CIP) and sterilizing-in-place (SIP) operations. Also, bioreactor turnaround periods and time spent with nonproductive culture phases are minimized, contributing to process efficiency (Figure 6.1b).

6.3
Cell Banking and Inoculum Development in the Context of Perfusion Processes

The quality and quantity of cryopreserved cells, as well as the seed-train expansion strategy to generate inoculum for the production bioreactor, are crucial issues that can determine the success of a production campaign. In the last decade, perfusion cultivations have been increasingly used to generate high-density cultures that can be preserved in cryobags, which in turn can later be thawed to directly inoculate seed bioreactors, eliminating small-scale culture flask cultivations. Also, perfusion has become increasingly popular for the operation of seed bioreactors, as a way of decreasing the number of seed-train steps and/or increasing inoculum density of the production bioreactor.

Working cell banks have traditionally been comprised of several hundreds of 1–2 ml vials, which are individually thawed to small-scale flasks and cultivated over many steps in increasing scales, until enough cell mass is obtained to inoculate a production bioreactor [6,7]. In the early 1990s, Ninomiya *et al.* [8] were pioneers in proposing large-scale, high-density freezing of mammalian cells using blood banking bags. They froze 25-ml aliquots of hybridoma suspensions at up to 150E6 cells ml^{-1} to later use in high-density cultures upon thawing. Heidemann *et al.* [9] carried out a deep investigation on this subject using recombinant CHO and baby hamster kidney (BHK) cells. They proposed freezing a total of 2E9 cells in 50 or 100-ml aliquots stored in cryobags of 250 or 500-ml nominal volume, respectively. The 1 : 5 ratio of working to nominal volume was intended to keep bag thickness low in order to better control the freezing and thawing rates. A standard −40 °C freezer showed as good results as a controlled-rate freezer for incubating the cryobags prior to vapor-phase nitrogen storage, and thawing at room temperature showed to be as adequate as at 37 °C. The use of the larger cryobags (100 ml) showed to be more adequate, since the cell suspension from a perfusion bioreactor could be directly frozen, with no need to centrifuge cells in order to concentrate them to get the target amount of 2E9 cells.

Heidemann *et al.* [9] further showed that large-scale freezing using 7.5% dimethylsulfoxide (DMSO) as cryoprotectant and its direct 20-fold dilution to a 2 l bioreactor upon thawing, with no need for DMSO wash steps, resulted in a quicker, more robust, and less labor-intensive seed-train strategy, which yielded equivalent cell viability, specific growth rate, specific productivity, and product quality as compared to the previous traditional seed-train based on 1-ml cryovials. A bioreactor with a small bottom, which can be inoculated directly from cryobags at 2-l initial working volume, then have its volume increased up to 12 l, and then be operated in perfusion, was proposed as a way to eventually enable inoculum generation for a 200-l production bioreactor in the same vessel in a single step.

Kleman *et al.* [10] used a design-of-experiment approach to study the conditions for large-scale freezing of CHO and HEK 293 cells in cryobags. Their results compare well with those by Heidemann *et al.* [9], since they found DSMO concentrations of 5–6% to be optimal when freezing cells at 30–40E6 ml^{-1}, and observed no need for DMSO wash post-thaw. DMSO concentrations in cultures post-thaw had no negative effects up to 0.3% [10] or 0.4% [9].

Application of perfusion to high-density cell cryopreservation was also evaluated by Clincke *et al.* [11], who developed an extremely high cell density perfusion process that allowed cell freezing at up to 100E6 cells ml^{-1}. Their process showed to be a reliable alternative for high-density cell bank manufacturing, with healthy recovery of cells upon thawing.

Seth [7] highlighted that, when using cryobags to freeze cells, filling of bags directly from a perfusion bioreactor could be done automatically using bag manifolds, reducing manipulation and contamination risks. Furthermore, in order to ensure optimized controlled rate freezing in the bags, customized rack configurations could be used in the freezers [12].

Tao *et al.* [13] developed a high-density cell bank and reported savings of 9 days in inoculum development by the use of cryopreserved aliquots containing 5E8 cells, which allowed direct inoculation of a Wave bioreactor, with no need for early cell expansion in flasks. The authors stressed that the high cell bank quality and the simplicity of the disposable perfusion system used to prepare it were key to successfully implement it in a manufacturing facility. According to Bonham-Carter [14], savings in seed-train expansion could be even larger (up to 2 weeks) when using 50–500 ml cryobags containing high-density cell suspensions propagated in perfusion bioreactors coupled to the ATF (alternating tangential filtration) system. Their strategy comprised thawing cells from a cryobag directly into a seed perfusion bioreactor, and inoculating the cells from the seed bioreactor directly into a fed-batch production bioreactor, enabling a period as short as 25–30 days between thawing and production harvesting.

Since most industrial processes are still carried out in fed-batch mode, different authors investigated the use of perfusion processes just to streamline seed-train expansion and/or to have a higher density at inoculation of the fed-batch production reactor. Kaisermayer and Yang [15] compared inocula developed in perfusion (48E6 cells ml^{-1}) and in batch mode (5E6 cells ml^{-1}). Perfusion allowed a sixfold higher split ratio (1 : 30 vs. 1 : 5), with a potential saving of at least one step in inoculum propagation, and enabled an 80% higher inoculation density (7.4E5 ml^{-1} vs. 4.1E5 ml^{-1}), so that maximum viable cell density was reached 2 days earlier in the fed-batch production bioreactor. Pohlscheidt *et al.* [16] reported that by carrying out a short 5 day perfusion cultivation in the $(n-1)$ seed bioreactor, a cell density of 16E6 cells ml^{-1} was attained, allowing a higher inoculation density of a 13.5-kl fed-batch production bioreactor. In this way, the duration of the fed-batch process was decreased by 3 days (−20%), allowing an increase in capacity utilization by 12–19% and a cost reduction by 7–9%.

The process acceleration reported by these authors for fed-batch processes receiving high-density inocula from seed perfusion bioreactors can also be experienced in production bioreactors ran in perfusion. Some companies are using perfusion in the $(n-1)^{th}$ seed bioreactor in order to be able to inoculate the nth bioreactor (i.e., the production bioreactor) at high cell densities (e.g., 5E6 ml^{-1}) and immediately start to perfuse.

6.4 Culture Conditions

In spite of the higher volumetric productivity that characterizes perfusion processes, establishing culture conditions to ensure stable, long-lasting high-cell-density processes is more labor-intensive and requires higher culture medium costs than to establish batch or fed-batch processes. Also, the time to develop a perfusion process and test/validate different batches from different culture time points can be considerably longer. In the past, when the concept of "time-to-market" dominated the biopharmaceutical arena, this was one of the main factors to move companies away from perfusion processes.

However, as discussed before, a change is being observed due to the new business context combined with new, simple laboratory tools that help carry out perfusion or perfusion-like processes at very small scale, decreasing medium consumption and allowing parallel operation of many units. There are nowadays a wide range of either commercial or in-house developed parallel small-volume or micro bioreactors [17], many of them capable of operating in perfusion, so that the low volume and the multiple units allow decreasing R&D time and costs.

Multiple noninstrumented small-scale flasks have been operated by different authors under "semicontinuous" or "semiperfusion" conditions in order to mimic perfusion processes [18–20]. For instance, the spin tubes (also known as tube-spin bioreactors), which became very popular in cell culture laboratories in the last years, can be easily used as low-cost devices, with working volumes as low as 5 ml, to study perfusion processes. After removal from CO_2 incubators, they can be placed directly into centrifuges to allow for medium exchange for one or more times a day, allowing intermittent perfusion to be studied at different dilution rates, which can be defined according to the instantly measured cell density and the cell-specific perfusion rate.

One key point to study when aiming at high-cell-density processes is the culture medium. Traditionally, perfusion processes have been carried out by feeding cultures with fresh nonmodified culture medium [21], at flow rates increasing with the growing cell density. However, this may not be the best solution when targeting high cell densities, for example, above 30E6 cells ml^{-1}, or when intending to get a very concentrated product stream.

After a comprehensive work to select a platform chemically defined medium for cultivation of different CHO cell lines at our laboratory [22], the CHO-MACS-CD medium was selected [23], which routinely gives us approximately 8–12E6 cells ml^{-1} in batch cultures ran from small spin-tubes up to 10 l bioreactors. However, in perfusion processes, even when applying perfusion rates in the range of 2–4 d^{-1}, cultures fed with this medium tended to undergo a sudden decrease in viability when viable cell densities approached 30E6 ml^{-1}. The medium supplier carried out spent media analyses and started supplying us a nutrient-balanced medium with a few additional supplements (which was named TC-LECC), which we use nowadays to run stable perfusion cultures at

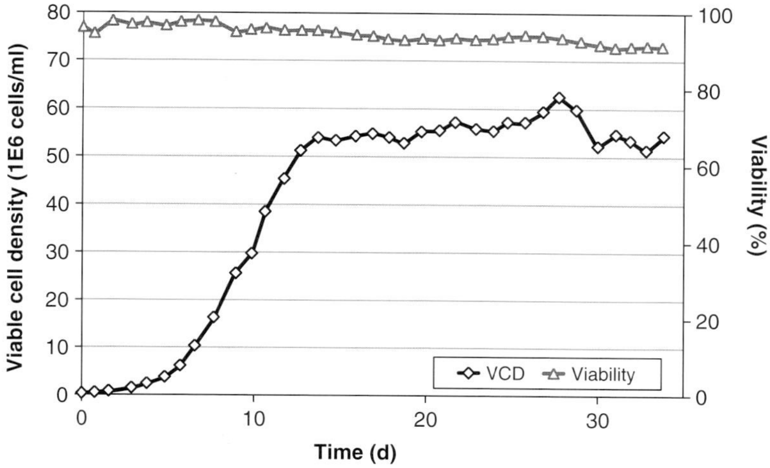

Figure 6.2 Perfusion cultivation of CHO cells in a benchtop bioreactor fitted with a marine impeller and a Rushton turbine, at 1-l working volume, using the customized chemically-defined TC-LECC medium (Xell AG, Germany). Dissolved oxygen was controlled at 30% air saturation and pH at 7.1 ± 0.05. Perfusion was carried out using a CS10 lamella settler (Biotechnology Solutions, USA) at a perfusion rate of 4 d^{-1}, being approximately 0.15 d^{-1} thereof removed through the cell bleed.

approximately 50E6 cells ml^{-1} using the aforementioned range of perfusion rates (Figure 6.2).

A different strategy proposed by some authors relies on using a special perfusion medium instead of the usual culture medium. The special medium differs from the usual one in that it is concentrated in some nutrients, in order to allow high cell densities to be supported at lower perfusion rates. Yang *et al.* [24] named this approach "controlled-fed perfusion" and reported a twofold increase in antibody volumetric productivity when compared to a conventional perfusion process, and an almost 10-fold increase when compared to a fed-batch process. Feng *et al.* [25] further investigated this strategy and proposed the amino acid feeding to be controlled according to the culture oxygen uptake rate (OUR). These authors reported a twofold increase in volumetric productivity over the conventional perfusion and the fed-batch process.

Since the higher product concentrations have long been considered a key advantage of fed-batch over perfusion processes, operating cultures at low cell-specific perfusion rates (CSPR) would allow increasing titers in perfusion. This strategy, also known as "push-to-low" optimization [26], is applicable to stable products that do not need to be readily removed from the bioreactor by a high dilution rate.

The CSPR concept, which was first introduced by Ozturk [27], was used by Dowd *et al.* [28] to optimize the perfusion feed rate. They evaluated a range of 0.05 to 0.4 nl $cell^{-1}$ d^{-1} and observed that product concentration was maximized at 0.2 nl $cell^{-1}$ d^{-1}, whereas volumetric productivity was maximum at

0.3 nl cell^{-1} d^{-1}. Warikoo *et al.* [2] reported 60-day stable perfusion cultures, which after starting cell bleeding were kept at steady-state concentrations of 50–60E6 cells ml^{-1} using cell-specific perfusion rates as low as 0.04–0.05 nl cell^{-1} d^{-1}. Assuming that a CSPR that showed good results at moderate cell densities would in principle provide an adequate environment for cells also at very high cell densities, Clincke *et al.* [29] adopted 0.05–0.06 nl cell^{-1} d^{-1} with separate on-demand supplementation of glucose and glutamine and were able to reach impressive cell concentrations in the range of 137–224E6 cells ml^{-1}. The separate glucose and glutamine addition aimed at keeping medium consumption low. According to Konstantinov [5], the challenge would be to decrease CSPR further to the order of 10–15 pl cell^{-1} d^{-1}.

A further alternative to enhance productivity of high-density perfusion cultures is to decouple cell growth and product formation, establishing a biphasic process comprising a first phase where growth is enhanced and a second phase where growth is arrested, but product formation is not affected. Altamirano *et al.* [20] and Vergara *et al.* [19] investigated to replace glucose in the medium by the slowly metabolizable sugar galactose as a way to decrease cell growth. Another approach was taken by Ibarra *et al.* [30]. They inducibly expressed the p21(CIP1) cyclin-dependent kinase inhibitor in NS0 cells to arrest the cell cycle in G1 phase and observed a fourfold increase in antibody production.

Another possibility of having a biphasic perfusion process is to apply mild hypothermia to decrease cell growth during the production phase. Over the last decade, a general trend has been observed in mammalian cell culture with the aim of increasing productivity by lowering culture temperature to arrest cell growth and improve culture longevity [31]. Chuppa *et al.* [32] were pioneers in manipulating temperature to optimize perfusion cultures, aiming at taking advantage of the lower oxygen consumption, lower perfusion rate, reduced glucose/lactate metabolism, simplified pH control, and reduced product degradation at lower temperatures. No previous studies on the effects of temperature on perfusion processes existed at that moment, but specially the lower cell-specific consumption of oxygen and nutrients at lower temperatures were claimed by the authors to be potentially important for perfusion, since higher cell densities would be achievable in a bioreactor with a given oxygen transfer rate and a given perfusion rate, thus potentially increasing product titer, facilitating cell retention and reducing volume for downstream operations. Indeed, decreasing culture temperature from 37 to 34 °C caused an almost twofold decrease in the glucose-specific consumption rate and a 25% reduction in the specific oxygen uptake rate. This in turn had as consequence that, when the authors operated the bioreactor at a constant oxygen transfer rate and dissolved oxygen was controlled through cell bleeding, a 23% higher steady-state cell density could be achieved at 34 °C. A 7-month long perfusion culture integrally carried out at 34 °C showed a very stable profile with very high viability and high cell productivity.

Bloemkolk *et al.* [33] had shown by flow cytometry a few years earlier that low temperatures retain cells longer in the G1 phase, thus decreasing specific growth rate. Chen *et al.* [34] characterized the cell cycle distribution of CL-11G cells cultivated in batch mode, and observed that while 56.4% of cells were in G0/G1 phase at 37 °C, this percentage increased to 74.9% at 34 °C and 82.8% at 31 °C. At the same time, a decrease in the percentage of cells in S phase was observed as a consequence of the lower temperatures. These adherent cells were then cultured in microcarriers in a perfusion spin filter-based bioreactor under two steady states, first at 37 °C and then at 34 °C. After the temperature down-shift, an increase in viable cell density and in pro-urokinase product concentration was observed, which led to an average 17% increase in viable cell density and an average 47% increase in product concentration at 34 °C, when both steady states were compared.

In the early work by Chuppa *et al.* [32], mild hypothermia was applied from the beginning during all processes, but in more recent publications the biphasic process strategy is usually chosen, starting cultivation at 37 °C and then shifting down temperature. A biphasic perfusion process for recombinant erythropoietin (EPO) production by CHO cells was reported by Ahn *et al.* [35], where perfusion was started and temperature was decreased (from 37 °C to temperatures in the range of 25 to 32 °C) when cells reached 10E6 ml^{-1}. The specific EPO formation rate was highest at 30 °C, but the cumulative EPO production was maximum at 32 °C, because at further lower temperatures the integral of viable cells decreased strongly. EPO glycosylation profile at 32 °C was comparable to the standard process at 37 °C, but was negatively affected at further lower temperatures, so that for this process the authors concluded 32 °C to be the optimal shift temperature. In the case of the production of follicle stimulating hormone (FSH), however, the first batch evaluations indicated a 13-fold increase in the specific production rate at 28 °C, so a perfusion process was carried out with a temperature shift down to 28 °C when cell concentration reached approximately 32E6 ml^{-1} [36]. However, in spite of a first sharp increase in FSH titer, viability, viable cell density, and product concentration started soon to decrease, indicating that at 28 °C probably the activities of cellular enzymes related to cell growth were too low. This hypothesis was supported by the fact that by shifting the perfusion run back to 37 °C the cell growth and viability were recovered.

The impact of hypothermia on product quality attributes, such as aggregation and glycosylation, was evaluated by Rodriguez *et al.* [37] for perfusion production of β-interferon by CHO cells. These authors started cultivation at 37 °C and decreased to 32 °C on day 3, still during the initial batch phase. Perfusion was started just on day 8. It was observed that product aggregation decreased from 42.9% on day 3 (temperature shift) to 28.7% on day 8 (perfusion start), and then to as low as 5.4% on day 16 (end of run). Specific production rate increased by 60% from day 3 to day 8, and by further 117% from day 8 to day 16, resulting in a 3.5-fold increase when comparing the low-temperature perfusion phase with the 37 °C batch phase.

The supplementation of cultures with short-chain fatty acids, such as sodium butyrate and sodium valerate, has been another strategy investigated in mammalian cell culture to decrease cell growth but enhance productivity [38,39]. In shake-flask semi-perfusion cultures, Hong *et al.* [40] observed that a 1-mM butyrate treatment led to a CHO cell growth decrease, but accompanied by an increase in culture longevity and specific productivity. Kim *et al.* [41] investigated a 5-mM butyrate treatment starting on day 16 (at 4.4E6 cells ml^{-1}) of a bioreactor perfusion culture. Although the relatively high butyrate concentration caused a sharp decrease in cell growth and viability, significant improvements in product titer and specific productivity were observed.

Some authors have investigated combining two factors that influence cell growth and productivity. Coronel *et al.* (unpublished results) combined sodium valerate treatment with temperature shift in a CHO perfusion process. Product titer and specific productivity were significantly higher during a steady state with 1 mM valerate at subphysiological temperature than during steady states at 37 °C either with or without valerate supplementation. In another study, Vergara *et al.* [19] did a combined temperature/nutrient shift in semi-perfusion cultures of CHO cells producing tissue plasminogen activator (tPA). By decreasing temperature from 37 to 34 °C and concomitantly switching from glucose to galactose, the authors obtained a 112% increase in the specific production rate.

A better understanding of protein expression and cell physiology has been enabled by the advances in genomics, proteomics and metabolomics. Klausing *et al.* [39] used a custom designed CHO cDNA microarray to investigate genes associated with increased productivity during sodium butyrate treatment, showing that transcriptomic analysis is an interesting tool to investigate effects of cultivation conditions on cell cultures. Jayapal and Goudar [42] carried out DNA microarray analysis on samples from laboratory- and manufacturing-scale BHK perfusion bioreactors that were operated under the same conditions. Transcriptomic fingerprints were similar for both bioreactor scales, but confirmed time-dependent changes to the cell physiological state. This study gave support to the comparability of laboratory and manufacturing-scale perfusion systems, so that transcriptomic analysis represents a tool to qualify scale-down models used in process characterization and for regulatory fillings.

Laboratory- and manufacturing-scale BHK perfusion bioreactors were also investigated by metabolomics [43]. Metabolic profiling captured physiological state shifts that occurred with process time/cell age but were independent of production scale, which is in agreement with the transcriptomic results by Jayapal and Goudar [42]. ^{13}C glucose and 2D-NMR spectroscopy have been used to quantify the physiological state of CHO cells in perfusion cultures and to validate a simplified metabolite balancing based model, which can be used for routine analysis, representing a valuable tool for bioprocess development [44].

Having established process conditions, a key point in perfusion processes is to ensure robust and stable steady-state operation over the long term. Thus, monitoring and automation are important tools both for process development and manufacturing-scale operation. Moreover, the higher the cell concentration in the process, the more important is the role of monitoring and automation.

Efficient control strategies allow keeping cells in a physiological steady-state as given by specific metabolic rates and metabolic rate ratios [45]. Online measurements or automated sampling platforms [28,46] are used to provide data for automated control strategies, which can be employed to control, for example, perfusion and bleed rates. Capacitance measurements and optical sensors have been used by Dowd *et al.* [28] and Gorenflo *et al.* [47], respectively, to control the perfusion feed rate based on the online cell concentration levels, maintaining a constant cell-specific perfusion rate. Online glucose measurements were used by Konstantinov *et al.* [48] and Castilho [49] to control perfusion feed rate in order to maintain glucose concentration at desired set-points, whereas Castilho [49] also adopted, in parallel, an automated bleed rate control based on oxygen consumption.

Real-time estimation of specific oxygen uptake and CO_2 production rates represent another tool to provide quantitative information on cell physiology, being useful both for process development and for monitoring of manufacturing-scale bioreactors [50]. However, dissolved CO_2 sensors are not routinely available in standard mammalian cell bioreactors, although high dissolved CO_2 levels can negatively affect growth, metabolism, productivity, and protein glycosylation [51]. Strategies to avoid CO_2 accumulation usually involve manipulating variables, such as gas sparging and bioreactor rocking rates (in wave-type bioreactors), yet this can be limited by cell sensitivity or system operational constraints, so that sometimes high dissolved CO_2 levels in high-density perfusion cultures cannot be avoided [11]. Goudar *et al.* [51] proposed reducing pCO_2 at the source through medium and base modification. By replacing $NaHCO_3$ in the medium with a MOPS-histidine buffer and $NaHCO_3$ in the pH control loop by Na_2CO_3, pCO_2 levels in BHK perfusion cultivations at 20E6 cells ml^{-1} were decreased by 63–70%, while specific growth rates and specific productivities increased by approximately 60–120%.

6.5 Cell Retention Devices

The core component of any perfusion system is the cell retention device used to separate cells from the medium to retain/recirculate them to the bioreactor [52–54]. The need for a cell separation device is only not true in exceptional cases either of fixed-bed bioreactors containing cells immobilized on microcarriers, such as the iCELLis™ bioreactor [55], or of bioreactors that confine the cells in a membrane-delimited compartment through which medium is perfused, such as miniPERM®, CELLine™, and hollow-fiber bioreactors. However, the application of the latter type of bioreactors seems to be confined to small-scale or niche applications, such as the production of monoclonal antibodies for diagnostic purposes [56].

Thus, in almost all applications the choice of the solid–liquid separation device is central in the design of a perfusion process. The separation principle of most traditional devices relies on the size of the cells and on the difference of the density of cells to that of the aqueous culture medium. However, since mammalian cells are relatively small particles (usually 10–20 μm in diameter), and their density (1.06–1.14 $g\,cm^{-3}$ according to [57]) is quite similar to that of aqueous media, their separation from the culture medium is not a trivial task. Since mammalian cells can be rather shear sensitive due to the lack of a cell wall, but must be kept viable upon separation, this makes cell separation operations in perfusion processes even more challenging. Furthermore, although the biopharmaceutical industry is mainly based on suspension-adapted cell lines, these keep a tendency to attach to surfaces, so that equipment fouling and clogging is a further concern in view of the high concentrations of cells, but also of proteins and nucleic acids.

To find a cell retention device that gives high separation efficiency, causes no cell damage, and operates reliably for a long time period has been usually seen as a challenge hampering perfusion processes from becoming more popular in the past decades.

The retention devices used in animal cell perfusion cultures rely basically on three different separation mechanisms (Table 6.1): (i) settling (under gravitational or centrifugal field), (ii) aggregation under ultrasonic waves (followed by settling), and (iii) filtration under different operation strategies (tangential-flow filters, alternating tangential-flow systems, floating membranes, spin-filters, and rotating cylindrical or disc filters). Cell retention devices can be placed either internally to the bioreactor or in an external recirculation loop (Figure 6.3). Internal devices have as advantage that the perfusion system seems less complex to the final operator, with less need for external tubings and pumps. However, external devices have the significant advantage of allowing to switch to a second device in case of failure (e.g., clogging) of the first one, and/or allowing longer process operation through an aforeplanned use of twin separators, which operate alternately and undergo periodical cleaning and sterilization (one device at a time), such as reported by Figueredo-Cardero *et al.* [58].

6.5.1 Gravitational Settlers

Gravitational settlers rely on cell settling by action of gravity to separate cells from the liquid phase, so that a liquid stream devoid or almost devoid of cells is removed by the top part of the equipment (Figure 6.4). However, due to the low density of cells and their reduced size, their settling velocities are in the range of 1–15 $cm\,h^{-1}$ [53] and decrease with increasing volumetric concentration [94,95].

As a consequence, sedimentation area of settlers for mammalian cell separation must be quite large to avoid cell drag and drop in separation efficiency. Although in other applications vertical settlers (Figure 6.4a) are quite common, in cell culture applications the most popular type is the inclined lamella settler

Table 6.1 Separation techniques employed for animal cell retention in perfusion bioreactors.

Separation mechanism	Device	Position relative to the bioreactor	Examples of suppliers	References
Gravitational settling	Lamella settlers	External	Biotechnology Solutions; Bayer Technology Services	[59–63]
Settling in the centrifugal field	Centrifuges (e.g., Centritech, kSep or Westfalia CSA1/CFA01)	External	Westfalia Separator; kSep Systems; Carr Centritech/Pneumatic Scale Corporation	[64–67]
	Hydrocyclones	External (internal also feasible)	Sartorius-Stedim; noncommercial prototypes	[68–74]
Aggregation under ultrasonic waves	Acoustic separators (Biosep®)	External, possibly directly attached to the bioreactor head plate	Applikon Biotechnology, Sonosep	[37,47,75–78]
Filtration	Tangential-flow filtration (e.g., ReadyToProcess™, Krosflo® or Microza)	External	GE Healthcare, Spectrum Labs, Pall Corp.	[11,29,79]
	Alternating tangential-flow (ATF®) systems	External	Refine Technology/Repligen	[2,11,29,59,77,78,80]
	Floating membrane devices	Internal	Almost all suppliers of wave-type bioreactors	[81–83]
	Spin-filters	Internal	Almost all bioreactor suppliers	[34,77,78,84–86]
	Rotating cylindrical filters (also known as vortex-flow filters or external spin-filters)	External	Bioengineering AG	[58,87–89]
	Rotating disc filters (also known as controlled-shear filters)	External	Noncommercial prototypes	[90–93]

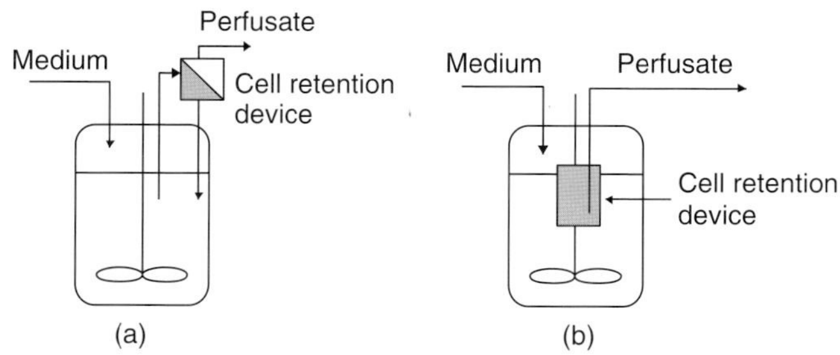

Figure 6.3 Coupling of a cell retention device to a bioreactor in a perfusion system: (a) internal device; (b) external device.

(Figure 6.4b). These are more compact devices, because a large number of inclined plates (known as lamellas) are placed inside the equipment (Figure 6.5), with a short distance (h) among them, so that the sedimentation path to be overcome by settling cells is reduced to ($h/\cos\alpha$), being α the inclination of the device and its lamellas.

The sedimentation area in a vertical settler corresponds to the cross-sectional area of its cylindrical part, whereas in a lamella settler it corresponds to the sum of the projected areas of all lamellas on the horizontal plane. However, according to Svarovsky [96], due to various inefficiencies only about 50% of this total area is usually effective. Because a lamella settler has a high sedimentation area packed in a compact volume, the residence time of cells inside it and outside the bioreactor is shorter, which is especially important for sensitive mammalian cells [97].

According to Castilho and Medronho [94], the sedimentation area needed for a given separation is based on the concept of the minimum sedimentation area ($A_{\min}$). In vertical settlers, $A_{\min}$ is calculated as the quotient of the perfusate flow

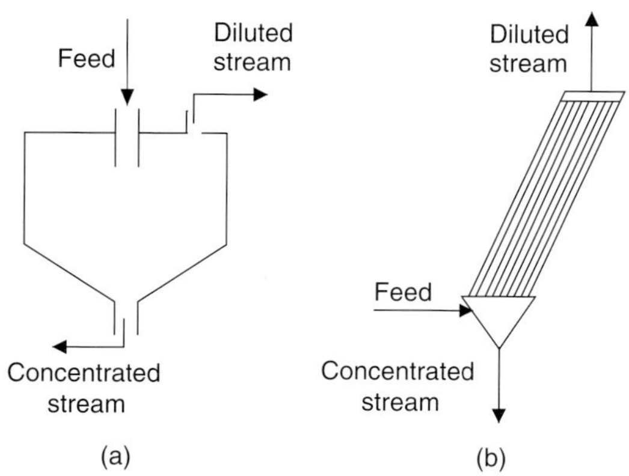

Figure 6.4 Types of gravitational settlers: (a) vertical settler; (b) inclined lamella settler.

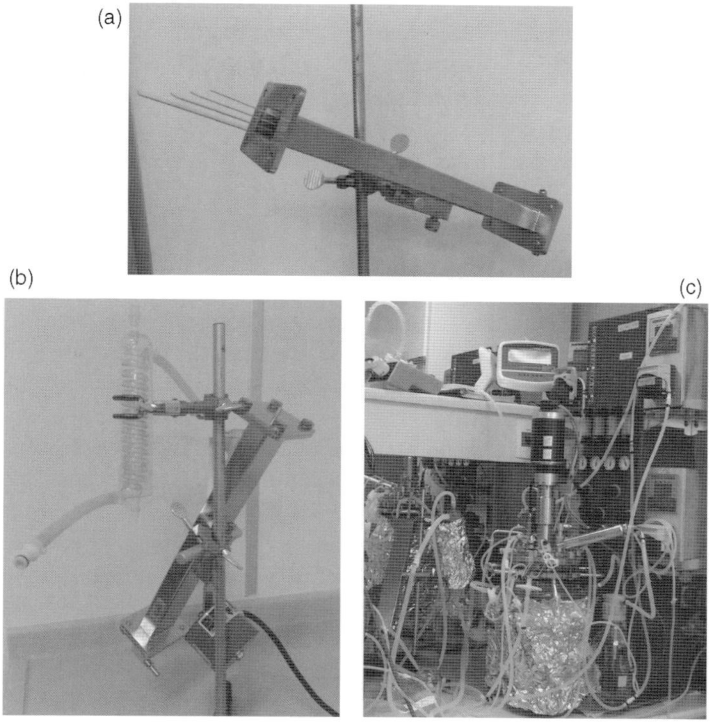

Figure 6.5 Laboratory-scale lamella settler system (CS10, Biotechnology Solutions) used at the Cell Culture Engineering Lab (LECC) of Federal University of Rio de Janeiro: (a) dismantled settler showing its lamellas; (b) settler setup including vibration device (red) and heat exchanger; (c) settler (on the left) operating as cell retention device (heat exchanger and bioreactor vessel are covered with aluminum foil to protect medium from light exposure).

rate (Q_{perf}) by the settling velocity of the smallest cell ($v_{t,min}$) present in the cell suspension, because in the limiting condition the ascending fluid velocity ($u = Q_{perf}/A_{min}$) will equal $v_{t,min}$. Attention should be paid to correct $v_{t,min}$ according to the actual cell volumetric concentration [97] and to multiply A_{min} by a factor of safety of 3 [94] to obtain the required settler area.

In lamella settlers, considering the 50% area effectiveness and the factor of safety of 3, the minimum sedimentation area (A_{min}), the area of each lamella (A_{lam}), the number of lamellas (n), and the inclination of the settler (α) are interrelated according to Equation 6.1:

$$n = 6 \cdot A_{min}/(A_{lam} \cdot \cos \alpha) \tag{6.1}$$

Inclined settlers are among the few cell retention devices that are successfully used both in lab-scale and industrial perfusion processes. They provide a low-shear environment for cells, and have no moving parts, which increases robustness, decreases contamination risks, and minimizes maintenance costs. A selective retention of viable cells can be achieved, since the settling velocities of nonviable cells have been reported to be 33–50% lower than of viable cells [98]. Undesired attachment of cells to the lamellas can occur, and this would lead to equipment clogging, but this can be successfully avoided by the use of a simple vibration system that shakes the settler either continuously or intermittently for short periods in periodic time intervals (e.g., for 15 s every 10 min). Also, undesired effects of cells being recirculated through a noncontrolled, nonoxygenated environment are successfully avoided by introducing a simple heat exchanger at the beginning of the recirculation loop (near the bioreactor outlet) to decrease temperature (e.g., to 20 °C) and so reduce cell metabolism. A complete laboratory-scale settler system, including the vibration device and the heat exchanger, is shown in Figure 6.5, and typical data from a perfusion run were shown in Figure 6.2.

Bayer was among the pioneers to industrially implement a perfusion process. The product (Kogenate) is a recombinant Factor VIII, which is a very unstable protein, and was approved for human use in 1993. The cell retention device used by Bayer is a lamella settler [60,63], and the perfusion technology established allows operation for 3–7 months (but virtually unlimited), operating at perfusion rates of up to 15 d^{-1} at viable cell concentrations of 20–60E6 ml^{-1} and cell viabilities in the range of 90–99% [63,99].

For some products that tend to adsorb to surfaces due to a large size and/or due to surface properties and charge, settlers have shown to present a performance superior to that of filtration-based devices. Coronel *et al.* [59] evaluated an inclined settler and a membrane-based device for perfusion of CHO cells, and observed that the perfusate stream in the latter was depleted of product, presumably to do adsorption of the product to the membrane surface, whereas the settler perfusate had the same product concentration as inside the bioreactor.

In spite of the successful reports on the use of settlers as a cell retention device for both laboratory and industrial perfusion processes, Shen and Yanagimachi [62] considered the need to improve the knowledge on the effects of geometric design and operational variables on settler performance. They developed a computational fluid dynamics (CFD) model to aid design and performance prediction of cell settlers, and used it to design a settler with twice the settling surface of the largest model commercialized by Biotechnology Solutions.

6.5.2
Centrifuges

Centrifugation is based on the sedimentation of particles under the action of a centrifugal field. As for gravitational sedimentation, the terminal settling velocity (v_t) can be calculated by the Stokes equation and then corrected according to the actual cell volumetric concentration [94]. However, the settling velocity in centrifuges is hugely higher than in settlers, since the intensity of the force field under centrifugal action ($\omega^2 R$) to be used in the Stokes equation is increased by several orders of magnitude over the gravitational field intensity (g). For animal cells, the ratio of centrifugal to gravitational field intensity ($\omega^2 R/g$) (also known as g-factor or relative centrifugal force, RCF), is usually adjusted to values in the range of 100–500, because it ensures efficient cell separation without generating too high shear stress that could damage the cells.

Centrifuges provide very high separation efficiencies, but are complex devices, with moving parts, and have both high capital and operational costs, impacting on the cost of goods.

Among the continuous centrifuges, those mostly employed in animal cell cultures are disc stack centrifuges and special centrifuge designs containing a single-use insert that gets in touch with the cell suspension. Similarly to the lamellas in gravitational settlers, the disc stacks in the bowl of centrifuges have the aim of decreasing the path that cells have to settle until they reach the underside of the discs and slide toward peripheral outlets, which are used to discharge the cells either continuously or intermittently. Disc stack centrifuges that have been mostly reported for mammalian cell separation are models CFA01 and CSA1 from Westfalia Separator AG [64,67]. However, clogging of outlet ports and discharge channels was observed during perfusion operation [67].

The specially designed centrifuges containing single-use inserts include the Centritech and the kSep models. The Centritech centrifuge has been in the market for over 20 years and is industrially used in the perfusion process of a marketed biopharmaceutical. This one is based on a disposable bladder and tubing system, mounted on top of a rotor, whereby the feed enters at one top end and the perfusate exits at the opposite top end, with the concentrated cell stream being collected at the bottom end of the insert. Although earlier works have reported successful results using this centrifuge [100], more recent works have reported difficulties in establishing a successful perfusion process based on either continuous, intermittent, or cell-once-through strategies [65,66].

6.5.3 Hydrocyclones

Hydrocyclones are simple mechanical devices comprised of a conical bottom part and a cylindrical upper part, containing one or more tangentially positioned inlets (Figure 6.6). There are no moving parts, and separation takes place due to the centrifugal field generated by the pressurized pumping of the cell suspension through the tangential inlets coupled directly to the cylindrical part. This causes a primary vortex to be formed, which leads the cells to settle under centrifugal action toward the wall and slide down to the underflow orifice, where the concentrated cell stream is collected. Because not all the fluid manages to leave the equipment through the narrow

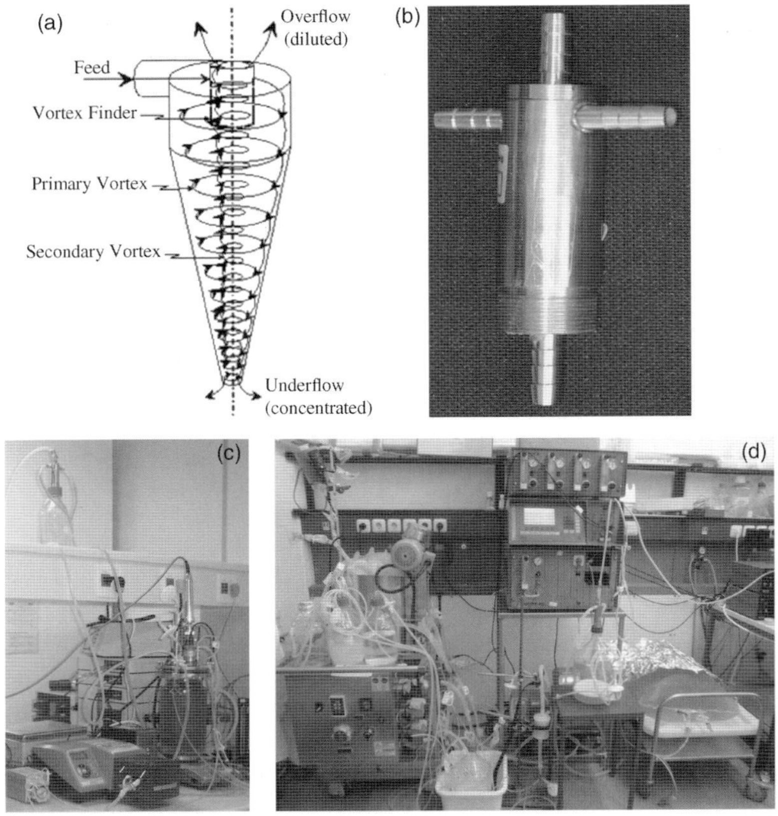

Figure 6.6 (a) General scheme of a conventional hydrocyclone, showing the primary and secondary vortices, as well as the underflow and overflow orifices; (b) stainless-steel protoype specially designed for mammalian cell separation according to Deckwer *et al.* [68]; (c) prototype being tested by our group at 2 l scale for intermittent perfusion at LECC/UFRJ; (d) prototype being tested at 50-l scale in a joint work of our group and the University of Bielefeld (Germany).

underflow orifice, a secondary ascending vortex is formed in the central part of the device, so that a stream devoid or almost devoid of cells is collected in the overflow orifice. Although hydrocyclones have been used for solid–liquid and liquid–liquid separation in several other industries since the late nineteenth century, only in the last decade a hydrocyclone geometry suited for mammalian cell separation was proposed [68,69] and its use for the separation of CHO, HeLa, BHK, and SP-2/0 cell lines was reported [70,101]. The patent of this specially designed hydrocyclone has been licensed to Sartorius Stedim.

When CHO cells were separated in batch experiments using the specially designed hydrocyclone with different combinations of underflow and overflow diameters, cell separation efficiencies above 97% were obtained for all configurations and no induction of apoptosis was observed within 48 h of hydrocycloning [70].

Hydrocyclone performance is mainly determined by the pressure drop across the device, by the diameter of its cylindrical part and by the inner geometrical proportions. The smaller the diameter of the cylindrical part, the more efficient the device is. Due to construction constraints that prevented scaling further down, the hydrocyclone specially designed for mammalian cell separation had a diameter of 1 cm [68]. In spite of the reduced size (the whole device fits in the pocket of a shirt), its processing capability is significant and at pressure drops of 1–1.15 bar flow rates through the device are as high as 1.4–1.5 l min^{-1} [70,73]. From that, depending on the diameters of the outlet orifices and on the operating pressure drop, up to 30% of the feed stream reports to the overflow (i.e., to the perfusate stream in a perfusion process). Therefore, investigation of the use of hydrocyclones for perfusion cultures using laboratory-scale bioreactors has to be carried out intermittently. This has hampered a much wider investigation of the use of these devices in continuous perfusion applications, but promising results have been obtained in tests carried out in biopharmaceutical companies in Cuba and the United States, in short-term experiments using a 15 l bioreactor [71] and in a 9 day perfusion run using a 300 l perfusion bioreactor [94].

Because of its simple construction out of different materials, compactness, and absence of moving parts, hydrocyclones are low-cost devices, need virtually no maintenance, and are very well suited for both disposable use or CIP/SIP operations in case of reusability. Its compactness allows having it incorporated into a disposable bag of a single-use bioreactor (Figure 6.7a). These features add to the high separation efficiencies and reduced cell damage, indicating the hydrocyclone as a promising cell retention device for perfusion processes.

(a) (b)

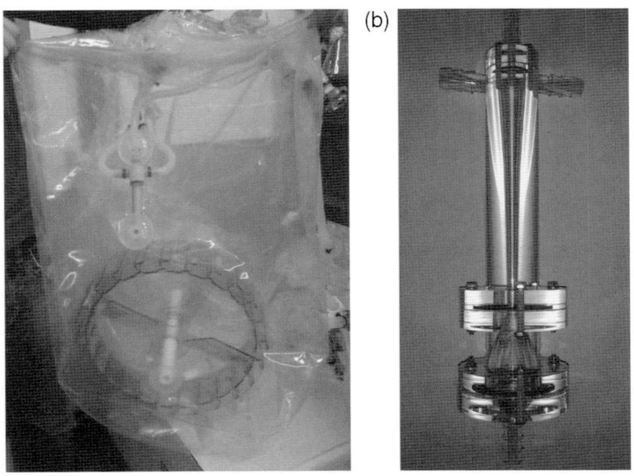

Figure 6.7 (a) Customized bag of an Air Wheel® bioreactor (PBS Biotech) incorporating a hydrocyclone (Sartorius); (b) Plexiglas® prototype of a hydrocyclone of novel geometry currently under development at LECC/Federal University of Rio de Janeiro.

However, its performance is very much dependent on operational conditions and specially on the internal geometry. Thus, special care should be taken when building a hydrocyclone, since imperfections in the inner geometry, for example, when built by extrusion out of plastic materials, can severely affect cell separation and cause shear stress peaks that damage the cells.

At the moment, studies are under way at the Cell Culture Engineering Laboratory (LECC) of the Federal University of Rio de Janeiro (Brazil) to develop novel geometries of hydrocyclones that can even improve their applicability in animal cell separation. Figure 6.7b shows a photo of a Plexiglas prototype that has been constructed for initial cell separation batch experiments under nonsterile conditions. After the tests with the Plexiglas prototypes, the aim is to build sterilizable prototypes (e.g., out of PEEK, polycarbonate or stainless steel) to test in perfusion processes.

6.5.4 Acoustic (Ultrasonic) Separators

Acoustic (or ultrasonic) separators are based on gentle acoustically induced cell aggregation, followed by sedimentation [102]. When under ultrasonic forces, the cells are first driven toward pressure nodes of the resonance field and then migrate laterally within these nodes, aggregating and forming relatively large, but loose clumps. The system operates in cycles, so that periodically the acoustic field is switched off and cells are allowed to settle back to the bioreactor, where upon agitation they get again dispersed and grow as single cells. The magnitude of the acoustic forces inside the apparatus, which is a function of the acoustic energy density distribution in the liquid, has a significant impact on retention efficiency of acoustic cell separation devices [53,76].

Commercial devices (Biosep®) are available for a wide range of perfusate flow rates ($1–1000\,l\,d^{-1}$) [103] and they can typically be mounted directly on the top of the bioreactor head plate, abbreviating the need for recirculation lines, tubings, and connectors, making the perfusion system simpler and more robust.

Shirgaonkar *et al.* [76] reported perfusion cultures of HEK 293S cells reaching viable cell densities up to $40E6\,ml^{-1}$ and operating up to 80 days. Dalm *et al.* [75] confirmed the suitability for simple and robust long-term operation (75 days) and reported separation efficiencies of 94–96% during the production phase. They used a pilot-scale separator ($200\,l\,d^{-1}$), but their results can be directly translated into the large-scale model ($1000\,l\,d^{-1}$), which in reality consists of a setup of five pilot-scale resonator chambers.

6.5.5 Tangential Flow-Filtration

Membrane-based separations present an interesting alternative for cell separation, yielding cell-free supernatants for downstream processing. Several commercial devices are available at different scales and, for a given device, scale-up can be modular. However, membrane fouling due to the high concentrations of cells, cell debris, proteins, and nucleic acids is a permanent concern in membrane-based bioseparations, and specially in perfusion processes, where the main goal is to ensure long-term bioreactor operation under steady-state conditions.

Feeding the cell suspension tangentially to the membrane surface significantly contributes to reduce this drawback and to increase the time interval before fouling levels become critical for process operation. The tangential flow generates high velocity gradients and, consequently, high shear rates at the membrane surface, avoiding fouling and minimizing flux decrease. In mammalian cell culture separations, however, a careful control of the shear rates, which in tangential-flow filtration (TFF) are intrinsically coupled to the feed flow rate and module/membrane geometry, is required to avoid cell damage.

Tangential-flow filtration can be accomplished using flat-sheet or hollow-fiber modules. The latter have become increasingly popular and consist of modules containing up to hundreds of small-diameter membrane tubings (usually 40–1500 μm in internal diameter) packed in a housing at highly compact configurations that can reach up to several thousands of square meters of membrane area per cubic meter of module volume [104,105].

Several recent papers report the use of hollow-fiber TFF devices to carry out perfusion of animal cells [11,29,79]. The most impressive data were reported by Clincke *et al.* [11,29], who demonstrated maximum viable cell densities as high as 214E6 ml^{-1} for the culture of recombinant CHO cells in a wave-type bioreactor. This extremely high cell density was seen as the limit of the system and corresponded to a theoretical null intercellular distance for the studied cell line. The authors considered that the system was limited by the high viscosity of the cell culture broth and by the high, inhibitory pCO_2 level (31 kPa) that was reached at such high cell concentration. Before testing the limit of the system, the authors were able to carry out a stable perfusion run, with daily cell bleed and a constant CSPR, at approximately 100E6 cells ml^{-1} for two weeks, demonstrating the feasibility of the wave-bioreactor/TFF perfusion system [29]. A comparison with fed-batch runs indicated a sixfold higher product harvest for the perfusion process after 12 days. The authors also compared the use of microfiltration (0.2 μm pore size) and ultrafiltration (50 kDa cut-off) hollow-fiber cartridges in the TFF system [11]. The monoclonal antibody product was retained within the bioreactor even when using the microfiltration cartridge, but product accumulation was much faster when using the ultrafiltration cartridge, reaching antibody concentrations of up to 3 g l^{-1} within 12 days post-inoculation. However, the amount of product daily discarded in the cell bleed turned out to be significant and such a process strategy would require recovering the product from the bleed line.

Product retention in perfusion culture is an intentional feature of the XD® Technology developed by the company DSM Biologics. Zijlstra [106] reported to be routinely operating over 150E6 cells ml^{-1}, getting titers 5- to 15-fold higher than in fed-batch processes. They preferentially use TFF to retain both cells and product, and cells are allowed to grow exponentially for 10–12 days. According to the author, a key point of the process is to use low-shear pumps. The product is harvested in the bleed line, and perfusate is waste. Record cell densities over 240E6 cells ml^{-1}, with a record product titer of $27\,g\,l^{-1}$ for a monoclonal antibody, have been obtained.

These process strategies that involve retaining the product in the bioreactor have been called "concentrated fed-batch" by some authors. However, since the process is characterized by cell retention, by continuous addition of nutrients in the medium and by continuous removal of metabolites in the supernatant, it seems more accurate to refer to this strategy as "concentrated perfusion."

6.5.6 ATF Systems

The Alternating Tangential Flow (ATF^{TM}) system uses conventional hollow-fiber modules operated within a housing. The cell suspension flows through the lumen of the fibers, whereby the flow direction is periodically inverted to ensure cleaning of the membrane surface [80]. The top of the ATF system is directly connected to the bioreactor through a single tubing with a large diameter to warrant low shear, resulting in a relatively simple perfusion setup. The bottom of the ATF housing is connected to two lines (vacuum and pressurized air), and contains a diaphragm that periodically moves downward and upward, as a consequence of a periodical switch between vacuum and overpressure dictated by the ATF controller unit. Each total cycle time (vacuum/overpressure) lasts approximately 10–20 s. The diaphragm movement causes the cell suspension to be drawn from the bioreactor and then back, generating a sort of periodical back-flushing that prevents membranes from fouling. Perfusate is pumped out from the extracapillary space of the housing. Figure 6.8 shows photos of the ATF-2 and ATF-4 systems, both dismantled and in perfusion operation.

Due to its relative simplicity and capacity to support extremely high cell densities (100–200E6 cells ml^{-1}), the ATF has experienced a large commercial success since its patenting [80]. It is currently employed in the commercial manufacture of two protein-based drugs [107] and is being used in a wide range of academic laboratories and R&D sectors of biopharmaceutical companies. Platform technologies, such as the continuous integrated manufacturing one developed at Genzyme [2], are based on the ATF system.

In several comparisons carried out with other cell retention devices, such as acoustic separators, spin-filters, Centritech centrifuges, and cell settlers, the ATF presented better results. Duvar *et al.* [78] reported CHO cell densities of 64E6 ml^{-1} and 130E6 ml^{-1} when using an ATF system fitted with 0.2 μm and 50 kDa membranes, respectively. Product was retained in the bioreactor by the 50 kDa membranes, turning this process into a "concentrated perfusion" process, and titers were fourfold higher than in fed-batch mode. The other four tested cell retention devices gave peak cell densities 4- to 6.5-fold lower than the 50 kDa ATF system. Crowley *et al.* [77] compared the ATF with a spin-filter and

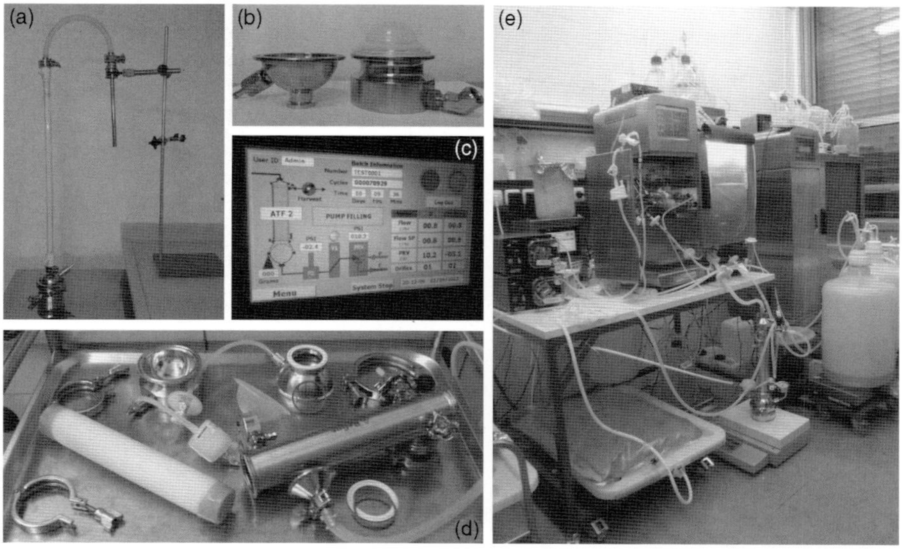

Figure 6.8 (a) ATF-2 system (Refine Technology); (b) detail of the diaphragm placed in the bottom part of the ATF-2 unit; (c) screen of ATF controller unit; (d) dismantled ATF-4 system showing its hollow-fiber cartridge; (e) ATF-4 system connected to a disposable Air-Wheel® bioreactor (PBS Biotech). Photos taken by our group at the Federal University of Rio de Janeiro and at the University of Bielefeld.

an acoustic separator for perfusion cultivation of PER.C6® cells producing a monoclonal antibody. Maximum viable cell densities were 3–5 times higher for the ATF, which resulted in a volumetric productivity of $0.9\,g\,l^{-1}\,d^{-1}$ as compared to $0.1–0.2\,g\,l^{-1}\,d^{-1}$ for the spin-filter and $0.6\,g\,l^{-1}\,d^{-1}$ for the acoustic separator.

However, when Clincke *et al.* [11,29] compared the ATF to a TFF system, employing the same hollow-fiber cartridges in both systems, the ATF, in spite of yielding very high cell concentrations (up to $132E6\,ml^{-1}$), showed a lower performance than the TFF. This was due mainly to the fact that the ATF was limited by the vacuum capacity failing to pull the highly viscous cell suspension after this cell density was attained. The TFF also presented limitations related to the high viscosity of high-density cell suspensions, but the onset of the ATF limitations was earlier.

For the production of a large protein, Coronel *et al.* [59] selected to use a cell settler over an ATF system, since the latter caused undesired product retention, also when hollow-fiber cartridges of different pore sizes were tested. Product retention was observed from the very beginning of perfusion, so it seemed to be due to product adsorption onto the large membrane area and not to membrane fouling. Therefore, the authors are at the moment investigating this further and testing membrane cartridges made of alternative materials. Other authors have also observed product retention, but in their case retention seemed to be due to fouling, since it appeared with time, increased gradually, and could be eliminated by exchanging the cartridge for a new one.

6.5.7 Floating Membrane Devices

Floating membrane devices have been developed to work as internal cell retention devices in wave-induced single-use bioreactors [81]. Due to the rocking motion of the bioreactor, the floating filter is quickly flicked across the surface, creating a tangential flow on the membrane surface that helps avoid filter clogging.

Tang *et al.* [83] reported the use of a 7-μm polyethylene membrane filter for perfusion cultivation of hybridoma cells. Maximum viable cell density was 20E6 ml^{-1}, approximately 10-fold higher than that obtained in batch cultures, and antibody volumetric productivity was 33 $mg\,l^{-1}\,d^{-1}$, approximately 16-fold larger than in the batch process. When cultivating PER.C6 cells in a wave bag fitted with the floating membrane and with single-use optical pH and DO probes, Adams *et al.* [82] also observed a 10-fold increase in maximum viable cell density over batch cultivations. However, they were able to achieve a very high cell density of 150E6 ml^{-1} at a viability of 99%, showing that for this cell line and culture medium the cell densities were 1 order of magnitude higher in both batch and perfusion than in the case of the hybridoma cells used by Tang *et al.* [83].

6.5.8 Spin-Filters

Spin-filters are internal cell retention devices comprised of a rotating cylindrical filter mesh placed inside the bioreactor. They are mounted either on the impeller shaft or driven by an independent motor [53]. The perfusate is pumped through a dip tube located inside the rotating cylinder.

After their introduction as early as in 1969 by Himmelfarb *et al.* [108], spin-filters became quite popular cell retention devices [109–112]. However, mesh fouling has always been a concern in spin-filter based processes, causing separation efficiency to vary along cultivation time and leading to early process interruption due to strong clogging of the mesh. In order to avoid this problem, which was seen as the main limitation for spin-filter use in animal cell perfusion cultures, Vallez-Chetreanu *et al.* [85] proposed using ultrasonic technology to vibrate the filter. An ultrasonic ceramic piezo-actuator was fixed on the filter axis and its use enabled achieving a threefold higher cell concentration in a 113% longer perfusion culture than without the filter vibration device. However, even when using the piezo-actuator, the culture had to be interrupted due to filter clogging within a relatively short process time (14.7 days as compared to 6.9 days without vibration).

Additionally, in spite of their decade-long use in animal cell perfusion cultures, the mechanism by which cells are separated in spin-filters has never been well understood, so that design and performance prediction of spin-filters have remained empirical over the decades.

In an attempt to contribute to a better understanding of the mechanism governing cell separation in such devices, Figueredo-Cardero *et al.* [84] developed a CFD model to study the flow field and particle dynamics in a spin-filter bioreactor system. They showed that flow pattern inside the spin-filter bioreactor resembled a Taylor–Couette flow, with the formation of vortices in the annular gap, which eventually transpassed the mesh, entering the spin-filter lumen. That was the most probable reason for the radial exchange flow that was detected in the CFD simulations, which had a magnitude up to 130-fold higher than the perfusion flow and was strongly influenced by the rotation rate. The radial exchange flow through the mesh had been experimentally observed by Yabannavar *et al.* [110], and the CFD model by Figueredo-Cardero *et al.* [84] enabled to understand and quantify it. This radial exchange flow is the probable reason why several authors have detected cell attachment also on the inner side of the filter mesh, as shown in Figure 6.9 in photos of the external and internal sides of a spin-filter mesh after a perfusion cultivation carried out at our laboratory.

Figure 6.9 (a) Spin-filter mounted inside a 1-l Bioflo 110 bioreactor (New Brunswick Scientific) before process start; (b) cell colonization on the outer surface of the spin-filter after end of run; (c) cell colonization on the inner surface of the spin-filter after end of run. Photos taken at LECC/Federal University of Rio de Janeiro.

It has long been postulated that cell separation in spin-filters is not solely due to the sieving action of the mesh, as evidenced by the high cell separation efficiencies that have been frequently reported for filter meshes with pore size larger than the cells [112,113]. In addition to the action of the centrifugal force due to mesh rotation and to the drag force due to radial flow arising from perfusion and exchange flow, some authors had postulated that the hydrodynamic lift would influence the probability of a cell to approach the mesh and eventually cross it or clog it [110,114]. Through their CFD model, Figueredo-Cardero *et al.* [84] were able to give evidence of the occurrence of particle lateral migration due to the lift force. Due to lateral migration, cells became depleted in the vicinity of the filter mesh, with an approximate reduction of 50% in cell concentration near the mesh. Because filter rotation significantly affected the magnitude of exchange flow and lateral migration, which in turn are important factors concerning separation efficiency and clogging, the CFD model provides a useful tool for process optimization.

6.5.9
Rotating Cylindrical Filters (Vortex-Flow Filters or External Spin-Filters)

Rotating cylindrical filters (RCF) are also known as vortex-flow filters or external spin-filters. These devices can be supplied in different scales and are currently successfully used in large-scale perfusion processes at industrial scale.

Together with rotating disc filters, RCF systems can be classified as dynamic filters. Dynamic filtration relies on creating a relative movement to generate shear stress at the filter surface and so minimize filter fouling and clogging [49].

As an advantage over tangential-flow filters, where feed flow rate and geometry determine the shear rates on the filter surface, in dynamic filters shear stress is not coupled to feed flow rate and transmembrane pressure, so that careful optimization of shear conditions can be carried out to minimize fouling without causing damage to cells [90].

Rotating cylindrical filter devices have been reported for harvesting [115] and perfusion [88,89,116] in animal cell processes. Fraune *et al.* [116] reported the use of a device based on a 10-μm mesh to carry out a perfusion cultivation of hybridoma cells for approximately 2 months. A rotation rate of 250 rpm was shown to provide favorable conditions that minimized mesh fouling and enabled prolonged operation. An RCF device was compared to a TFF system by Mercille *et al.* [88] for perfusion of hybridoma cells. Retention of the large IgM product by the RCF occurred, indicating incidence of fouling, and addition of DNAse to the medium resulted in complete elimination of product retention. This in turn gave evidence that DNA was involved in mesh fouling. Successful perfusion cultivations were carried out for approximately 100 days.

Perfusion processes with several cell lines (HEK 293, HeLa, mouse myeloma, and CHO) were carried out at 3-l scale for 30–60 days by Roth *et al.* (2001), using a 10-μm filter. Separation efficiencies were ≫99% and no negative effects on cell viability were observed. Cultures became less aggregated and more monodisperse with time, which was seen as an advantage of the RCF.

As for internal spin-filters, design and determination of operational conditions for RCF systems remain largely empirical due to the lack of understanding of the mechanism governing fluid flow and particle dynamics. In recent works, Figueredo-Cardero *et al.* [58,87] used experimental particle imaging velocimetry (PIV) and CFD simulation tools to investigate RCF systems at different scales. Both studies together revealed that, in spite of the turbulent regime and of the thin, highly permeable meshes applied in animal cell applications, which differ from the conditions employed in other well-studied RCF applications, Taylor–Couette vortices are formed and give rise to a radial exchange flow similar to that observed in internal spin-filters. Particle lateral migration was also shown to occur in RCF, although in less extent than in spin-filters.

6.5.10
Rotating Disc Filters (Controlled-Shear Filters)

As mentioned earlier, rotating disc filters (RDF) can be classified as dynamic filters. A careful choice of the rotation rate and the geometry allows optimization of shear stress levels, in order to find a compromise that successfully avoids membrane fouling and does not damage cells. Similar filters that have a smoothly conical rotor instead of a disc rotor have been called controlled-shear filters and have been used for harvesting of BHK cells [93].

Castilho and Anspach [90] designed an RDF for animal cell separation based on experimental determinations of shear stress resistance of CHO and BHK cells and on CFD simulations of different geometries and rotation rates. A sterilizable prototype with the final selected geometry (Figure 6.10) was built and tested at first in batch separations, operating at the best rotation rate predicted by the CFD simulations. These batch tests showed that the designed RDF was effectively able to prevent both cell damage and membrane fouling. Stable fluxes of $61\,\mathrm{l\,m^{-2}\,h^{-1}}$ could be established at transmembrane pressures as low as 1.9 kPa, with no cell viability losses. Castilho *et al.* [91] evaluated the prototype shown in Figure 6.10 for perfusion application. It was connected to a running perfusion bioreactor (by replacing the previous cell retention device) and operated for further 16 days with no problems of sterility and no indications of membrane fouling. The CHO cell line under study usually formed large cell clumps. Upon start of RDF operation, there was a first apparent drop in cell viability due to disaggregation of clumps, followed by a quick recovery in viability, which then remained above 90% until the end of the experiment. Microscopic observations confirmed that the aggregating culture became a monodisperse cell suspension due to the controlled shear action of the RDF.

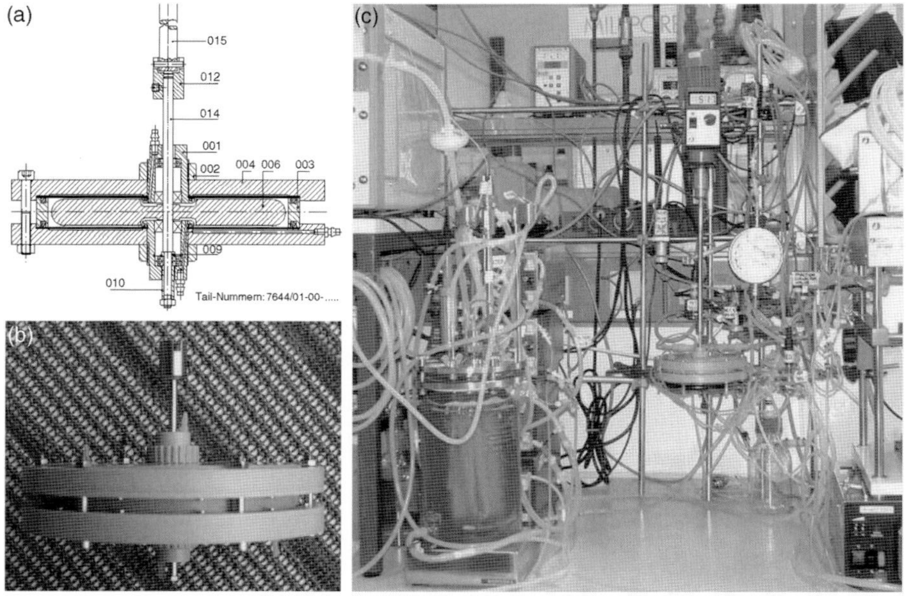

Figure 6.10 (a) Geometry selected using CFD; (b) prototype built and used in the batch filtration experiments [90] and in perfusion mode [91]; (c) prototype in perfusion operation [49].

6.6 Integrated Perfusion–Purification Processes for Continuous Biomanufacturing

The advances in protein expression, culture media, and cell retention devices experienced over the last decade have enabled significant improvements in titer and productivity of upstream processes. This has by far not been accompanied by an increase in adsorption capacity of chromatography media and productivity of purification processes. Thus, downstream processing remains accounting for up to 80% of total production costs [117], and purification – specially the capture chromatography step – has turned into a limiting factor in facility throughput, shifting the capacity bottleneck in biopharmaceutical manufacturing from upstream to downstream processes [118].

Continuous and semi-continuous chromatography techniques, which have been applied in the fine chemical and pharmaceutical industry since the 1990s [119], have the potential to increase resin capacity utilization, decrease column sizes and process footprint, improve throughput, and reduce costs.

Thus, several strategies based on multicolumn chromatography systems and/or membrane adsorbers, including continuous, semi-continuous, repeated, or cyclic operation modes, have been proposed in the last years in order to extend the benefits of continuous upstream processing also to downstream biomanufacturing [63,91,118,120–123]. Additionally, nonchromatography techniques, such as precipitation and flocculation, have been proposed as alternative technologies that can be implemented continuously and scale with processed volume [124].

Periodic countercurrent chromatography, which can be carried out in three- or four-column configurations (3C-PCC, 4C-PCC), has been shown to enable up to 30% increases in productivity (g l_{resin}^{-1} h^{-1}) and to decrease buffer consumption by also up to 30% [125]. Godawat *et al.* [120] investigated the use of PCC for the continuous capture step of different proteins and compared it with the existing batch chromatography processes. With PCC, process economics was improved due to lower buffer consumption and better resin utilization efficiency, harvest hold vessels could be eliminated, and capture column size could decrease by 1–2 orders of magnitude.

The PCC concept was successfully applied in the integrated continuous production of a monoclonal antibody (3C-PCC) and a recombinant enzyme (4C-PCC) [2]. The harvest obtained from a bioreactor perfused by an ATF system was pumped through a disposable surge bag and directly loaded onto the PCC chromatography system, which was fully closed and could operate under sterile conditions over prolonged periods of time. The direct load of the ATF perfusate eliminated the need for a clarification step and for harvest hold vessels, allowing for a significantly streamlined process train. When the continuous capture process for the antibody and the enzyme were compared to the corresponding batch processes, the data revealed to be quite impressive: resin capacity was increased by 20–50%, buffer usage was decreased to 54–75% of the batch consumption, column residence time was approximately halved, and column volume was decreased to 4–8% of the batch column volume.

Another useful tool for integrating upstream operations and capture step are membrane adsorbers. The controlled-shear affinity filtration (CSAF) concept investigated by Vogel *et al.* [126] to carry out simultaneous batch cell harvesting and product adsorption was further extended by Castilho *et al.* [91] to develop a continuous integrated perfusion/purification process.

Using the RDF shown in Figure 6.10 fitted with Protein A membranes [127], an automated system was built, which integrated the features of an automated bioreactor and an automated liquid chromatography system [49]. Using this system, IgG produced by CHO cells was continuously adsorbed during perfusion cultivation onto the affinity membranes inside the RDF, directly from the cell suspension, and periodically eluted through intermittent elution cycles that lasted 40 min. The IgG eluate was 14-fold more concentrated than inside the bioreactor and SDS-PAGE analysis (Figure 6.11) showed that it had high purity, containing only the two bands corresponding to the heavy and light antibody chains and a third contaminating band at about 22 kDa [91]. Such a system could be further developed to become truly continuous, without stops for periodical elution cycles, by using a twin RCF system, alternating continuous cell separation and product adsorption in one unit and product desorption, membrane regeneration, and equilibration in the other unit. The periodical membrane regeneration, which can be carried out in reverted direction, could further contribute to a stable long-term operation of this membrane-based perfusion/purification system.

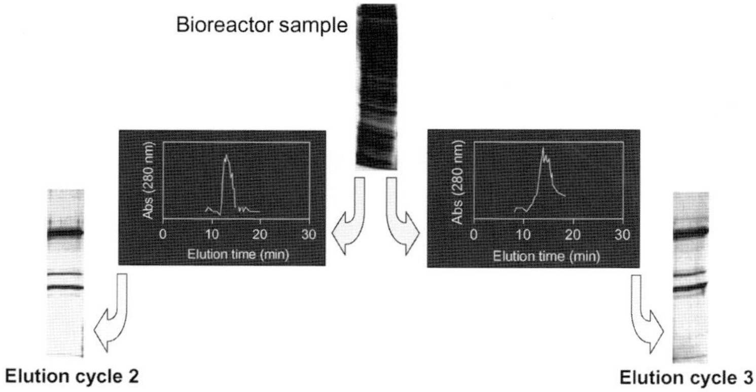

Figure 6.11 SDS-PAGE analysis under reducing conditions of eluates obtained in different elution cycles carried out during perfusion cultivation of CHO cells using a rotating disc filter fitted with Protein A membrane adsorbers to accomplish integrated perfusion and product capture.

In an attempt to go beyond capture, carrying out an end-to-end continuous integrated process, Tiainen *et al.* [128] automated a perfusion–purification process using the ATF and standard Äkta systems. A six-step purification process was run and each cycle lasted 14 h. Only the capture step used a dual column setup to allow one column to be loading and the other to be undergoing washing, viral inactivation, elution, and regeneration. There were no hold tanks, in no steps, and the authors showed that the new concept could run uninterruptedly for at least 7 days. Based on this experience, the authors concluded that perfusion cultivation combined with continuous multistep purification enables flexible and highly productive manufacturing with minimal footprint. Removal of hold stages between chromatography steps was a further advantage of the proposed process.

6.7 Concluding Remarks

As stated by Gottschalk *et al.* [129], innovations in the biomanufacturing industry are usually incremental, but sometimes existing technologies reach their limits and additional constraints are imposed by market forces or regulatory bodies, enabling occasional major technological shifts.

At the moment, a technological shift toward continuous bioprocessing seems to be starting in the biopharmaceutical industry. According to Sinclair [130] almost all innovative companies and suppliers are studying continuous processing. It is expected that in the near future a unified platform technology, applicable for monoclonal antibodies and nonantibody proteins, will exist, which will be efficient, simple, flexible, compact, automated, mobile, and cost-effective, with extra-low production cycles, and offering multiproduct and multiphase (clinical/commercial) manufacturing capability [2,5]. Quoting a case study on the production of a monoclonal antibody by an integrated continuous process, it was reported that the new technology led to a time interval from culture medium to purified protein of only 22 h (10 h for upstream and 12 h for downstream processing) [5], and this could further decrease in the future.

The shift toward continuous biomanufacturing is partly interrelated with the recent advances in disposable technology, which became very abundant and generally accepted over the last decade: (i) disposable devices are sterile closed systems, so that their use significantly decreases bioburden risks that were in the past a concern regarding continuous-flow processes; (ii) the smaller scales enabled by high-productivity continuous processes fit well to the scales of disposable units currently available in the market.

In regulatory terms, the US Food and Drug Administration (FDA) seems to be encouraging the developments toward continuous biomanufacturing. In continuous integrated processes, the steady-state operation has the potential to decrease product heterogeneity, and lot definition is not an issue – in current perfusion processes it is already well defined, based either on time or amount [131]. Furthermore, the use of disposable, closed systems end-to-end might eliminate the need for class C rooms [132] and might open up the possibility of having upstream and downstream operations placed in a single ballroom-type area, contributing to a decrease in capital investment for building new continuous-flow facilities.

Regarding the upstream processing, which is the starting point for any continuous integrated bioprocessing strategy and the focus of this chapter, advances in recent years in cell retention devices, cell culture media, and process strategies have enabled extremely high cell densities to be achieved under stable conditions, enabling a desired combination of high volumetric productivities and high titers.

However, although steady-state perfusion processing has undoubtedly positive impacts on product quality, higher-cell-density and/or longer processes also imply a continuously growing need for:

- establishing more and more robust control strategies;
- implementing plant designs that allow at-line sampling;
- giving regulators evidence that processes operate under steady state;
- confirming the genetic stability of cells with a focus on *in vitro* cell age;
- evaluating end-of-production cells to confirm viral safety and absence of contaminations;
- etc.

Thus, there are still many challenges to face, but the path to the technological shift toward continuous biomanufacturing is being currently paved.

References

1 Mellado, M.C.M. and Castilho, L.R. (2008) Recombinant therapeutic proteins, in *Animal Cell Technology: From Biopharmaceuticals to Gene Therapy* (eds L.R. Castilho, A.M. Moraes, E.F.P. Augusto, and M. Butler), Taylor & Francis, New York, pp. 389–408.

2 Warikoo, V., Godawat, R., Brower, K., Jain, S., Cummings, D., Simons, E., Johnson, T., Walther, J., Yu, M., Wright, B., McLarty, J., Karey, K.P., Hwang, C., Zhou, W., Riske, F., and Konstantinov, K. (2012) Integrated continuous production of recombinant therapeutic proteins. *Biotechnol. Bioeng.*, **109**, 3018–3029.
3 Gottschalk, U. (2013) Biomanufacturing: time for change? *Pharm. Bioprocess.*, **1**, 7–9.
4 Konstantinov, K.B. (2012) Implementation of integrated continuous bioprocessing in the biopharmaceutical industry. *Proceedings of the XIX Congresso Brasileiro de Engenharia Química (Brazilian Chemical Engineering Congress), September 9–12, 2012, Búzios, Brazil.* Associação Brasileira de Engenharia Química, São Paulo.
5 Konstantinov, K.B. (2013) The promise of continuous bioprocessing. *Proceedings of the Integrated Continuous Biomanufacturing Conference, October 20–24, 2013, Barcelona, Spain.* Engineering Conferences International, New York.
6 Chico, E., Rodriguez, G., and Figueredo-Cardero, A. (2008) Bioreactors for animal cells, in *Animal Cell Technology: From Biopharmaceuticals to Gene Therapy* (eds L.R. Castilho, A.M. Moraes, E.F.P. Augusto, and M. Butler), Taylor & Francis, New York, pp. 273–294.
7 Seth, G. (2012) Freezing mammalian cells for production of biopharmaceuticals. *Methods*, **56**, 424–431.
8 Ninomiya, N., Shirahata, S., Murakami, H., and Sugahara, T. (1991) Large-scale, high-density freezing of hybridomas and its application to high-density culture. *Biotechnol. Bioeng.*, **38**, 1110–1113.
9 Heidemann, R., Mered, M., Wang, D.Q., Gardner, B., Zhang, C., Michaels, J., Henzler, H.J., Abbas, N., and Konstantinov, K. (2002) A new seed-train expansion method for recombinant mammalian cell lines. *Cytotechnology*, **38**, 99–108.
10 Kleman, M.I., Oellers, K., and Lullau, E. (2008) Optimal conditions for freezing CHO-S and HEK293-EBNA cell lines: influence of Me_2SO, freeze density, and PEI-mediated transfection on revitalization and growth of cells, and expression of recombinant protein. *Biotechnol. Bioeng.*, **100**, 911–922.
11 Clincke, M.F., Mölleryd, C., Samani, P.K., Lindskog, E., Fäldt, E., Walsh, K., and Chotteau, V. (2013) Very high density of Chinese hamster ovary cells in perfusion by alternating tangential flow or tangential flow filtration in WAVE Bioreactor^{TM}. Part II: Applications for antibody production and cryopreservation. *Biotechnol. Prog.*, **29**, 768–777.
12 Seth, G., Hamilton, R.W., Stapp, T.R., Zheng, L., Meier, A., Petty, K., Leung, S., and Chary, S. (2013) Development of a new bioprocess scheme using frozen seed train intermediates to initiate CHO cell culture manufacturing campaigns. *Biotechnol. Bioeng.*, **110**, 1376–1385.
13 Tao, Y., Shih, J., Sinacore, M., Ryll, T., and Yusuf-Makagiansar, H. (2011) Development and implementation of a perfusion-based high cell density cell banking process. *Biotechnol. Prog.*, **27**, 824–829.
14 Bonham-Carter, J. (2011) Upstream process intensification. *Proceedings of the 4th International School on Production of Biologicals in Animal Cell Cultures, November 7–11, 2011, Rio de Janeiro, Brazil.* COPPE-Federal University of Rio de Janeiro, Rio de Janeiro.
15 Kaisermayer, C. and Yang, J. (2013) Highly efficient inoculum propagation in perfusion culture using WAVE Bioreactor^{TM} systems. *BMC Proc.*, 7 (Suppl. 6), P7.
16 Pohlscheidt, M., Jacobs, M., Wolf, S., Thiele, J., Jockwer, A., Gabelsberger, J., Jenzsch, M., Tebbe, H., and Burg, J. (2013) Optimizing capacity utilization by large scale 3000 L perfusion in seed train bioreactors. *Biotechnol. Prog.*, **29**, 222–229.
17 Cui, Z.F., Xu, X., Trainor, N., Triffitt, J.T., Urban, J.P., and Tirlapur, U.K. (2007) Application of multiple parallel perfused microbioreactors and three-dimensional stem cell culture for toxicity testing. *Toxicol. In Vitro*, **21**, 1318–1324.

18 Henry, O., Kwok, E., and Piret, J.M. (2008) Simpler noninstrumented batch and semicontinuous cultures provide mammalian cell kinetic data comparable to continuous and perfusion cultures. *Biotechnol. Prog.*, **24**, 921–931.

19 Vergara, M., Becerra, S., Díaz-Barrera, A., Berrios, J., and Altamirano, C. (2012) Simultaneous environmental manipulations in semi-perfusion cultures of CHO cells producing rh-tPA. *Electron. J. Biotechnol.*, **15** (6), doi: 10.2225/vol15-issue6-fulltext-2.

20 Altamirano, C., Cairó, J.J., and Gòdia, F. (2001) Decoupling cell growth and product formation in Chinese hamster ovary cells through metabolic control. *Biotechnol. Bioeng.*, **76**, 351–360.

21 Fike, R. (2009) Nutrient supplementation strategies for biopharmaceutical production. Part 1: Identifying a formulation. *BioProcess Int.*, **7**, 44–51.

22 Castilho, L.R., Heinrich, C., Northoff, S., and Noll, T. (2012) Screening of animal-component-free media for the culture of CHO cells in shaken tubes and stirred-tank bioreactors. *Proceedings of the Cell Culture Engineering XIII Conference, April 21–27, 2012, Phoenix, the United States*. Engineering Conferences International, New York.

23 Northoff, S., Heinrich, C., Büntemeyer, H., Hübel, T., and Schröder, B. (2012) Entwicklung von Zellkultur- und Feed-Medien. *BIOspektrum*, **4**, 413–414.

24 Yang, J.D., Angelillo, Y., Chaudhry, M., Goldenberg, C., and Goldenberg, D.M. (2000) Achievement of high cell density and high antibody productivity by a controlled-fed perfusion bioreactor process. *Biotechnol. Bioeng.*, **69**, 74–82.

25 Feng, Q., Mi, L., Li, L., Liu, R., Xie, L., Tang, H., and Chen, Z. (2006) Application of "oxygen uptake rate-amino acids" associated mode in controlled-fed perfusion culture. *J. Biotechnol.*, **122**, 422–430.

26 Konstantinov, K.B., Tsai, Y., Moles, D., and Matanguihan, R. (1996) Control of long-term perfusion Chinese hamster ovary cell culture by glucose auxostat. *Biotechnol. Prog.*, **12**, 100–109.

27 Ozturk, S.S. (1996) Engineering challenges in high density cell culture systems. *Cytotechnology*, **22**, 3–16.

28 Dowd, J.E., Jubb, A., Kwok, K.E., and Piret, J.M. (2003) Optimization and control of perfusion cultures using a viable cell probe and cell specific perfusion rates. *Cytotechnology*, **42**, 35–45.

29 Clincke, M.F., Mölleryd, C., Zhang, Y., Lindskog, E., Walsh, K., and Chotteau, V. (2013) Very high density of CHO cells in perfusion by ATF or TFF in WAVE bioreactor^{TM}. Part I. Effect of the cell density on the process. *Biotechnol. Prog.*, **29**, 754–767.

30 Ibarra, N., Watanabe, S., Bi, J.X., Shuttleworth, J., and Al-Rubeai, M. (2003) Modulation of cell cycle for enhancement of antibody productivity in perfusion culture of NS0 cells. *Biotechnol. Prog.*, **19**, 224–228.

31 Becerra, S., Berrios, J., Osses, N., and Altamirano, C. (2012) Exploring the effect of mild hypothermia on CHO cell productivity. *Biochem. Eng. J.*, **60**, 1–8.

32 Chuppa, S., Tsai, Y.S., Yoon, S., Shackleford, S., Rozales, C., Bhat, R., Tsay, G., Matanguihan, C., Konstantinov, K., and Naveh, D. (1997) Fermentor temperature as a tool for control of high-density perfusion cultures of mammalian cells. *Biotechnol. Bioeng.*, **55**, 328–338.

33 Bloemkolk, J., Gray, M., Merchant, F., and Mosmann, T. (1994) Effect of temperature on hybridoma cell cycle and MAb production. *Biotechnol. Bioeng.*, **40**, 427–431.

34 Chen, Z.L., Wu, B.C., Liu, H., Liu, X.M., and Huang, P.T. (2004) Temperature shift as a process optimization step for the production of pro-urokinase by a recombinant Chinese hamster ovary cell line in high-density perfusion culture. *J. Biosci. Bioeng.*, **97**, 239–243.

35 Ahn, W.S., Jeon, J.J., Jeong, Y.R., Lee, S.J., and Yoon, S.K. (2008) Effect of culture temperature on erythropoietin production and glycosylation in a perfusion culture of recombinant CHO cells. *Biotechnol. Bioeng.*, **101**, 1234–1244.

36 Yoon, S.K., Ahn, Y.H., and Jeong, M.H. (2007) Effect of culture temperature on follicle-stimulating hormone production by Chinese hamster ovary cells in a perfusion bioreactor. *Appl. Microbiol. Biotechnol.*, **76**, 83–89.

37 Rodriguez, J., Spearman, M., Tharmalingam, T., Sunley, K., Lodewyks, C., Huzel, N., and Butler, M. (2010) High productivity of human recombinant beta-interferon from a low-temperature perfusion culture. *J. Biotechnol.*, **150**, 509–518.

38 Kumar, N., Gammell, P., and Clynes, M. (2007) Proliferation control strategies to improve productivity and survival during CHO based production culture. *Cytotechnology*, **53**, 33–46.

39 Klausing, S., Krämer, O., and Noll, T. (2013) Bioreactor cultivation of CHO DP-12 cells under sodium butyrate treatment: comparative transcriptome analysis with CHO cDNA microarrays. *BMC Proc.*, **5** (Suppl. 8), P98.

40 Hong, J.K., Lee, G.M., and Yoon, S.K. (2011) Growth factor withdrawal in combination with sodium butyrate addition extends culture longevity and enhances antibody production in CHO cells. *J. Biotechnol.*, **155**, 225–231.

41 Kim, J.-S., Ahn, B.-C., Lim, B.-P., Choi, Y.D., and Jo, E.-C. (2004) High-level scu-PA production by butyrate-treated serum-free culture of recombinant CHO cell line. *Biotechnol. Prog.*, **20**, 1788–1796.

42 Jayapal, K.P. and Goudar, C.T. (2013) Transcriptomics as a tool for assessing the scalability of mammalian cell perfusion systems. *Adv. Biochem. Eng. Biotechnol.*, **139**, 227–243.

43 Vernardis, S.I., Goudar, C.T., and Klapa, M.I. (2013) Metabolic profiling reveals that time related physiological changes in mammalian cell perfusion cultures are bioreactor scale independent. *Metab. Eng.*, **19**, 1–9.

44 Goudar, C., Biener, R., Boisart, C., Heidemann, R., Piret, J., de Graaf, A., and Konstantinov, K. (2010) Metabolic flux analysis of CHO cells in perfusion culture by metabolite balancing and 2D [13C,1H] COSY NMR spectroscopy. *Metab. Eng.*, **12**, 138–149.

45 Konstantinov, K.B. (1996) Monitoring and control of the physiological state of cell cultures. *Biotechnol. Bioeng.*, **52**, 271–289.

46 Chong, L., Saghafi, M., Knappe, C., Steigmiller, S., Matanguihan, C., and Goudar, C.T. (2013) Robust on-line sampling and analysis during long-term perfusion cultivation of mammalian cells. *J. Biotechnol.*, **165**, 133–137.

47 Gorenflo, V.M., Ritter, J.B., Aeschliman, D.S., Drouin, H., Bowen, B.D., and Piret, J.M. (2005) Characterization and optimization of acoustic filter performance by experimental design methodology. *Biotechnol. Bioeng.*, **90**, 746–753.

48 Konstantinov, K., Goudar, C., Ng, M., Meneses, R., Thrift, J., Chuppa, S., Matanguihan, C., Michaels, J., and Naveh, D. (2006) The "push-to-low" approach for optimization of high-density perfusion cultures of animal cells. *Adv. Biochem. Eng. Biotechnol.*, **101**, 75–98.

49 Castilho, L.R. (2001) *Development of a Dynamic Filter for Integrated Perfusion Cultivation and Purification of Recombinant Proteins from Mammalian Cells*, VDI Fortschritt-Berichte Reihe 17 Nr. 212, VDI Verlag, Düsseldorf.

50 Goudar, C.T., Piret, J.M., and Konstantinov, K.B. (2011) Estimating cell specific oxygen uptake and carbon dioxide production rates for mammalian cells in perfusion culture. *Biotechnol. Prog.*, **27**, 1347–1357.

51 Goudar, C.T., Matanguihan, R., Long, E., Cruz, C., Zhang, C., Piret, J.M., and Konstantinov, K.B. (2007) Decreased pCO_2 accumulation by eliminating bicarbonate addition to high cell-density cultures. *Biotechnol. Bioeng.*, **96**, 1107–1117.

52 Woodside, S.M., Bowen, B.D., and Piret, J.M. (1998) Mammalian cell retention devices for stirred perfusion bioreactors. *Cytotechnology*, **28**, 163–175.

53 Castilho, L.R. and Medronho, R.A. (2002) Cell retention devices for suspended-cell perfusion cultures. *Adv. Biochem. Eng. Biotechnol.*, **74**, 129–169.

54 Voisard, D., Meuwly, F., Ruffieux, P.A., Baer, G., and Kadouri, A. (2003) Potential of cell retention techniques for large-scale high-density perfusion culture of suspended mammalian cells. *Biotechnol. Bioeng.*, **82**, 751–765.

55 Drugmand, J.C., Havelange, N., Collignon, F., Castillo, J., and Girod, P.-A. (2012) 4 g/l·day: Monoclonal antibody volumetric productivity in the iCELLis^{TM} disposable fixed-bed bioreactor. *Proceedings of the 21st Annual Meeting of the European Society for Animal Cell Technology (ESACT), June 7–10, 2009, Dublin, Ireland.* ESACT Proceedings, vol. 5, Springer, The Netherlands, pp. 375–378.

56 Vermasvuori, R. and Hurme, M. (2011) Economic comparison of diagnostic antibody production in perfusion stirred tank and in hollow fiber bioreactor processes. *Biotechnol. Prog.*, **27**, 1588–1598.

57 Medronho, R.A. (2003) Solid–liquid separation, in *Isolation and Purification of Proteins* (eds B. Mattiasson and R. Hatti-Kaul), Marcel Dekker, New York, pp. 131–190.

58 Figueredo-Cardero, A., Martinez, E., Chico, E., Castilho, L.R., and Medronho, R.A. (2014) Rotating cylindrical filters used in perfusion cultures: CFD simulations and experiments. *Biotechnol. Prog.*, doi: 10.1002/btpr.1945.

59 Coronel, J., Heinrich, C., Figueredo-Cardero, A., Northoff, S., and Castilho, L.R. (2013) Process evaluation for the production of a labile recombinant protein. *Proceedings of the 23rd ESACT Meeting, June 23–26, 2011, Lille, France.* European Society for Animal Cell Technology (ESACT), Frankfurt.

60 Henzler, H.J., Kauling, J., Schmitt, F., Beckers, E., Bödeker, B., Von Hugo, H., Konstantinov, K., Naveh, D., and Steiner, U. (2011) A unit and a process for carrying out high cell density fermentation. EP Pat. EP1451290 B1.

61 Barngrover, D.A., Jaeobsen, W.J., Nicolakis, D.P., and Fleury, J.E. (1998) Continuous settling apparatus. US Pat. 5733776 A.

62 Shen, Y. and Yanagimachi, K. (2011) CFD-aided cell settler design optimization and scale-up: effect of geometric design and operational variables on separation performance. *Biotechnol. Prog.*, **27**, 1282–1296.

63 Vogel, J.H., Nguyen, H., Giovannini, R., Ignowski, J., Garger, S., Salgotra, A., and Tom, J. (2012) A new large-scale manufacturing platform for complex biopharmaceuticals. *Biotechnol. Bioeng.*, **109**, 3049–3058.

64 Iammarino, M., Nti-Gyabaah, J., Chandler, M., Roush, D., and Göklen, K. (2007) Impact of cell density and viability on primary clarification of mammalian cell broth. *BioProcess Int.*, **5**, 38–50.

65 Kim, B.J., Chang, H.N., and Oh, D.J. (2007) Application of a cell-once-through perfusion strategy for production of recombinant antibody from rCHO cells in a Centritech Lab II centrifuge system. *Biotechnol. Prog.*, **23**, 1186–1197.

66 Kim, B.J., Oh, D.J., and Chang, H.N. (2008) Limited use of Centritech Lab II Centrifuge in perfusion culture of rCHO cells for the production of recombinant antibody. *Biotechnol. Prog.*, **24**, 166–174.

67 Björling, T., Dudel, U., and Fenge, C. (1995) Evaluation of a cell separator in large scale perfusion culture, in *Animal Cell Technology: Developments Towards the 21st Century* (eds E.C. Beuvery, J.B. Griffiths, and W.P. Zeijlemaker), Kluwer Academic Publishers, Dordrecht, pp. 671–675.

68 Deckwer, W.-D., Medronho, R.A., Anspach, F.B., and Lübberstedt, M. (2001) Method for separating viable cells from cell suspensions. US Pat. 6878545 B2.

69 Medronho, R.A., Schütze, J., and Deckwer, W.-D. (2005) Numerical simulation of hydrocyclones. *Lat. Am. Appl. Res.*, **35**, 1–8.

70 Pinto, R.C.V., Medronho, R.A., and Castilho, L.R. (2008) Separation of CHO cells using hydrocyclones. *Cytotechnology*, **56**, 57–67.

71 Medronho, R.A., Matanguihan, C., Konstantinov, K., and Zhang, C. (2008) Evaluation of hydrocyclone in high density mammalian perfusion processes.

Proceedings of XI Cell Culture Engineering Conference, April 13–18, 2008, Sunshine Coast, Australia. Engineering Conferences International, New York.

72 Elsayed, E.A. and Wagner, R. (2011) Application of hydrocyclones for continuous cultivation of SP-2/0 cells in perfusion bioreactors: effect of hydrocyclone operating pressure. *BMC Proc.*, **5** (Suppl. 8), P65.

73 Elsayed, E.A., Medronho, R.A., Wagner, R., and Deckwer, W.-D. (2006) Use of hydrocyclones for mammalian cell retention: separation efficiency and cell viability (Part 1). *Eng. Life Sci.*, **6**, 347–354.

74 Lübberstedt, M., Medronho, R.A., Anspach, F.B., and Deckwer, W.-D. (2000) Abtrennung tierischer Zellen mit Hydrozyklonen. *Chem. Ing. Tech.*, **72**, 1089–1090.

75 Dalm, M.C., Jansen, M., Keijzer, T.M., van Grunsven, W.M., Oudshoorn, A., Tramper, J., and Martens, D.E. (2005) Stable hybridoma cultivation in a pilot-scale acoustic perfusion system: long-term process performance and effect of recirculation rate. *Biotechnol. Bioeng.*, **91**, 894–900.

76 Shirgaonkar, I.Z., Lanthier, S., and Kamen, A. (2004) Acoustic cell filter: a proven cell retention technology for perfusion of animal cell cultures. *Biotechnol. Adv.*, **22**, 433–444.

77 Crowley, J., Wübben, M., and Coco Martin, J.M. (2013) Perfusion cell culture. European Pat. 2540815.

78 Duvar, S., Hecht, V., Finger, J.J., Gullans, M., and Ziehr, H. (2013) Developing an upstream process for a monoclonal antibody including medium optimization. *BMC Proc.*, **7** (Suppl. 6), P34.

79 Gálvez, J., Lecina, M., Solà, C., Cairó, J.J., and Gòdia, F. (2012) Optimization of HEK-293S cell cultures for the production of adenoviral vectors in bioreactors using on-line OUR measurements. *J. Biotechnol.*, **157**, 214–222.

80 Shevitz, J. (2003) Fluid filtration system. US Pat. 6544424 B1.

81 Singh, V. (2003) Disposable perfusion bioreactor for cell culture. US Pat. 6544788 B2.

82 Adams, T., Noack, U., Frick, T., Greller, G., and Fenge, C. (2011) Increasing efficiency in protein and cell production by combining single-use bioreactor technology and perfusion. *BioPharm Int. Suppl.*, **24**, s4–s11.

83 Tang, Y.J., Ohashi, R., and Hamel, J.F. (2007) Perfusion culture of hybridoma cells for hyperproduction of IgG(2a) monoclonal antibody in a wave bioreactor-perfusion culture system. *Biotechnol. Prog.*, **23**, 255–264.

84 Figueredo-Cardero, A., Chico, E., Castilho, L.R., and Medronho, R.A. (2009) CFD simulation of an internal spin-filter: evidence of lateral migration and exchange flow through the mesh. *Cytotechnology*, **61**, 55–64.

85 Vallez-Chetreanu, F., Fraisse-Ferreira, L.G., Rabe, R., von Stockar, U., and Marison, I.W. (2007) An on-line method for the reduction of fouling of spin-filters for animal cell perfusion cultures. *J. Biotechnol.*, **130**, 265–273.

86 Liu, H., Liu, X.M., Li, S.C., Wu, B.C., Ye, L.L., Wang, Q.W., and Chen, Z.L. (2009) A high-yield and scaleable adenovirus vector production process based on high density perfusion culture of HEK 293 cells as suspended aggregates. *J. Biosci. Bioeng.*, **107**, 524–529.

87 Figueredo-Cardero, A., Chico, E., Castilho, L.R., and Medronho, R.A. (2012) Particle image velocimetry (PIV) study of rotating cylindrical filters for animal cell perfusion processes. *Biotechnol. Prog.*, **28**, 1491–1498.

88 Mercille, S., Johnson, M., Lemieux, R., and Massie, B. (1994) Filtration-based perfusion of hybridoma cultures in protein-free medium: reduction of membrane fouling by medium supplementation with DNAse-I. *Biotechnol. Bioeng.*, **43**, 833–846.

89 Roth, G., Smith, C.E., Schoofs, G.M., Montgomery, T.J., Ayala, J.L., Monica, T.J., Castillo, F.J., and Horwitz, J.I. (1997) Vortex flow filtration for cell separation in bioreactor operations, in *Membrane Separations in Biotechnology* (ed. W.K. Wang), Marcel Dekker, New York, pp. 63–83.

90 Castilho, L.R. and Anspach, F.B. (2003) CFD-aided design of a dynamic filter for mammalian cell separation. *Biotechnol. Bioeng.*, **83**, 514–524.
91 Castilho, L.R., Anspach, F.B., and Deckwer, W.D. (2002) An integrated process for mammalian cell perfusion cultivation and product purification using a dynamic filter. *Biotechnol. Prog.*, **18**, 776–781.
92 Francis, P. (2011) Modeling of controlled-shear affinity filtration using computational fluid dynamics and a novel zonal rate model for membrane chromatography. PhD thesis. The University of British Columbia.
93 Vogel, J.H. and Kroner, K.H. (1999) Controlled shear filtration: a novel technique for animal cell separation. *Biotechnol. Bioeng.*, **63**, 663–674.
94 Castilho, L.R. and Medronho, R.A. (2008) Animal cell separation, in *Animal Cell Technology: From Biopharmaceuticals to Gene Therapy* (eds L.R. Castilho, A.M. Moraes, E.F.P. Augusto, and M. Butler), Taylor & Francis, New York, pp. 273–294.
95 Henzler, H.J. (2012) Kontinuierliche Fermentation mit tierischen Zellen. Teil 1. Aspekte der kontinuierlichen Prozessführung. *Chem. Ing. Tech.*, **84**, 1469–1481.
96 Svarovsky, L. (2000) *Solid–Liquid Separation*, 4th edn, Butterworth-Heinemann, Oxford.
97 Henzler, H.J. (2012) Kontinuierliche Fermentation mit tierischen Zellen. Teil 2. Techniken undMethoden der Zellrückhaltung. *Chem. Ing. Tech.*, **84**, 1482–1496.
98 Wang, Z. and Belovich, J.M. (2010) A simple apparatus for measuring cell settling velocity. *Biotechnol. Prog.*, **26**, 1361–1366.
99 Konstantinov, K.B. (2008) Development of processes for manufacturing of therapeutic proteins. *Proceedings of the 4th International School on Production of Biologicals in Animal Cell Cultures, July 18–22, 2008, Rio de Janeiro, Brazil.* COPPE-Federal University of Rio de Janeiro, Rio de Janeiro.
100 Apelman, S. (1992) Separation of animal cells in continuous cell culture systems, in *Animal Cell Technology: Basic & Applied Aspects* (eds H. Murakami, S. Shirahata, and H. Tachibana), Kluwer Academic Publishers, Dordrecht, pp. 149–154.
101 Elsayed, E.A. (2005) Application of hydrocyclone for cell separation in mammalian cell perfusion cultures. PhD thesis. Technical University of Braunschweig.
102 Sonosep (2014) www.sonosep.com/biosep.pdf (January 10, 2014).
103 Applikon (2014) www.applikon-bio.com/index.php?option=com_content&view=article&id =247:general&catid=75:biosep&Itemid=144&Itemid=236 (January 10, 2014).
104 Nobrega, R., Borges, C.P., and Habert, A.C. (2005) Processos de separação com membranas, in *Purificação de Produtos Biotecnológicos* (eds A. Pessoa, Jr. and B.V. Kilikian), Editora Manole, Barueri, Brazil, pp. 37–88.
105 Rautenbach, R. (1997) *Membranverfahren: Grundlagen der Modul- und Anlagenauslegung*, Springer, Berlin.
106 Zijlstra, G. (2013) New approaches in continuous biomanufacturing: continuous XD® cell cultures (at 100 million cells/ml and beyond) coupled to the Rhobust® EBA integrated clarification and purification technology. *Proceedings of the Integrated Continuous Biomanufacturing Conference, October 20–24, 2013, Barcelona, Spain.* Engineering Conferences International, New York.
107 Refine Technology (2014) www.refinetech.com/company.php (January 10, 2014).
108 Himmelfarb, P., Thayer, P.S., and Martin, H.E. (1969) Spin filter culture: the propagation of mammalian cells in suspension. *Science*, **164**, 555–557.
109 Deo, Y.M., Mahadevan, M.D., and Fuchs, R. (1996) Practical considerations in operation and scale-up of spin-filter based bioreactors for monoclonal antibody production. *Biotechnol. Prog.*, **12**, 57–64.

110 Yabannavar, V.M., Singh, V., and Connelly, N.V. (1992) Mammalian cell retention in a spin filter perfusion bioreactor. *Biotechnol. Bioeng.*, **40**, 925–933.
111 Yabannavar, V.M., Singh, V., and Connelly, N.V. (1994) Scaleup of spinfilter perfusion bioreactor for mammalian cell retention. *Biotechnol. Bioeng.*, **43**, 159–164.
112 Iding, K., Lütkemeyer, D., Fraune, E., Gerlach, K., and Lehmann, J. (2000) Influence of alterations in culture condition and changes in perfusion parameters on the retention performance of a 20 µm spinfilter during a perfusion cultivation of a recombinant CHO cell line in pilot scale. *Cytotechnology*, **34**, 141–150.
113 Avgerinos, G.C., Drapeau, D., Socolow, J.S., Mao, J.I., Hsiao, K., and Broeze, R.J. (1990) Spin filter perfusion system for high density cell culture: production of recombinant urinary type plasminogen activator in CHO cells. *BioTechnology*, **8**, 54–58.
114 Vallez-Chetreanu, F. (2006) Characterization of the mechanism of action of spin-filters for animal cell. PhD thesis. École Polytechnique Fédérale de Lausanne.
115 Hawrylik, S.J., Wasilko, D.J., Pillar, J.S., Cheng, J.B., and Lee, S.E. (1994) Vortex flow filtration of mammalian and insect cells. *Cytotechnology*, **15**, 253–258.
116 Fraune, E., Meichsner, S., and Kamal, M.N. (1997) A new spinfilter design, in *Animal Cell Technology: From Vaccines to Genetic Medicine* (eds M.J.T. Carrondo, B. Griffiths, and J.L.P. Moreira), Kluwer, Dordrecht, pp. 283–288.
117 D'Souza, R.N., Azevedo, A.M., Aires-Barros, M.R., Krajnc, N.L., Kramberger, P., Carbajal, M.L., Grasselli, M., Meyer, R., and Fernández-Lahore, M. (2013) Emerging technologies for the integration and intensification of downstream bioprocesses. *Pharm. Bioprocess.*, **1**, 423–440.
118 Bisschops, M. and Brower, M. (2013) The impact of continuous multicolumn chromatography on biomanufacturing efficiency. *Pharm. Bioprocess.*, **1**, 361–372.
119 Zobel, S., Helling, C., Ditz, R., and Strube, J. (2014) Design and operation of continuous countercurrent chromatography in biotechnological production. *Ind. Eng. Chem. Res.* doi: 10.1021/ie403103c
120 Godawat, R., Brower, K., Jain, S., Konstantinov, K., Riske, F., and Warikoo, V. (2012) Periodic counter-current chromatography: design and operational considerations for integrated and continuous purification of proteins. *Biotechnol. J.*, **7**, 1496–1508.
121 Napadensky, B., Shinkazh, O., Teella, A., and Zydney, A.L. (2013) Continuous countercurrent tangential chromatography for monoclonal antibody purification. *Sep. Sci. Technol.*, **48**, 1289–1297.
122 Angarita, M., Baur, D., Müller-Späth, T., Lievrouw, R., Lissens, G., Ströhlein, G., and Morbidelli, M. (2013) Twin column column CaptureSMB: a novel cyclic process to increase the capacity utilization in protein A chromatography. *Proceedings of the Integrated Continuous Biomanufacturing Conference, October 20–24, 2013, Barcelona, Spain.* Engineering Conferences International, New York.
123 Rousset, F. (2013) Continuous chromatography: disruptive technology for downstream processing. *Proceedings of the Integrated Continuous Biomanufacturing Conference, October 20–24, 2013, Barcelona, Spain.* Engineering Conferences International, New York.
124 Hammerschmidt, N., Tscheliessnig, A., Satzer, P., Schulz, H., Helk, B., and Jungbauer, A. (2013) A process for next-generation antibody production; cold ethanol precipitation and calcium-phosphate flocculation of recombinant antibodies. *Proceedings of the Integrated Continuous Biomanufacturing Conference, October 20–24, 2013, Barcelona, Spain.* Engineering Conferences International, New York.
125 Jagschies, G. (2008) Operational excellence: the future of

biopharmaceutical manufacturing. *Innov. Pharm. Technol.*, **26**, 57–60.

126 Vogel, J.H., Anspach, F.B., Kroner, K., Piret, J.M., and Haynes, C.A. (2002) Controlled shear affinity filtration (CSAF): a new technology for integration of cell separation and protein isolation from mammalian cell cultures. *Biotechnol. Bioeng.*, **78**, 806–814.

127 Castilho, L.R., Anspach, F.B., and Deckwer, W.D. (2002) Comparison of affinity membranes for the purification of immunoglobulins. *J. Membr. Sci.*, **207**, 253–264.

128 Tiainen, P., Bjelke, J.R., Skibstrup, D., Heitmann, M., and Akesson, M. (2013) End-to-end continuous production of complex recombinant proteins: integration of perfusion cultivation and automated multi-step purification. *Proceedings of the Integrated Continuous Biomanufacturing Conference, October 20–24, 2013, Barcelona, Spain.* Engineering Conferences International, New York.

129 Gottschalk, U., Brorson, K., and Shukla, A.A. (2013) Innovation in biomanufacturing: the only way forward. *Pharm. Bioprocess.*, **1**, 141–157.

130 Sinclair, A. (2013) Addressing the process and economic dimensions (workshop introductory talk). *Proceedings of the Integrated Continuous Biomanufacturing Conference, October 20–24, 2013, Barcelona, Spain.* Engineering Conferences International, New York.

131 Warikoo, V. (2013) Cost analysis of continuous bioprocessing over a product's lifecycle (talk during workshop on Process and Economic Dimensions). *Proceedings of the Integrated Continuous Biomanufacturing Conference, October 20–24, 2013, Barcelona, Spain.* Engineering Conferences International, New York.

132 Cazeault, C. (2013) Integrated continuous biomanufacturing: quality and regulatory considerations. *Proceedings of the Integrated Continuous Biomanufacturing Conference, October 20–24, 2013, Barcelona, Spain.* Engineering Conferences International, New York.

7
Perfusion Process Design in a 2D Rocking Single-Use Bioreactor

Nico M.G. Oosterhuis

7.1
Introduction

Nowadays, the application of single-use bioreactors has become more and more common in biopharmaceutical bioprocesses. Single-use equipment is introduced not only for mammalian cell culture processes but also for microbial-based processes [1].

The advantages of applying single-use bioreactors like reduction of contamination risk, reduction of operational costs (no cleaning needed, simple validation, short turn-around), and higher flexibility has led to the full acceptance of this new technology over the last 10 years.

Most single-use bioreactors are limited to the application in mammalian cell culture processes due to restrictions in oxygen mass-transfer. This is because of construction constraints limiting the power input into the bioreactor needed for sufficient mass transfer and mixing.

Especially when cell densities become high, oxygen limitation might become an issue. Even more important, but generally overlooked, is the transfer of the carbon dioxide produced. At higher cell densities, CO_2-transfer limitation may result in lowering of the pH, which leads to higher amounts of alkaline used and therefore to too high Na^+ levels in the medium.

Recently, the CELL-tainer® single-use bioreactor has been introduced, which overcomes this limitation, as has clearly been shown in microbial applications [2]. As such, this reactor also makes higher cell densities possible in mammalian cell culture processes and therefore is very well suited to support perfusion processes as well.

7.2
Production Costs

Among others, the introduction of biosimilars has led to more focus on the reduction of production costs. The application of single-use bioreactors can

Continuous Processing in Pharmaceutical Manufacturing, First Edition. Edited by Ganapathy Subramanian.

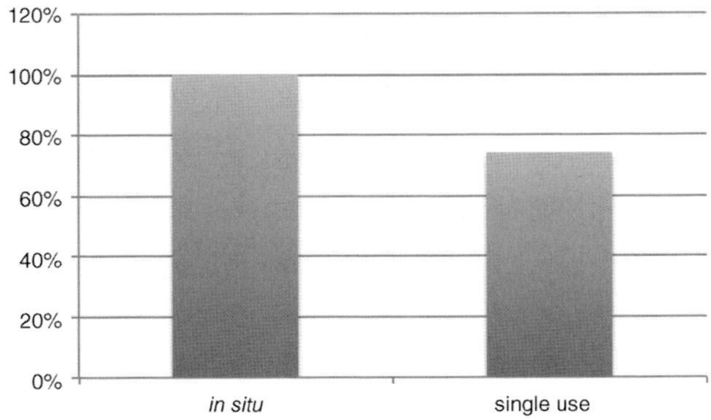

Figure 7.1 Cost reduction due to application of single-use bioreactors (fed-batch mammalian cell process at 150 l scale, incl. preculture costs).

lead to a significant cost reduction, not only due to direct operational costs (Figure 7.1), but also due to significant lower investment levels (less infrastructure needed), absence of complex validation studies (no cleaning validation, no validation of infrastructure like sterilizing-in-place and cleaning-in-place), and short turn-around times of equipment (for a 20 day fed-batch process, 10% more runs/year can easily be achieved).

Besides by introduction of single-use technology, upstream costs also can be reduced by the application of perfusion processes. A comparison of different process types in which an ATF system (alternating tangential flow system, Refine Technologies) is applied shows a potential of 50% reduction of upstream costs when applying a perfusion process (Figure 7.2) (www.refinetech.com). An overview by BioPharm Services [3] shows the effect on costs-of-goods when applying continuous processing at various scales of production (Figure 7.3). As can be concluded from this analysis, the impact of continuous processing (perfusion) is mainly on the cost of goods. Due to the higher complexity of equipment, the

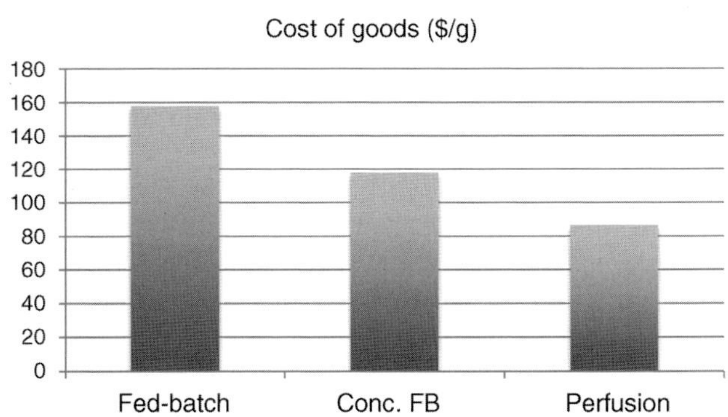

Figure 7.2 Cost comparison of different process types (www.refinetech.com).

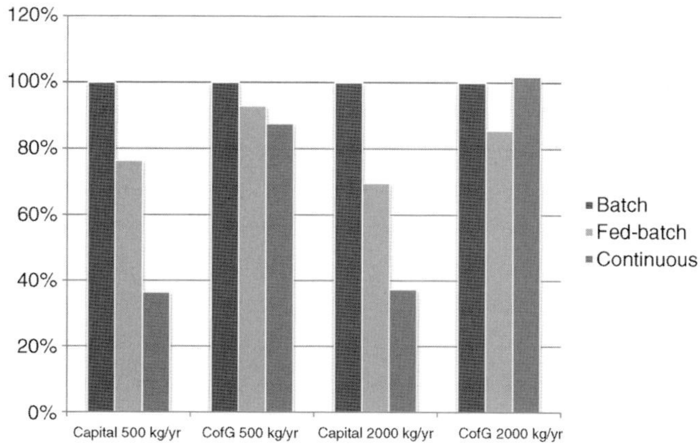

Figure 7.3 Cost analysis of different process types, comparison of capital costs, and cost of goods [3].

capital costs (including those for downstream processing) are almost equal for the various process types.

Summarizing, it can be concluded that the combination of single-use bioprocessing and operating a perfusion process will lead to significant operational cost savings and savings in investments.

7.3 Equipment Requirements for a Single-Use Perfusion Process

First of all, the bioreactor must be able to support higher cell densities, which has consequences for mass transfer properties. Assuming a cell density of 20×10^6 cells, with a specific oxygen uptake rate of 5–10 pmol $cell^{-1}$ day^{-1} (average value for Chinese hamster ovary (CHO) cells) [4], the required oxygen mass transfer rate should be at least 30–60 h^{-1} (Figure 7.4). As for CO_2 the mass transfer rate is approximately 70% of that of O_2, at a specific carbon dioxide production rate of 4–6 $pmol^{-1}$ $cell^{-1}$ day^{-1} [4], the k_La for CO_2 needs to be at least 50–70 h^{-1}.

Based on supplier information as well as on literature, it may be concluded that the k_La for most single-use bioreactors is in the range of 20–40 h^{-1}, which is not sufficient to support mass transfer for higher cell densities. Applying special type of spargers (microspargers) in stirred bioreactors and enriching the air with oxygen to control DO at acceptable levels may result in sufficient mass transfer. Usually, this is the strategy followed. However, stripping of CO_2 requires a steady bubble flow using standard spargers. In order to increase mass transfer capacity, more complex systems are needed, including more complex control strategies.

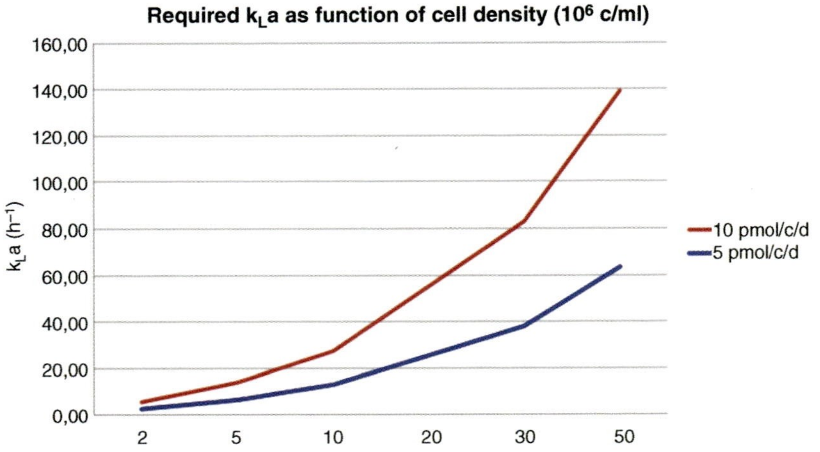

Figure 7.4 Required oxygen transfer rate k_La as function of cell density at different specific oxygen uptake rates for CHO-cells at a DO-level of 30% (air saturation).

A study by Bonham-Carter *et al.* [5] shows the effect of high cell densities (up to 35×10^6 cells ml^{-1}) in a CHO-culture on the DO-levels in a Wave-type bioreactor connected to an ATF device. DO-levels start to be below 20% oxygen saturation at cell densities of $25–30 \times 10^6$ cells $ml^{-1,}$ which confirms our earlier statement.

The CELL-tainer® single-use bioreactor (Figure 7.5) applies an innovative way of shaking the bag (2D rocking), ensuring a significant increase of mass transfer also under conditions applicable for cell culture (Table 7.1). The application of the CELL-tainer® in higher cell density processes reduces the complexity of operation.

Many perfusion devices have been introduced over the years. An extensive overview of different available perfusion devices, their advantages, and

Figure 7.5 CELL-tainer® single-use bioreactor at 20 and 200 l scale.

Table 7.1 k_La Values for different types of equipment.

	Shake-flask	Stirred single-use bioreactor	Wave-type bioreactor	CELL-tainer® (2D rocking)
k_La (h^{-1})	<50	2–20	<30	50–150[a)]

a) Under cell culture conditions. For microbial applications, k_La values of $>400\,h^{-1}$ have been reported [2].

drawbacks has been published by Castilho and Medronho [6]. Table 7.2 summarizes the properties of different available perfusion devices.

Most cell retention systems applied for perfusion processing are based on size exclusion, like cross-flow filters and spin filters, or are a combination of separation on basis of size and density difference like settlers, centrifuges, and hydrocyclones. Acoustic separation has been applied as well [7].

Nowadays, the ATF system (www.refinetech.com) has become more and more accepted in bioprocessing, mainly due to its positive properties in terms of reduction of fouling of the filters and the ability to define the filter cut-off. This makes it also possible not only to concentrate cells, but even the product [8].

Despite the frequently applied combination of the ATF with single-use bioreactors (www.refinetech.com) [5], the housing of the filter still has to be autoclaved and sterile connections have to be made with the bioreactor. The process control of the ATF is rather complex as well.

An internal filter device is available for rocking bags (GE). This filter floats on the surface of the liquid [9]. The disadvantage of such floating filter is that the filter reduces the surface for mass transfer. Also, the fouling of these filters seems to be significant (Frohlich, B. (2013) personal communication).

Based on this evaluation of properties it has been decided to evaluate two different technologies of perfusion in combination with the CELL-tainer® single-use bioreactor. An important requirement is that the perfusion device be fully disposable as well.

7.4 Testing Results Single-Use Perfusion Process

In order to overcome the mass transfer restriction by using a floating filter, we have decided to test a filter that can be sealed at the bottom of the bag. As filter material, Solupor®, a hydrophilic, ultrahigh-molecular-weight polyethylene (UHMPE) has been applied (http://www.lydallfiltration.com/app/liquid/bio_pharm.shtml). This membrane material is a USP class VI material, gamma

Table 7.2 Properties perfusion devices.

Property	Device						
	Spin-filter	**Centrifuge**	**Settler**	**Hydrocyclone**	**Internal membrane**	**ATF**	**Acoustic**
Construction	Simple	Complex	Simple	Simple	Simple	Complex	Complex
Separation	Size	Gravity	Gravity	Gravity	Size	Size	Gravity
Capacity	$>1\ m^3\ d^{-1}$	$>2\ m^3\ d^{-1}$	$>1\ m^3\ d^{-1}$	$<200\ l\ d^{-1}$	$<20\ l\ d^{-1}$	$<1\ m^3\ d^{-1}$	$<200\ l\ d^{-1}$
Retention (%)	>90	>98	<90	<90	>98	>95	>95
Cell density ($\times 10^6$ c ml^{-1})	<20	>20	<20	<20	<20	>100	>50
Shear	Average	High	Low	High	Low	Average	Average
Fouling	Average	Low	Average	Low	High	Average	Low
Investment	High	High	Average	Low	Low	High	Average
Operational cost	Low	Low	Low	Low	High	High	Low
Availability	Wide	Limited	Limited	No	Wide	Limited	Limited
Main issues	Clogging	Complexity	Patents	Patents	Fouling	Product loss	Agglomeration
Single use	No	No	Maybe	Maybe	Yes	No	Yes

stable, and can be sealed with the polyethylene film of the bags. Solupor® also has excellent clear water fluxes even at low pressure-drops.

In first instance tests have been done with a filter surface of 16 cm^2 and a filter pore size of 5–7 μm. In these tests, in a culture of CHO cells, in 24 days, 76 l has been perfused through the filter. When the pore size was reduced (2 μm), but the filter surface increased (64 cm^2), in 28 days, 60 l has been perfused. However, in both cases after perfusion during these 20–24 days, the filter started to block due to fouling of the membrane. Despite the positive properties of the filter material and increase of filter size, obviously membrane type perfusion systems are less suitable for running long-term perfusion processes.

7.5 Simplified Seeding Process

A typical standard seeding process for mammalian cell culture requires many steps and various equipment to finally seed a 200 or 2000 l bioreactor. After thawing of the vial into a 40 ml shake-flask or spinner-flask, at least another 1–2 steps are needed before a (single-use) bioreactor with a 1 l working volume can be inoculated. Thereafter, 2–3 steps are needed in wave bags to expand the cells to 25 l, which might be sufficient to seed at least a 200 l (100 l working volume) bioreactor. So, all together at least six steps (including handling and risk of contamination) are needed.

When applying the CELL-tainer® expansion set, one can go directly from a 40 ml flask into the 25 l (working volume) bag. As such, 3–4 steps can be reduced, resulting in less handling and less equipment to be used (Figure 7.6). The overall time for seeding depends on the doubling time of the cells. As can be concluded from Table 7.3, comparable doubling times are found in a comparison with a traditional seeding scheme.

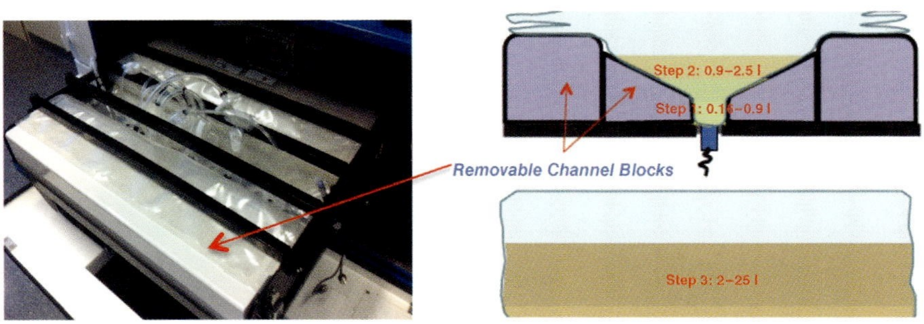

Figure 7.6 Expansion set CELL-tainer®.

Table 7.3 Typical growth rates in different seeding processes [10].

Step	Vessel (current process)	Growth rate (d^{-1})	
		Current process[a)]	CELLtainer process
640 ml	2 × 1 l shake-flask	0.47 ± 0.09	0.21
2.5 l	10 l Wave	0.44 ± 0.06	0.53
5 l	10 l Wave	0.41 ± 0.04	0.49
25 l	50 l Wave	0.42 ± 0.05	0.39
All steps		0.44 ± 0.07	0.47 ± 0.14

a) Obtained from a set of 26 expansions done using the current process; values are mean and standard deviation.

Data show that the CELL-tainer® expansion set simplifies the seeding process. Saving bags and reduction of handling is the main benefit of such approach (Figure 7.7).

Further optimization is possible when the last steps are combined with a perfusion device. Combination of a perfusion device with the CELL-tainer® expansion set opens the potential to develop a very simplified seeding process where only one bioreactor is needed to seed a large culture vessel. In one and the same bag the culture can be expanded from 0.15 to 25 l working volume. Assuming a cell density of 30×10^6 cells ml^{-1} at 25 l, the amount of cells is sufficient to seed a volume of at least 600–1000 l. In such a way, the seed process can be simplified to a one-step process.

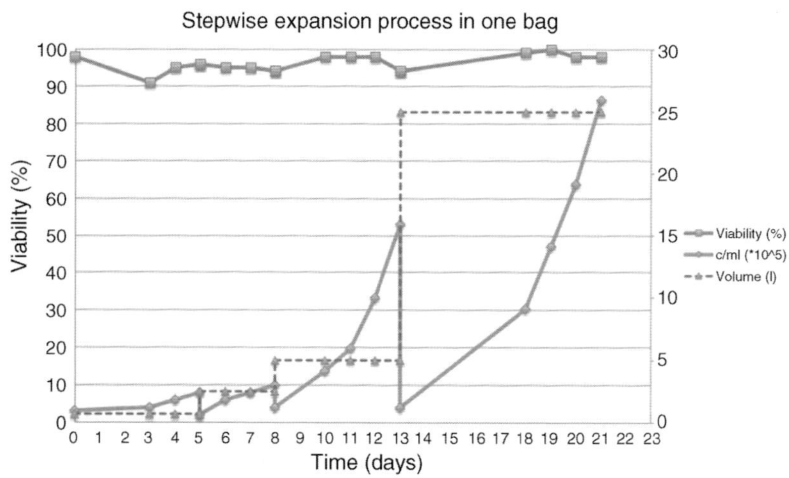

Figure 7.7 Cell culture results using the CELL-tainer® expansion set.

7.6 Future Outlook

Perfusion processes can clearly lead to lower investments (due to smaller scale) which, in combination with single-use technologies, make the industry more flexible. A survey by Langer (BioPlan Associates) [11] shows that there is a strong interest by the industry to apply perfusion culture as a commercial manufacturing tool. However, respondents of the survey showed to be hesitating to apply this technology due to concerns about certain aspects, such as process complexity, contamination risks, and ability to scale-up.

Application of a single-use device that is already connected to the single-use bioreactor (bag) before use would reduce the sterility risks.

A promising single-use perfusion device is the "Cytoperf" (http://www.iprabio.be/coretechnologies/cytoperf/about-cytoperf) (see elsewhere in this book), which can be fully gamma sterilized and preconnected to the bag. This will contribute to the further acceptance of single-use perfusion processes. Because the CELL-tainer® single-use bioreactor supports high cell density cultures, the combination of these technologies shows a high potential for further intensifying cell culture processes as well as seeding processes, which leads to significantly lower costs of production of biopharmaceuticals and reduction of contamination risks.

References

1 Oosterhuis, N.M.G., Neubauer, P., and Junne, S. (2013) Single-use bioreactors for microbial cultivation. *Pharm. Bioprocess.*, **1** (2), 167–177.

2 Junne, S., Solymosi, T., Oosterhuis, N.M.G., and Neubauer, P. (2013) Cultivation of cells and microorganisms in wave-mixed disposable bag bioreactors. *Chem. Ing. Tech.*, **85** (1–2), 1–11.

3 Sinclair, A. and Brown, A. (2013) Continuous process economic evaluation. *Continuous Bioprocessing, Current Practice & Future Potential.* Refine Technology, pp. 73–81.

4 Goudar, C.T., Piret, J.M., and Konstantinov, K.B. (2011) Estimating cell specific oxygen uptake and carbon dioxide production rates for mammalian cells in perfusion culture. *Biotechnol. Prog.*, **27** (5), 1347–1357.

5 Bonham-Carter, J., Weegar, J., Nieminen, A., Shevitz, J., and Eliezer, E. (2011) The use of the ATF system to culture Chinese hamster ovary cells in a concentrated fed-batch system. *BioPharm Int.*, **24** (6), 42–48.

6 Castilho, L.R. and Medronho, R.A. (2002) Cell retention devices for suspended-cell perfusion cultures. *Adv. Biochem. Eng.*, **74**, 129–169.

7 Gorenflo, V.M., Smith, L., Dedinsky, B., Persson, B., and Piret, J.M. (2002) Scale-up and optimization of an acoustic filter for 200 l/day perfusion of a CHO cell culture. *Biotechnol. Bioeng.*, **80** (4), 438–444.

8 Zijstra, G.M., Hof, R.P., and Schilder, J. (2007) Improved process for culturing cells. WO2008/006494 A1 (July 4, 2007).

9 Singh, V. (2003) Disposable perfusion bioreactor for cell culture. US Pat. US2003/0036192 A1.

10 Frohlich, B., Bedard, C., Gagliardi, T., and Oosterhuis, N.M.G. (2012) Co-development of a new 2-D rocking single-use bioreactor to streamline cell expansion processes. IBC BioProcess International Conference (2012), Rhode Island.

11 Langer, E.S. (2011) Trends in perfusion bioreactors. *BioProces Int.*, **9** (10), 18–22.

8
Advances in the Application of Perfusion Technologies to *Drosophila* S2 Insects Cell Culture

Lars Poulsen and Willem A. de Jongh

8.1
Introduction

The choice of expression system and production method is a vital strategic decision in recombinant subunit vaccine development. *Drosophila* S2 insect cells have been used in research for almost 40 years and over the last 10 years several clinical development programs have employed the system for antigen production. Dr. Schneider derived the cell line from late-stage *Drosophila melanogaster* (fruit fly) embryos in 1972. She named the cell line *Drosophila* Schneider line 2 (synonyms: S2, SL2, D.mel. 2). The S2 system has unique advantages for low-cost production compared to other insect cell expression systems. A wide variety of upstream processing options are possible as the S2 system is a stable cell line-based, nonviral, and nonlytic expression system. This is in contrast to the broadly used lytic Baculovirus Expression Vector System (BEVS), which is an obligatory batch process approach. Compared to BEVS, S2 enables advanced processing options beyond batch, for example fed-batch and perfusion and concentrated perfusion (where the protein of interest is retained in the bioreactor).

Insect cell expression systems are generally known for their ability to succeed with difficult to express protein challenges. Table 8.1 lists a limited set of examples from the literature for proteins and protein classes that have been expressed in S2 cells.

The *Drosophila* S2 system is particularly well suited to vaccine manufacture and has been applied for clinical development projects. These projects include a Her2 positive breast cancer subunit vaccine (Pharmexa A/S) and as a component in a Crohn's disease cellular therapy (TxCells), both tested in Phase II clinical trials. Furthermore, Phase I clinical trials for a West Nile virus vaccine by Hawaii Biotech, and a dengue virus vaccine by Merck, Inc. have been performed. Among other projects, there are also two malaria subunit vaccines currently in preclinical development.

Continuous Processing in Pharmaceutical Manufacturing, First Edition. Edited by Ganapathy Subramanian.

Table 8.1 Examples of S2 expressed proteins from the literature, reviewed in Ref. [1].

	Family	S2 Produced
Secreted	Anti-angiogenic	Endostatin, Canstatin
	Cytokines and growth factors	VEGF, IL5, IL12, EPO, RANKL, TNF, lymphotactin
	Enzymes	Sea raven type II anrifreeie protein
	Plasma proteins	Human transferrin
	Monoclonal antibodies	IgG, IgM, scFv, Fc, chimeras and Fab fragments
Viral	Viral Proteins	JEV, rabies virus. West Nile virus, Influenza, Dengue fever
	Virus like particles	JEV glytoprot [Fj, HIV, Rotavirus
Complex surface	Receptors	CD23*, EGFR*, Her2*, ADAM33*, glucagon rec., MHC class II I-Ed
	Integrins and related receptors	αIIβ3, suPAR
	GPCRs	D1 and D2 dopamine receptors, human mu opioid receptor, IL-5 receptor α, chemokine CxCR3, CXCL11 receptors

Traditionally, three cultivation strategies have been applied for cell culture: batch, fed-batch, and continuous cultivation. Each approach has their distinct advantages and disadvantages, as highlighted in Table 8.2.

Within the field of continuous cultivation, advances in retention technologies have allowed for specialized continuous cell culture bioprocesses termed perfusion processes. A perfusion culture is a continuous process in which a culture is continuously supplied with fresh medium to the bioreactor, while the cells are retained and clarified culture media is continuously harvested. With this, perfusion systems combine the high cell densities from a fed-batch with the continuous product harvesting/byproduct removal from the continuous reactor. This gives the advantage of high productivity in a relatively small-sized bioreactor.

Table 8.2 An overview of cell culture strategies [2].

Type	Positive	Negative
Batch	Simple, low risk of infection (contamination)	Potential issues with proteases, low yields
Fed-batch	Simple, high yields and titer, dilution of bi-products	Potential issues with proteases and protein instability, risk of infection
Continuous cultivation	High yields, low protein instability/ protease degradation issues, removal of biproducts/Addition of complete medium, small reactor demand	Risk of infection and equipment failure, high equipment cost, complex compared to (fed)-batch

Table 8.3 Scalable perfusion technologies.

Technology	Commercialized available from	Perfusion rate ($l\ d^{-1}$)
Hollow fiber	Spectrum Microgon INC., Refine Technology	0–1000
Spin filter	B. Braun Biotech, Bioengineering AG	0–500
Centrifuge	Kendro, Westfalia Separator AG	1–2600
Acoustic	Applikon	1–1000

The center of a perfusion setup is the cell retention device. Many technologies exist applying just as many principles, as reviewed in Ref. [3]. However, only two separation principles have been proven scalable, thus will only be addressed in this chapter. These are retention based on particle size (filtration) and on particle density (Table 8.3).

These principles can be demonstrated by the following two *Drosophila* S2 vaccine development case studies.

8.2 Case Study 1: Acoustic Separation

The objective of this development work was to develop and improve a RANK Ligand (RANKL)-based vaccine production process. The process was required to be reproducible, robust, and meet acceptable product expression levels to facilitate transfer of the RANKL upstream process to a CMO.

Two B. Braun Biostat B-DCU Quad systems were employed for the development work. Each system was equipped with four bioreactors, with 1.5 or 4.5 l working volume. The reactors were assembled according to the manufacturer's instructions and sterilized by autoclaving.

8.2.1 The Perfusion Setup (BioSep)

The perfusion system used in this case study was based on the BioSep system from Applisens (Figure 8.1). Acoustic particle separation applies resonant ultrasonic standing waves to separated particles from the fluid. When an acoustic resonance field is applied in a cell suspension, cell agitation is promoted primarily by the second retention force and the Bernoulli force [5] and clarified medium can be removed by a harvest pump. Both the retention device and the harvest pump are turned off in parallel at given time intervals to allow for retained cells to reenter the bioreactor and become resuspended by the impeller. This technology was commercialized by Applikon and can treat from 1 to 1000 l culture per day, dependent on the resonator (BioSep) model. The model used in this case study was the BioSep 10 l per day resonator chamber for the 1.5 and 4.5 l runs and the 50 l per day resonator chamber for the 20 l production run.

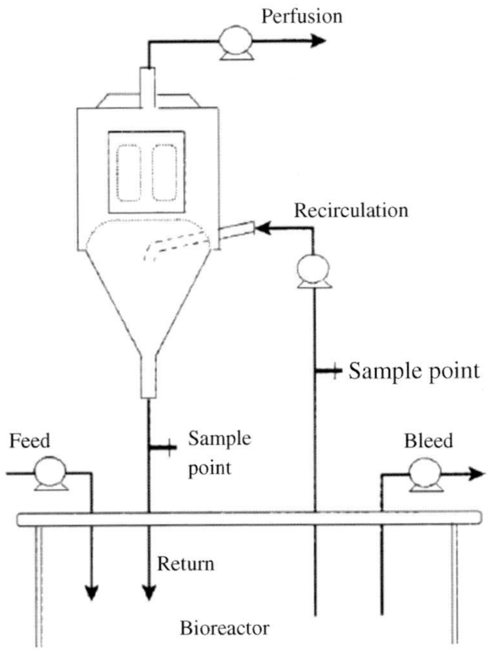

Figure 8.1 A typical setup of the BioSep perfusion setup. Figure adapted from Ref. [4].

8.2.2 Results and Discussion

8.2.2.1 Development

The cultivations were continued for up to 14 days to determine the effects of different process parameters on the perfusion process. The main parameters of interest were (i) the variation in the cell count and cell viability in the fermenter; (ii) the concentration of RANKL in the perfusate; (iii) the final titer of RANKL produced during the process; and (iv) RANKL protein cleavage.

The initial process development was based on the already established Phase II production process for a Her2 positive breast cancer vaccine produced in S2 cells. Based on experience from this process, it was decided that the maximum cell count should not exceed 90E6–100E6 cells ml^{-1}, since in doing so cell culture viability was negatively influenced. This necessitated the development of different bleed rate control strategies to prevent the cell concentration in the culture from becoming too high.

8.2.2.2 Cell Count in the Bioreactor

Two specific issues in controlling the cell count were the establishment of a transferable bleed rate control strategy, and the loss of cells through the BioSep.

The control of the bleed rate was complicated by the variable nature of the culture growth rate during the perfusion process, while uncontrolled cell loss led to an inherently unstable system.

8.2.2.3 Effects of BioSep Settings on Cell Loss and Viability

The problem of cell loss through the BioSep was addressed by testing the impact of the main settings, these being regular in-process flushing of the BioSep, power, run time/stop time, and recirculation pump rate. For 1.5 l fermentation volumes cell loss could be prevented by using an increased run time/stop time ratio on the BioSep.

It was observed that long stop times (60 s), followed by short run times (4.5 s) led to a situation where the BioSep was not operating efficiently, with high levels of cell loss though the BioSep as a result. A more efficient setting was found to be a run time of 15 s, followed by a stop time of 4.5 s. Although this appeared to be an optimal setting for lower flow rates, it was not directly scalable for higher flow rates. A high level of cell loss occurred when the flow rate through the BioSep was increased above 3 l per day. This occurred when the fermentation scale was increased to 4.5 l for the consistency run. It was later found that the power setting had no effect on cell viability in the tested range (5–8 W), while the cell separation improved dramatically. A power setting of 8 W was therefore used for the 4.5 l fermentation runs.

The effect of increasing the BioSep recirculation pump rate was found to increase cell loss. The original pump rate was therefore maintained.

Finally, the problem of BioSep fouling during the run was solved by instituting regular flushing of the BioSep during the run. This was done by extracting 20–60 ml of media directly through the BioSep at a fast flow rate, once daily.

8.2.2.4 Controlling the Cell Concentration Through Bleed Rate Control

With the uncontrolled cell loss through the BioSep resonator solved, implementation of a consistent and robust control of the cell concentration in the bioreactor was possible. The acceptable cell concentration was established to 50E6–90E6 cells ml^{-1}, yielding high product purity and acceptable titers. However, the optimal cell concentration was determined to be in the range of 65E6–80E6 cells ml^{-1} resulting in high yields as well as product purity.

The perfusion process is not in a steady state, thus it is necessary to constantly control the cell concentration. This was achieved by having a bleed on the fermenter. The bleed should ideally remove cells at a rate that equals the growth rate, thereby stabilizing the cell concentration in the fermenter. The perfusion flow is not completely cell-free as the acoustic cell-retention device does not retain all cells. Consequently, the Bleed can be defined as

$$B = \mu = B_{\text{total}} - P \cdot \left(1 - \frac{\text{SE}}{100}\right), \tag{8.1}$$

where μ is the growth rate, P is the perfusion rate, SE is the separation efficiency (%) and B_{total} is the total cell bleed of the reactor. With the relationship

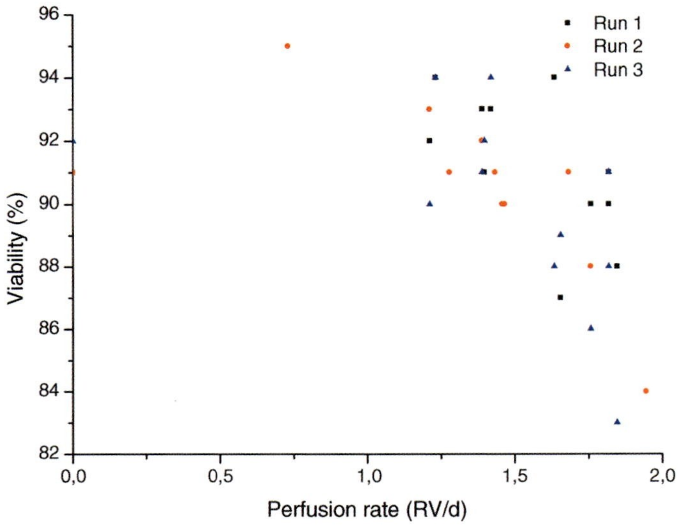

Figure 8.2 Culture viability vs. total dilution rate.

in Equation 8.1, it can be observed that the bleed rate cannot be defined by using an average cell loss for a specific bleed rate.

8.2.2.5 Effect of Total Dilution Rate on Culture Viability

Issues with the cell culture viability were observed for certain perfusion runs. To investigate this issue, data from several runs at varying perfusion rates were compiled to test the effect of different dilution rates on viability. This resulted in Figure 8.2.

It can be observed that total dilution rates should not be increased above 1.5 RV d^{-1}, as this leads to decreases in culture viability.

8.2.2.6 Development of the Perfusion Rate Profile

The perfusion rate was increased through two steps, over two days, to the final perfusion rate. This was done to minimize the possible effects on product yield and quality of abruptly changing the perfusion rate. Also, by increasing the perfusion rate in this way, the cell count at the beginning of the product harvest period (day 6–14) was less variable between different cultivations and through the harvest period. Another effect was that the glucose concentration in the bioreactor did not increase significantly as previously observed (data not shown).

8.2.2.7 Initial Testing of Robustness of Upstream Process in 1.5 l Fermentations

The robustness of the process was examined by running three fermentations using a monoclonal RANKL-producing (mRANKL) cell line. The process was not finalized at this point and certain parameters were still altered during the

Table 8.4 Results from initial robustness tests using the mRANKL cell line.

	Average cel count (E6 cells ml^{-1}) (StDev [%])	Average production perfusion ($mg\ l^{-1}$)	Total RANKL produced (g)	Avg. perfusion rate ($RV\ d^{-1}$)
Run 1	65 (20%)	70	1.2	1.4
Run 2	71 (13%)	54	0.9	1.4
Run 3	89 (20%)	114	1.7	1.2
Average	75	79	1.3	1.3
StDev %	17	39	32	9

cultivation run. These parameters were BioSep run time/stop time settings and the perfusion rate profile. The results from the experiments can be seen in Figure 8.3 and Table 8.4.

The initial test of the process was used to further optimize the upstream standard operating procedure (SOP) as well as to decrease the problems observed with the cell loss through the BioSep. The first two cultivation runs resulted in cell loss through the BioSep, thus the settings of cultivation three were applied for the consistency runs. The second cultivation (Figure 8.3 and Table 8.4) had a different perfusion rate profile, skipping the initial 0.5 RV d^{-1} setting. As seen in the table, this contributed to a lower average titer in the perfusate. The best producing fermentation was the third cultivation, featuring low cell loss through the BioSep and a two-step perfusion rate increase, resulting in the best control.

The levels of variation between the fermentations were found to be acceptable, and it was therefore decided to proceed to the consistency runs for the final test of the process.

8.2.2.8 Scaling Up and Consistency in 4.5 l Fermentations

The process was scaled up from 1.5 to 4.5 l in order to transfer the process to the CMO. The up-scaling formed part of the consistency runs and involved designing the runs to be equivalent to the development runs to be done at the CMO in 5 l fermentations. The only process variable that needed to be changed because of the scale-up was the power setting on the BioSep. The power had to be increased from 5 to 8 W to ensure that the cell loss through the BioSep remained acceptable.

The results from the consistency run can be observed in Figures 8.4 and 8.5.

This level of production would allow 9.5 to 14 g to be produced using the 20 l bioreactor for the 14 day process planned at the CMO from the upstream process.

The upstream process was shown to be consistent within acceptable standard deviations. Consistency runs yielded reproducible cell counts (10% standard deviation), viabilities (>88%), RANKL production (3 g ± 20%), throughout the process. Based on these results, the process was transferred to the CMO.

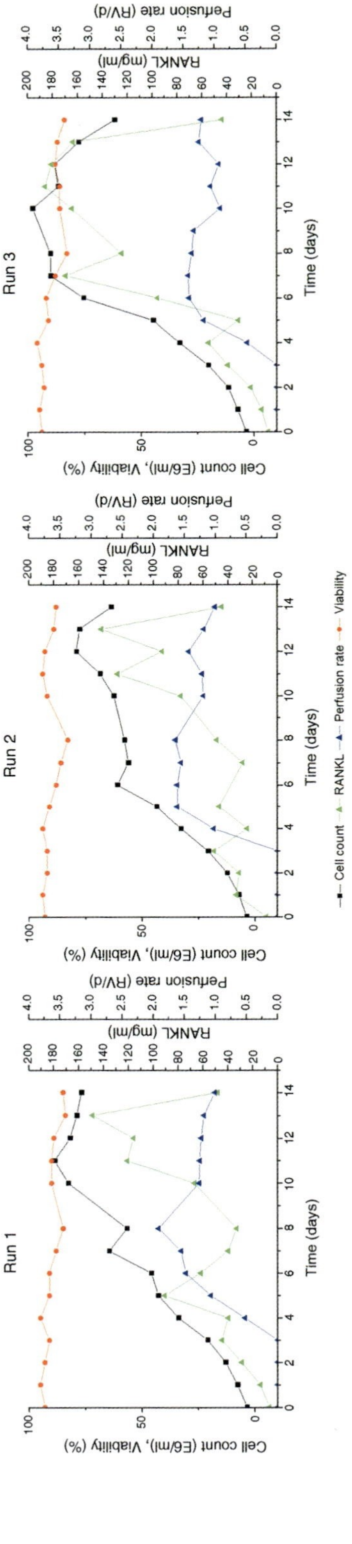

Figure 8.3 Cultivation profiles of cell count, viability, perfusion rate, and RANKL titer during initial robustness tests.

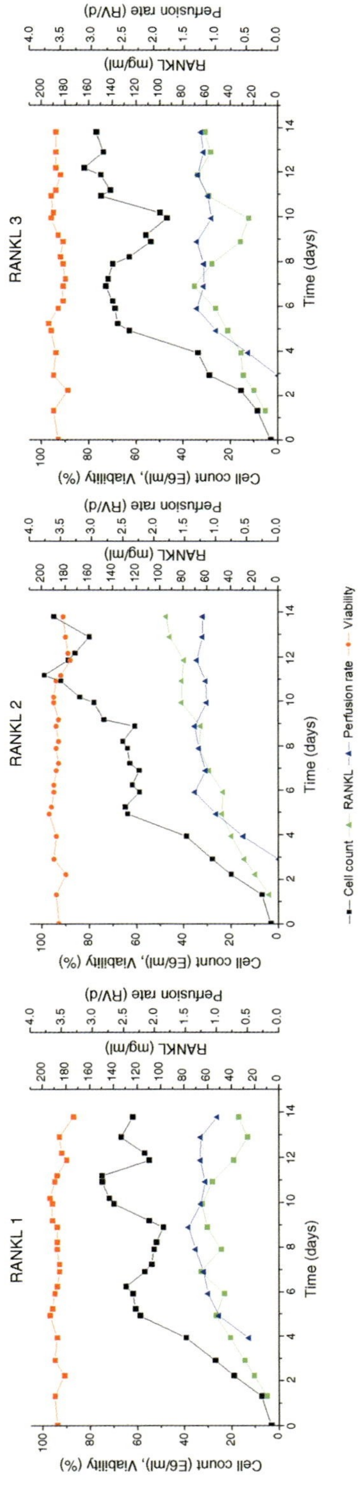

Figure 8.4 Cultivation profiles of cell count, viability, perfusion rate, and RANKL titer during the consistency runs.

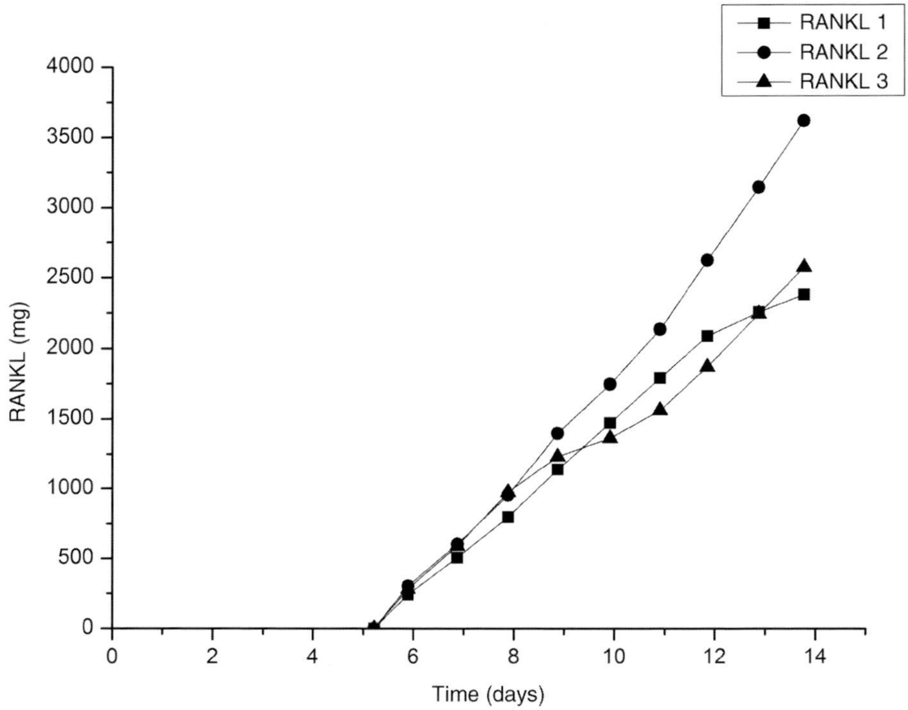

Figure 8.5 Total accumulated RANKL during the consistency runs.

8.2.2.9 **Process Scale-Up**

At the CMO the process was scaled up to 20 l working volume using a 30 l stainless steel reactor, BioSep 50 l per day resonator chamber combined with a BioSep Controller 10–50 l. The results from the process run can be found in Figure 8.6.

During the 14 days, a total of 227 l was harvested. The average titer was measured to 63 mg l^{-1}, yielding a total of 14.3 g RANKL produced in the upstream process. No scaling issues were observed relating to cell growth, viability or production. However, as seen from the scale up to 4.5 l, the BioSep power setting did not scale well. This led to a high degree of cell loss through the BioSep when the power setting was kept at the same level as was used for the 10 l Biosep.

8.2.3 Conclusions for Case Study 1

Throughout the upstream process development, issues with scalability of the BioSep were observed, with uncontrolled cell loss as a result. An overview of cell losses at various scales can be found in Figure 8.7.

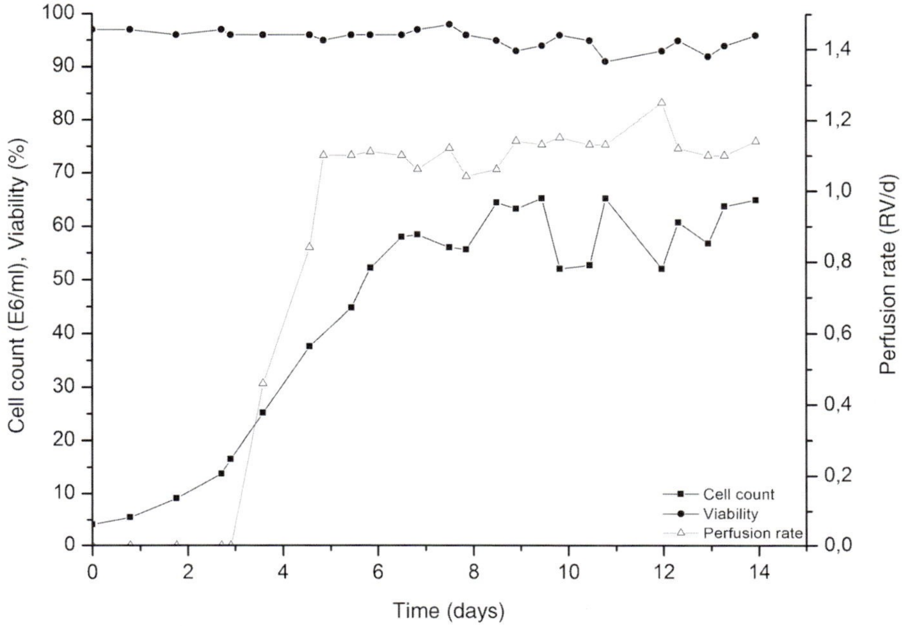

Figure 8.6 Cell count, viabilities and perfusion rate for 20 l perfusion production.

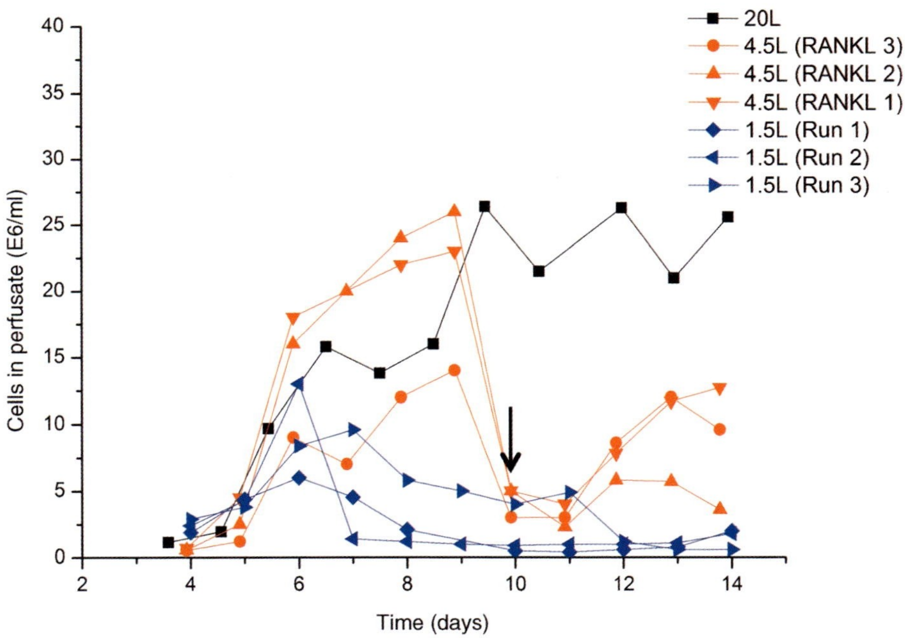

Figure 8.7 Cells in the perfusate over time at 1.5, 4.5, and 20 l working volume. The black arrow indicates a change in the power setting for the 4.5 l bioreactor runs.

The cell loss was however to some degree controlled by optimizing the settings of the BioSep controller. We experienced that increasing the power setting dramatically increased the cell retention. This is demonstrated in Figure 8.7, where a drastic decrease in cell loss was attained by increasing the power setting from 5 to 8 W on day 9 for the three 4.5 l bioreactor runs. Similarly, optimizing the run time/stop time ratio also gave a significant increase in cell retention. It has to be noted that S2 cells, contrary to other insect and mammalian cells, are small (9–10 μm) and grow to very high densities. Based on this, it appears that the BioSep has some challenges in scalability when it is combined with S2 cells. This issue can likely be solved by further increases in the power input settings at larger scales. Nevertheless, a perfusion process was successfully developed and performed in 20 l scale, with a final titer of 14.3 g of RANKL protein.

8.3 Case Study 2: ATF-Based Cell Retention

The field of neglected diseases is particularly relevant for the application of process-intensifying and cost-reducing processing production modes. Specifically, the mostly developing nation location of malaria and the nonprofit funding sources involved requires optimal cost-effective production. Single-use bioreactors combined with perfusion technology provide manufacturing flexibility and cost reductions. The aim in this project was to develop a cost-effective *Drosophila* S2 based production processes combining the constitutive S2 expression system with single-use bioreactor and perfusion technology.

ExpreS^{2}ion has established collaborations with The Jenner Institute, Oxford University, and The Center for Medical Parasitology, Copenhagen University, to develop the protein production processes for the blood-stage malaria vaccine candidate antigen PfRH5 [6], and the placental malaria vaccine antigen VAR2-CSA, respectively. Malaria antigens are particularly difficult to produce, and successful high-level production in the S2 system provides a solution to this urgent need. Furthermore, production of these complex protein vaccine antigens provides an ideal opportunity to apply advanced processing technologies.

8.3.1 ATF Technology

The alternating tangential flow (ATF) is a filter-based perfusion technology developed to prevent filter fouling, an inherent drawback when using filters for cell retention. The ATF setup consists of a hollow fiber module and a back-flush pump (Figure 8.8). Standard cell separation by filtration occurs in a one-directional flow, resulting in fouling, but with ATF this problem is solved by constantly cleaning the fibers with a back-flush motion, every 5–10 s. The technology has some distinct advantages including nearly linear scale-up and cell-free perfusate.

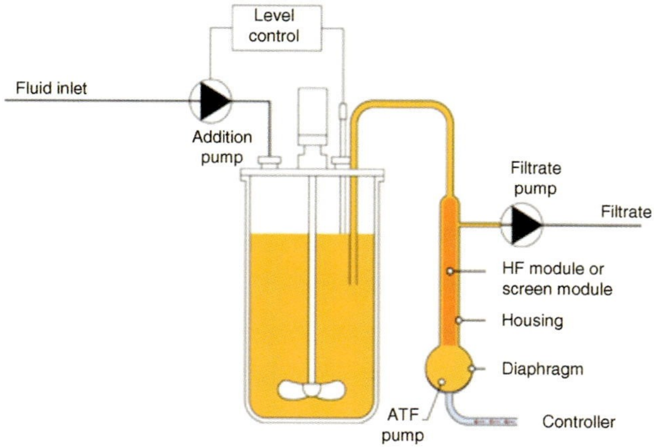

Figure 8.8 The ATF setup. Figure adapted from Ref. [6].

8.3.2 Methods

The growth profiles and product yield for batch, fed-batch, and perfusion production methods were compared. A truncation variant of the **VAR2CSA** placental malaria vaccine antigen and full-length **PfRH5** were cloned into a pExpreS^2 vector. The vectors were transfected into *Drosophila* S2 insect cells and stable cell lines were established using antibiotic selection for 3 weeks. The cells were inoculated at between 5E6 and 8E6 cells ml^{-1} for batch, fed-batch, or perfusion experiments in either 1 l DasGip, 2 l B. Braun or CellReady3 L bioreactors. The production runs were harvested at different time points depending on production mode. The batch process was harvested after 3 days, the fed-batch process on day 7, and the perfusion cultures on either day 6 or 9.

Alternating tangential flow technology from Refine was employed for concentrated perfusion production using a 50 kDa membrane, which results in retention of the proteins in the bioreactor. The bioreactor conditions were performed at 25 °C, pH 6.5, and the stirrer speed was set to 110–150 rpm. The perfusion rates were set to 0.5 to 3 reactor volumes (RV) per day. The perfusion rate was increased significantly faster for the CellReady3 L perfusion, with 3 RV day^{-1} reached by day 6 versus day 9 for the B. Braun runs.

8.3.3 Results

8.3.3.1 Cell Counts Achieved Using Perfusion Technology

S2 cells easily grow to cell densities of 40–50E6 cells ml^{-1} in shake-flask culture and batch mode in bioreactors. A fed-batch approach increased maximum cell density to 60–80E6 cells ml^{-1} and cell counts of up to 104E6 cells ml^{-1} was

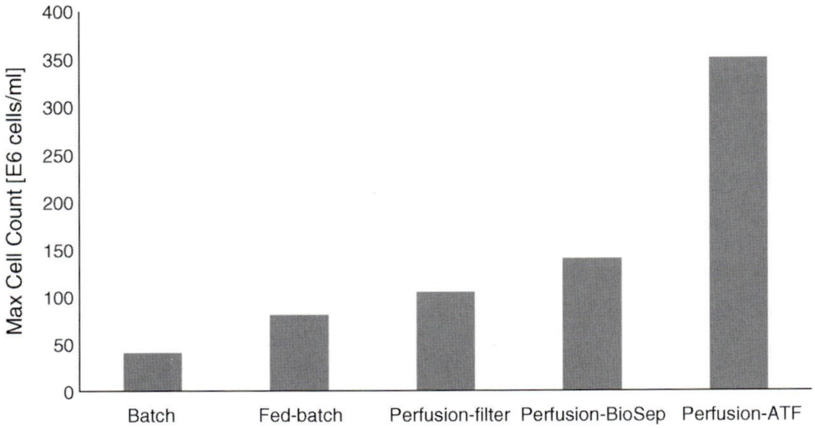

Figure 8.9 The effect of different production modes on maximum cell counts. The Perfusion-BioSep run was performed using the 10 L BioSep (Applikon) in a 2 l B. Bruan bioreactor and the Perfusion-ATF run was performed using the ATF2 (Refine) in a CellReady3 L (Merck-Millipore). The perfusion-filter experiment [5] was performed using the Wave system (GE Healthcare) in a 2 l CellBag using a floating filter with nominal pore size of 7 μm. Figure modified from Ref. [8].

reported in Ref. [7], for a floating filter in a wave bioreactor. ExpreS^{2}ion has achieved 140E6 cells ml^{-1} using the BioSep perfusion technology in 2 and 5 l B. Braun bioreactors. Applying the ATF perfusion technology further increased cell counts to 300–350E6 cells ml^{-1} in both B. Braun 2 l and CellReady3 L bioreactors (Figure 8.9).

8.3.3.2 Effect of Feed Strategy

Feed strategy can have significant effects on specific productivity and growth rate. Figure 8.10a demonstrates the effects on growth and viability of using a

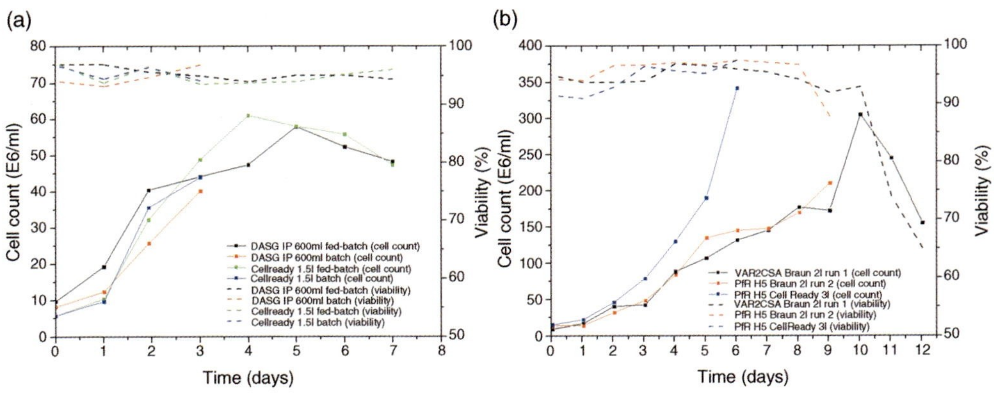

Figure 8.10 (a) Growth curves for batch and fed-batch S2 cultures cultivated in either CellReady3 L or 1 l DasGIP bioreactors. (b) Growth curves for perfusion runs using the ATF2 in 2 l B. Braun or CellReady3 L bioreactors for either a VAR2CSA or PfRH5 producing cell line. (Figure modified from Ref. [8]).

fed-batch strategy of daily single-shot feed additions. The effect of perfusion feed profile was tested by increasing the feed rate to the maximum achievable feed rate of 3 RV day^{-1} in 6 or 9 days. It can be seen in Figure 8.10b that the CellReady 3 L run had a significantly higher growth rate compared to the two B. Braun runs. The reason for this was that the feed rate was increased gradually over 9 days for the B. Braun runs, while the feed rate for the CellReady 3 L run was increased to the same level in only 6 days. Furthermore, the feed rate was increased in such a way that the culture was never nutrient limited, remarkably leading to an exponential growth curve to a cell count of 350E6 cells ml^{-1}. The production run was stopped when the maximum flow rate of the ATF was reached. However, it is clear that the specific productivity of the S2 cells under exponential growth conditions was significantly lower when compared to the linear growth conditions. Similar yields were achieved by day 6 in both bioreactors, even though the cell counts were up to threefold higher in the exponential growth experiment (Figure 8.10b).

Similarly, a linear growth profile was maintained for the VAR2CSA concentrated perfusion run. The growth rate was then increased from 2RV to 3RV per day in one step on day 9. This led to a very large increase in cell count, but as the perfusion rate could not be further increased the viability started to decrease. Both cell count and viability drastically decreased when the culture became nutrient limited. This demonstrates the importance of maintaining a minimum perfusion rate to achieve high viability. ExpreS^{2}ion estimates the needed perfusion rate using the standard approach of attempting to maintain a constant flow rate per cell per day throughout the run.

8.3.3.3 Yield Improvements Achieved Using Fed-Batch and Concentrated Perfusion

The VAR2CSA truncation variant was expressed in batch and fed-batch culture in 1 l DasGip Bioreactors. Yield increases of higher than 30% were achieved when using fed-batch versus batch production. Furthermore, concentrated perfusion led to cell counts of more than 300E6 cells ml^{-1}. Unfortunately, no quantitative analysis technique was available to determine the actual yields. However, by Western dot blot analysis, significant yield increases were observed compared to fed-batch culture.

The production of the blood-stage malaria antigen (PfRH5) was also compared in batch, fed-batch, and concentrated perfusion using both CellReady3 L and glass bioreactors. Through the use of fed-batch the yield was increased by 300% compared to batch culture. Comparable yields of 210 mg l^{-1} were obtained in both CellReady3 L and B. Braun bioreactors at day 6 of cultivation. Furthermore, *350E6 cells* ml^{-1} were achieved in concentrated perfusion mode using the ATF and CellReady3 L. The final PfRH5 yield using concentrated perfusion was *500 mg* l^{-1} after 9 days of production (Figure 8.11).

8.3.3.4 Protein Stability

Strikingly, product degradation was observed when the cell count and culture viability decreased during the last two days of the Var2CSA perfusion

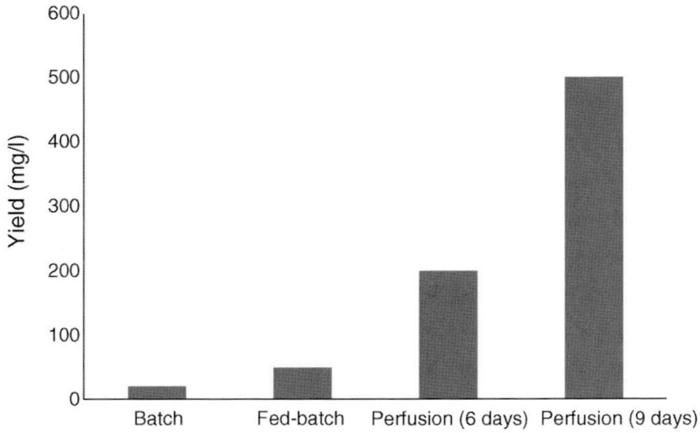

Figure 8.11 PfRH5 yield from batch, fed-batch, and concentrated perfusion cultures [8].

culture. However, it is assumed that since product degradation was not observed during production before this point, degradation could be avoided by maintaining high cell viability. A similar issue was encountered for the PfRH5 concentrated perfusion runs. Analysis of purified protein from day 6 or 10 harvests showed significant cleavage corresponding to a natural cleavage product of PfRH5. This cleavage product was not present during batch culture, but was also observed to a limited extent in fed-batch culture. In this latter case product cleavage was less extensive compared to VAR2CSA. However, cleavage was present independent of culture viability and appeared to correlate more with culture duration.

8.3.4
Conclusions for Case Study 2

The key weakness of concentrated perfusion is the potential for protein cleavage or degradation caused by the extended protein residence time in the bioreactor. This was demonstrated in case study 2 for PfRH5 and to a lesser extent VAR2CSA. However, performing standard perfusion using the ATF offers a simple solution through reduction of product residence time to less than a day. Each protein should therefore be evaluated for stability before embarking on developing a concentrated perfusion process. For instance, the VAR2CSA truncation variant could be successfully produced using concentrated perfusion on the condition of high cell viability. Significant yield increases through increased cell counts, and consequent production-scale reductions are possible for both concentrated perfusion and standard perfusion. These two perfusion options therefore offer attractive process intensification approaches for both degradation-sensitive, as well as inherently stable, proteins.

8.4 Final Remarks

Perfusion technology offers unique advantages for the production of cost-sensitive vaccine antigens. The technologies and case studies discussed in this chapter gives a practical overview of the advantage and potential pitfalls in using perfusion in combination with the *Drosophila* S2 expression system. It was also demonstrated that these technologies could be successfully employed using single use bioreactors such as the CellReady3 L from Merck-Millipore and the Wave system from GE Healthcare. Combining these three technologies enables production of challenging proteins at high yields, using small footprint production facilities, with the flexibility and cost advantages inherent in single-use technologies.

Acknowledgments

The authors thank M. dos Santos Marques Resende, B. Berisha, and M. Nielsen from the Centre for Medical Parasitology, Faculty of Health, Copenhagen University, Denmark; C. Leisted, A. Strøbæk, and C. Dyring from ExpreS2ion Biotechnologies ApS, Agern Allé 1, Hørsholm, DK-2970, Denmark (wdj@expres2ionbio.com); K. A. Hjerrild, A. D. Douglas, and S. J. Draper from The Jenner Institute, University of Oxford, United Kingdom; and K. E. Wright and M. K. Higgins from the Department of Biochemistry, University of Oxford, United Kingdom.

References

1 de Jongh, W.A., Salgueiro, S., and Dyring, C. (2013) The use of *Drosophila* S2 cells in R&D and bioprocessing. *Pharm. Bioprocess.*, **1**, 197–213. doi: 10.4155/pbp.13.18

2 Kadouri, A. and Spier, R.E. (1997) Some myths and messages concerning the batch and continuous culture of animal cells. *Cytotechnology*, **24**, 89–98. doi: 10.1023/A:1007932614011

3 Voisard, D., Meuwly, F., Ruffieux, P.-A., Baer, G., and Kadouri, A. (2003) Potential of cell retention techniques for large-scale high-density perfusion culture of suspended mammalian cells. *Biotechnol. Bioeng.*, **82**, 751–765. doi: 10.1002/bit.10629

4 Dalm, M.C.F., Jansen, M., Keijzer, T.M.P., van Grunsven, W.M.J., Oudshoorn, A. *et al.* (2005) Stable hybridoma cultivation in a pilot-scale acoustic perfusion system: long-term process performance and effect of recirculation rate. *Biotechnol. Bioeng.*, **91**, 894–900. doi: 10.1002/bit.20552

5 Trampler, F., Sonderhoff, S.A., Pui, P.W., Kilburn, D.G., and Piret, J.M. (1994) Acoustic cell filter for high density perfusion culture of hybridoma cells. *Biotechnology*, **12**, 281–284.

6 Douglas, A.D., Williams, A.R., Illingworth, J.J., Kamuyu, G., Biswas, S. *et al.* (2011) The blood-stage malaria antigen PfRH5 is susceptible to vaccine-inducible cross-strain neutralizing antibody. *Nat. Commun.*, **2**, 601. doi: 10.1038/ncomms1615

7 Wang, L., Hu, H., Yang, J., Wang, F., Kaisermayer, C. *et al.* (2012) High yield of

human monoclonal antibody produced by stably transfected *Drosophila* Schneider 2 cells in perfusion culture using wave bioreactor. *Mol. Biotechnol.*, **52**, 170–179. doi: 10.1007/s12033-011-9484-5

8 de Jongh, W.A. (2012) Process intensification approaches for cost sensitive protein application. *Continuous Bioprocessing: Current Practice and Future Potential*, Refine Technology, pp. 47–53.

9 Single-Use Systems Support Continuous Bioprocessing by Perfusion Culture

William G. Whitford

9.1 Introduction

Many improvements have been made in biopharmaceutical manufacturing since its inception in the 1980s. They have involved each individual operation, and include such diverse advances as improved cloning and selection methods, removal of animal-derived materials, implementation of single-use systems, and improved purification resins and columns. Currently, the most common approach to upstream large-scale biopharmaceutical manufacturing is the fed-batch mode applied to suspension culture. This is not to say that other approaches have not been tried, even with great success. For example some have very successfully employed perfusion culture in upstream processes of approved biopharmaceutical manufacturing. Nevertheless, despite numerous performance and safety improvements, the overall paradigm of a severely discrete batch process has not evolved a great deal.

While the batch process is still by far the most popular, recent studies signal that this may be changing. Such sponsors as Genzyme and Amgen have very publicly announced their intent to pursuing radical new technologies to improve and streamline processes. Others are more quietly pursuing similar goals. This kind of major change to biopharmaceutical production is critical if sponsors are expected to maintain reasonable drug costs and continue to improve upon current productivity levels.

Continuous processing (CP) is a manufacturing approach in which raw materials constantly flow in and out of equipment as they are continually processed into an intermediate or final product. In CP, production occurs at a single location, without interruption. It proceeds in that way for variable lengths of time – from days to months to years – and is only interrupted for such reasons as cleaning of equipment or the incremental deterioration of enzymes, catalysts, or cultures. This is in contrast to the discontinuous “batch” production, where a specific quantity of product is manufactured in a single, discrete volume during the same cycle of manufacture. The batch production mode is frequently segmented into many individual steps that are often

Continuous Processing in Pharmaceutical Manufacturing, First Edition. Edited by Ganapathy Subramanian.

performed at separate facilities (suites, buildings, or cities). In continuous processing, on the other hand, production occurs at a single location, without interruption. In CP, manufacturing is often conducted with more automation and fewer human operators and is now used in many types of processes in many industries. It is really quite fascinating to see; for example, dough constantly assembled in the front of the plant, biscuits baked in a long linear oven, cooled on a conveyer belt, and finally boxed and shipped out the back without pause or interruption. In pharmaceutical manufacturing, this process generally incorporates a chemical reactor or bioreactor. Although many (semi)continuous processes for either suspended or adherent animal cells are known to be used in biopharmaceutical production, details on their design and operation are not always publicly available. It should be considered that terminology in this dynamic field can sometimes get fuzzy – for example, continuous processing is also referred to as continuous production, continuous flow processing, or continuous manufacturing. Furthermore, minor (to nonspecialists) distinctions are often made between different implementations and styles. In fact, few processes are absolutely and exquisitely "continuous" in a strict sense. Consider that most materials arrive in packages by truck or railroad car, and that most processes employ tanks or hoppers that must be filled. Depending on the periodicity of entire production episodes, or the specific nature of more discrete individual component operations, some apply such terms as semi- and pseudocontinuous or even microbatch operation. Nevertheless, the characteristics and values described here do apply to many such incompletely continuous processes.

Interest in the use of CP techniques in large-scale biomanufacturing has increased dramatically in the past few years, to the extent that many are now predicting its eventual dominance in the industry [1,2]. This is due to the many specific benefits either continuous manufacturing, or operations contributing to it, provide (Table 9.1). An accurate picture of the status of CP in biopharmaceutical manufacturing is difficult to develop for a few reasons:

- Many upstream CP process, such as perfusion culture, have actually been in use for decades.
- New and disparate CP-enabling technologies appearing are in various stages of acceptance.
- While interest is currently high, much incorporation accomplished is still held confidentially.

It has been over 10 years since the US Food and Drug Administration (FDA) articulated – in its guidance for process analytical technology (PAT) – the goal of "facilitating continuous processing to improve efficiency and manage variability" [3]. Since that time, regulators and industry have worked toward applying CP to all facets of pharmaceutical manufacturing, including bioproduction [4,5]. Janet Woodcock (FDA's CDER director) has expressly predicted the obsolescence of batch processing in favor of a CP approach to pharmaceutical

Table 9.1 Values in continuous processing for pharmaceutical manufacturing.

Feature or attribute	Example or benefit
Supported by regulators/agencies	FDA and EMA publications generally silent on manufacturing mode and lot definition Expressly advocated by leaders and in some guidance Janet Woodcock (FDA CDER) predicts obsolesce of batch Allowed by EMA validation guideline and FDA PAT guidance
PAT and QbD friendly	Promotes both enabling tools and goals Supports online, in-line monitoring, real-time QA and heightened process understanding Amenable to CQV, CPV and RTR initiatives
A well-established technology	From cracking oil to cooking Oreos
Limitations and negative perceptions alleviated by	Heightened process understanding and control techniques Better in-process monitoring and feedback control Incorporating improved mixing and product flow systems New and enabling biopharma technologies, for example, SUT
Faster and more robust PD	PD at the scale of manufacturing Simplifies scale-up/tech transfer Clinical material in same equipment as final product
Heightens processing parameter consistency	Greatly simplifies process flow and control strategy Operating parameters fixed around one (optimized) point Materials, intermediates and product in consistent conditions/steady states No gradients of decreasing materials/increasing waste over time Eliminates microheterogeneities from late stage batch reactions/culture Heightens product quality and homogeneity Reduces out-of-specification product
Less failure from stressed mulitplex PID control in complex design space	Reduces product loss and reprocessing
Increases process efficiency/capability	Reduceds process variability Increases production rate control Shortens process stream/processing times Supports integrated processing w/fewer steps Inherently supports closed processing Reduces set-up and downtime
Accepts materials/activities/chemistries unavailable in batch	Product or material residence time–sensitive conditions can be entertained Non-nominal condition sensitivities are avoided

(continued)

Table 9.1 (*Continued*)

Feature or attribute	Example or benefit
Operates at higher molecular efficiency	Can reduce material consumption Produces more concentrated raw product
Lowers process/reaction volume and times	Reduces reactor residency times Reduces process container sizes Batch/lot determined by, mass, volume, throughput, time–stamp Can promote increased safety
Provides more process flexibility	Ease of product change over Modular/portable/transferable equipment Variable range of throughputs for capacity control and production balancing in, for example, market response Provides interchangeability for different plug and play units ops and multiproduct facilities Supports hybrid designs: For example, classical and single-use systems; semicontinuous or microbatch.
Reduces equipment footprint and facility extent	Increases volumetric productivity Lot determined by run time and not containment size Greatly simplifies production train Unit operations can be contiguous
Reduces operator intervention	Process tuned to run at unchanging process inputs Integrated process with fewer steps Amenable to process automation Easy to clean, inspect and maintain Reduces handling of intermediates
Increases overall facility utilization efficiency	Supports a "platform" approach: 1 process supporting >1 product Reduces development/transfer steps and equipment Ameliorates future facility expansion requirements Many existing small-molecule CP operations apply to biopharm Supports demands by biosimilars, globalization and drug shortages
Increases profitability	Reduces CPA and COG Reduces capitol expense Always operating at peak efficiency Simplifies process/reduces wasteage and loss Reduces operator activity and personnel need Reduced material usage in development Heightens raw materials utilization efficiency Reduces intermediate and final product inventory
Supports many sustainability/green initiatives	Reduces equipment to be cleaned/steamed Reduces service and energy consumption Reduces processing footprint and operator requirements

Table 9.2 Upstream single-use technology features and functions.

Features provided by SU	Upstream operations supported by SU
Reduced contamination risks	Cell culture for seed expansion and production
Lower initial investment costs	Media, buffer and process liquid preparation
Lower facility and operating cost	Liquid pumping, filtration, collection, shipping
Reduced operator requirement	On-line contents monitoring sensors/samplers
Process efficiency and flexibility	Transport/storage of intermediate and product
Time to market and ease of use	Cryopreservation of seeds and intermediates

manufacturing. Along with increased monitoring, automated process control, and new statistical approaches, CP is one of the main goals of quality by design (QbD). As such, it is supported by the FDAs initiatives for flexible regulatory approaches and science-derived quality and control specifications. The European Medicines Agency (EMA) referred to CP in its draft *Guideline on Process Validation*, and the FDA released a strategic plan, *Advancing Regulatory Science*, which includes an advocacy of CP [6,7]. In 2012, Genzyme (a subsidiary of Sanofi), reported on their interest in the development of an integrated continuous bioprocessing approach as a potential universal platform exploiting the values of single-use technology (Table 9.2) for manufacturing protein biologicals [8]. Amgen and GlaxoSmithKline have similarly announced significant commitments to CP in an effort to improve efficiency and reduce costs [9,10].

9.2 Potential Advantages in Continuous Processing

9.2.1 Improved Product Quality

Improved product quality is a major argument for considering continuous processing. One factor is that, unlike in many batch procedures, CP reactions are not "warmed-up," materials (or primary metabolites) are not exhausted, and bolus reactions (or cultures) are not run to the point of inefficiency. In bioproduction, such consistencies as media nutrient level maintenance allow the cells to be kept in one or more "steady states." Cultures do not experience such stresses as lags at seedlings, or drop-off at the end of culture where cell viability is greatly reduced while inefficient and uncharacterized reactions occur. The lack of gradients in materials and conditions (as they exist in early and late-stage batch cultures) reduces intra-lot entity heterogeneities in the product population. This heightens quality and reduces out-of-specification product. Furthermore, lot-to-lot heterogeneities are reduced when this same operational consistency extends throughout and across production campaigns. Processing delays are greatly reduced in a continuous processing system as product is moved in a constant flow from one step to the next. In batch processing, product intermediates are often stored or kept on hold as they are examined and moved through the many steps of the process. These delays, transfers, and exposures can lead to product degradation, increase risks of contamination, and present other product safety concerns. In continuous processing, intermediates are kept in a more consistent condition for a much shorter period of time. This adds the feature of improved product quality to such other CP benefits as productivity and process flexibility.

9.2.2 Ease in Process Development

In manufacturing process development (PD), CP has contributed to a faster, cheaper, and more robust approach to many processes than such traditional discontinuous modes as batch could provide. CP places less demand on material use in PD because of its reduced reaction volumes and process modeling as well as its time-controlled materials mass consumption. The scale of operation can remain constant from PD to manufacturing, therefore, many issues in technology transfer are prevented and scale-up concerns reduced or even eliminated. For example, a CP reactor can operate very economically for a few hours for PD, and that same unit can later provide "large-scale" production by simply operating for weeks to months on the manufacturing floor. This feature also has implications for the production of clinical trial material in that it too can be manufactured in the exact same equipment that will be employed for final product. CP PD is supported by technological developments in mixing/mass-flow systems, and CP-based processes can often accept activities or chemistries unavailable in the more episodic batch-style manufacturing. Finally, some previously unavailable reactor residency time-sensitive processes may even be entertained. Consider a product that breaks down at conditions of formation. A CP approach may get that product out of the reactor before it is compromised. In some circumstances, such advantages can even contribute to increased operator safety.

Continuous processing actually supports a significantly simplified control strategy. It presents a more integrated processing opportunity with fewer steps, and thus can provide reduced process variability with (ultimately) increased comprehensive system control. It heightens process parameter consistency in a few ways, primarily in that operating conditions remain set around single optimized points throughout a manufacturing lot. In CP, materials and intermediates exist in consistent conditions and that provides a number of benefits, including reducing the control activities to maintain steady states.

9.2.3 Improved Scalability

Continuous processing provides for easier scalability and allows for more immediate control and balancing of production capacity following changing demand requirements. As production rate is determined primarily by time and not volume, production increases can be accomplished simply by implementing longer campaigns. For even greater demand, due to the smaller footprint, "scaling out" or "numbering-up" by adding additional continuous processing units can be easily accomplished. It is of note that scalability is a key health issue as drug shortages have become a higher concern with the FDA. Also, such recent business imperatives as risk mitigation through increasing manufacturing depth and redundancy in facilities make this feature even more potent and practical. The time versus reactor volume operator in CP product mass generation has implications in the agility and flexibility of production it can supply in response to market forces.

9.2.4
Increased Profitability

There are two major components driving increased profitability through continuous processing. Profits can be increased through (1) more efficient and economical facility design/utilization and (2) a reduction in the cost of goods. One of the primary advantages to utilizing CP in biopharmaceutical manufacturing is the improvement in manufacturing facility utilization. Continuous processing employs equipment that has a smaller footprint than required in fed-batch processing, and typically requires less energy. The smaller footprint allows for a reduction in the size of manufacturing facilities and allows for a number of added features, such as a system that is more "portable." This, in turn, provides for reduced initial capital investment and easy capacity expansion capability. CP supports this without maintaining a large (and potentially highly controlled) manufacturing facility, or having to consider either incremental build-out or outsourcing. Also, by reducing non–value-added steps such as intermediate and final-product inventory, CP reduces the facility requirement for their storage. This is all because, by definition, an integrated continuous process dramatically reduces or eliminates the need for WIP and production quarantines.

Cost of goods is reduced by CPs shorter processing times, as well as a simplified process stream with fewer opportunities for product loss or reprocessing, contributing to better material utilization. The (bio)reactor volumetric productivity and increased process efficiency results in reduced cost per action (CPA) through such factors as higher product yields per square foot. A number of efficiencies and economies (including some appreciated downstream) result from CP often operating at a significantly higher molecular efficiency and (in some manufacturing cases) providing more concentrated bulk intermediate product. This determines that should there be a need for product intermediate containment, smaller containers and storage suites are required.

Continuous processing's increased process efficiency and capability results in reduction in both contamination risk and process cycle times, each influencing manufacturing expense. Other cost savings occur through an increase in automation as well as reductions in service requirement and operator labor demand.

Heightened process automation is supported by, for example, its potential for being tuned to run at unchanging process inputs. One way it lessens the need for operator intervention (and therefore support personnel) is its generally simplified process and optimization of the process flow.

9.2.5 Sustainability

Corporate social responsibility (CSR) has been gaining traction as a very real and desirable endeavor by pharmaceutical sponsors. Within the manufacturing arena, the discipline has taken on a much more sincere and significant priority of late. The related field of social accounting refers specifically to the communication of the social and environmental effects of a company's activities. So, regardless of a sponsor's effort to change the nature of either their product or manufacturing processes to accommodate sustainability demands, it is becoming a specific goal to adhere to a growing set of guidelines for social accounting and reporting.

In this consideration, it is of note that for many processes and implementations CP inherently provides a smaller ecological footprint than platforms based upon batch processes. For example, without any specific engineering or optimization toward sustainability-specific goals, many of the increased efficiencies mentioned earlier translate into reduced energy and service demands – resulting in reduced ecological pressure. Its extended intracleaning operation process duration results in a reduction of fresh water and fuel consumption, as well as foul water and carbon emission. The reduced operator demand contributes to such sometimes hidden ecological sustainability values as reduced hydrocarbon fuel consumption due to personnel commuting. While individual manufacturing steps or general implementations can always be improved, there appear to be no CP-specific principles that inherently contribute to a greater ecological footprint.

9.3 Challenges in Adoption of Continuous Processing

In fact, the general values of CP have been so accepted that the focus on implementation in biomanufacturing is now on particular (mostly biopharma-specific) perceived limitations. Justified or not, quite a few concerns have been expressed regarding the implementation of continuous biomanufacturing (CB). They fall into the areas of

- Performance reliability (incidence of failure)
- Economic justifications and investment risks
- Implementing: control and validation needs regulatory body dispositions/filing concerns.

For many processes, such previous limitations – or their perception – are being alleviated by either advances in CB technologies or by OpEx-driven advances in bioprocess understanding and control in general. Examples of the latter include advances in cellular systems biology, bioreactor monitoring technologies, and advanced feedback control.

Specifically in bioproduction, some readily acknowledge the technical feasibility of continuous approaches, but express business-based concern for potentially limited bottom-line financial savings (ROI/NPV). They cite such factors as model-based revelation of the relatively small contribution of active biopharmaceutical ingredient manufacturing costs to total costs. Also, they point out that this is aggravated by the significant existing batch process capacity and capability in biopharma. To this it is argued that in such considerations biopharmaceuticals are a different animal in general and many of the mechanistic and other models or formulae that apply to food or small-molecule pharma must be significantly modified to be of any value here. And, as recent manufacturing and regulatory trends alter the picture even further, the financial benefits of CB should become even stronger. These trends include

- Biosimilars and biobetters
- Manufacturing globalization
- Nationalized supply demands
- Personalized product response
- Drug shortage/supply protection.

Some still have concerns regarding the response by regulators (despite some even expressing support of the initiative), or how CP systems interface with such ongoing initiatives as the *Design Space* concept. Others raise such CP-specific process management concerns as

- Effects upon batch definition and control
- Elimination of nonfinished intermediates
- Change control, deviations, OOS, failures
- CAPA (corrective action/preventive action)
- FMEA (failure mode and effects analysis)
- Other critical compliance-based processes.

In reply, it is pointed out that there has been regulated biomanufacturing employing perfusion culture for decades and the development of a CP approach is now actively supported by regulators. Furthermore, existing FDA and EMA regulations and guidance are generally neutral (silent) on existing modes of manufacturing – and (at least) accommodating in the means of lot definition. It is of note that 21 CFR 210.3 expressly acknowledges CP in pharmaceutical manufacturing in its definition of a lot:

> "Lot means a batch, or a specific identified portion of a batch, having uniform character and quality within specified limits; or, in the case of a drug product produced by continuous process, it is a specific identified amount produced in a unit of time or quantity in a manner that assures its having uniform character and quality within specified limits."

Also, 21 CFR 211.150(b) speaks of "*a system by which the distribution of each lot of drug product can be readily determined*" (author's emphasis). All in all, it appears that any legitimate concern for hurdles in implementing CP in biomanufacturing might be properly designated as a lack of experience and filing precedent, as opposed to a true conflict in technology or regulation.

While some CB attributes inherently provide immediate advantages (such as reduced reactor residency time) others do present challenges (such as cell-line stability concerns). The latter issue is that no matter how a perfusion reactor is maintained, if cells are dividing the number of generations from original cloning or validation is increasing. This introduces at least two distinct issues: (1) many cell lines deteriorate in some way(s) after some tens of generations from production, and (2) even if productivity or product quality is unaffected by generation number, this fact would have to be validated for the duration of continuous production. One development mitigating this concern is the fact that newer cloning methods and vectors are supporting producer strains of higher molecular characterization and more stable rDNA integration.

Some industry experts have wondered how it is that CB can reduce required reactor volume or footprint. After all, the peak-specific productivity of a cell is not necessarily changed. In CP culture, lag phases are eliminated because a culture is always operating at its peak efficiency. Moreover, the constant flow of fresh media supports productive operation at cell densities of 3–10× the density normally observed in more episodic approaches, such as fed-batch. Combined with other operational efficiencies just mentioned, the increased volumetric productivity of "concentrated" or "enhanced" perfusion culture can significantly reduce footprint and increase overall reactor-specific volumetric efficiency up to 100-fold.

Beyond narrow technical challenges, an objective and thorough analysis of the value of any manufacturing platform requires a number of physical, operational, quality, temporal, economic, and even environmental parameters to be considered. The best approaches to fit and benefit analysis now include a comprehensive overall ranking strategy considering the most current technologies employing a multi-attribute risk-based approach. New strategies are also needed in regulatory applications, knowledge management, and compliance software supporting regulatory and quality operations. While some biomanufacturing unit operations can be very readily converted to CP, for others the means of some required parameter monitoring is not yet adequate.

Also, there are processes relying upon non-CP amenable steps, such as significant "rest periods" for intermediates between operations. Although often in such cases a means of accelerating the effect of storage (such as the process of cooling) can be readily prescribed. The number of measurement points and sufficient understanding of true critical process parameters (CPPs) for many new bioproduction CP processes are yet to be determined, and this is notable because transition from existing batch to CP does require both clear product CQA and CPP understanding. Example concerns here include material blending uniformity, real-time sampling accuracy, and the quality or efficiency implications of process intermediate values.

Raw materials concerns in CP range from changes in the basic control of incoming supply, to a requirement to provide either higher materials properties consistency or increased process robustness in order to accommodate known materials variability. CP usually also demands very accurate and precise materials feeding or dispensing technologies to be specified, or even developed. However, new developments, such as automated dispensing apparatus, prequalified raw materials, and PAT-controlled staging are certainly of value here. Well-founded or not, process-related concerns include those regarding

- Start-up and shut down material loses and costs
- The means of achieving the required robust process throughput balancing
- Fears that equipment cleaning may be more difficult or complicated then in batch
- Potential requirements for fully or semiautomated intra- or postproduction quarantine
- The fact that when any unit-op in CP is down for any reason, the whole process can be down.

Finally, distinct concerns exist in developing highly vertically integrated CP processing trains. These are processes in which many continuous operations are concatenated into nearly completely contiguous manufacturing workflows. One issue is the physical control of the interfaces between unit operations, such as the incorporation of appropriate material flow connectors and surge or break protection. Another is the need to characterize the propagation and implications of changes and disturbances through the entire system. Finally, we should consider the required supervisory control systems required. Here, new and more comprehensive adaptive/closed loop (hierarchical or otherwise networked) enterprise control systems must not only be instituted, but in many cases developed. This is being actively addressed by not only advances in control algorithms and information management systems, but by a number of hardware advances. For example, there are continued developments in SCADA-based higher-level distributed process control supported by fieldbus two-way network systems supporting integrated device-side control.

9.4 Continuous Biomanufacturing

Many modern bioproduction approaches currently employ continuous processing amenable underlying processes and technologies. CB is supported by pharmaceutical regulatory agencies and provides many specific benefits in bioprocessing. A growing number of biopharmaceutical manufacturers currently employ continuous processes in unit operations and recent developments promise to stimulate even more interest in them.

Quite a number of culture mode options that can support a continuous or semicontinuous manufacturing approach have existed for decades. Recently, a number of manufacturing-scale perfusion or perfusion-capable bioreactors have been launched (Table 9.3), and this includes the currently popular stirred tank single-use bioreactor (SUB). Successful implementations have now been achieved in a number of good manufacturing practice (GMP) installations of premiere biopharmaceutical sponsors, including for approved product. For example, Genzyme's continued commitment to perfusion-based production is demonstrated by their expansion of such perfusion cell culture capacity at their Geel, Belgium plant involving 4000 l perfusion bioreactors, with dedicated seed and purification trains.

It is important to consider that even the best models examining the relative efficiencies and values of CB to batch employ the currently observed operational parameters and outputs of each. As many continuous biomanufacturing procedures and installations are either in their infancy, or yet-to-be-implemented, this can be regarded as supplying worst case values for unoptimized CB processes.

There are ongoing EU GMP Guideline/ICH Q3C (R4) issues concerning new toxicological models and more science-based dispositions toward contamination, cross-contamination, and multiproduct manufacturing. This has often been invoked in regard to closed manufacturing, but also has implications in continuous biomanufacturing. Its resolution should clarify synergies and paths forward in creative processing modes, process flow, as well as facility design and classification. It is apparent that many of the concerns mentioned have already been addressed at length, even in the public forum, and have been in many cases resolved. Furthermore, many of the features of CP can actually reduce failure risk, or assist in its mitigation (see Section 9.2.3).

In summary, other than the usual hesitation regarding anything new, there really are a few real financial, engineering, or regulatory concerns to preclude the serious consideration of CB in pharmaceutical manufacturing. Industry leaders see the design of closed, disposable, integrated, and continuous biomanufacturing systems for biopharma on the near horizon.

Table 9.3 Single-use and hybrid perfusion-type culture enabling products.

SU perfusion support	Commercial examples	SU/Hybrid PC application
Stirred tank	Xcellerex XDR Single-Use Bioreactor System (GE Healthcare) and PBS Air-Wheel® (PBS Biotech)	SU PC when combined with perfusion-enabling technology. Suspension and adherent (e.g., microcarrier) culture.
Roller bottle	Nunc™ TufRol™ Roller Bottles (Thermo Scientific) in RollerCell 40 (CELLON S.A)	SU PC closed media exchange with some CPP control. Adherent culture.
Stacked array flask	RepliCell (Aastrom) and Xpansion (Artelis)	SU PC closed media exchange with some CPP control. Adherent culture.
Wave-action based	BIOSTAT® RM (Sartorius Stedim) and WAVE (GE Healthcare)	SU PC with perfusion-enabling technology. Suspension and/or adherent (e.g., microcarrier)
Hollow Fiber	LSBR (FiberCell Systems)	SU fully controlled PC. Suspension/adherent
Moving packed-bed	BioCell MB & MBS (Bioreactor Sciences)	SU fully controlled PC. Suspension/adherent
Fixed packed-bed	iCELLis™(ATMI) and Celligen FibraCel (NBS)	SU or hybrid fully controlled PC. Adherent and/or some suspension culture.
Perfusion enabling tech	**Commercial examples**	**Perfusion application**
Hollow fiber media exchange	ATF System (Refine Technology) and KrosFlo® (Spectrum)	Hybrid or full SU PC when combined with certain bioreactors. Suspension or adherent (e.g., microcarrier) culture.
Centrifugal media exchange	Centritech (Carr) and kSep® (KBI Biopharma)	SU PC as combined with certain bioreactors. Suspension or adherent (e.g., microcarrier)
Sonic wave media exchange	CYTOPERF (APIcells), BioSep (Applikon) and (FloDesign Sonics)	SU or hybrid PC when combined with certain bioreactors. Suspension culture.
Hydrocyclone media exchange	Hydrocyclone (Sartorius)	SU PC. Suspension or adherent.
Spin filter media exchange	Spin filter P(Sartorius)	SU PC. Suspension or adherent.

9.5
Single-Use Systems

The biopharmaceutical industry now incorporates significant levels of single-use (SU) technology and systems in the majority of cell-culture based production processes [11,12]. This is due to the remarkable benefits the technology affords to the majority of popular production platforms and particular implementations (Table 9.4) [13,14]. The most important reasons for their extensive adoption include faster

Table 9.4 Developments in single-use technologies (SUT).

Demand	Current status
Cost and financial advantages	Rigorous modeling and published studies delineate the significant savings single-use technologies provide in many implementations.
Unit operations support	Single-use technologies exist for most ops in bioproduction. Many have seen industry acceptance or been used to manufacture approved products.
Products and platforms support	Success has been demonstrated in the production of significant product categories and for all major production modes and formats.
Component offerings	Multiple vendors support diverse products for many operations, and multiple technologies support distinct processes (e.g., mixing, sensing and connectivity).
Materials acceptability	Single-use technologies have overcome classification and scale-influenced qualification demands, including mechanical strength and leachables.
Process development and control	Supported by applicability of production-scale control in development. Formats comparable to conventional systems are available.
Technical transfer	Overlapping system capacity ranges with uniformity of component materials and configurations support efficient transfer.
Scale-up	Case studies have established practical comparability (e.g., mixing, flow, power/volume, and k_La explained through computational fluid dynamics, stochastic and empirical multiscale modeling).
Regulatory	FDA prefers SUT reduced qualification/validation demands and contamination potential, with increased design flexibility. SUTs are now being used in approved product manufacturing.
Probes, sensors, and monitoring	SUT mixers, bioreactors and columns support both traditional and an increasing number of single-use sensors and samplers.
Connectivity	Continued development has increased flow rates, improved ease of use and reliability, and increased the number of distinct technologies and product vendors.
Ecological footprint	Significant studies have concluded the environmental impact of many applications of SUT is equivalent to or less than traditional systems.
Performance	SUT can show scalability, reliability, flexibility and productivity equivalent or superior to traditional systems.
QbD and PAT	In general, SUT capabilities here are equal to traditional systems, with some unique advantages.

Table 9.5 Commercially available upstream single-use bioprocessing components.

- Preparation and storage of media/buffers in SU mixers
- SU liquid and gas filtration of many types, including TFF
- SU valving and SU peristaltic or diaphragm pumps
- SU process fluids heat exchange and manifold distribution
- Storage of media and buffers for CP feeding in SU BPC
- SU storage and metered distribution of dry powders
- SU or hybrid bioreactor cell culture in seed generation
- Production in SU or hybrid-SU perfusion bioreactors
- Continual appearance of new SU probes and sensors
- SU real-time automated online multi-analysis interface
- SU flow-path online real-time controlled feed porting
- Clarification by SU centrifugation or filtration into BPC

install and turnaround times, lower capital and utility costs, and reduced concern for cross-contamination. In the past decade, multilaminate sterile bags, with either impellers (modeled after the classical stirred tank) or an external rocker-type platform (i.e., wave-type bioreactors) have allowed the preparation of media and process fluids and the culture of cells in disposable, single-use, and presterilized assemblies [15]. Implementation of these technologies has resulted in prepackaged and sterilized systems, complete and ready for use with preinstalled mixers and monitoring probes (Table 9.5) [16]. A commonly used industry definition for single-use systems from the Bio-Process Systems Alliance is as follows:

> "Single-use systems consist of fluid path components to replace reusable stainless steel components. The most typical systems are made up of bag chambers, connectors, tubing and filter capsules. For more complex unit operations such as cross flow filtration or cell culture, the single-use systems will include other functional components such as agitation systems, and single-use sensors" [17].

Single-use bioreactors are now available from multiple suppliers, with several offering sizes up to a 2000 l working volume [18–21]. A variety of sparging mass-transfer and cell suspension designs are available from rocker-style to top- or bottom-mounted impellers to innovative packed bed or even "air-wheel" impelled stirred-tank reactors [22]. In fact, the overall world market for single-use bioreactors has been calculated to approach $80M by 2017. Well over 20 distinct SU bioreactor offerings are now available, including technologies from such companies as

- BioReactor Sciences
- Thermo Scientific
- FiberCell Systems

- Sartorius Stedim
- GE Healthcare
- PBS Biotech
- Cellexus
- ATMI.

From upstream process material preparation through final product formulation, biopharm sponsors are increasingly presented with numerous SU solutions supporting all major production platforms [23–25]. SU flow-path centrifuges, depth and diafiltration (including tangential-flow filtration (TFF) or cross-flow filtration (CFF)), and heat exchangers allow disposable downstream processing to begin directly from the bioreactor harvest. The disposable, prepacked, and ready-to-use capture chromatography columns now available are often regarded as too costly to be single use in batch culture, yet do eliminate the time and effort of packing and column testing [26]. We can therefore see that CB applications of existing SU products can significantly change their economic considerations. Furthermore, a number of creative and entirely SU flow-path technology options, such as simulated moving bed (SMB) are increasingly available [27]. Recent offerings even include SU systems for virus clearance and drug formulation/filling applications. A single-use product-contact train in this step provides solid assurance of no cross- or processing contamination from either other products filled using the same equipment or the equipment processing and maintenance activities.

While providing many unique added benefits, such as ease and economy of process reconfiguration, disposables also well support such generally required production capabilities as the use of existing reusable sensing and monitoring systems. Other discovered benefits provided by SU include multiple-wrapped sterile liquid containment bags providing an ease of transfer between areas of diverged classification or bio-safely level.

Despite the many advantages afforded by disposable systems, a few challenges have been reported [28,29], such as the need to design novel process flow paths for SU implementation. However, this is usually more than compensated by such factors as the concomitant reduction in facility design and implementation time, capitol expense, plant footprint, and service requirements [30].

Another issue has been that while most production cell lines will grow well in most plastic films, there have been some exceptions. These have sometimes been traced to a necessary medium component being removed by absorption in to the plastic, such as cholesterol absorption into plastic bags preventing growth of some NS0 cell lines. Also, some recent studies have indicated that for some particular clones, inhibitory substances can leach from plastic components to the culture medium resulting in reduced cell growth. Activities on these examples illustrate the attention now given to the practicality of SU systems and components, and how the industry is aggressively addressing such challenges [31–33].

The industry is now working on standardizing many parameters surrounding SU system risk assessment and qualification. This is because many tests currently used in such activities are often specified or even designed by each customer individually with their supplier. For example, there is much effort now to standardize the extractables and leachables testing applied to the plastics used in the manufacturing of SU products. Standards setting organizations, supplier, and user groups currently interested in this effort include the BPSA, BPOG, PSA, PDA, ASTM, SIVB, ISPE, USP, PQRI and, rather remarkable, many more [32]. Current packages also typically include testing for such factors as tensile properties, tear resistance, and gas transmission rate. Relevant here is that this author is not aware of the consideration of continuous processing in this effort at this time.

Concern for the environmental impact of particular materials and components from waste generation in biomanufacturing operations has been specifically addressed [34,35]. As in other industries, the final answers to concerns, such as the relative aggregate carbon footprint, here are troublesome due to such issues as model assumptions and implementation-specific considerations [36]. However, the growing conclusion is that the most accurate picture is developed by employing strict life-cycle analysis techniques [37–39]. By this, the transition to disposables-based operations is seen as providing a net reduction in environmental impact for most any particular parameter examined.

There are now a number of publications providing comprehensive modeling results, applications data, and case studies by either disposable systems providers, or better yet, the industry's premier SU adopters [40]. These reports present the actual results obtained in implementing commercially available systems in real-life operations and can reveal implementation details, observations, and summaries of particular value for those just getting started. They frequently include examination of some of the considerations presented in Table 9.6, and often provide detailed information on subtopics, such as product contact leachables, practical flow rates, and disposable bioreactor oxygen transfer coefficient (k_La). Other sources of information on the implementation of disposables include patents and reports from government-commissioned studies [41].

Single-use system requirements that sponsors have identified include

- Cell culture performance/productivity
- Assurance of consumables supply
- Robust operational reliabilities
- Ease of use and modification
- Ease of transfer and scaling
- Buffer/media transfer rate
- Gas mass transfer rates
- Final product safety.

Table 9.6 Single-use technology gap analysis.

Concern	Progress
Scalability limitations: 2000 l max working volumes	Higher specific productivity, new entity types and globalization of both manufacturing and markets are reducing required process volumes.
Newer processes and models in infancy	Publications, filings and case studies are appearing in greater numbers.
"Robustness" concerns	Now, years of experience and numbers of examples have been established.
Disposable materials storage requirements	True, but more than compensated by reduction in operational footprint and service requirements
Questions regarding product and process materials compatibility	Few questions remain as has been generally established through for example, BPOG/BPSA and contracted studies.
Inventory, storage and repetitive purchases required	If anticipated, these incremental activities are compensated for by reduced operational and service footprint/demands.
Potential for vendor dependency (single-source equipment)	For many products, multiple vendors have emerged.
Potential for dependency on single or novel systems	For many systems, multiple related technologies have emerged.
Observed variability in vendor "maturity" and capabilities	Most vendors are advancing as SUT use and acceptance continues.
New vendor audit issues.	Better understanding and informed planning are progressing rapidly.
Availability: Generic, standard or specialized	Less of a concern as this issue is becoming generally understood. However, ideally, all desire every product to be generic.
Novel validation demands	For example, BPOG, BPSA and contracted studies are establishing methods.
Novel engineering and process layout/flow design requirements	Issue has been addressed (e.g., through a number of experienced and specialized consultants).
Developing industry and regulatory standards	Standards are in progress through aggressive sponsors, FDA and BPOG/BPSA activity.
Contents transfer flow rate limitations	Advanced designs (e.g., larger ports, improved connectors) are resolving this issue.
Connectivity issues: standardization and solutions desired	Numerous new connection solutions are appearing in the market.
Questions regarding new materials: leachables and extractables	Questions are being answered by for example, vendors, BPOG/BPSA and contracted studies.
Questions regarding the carbon footprint and fate of used materials	Overall, the environmental footprint and sustainability issues have been affirmatively addressed. Even so, consumable disposal remains a challenge.

While existing systems for disposable processing have been accepted in bioproduction for many operations, new developments in the technology and scale of application continue to be presented. This includes SU applications in vaccine manufacturing [42–44] and cell-based therapies [45–47]. Exciting advancements continue in the areas of connectivity, sampling and monitoring [48]. Aseptic sampling ports and means of accommodating classical dissolved oxygen and pH probes have long been available in disposable containers. Sensing technologies, from pH to pressure, continue to be introduced from a number of suppliers and include those that are either noninvasive or disposable themselves [49]. One that has been very well received is a means of providing dissolved oxygen and temperature sensing that employs a single-use sheath premolded in a disposable bioreactor bag port prior to irradiation sterilization. Its optical reader provides accurate *in situ* measurement of dissolved oxygen using phase fluorometric detection. Concurrent temperature measurements are obtained by a stainless steel thermal window embedded in the sheath. There is also a growing excitement regarding the use of near- and mid-infrared technologies in many bioprocessing applications from QC analysis of raw materials to final product measurement [50]. They can even potentially provide on-line information on bioreactor levels of substrate, biomass, product, and metabolite concentrations – which could be useful for improved process monitoring or control. Such real-time in-process component monitoring is being supported not only by PCL-enabled SU probes, but by the development of on-line and at-line cell-free autosamplers and disposable noninvasive porting.

Single-use systems in general have become an accepted component of animal-cell based bioproduction. Having been examined for years in less regulated environments, off-the-shelf SU systems are now in regular use to some extent in nearly every segment of the production train by CMOs and biopharma in regulated production applications (Figure 9.1) [51–53]. In fact, for many operations the question has evolved from "Is there an SU technology available that can support my operation?" to "Which advanced SU system best supports my needs?" [54]. The field has progressed to the point that there now even exist pre-engineered, modular and turn-key facilities. Modular SU systems involve housing SU bioprocessing equipment within discrete and limited areas of classified space. They can exist within dedicated isolator cabinets housed within rooms of reduced classification, or even within prefabricated trailers. The advantages of these facilities are such that significant adoption of flexible bioprocessing modules and plug-and-play factories seems likely, and vaccine sponsors are already reported to be early adopters of such. Modular technology facilitates the trend toward globalization, including transfer of bioprocessing to lesser-developed countries. The present values of SU-based operations are now well known, but such modular systems will allow entire plants to be essentially cloned. This will provide many economies to major manufacturers as well as assist in the establishment of ISO and cGMP manufacturing in developing countries. As this trend continues, we anticipate such modular systems and facility design to become available with higher-level integrated system management [55,56].

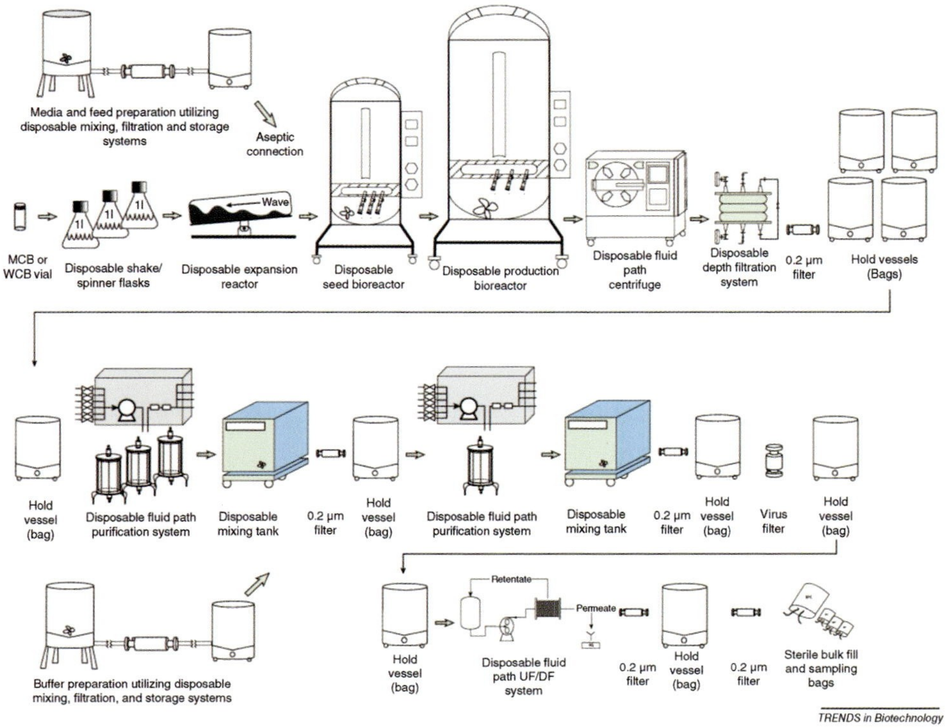

Figure 9.1 Example single-use (or disposable) systems throughout the bioproduction train. From Ref. [56], reprinted with permission.

9.6
Hybrid Systems

Processes, unit operations, or individual instrumentation composed of both single-use and reusable components remain quite common. This will likely remain true in the context of CB, with the implication of more than one operation in a contiguous, if not functionally closed, implementation. For a number of reasons, including component availability, individual reusable components are often employed in hybrid implementations of otherwise single-use flow paths. One example of this is the use of classical poloragraphic DO probes in single-use bioreactors. Here, the cleaned and sterilized probes are aseptically inserted into the SU bioreactor using specialized SU connectors. Even though more and more process components are becoming available as SU, the trend toward multi-op skids, system modularity, and more integrated processes portends the use of hybrid components to continue for some time. Hybrid systems present a few particular issues to be addressed, including the connection of the reusable component to the commonly preassembled, gamma-irradiated ready-to-use single-use components – as well as such QS issues as operational qualification and process validation.

9.7
Perfusion Culture

Virtually the only CB-supporting upstream processes are variations of large-scale perfused cultures, most often operating in some type of chemostat [57,58]. In perfusion mode, cells are retained through immobilization, isolation or concentration in some way to allow older culture medium (perfusate) to be withdrawn and replaced by fresh medium. Depending upon the type of cell, nature of the cell retention, and type of culture density control employed, a variety of cell densities and production states can be achieved. Platforms by which a perfused culture is driven to unusually high densities is referred to an intensified perfusion, and this has become quite popular of late. Principal values afforded by perfusion culture in general include

- Products significantly reduced reactor residency duration
- Potential for establishing steady states during production
- Dramatic and sustained growth in volumetric productivity.

In chemostat, a "steady state" is maintained by a balance of such parameters as cell growth, metabolism, feeding, and dilution. It can be important to realize that operating at steady state conditions can diverge from a true equilibrium and that especially in biomanufactruing we actually do not achieve all properties of the culture to maintain true steady states. This, as well as adaptation and innovation in the physical reactor technologies of the field, have caused some ambiguity in the application of the terminology describing the types of perfused bioreactors in use today (Table 9.7). Quite a number of creative solutions to the earlier challenges encountered (especially in scale-up) have been engineered, including for both adherent and suspension cultures [59–61]. They include many flavors of fluidized bed, centrifugal concentrators, gravity-based (conical and inclined ramp) settlers, packed-bed, spin-filters, ultrasonic resonators/filters, as well as crossflow membrane and diverse (internal and external) hollow fiber based systems. Many of these approaches have been employed for years and have been well described and reviewed [62,63]. Pertinent here are those systems supported by, or engineered in, single-use components (Table 9.3). Finally, it is important to consider that continuous processing, including perfusion culture, can place increased or unique pressures upon manufacturing systems, and especially for single-use systems. Examples include validation of operational consistency throughout the duration of extended culture, unique stresses that the extended time of operation continuous processes place upon the equipment (Table 9.8), and the increased mass transfer demands intensified perfusion

Table 9.7 Concepts in upstream continuous processing in techniques. Some with overlapping features.

System	Description
Dialysis	Primary/secondary metabolites are swapped across a membrane
Extraction	A two-phase system that lowers some secondary metabolites
Perfusion	Media continuously exchanged (by, e.g., gravity/filter/centrifuge)
Filtration	Media changed and cells retained by a (static/spin/virtual) filter
External Filtration	Media continuously exchanged through an external filtration unit
Hollow fiber perfusion	Media changed and cells retained within a hollow fiber cartridge
Enhanced perfusion	Media continuously exchanged with cells greatly concentrated
Continuous	Prolonged control of feeding/harvest maintaining a steady state
Chemostat	A steady state type where culture expansion equals dilution rate
Repeated	A fraction of the biomass provides seed for the next culture cycle
Attached continuous	2-D surface stacked array multiplate reactor/medium exchange
	3-D fixed-scaffold/packed-bed reactors and medium exchange

mode places upon bioreactors. While some perfusion technologies could theoretically be operated indefinitely, such practical considerations effectively limit the culture durations currently approached to between 20 and 60 days. However, in time effective culture durations of from 2 to 4 months are not inconceivable. Presented later is an introduction to some of the more popular technologies commercially available to support large-scale single-use perfusion culture of animal cells in bioproduction.

Table 9.8 CB modifies operational qualification concepts. CB can dramatically increase the duration and throughput volumes involved in each "use." Review of the (pre) validation requirements advised.

Concept	Definition
Reusable	Equipment or material intended for use for an indefinite number of times: especially in different production cycles or batches, and after salvaging or preparation by special treatment or processing.
Multi- or limited use	Equipment or material intended for use in a process for a limited number of cycles: determined by validated procedure or subsequent testing.
Single use	Equipment or material intended for use in a process for one cycle and then retired from use.
Hybrid	Equipment, material or operation composed of both reusable and single-use components.
Disposable	Equipment or material intended for use either for one time or for use in a process in a limited number of times, and then retired as waste.

9.8 Single-Use in Continuous Biomanufacturing

Single-use technologies provide distinct value to each mode of bioprocessing, as well as specific and enabling features in continuous biomanufacturing (CB) implementations [64]. SU features that complement CB range from low initial investment costs, to contributing reduced time-to-market, to support of heightened process control [65,66]. Most individual operations in a proposed CB process now have commercially available SU or hybrid solutions. To begin with, much of the SU equipment offerings for batch bioproduction have the same or related application in CB systems. Examples range from such simple equipment as tubings and connectors, to more complex assemblies such as bioprocess containers (BPCs) for the cryopreservation of large working stock aliquots. SU supports such early upstream activities as SU metered distribution of liquids through SU manifolds, as well as the storage and distribution of dry powders. Further down the process single-use mixers (SUMs) aid in the preparation of media or buffers, which can then be stored in SU BPCs. It is clear how the introduction of SU technologies in bioprocessing mixing and filtration operations can increase the convenience and speed of lot turnaround and product change-over in such applications. There are now even SU heat exchangers supporting such activities as the modification of the temperature of culture media from its formulation and/or storage into the bioreactor, and of the raw harvest from the bioreactor post culture [67]. Around the perfusion bioreactor itself there are SU liquid and gas filtration materials of many types. There is a continually growing number of SU product-contact manufacturing-scale bioreactor types to support batch cell culture in the generation of perfusion reactor seed generation [68].

As introduced previously, perfusion-supported modes of culture are the only practical CB supporting upstream process for cell-based biomanufacturing. Most commercially available large-scale SU bioreactors are capable of supporting perfusion culture of some type, when fitted with appropriate ancillary equipment. Some, such as packed-bed reactors, inherently lend themselves to perfusion operation without modification. A number of perfusion-capable bioreactors either now exist with an SU flow path, or are in the process of being converted to SU by their manufacturers (Figure 9.2) [69,70]. Other bioreactor styles, such as impeller-driven stirred tank reactors, have SU perfusion culture-supporting accessory equipment available for incorporation in CB implementations. This equipment is also either currently available in an SU format, or now being developed as such by the manufacturers. CB is supported by ongoing technological developments in mixing and mass-flow systems and (even *more* importantly) by the many recent advances in process monitoring and feedback/feed-forward manufacturing process control. It should be noted that CB efficiently promotes both the tools and goals of such operational excellence, thereby enabling such initiatives as PAT and

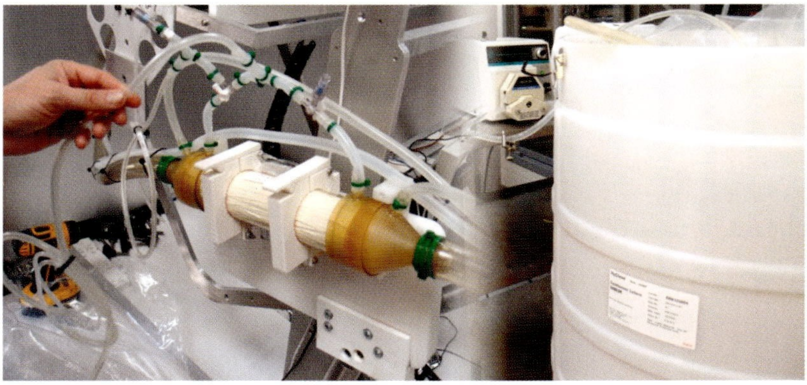

Figure 9.2 Single-use, continuous bioproduction with a single-use Thermo Scientific HyClone BioProcess Container and Drum (right) supporting culture in a FiberCell Systems LS-HFBR bioreactor (left).

QbD. It readily accepts most new on-line monitoring approaches and real-time quality assurance developments. Moreover, because high-throughput and reduced facility residency of intermediates are its hallmark, CB actually *requires* such advances. Combined with the industry's growing bioprocess understanding, CB extends such capabilities to advancing continuous quality verification (CQV), continuous process verification (CPV), and real-time release (RTR) enabling initiatives. No limitations to such activities have been reported from the coincident employment of SU materials.

Continuous biomanufacturing therefore demands increased near real-time *in situ* monitoring or process sampling in support of the comprehensive control procedures required to maintain the steady states involved. SU flow-path systems in sampling include those for the withdrawal, transport, and storage of cell-free, microcarrier-free, or raw cell-containing samples for analysis. For such sampling, currently commercially available products include

- Open/cell-free sampling probes
- Online multianalysis interfaces
- Small depth filtration cartridges
- Diverse plumbing solution styles
- <50 ml capacity BPC manifolds.

There are vendors of commercially available SU apparatus for sampling in real-time to support automated, online, multianalyte, or multivariate monitoring [71,72]. The continued appearance of new SU monitoring probes and sensors of various styles have provided significant support of this initiative. Recently, John Carvell of ABER Instruments remarked that "We are seeing advanced monitoring techniques and single-use systems empowering the development of continuous processing in biotechnology" [73].

A variety of fluids are supplied to, and collected from, perfusion culture systems throughout operation – and SU flow-path solutions exist for each of them. A number of products exist to support the controlled production and distribution of sterile SU reactor charge, feed, sampling, and recycling of fluids for perfusion culture. Large-volume activities, such as culture media support, are facilitated by products of various designs and sources including SUMs, SU manifolds, SU aseptic connection solutions, and SU pumps and valves [74]. While the demand for many services and consumables are reduced in CB, one that is not is cell culture media. Large quantities of media are required to be supplied continuously to the perfusion bioreactor. Surprisingly, the "topping-up" of large-scale SU fluid containers with newly prepared buffer to provide a virtually unlimited and constant supply of each buffer/media type can be validated for GMP procedures, including perfusion culture. Culture media and buffers are typically prepared in SU mixing/hydration/dilution systems composed of a rigid containment system with a motor and controls driving radiation-sterilized SU bags equipped with disposable impeller assemblies.

Furthermore, continuous, automated in-line culture media and buffer dilution, conditioning, and dispensing have been attempted for decades, and interest in them remains high. Advancements in the mass flow technology, monitoring, and feedback control required to establish and maintain process fluid specifications are now allowing such approaches to become a reality. This is due in part to advances in related technologies already accomplished in support of the ink and cosmetics industries. The compact size and portability of such equipment involved allows it to produce fluids at the "point of use" and is now supported by the incorporation of SU technologies. Thus, in-line fluid preparation and conditioning provides benefits to bioprocessing in general, supports CB in particular and provides specific features supporting SU technology application in CB. For example, its significantly reduced buffer prep tank size requirement in CB supports application of SU mixers, BPCs, and manifolds.

Moving further down the process, the large-scale collection and initial processing of product-containing harvest can be accomplished by SU centrifugation or SU depth filtration directly into CB downstream operations, through SU fluid transport. It should be noted here that even though, by definition, a CB process line moves intermediate product from operation to operation in a continuous fashion, BPCs are still required throughout the process stream for such purposes as process fluid formulation, surge or break protection, sampling, and emergencies (Figure 9.3).

As introduced earlier, CB contributes to reduced process development times in a number of ways. These support SU-specific efficiencies provided by, for example, elimination of the requirement to develop services supplying cleaning and steaming steps. Other SU advantages in CB process development are its support of an open architecture approach as well as a number of hybrid designs. Such design flexibility includes equipment combinations of between reusable

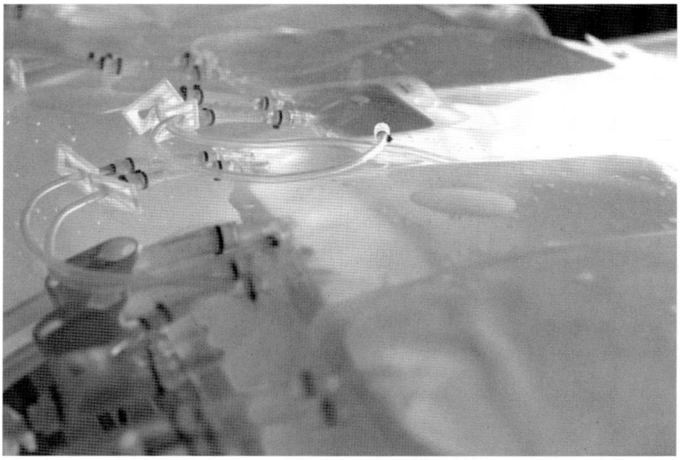

Figure 9.3 Continuous biomanufacturing capable Thermo™ Scientific™ BioProcess Container assembly.

and disposable systems, divergent suppliers and locations, or of particular equipment styles. As applied to CB we can see the many flexibilities of SU support a manufacturing platform of exceptional efficiency, adaptability, and operational ease [75]. Advances in the engineering of SU transfer tubing, distribution manifolds, and container porting also support creativity in process design. This is of particular value in designing a process with such demands as an entirely new flow path, process monitoring and control, or lot designations – such as for CB. Creative development in process flow and flexible configurations in perfusion culture is required in CB for many reasons, including

- Commercially available CB solutions are still in development
- Procedures for optimal production have not been discovered
- Refined procedures that do exist are generally not published
- New development in such CB support as intensified perfusion
- New understandings in perfusion culture metabolic demands
- Developments in solutions for perfusion mass transfer needs.

Operationally, CB contributes to overall process flexibility in that its equipment tends to be easy to clean, inspect, and maintain. It inherently promotes simple and rapid product changeover, "scaling-out," or "numbering-up" to increase maxim capacity, and a time-effected product mass accumulation providing a continuously variable manufacturing rate. SU systems can provide concomitant flexibility and ease of product changeover because they tend to be more modular, reconfigurable, and transportable than much of the older stainless equipment [75]. In fact, the size, configuration, and reduced service requirements of SU systems actually encourage diversity of physical location within a suite or plant, as well as relocation to other manufacturing sites. During production, CBs reduction or elimination of such non–value-added steps as bioreactor harvest and intermediate product storage (or hold), its testing, as well as related equipment maintenance, complements the ease of SU product component installation during setup.

What has been presented so far relates to existing products and manufacturing platforms. Recent trends in manufacturing demands synergize with many of the SU and CB coincident values and features described here. These new manufacturing goals and considerations include

- Development of more personalized medicines
- Anticipated lower mass "next-gen" products
- Globalization of production competition
- Trend toward contract manufacturing
- Explosion in biosimilar development
- Price-sensitive/controlled markets
- Trends for local manufacturing
- Demand for process flexibility
- Need for pandemic response
- Increased volumetric yield.

Although CB will not be feasible for all products and processes, many implementations well-support a "platform" approach in which a single process supports more than one product. CB nearly always shortens the process stream and its duration, reduces downtime, and greatly reduces (manual) handling and storage of intermediates. These features complement related operational efficiencies of SU systems. For example, processes with SU technology benefit from ease and speed of process setup due to the modular and presterilized nature of each SU commodity resulting in the elimination of cleaning, sterilization, and testing of process equipment.

The cumulative benefit from an SU and CB process contributes greatly to a reduced overall processing time for the active pharmaceutical ingredient. As CB processes have greatly simplified production trains, they inherently facilitate the application of closed processing approaches to individual operations and even processes. Especially in bioproduction, the modularity and integral gamma irradiation sterility of SU combined with the simplicity and sustained operation of CB promise the appearance of platforms of unparalleled operational ease and convenience [76,77].

Beyond CB's higher inherent operational efficiency, coincident benefits from the improvements in recombinant clone generation and intensified feeding strategies are determining that more concentrated perfusion bulk intermediate product is being generated. For both surge protection and product intermediate containment, smaller containers and storage suites are now required – both of which plays right into the efficient application of SU systems and technologies. These values contribute to promoting the common goals of reducing capital expenditures, minimizing project timelines, and increasing operational flexibility – while minimizing operational costs. But the advantages here go even beyond this. Employment of SU equipment in a continuous bioprocess flow supports the design of closed and highly integrated operations. This is enabling such initiatives as the growing "Factory-of-the Future" initiative of manufacturing even divergent product types in grey space "ballroom" suites of reduced environmental classification.

Room classifications are a heavy burden for biopharmaceutical sponsors. Controlled nonclassified (CNC) is a designation often used in noncritical areas in GMP manufacturing facilities. The International Society of Pharmaceutical Engineering (ISPE) defines CNC as a nonclassified room environment where closed processes and their immediate support systems may be located. CNC spaces are cleanable and controlled, but do not have the rigid procedural controls and personal gowning requirements of classified areas. In regulated closed-system processing, the status of the manufacturing suite becomes secondary to the integrity of the closed systems. Biomanufacturing processes employing closed operations in an environment of reduced classification is currently a goal being actively pursued in the industry [78]. For maintaining sterility, many biomanufacturing operations are already intrinsically functionally closed. For the same reason, presterilized single-use biomanufacturing systems are necessarily closed upon delivery. Continuous manufacturing processes, due to the integral nature of its contiguous operations, inherently lend themselves to closed operation. Surprisingly, there is ongoing work regarding the precise nature of a "closed process" within biomanufacturing for CMC purposes. For example, the ISPE currently advises within its definition of the term "It is the manufacturer's responsibility to define and prove closure for a process step" [79]. Nevertheless, by exploiting these system feature correlations and designing a *functionally* closed manufacturing flow path, a facility can be envisioned with combined work areas not requiring classification. Such a facility offers many potential benefits, including a reduction in

- Construction costs
- Start-up schedule extent
- Utilities (clean water and steam)
- Manufacturing suite area and barriers
- Suite classification (and maintenance costs)
- Manufacturing suite operation steps and costs
- HVAC (and related plant and quality maintenance).

Continuous biomanufacturing promotes increased profitability, beginning with reduced capital expense, by invariably reducing equipment footprint and facility extent [80]. This is a consequence of a CB batch being primarily determined by run time rather than reaction container size, thereby reducing the size of a bioreactor. However, there are a number of other features contributing to this (Table 9.1). CB can lessen the need for operator intervention (and therefore support personnel) because it simplifies a process and optimizes process flow. Also, by reducing non–value-added steps, such as intermediate product hold and final product inventory, CB reduces the facility requirement for their storage. This completely harmonizes with SU technology and systems, which themselves present reduced validation requirements, quality systems maintenance, controlled environment extent, and operations personnel. Perfusion culture requires an inherently smaller reactor volume and independence from cleaning and sterilization for extended periods of time. This complements SU systems scale limitations as well as total independence from any cleaning or sterilization service. The synergy of employing a process that requires cleaning-in-place (CIP)/sterilizing-in-place (SIP) only once each 1–3 months, with a format that does not require the service at all, is obvious. In addition to promoting such advanced process development and operational goals, for many of the values described earlier, both SUS and CB require a significantly simplified process control strategy. They present more integrated processing, with fewer steps or operations, and thus can also provide reduced process variability, HMI activities, and provide (ultimately) a more integral comprehensive system control. Such correlative features result in dramatically increased overall facility efficiencies, further reducing both capital and operational expenses. John Bonham-Carter of RepliGen has remarked that although such factors as existing facility configuration and capacity must be considered, "savings can be obtained from the implementation of single-use equipment and continuous processing through more efficient trained personnel and facility use" [81].

The heart of an upstream CB approach is the bioreactor, and perfusion bioreactors have been successfully employed in biopharmaceutical production for decades. At the research scale there have been SU hollow fiber perfusion bioreactors available from a variety of vendors for over 40 years. At even the production scale there have been steel construction perfusion bioreactors in use for over 20 years. However, only recently have commercially available SU and hybrid production-scale perfusion-capable equipment appeared [14]. Their coordinated implementation in actual production settings with appropriate control is just now beginning. Such systems are essentially composed of

- SU and inherently designed perfusion-capable bioreactors
- SU batch reactors with SU/classical ancillary perfusion devices
- A growing variety of SU and hybrid monitoring probes and sensors
- SU pumps and automated fluid modification/delivery of various design
- Automated SU online sampling, interface, valve, and feeding technologies.

The fact that many SU systems are constructed from materials that are compliant with pharmaceutical standards and are free from animal products supports CB application in a wide variety of product types and classification. In fact, SU systems are available for most any process format (e.g., microcarriers and suspension), platform (e.g., cell line, vectors, and culture media), mode (e.g., dialysis or intensified perfusion) or scale (e.g., through rapid, inexpensive horizontal scale-out). "Future proofing," or supporting the sustainability of a new CB process in the face of product lifecycle or emerging technology imperatives, is supported by many SU features. Examples here include low initial facility, service, and equipment costs – and especially, their need for undedicated manufacturing suites and ease of process train reconfiguration. CB has, however, introduced an interesting twist on the standard paradigm of the concept of iterations of equipment usage. There has always been a bit of wiggle room in the distinction between the concept of "single-use" and such terms as "disposable" or "limited-use," and it is important to consider how CB has determined a re-examination of a few related concepts in this regard. For example, in CB one may employ a piece of equipment or material "once" for many weeks or months, which had been originally designed to be used "once" for a matter of hours or days (Table 9.8).

One can see why processes that are CB as well as SU are being adopted for the production of many existing protein biological and vaccines. However, there are many developing cell culture formats and expression systems serving a growing number of entirely new entities and product types. It is valuable to consider how SU CB approaches serve not only today's demands, but upcoming products and manufacturing technologies as well (Table 9.9). For example, we know there are over 20 antibody conjugates now in development. As the preconjugate antibodies are generally produced in Chinese hamster ovary (CHO)/NS0 type suspension transfectoma, we see them as amenable to single-

Table 9.9 Single-use continuous biomanufacturing potential in next-gen products.

Next-generation technology	SU potential	CB potential
Biosimilars, biobetters	Yes – CB	Yes
Cocktails/polyclonals	Yes – CB	Yes
Next Generation antibodies	Yes – CB	Yes
• Bi- and multispecific antibodies (bisAbs, BiTEs, DARTs)	Yes – CB	Yes
• New CD20, HER2 and EGFR Ab's	Yes – CB	Yes
• ADCC – enhanced MAb oncotherapeutics	Yes – CB	Yes
• Recombinant antibody mixtures	Yes – CB	Yes
• Glycoengineering, Fc AA mutations	Yes – CB	Yes
• Engineered Ab (e.g., scFv, VH/VL, mini-Abs)	*Yes – CB/CF*	Yes
• Fragments and Ab–like proteins (FAb, Fcab, nanobody)	*Yes – CB/CF*	Yes
• Immunoconjugates, for example, ADCs	*Yes – CB/CF*	*Preconjugate*
New protein biologics for cancer, osteoporosis, ophthalmic . . .	*Yes – CB/CF*	Yes
Designed Ankyrin Repeat Proteins (DARPins)	*Soon – CF*	Yes
Domain antibodies, dAbs, other next–generation fragments	*Soon – CF*	Yes
Anticalins, Adnectins and other alternative scaffolds	*Soon – CF*	Yes
Dual ligand peptides and assemblies	*Soon – CF*	Yes
Viral vectors and vaccines	Yes – CB	*Nonlytic*

use perfusion approaches. Interestingly, we also see SU and CP technologies now being applied in even novel bacterial vaccine production [82].

As an implementation of CP, environmental objectives are supported by the fact that CB itself can reduce the

- Amount of equipment to be processed in cleaned or steam sterilization
- Process steps, footprint, service requirements, and energy consumption
- Number of support personnel (and their commuting to work) required.

Finally, advanced means of environmental impact assessment and reporting for each of SU materials and CP manufacturing approaches have been reviewed (shown earlier), but *it* is of note that none appear to be, or have been reported as, in conflict with each other.

9.9 Roller Bottles

Roller bottle systems of many styles have traditionally been the most popular bioreactor system for the production of biologics and viruses using adherent cells. Though simple and reliable, it is extremely labor intensive and requires a large physical footprint. Nunc™ TufRol™ Roller Bottles (Thermo Scientific) in a RollerCell 40 (CELLON S.A.) offers single-use, somewhat continuous operation solutions for attached cell roller bottle culture. It can also support arrays of tens of roller bottles in large-scale batch suspension culture. However, perfused suspension culture or microcarrier-based continuous operation does not appear to be practical here.

9.10 Mechanically Agitated Suspension Reactors

Mechanically agitated (often *stirred-tank*) bioreactors, containing either suspension or anchorage-dependent cultures on a support matrix, have dominated the industry in large-scale production. In this system, suspension or matrix-attached cultures are agitated through a number of mechanical mechanisms, from marine impellers to paddles to airwheels. The stirred tank bioreactor (STR) is the most popular of the suspension systems for such reasons as it is simple to operate, easy to scale up, and well understood. One advantage here is that suspension cell systems do not depend on constrained surface area. This allows operational cell densities obtainable to be quite variable and amenable to intensified perfusion mode culture increases to over 10^8 cells ml^{-1}. Depending on the mode of operation and culture platform, STRs can provide very efficient mass transfer. This is accomplished by a variety of sparge mechanisms and the use of marine or pitched blade impellers. For attached cultures, several types of commercially

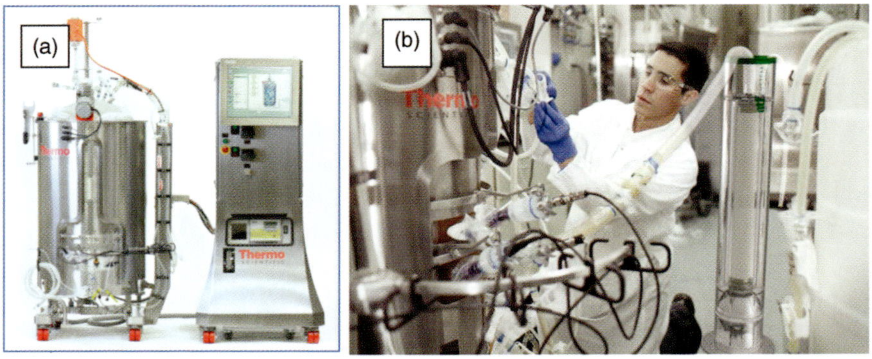

Figure 9.4 Single-use, perfusion bioproduction accomplished in a single-use Thermo Scientific HyPerforma S.U.B. TK 250L (a) depicted with a Refine Technology single-use ATF6 System (b).

available microcarriers include dextran-based microcarriers from GE Healthcare, and a variety of offerings from Paul Life Sciences (SoloHill). Each product differs in such diverse characteristics as their porosity, specific gravity, optical properties, regulatory classification, and surface chemistries [44].

Suspension culture requires vigorous agitation, which can be problematic. Another issue to be considered is the separation of cell-encoated microcarriers from the ambient media. STRs are easily converted to culture systems supporting continuous processes through the addition of ancillary perfusion devices (Figure 9.4). Either freely floating cells or microcarriers can be employed in an entirely single-use or hybrid perfused culture process. Examples here include an Xcellerex XDR Single-Use Bioreactor (GE Healthcare) employing an ancillary filtering apparatus, such as the ATF System (Refine Technology) or KrosFlo® System (Spectrum Instruments). Such apparatus can provide fully single-use flow-path perfusion culture capability for suspension cell or microcarrier culture (*see individual system descriptions later*). They can also be employed in the separation of cells or microcarriers at harvest.

9.11
Hollow Fiber Media Exchange

RepliGen's ATF™ System is a filtration-based cell separation system using alternating tangential flow through hollow fibers of a filter module. The benefits of the ATF System include nearly linear scale-up (from <1 to >2000 l), simplicity of operation and validation, plus a choice of filter materials and pore sizes. Traditional TFF in comparison can become clogged over time from cell aggregates in the pores or accretion of debris across the membrane surface. In a one-directional flow system, aggregates lodging in the hollow fiber will diminish filtration capacity by the degree of blockage. In contrast, the alternating flow has an inherent self-cleaning ability allowing a filter to perform significantly longer than one would expect. This transient reversible flow is actuated by a large surface area (minimum shear) diaphragm. The ATF4 pump head displaces about 400 ml of liquid with each exchange, generating a flow of about 3–4 l min^{-1}. The combination of a reversible flow through the filter with high and low pressure cycles results not only in an efficient tangential flow effect, but also in significant trans-membrane fluxes to prevent fouling even at cell concentrations in the order of 200×10^6 cells ml^{-1}. Offered mostly as a standard product, and using a single vessel connection having little or no customization, it has been shown to be robust and adaptable to most production requirements, including either classical stainless steel or SU platforms. Many "instigator" or premiere biopharmaceutical sponsors are currently employing the ATF with single-use bioreactors in hybrid enhanced perfusion and continuous culture applications. A single-use ATF is currently in late-stage development by the manufacturer, and when employed with SUBs will provide for an entirely SU flow-path enhanced perfusion system.

Spectrum Laboratories KrosFlo Perfusion System is an entirely single-use flow path system also enabling external hollow-fiber based perfusion culture. This cultured cell and microcarrier filtration accessory product comes sterile and ready-to-use, providing such benefits as a dramatically reduced set-up time. It employs single-use low-shear levitating pumps, reducing impact on cell viability. The manufacturer advertises up to 400×10^6 cells ml^{-1} in a noninvasive flow path with inline pressure sensors and cartridges containing polyethersulfone or polyethersulfone hollow fibers. It is scalable, with commercial implementations from 2 to 2000 l in application with either reusable or single-use bioreactors. The automated KrosFlo Perfusion System (aKPS) is a more comprehensive solution featuring feedback control loops, control of the recirculation pumps, back-pressure valves, permeate pump and high-pressure circuits, touchscreen HMI, permeate scale, and DCS hardware.

9.12 Packed Bed Bioreactors

Packed bed (PB) bioreactors provide yet another approach to a continuous culture enabling upstream process. They are capable of supporting a variety of cell lines for long periods of time while providing some rare and valuable performance features. One example is the extremely low shear established due to the immobilization of cells within the macroporous matrices. This concept has been applied for decades in a number of implementations, many of which failed due to inherent design faults. Performance limitations, such as suboptimal properties in both fluid flow and diffusive mass transport had been an endemic problem for PB. The newest configurations have specifically addressed these issues traditionally associated with immobilized cell culture, as well as introducing such improvements as single-use flow paths. PB reactors are currently employed in a number of diverse manufacturing, research, and therapeutic applications, such as bioartificial organs and the *ex vivo* expansion of a variety of human cells from differentiated organ cells to stem cells. The successful implementation of commercial PB reactors in support of large-scale recombinant biologic and vaccine manufacturing has been accomplished [83]. Of the commercialized PB reactors on the market, those with large-scale SU flow path perfusion capability include the Celligen BLU (NBS), iCellis (ATMI), TideCell (CESCO), and MBS (Bioreactor Science).

Packed bed type systems can be further classified into two types: fixed bed and moving bed. Most PB bioreactors for cell culture are fixed bed systems, including NBS' Celligen basket bioreactor, ATMIs iCellis, and CESCOs TideCell bioreactor. The BioCell MB(S) bioreactor is the only commercial product with a moving bed, and this provides some rather unique flexibility and functionality. All PB bioreactors use similar macroporous nonwoven PET fiber carriers that differ principally in surface treatment, configuration, and structure. The carriers' most common characteristic is their high surface area, which allow for high-density cell cultures. The use of carriers also supports easy separation of the ambient media from the attached cells, supporting convenient media replacement, perfusion culture, or final harvest.

The cells in both the iCellis and Celligen bioreactors are continually submerged in media, relying upon aeration mechanisms to supply oxygen. Diffusive mass transfer in the Celligen depends on agitation as well as sparging, while the iCellis relies on its defined waterfall surface area. The TideCell and BioCell MB(S) use the principle found in roller bottles, exposing cells directly to air for oxygen transfer. Employing this direct-to-air principle provides for a number of features. For example, it simplifies production scale-up and eliminates the foaming and shear issues commonly encountered with other approaches to aeration. Schematic diagrams of two PB bioreactors are depicted in Figure 9.5.

The Celligen bioreactor has factors to consider in scaling-up due, for example, to the increasing depth or height of a bioreactor bed as scale increases. The TideCell uses bidirectional flow and multiple internal tubes to mitigate this particular challenge, but is nevertheless limited by the media's flow rate as production is scaled up. Both the iCellis and the BioCell MB use shallow beds and unconstrained flow rate to resolve these scale-up issues. Both the iCellis and the Celligen have an additional concern of using less than twice the volume of medium around their bed, which determines a requirement or frequent/continual medium replacement/feeding to maintain nutrient and oxygen supply. The medium volume cannot be further adjusted during cell seeding, infection, or transfection procedures. Furthermore, the media volume for the TideCell and the BioCell MB(S) is variable, supporting over 5× the bed volume and creating a more robust environment for the culture. This also provides for less frequent medium replacement and provides increased efficiency in cell attachment for virus infection processes.

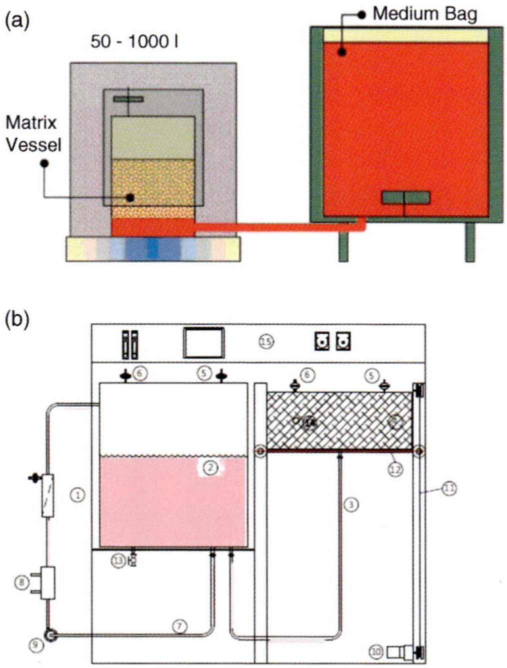

Figure 9.5 Schematic diagrams of two packed bed bioreactors.

9.13 Hollow Fiber Perfusion Bioreactors

Hollow fiber perfusion bioreactors (HFPB) are a high-density, continuous perfusion culture system. While not a stirred tank suspension mode, they are not truly packed bed reactors either. Animal cells are generally seeded within a cartridge but outside the internal hollow fibers in what is referred to as the extracapillary space (ECS). Culture medium is pumped through the lumen of the hollow fibers, allowing nutrients and metabolic products to diffuse both ways across the fiber walls. Having passed through the cartridge, the medium can be either oxygenated and returned to it or collected as a harvest while fresh medium is introduced. The four fundamental characteristics of an HFPB system are as follows:

- Extremely high culture binding surface-to-volume ratios
- Immobilization of cells at very high (biomimetic) density
- Culture on a porous matrix supporting prolonged culture
- Selectable fiber porosity providing segregation of solutes.

The high-density culture in such controlled hydrodynamic conditions as an HFPB can provide a microenvironment of directional flow, establishing a gentle interstitial gradient within the cell mass for autocrine stimulation, cell alignment, and desirable cell–cell or cell–surface interactions. Because an HFPB cell culture (on the ECS side of the fibers) can exist at concentrations ≥100× that of standard suspension cultures, it was discovered early on that continuous culture in less animal serum may be more easily established and provide several benefits over classical culture modes [84–86]. To support this, a serum replacement (CDM-HD, FiberCell systems) was designed to take advantage of the unique cell culture conditions found within a hollow fiber bioreactor. Besides being optimized for continuous culture, this chemically defined serum-free supplement is surfactant-, protein-, and animal component-free. Especially relevant to this report is that the formulation was specifically designed for compatibility with the entirely single-use flow path provided by the system. In SU perfusion culture this formulation provides consistency in culture performance and protein production, including in such posttranslational modifications as glycosylation. Another feature presented is a reduction in both protein and DNA contamination of the harvest. HFPB systems allow for the long-term support of divergent cell types in coculture at even extreme ratios [45]. The FiberCell Duet and the new large-scale LSHFBR from FiberCell Systems have demonstrated performance in providing single-use flow-path perfusion culture with a diverse array of adherent or even suspension cell lines [45].

9.14 Continuous Flow Centrifugation

High-capacity continuous flow centrifuges are available with a wide variety of rotor designs. Designs supporting perfusion are commonly referred to as "zonal" (because of the dominant principle of particle separation employed). They contain a large volume of sample in a single central cavity that is capable of dynamic loading and unloading while rotor is spinning. Many existing centrifugation systems cannot be used for high-density fed-batch animal cell processes for technical reasons, including unacceptable losses in cells product. While they can support a number of functions, from cell washing to transfection to cell-based therapy, we focus here on those enabling a perfusion mode of cell culture.

Each is economical to use, as even the disposable components have robust longevity within a run. They can provide consistent performance with no mid-run degradations, such as filter aging or clogging. The systems support processes that are simple to transfer and scale up. Since the parameters that control the separation are G-force, time, and flow rate, such things as filter capacity or surface areas are not a concern.

Cell separation takes place in a presterilized module constructed from Class VI pharmaceutical-grade materials. Once the module is installed and tubing connected using an aseptic technique or sterile welding, the systems are virtually closed, providing a high degree of aseptic or sterile reliability without the need for CIP or SIP (Figure 9.6). While different products employ distinct separation

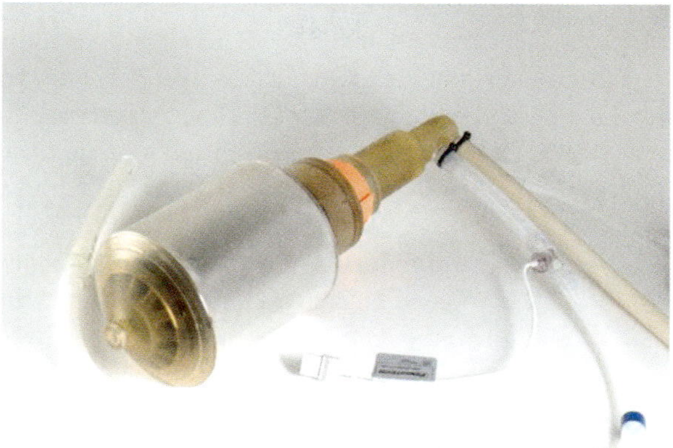

Figure 9.6 The single-use module from a *CARR Centritech* closed, continuous bioprocessing capable centrifuge.

principles, essentially the cell suspension is fed into an inlet at one end of the module and the cells are centrifugally concentrated or separated from the media. Clarified supernatant is discharged from one outlet and cell concentrate from yet another outlet, possibly in a distinct cycle. These devices can support both perfusion culture and bioreactor harvest operations.

CARR Centritech's CELL8 from PneumaticScaleAngelus utilizes a gamma irradiation sterilized single-use module. All process contact surfaces are easy to install and are 100% replaceable after each run. Low-shear isolation of mammalian and insect cells is possible and minimal reduction in viability of recovered cells achievable. When employed in harvest functions, minimal cell debris is produced within the centrifuge. CELL8's modules contain no rotating seals and are readily connected to a single-use bioreactor to establish either perfusion culture or clarified harvest. Customer-specified single-use connectors are available.

The CELL8 presents a completely automated three-step process of separation, isolation, and discharge with a flexible cycle parameter entry. The basics of perfusion operation are that the cell suspension is gently pumped to the module and the cells settle to the lower outer radius via low G-force while debris and supernatant are continuously discharged. In the cell discharge phase, concentrated cells are isolated by inflating an air barrier behind the module, cutting off feed from the concentrated cells, which are discharged via a pump. This cycle is repeated until the bioreactor volume has been processed. Several modes of operation are available to completely eliminate the need for extremely sensitive cells from being processed through the peristaltic pump. The CELL8 has a demonstrated track record in the perfusion of cell cultures as well as the differential harvest of supernatant, cells, and debris. The system is very versatile and can accommodate a variety of applications and cell culture requirements. The whole system operates in a totally closed, presterilized bladder, which can be programmed to run continually or intermittently to turn over a fixed volume from the bioreactor.

The manufacturer contends that the CELL8 is the only commercial perfusion technology that can remove dead cells from a bioreactor. By reducing the rotor speed, dead cells can be separated from the cell concentrate that is processed back to the bioreactor. They recommend that a process should be optimized to remove dead cells periodically throughout the cell culture production run. The CELL8 can operate at 36 to $320 \times g$ and support bioreactor volumes of up to 3000 l working at flow rates of 6–120 l h^{-1}.

The kSep6000S from kSep Systems also provides automated class VI single-use flow-path perfusion support, yet through an entirely different technology. In this GMP closed system unit, a fluid flow force counteracts the centrifugal force and creates a fluidized bed of cells that remain in suspension throughout the process. The chamber's seamless rotation along the horizontal axis determines that there is no gravitational activity in the process and therefore no slant effect. There is a continuous operation with chamber emptying by reversal of flow, and the chamber never stops rotating. The manufacturer emphasizes the extremely low shear of this filterless system providing constant oxygen and nutrient supply in the 6 l (6×1000 ml) volume chamber. It advertises an over 10 l min^{-1} flow rate with a total processing volume of from 100 to 6000 l.

Features championed in the 6000s include easy process scale-up, reduced validation procedures, and practical separation and removal of dead cells. The single-use system enabling feature promoted include ease of interface with a SUB and the concomitant removal of plastic particles from single-use plastic products. Performance values include a noise level <62 dBA, flow rates ranging from 0.5 to 10.8 l h^{-1} and a 600–1200 billion cell capacity per cycle. The manufacturer contends that the kSep® technology provides significant advantages for users who want to either harvest cells as product or discard cells as by-product during manufacturing. They explain that through the balance of centrifugal and fluid flow forces, the kSep® retains particles, such as cells or microcarriers as a concentrated fluidized bed under a continuous flow of media or buffer. This automated sequence available is advertised being used in cell-based therapy manufacturing, cell banking, and vaccine manufacturing processes.

9.15 Acoustic Wave Separation

Separation by ultrasound is a technique for the isolation of small particles from fluids without the need for invasive components, such as membranes, or the moving components required by centrifuges or spin filters. It is a nonfouling and nonclogging retention device for perfusion applications. Through what are variously referred to as ultrasonic resonators, separators or filters, acoustic wave separation (AWS) has been essentially demonstrated for decades – but only recently successfully applied to practical large-scale animal cell separation in perfusion culture and reactor harvest applications.

Ultrasonic separators are comprised of two components: (1) an ultrasonic controller generating an electric driving signal of defined power and frequency, and (2) a chamber of a particular geometry where the driving signal is converted into an ultrasonic standing wave field that inhibits the dispersion of cells flowing through the chamber. Perfusion culture processes using an acoustic separator typically involve continuous addition of fresh medium to the bioreactor, while cells are filtered from the harvest stream by the separator and returned to the bioreactor. Several modes of operation are available, making acoustic perfusion generally applicable for suspended animal cell culture as well as for anchorage-dependent cell lines and even for the perfused culture of plant cells. An important aspect of the system is that (in distinction to some physical sieve systems) it produces virtually no shear or hydrodynamic stress on the cells whatsoever. In contrast to other cell separation techniques, the acoustic energy constitutes a "virtual" screen or mesh, and thus provides a superior noncontact, nonfouling, nonmoving means of cell separation. Product concentration has been reported to increase up to fivefold, allowing a practical reduction of the required bioreactor volume of up to 100-fold. This fact, and that the technology has been demonstrated to allow for up to thousands of hours of continuous operation, illustrates its potential in supporting continuous bioproduction processes. One commercialized product, the AppliSens Biosep Acoustic Separator, which has been optimized for the separation and retention of cells in perfusion cell culture processes, is marketed by Applikon Biotechnology BV.

Acoustic wave separation is also being investigated in new approaches to cell clarification providing heightened efficiency and product quality. The Wave D3TM separation technology developed and patented by FloDesign Sonics, Inc. is now of interest in such applications. Its performance was recently reviewed by Merrimack Pharmaceuticals in the context of the popular depth-flow filtration (DFF), centrifugation, and TFF approaches. In the report, this nonoptimized AWS process favorably compared to a full-scale DFF GMP process [87].

Another product, the Cytoperf from APIcells, Inc., is the first commercially available fully disposable AWS device addressing single-use flow path demands in high-density perfusion culture. As a nonfouling and nonclogging retention device this disposable acoustic perfusion system becomes a powerful solution for perfusion cultures in single-use continuous or semicontinuous operations. It can also be used for cell concentration and washing, including in harvest. The Cytoperf has an adjustable acoustic frequency to minimize heat energy to be dissipated and requires no complex cooling loop (which can create a gradient temperature across the field). There is no operator-required adjustment of the acoustic waves, meaning it does not require an expert operator or adjustment protocol. This gamma-sterilized or autoclavable single-use devise employs a unique nonrecalculating loop in its movement of cells.

9.16 Conclusion

Continuous processing is a well-established and fundamental mode of modern manufacturing. Recent trends in manufacturing demands synergize with many of the single-use and continuous biomanufacturing values and features. The recent heightened interest in CB is coincident with the maturing of SU manufacturing, and a growing number of biopharmaceutical companies currently employ some CB-enabling and/or SU operations. CB and SU technology provide manufacturers with many complementary benefits. CB processes have greatly simplified production trains and inherently facilitate application of closed processing approaches to individual operations and even processes. CB also provides such benefits as shortening the process duration and reducing handling of intermediates. These features complement the operational efficiencies of SU systems, contributing to a greatly reduced cumulative processing time and personnel activity in production. The modularity and integral gamma irradiation sterility of SU systems combined with the reduced footprint, simplicity, and sustained operation of CB yield significant promise for the future. Primarily, industry innovators are now developing vertically integrated, closed, and disposable continuous upstream bioproduction systems. However, we can also envision in the near future such systems implemented in flexible modular skids within unclassified "ballroom" CNC suites. These are envisioned as employing so-called "pod" technology featuring fully integrated scheduling and management of

- Raw material supply
- Media and buffer preparation
- Equipment maintenance and calibration
- Facility, mechanical systems, and process control systems.

The ultimate goal for many is to see the SU CB process with the above features implemented in "Factories-of-the-Future" consisting of pre-engineered, turn-key, and multiproduct manufacturing facilities.

References

1 Schaber, S.D., Gerogiorgis, D.I., Ramachandran, R., Evans, J.M., Barton, P.I., and Trout, B.L. (2011) Economic analysis of integrated continuous and batch pharmaceutical manufacturing: A case study. *J. Ind. Eng. Chem.*, **50** (17), 10083–10092.

2 Konstantinov, K., Goudar, C., and Titchener-Hooker, N. (2013) ECI's Integrated Continuous Biomanufacturing Castelldefels, Spain, October, 20–24.

3 FDA (2003) PAT: A Framework for Innovative Pharmaceutical Development, Manufacturing, and Quality Assurance. FDA Guidance for Industry.

4 Langer, E.S. (2011) Trends in perfusion bioreactors: will perfusion be the next revolution in bioprocessing? *BioProcess Int.*, **9** (10), 18–22.

5 Whitford, W.G. (2012) Continued progress in continuous processing for

bioproduction. *Life Science Leader*, June, 62–64.
6 EMA (2012) Draft Guideline on Process Validation EMA/CHMP/CVMP/QWP/70278/2012-Rev1, 29 March 2012. http://www.ema.europa.eu/docs/en_GB/document_library/Scientific_guideline/2012/04/WC500125399.pdf.
7 FDA (2011) Advancing Regulatory Science at FDA: a strategic plan. http://www.fda.gov/regulatoryscience (accessed August 2011).
8 Warikoo, V., Godawat, R., Brower, K. *et al.* (2012) Integrated continuous production of recombinant therapeutic proteins. *Biotechnol. Bioeng.*, **109** (12), 3018–3029.
9 Palmer, E. (2013) GSK commits to continuous processing. FiercePharma Manufacturing, February 19, 2013. http://www.fiercepharmamanufacturing.com/story/gsk-commits-continuous-processing/2013-02-19.
10 Karen, W. (2013) Biotech firms in race for manufacturing breakthrough. *MIT Technology Review*, January 30, 2013. http://www.technologyreview.com/news/509336/biotech-firms-in-race-for-manufacturing-breakthrough.
11 BioPlan Associates, Inc. (2013) *10th Annual Report and Survey of Biopharmaceutical Manufacturing Capacity and Production*, BioPlan Associates, Inc., ISBN 978-1-934106-23-5.
12 Whitford, W.G. (2010) Single use systems as principal components in bioproduction. *BioProcess Int.*, **8** (11), 34–42.
13 Whitford, W.G. (2010) Using disposables in cell-culture-based vaccine production. *BioProcess Int.*, **8** (S4), 20–27.
14 Langer, E.S. and Rader, R.A. (2013) Advances in techniques and single-use systems are revolutionizing vaccine manufacturing. *BioPharm Int.*, **26** (8), 14–17.
15 Jones, S.D. and Ransohoff, T.C. (2011) Single use products for bioproduction: available options for cell culture and downstream processing. *Am. Pharm. Rev.*, **14** (4), 12–20.
16 Whitford, W.G. (2013) Current drivers and directions in bioprocess monitoring, *Bioresearch Online Newsletter*, July 22, 2013.
17 Bio-Process Systems Alliance (2012) FAQ 1. http://www.bpsalliance.org/faq.html.
18 Polès-Lahille, A., Richard, C., Fisch, S., Pedelaborde, D., Gerby, S., Nora Kadi, N., Perrier, V., Trieau, R., Balbuena, D., Valognes, L., and Peyret, D. (2011) Disposable bioreactors: from process development to production. *BMC Proc.*, **22** (5), S2.
19 Whitford, W.G. (2010) Single use systems as principal components in bioproduction. *BioProcess Int.*, **8** (11), 34–42.
20 Smelko, J.P., Wiltberger, K.R., Hickman, E.F., Morris, B.J., Blackburn, T.J., and Ryll, T. (2011) Performance of high-intensity fed-batch mammalian cell cultures in disposable bioreactor systems. *Biotechnol. Prog.*, **27** (5), 1358–1364.
21 Eibl, R., Kaiser, S., Lombriser, R., and Eibl, D. (2010) Disposable bioreactors: the current state-of-the-art and recommended applications in biotechnology. *Appl. Microbiol. Biotechnol.*, **86** (1), 41–49.
22 PBS Biotech, Inc. (2012) PBS Biotech: Products and Technology. PBS Biotech, Inc., Camarillo, CA pbsbiotec.com/products-technology.
23 McLeod, L. (2009) The road to a fully disposable protein purification process: single-use systems eliminate time-consuming, non–revenue-generating activities. *BioProcess Int.*, **7** (4), S4–S8.
24 Eibl, R. and Eibl, D. (2011) *Single-Use Technology in Biopharma Manufacturing*, John Wiley & Sons, Inc., Hoboken, NJ, ISBN: 978-0-470-92276-7.
25 Lajmi, A.R., Nochumson, S., and Berges, A. (2010) Impact of antibody aggregation on a flow-through anion exchange membrane process. *Biotechnol. Prog.*, **26** (6), 1654–1661.
26 Bisschops, M., Frick, L., Fulton, S., and Ransohoff, T. (2009) Single-use, continuous-countercurrent, multicolumn chromatography. *BioProcess Int.*, **7** (6), S18–S23.
27 Brown, S. (2012) The challenges of adopting single-use technology. *BioPharm Int. Suppl.*, **25** (11), s4–s8.
28 Whitford, W.G. (2012) Single-use systems in animal cell culture bioproduction, in

Antibody Mediated Drug Delivery Systems (ed. P.Y. Pathak), John Wiley & Sons, Inc., Hoboken, NJ, pp. 209–227.
29 Richardson, N.E. and Chiang, B. (2007) Equipment design and process challenges with running a perfusion process in a disposable stirred-tank: a case study. Centocor R&D, Spring House, PA, http://www.refinetech.com/media/downloads/centocor-ibc2007-nr-final.pdf.
30 Levine, H.L., Stock, R., Lilja, J.E., Gaasvik, Å., Hummel, H., Ransohoff, T.C., and Jones, S.D. (2013) Single-use technology and modular construction. *BioProcess Int.*, **11** (S4), 40–45.
31 Craig, J. and Bhella, R. (2011) A step toward standardizing films for single-use bioprocessing vessels. *BioProcess Int.*, **9** (5), S42–S46.
32 Bio-Process Systems Alliance (2012) Technical Guide on Extractables and Leachables, http://www.bpsalliance.org/guides.html.
33 Littlefield, B. (2009) Determination of extractables/leachables from integrated single-use systems. PDA Conference on Biopharmaceutical Development and Manufacturing (Munich).
34 Levine, H.L., Lilja, J.E., Stock, R., Hummel, H., and Jones, S.D. (2012) Efficient, flexible facilities for the 21st century. *BioProcess Int.*, **10** (S11), 20–30.
35 Rawlings, B. and Pora, H. (2009) A prescriptive approach to management of solid waste from single-use systems. *BioProcess Int.*, **7** (4), S40–S47.
36 Searchinger, T. (2009) Fixing a critical climate accounting error. *Science*, **326** (5952), 527–528.
37 Rawlings, B. and Pora, H. (2009) Environmental impact of single-use and reusable bioprocess systems. *BioProcess Int.*, **7** (2), 18–26.
38 Mauter, M. (2009) Environmental life-cycle assessment of disposable bioreactors. *BioProcess Int.*, **8** (4), 18–28.
39 Pietrzykowski, M., Flanagan, W., Pizzi, V., Brown, A., Sinclair, A., and Monge, M. (2011) An environmental life cycle assessment comparing single-use and conventional process technology. *BioPharm. Int.*, **24** (S1), 30–38.
40 Sinclair, A. and Monge, M. (2010) Influence of process development decisions on manufacturing costs. *BioProcess Int.*, **8** (8), 36–40.
41 Fuerst, T., Wallace, K., Gomez, P., Gambale, P., Baird, A., and Thomas, S. (2009) Ensuring biologics advanced development and manufacturing capability for the United States government: a summary of key findings and conclusions. http://oai.dtic.mil/oai/oai?verb=getRecord&metadataPrefix=html&identifier=ADA506569.
42 Robinson, J.M. (2009) An alternative to the scale-up and distribution of pandemic influenza vaccine. *BioPharm. Int.*, **22** (1), S12–S20.
43 Lee, E.K. (2010) Single-use technologies in biologics and vaccines manufacturing industries. Fourth National Conference on Clinical Research Vaccines and Biologics Summit 2010, Kuala Lumpur, Malaysia.
44 Whitford, W.G. and Fairbank, A. (2011) Considerations in scale-up of viral vaccine production. *BioProcess Int.*, **9** (S8), 16–28.
45 Whitford, W.G., Hardy, J., and Cadwell, J.J.S. (2014) Cell-based therapy supported by single-use enhanced perfusion culture. *BioProcess Int.*, **12** (S3), 26–33.
46 Spanholtz, J., Preijers, F., Tordoir, M., Trilsbeek, C., Paardekooper, J., de Witte, T., Schaap, N., and Harry Dolstra, H. (2011) Clinical-grade *generation* of active NK cells from cord blood hematopoietic progenitor cells for immunotherapy using a closed-system culture process. *PLoS One*. doi: 10.1371/journal.pone.0020740
47 Whitford, W.G. and Cadwell, J.J.S. (2011) The potential application of hollow fiber bioreactors to large-scale production. *BioPharm Int. Suppl.*, **24**, s21–s26.
48 Whitford, W.G. (2011) Improving process monitoring capabilities in SUB bioprocess development. IBC Life Sciences' Antibody Development and Production Week, 16–18 March 2011, Bellevue, WA.
49 Whitford, B. (2010) Single use systems support of PAT and QbD in bioproduction. *Life Science Leader*, **2**, 36–38.
50 Cervera, A.E., Petersen, N., Lantz, A.E., Larsen, A., and Gernaey, K.V. (2009) Review article: process sensing and

control. Application of near-infrared spectroscopy for monitoring and control of cell culture and fermentation. *Biotechnol. Prog.*, **25** (6), 1561–1581.
51 Witcher, M.F. and Odum, J. (2012) Biopharmaceutical manufacturing in the twenty-first century: the next generation manufacturing facility. *Pharm. Eng.*, **32** (2), 10–22.
52 Shanley, A. and Thomas, P. (2012) Facilities of the future. http://www.pharmamanufacturing.com/whitepapers/2012/012.html.
53 Levine, H.L. (2011) Vaccine manufacturing in the coming decade. The World Vaccine Manufacturing Congress, Lyon, France.
54 Langer, E. (2012) Biomanufacturing innovation. *BioPharm. Int.*, **25** (6), 22–25.
55 Abhinav, A., Shukla, A., Mostafa, S., Wilson, M., and Lange, D. (2012) Vertical integration of disposables in biopharmaceutical drug substance manufacturing. *BioProcess Int.*, **10** (6), 34–47.
56 Shukla, A. and Gottschalk, U. (2012) Single-use disposable technologies for biopharmaceutical manufacturing. *Trends Biotechnol.*, **31** (3), 147–154.
57 Acuna, J., Hewitt, M., Johnston, R., Kirkland, D., Shikibu, T., and Zhang, D. (2011) Modeling perfusion processes in biopharmaceutical production. *BioProcess Int.*, **9** (2), 52–58.
58 Bonham-Carter, J. and Shevitz, J.A. (2011) Brief history of perfusion biomanufacturing. *BioProcess Int.*, **9** (9), 24–30.
59 Voisard, D., Meuwly, F., Ruffieux, P.A., Baer, G., and Kadouri, A. (2003) Potential of cell retention techniques for large-scale high density perfusion culture of suspended mammalian cells. *Biotechnol. Bioeng.*, **82** (7), 751–765.
60 Pollock, J., Ho, S.V., and Farid, S.S. (2013) Fed-batch and perfusion culture processes: economic, environmental, and operational feasibility under uncertainty. *Biotechnol. Bioeng.*, **110** (1), 206–219.
61 Langer, E.S. (2011) Perfusion bioreactors are making a comeback, but industry misperceptions persist. *BioProcess. J.*, **9** (2), 49–52.
62 Kuystermans, D. and Al-Rubeai, M. (2011) Bioreactor systems for producing antibody from mammalian cells, in *Cell Culture Engineering, Antibody Expression and Production* (ed. M. Al-Rubeai), Springer, New York, NY, pp. 25–52.
63 Dhinakar, S., Kompala, D., and Ozturk, S.S. (2006) Optomization of high cell density perfusion bioreactors, in *Cell Culture Technology for Pharmaceutical and Cell-Based Therapies* (ed. S. Ozturk), Taylor & Francis, Boca Raton, FL, pp. 387–411.
64 Whitford, W.G. (2013) Supporting continuous processing with advanced single-use technologies. *BioProcess Int.*, **11** (4 Suppl.), 46–52.
65 Whitford, W.G. (2013) Impact of single-use technology on continuous processing, in *Continuous Bioprocessing Current Practice & Future Potential* (ed. J. Bonham-Carter), Refine Technology, pp. 55–63.
66 Whitford, W.G. (2013) Single-use technology supporting upstream continuous bioprocessing. ECI's Integrated Continuous Biomanufacturing, Castelldefels, Spain.
67 (2014) DHX Single-use heat exchanger. http://www.asisus.com/life-sciences/bioprocessing-products/heat-transfer (July 16, 2014).
68 Weber, A., Husemann, U., Chaussin, S., Adams, T., De Wilde, D., Gerighausen, S., Greller, G., and Fenge, C. (2013) Development and qualification of a scalable, disposable bioreactor for GMP-compliant cell culture. *BioProcess Int.*, **11** (4), 6–17.
69 Whitford, W.G. (2013) Single use technology supporting the comeback of continuous bioprocessing. *Pharm. Bioprocess.*, **1** (3), 249–253.
70 Refine Technology (2013) www.refinetech.com/product-technology.php (January 6, 2013).
71 SAW Instruments GmbH (2013) http://saw-instruments.com/products/samx.php (January 6, 2013).
72 Flownamics® (2013) www.flownamics.com/products_segflow.php (January 6, 2013).
73 Carvell, J. (2013) Insights into monitoring changes in the viable cell density and cell

physiology using scanning, multifrequency dielectric spectroscopy. 2nd Biotechnology World Congress, 18–21, 2013, Dubai, UAE.

74 Quattroflow-4400 (2013) Single Use http://www.psgdover.com/en/quattroflow/catalogue/qf-4400-series (January 6, 2013).

75 Whitford, W.G. (2012) Single-use bioreactor flexibility reduces risk, costs, and delays in bioproduction. Biosimilars and Single-Use Bioreactors, London, UK.

76 Whitford, W.G. (2012) Single-use systems support continuous processing in bioproduction. *PharmaBioWorld*, **10** (10), 40–52.

77 Whitford, W.G. (2013) Single-use systems support continuous processing in bioproduction. World Biopharm Forum, Continuous Processing in Biopharmaceutical Manufacturing, Robinson College, Cambridge, UK.

78 Chalk, S., Probst, S., Green, K., Moser, R., Urbanski, F., Zicaro, M., Smock, P., Pranzo, L., Dooley, L., and McDuff, P. (2011) New challenges to the cleanroom paradigm for multi-product facilities. *BioPharm Int.*, **24** (8), 44–65.

79 ISPE (2010 *Risk-Based Manufacture of Pharmaceutical Products: A Guide to Managing Risks Associated with Cross-Contamination*, vol. 7, International Society for Pharmaceutical Engineers, Tampa, FL.

80 Langer, E.S. (2011) Better upstream technologies. *BioPharm Int.*, **24** (6), 24.

81 Bonham-Carter, J. (2013) Implementing continuous processing in a single-use facility of the future. Second Biotechnology World Congress, Dubai, UAE.

82 Plješa, T. (2013) Single use technologies in bacterial vaccines production: current state of the art and future directions. VIC Congress Vaccines: Formulation, Development, Manufacturing and Novel Production Techniques, Brussels, Belgium.

83 Warnock, J.N., Bratch, K., and Al-Rubeai, M. (2005) Packed bed bioreactors, in *Bioreactors for Tissue Engineering* (ed. J. Chaudhuri), Springer, New York, NY, pp. 87–113.

84 Cadwell, J.J. (2013) Novel large-scale bioreactor supports continuous manufacturing. Second Biotechnology World Congress, Dubai, UAE.

85 Whitford, W.G. and Cadwell, J.J.S. (2009) Interest in hollow-fiber perfusion bioreactors is growing. *BioProcess Int.*, 7 (9), 54–63.

86 Whitford, W.G. and Cadwell, J.J.S. (2011) The potential application of hollow fiber bioreactors to large-scale production. *BioProcess Int.*, **24** (5), s21–s26.

87 Rozembersky, J. (2013) Merrimack pharmaceutical evaluating acoustic wave separation for Mab harvest CHO cell clarification. IBC's Bioprocess International Conference and Exhibition, Boston, MA, USA.

10
Multicolumn Countercurrent Gradient Chromatography for the Purification of Biopharmaceuticals

Thomas Müller-Späth and Massimo Morbidelli

10.1
Introduction to Multicolumn Countercurrent Chromatography

These days, many downstream purification processes of biopharmaceuticals are based on a sequence of two or more chromatography steps, run in discontinuous, single column mode, also referred to as batch chromatography. The first chromatography step is generally called the capture step while additional chromatography steps are called polishing steps. Batch chromatography can be either run in bind/elute mode with the product adsorbing on the stationary phase and the impurities passing through the chromatographic bed, or in flow-through mode with the impurities adsorbing on the stationary phase and the product passing through. A concentration increase of the product is only possible with bind/elute chromatography. The purpose of the capture step is the concentration of the product and the removal of a large part of the non–product-related impurities. Polishing steps are generally employed for removal of product-related impurities, such as aggregates or host cell DNA, and are run either in bind/elute mode or in flow-through mode.

Multicolumn countercurrent chromatography is capable of improving the performance of many chromatographic batch separations; however, the right process has to be selected for the right purpose. In capture applications, improvements can be expected through multicolumn countercurrent chromatography if the product exhibits a broad, diffuse breakthrough curve; in polishing applications improvements can be expected for "difficult" separations, where product and impurities partially overlap in the corresponding chromatogram. Obviously the shape of the breakthrough curve and the "difficulty" of the separation depend on a number of parameters and constraints. A rough estimate can be obtained by the following considerations for batch chromatography that are summarized in the mathematical expression in Equation 10.1: The volume of feed to be purified by chromatography, V_{feed}, and the transit time for the downstream step, t_{transit}, (i.e., the time available to process a certain amount of feed material, e.g., a harvest batch) are given. Also, the batch linear feed flow rate,

Continuous Processing in Pharmaceutical Manufacturing, First Edition. Edited by Ganapathy Subramanian.

u_{feed}, is known. From small-scale experiments, feed time, t_{feed}, and cycle time, t_{cycle}, of a single run are known. From these constraints the required column diameter d can be estimated. In this regard it is important to identify the feed duration in comparison to the duration of a typical batch experiment:

$$\frac{V_{\text{feed}}}{t_{\text{transit}}} = u_{\text{feed}} \times \frac{\pi d^2}{4} \times \frac{t_{\text{feed}}}{t_{\text{cycle}}} \times n \times \frac{1}{1000} = \frac{\text{Prod} \times V_{\text{col}}}{c_{\text{feed}} \times Y} \times n \tag{10.1}$$

With

$$\text{Prod} = \frac{u_{\text{feed}} \times \frac{\pi d^2}{4} \times c_{\text{feed}} \times t_{\text{feed}} \times Y}{V_{\text{col}} \times t_{\text{cycle}}} \tag{10.2}$$

With V_{feed}: [l] volume of feed to be processed by downstream operation; t_{transit} [h]: transit time, the time available to process the entire feed volume; u_{feed} [cm h^{-1}]: linear feed flow rate (average feed flow rate); d[cm]: column inner diameter; t_{feed} [h]: time during which the feed is loaded onto the column; t_{cycle} [h]: duration of the chromatographic run (cycle); n [-]: number of cycles run within transit time; Prod [g l^{-1} h^{-1}]: productivity; c_{feed} [g l^{-1}]: feed concentration; Y [%]: Yield.

Constraints: $n \times t_{\text{cycle}} \leq t_{\text{transit}}$, $u \leq u_{\max}$, $t_{\text{feed}} \leq t_{\text{cycle}}$.

From Equation 10.1, a few important aspects are highlighted here regarding the "difficulty" of the separation. In polishing applications, the separation of product and impurities can be generally improved by increasing the separation (cycle) time, turning in a "difficult" separation into a "less difficult" one. However, this needs to be balanced by a larger column diameter or feed time to achieve the same volumetric throughput. There are manufacturing constraints with respect to maximum column diameters. Today in industry maximum column diameters are 100–200 cm. Thus, by prolonging the cycle time the productivity decreases since the same amount of material is processed using a larger resin volume. Increasing the feed time (i.e., the load) generally leads to a worse separation.

The same holds true for the case where the feed duration or the flow rate are decreased. Both factors generally lead to an improvement of the separation but lower the productivity.

Summarizing these considerations, there is a tradeoff between productivity and separation or purity.

In capture chromatography there is a tradeoff between the sharpness of the breakthrough curve (caused by mass transfer effects) and the productivity. Decreased loading flow rates lead to sharper breakthrough curves but lower the productivity by requiring larger columns.

Taking into account the aforementioned productivity considerations and manufacturing constraints, in practice many separations cannot be modified to the point where they are not "difficult" anymore/where the breakthrough curve shape is rectangular. For these processes, multicolumn countercurrent chromatography represents the optimal solution.

Figure 10.1 shows a schematic guideline for the selection of the optimal chromatography process (in terms of productivity) for the most common

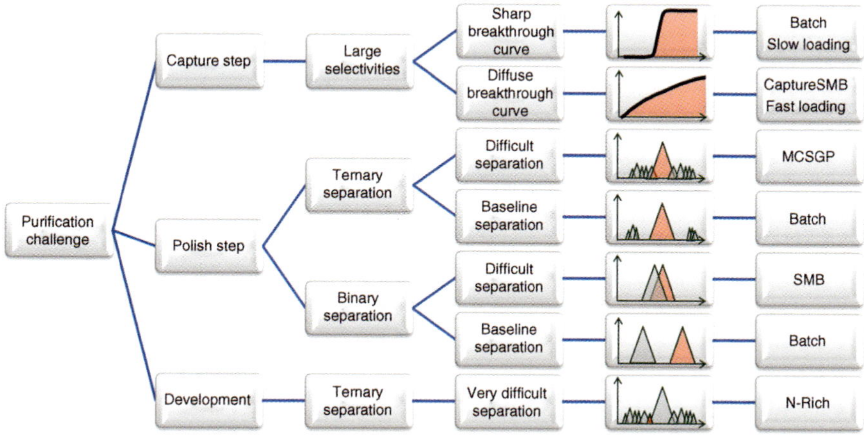

Figure 10.1 Decision tree for the selection of the optimal downstream process.

chromatography challenges. The schematic chromatograms illustrate the different cases that are encountered in downstream processing.

In the case of the capture step, sharp or diffuse breakthrough curves may occur. In case of sharp breakthrough curves, batch chromatography is the method of choice. In case of diffuse breakthrough curves, multicolumn sequential loading processes are optimal.

In binary and ternary separation polishing applications, where baseline separation is present, batch chromatography is the optimal process delivering product with maximum yield and purity. In difficult ternary separations, where the product of interest is overlapping with closely eluting impurities in the front and in the tail and is a major component compared to the closely eluting impurities, the MCSGP (multicolumn countercurrent solvent gradient purification) process is the optimal separation process.

For very difficult ternary separations in a manufacturing scenario (where the product of interest is a minor component compared to the closely eluting impurities) also the MCSGP process is the optimal choice. If only relatively small amounts of product are required for characterization purposes and the product recovery is not of primary importance, the N-Rich process presents a better option than the MCSGP process. However, the N-Rich process is not ideal for manufacturing purposes since, in contrast to MCSGP, it does not reach a cyclic steady state.

In difficult binary separations where the product of interest is overlapping with closely eluting impurities in the front or in the tail and the separation can be run under isocratic conditions, the four-zone or three-zone simulated moving bed (SMB) process is the optimal separation process. Four-zone or three-zone SMB is also applicable for pseudoternary separations where the product is overlapping with impurities in the front or in the tail and the remaining impurities are baseline-separated on the respective other side of the product peak.

Thus summarizing, multicolumn processes are beneficial in the capture step in case of a diffuse breakthrough curve and in polishing steps when an overlap between the product and the impurities is present.

The CaptureSMB, MCSGP, SMB, and N-Rich processes will be presented next.

10.2 Introduction to Multicolumn Simulated Moving Bed (SMB) Chromatography

In countercurrent chromatography, mobile and stationary phases are moved in opposite directions relative to each other. In other thermal separation processes, like distillation or extraction, a continuous mode of operation with continuous flow of both phases is common. In chromatography, while it is straightforward to generate a continuous flow of liquid, it is problematic from an engineering point of view to continuously move the solid stationary phase in order to implement a "true moving bed" (TMB). In practice the chromatographic bed is split into multiple columns of identical size and the movement of the stationary phase is realized in steps with the columns maintaining their position for a certain period of time before moving to the next position. Thus, since the stationary phase movement occurs in increments and is only simulated. This concept is called simulated moving bed [1,2]. Physical movement of the columns can be realized for instance by mounting the columns in a revolver as demonstrated in the cSEP and iSEP processes [1]. However, in most cases, instead of actually moving the columns, the column inlets are switched to the next column with the same effect. In terms of hardware, column inlet switching can be achieved by changing the flow path by means of valves, avoiding the use of special hardware and allowing for greater flexibility with regards to individual switching times than a revolver-type setup [1].

It is obvious that for simulated movement of the stationary phase, and thus for countercurrent chromatography, at least two columns are required. Thus, in the absence of TMB chromatography, today countercurrent chromatography processes are based on the simulated moving bed concept and always use at least two columns. With regard to the fluid path, the columns can be run either in interconnected mode where a mobile phase stream exiting one column is supplied to another column, or in batch mode where the columns are supplied with mobile phase independently. In case where multicolumn countercurrent chromatography is used with three or more columns, interconnected and batch states may be present at the same time.

Historically, the four-zone SMB process (Figure 10.2) for binary separations was the first multicolumn process to be introduced to the pharmaceuticals production in the 1990s [3]. It was very successfully applied to the separation of chiral compounds with two enantiomers, which represent a difficult binary

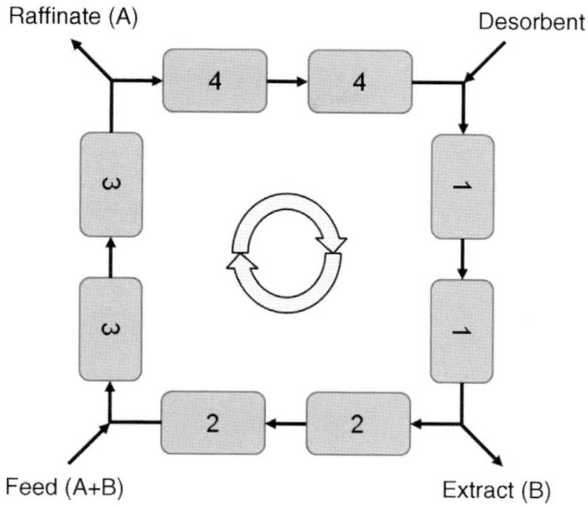

Figure 10.2 Schematic of an eight-column four-zone SMB. Each zone comprises two columns. The circular arrow indicates the direction of port switching and the remaining arrows represent liquid flows.

separation according to Figure 10.1. Improvements of up to factor 10 in productivity have been reported for a chiral separation in comparison with batch chromatography, accompanied by up to 80% reduction in solvent consumption [4]. Four-zone SMB has successfully been scaled up to large-scale production (see case study in [5]). Despite these advantages, four-zone SMB has never found entry in biopharmaceuticals production, which is mainly due the following limitations: four-zone SMB cannot perform difficult ternary separations, which are very common in biopharmaceutical production, and it is not capable of running linear gradients, which are required to reproducibly separate biomolecules. The option of running two 4-zone SMBs in series (SMB cascade) performing two binary separations in a row to obtain a ternary separation have also not found applications in biopharmaceutical manufacturing due to high dilution of the product potentially requiring an intermediate concentration step and the persistent incapability of running linear gradients. Gradient capabilities are not required in size exclusion chromatography (SEC) allowing for potential applicability of SMB. An interesting concept of applying SEC-SMB has been presented by Park *et al.* for the matrix-assisted refolding of protein from solubilized inclusion bodies [6]. Thereby the countercurrent movement of stationary and mobile phase is used to achieve high refolding yield of the target protein at significantly reduced refolding buffer consumption compared to the batch refolding process.

In the following, different countercurrent chromatography processes are presented according to their applicability in biopharmaceuticals production.

10.3 Capture Applications

10.3.1 Introduction

The purpose of the capture step in the downstream processing of biopharmaceuticals is the removal of non–product-related impurities and the concentration of the product. Typically the process has to deal with large volume streams from the upstream fermentation. Therefore, typically stationary phases with high capacities for the target molecule and large particle diameters are used. Large particle diameters exhibit low backpressure at high flow rate allowing for high throughput. On the other hand, large particles lead to increased mass transfer phenomena translating into fronting and tailing of the internal product profiles in the columns. For chromatographic breakthrough (BT) curves, increased mass transfer effects lead to shallower BT curves [6]. Because of these effects it is important to distinguish among the static binding capacity (SBC), corresponding to the maximum binding capacity and the dynamic binding capacity (DBC), which corresponds to the capacity under flow conditions. DBC values are frequently used as a measure to compare resin capacities and different standards are used, for example, 1% DBC values or 10% DBC values. These values refer to the amount of product that has been loaded onto the column when the value of 1 or 10%, respectively, of the feed concentration has been reached at the column outlet.

In single-column chromatography, DBC values are used as indicators for the column load. Exceeding the load corresponding to 1% DBC is generally not desired in order to minimize product losses. In fact, in order to account for resin degradation over time it is common practice to load the column only up to 80 or 90% of the load that corresponds to 1% DBC (10–20% load safety margin). This loading restriction entails that a large fraction of the SBC remains unused during column loading.

Using multicolumn countercurrent chromatography, the capacity utilization can be drastically increased. During the loading step of the multicolumn capture process, at least two columns are interconnected and loaded in series. Thereby the product breaking through from the first column is captured in a second column. The first column is loaded up to high breakthrough values, for instance up to 70% DBC [7]. Consequently, the capacity of the first column is used to a large extent and values of 90% or larger of the SBC have been reported [8]. The increased capacity utilization decreases resin costs and increases productivity. In the case of monoclonal antibody (mAb) capture using protein A affinity, 40% resin cost reduction and up to 40% productivity increase have been found [7,9].

Figure 10.3 schematically illustrates the concept of increasing stationary phase capacity utilization by sequential capture processes. In the following, we assume that the x-axis shows all elution volumes after subtraction of the dead volume, that is, the elution volume of unretained target compound. In Figure 10.3 the area A represents the mass that can be loaded on a single column before

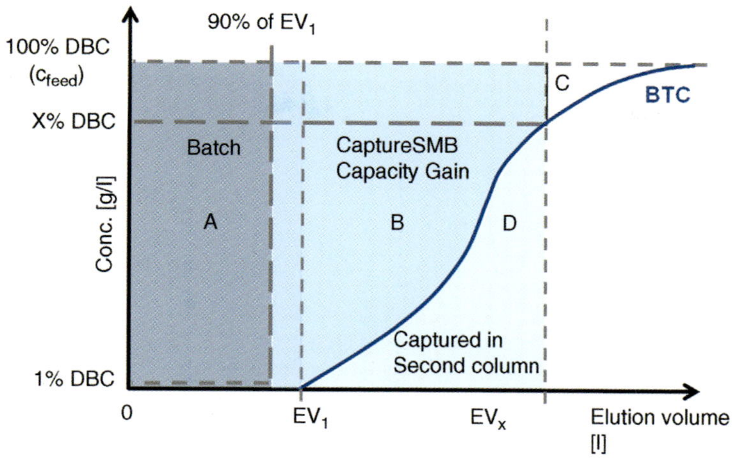

Figure 10.3 Schematic illustration of a breakthrough curve. EV_1, EV_X: Elution volumes corresponding to 1% feed concentration (1% DBC), and X% feed concentration, respectively (X% DBC). The elution volume value of 90% of the elution volume EV_1 is also indicated schematically.

reaching the 1% DBC value. On the right-hand side the area is limited by the volume of 90% of EV1, whereby EV1 is the elution volume corresponding to 1% DBC. As said, the 90% is a loading safety factor accounting for column aging. When loading two columns in series until reaching a desired breakthrough value of X% of the feed concentration, the upstream column contains the additional mass corresponding to area B and the downstream column contains the mass corresponding to area D in Figure 10.3. The total area $A+B+C$ corresponds to the static capacity. Thus, the capacity utilization of batch capture chromatography is $A/(A+B+C)$ and the capacity utilization of CaptureSMB is $(A+B)/(A+B+C)$ according to Figure 10.3. An important consequence of these findings is that in single-column chromatography, the DBC determines the effective column loading and the SBC is not relevant. In contrast, in CaptureSMB the capacity utilization can be extended closer to the static capacity and therefore the static capacity is more important.

The increased capacity utilization of CaptureSMB leads to significant resin cost savings, which is particularly relevant in the case of capture with expensive affinity materials with low resin lifetime. In this regard, Protein A affinity chromatography plays a special role since the stationary phases have been optimized within the last decades for high capacity and caustic stability, allowing for running Protein A columns for hundreds of cycles without significant loss of capacity. In contrast, most other affinity materials that are available today have much lower capacity and caustic stability making capacity utilization improvement even more important.

In sequential loading processes the number of columns required to accommodate the internal product concentration profile (from zero close to the feed concentration) is dependent on the stationary phase, the product to be captured, the bed height, and the flow velocity. In the case of monoclonal antibody capture using Protein A chromatography two sequentially loaded columns are sufficient [7–9] while for other cases like the capture of an enzyme using hydrophobic interaction chromatography (HIC), the use of three sequentially loaded columns has been reported [8].

10.3.2 Process Principle

In the following the sequential loading process is explained for a twin-column sequential loading process (CaptureSMB), see Figure 10.4 [9].

The process comprises interconnected phases I1, I2, where the columns are loaded and washed sequentially, and batch phases B1, B2, where the formerly upstream column is washed, eluted, and regenerated, and the formerly downstream column is continued to be loaded. The elution may be achieved through a step gradient but also linear gradients are possible.

In the subsequent interconnected phase the regenerated column is placed in the downstream position and the previously loaded column is placed in the upstream position.

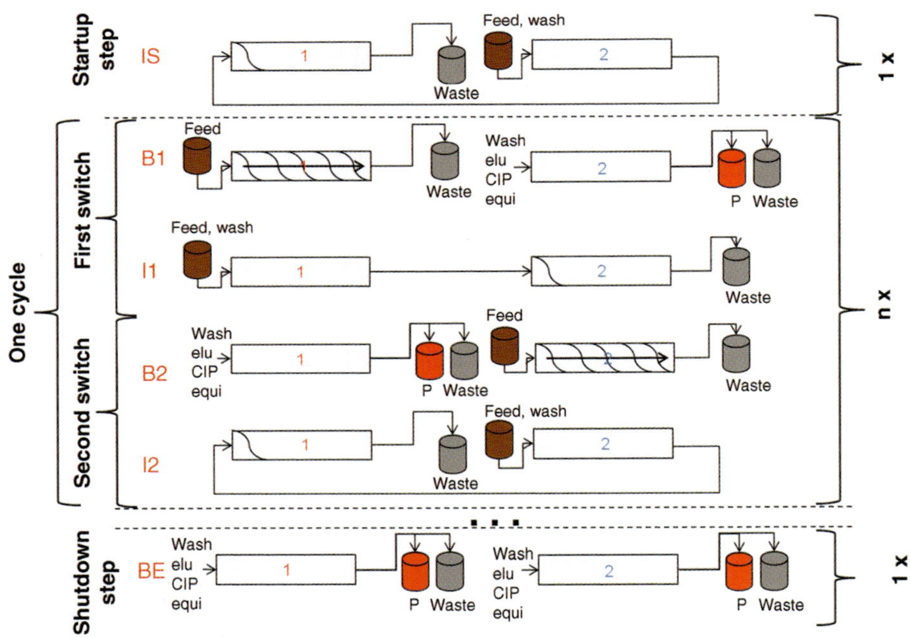

Figure 10.4 Schematic illustration of the twin-column CaptureSMB process. The letters indicate the following: "IS" – Interconnected startup phase, "B1" – first batch phase, "I1" – first interconnected phase, "B2" – second batch phase, "I2" – second interconnected phase, "BE" – final batch elution phase, "Wash" – washing buffer, "elu" – elution buffer, "CIP" – CIP buffer, "equi" – equilibration buffer, "P" – product.

The process applies a dual loading flow rate strategy to optimize the overall process performance. In the interconnected phase the columns are operated at maximum possible feed flow rate, while in the batch phase the column that previously was in the downstream position is continued to be loaded at a lower flow rate. The lower feed flow rate ensures that no breakthrough of feed from the single column occurs while the other column performs the tasks of washing, recovery, and regeneration (wash, elute, clean-in-place (CIP), re-equilibration in Figure 10.4). Moreover, the lower feed flow rate leads to an improved dynamic capacity for the batch feeding step. In twin-column CaptureSMB the duration of the batch phases B1 and B2 is determined by the overall duration of the washing, recovery, and regeneration tasks. An increased duration of these tasks may lead to a very low loading flow rate in the batch phase. However, the advantages of the process versus batch chromatography in terms of capacity utilization persist, since these are due to the sequential loading in the interconnected phase where the upstream column is loaded to X% DBC (X is typically in the range of 60–90). In the interconnected step, following the loading, the columns are washed sequentially to adsorb unbound protein on the downstream column. The washing, recovery, and regeneration tasks are identical in batch and in CaptureSMB chromatography except for the first washing step. In CaptureSMB the first washing step is split into two parts with the first part of the washing step taking place as interconnected wash (typically three-column volumes) during the phases I1, I2 following the load and the second part taking place in the subsequent batch phase. The stationary phase and buffers are the same as in batch capture chromatography.

A closer look at the internal chromatograms, that is, UV signals recorded at the outlet of each column of a CaptureSMB run for mAb purification at cyclic steady state helps in visualizing the process principle (see Figure 10.5, data reported in Ref. [9]). The disconnected phases B1 and B2 and interconnected phases I1 and I2 are clearly distinguishable. Toward the end of the interconnected phase the UV signal of the upstream column increases from the elevated baseline that corresponds to the impurities in the flow through. The rise of the UV signal is due to the mAb breaking through from the upstream column. The downstream column does not exhibit this rise indicating that the mAb entering the downstream column is fully adsorbed. Process analytical technologies (PAT) for monitoring and process control based on breakthrough data has been presented by Warikoo *et al.* and Godawat *et al.* [8,10] and validated for the twin-column CaptureSMB process.

Processes with more columns are based on the same principle that is illustrated in Figure 10.3 and feature a mix of interconnected and batch states. Three ways of running a three-column capture process (3C-PCC) are reported in the literature [7,8,10]. It was found that in sequential loading processes a washing step in the interconnected phase following the interconnected loading phase is important to ensure a high process yield. The interconnected washing step is typically 3–5 single-column volumes. The washing step is important to wash unbound biomolecules and molecules desorbing due to isotherm effects from

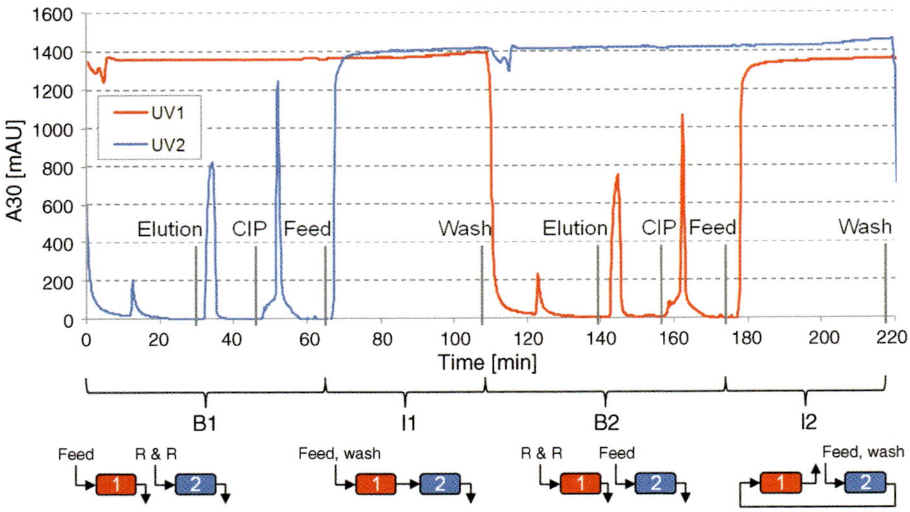

Figure 10.5 Chromatograms of a batch capture cycle (left) and a CaptureSMB cycle (right) in cyclic steady state. The markers indicate the beginning of feed, wash, elution and CIP phases, respectively. In the first interconnected phase of the process column 1 (red UV signal) is upstream of column 2 (red UV profile) and in the second interconnected phase vice versa. The small disturbances in the UV1 at the beginning of the cycle and UV2 at the beginning of the second switch are due to the interconnected phase wash. The small process flow sheets at the bottom of the figure show the fluid connections of the columns.

the interstitial void volume of the upstream column into the downstream column for re-adsorption.

It is worth mentioning that theoretical optimizations of multicolumn countercurrent capture processes may lead to optimal column bed heights below 7–10 cm. These bed heights are difficult to pack in large scale, and it is recommended to include minimal bed height constraints of 10 cm bed height or larger in optimization considerations. It was shown that under these constraints for mAb capture using Protein A the twin-column capture process was equal or better in terms of productivity than setups with three or more columns [9].

Equipment for countercurrent chromatography capture processes is available from a number of suppliers. Two-column equipment is available from ChromaCon (CaptureSMB process), three-column equipment from GE (3C-PCC) process, and equipment with more columns from Tarpon, Novasep, and Semba.

10.3.3 Application Examples

For production of mAbs, purification platforms have been developed based on Protein A affinity capture followed by one or two additional polishing steps. With sequential loading processes the performance of the Protein A capture step can be improved without changing the stationary phases or buffers used in the downstream process.

The application of multicolumn sequential loading processes for mAb capture has been evaluated by Genentech and Genzyme/Sanofi. In both cases a three-column setup was used (with at most two columns loaded in series) [7,8,10]. Genzyme/Sanofi have also evaluated a four-column setup for the capture of enzymes using pseudo-affinity and HIC stationary phases [8]. Godawat *et al.* have also reported design criteria for three-column processes and the use of a UV-based process control strategy [8]. They carried out a comparison between a batch process and the multicolumn process showing significant advantages of the multicolumn process in terms of column size reduction (factor 23–35), resin capacity utilization (1.3- to 3.3-fold), and buffer savings (20–70%). This analysis included process integration with continuous fermentation instead of batch fermentation, which contributed to a large extent to the savings.

Mahajan *et al.* have evaluated the improvements of the single processing step alone [7]. They concluded that the multicolumn chromatography and modified batch processes have the potential to save approximately 40% on the cost of resin, buffer, and processing time.

A twin-column sequential loading process, CaptureSMB, was evaluated by Müller-Späth *et al.* for mAb capture using Protein A affinity chromatography and similar improvements were found in terms of resin capacity utilization and productivity (up to 30–40%) [9]. The advantages were larger for increased interconnected state feed flow rates, which is expected as the dynamic binding capacity of the stationary phase decreases with increasing flow rate. This affects the batch chromatography load to a much greater extent than the CaptureSMB load.

All authors have reported comparable product quality of sequential loading processes and batch processes [7–9].

Cost modeling revealed 30–40% resin cost savings for three different scenarios (proof-of-concept, clinical phase III, and commercial manufacturing) [9]. A detailed cost modeling analysis for a 3C-PCC process was carried out by Pollock *et al.* [11] showing savings of 30% in the proof-of-concept scenario, while savings in phase III and commercial phases scenarios were lower. This was attributed to the fact that in commercial scale the full lifetime of the stationary phase is exploited while the resin is discarded after a few cycles in the proof-of-concept scenario, leading to high relative resin costs [$ resin cost/g product] so that resin cost savings by sequential loading processes have a larger impact.

10.4 Polishing Applications

10.4.1 Introduction

One of the major tasks in chromatographic polishing applications is the clearance of product-related impurities, such as protein fragments, isoforms, or

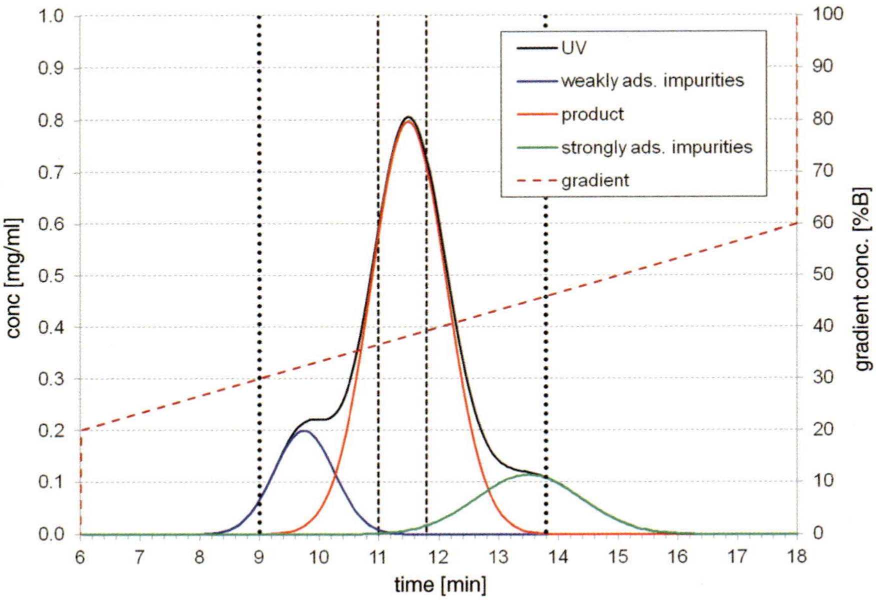

Figure 10.6 Schematic illustration of a typical bioseparation problem where the product (P) is flanked by weakly (W) and strongly (S) adsorbing impurities with similar adsorptive properties. The overlapping regions of product and impurities are clearly visible. The dashed vertical lines confine an interval where the product has high purity while the dotted vertical lines confine an interval that includes the entire product.

aggregates. A typical ternary polishing separation challenge is illustrated in Figure 10.6 (simulation data). The figure shows simulation data that mimic a real situation. A representative UV signal is shown as it would be recorded by the UV detector in a preparative batch chromatography run. The signal was mathematically deconvoluted in order to visualize the weakly adsorbing impurities W, the product P and the strongly adsorbing impurities S. In practice the W, P, S concentrations could be obtained by fractionation and offline analysis. The overlap between W/P in the front and P/S in the tail of the profile are clearly visible in the deconvoluted signal, indicating a "bad" separation. The dashed vertical lines in Figure 10.6 confine a narrow product fraction with high purity but low yield. The dotted lines confine a much wider fraction, including the entire product, thus corresponding to maximum yield but very low purity. This situation where high purity is possible only at the cost of yield and vice versa is called yield/purity trade-off. As outlined earlier it is detrimental to productivity to prolong the gradient to improve the separation. Also, it is detrimental to productivity to decrease the load. The overlap of product and impurities that persists after reasonable batch chromatography optimization effort inevitably leads to a yield/purity trade-off.

Multicolumn countercurrent chromatography in the form of MCSGP is the only process capable of resolving the yield/purity tradeoff, performing a ternary separation and preserving the gradient that was used in the reference batch run. The idea behind the MCSGP process is the internal reprocessing of the impure side fractions where the product and impurities overlap.

10.4.2
Multicolumn Countercurrent Solvent Gradient Purification Principle

The process principle of MCSGP is shown here for a twin-column setup in Figure 10.7. The schematic chromatogram at the bottom of Figure 10.7 represents a batch chromatogram that has been divided into different sections (vertical dashed lines) according to the tasks that are carried out in the batch chromatography run (equilibration in zone 1, feeding in zone 2, washing in zone 3, elution in zones 4–7, cleaning and re-equilibration in zone 8). The elution is subdivided into additional zones according to the elution order of W, P, and S in the chromatogram (elution of weakly adsorbing impurities W in zone 4, elution of the overlapping part W/P in zone 5, elution of pure P in zone 6, elution of the overlapping part of P/S in zone 7). In the twin-column MCSGP process these individual tasks are carried out in a similar fashion, with the decisive difference that the W/P and the P/S eluate are directed to a second column for recovery of P. Thus, the process tasks of the single-column batch process and the MCSGP process are analogous and it is possible to derive the operating parameters for MCSGP from the batch operating parameters and the corresponding chromatogram. The MCSGP process design procedure is outlined in the next chapter.

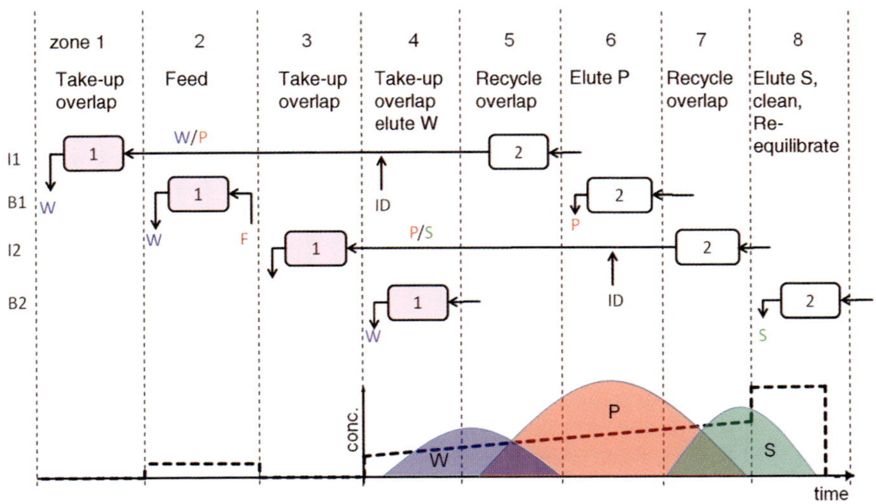

Figure 10.7 Schematic illustration of the twin-column MCSGP process principle (first switch). The dashed vertical lines separate the different MCSGP process tasks corresponding to the zones of the schematic batch chromatogram shown in the lower part of the figure. Phases I1, B1, I2, B2 are carried out sequentially.

A complete cycle of a twin-column MCSGP process comprises two "switches" with four pairs of tasks each (I1, B1, I2, B2) as illustrated in Figure 10.7. The phases in each switch are identical; the difference is only in the column position: In the first switch, column 1 is downstream of column 2 while in the second switch (not shown in Figure 10.7) column 2 is downstream of column 1. The four phases include the following tasks:

- Phase I1: The overlapping part W/P is eluted from the upstream column (zone 5), and internally recycled into the downstream column (zone 1). In between the columns, the stream is diluted inline with buffer/solvent to re-adsorb P (and overlapping W) in the downstream column. At the end of phase I1, pure product is ready for elution at the outlet of the upstream column (zone 5).
- Phase B1: Pure P is eluted and collected from the column in zone 5 (column 2 in Figure 10.4), keeping the overlapping part P/S and S in the column. At the same time, fresh feed is injected into the column in zone 2.
- Phase I2: The overlapping part P/S is eluted from the upstream column (zone 7), and internally recycled into the downstream column (zone 3). In between the columns, the stream is diluted inline with buffer/solvent to re-adsorb P in the downstream column. At the end of the step, all remaining P has been eluted from the upstream column and only S is left in the upstream column.
- Phase B2: The column in zone 8 (column 2 in Figure 10.4) is cleaned to remove S and re-equilibrated. At the same time, W is eluted from the other column in zone 4.

After having completed these tasks, the columns switch positions and in the next phase I1 (not shown in Figure 10.7), column 2 is in the downstream position (zone 1) and column 1 is in the upstream position (zone 5). At the beginning of this I1 phase, column 2 is cleaned and re-equilibrated and ready for uptake of the W/P fraction from column 1. After having completed B1, I2, and B2 for the second time the columns are returning to their original positions and one cycle has been completed. Column 1 is now clean and ready for uptake of W/P from column 2 in phase I1 (as shown in Figure 10.7).

As in other countercurrent chromatographic processes, in practice in MCSGP the column movement is simulated by connecting and disconnecting column inlets and outlets through valve switching and not by physical movement of the columns.

The process reaches a cyclic steady state, in which the amount of product withdrawn in each cycle is equal to the amount of product fed and the product quality is the same from cycle to cycle. Figure 10.8 shows startup and achievement of cyclic steady state for an example of Lysozyme purification. Through loading of an increased amount of feed in the first cycle the startup time can be significantly reduced such that the process is in cyclic steady state from the

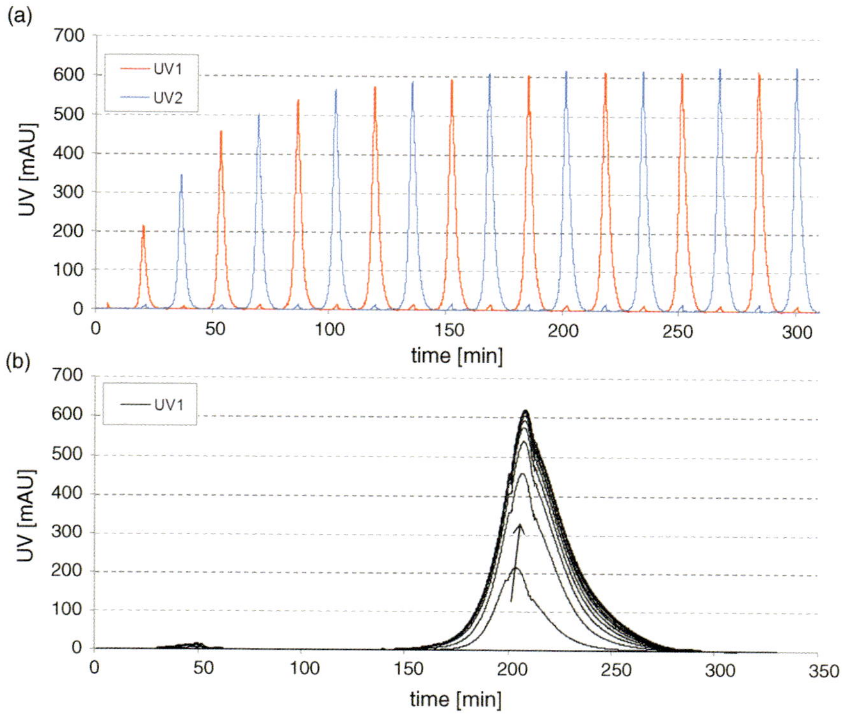

Figure 10.8 Start-up and steady state of MCSGP for Lysozyme purification. (a) Internal chromatograms measured by the UV detectors located at the outlet of each column. Each peak corresponds to a product elution. (b) Overlay of the internal chromatograms of UV1. The arrow indicates the increase in concentration from cycle to cycle until a cyclic steady state is reached where peak height and shape remain constant from cycle to cycle.

second cycle onward. By overlay of the UV signals of subsequent cycles, it can be determined if the process has reached cyclic steady state. In cyclic steady state, the UV signals of subsequent cycles match exactly and the process delivers product of constant quality. For typical applications of MCSGP, differences in bed height or packing quality can be tolerated within certain limits (approximately up to 10% bed height difference). However, it has to be ensured that the product quality is analyzed as average from both columns, that is, product collected over one complete cycle (corresponding to one product elution per column) or multiple complete cycles should be analyzed.

Although the average residence time of the product in the MCSGP process is longer than in batch chromatography, no detrimental effect on product quality has been observed or reported in the literature so far. A simulation analysis using typical MCSGP operating conditions has shown that a population of tracer product molecules is reduced to 0.01% approximately within five cycles.

10.4.3 Multicolumn Countercurrent Solvent Gradient Purification Process Design

As stated earlier, the MCSGP process operating parameters can be determined from a single column batch chromatogram. In the "design" chromatogram, from which the MCSGP operating parameters are derived, at least part of the product (20–50%) fulfills the purity specifications. If this is not the case, a new "design" batch run with improved conditions should be recorded. The regions of pure product P and the overlapping regions with weakly adsorbing impurities W/P, (phase 5 in Figure 10.7) and strongly adsorbing impurities P/S, (phase 7 Figure 10.7) have to be known approximately, for instance by offline analysis. From the analyzed batch process, MCSGP operating parameters can be determined based on the schematic shown in Figure 10.9.

The MCSGP design is done based on the previously evaluated "design" batch chromatogram along the following lines:

- The width of the zone intervals is known since the time span and the flow rate of the batch chromatogram is known. From this the volume to be delivered by the pumps to the upstream column (column 2 in Figure 10.7, phases 5, 6, and 7) is known. The volume corresponding to phase 4 is defined by the start of the gradient and the start of phase 5. Phase 8 parameters (cleaning and re-equilibration) can be chosen the same as in batch chromatography.

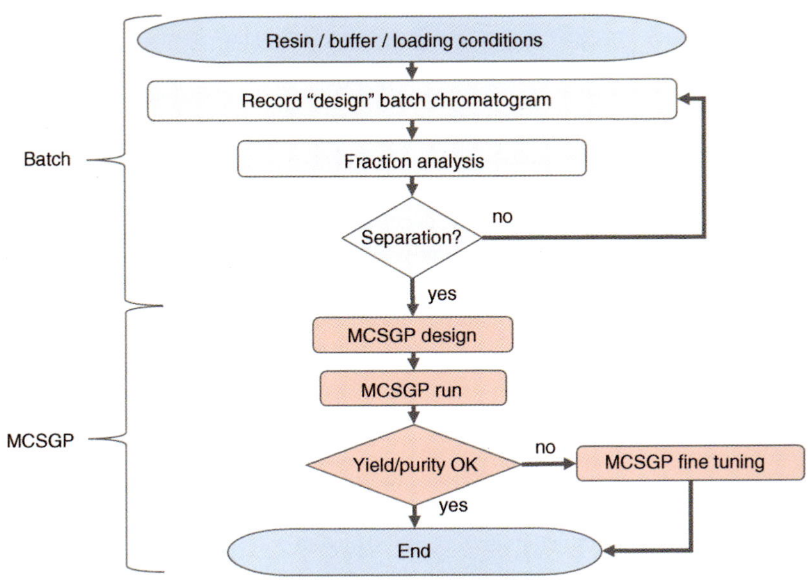

Figure 10.9 MCSGP process design schematic.

- The gradient concentrations [%B] at the start and the end of each zone are known. Therefore, the gradient to be delivered by the pump to the upstream column (column 2 in Figure 10.7, phases 5, 6, and 7) is known.
- The magnitude of the inline dilution streams in phases 1 and 3 is chosen such that the maximum concentration occurring in W/P and P/S, respectively, is diluted to the starting concentration of the gradient or to conditions corresponding to the adsorptive strength of the feed, whichever is higher.
- The amount of feed added in phase 3 corresponds to the amount of feed that is removed via the product elution window. This determines the feed volume to be added each cycle.

Thus, summarizing the process design, the procedure aims at reproducing the underlying batch chromatogram within the twin-column system with the key difference that the impure side fractions are internally recycled in MCSGP whereas they are collected and discarded in batch chromatography.

The initial operating point is designed to deliver the product with the same productivity as the underlying "design" batch chromatography run. For process optimization, further MCSGP runs are carried out in order to improve productivity for instance by increasing the load or running a steeper gradient. In batch chromatography these actions would lead to an increased overlapping of product and impurities, causing a decrease in yield for the desired purity. In contrast, the MCSGP process can afford having increased overlaps between product and impurities due to its internal recycling capabilities. Since the MCSGP can transform low-yield batch processes into high-yield process it can help speeding up process development timelines. Required product and process quality thresholds (e.g., in terms of purity, yield, productivity) can be reached much earlier using MCSGP than by optimizing the batch process. This factor can be very important in an industrial setting for both originator and biosimilar producers.

The operating parameter determination procedure has been automated in a software tool ("MCSGP wizard," ChromIQ software, ChromaCon AG, Switzerland) that allows simple MCSGP design.

10.4.4 Multicolumn Countercurrent Solvent Gradient Purification Case Study

Multicolumn countercurrent solvent gradient purification has been successfully applied in protein and peptide purifications using a variety of stationary and mobile phases including ion exchangers, hydrophobic interaction and reverse phase chromatography using aqueous buffers (proteins) and reverse phase solvents (peptides), respectively. Application examples include the purification of mAbs, of mAb isoforms, bispecific antibodies, fusion proteins, PEGylated proteins, and peptide hormones.

Historically, the first MCSGP processes were operated with six columns. Aumann *et al.* have shown the purification of Calcitonin using reverse phase chromatography using six- and three-column setups [12–14].

The isolation of mAb isoforms was shown by Müller-Späth *et al.* [15,16]. Apart from removing unwanted isoforms, antibody isoform separation is of interest for characterization purposes or potentially for production of biobetters. MCSGP can also be useful to straighten out product isoform patterns resulting from variations in upstream fermentation. This capability can be potentially of high interest for biosimilar manufacturers. An illustration of mAb isoform straightening is shown in Figure 10.10 (data from Ref. [16]) for the case of Herceptin®, a mAb manufactured by Roche for cancer treatment. Figure 10.10a shows the isoform patterns obtained by analytical cation exchange chromatograms of two different feed materials: Herceptin® obtained from the pharmacy and Herceptin®, spiked with weakly adsorbing isoforms. Figure 10.10b shows the analytical chromatograms of the product pools obtained using cation-exchange MCSGP running exactly the same operating parameters. It is obvious that the product isoform pattern is identical despite the large variations in the feed pattern.

The purification of bispecific antibodies using cation-exchange MCSGP has been shown by Müller-Späth *et al.* [17]. The purification of a bispecific antibody represents a classical ternary difficult separation since the target bispecific antibody is accompanied by a number of undesired antibody forms that are coexpressed by the host cells, for instance the parental monoclonal antibodies.

The application of MCSGP for monoclonal antibody capture from clarified cell culture harvest using a cation exchange stationary phase was demonstrated by Müller-Späth *et al.* [18] as well as the purification of a therapeutic peptide [19].

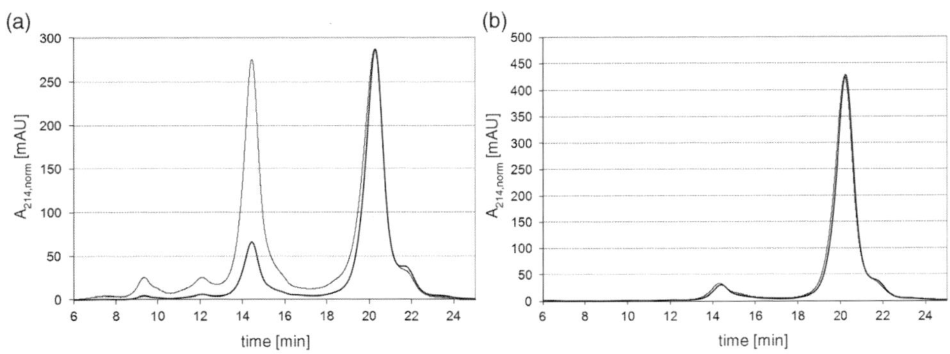

Figure 10.10 mAb isoform separation capabilities of MCSGP visualized for the case of Herceptin® using analytical cation exchange chromatograms. (a) Overlay of original Herceptin® (blue) and Herceptin® spiked with weakly adsorbing isoforms (red) chromatograms. (b) Overlay of product pools obtained using the same MCSGP operating conditions for the two feed materials.

The application of MCSGP to PEGylated protein purification is outlined in the following in greater detail. The case can be regarded as representative for a "difficult" purification of a product from product-related impurities. The purification target was mono-PEGylated α-Lactalbumin. α-Lactalbumin has a molecular weight of 14.2 kDa and an isoelectric point (pI) in the range from 4.2 to 4.5 [20]. Mono-methoxy-poly ethylene glycol-*N*-succinimidyl-propionate (mPEG-SPA) reagents of nominal molecular weights of 5000 Da were used for PEGylation via the primary amines present on Lysine to form stable amides [21]. Due to the presence of multiple accessible Lysines in the protein, mono-PEGylated, di-PEGylated, tri-PEGylated, and higher order PEGylated protein was formed. The reaction was stopped by acidification using 0.1 M HCl. Apart from the PEGylated proteins the reaction mixture also contained native, un-PEGylated protein and mPEG-SPA breakdown products.

The PEGylation reaction mixture was separated using preparative anion-exchange chromatography (Poros 50 HQ) with a load of $4\,g\,l^{-1}$ and a linear salt gradient including fractionation of the elution peak. The fractions were analyzed by size exclusion chromatography (SEC)-HPLC and product (P) and impurities were identified (see Figure 10.11). For MCSGP design, the product pool corresponding to a SEC purity of >90.0% was defined as product elution window and

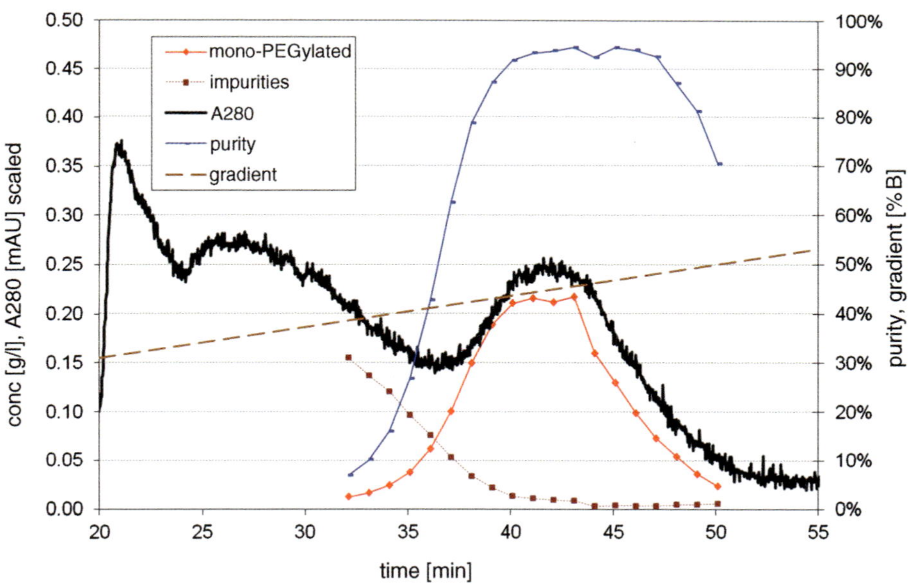

Figure 10.11 Preparative batch linear gradient run for the purification of mono-PEGylated α-Lactalbumin. The concentrations of product (mono-PEGylated) and impurities as determined by offline SEC analysis are shown as diamonds and squares, respectively. The product purity is indicated by the thin blue line. The product collection window for MCSGP is represented by a red transparent rectangle and the overlapping regions of product and impurities W/P and P/S intended for internal recycling in the MCSGP process are represented by grey transparent rectangles.

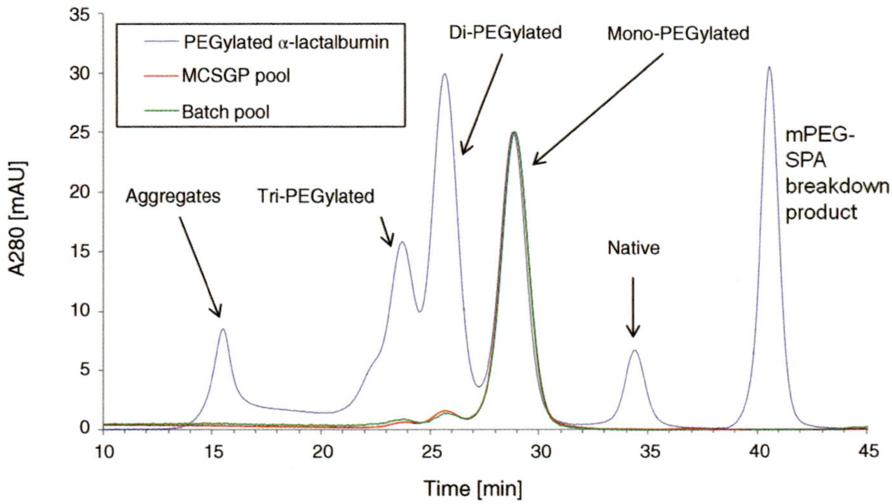

Figure 10.12 SEC chromatograms of PEGylated protein feed (blue) and product pools from batch (green), and MCSGP chromatography (red). Chromatograms were normalized for the mono-PEGylated product species.

the impure, product-containing side-fractions W/P and P/S indicated in Figure 10.11 that contained significant amounts of product were selected for internal recycling. The MCSGP process was designed according to the procedure outlined in Chapter 9 and run over multiple cycles into cyclic steady state, where MCSGP product pool fractions were collected.

The MCSGP product pool, the high purity batch pool, and the PEGylated reaction mixture were analyzed using SEC-HPLC and the resulting chromatograms are shown in Figure 10.12. The chromatograms demonstrate that the same product quality (93% purity) can be obtained using batch and MCSGP chromatography. However, the yield of the batch run was only 56% while the yield for MCSGP was 83%; so almost 50% more product could be recovered using MCSGP. A batch product pool with the same yield as MCSGP would have a purity of only 82% and include more than the double amount of impurities. Furthermore, the buffer consumption in this case was reduced by 50% using MCSGP.

The results of the comparison are summarized in Figure 10.13, where the yield/purity trade-off of batch chromatography and the simultaneous achievement of high yield and purity become evident.

The presented example additionally shows that potential benefits in process development time can be achieved through the use of MCSGP. Of course, it would be possible to produce the desired mono-PEGylated species by other means. One could genetically engineer the host cell to eliminate all but one of the relevant lysines or one could optimize the PEGylation reaction or improve the batch chromatography. However, all of these options require significant process development time.

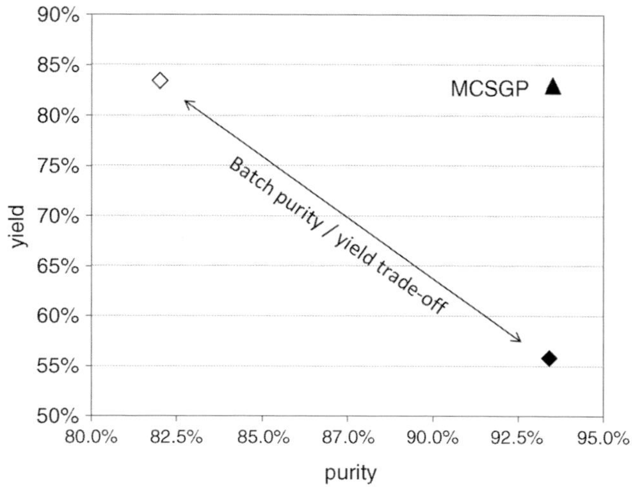

Figure 10.13 Yield/purity chart showing the results of a high-purity batch pool (full diamond), a high yield batch pool (empty diamond), and an MCSGP pool (triangle).

10.5
Discovery and Development Applications

Multicolumn countercurrent chromatography is also applicable in the case of drug identification and drug development for the isolation of minor compounds in a complex mixture. Similarly as MCSGP, the N-Rich process, developed by ChromaCon, uses the concept of internal recycling to recycle a portion of the chromatogram from one column to the other. However, the fundamental difference to MCSGP is that all fractions except the product fraction (phase 6 in Figure 10.1) are discarded and only the product fraction is internally recycled (Figure 10.14). Since the amount of product that is removed per cycle (through the discarded W/P and P/S fractions) is smaller than the amount of product that is fed, the product P accumulates within the system while the other components are removed. The duration of one cycle is similar as the duration of a batch chromatography run. Using the N-Rich process principle, enrichments of up to 1000-fold can be achieved. The enrichment comprises a simultaneous increase of the concentration and improvement of the purity. Once the process has been operated over a number of cycles and sufficient enrichment has been achieved, the product of interest is recovered through a very shallow isocratic or gradient elution with fine fractionation. The fractionation ensures the recovery of the compound of interest and potentially also neighboring compounds. The N-Rich process amplifies an entire region of the underlying "design" chromatogram; therefore, the exact position of the compound in the chromatogram does not need to be known. Since the process does not operate with maximum yield and does not reach a cyclic steady state it is not suited to continuously or periodically

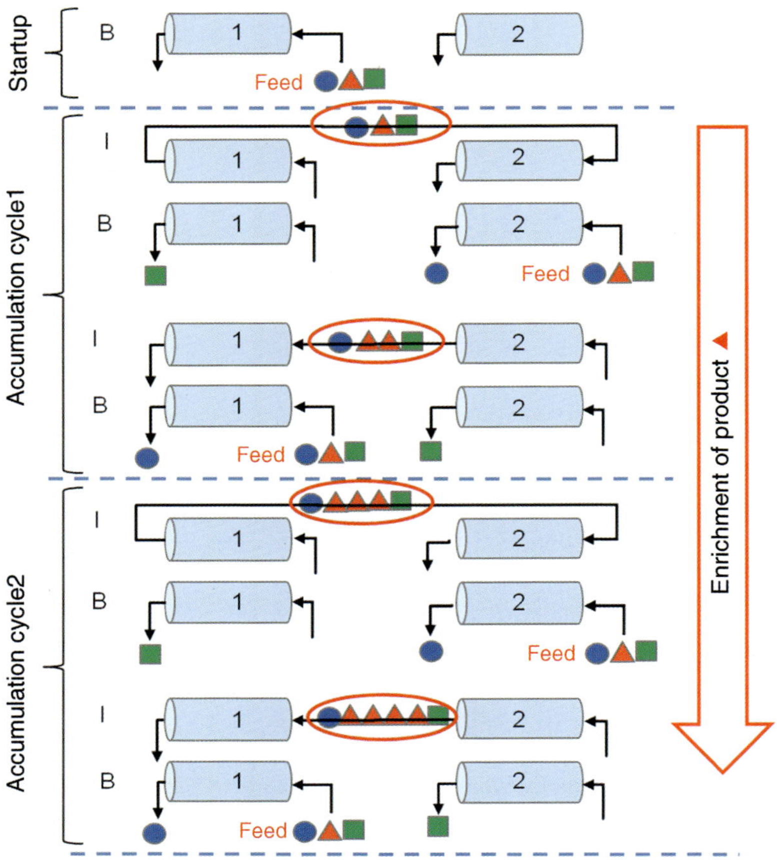

Figure 10.14 N-Rich process principle. The compound of interest (red triangles) is accumulated over multiple cycles by internal recycling from one column to the other. The re-adsorption of the product in the downstream column is ensured by inline dilution (not shown). The weakly adsorbing impurities (circles) and the strongly adsorbing impurities (squares) are removed every cycle.

manufacture a product. In fact the process is used for the one-time production of compounds of interest. Possible applications include the identification of potential drug candidates or the isolation of product-related impurities in milligram to gram amounts for characterization purposes (e.g., product isoforms). Through the N-Rich process, the effort of repeated HPLC runs, fractionation, manual handling, and pooling can be significantly reduced and replaced by a fully automated process.

The N-Rich process has been demonstrated for the isolation of product-related impurities of Fibrinopeptide A, produced by chemical synthesis [22]. Enrichment factors of 600-fold were achieved by improving the purity from 0.13% to over 80%. The concentration of the target compound was increased 10-fold.

10.6
Scale-Up of Multicolumn Countercurrent Chromatography

The scale-up of multicolumn countercurrent chromatography is straightforward since chromatography as such is a scalable technique (scale-up is usually done by increasing the column diameter) and in most cases (MCSGP, CaptureSMB) no specialized equipment is required. Existing pump, valve, and detector technology is suited for large-scale multicolumn countercurrent chromatography. The ratio of dead-volumes to column volume decreases when scaling up from the lab scale and a negative impact is not expected in that regard.

The scale-up of multicolumn countercurrent processes in pharmaceuticals production has been successfully demonstrated for four-zone SMB processes [5].

An MCSGP scale-up cost calculation has been carried out by Takizawa in collaboration with Sandoz for a biosimilar manufacturing process showing significant cost savings of the multicolumn countercurrent process [23].

Pilot and large-scale equipment for multicolumn countercurrent chromatography in biopharmaceuticals manufacturing has to be GMP-production capable, allowing for cleaning and sanitization or comprising a fully disposable presterilized fluid path. Today equipment solutions fulfilling these requirements are available or in development by various manufacturers.

10.7
Multicolumn Countercurrent Chromatography as Replacement for Batch Chromatography Unit Operations

As outlined in the previous chapters multicolumn countercurrent processes are suited for all chromatographic unit operations. Therefore, in existing or planned chromatographic downstream processes, they can be used as replacement for any batch chromatography step, thereby significantly improving productivity and process economics.

Reflecting the productivity Equation 10.2, an elevated productivity allows the following production options:

1) More product can be produced within the same timeframe and the same bed volume.
2) The same amount of product can be produced within the same timeframe using smaller columns.
3) The same amount of product can be produced using the same bed volume within a shorter time frame.

If resin costs are a key economic parameter, option (2) would be very attractive; in the case of purification of an instable product, option (3) would be most interesting.

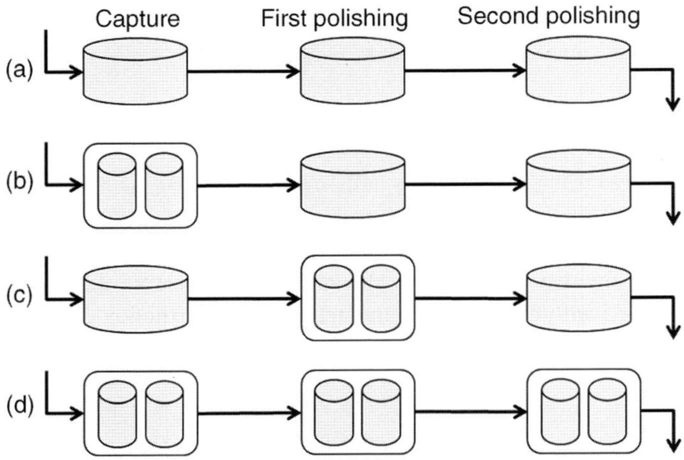

Figure 10.15 Examples for downstream processes with varying degree of multicolumn countercurrent process implementation. (a) Traditional downstream process with three batch steps. (b) Hybrid process with multicolumn countercurrent capture step and batch polishing steps. (c) Hybrid process with batch capture step, one multicolumn countercurrent polishing step and one batch polishing step. (d) Downstream process with three multicolumn countercurrent step.

When replacing batch steps by multicolumn countercurrent processes, the economic advantages of multicolumn countercurrent processes are cumulative and improve with the number of batch steps replaced. Also, hybrid processes are possible. For instance a multicolumn countercurrent capture step using an affinity stationary phase can be used instead of a batch capture step, while the polishing steps remain in batch mode. Obviously, independent of the capture step, a multicolumn countercurrent step can be used for polishing (e.g., MCSGP in Ion exchange or HIC mode). Four of the eight possible combinations of batch and multicolumn countercurrent processes for a three-chromatography step downstream process are shown in Figure 10.15. Intermediate nonchromatographic steps are omitted in the figure for the sake of simplicity.

Independent of the type of process used in the single chromatographic unit operation (batch or multicolumn countercurrent), the downstream process may be optimized by process integration. In traditional downstream processing the entire product resulting from a single unit operation is pooled and processed further not before completion of the last run of the unit operation. Thus, the later unit operation has to wait for all runs of the earlier unit operation to be completed before starting, causing a high degree of inactivity. By process integration the scheduling of the chromatographic steps is improved such that the later chromatographic unit operation starts as soon as enough material is available from the earlier unit operation. Consequently also the size of the intermediate hold tanks can be reduced or hold tanks can be even completely eliminated. As mentioned, multicolumn countercurrent are very suited for integrated processes, particularly since they produce product in smaller intervals than batch chromatography, which allows for further improvement of the scheduling.

10.8 Multicolumn Countercurrent Chromatography in Continuous Manufacturing

The cyclic nature of multicolumn countercurrent processes has a number of operational implications that need to be addressed when evaluating these technologies in the context with continuous manufacturing. The orthodox definition of continuous manufacturing implies that the feed stream is uninterrupted [24]; according to this definition even small interruptions for valve switching are not allowed, as present in the simulated moving bed concept. The only chromatographic technique fulfilling this strict condition is continuous annular chromatography (pCAC) [25]. However, this technique requires specialized equipment, and operational issues regarding packing quality have been reported [26]. Most importantly, the technique is not countercurrent but cross-current, which limits its applicability for difficult separations.

A downstream concept where the feed is delivered in packages with small interruptions is considered to be quasicontinuous or periodic but nevertheless compatible with continuous upstream.

When coupled to continuous fermentation and operating over a prolonged time period in the range of weeks or months, the sterile coupling of the equipment needs to be warranted. Since all currently available lab-scale systems are not suited for sterile operation, at least the back-growth of microbes through the harvest line needs to be avoided for instance by means of sterile filters. On larger-scale sterile equipment is needed with a CIP or SIP (steam-in-place) option.

The reduction of the number of columns and equipment of multicolumn countercurrent chromatography in order to reduce equipment complexity and decrease the risk of hardware failure also bears operational implications with respect to uniformity of the feed supply: For high titer applications, twin-column CaptureSMB processes use a dual loading flow rate strategy instead of continuously feeding at a uniform feed flow rate, which is possible in many cases in setups with more columns. Due to the discontinuous feed flow rate nature they require an intermediate surge bag that matches the downstream net feed flow rate to the harvest flow rate. Also, twin-column MCSGP requires an intermediate surge bag, whereas six-column MCSGP does not. However, it is questionable if this feature is actually a disadvantage or if a surge bag would be required anyway also in continuous downstream. Most likely a surge bag would be continued to be used to de-risk the downstream process by avoiding a chain reaction of failures in case one of the unit operations in the downstream or upstream process experiences a failure. This would be done even in the case when a downstream process with more columns was used that theoretically would allow continuous feeding.

In continuous manufacturing the columns can be significantly downsized as the product is withdrawn continuously at a low flow rate. Current cell-specific perfusion rate values in the range of 0.025 nl cell day^{-1} have been reported. Assuming a cell density of 150 million cells ml^{-1} the flow rate exiting a 200 l fermenter would be 31 l h^{-1} or 520 ml min^{-1}, which could be handled by equipment considered "pilot scale" in existing processes [24].

This means that equipment with relatively small column diameter is sufficient for production purposes. In this case twin-column equipment with 10 cm inner diameter columns would be capable of handling the volume flow, which would be considered a pilot-scale equipment in traditional large-scale antibody manufacturing based on fed-batch fermentation.

The definition of a "product batch" in continuous manufacturing has been the matter of ongoing discussions in the industry. In fact regulatory authorities have shown a very flexible attitude toward this topic allowing for mass-based, time-based, or raw-materials-based definitions [25].

10.9
Process Analytical Tools for Multicolumn Countercurrent Processes

Multicolumn countercurrent processes in continuous manufacturing are predestined for the implementation of process analytical tools (PAT) since online information on product quality can be obtained more regularly and over longer periods of time compared to batch- or fed-batch-based processes that have to be completed within a certain transit time. Cyclically continuous processes in continuous manufacturing deliver a steady output of microbatches that can be subject to state-of-the art analytical tools.

Also in fed-batch-based manufacturing processes the cyclical nature allows for obtaining this online information; however, the number of microbatches is capped by the maximum allowed transit time.

Reported online analytics for multicolumn processes for biopharmaceuticals have been mainly employing UV-based monitoring and control strategies. By overlaying UV signals of subsequent cycles steady state information can be obtained. In cyclic steady state, the UV signals of subsequent cycles should match when overlain. Nonmatching of UV signals indicate that the process has either not yet reached cyclic steady state or that it is exiting cyclic steady state. Even more information, potentially even on product purity, may be obtained online if more UV wavelength signals are compared or UV spectral data are evaluated. Also, other spectroscopic techniques such as NIR may become important tools to obtain a cyclic steady state "fingerprint." If properly calibrated, purity information may be extracted from the online signals. Next to UV, conductivity and pH are routinely checked to monitor cycle-to-cycle buffer and gradient reproducibility.

Once the online information (e.g., UV) has been obtained it is obvious to use it for feedback control. Excursions from cyclic steady state, which may occur for instance due to column aging, can be balanced by changing process operating parameters, for instance the switch time [27].

The determination of the product purity can be realized effectively using an at-line HPLC and analyzing the product from each cycle; however, it is elaborate in terms of equipment setup and integration. The use of the purity information from an at-line HPLC for process feedback control has been described for a twin-column MCSGP process by Krättli *et al.* [28].

References

1 Schulte, M., Wekenborg, K., and Wewers, W. (2005) Process concepts in preparative chromatography, in *Preparative Chromatography*, 1st edn (ed. H. Schmidt-Traub), Wiley-VCH Verlag GmbH, Weinheim, p. 191.

2 Ruthven, D.M. and Ching, C.B. (1989) Counter-current and simulated counter-current adsorption separation processes. *Chem. Eng. Sci.*, **44**, 1011.

3 Nagamatsu, S., Murazumi, K., and Makino, S. (1999) Chiral separation of a pharmaceutical intermediate by a simulated moving bed process. *J. Chromatogr. A*, **832** (1–2), 55–65.

4 Grill, C.M., Miller, L., and Yan, T.Q. (2004) Resolution of a racemic pharmaceutical intermediate: a comparison of preparative HPLC, steady state recycling, and simulated moving bed. *J. Chromatogr. A*, **1026**, 101–108.

5 Hamende, M. (2005) Case study in production-scale multicolumn continuous chromatography, in *Preparative Enantioselective Chromatography* (ed. G.B. Cox), Blackwell Publishing Ltd., p. 253.

6 Park, B.J., Lee, C.H., Mun, S., and Koo, Y.M. (2006) Novel application of simulated moving bed chromatography to protein refolding. *Process Biochem.*, **41**, 1072–1082.

7 Mahajan, E., George, A., and Wolk, B. (2012) Improving affinity chromatography resin efficieny using semi-continuous chromatography. *J. Chromatogr. A*, **1227**, 154–162.

8 Godawat, R., Brower, K., Jain, S., Konstantinov, K., Riske, F., and Warikoo, V. (2012) Periodic counter-current chromatography – design and operational considerations for integrated and continuous purification of proteins. *Biotechnol. J.*, **7** (12), 1496–1508.

9 Müller-Späth, T., Angarita, M., Baur, D., Lievrouw, R., Lissens, G., Strohlein, G., Bavand, M., and Morbidelli, M. (2013) Increasing capacity utilization in Protein A chromatography. *BioPharm Int.*, **26** (10), 33–38.

10 Warikoo, V., Godawat, R., Brower, K., Jain, S., Cummings, D., Simons, E., Johnson, T., Walther, J., Yu, M., Wright, B., McLarty, J., Karey, K.P., Hwang, C., Zhou, W., Riske, F., and Konstantinov, K. (2012) Integrated continuous production of recombinant therapeutic proteins. *Biotechnol. Bioeng.*, **109** (12), 3018–3029.

11 Pollock, J., Bolton, G., Coffman, J., Ho, S. V., Bracewell, D.G., and Farid, S.S. (2013) Optimising the design and operation of semi-continuous affinity chromatography for clinical and commercial manufacture. *J. Chromatogr. A*, **1284**, 17–27.

12 Aumann, L. and Morbidelli, M. (2007) A continuous multicolumn counter-current solvent gradient purification (MCSGP) process. *Biotechnol. Bioeng.*, **98** (5), 1043–1055.

13 Aumann, L., Stroehlein, G., and Morbidelli, M. (2007) Parametric study of a 6-column counter-current solvent gradient purification (MCSGP) unit. *Biotechnol. Bioeng.*, **98** (5), 1029–1042.

14 Aumann, L. and Morbidelli, M. (2008) A semicontinuous 3-column counter-current solvent gradient purification (MCSGP) process. *Biotechnol. Bioeng.*, **99** (3), 728–733.

15 Müller-Späth, T., Aumann, L., Melter, L., Ströhlein, G., and Morbidelli, M. (2008)

Chromatographic separation of three monoclonal antibody variants using multicolumn counter-current solvent gradient purification (MCSGP). *Biotechnol. Bioeng.*, **100** (6), 1166–1177.

16 Müller-Späth, T., Krättli, M., Aumann, L., Ströhlein, G., and Morbidelli, M. (2010) Increasing the activity of monoclonal antibody therapeutics by continuous chromatography (MCSGP). *Biotechnol. Bioeng.*, **107** (4), 652–662.

17 Müller-Späth, T., Ulmer, N., Aumann, L., Ströhlein, G., Bavand, M., Hendriks, L.J.A., de Kruif, J., Throsby, M., and Bakker, A.B.H. (2013) Purifying common light-chain bispecific antibodies: a twin-column, counter-current chromatography platform process. *BioProcess Int.*, **11** (5), 36–45.

18 Müller-Späth, T., Aumann, L., Ströhlein, G., Kornmann, H., Valax, P., Delegrange, L., Charbaut, E., Baer, G., Lamproye, A., Jöhnck, M., Schulte, M., and Morbidelli, M. (2010) Two step capture and purification of IgG2 using multicolumn counter-current solvent gradient purification (MCSGP). *Biotechnol. Bioeng.*, **107** (6), 974–984.

19 Müller-Späth, T., Ströhlein, G., Lyngberg, O., and Maclean, D. (2013) Enabling high purities and yields in therapeutic peptide purification using multicolumn counter-current solvent gradient purification. *Chim. Oggi*, **31** (5), 56–60.

20 Bramaud, C., Aimar, P., and Daufin, G. (1995) Thermal isoelectric precipitation of α-lactalbumin from a whey-protein concentrate – influence of protein–calcium complexation. *Biotechnol. Bioeng.*, **47** (2), 121–130.

21 Fee, C.J. and Van Alstine, J.A. (2006) PEG-proteins: reaction engineering and separation issues. *Chem. Eng. Sci.*, **61** (3), 924–939.

22 Müller-Späth, T., Ströhlein, UlmerN., Bavand, G., and N-Rich, M. (2013) A novel automated enrichment process for the isolation of product-related impurities from active pharmaceutical ingredients. Poster presentation at the PREP Symposium 2013, Boston, MA.

23 Takizawa, B.T. (2011) Evaluation of the financial impact of continuous chromatography in the production of biologics. Available at http://hdl.handle.net/1721.1/66045 (last accessed August 27, 2014).

24 Konstantinov, K. (2013) The promise of continuous bioprocessing. Integrated Continuous Biomanufacturing, October 20–24, Castelldefells, Spain.

25 Jungbauer, A. (2013) Continuous downstream processing of biopharmaceuticals. *Trends Biotechnol.*, **31** (8), 479–492.

26 Vogel, J.H., Nguyen, H., Pritschet, M., Van Wegen, R., and Konstantinov, K. (2002) Continuous annular chromatography: general characterization and application for the isolation of recombinant protein drugs. *Biotechnol. Bioeng.*, **80**, 559–568.

27 Krättli, M., Strohlein, G., Aumann, L., Muller-Spath, T., and Morbidelli, M. (2011) Closed loop control of the multi-column solvent gradient purification process. *J. Chromatogr. A*, **1218**, 9028–9036.

28 Krättli, M., Steinebach, F., and Morbidelli, M. (2013) Online control of the twin-column counter-current solvent gradient process for biochromatography. *J. Chromatogr. A*, **1293**, 51–59.

11
Monoclonal Antibody Continuous Processing Enabled by Single Use

Mark Brower, Ying Hou, and David Pollard

11.1
Introduction

The growth of therapeutic proteins and vaccines continues to gain momentum in the marketplace with biologically derived molecules owning a predominant position among the top 10 selling drugs. Biotherapeutics remains the largest and fastest growing class of novel pharmaceuticals entering the market where in 2012 approximately 28 biomolecules were approved and 350 biomolecules were in the clinical development phase [1]. The annual growth is expected to continue at a rate of 9.5% for the period between 2010 and 2016 [2] equating to a US $58 billion industry [3]. While the economic success has been dominated by full-length humanized monoclonal antibodies (mAbs), expansion into new modalities is accelerating including antibody drug conjugates, multispecific antibodies, glycan engineered proteins, and novel fragments and scaffolds.

Despite this growing success, the biopharmaceutical industry faces strict competitive challenges from multiple pressures including economic, regulatory, and political [4]. As a result, there is a significant drive to boost the overall productivity of biotherapeutic programs by shortening development timelines and lowering both development and production costs, while maintaining product quality [4]. Recently, progress has been made to significantly accelerate process development timelines by innovative, high throughput, technology solutions for the cell line development and upstream process (USP) characterization spaces [5,6]. High throughput methods for chromatography development have also been demonstrated in the downstream space [7]. However, the inherent inefficiency of those batch-based chromatographic separations leads to relatively unproductive downstream purification processes (DSP) as a whole.

The expanding diversity of biotherapeutic pipelines with novel modalities is pressuring the industry away from the traditional fixed 10–20 kl stainless steel manufacturing facilities built in the last two decades toward more flexible approaches that can easily accommodate both large and small drug demands from the diverse modality platforms each of which may require specialized technologies in the production process. This evolving competitive business

Continuous Processing in Pharmaceutical Manufacturing, First Edition. Edited by Ganapathy Subramanian.

environment is driving the biopharmaceutical industry toward a tipping point for radically improved, lower cost bioprocessing options [8]. Because of the large number of full length antibodies in development, and their relatively high dosing requirements, low-cost mAb production solutions must be aggressively pursued. Therefore, the strategies presented herein are focused on monoclonal antibody production; however, the basic principles can be applied to other therapeutic protein classifications.

11.1.1
Single-Use Revolution to Enable Process Intensification and Continuous Processing

The benefits of single-use technology with disposable components is well understood to provide the much needed flexibility while significantly reducing the up-front investment in a facility [9]. The elimination of clean- and sterilize-in-place procedures reduces equipment complexity that can dramatically lower capital cost, facility footprint, and increase turnover time/throughput [10]. For example, the economic analysis presented in Figure 11.1 shows that up to a modest

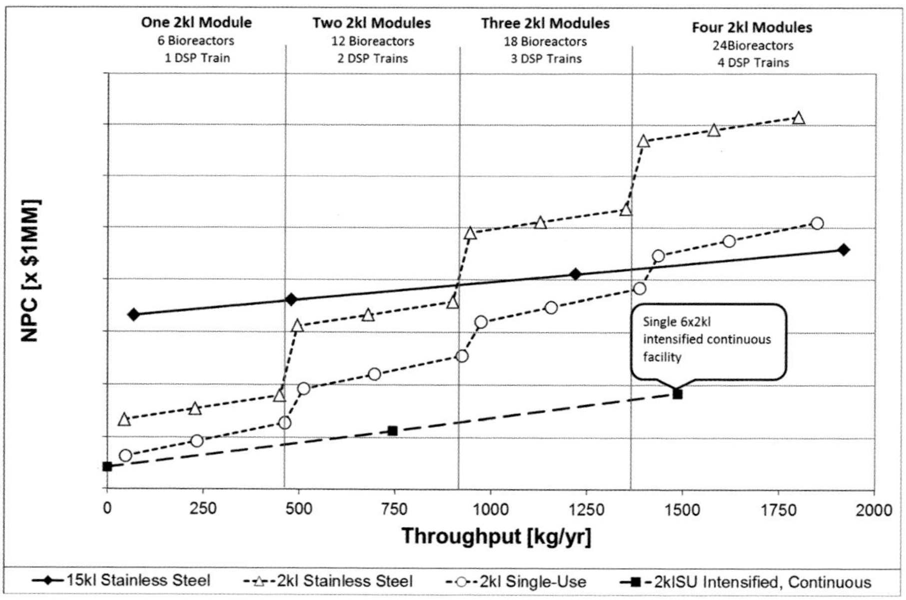

Figure 11.1 Comparison of single-use (complete end-to-end process) and stainless steel facility economics for the production of monoclonal antibody drug substance assuming a fed-batch bioreactor titer of $3\ g\ l^{-1}$. It is noted that the lowest value of net present cost (NPC) is the preferred outcome and recognizes the total expense associated with the facility including construction, capital, and operating costs for a brownfield facility assuming 20 years of operation. A 15 000 l stainless facility base case is compared to: one module consisting of six bioreactors and one purification train at 2000 l scale either stainless or single use. The capacity is increased by adding identical 2000 l modules.

1300 kg $year^{-1}$ and at 3 g l^{-1} upstream titer the fully single-use mAb facility at 2000 l is the preferred option (i.e., lowest net present cost) over either the 2000 or 15 000 l stainless steel configurations. At higher upstream titers, such as 10 g l^{-1}, the 2 kl single-use is always the lower-cost option compared to stainless steel. Furthermore, intensified continuous processes represent a game-changing strategy, which shows economic advantages on the order of net present cost (NPC) difference NPC of $200MM over the lifetime of a facility.

This realization has driven the industry to define upstream intensification processes [11] to concentrate product throughout the course of the cell culture. Here, an ultrafiltration membrane is used on the bioreactor to retain cells and product while media is perfused through the bioreactor. This has taken the molecular biology and fermentation advancements in fed-batch expression from 3–5 g l^{-1} titers to intensified processes with titers of 10–15 g l^{-1}. As such a 2000 l single-use bioreactor with intensification can generate a similar volumetric productivity as a 6000 to 10 000 l stainless steel bioreactor. This substantial increase in upstream productivity must be matched by the downstream to realize highly productive protein production facilities. To date however, protein purification processes have been comprised of relatively low productivity unit operations, such as batch-based chromatography (~15 g l^{-1} h^{-1}) and tangential-flow filtration strung together in a linear manner resulting in relatively low throughputs. As bioreactors

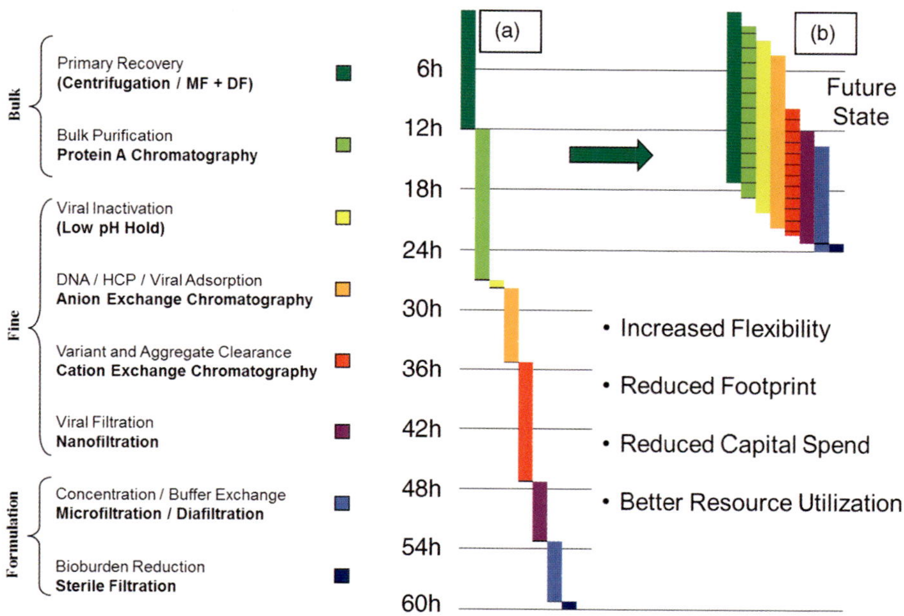

Figure 11.2 Example of (a) batch-based DSP processing time with linear processing for a generic three-column purification process as (b) the productivity gain, which can be realized if all of the unit operations are run concurrently.

have become smaller with intensified processing, the chromatography columns have become larger with multiple cycles and longer processing times that impact the facility output [12]. Therefore, obvious benefits exist for an intensified, continuous process that can handle changing upstream capacity without dramatic changes in chromatography column size and processing time.

In a standard three-column monoclonal antibody purification process shown in Figure 11.2a) it is common practice to pool the entire product stream from the preceeding unit operation prior to moving on to the next. This not only requires the installation of large interoperation holding vessels where the intermediate is sampled for purity and quality, but also leads to lengthy processing times, on the order of 40–80 h in-suite, before arriving at purified drug substance. A future state is also presented in Figure 11.2b with a fully continuous downstream purification train. This future state offers increased flexibility, reduced footprint, reduced capital expenditure, and better resource utilization compared to traditional batch processing in stainless steel facilities.

A high-level gap analysis of traditional batch-based downstream processing is presented in Figure 11.3 where nondisposability and low productivity are

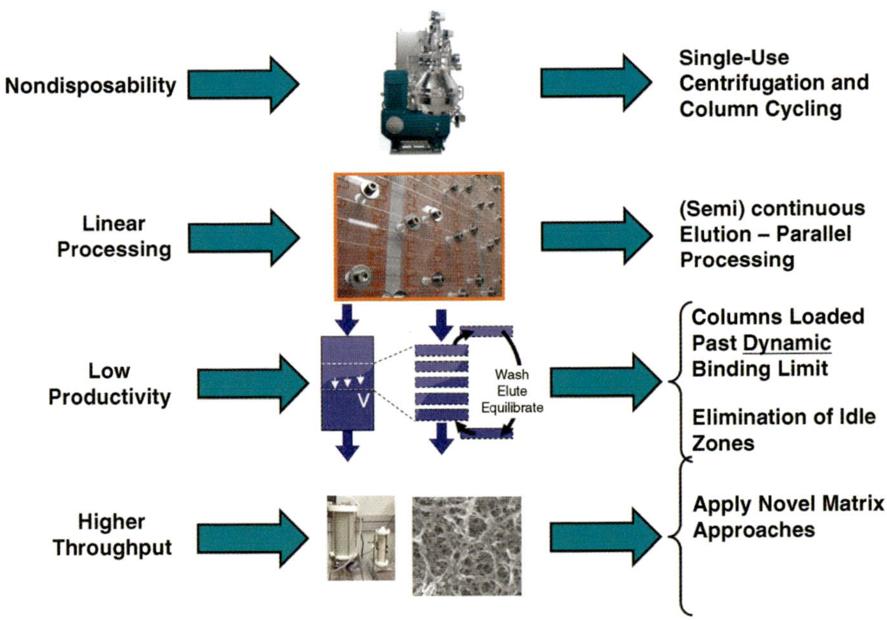

Figure 11.3 A summary of the existing challenges to batch processing and answers that provide a continuous solution: (1) Single-use centrifugation allows a disposable flow path for cell removal; (2) CMCC incorporates heavy column cycling, which transforms columns into single-use components and allows for an integral approach to the product pool; (3) countercurrent column loading of CMCC increases the specific productivity of chromatography steps; and (4) next-generation single-use matrices that allow for further specific productivity enhancements in chromatography steps.

identified as key technological challenges. With the use of emerging technologies designed to fill these gaps, such as continuous single-use centrifugation integrated with continuous multicolumn chromatography (CMCC) and single-pass tangential-flow filtration (SPTFF), the fully continuous DSP becomes a feasible option. This enables the continuous processing benefits to be recognized, such as short processing times, reduced capital cost, high productivity, and streamlined process [13]. One chief obstacle in transitioning from batch to continuous operations is the cleaning and sanitization validation on complex dedicated continuous processing skids, which may require such vigor as the complete disassembly, cleaning, and reassembly of hardware. With the use of fully single-use wetted paths, including the highly cycled CMCC chromatography columns, this concern is largely alleviated. Additional productivity benefits are realized from the elimination of lengthy clean-in-place and sanitize-in-place steps, as well as from loading enhancements made during the CMCC steps (see Section 11.1.2).

The evolution of the DSP to continuous processing can be thought of as stepwise transformation from (i) the current 15 kl scale batch-based processes to (ii) 2 kl intensified, single-use enabled, to (iii) continuous end to end processing, to finally (iv) commodity processing with next-generation materials and streamlined DSP train as seen in Figure 11.4. The envisioned future state with a fully single-use, continuous purification approach provides a flexible low-cost solution to integrating all the unit operations in a closed process. Closing the system allows facility air handling classification to be reduced compared to current practices (Grade C and B space) as well as transitioning away from individual containment suites to a low-cost, single-room suite

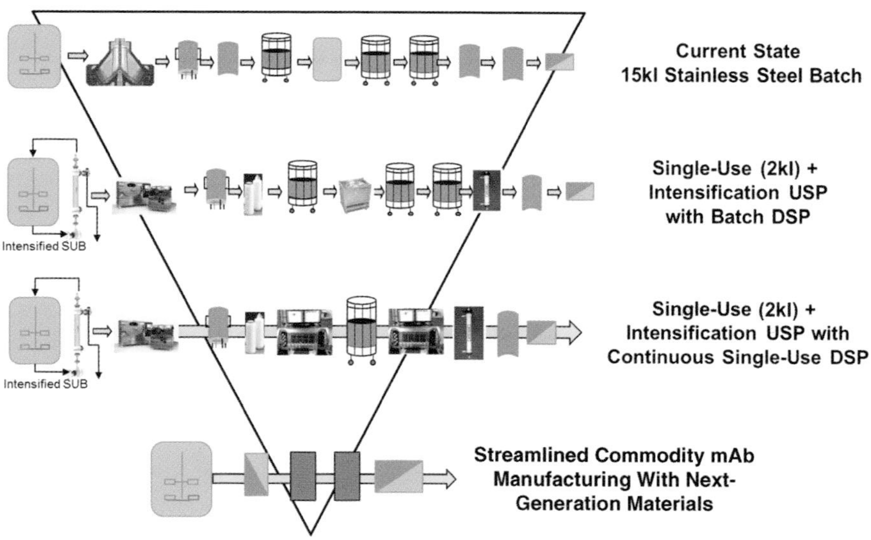

Figure 11.4 The transition from batch processing to continuous enabled by single-use technologies.

housing multiple unit operations, which ultimately facilitates a multiproduct facility [14].

11.1.2 Principles of Continuous Multicolumn Chromatography for Biological Production (BioSMB)

The proposed continuous downstream process relies most heavily on transforming batch-based chromatographic steps into a pseudo steady-state process with periodic column elutions. As such, this section provides a summary of the principles governing continuous multicolumn chromatography operation and the chromatography skid used to perform the methods described herein (Tarpon Biosystem BioSMB^{TM}). A more detailed description can be found in Chapter 10 of this book and by Bisschops. For clarification, CMCC steps are referred to as continuous due to the uninterrupted flow of feed, not to imply that a continuous stream of product is generated.

Classic steady-state countercurrent chromatography, a subset CMCC process and termed simulated moving bed (SMB) chromatography, has been adopted for industrial applications including amino acid, sugar, and chiral separations to overcome capacity bottlenecks [15–18]. In these systems, a stationary phase flow in a direction opposite to the isocratic mobile phase flow is simulated through valve switching between columns connected in a circuit. The result is a steady stream of enriched extract and depleted raffinate leaving different columns in the circuit due to differences in the partition coefficient for the stationary phase for each component in the binary feed solution.

Typically the adsorbent flow is simulated by switching column inlet and outlets by sophisticated stainless steel valve manifolds up to 100 000 l in scale in industries where sanitary processing is not a requirement. These applications have shown 20% resin reduction and 50–55% buffer savings [19]. The benefits of reduced resin and buffer usage can now be applied to bind and elute biologics systems by implementation of a single-use wetted path including a zero-dead volume valve manifold system from Tarpon Biosystems Inc. [20]. The valve block accommodates 240 individually addressable diaphragm valves that provide asynchronous switching and other flexibility in method generation. The single-use aspect of the wetted path negates the need to validate cleaning of the pump heads, valve block, or sensor array between batches or campaigns.

In contrast to a classic SMB process, bind and elute chromatography common to the biopharmaceutical industry is not typically operated isocratically (as is the case with affinity and ion-exchange chromatography), and as a result, it is necessary that a column must undergo discrete steps within the chromatography process, such as loading, washing eluting regeneration, and equilibration. To maximize the dynamic binding capacity and specific productivity of bind and elute steps, the user creates countercurrent flow in only the "loading zone" where simulated stationary flow is in the opposite direction to the incoming crude feed stream using a comparatively small columns number (ranging from

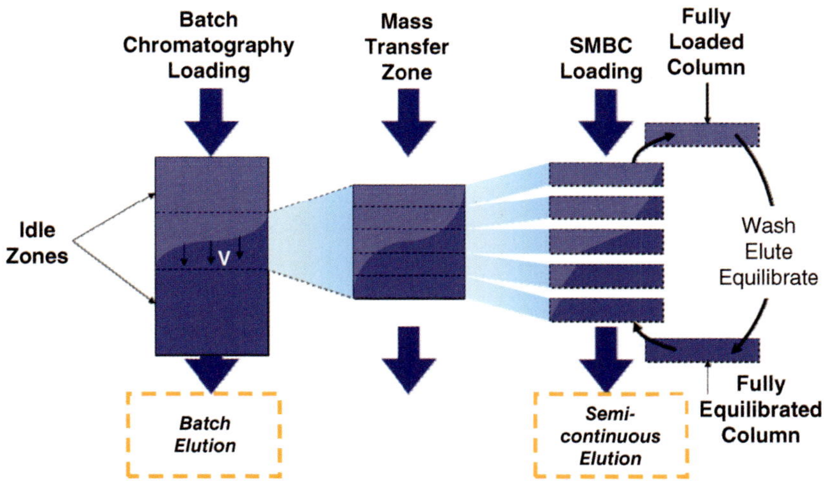

Figure 11.5 Comparison of the loading zone from batch chromatography where idle mass transport zones are present to continuous multicolumn chromatography where those idle zones are eliminated by allowing product breakthrough in the leading column(s) to be captured by the next small column in series.

2 to 6). As such, the first column in a series in this zone is loaded to saturation before the feed stream is switched to the next column in series to continue loading while the first column undergoes the washing and elution cycle. The other steps in the chromatographic process are then carried out on an individual column, or columns, through asynchronous valve switching. Upon regeneration and equilibration, the column is finally reintroduced to the loading zone as the last column in the series [21].

During the loading step in traditional batch chromatography, a mass transfer zone develops as a wave front traveling through the column, which corresponds to a small fraction of the entire column volume as shown in Figure 11.5. In front of the mass transfer zone, the chromatography media remains saturated and at equilibrium with the feed solution so limited mass transfer occurs. Beyond the mass transfer zone, the feed solution is lean in product and again, the mass transfer is limited. As such a majority of the column is underutilized for the physical adsorption process during the time spent loading the column, which contributes to the low specific productivity of chromatographic separations. In addition, the column loading is typically stopped well before the mass transfer zone reaches the outlet of the column to prevent product loss to the flow-through fraction. This leaves a signification portion of the static binding capacity of the column underutilized such that large-scale columns may only be loaded to 65% of their potential capacity, another contributing factor to low specific productivity [20]. In contrast, countercurrent contact of the feed solution with the stationary phase in CMCC applications provides improved driving force for mass transfer, which is now occurring over the entire bed volume of the loading zone [20]. Practically speaking, this requires that the first column(s) in the loading zone is loaded past its dynamic binding capacity and as a result, product will be found in the effluent. This product, which would have been lost to the flow-through fraction in a batch process, adsorbed in the next column in series in the loading zone of CMCC. As such, specific productivities of for CMCC range from 2 to 10× compared to an equivalent batch-based process.

The BioSMB skid not only facilitates the countercurrent flow in the loading zone, but also carries out other chromatographic steps on separate columns simultaneously. These complex methods can be visualized using a circular chronogram as shown in Figure 11.6, where the outer ring displays the feed to each individual column and the inner ring shows where the effluent of each column is directed. In the example presented in Figure 11.6 for an eight-column affinity adsorption example, the loading zone is shown in green where crude feed is introduced to three columns starting with column 6. The effluent of column 6 is fed to column 7, the effluent of column 7 is fed to column 8, and the effluent of column 8 is sent to the flow-through fraction. All other chromatographic steps in the process are occurring simultaneously.

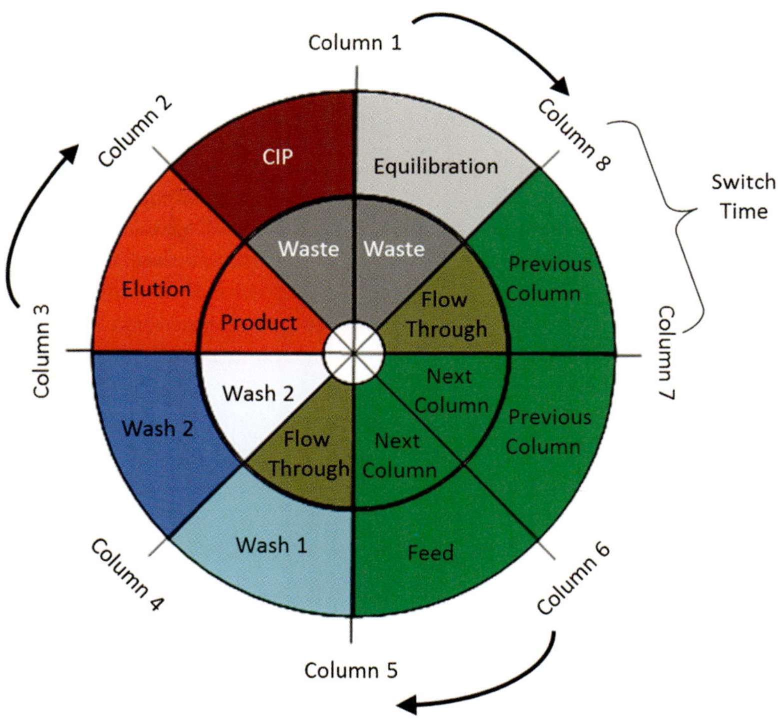

Figure 11.6 Circular chronogram example for bind and elute step with eight columns. The outer ring shows the feed solution of each column with columns 6, 7, and 8 in the loading zone (green) and columns 4 and 5 are in the wash zone and so on. The inner ring shows where the effluent of a column is directed.

The time it takes for a column to switch positions in the load zone is referred to as the switch time (t_S) and can be calculated from Equation 11.1.

$$t_S = \frac{(DBC_{CMCC} \times V_{col})}{Q_F \times c_0} \tag{11.1}$$

where DBC_{CMCC} is the dynamic binding capacity achieved in the CMCC loading zone, V_{col} is an individual column volume, Q_F is the feed flow rate, and c_0 is the concentration of product in the feed.

A full process cycle requires that all columns spent must undergo all of the steps in the chromatographic process and is equal to the number of columns in a CMCC process times the switch time. The time dedicated for each nonloading step is based upon the required buffer volume and a flow rate limitation. An additional constraint imposed on the system is that all nonloading steps must be completed in a time referred to as residual processing time (RPT), which can be calculated from Equation 11.2. This constraint may require that the loading steps are run at different linear velocities from the remaining steps of the process.

$$RPT = (Col_T - Col_L) \times ST \tag{11.2}$$

where Col_T and Col_L refer to the total number of columns in the process and the number of columns in the loading zone, respectively.

Incremental changes in the upstream titer can be compensated for in the CMCC process by adjusting the switch time as per Equation 11.1. If large changes in the titer occur additional columns of the same size can be added to the process as per Equation 11.2 to keep the RPT consistent resulting in similar process kinetics between a $2\,g\,l^{-1}$ or $10\,g\,l^{-1}$ feed stream. Typically a design model is created for the capture step that relates capture efficiency to the required resin volume and flow rates in the load zone that allows optimization of specific productivity. Typical models show that 2–4 columns can be used in the load zone with using 6–8 total columns for a $3\,g\,l^{-1}$ titer process or between 8 and 10 columns for a $10\,g\,l^{-1}$ process. The CMCC system offers a degree of freedom in the processing time (i.e., Q_F) to accomplish the same separation. The user may choose to minimize the column volume (and thus operate at a large number of cycles for a given separation), or to minimize processing time (and thus increasing column size).

11.2 Continuous Downstream Processing for Monoclonal Antibodies Unit Operation Development

To realize a truly continuous, integrated downstream purification process each unit operation feeds directly into the next as summarized in a block-flow diagram shown in Figure 11.7. All of the familiar unit operations are represented starting with crude cell culture broth from a single-use bioreactor,

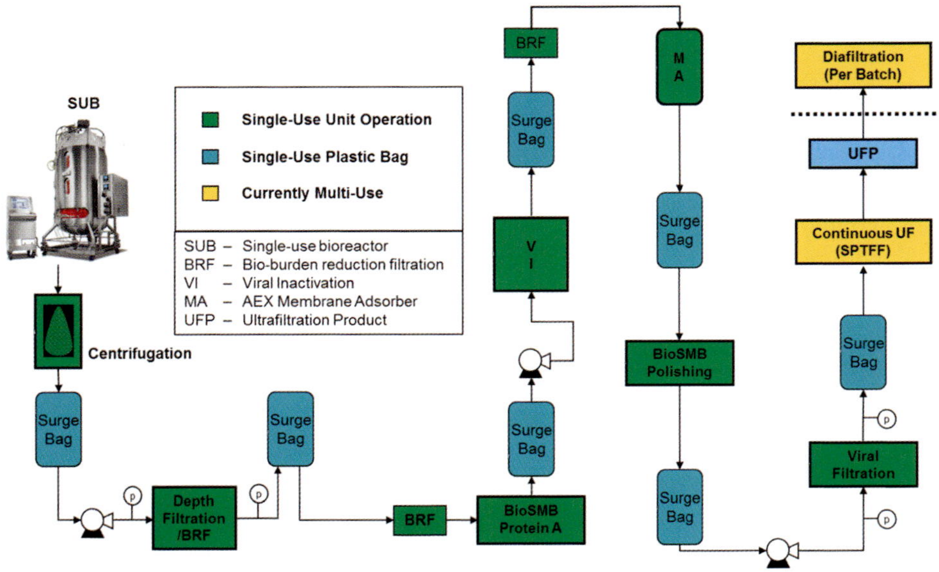

Figure 11.7 Block flow diagram of a continuous downstream purification process. All of the unit operations in the downstream are run at the same time using surge vessels as a place for stream conditioning for feed to the next step.

which is fed through a single-use centrifuge to remove biomass, and then a bank of depth and sterilizing grade filters to remove remaining particulates from the centrate. The clarified feed stream is then processed by a CMCC affinity protein A capture step for bulk purification. The protein A effluent is treated to a low pH viral inactivation step for a specified period of time prior to loading on an anion exchange membrane. The anion exchange product is polished through a second capture chromatography step prior to viral filtration. The viral filtrate is concentrated to an intermediate concentration using single-pass tangential-flow filtration and the retentate is collected for a specified period of time. Finally, the ultrafiltration product (UFP) is diafiltered into formulation buffer in discrete lots, which can be used as a point for batch definition. Due to the interdependency of each unit operation on the others, the individual steps were studied and characterized around a center point separately (described in Sections 11.2.3–11.2.6) before integrating them together for the demonstration of a continuous process.

This continuous process is said to be at pseudo steady state after a startup period required for feed to reach each individual unit operation and before a shutdown period when there is no longer feed available for each unit operation. This pseudo steady state refers only to the flows into and out/of each unit operation and is not intended to assume that the properties of these streams are constant (such as concentration, pH, and conductivity). In fact gradients in these properties are expected in the effluent of several unit operations. These gradients in the incoming surge stream are largely dampened out by choosing an appropriate volume of surge material to act as a buffer going into the next unit operation. More discussion on this topic will be given in Section 11.2.3.

11.2.1
Surge Vessels and Balancing Flows

In the continuous paradigm the familiar large pooling vessels used in batch operation between each unit operation have been replaced by small single-use mixing bags used as surge vessels. During the pseudo steady state operation, each surge bag must maintain a constant volume where the feed rates to that vessel directly matches take-off rate over a long period of time. Conductivity and pH adjustments for the next unit operation are also made in the surge vessels by adding an appropriate acid, base, or other component for stream conditioning. These additions must be accounted for in take-off rate so that accumulation for each surge vessel is avoided according to Equation 11.3.

$$0 = Q_{\text{out}} - Q_{\text{in}} - \sum_i Q_i \tag{11.3}$$

where Q_{out} is the takeoff flow rate, Q_{in} the incoming flow rate, and Q_i are the flow rates for any component added for stream conditioning.

One factor that aids in the design of the surge vessels for a continuous process is that the target length of each unit operation is increased from 4 to 8 h to the desired continuous processing time. Table 11.1 shows how effluent flows are affected by transforming batch processes into continuous processes.

Table 11.1 Comparison of typical flow rates in downstream unit operations run in both batch and continuous modes assuming a 2000 l bioreactor harvest at 3 g l^{-1} titer.

Step	Target batch processing time [h]	Batch flow rate [l min^{-1}]	Continuous processing time [h]	Continuous flow rate [l min^{-1}]
Centrifugation/depth filtration	4	8	23	1.5
Protein A chromatography	8	15	23	0.5
Anion/cation exchange chromatography	8	8	23	0.6
Viral filtration	8	1	23	0.3
Ultrafiltration (cross-flow rate)	8	25	23	0.3

11.2.2
Primary Recovery: Centrifugation and Depth Filtration

The removal of cells and particulates from cell culture media is traditionally accomplished by stainless steel disc stack centrifugation followed by a relatively small bank of depth and sterilizing-grade filters. For continuous processing limited to the 2000 l scale, alternatives to replace the difficult to clean, and capital intensive stainless steel centrifugation are a disposable depth filtration train and single-use centrifugation. A two-stage depth filtration run in series where the pore size of the media is stepped down from stage 1 to stage 2, followed by a sterilizing-grade filter is an effective way to clarify cell culture fluid [22]. This approach to clarification has two limitations. First, depth filter configurations across cell types and specific fermentation processes have proven to be nonplatformable, resulting in a significant rescreening and optimization effort for each new pipeline product. Second, the required membrane area for clarification is proportional to the percentage of biomass in the feed. As a result, intensified fermentation processes with significantly higher biomass will require increasingly more membrane area for an equal volume harvest. Centrifugation provides a more platformable approach and requires minimal optimization for each mAb product.

The single-use kSep centrifuge provides a solution to lengthy steam-in-place cycles utilized in disc-stack centrifuges by providing a fully disposable fluid flow path enabling continuous centrifugation. A typical pilot-scale system consists of 4 × 100 ml pear-shaped chambers as shown in Figure 11.8 while the scale-up skid for harvesting a 2000 l bioreactor consists of 6 × 1000 ml chambers. The operating g-force of the lab- and pilot-scale kSep centrifuges are 1000 × g and 2000 × g, respectively. The centrifuge is prepared in three steps: (1) inserting a gamma-sterilized chamber set into the rotor, which is utilized to collect the cells, (2) inserting a gamma-sterilized tubing manifold into a bank of pinch valves, which directs flows on the skid throughout the automated load and discharge cycles, and (3) aseptically joining the chamber and tubing sets using a tubing welder. The total time it takes a trained operator to turn around the kSep centrifuge is approximately of 0.5 h whereas the cleaning and sanitization cycles for the disc-stack centrifuge is on the order of 8 h.

Cell solids are trapped in the kSep chambers by balancing the centrifugal force, created by the unique carrousel design of the rotor, and the drag forces associated by fluid flow into the chamber in the opposite direction resulting in a zero-shear environment. As a result of the balanced forces, cells are retained in a fluidized bed inside each of the chambers, which enables efficient washing of the intracellular space to either the centrate or waste streams once the chambers have been loaded to capacity. Washed cells are flushed out of the chambers to waste by reversing the wash buffer flow into the direction of the centrifugal force. More details on the mode of operation of the kSep centrifuge can be found in Chapter 10 of this book. The kSep centrifugation step is a discontinuous approach where <3 min out of a 10–20 min cycle are spent washing

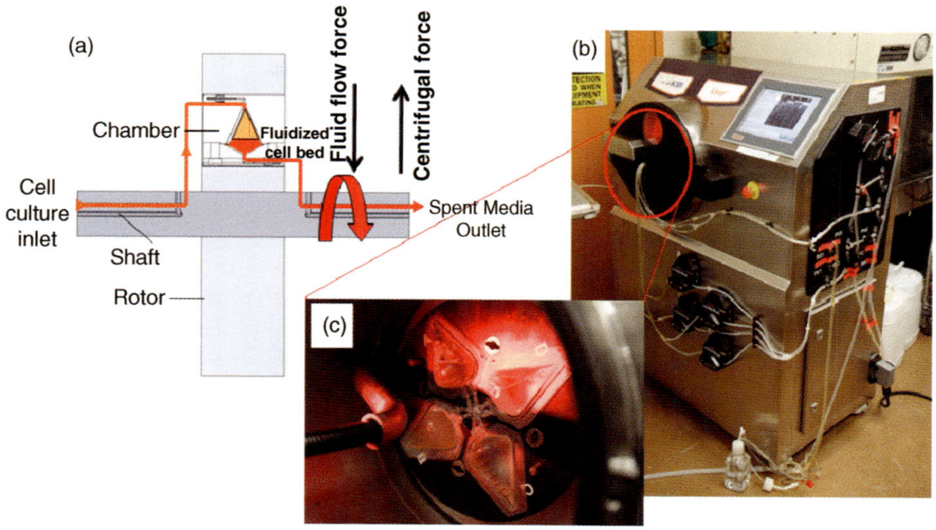

Figure 11.8 Single Use Centrifugation: Panel A describes the mode of cell capture in the kSep centrifuge where the centrifugal force is in the opposite direction to the incoming fluid flow. In this figure, the axis of rotation is in the plane of the page such that the rotor would be spinning out of the page toward the reader. Panel B shows the kSep centrifuge in operation with the bank of pinch valves directing fluid flows on the skid. Panel C is a close-up view of the rotor housing the 4 × 100 ml pear-shaped chamber set.

and discharging cells. The time spent when centrate and wash buffer are not being sent forward must be accounted for in flow rate calculation as per Equations 11.4 and 11.5:

$$Q_{\text{kSep Feed}} = \frac{V_{\text{Batch}}}{t_{\text{Batch}} \times \theta_{\text{ksep}}} = \frac{V_{\text{Batch}}}{t_{\text{Batch}}} \times \frac{t_{\text{ksepCT}}}{t_{\text{kSepFeed}}} \tag{11.4}$$

$$Q_{\text{kSep Out}} = \frac{V_{\text{Centrate+}} V_{\text{Wash}}}{t_{\text{ksepCT}}} \tag{11.5}$$

Where Q_{kSep} is the feed-flow rate to the centrifuge; V_{Batch} is the volume of the incoming batch to be processed; t_{Batch} is the desired time to process the batch and θ is the fractional time spent in the loading phase of the centrifugation cycle; T_{kSepCT} is the kSep cycle time and t_{kSepFeed} is the time spent in the feeding phase of the kSep cycle; V_{Centrate} is the volume of centrate collected per cycle; and V_{Wash} is the volume of wash collected per cycle.

Performance of the centrifuge is characterized by the turbidity of the centrate measured in nephelometric turbidity units (NTU). As the chamber reaches its physical limitation for the volume of solids it can hold, particulates start exiting the chamber and causing contamination of the centrate stream. Charting the NTU over loading time allows the operator to determine how many cells a chamber can hold and when to trigger the washing and dumping phases of the

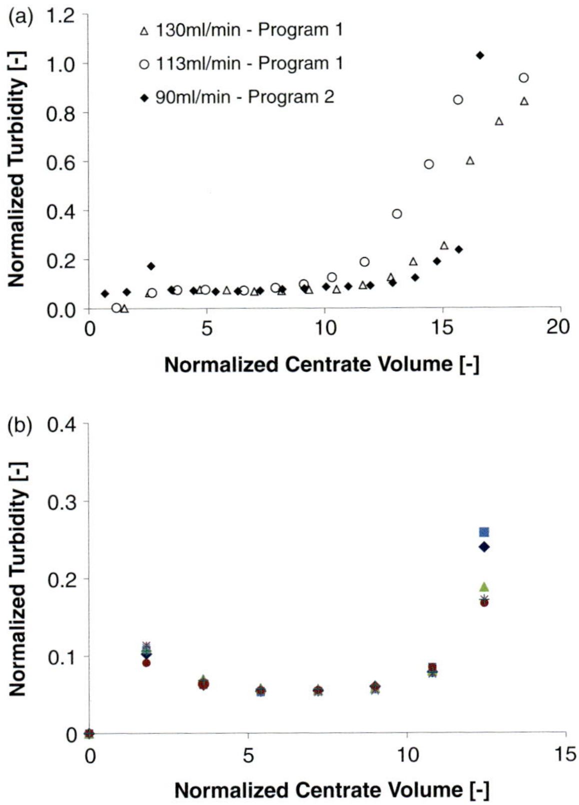

Figure 11.9 (a) Turbidity breakthrough profiles from the kSep centrifuge normalized to the turbidity of the feed stream and to the chamber volume (100 ml) at $1000 \times g$. Two different mAb programs using CHO cells for expression show the similar characteristic breakthrough shape. (b) Seven repeated cycles for program 1 at $90\,ml^{-1}\,min^{-1}$ $chamber^{-1}$ flow rate, and $1000 \times g$. Curves in Figure 11.9a and b were generated from different batches of the same program with different initial cell densities.

cycle. These particulate breakthrough curves have a characteristic shape, displaying a period of low turbidity when solids are being efficiently captured, followed be an exponential rise in turbidity once the chamber capacity has been exceeded. Figure 11.9a shows the turbidity breakthrough curves with the 100 ml chamber skid for two different mAb products, each with cell concentrations of $40–100 \times 10^6\,cells\,ml^{-1}$ in the feed. This equates to roughly 10–15 chamber volumes of feed prior to a wash and cell discharge cycle. With the same feed stream (project 1), it can be seen that at a given g-force, higher solids retention and a steeper breakthrough curve is seen at lower flow rates where the centrifugal force becomes more dominant. The separation has been shown to be robust by demonstrating consistent breakthrough curves for >7 cycles as shown in

Table 11.2 Comparison of key operation parameters for the kSep centrifuge and a standard disc-stack centrifuges.

Parameter	kSep performance	Historical disc stack performance
g-force	1000–2000 × *g*	4000–10 000 × *g*
Clarification efficiency	>90%	>95%
Centrate pool turbidity	<90NTU	<40NTU
Viability reduction	Negligible over individual cycle <3% over 8 h	Not available
Yield	98%	96%
Turnaround time	0.5 h	8 h
Depth filtration performance Post centrifugation	200 l m^{-2}, 220 LMH, <20 psi[a)] to 200 l m^{-2}, 20 LMH, <20 psi[b)]	500 l m^{-2}, 150 LMH, <20 psi[a)]

a) Using a platform depth filter media.
b) Using optimized depth filter media for kSep centrate.

Figure 11.9b and as many as 80 cycles in data not shown. Disc-stack and kSep centrifugation performance is compared in Table 11.2.

The relatively low g-force generated by the kSep centrifuge compared to a disc-stack centrifuge, results in a more turbid centrate pool, which may impact loading volume on the subsequent depth filtration step. Using the same grade depth filter media, the loading was shown to be reduced from of 500 l m^{-2} at a constant flux (150 LMH) with disc stack centrate to just 200 l m^{-2} using kSep centrate at a similar flux (220 LMH) and the same maximum pressure (20 psi). However, it must be noted that the relatively low g-force of the kSep centrifuge may result in a lower threshold for the diameter of particulates, which are retained by the centrifuge and as a result a more open depth filter media may be more appropriate for use with kSep centrate. Figure 11.10 shows the pressure versus loading profiles seen using the same kSep centrate as feed using two different depth filter media for fluxes of 150 and 20 LMH. These two fluxes were chosen to represent typical first flow rates for batch processing and continuous processing, respectively. It can be seen that the optimized depth filter media outperformed the standard depth filter media at both fluxes. In addition, reduced pressures were observed in the low flux regime consistent with lengthened step times associated with continuous processes. The depth filter effluent is passed through a sterilizing grade filter to remove any remaining particulates in the stream that may plug the downstream chromatography column and to reduce as a means for bioburden reduction. In conclusion, although the kSep may result in a more turbid centrate stream, there is little impact on the subsequent depth filtration polishing step once an appropriate depth filter medium is selected for the application.

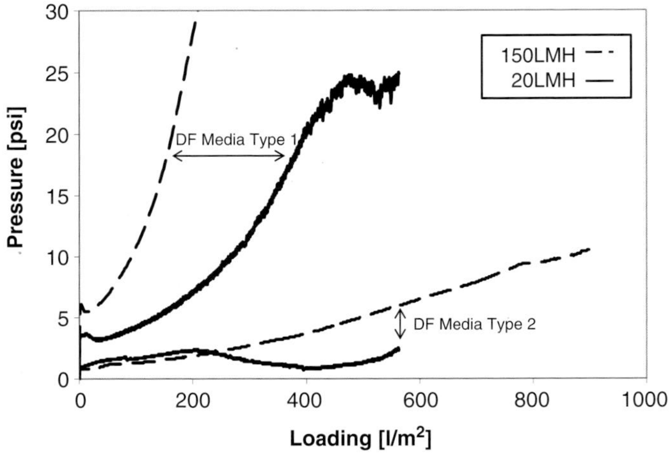

Figure 11.10 Pressure versus loading curves generated using kSep centrate on two different depth filter media. The loading was conducted at constant flow rates at two different flux values: 150 LMH to represent batch type processing, and 20 LMH to represent continuous type processes.

11.2.3
Bulk Purification: Continuous Multicolumn Chromatography – BioSMB Protein A Capture and Viral Inactivation

The clarified cell culture stream exiting the depth filter/sterile filtration train is fed to a Tarpon BioSMB continuous chromatography skid for protein A affinity antibody capture. Protein A is an affinity ligand that captures the constant domain of most monoclonal antibodies subclasses (near neutral pH and over a broad conductivity range). Elution of the product is achieved by an acidic pH shift. Protein A serves as a bulk purification step and raises the antibody purity to >95%.

Due to the increased number of columns in continuous chromatography, and the need to achieve a steady state over a number of cycles, significant feed is required for each experiment compared to traditional batch chromatography carried out on 0.5 or 1 cm diameter packed columns. As such, it becomes critical that the underlying method development be carried out on small batch columns to provide for the necessary separation. Predicated on that notion, continuous chromatography development focuses on transforming an optimized batch method into a continuous method while maintaining the desired separation. Therefore, continuous method development focuses on two main areas – the feeding phase where columns are typically loaded past the capacity demonstrated for batch chromatography, and the elution phase which is critical yield and purity of the product. It may happen that as a result of overloading of the columns, a different purity profile is seen in the CMCC effluent pool after optimization. In these scenarios, the method must be further adjusted to meet the purity targets by altering either how the columns are loaded or

Table 11.3 Batch protein A process used for transformation into a CMCC step.

Step	Buffer	Volume	Flow rate (cm h^{-1})
Equilibration	Low conductivity	5CV	300
Loading	Clarified culture fluid	<35 g l^{-1}	250
Wash 1	Low conductivity	3CV	300
Wash 2	High conductivity	3CV	
Wash 3	Low conductivity	3CV	
Elution	Low pH	5CV	
Strip	Acidic	3CV	
Sanitization	Basic	5CV	

how the columns are washed prior to the elution. The protein A process described next was derived from a standard batch process given in Table 11.3.

11.2.3.1 Protein A Loading Zone Optimization

To maximize protein loading on the adsorbent in continuous multicolumn chromatography, columns are often configured in a series configuration in the loading zone. To further increase the specific productivity of the step, columns may also be arranged in parallel, thus splitting the feed stream and increasing the residence time in the bed. Each column or group of columns arranged in series is referred to as a stage in the adsorptive zone.

The first column in the adsorption zone (receiving fresh feed) is loaded until it is approaching its absolute capacity for protein as it exits the loading zone while each subsequent stage contains columns at reduced loadings. As such, the liquid solution contained in the interstitial space of the first column retains a considerable concentration of product, which is displaced during wash 1. To prevent this product from being lost, wash 1 is sent through either a freshly equilibrated column just entering the feeding zone, or is combined with flow-through of previous stage's effluent and sent to the final stage in the adsorption zone. BioSMB methods are typically written in the later style. There are many permutations for the loading zone configuration bounded by practical limitations, most notably pressure drop over the bank of columns, which is typically limited to 3 bar with agarose-based media due to its limited mechanical stability. Two such configurations are presented in Figure 11.11.

A design model for the protein A capture using multiple columns in the loading zone on the BioSMB has been described by Bisschops and Brower [20] and is characterized by two main parameters. The first parameter is the separation factor, S, which is the flow rate ratio of binding sites in the adsorbent (simulated) to the antibody product in the feed and represents the dimensionless loading of the adsorbent. At $S=1$, the adsorbent is loaded exactly to its static binding capacity at equilibrium, and at values less than one, the column is loaded past its saturation point. The second parameter is the number of transfer units, NTU, which is a dimensionless unit associated with the mass transfer properties of the chromatography system. NTU can be described as the ratio between the residence time

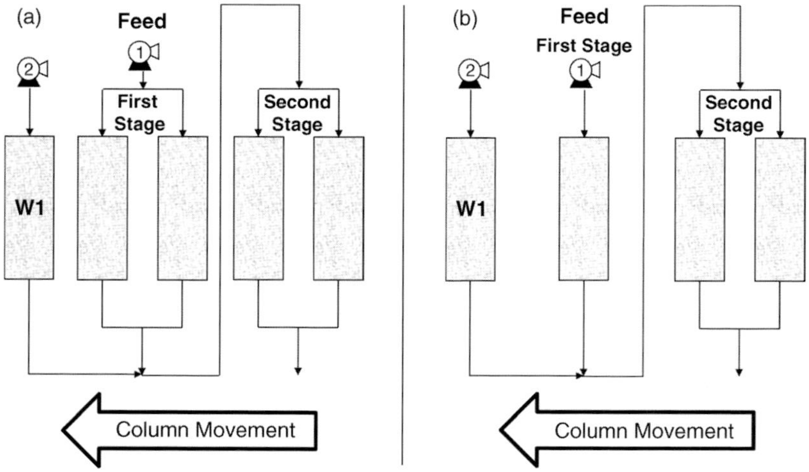

Figure 11.11 Load zone configurations for protein A monoclonal antibody capture: (a) 2 in series, 2 in parallel configuration with (4) total columns and (b) (1) column stage 1 and (2) column stage 2 with (3) total columns. In both configurations, Wash 1 is combined with the effluent from the first stage and sent to the second stage for protein recovery.

of the liquid in the feeding zone and the characteristic time associated with the mass transfer kinetics [20]. Equations for the separation factor and the number of transfer units are given in Equations 11.6 and 11.7, respectively. The separation factor and NTU can then be used to estimate the capture efficiency, CE, or adsorption yield of the system using Equation 11.8 [23]

$$S = \frac{Q_{\text{bed}} \cdot q_{\text{m}}}{Q_{\text{f}} \cdot c_0} = \frac{V_{\text{col}} \cdot q_{\text{m}}}{t_{\text{S}} \cdot Q_{\text{f}} \cdot c_0} \tag{11.6}$$

$$\text{NTU} = k_{\text{oL}}a \sum \frac{N_i V_{\text{col}}}{Q_i} = k_{\text{oL}}a \left[\frac{N_1 V_{\text{col}}}{Q_{\text{f}}} + \frac{N_2 V_{\text{vol}}}{Q_{\text{f}} + Q_{\text{W1}}} \right] \tag{11.7}$$

where $Q_{\text{bed}} \equiv V_{\text{col}}/t_{\text{S}}$ is the simulated adsorbent phase flow rate, q_{m} is the static binding capacity at equilibrium, k_{oL} is the overall liquid phase mass transfer coefficient, a is the area for mass transfer, i is pass number when loading columns in series, N is the number of columns in each stage of adsorption when loading columns in series, and Q_{W1} is the flow rate of first column wash step.

$$\text{CE} = 1 - \left[\exp\left(-\text{NTU} \cdot \left(1 - \frac{1}{S}\right)\right) \cdot \left(1 - \frac{1}{S}\right) / 1 - \left(\frac{1}{S} \cdot \exp\left(-\text{NTU} \cdot \left(1 - \frac{1}{S}\right)\right)\right) \right] \tag{11.8}$$

Examination of Equations 11.6–11.8 reveals several important concepts. First, q_m and $k_{\text{OL}}a$ are the only unknown terms needing to be defined in the system. The classic chromatography concepts of adsorption isotherm analysis and frontal analysis may be employed to estimate q_m and $k_{oL}a$, respectively. Second, the theoretical adsorption yield can be easily estimated at different operating conditions by changing the operational parameters c_0, a function of the fermentation process, t_S, which influences S, and Q_f, which influences NTU. Q_{W1} also has a small effect on NTU.

Using this approach several theoretical operating lines have been constructed for antibody capture. The model was then validated by comparing the theoretical results with CMCC data derived from BioSMB experimental results repeated at low feed titers of $2\,g\,l^{-1}$ and high feed titers of $10\,g\,l^{-1}$. The results are shown in Figure 11.12. The BioSMB data were generated using 1.6 cm diameter columns with a bed height of 2.5 cm packed with

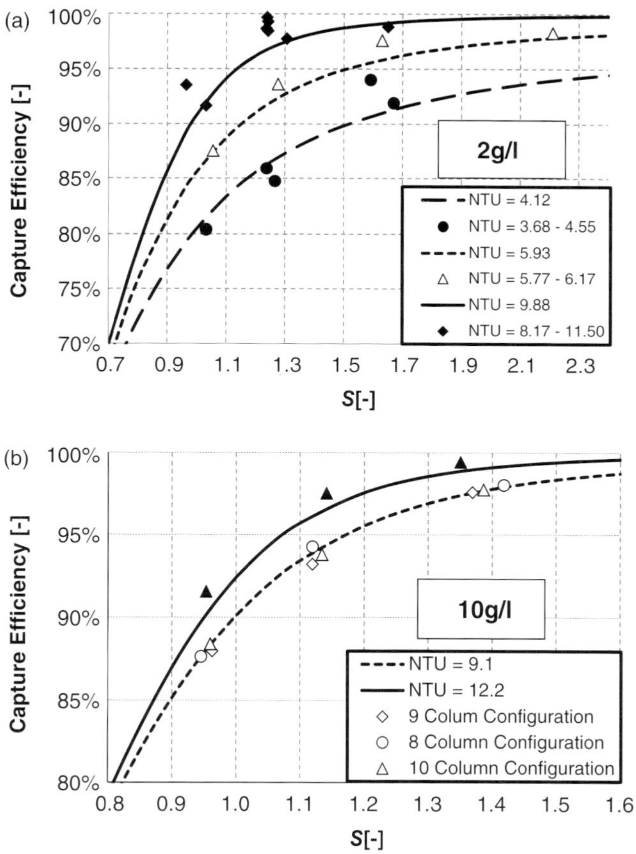

Figure 11.12 Theoretical capture efficiency curves (lines) for a monoclonal antibody on a protein A adsorbent (MabSelect SuRe™) plotted as lines with corresponding experimental data for (a) $2\,g\,l^{-1}$ mAb feed stream using an 8-column (1.6 cm × 2.5 cm) method and (b) $10\,g\,l^{-1}$ mAb feed stream for 8-, 9-, and 10-column methods (1.6 cm × 2.5 cm). The predictive design models for BioSMB show a reasonable fit to the BioSMB experimental data within 2% as well as operational ranges where >99% capture efficiency can be achieved.

Mabaselect SuRe™ adsorbent. The low titer experiments were all conducted with a (4) column load zone shown in Figure 11.11a and a total of (8) columns in the method. Due the higher titer (i.e., faster switch times), and the desire to use the same column dimensions with the $10\,g\,l^{-1}$ feed, (9) and (10) column methods were conducted utilizing the (4) column load zone as well as an (8) column method using the (3) column load zone shown in Figure 11.11b. Both adding columns to the entire process, and removing a column from the loading zone, have the same effect on the method – lengthening the time available to accomplish all reaming chromatographic steps other than loading and consequently reducing the linear velocity for each of those steps.

Figure 11.11a and b demonstrate several key concepts. First, that the design equations can be used to estimate BioSMB capture performance over a wide range of *NTU* and *S* values and can be used as a starting point for experimental design. Second, that at a given flow rate, a switch time can be chosen to provide for >99% capture efficiency for either $2\,g\,l^{-1}$ or $10\,g\,l^{-1}$ feed streams. Practical considerations must always be taken into account, most importantly that as the switch time is reduced, the linear velocity of the remaining processing steps increases and the residence time decreases. The appropriate number of columns in the method must be chosen to allow for linear velocities of those remaining steps to be in the range of $300–600\,cm\,h^{-1}$. It can be seen that for a $10\,g\,l^{-1}$ feed stream, the capture efficiency is consistent regardless of the column configuration. Finally, the design equations can also be used as a basis for scale-up. Once the final titer and volume of the upstream process is known, and the desired processing time is set, the columns can be sized, and switch times chosen to give a specific NTU and *S*.

The degree of freedom in the BioSMB design space that allows for achieving the same capture efficiencies with multiple flow rate and switch time combinations allows for operation in different regimes. The first is characterized by heavy column cycling at separation factors between 1.25 and 1.4, and would be appropriate for clinical campaigns where it is desirable to exhaust a column's lifetime in a single campaign. The second regime operates at separation factors in the range of 1.05–1.20 where columns are loaded very close to their static binding capacity. Here cycling is less frequent and columns can support multiple campaigns, such as in the manufacturing environment. For reference, batch chromatography typically operates at separation factors between 1.5 and 1.6. It should be noted that for scale up considerations, an optimized process should hold linear velocity and residence time in each step in the process constant as is the case with traditional batch-based chromatography processes. As a result, by changing operational regimes, one would need to revalidate the process such that critical product attributes and purity requirements are maintained.

Based on the experimental data, the CMCC step was compared to the original optimized batch process on the basis of processing 2000 l of clarified cell culture fluid at different titers and the benefits are summarized in Table 11.4. The

Table 11.4 Demonstration of the options of BioSMB approaches that can provide productivity and step time improvement to conventional resin chromatography.

Protein A process	Batch	BioSMB	BioSMB	Batch	BioSMB	BioSMB	BioSMB
Titer	$2\,g\,l^{-1}$	$2\,g\,l^{-1}$	$2\,g\,l^{-1}$	$10\,g\,l^{-1}$	$10\,g\,l^{-1}$	$10\,g\,l^{-1}$	$10\,g\,l^{-1}$
Step time [h]	24	20	12	48	20	12	20
Relative total adsorbent volume [l]	1	0.26	0.43	5	0.32	0.54	0.88
Relative individual Column volume [l]	1	0.03	0.05	5	0.03	0.05	0.22
Number of columns	1	8	8	1	10	10	4
Number of cycles	4	14	9	4	54	32	17
Loading linear velocity [$cm\,h^{-1}$]	250	440	470	250	440	470	140
Relative specific productivity [g/(l·h)]	1	3.2	3.2	0.75	14.0	14.0	4.8

CMCC process uses multiple columns 2 orders of magnitude smaller than that required for the batch process, and the CMCC process can be adapted to high titers by adding additional columns of the same dimensions as an analogous method at low titer. In addition, there are significant step time and specific productivity enhancements associated with the continuous processing scenario that are magnified at high titer. Finally, column dimension, arrangements, and step time may be manipulated to meet the desired goal of the step whether it be reduced complexity or increased cycle numbers.

11.2.3.2 Protein A Elution Zone Considerations

Protein A is bulk purification step and is not used for fine separation of closely related species. It may occur that a prepeak or tail contains the majority of impurities and should be omitted for the elution pool; however, in most instances, protein A pool cutting is designed to deliver a high recovery yield of the product. The effect of optimizing the loading zone by changing switch time in BioSMB methods results in varied flow rates and residence times for the other steps in the chromatographic process. This is of primary importance in the elution zone where mass transfer limitations exist for transporting product out of the pore structure and into the eluate stream. It may occur that the residence time is reduced to such an extent that the recovery yield is sacrificed. Figure 11.13 shows the recovery yield plotted against the residence time in the elution zone. It can be seen that at high residence times the recovery yield remains close to 100%; however, there is a critical residence time at 5 min below which yield is sacrificed. As a result, a

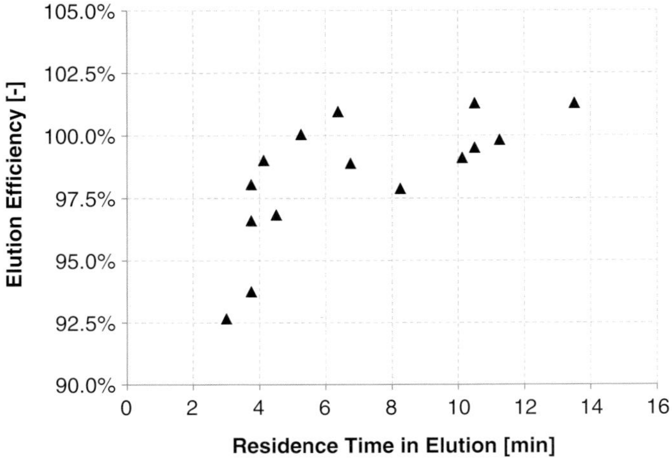

Figure 11.13 Elution efficiency of the mAb product plotted as a function of residence time in the elution zone. For this monoclonal antibody, a minimum of 5 min residence time is required to fully recover the product.

constraint is placed on the process for this molecule that the switch time must be sufficiently large to allow for 5 min residence time in the elution zone.

Processes robustness and reproducibility over a long number of cycles and multiple columns is critical to the success of a continuous multicolumn chromatography step. To ensure that the BioSMB method can accomplish a reproducible separation, a method was run across 8 days and 144 cycles. The experiment used eight 2.5 cm diameter × 2.5 cm MabSelect SuRe™ columns performing the optimized method with the four-column load zone presented in Figure 11.11a. Each individual column elution was collected every 6 cycles and was assayed for yield and process residuals. The capture efficiency and elution yield were constant across the 144 cycle experiment at >99%. In addition, the clearance of process residuals also remained constant across the large number of cycles as shown in Figure 11.14. Here the data are averaged across the eight columns for each assayed cycle and there is no trend at indicating that either Chinese hamster ovary (CHO) host cell protein (CHOP) or DNA is compromised at large cycle numbers. In data not presented, it was shown that eight individual columns performed very similarly with a standard deviation of 0.06 for the average LRV DNA and CHOP clearance over the course of the experiment.

Column elutions are discrete events and as such they do not provide a constant flow rate into the next unit operation. If the peak is being collected based on UV or time triggers, portions of the eluate stream will not be brought forward into the subsequent unit operation. As such, Equation 11.9 may be used to calculate the appropriate eluate flow rate for use in the continuous process.

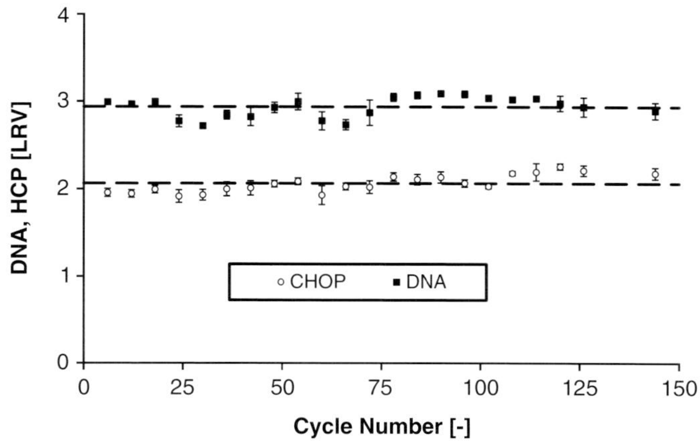

Figure 11.14 The LRV value averaged over the eight columns in the BioSMB method taken every 6 cycles for 144 cycles. Consistent residual DNA and host cell protein clearance was observed over the course of the 144 cycles of BioSMB protein A capture.

$$Q_{PAP} = \frac{V_{El}}{t_S} \tag{11.9}$$

where Q_{PAP} is the protein A product flow rate into the next unit operation and V_{El} is the total volume of protein A product brought forward into the next step.

11.2.3.3 **Viral Inactivation**

The US Food and Drug Administration (FDA) guidance mandates two orthogonal viral reduction processing steps in purification processes for proteins derived from mammalian cell culture [24]. Inactivation of the viral load is typically included as one of these dedicated steps and may be accomplished by several means. Effective inactivation has been shown by heat treatment and exposure to UV-C light, detergents, and solvents; however, the most common method employed in mAb purification process is a low pH shift and hold [25,26]. In typical batch processing the protein A product pool, eluted at low pH, is collected in a vessel and the pH is adjusted further down typically to <pH = 4.0. The pool is held at that pH for defined residence time, τ_{VI}, a period of 30–60 min depending on specific viral inactivation kinetics. After the low pH hold, the inactivated protein A eluate pool is adjusted to a safe pH for protein stability.

The traditional viral inactivation process just described may be transformed into either a periodic process by repeating the batch process on a discrete number of elutions from the CMCC step, or it must be rethought of for continuous operation. One truly continuous option relies on principles developed for continuous sterilization of media into a bioreactor as shown in Figure 11.15. In such systems, nonsterile media are heated to the sterilization temperature through a heat exchanger and is maintained at that temperature

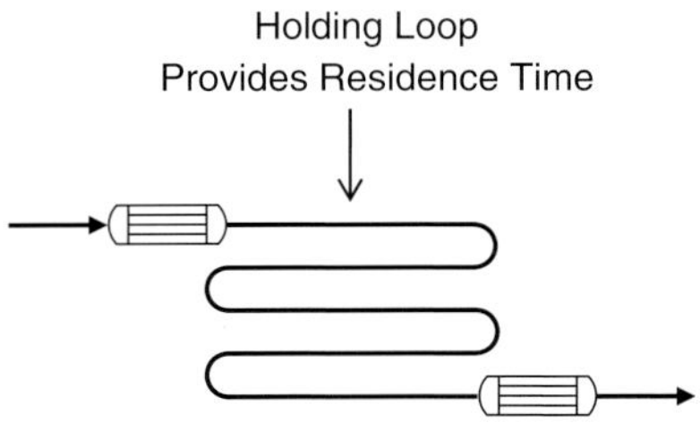

Figure 11.15 Basic schematic of a continuous sterilizer with heat exchangers to adjust the temperature of the incoming and outgoing media, and a coil to provide the desired residence time.

in a holding loop consisting of insulated lengths of pipe connected by U-bends [27]. The tube is designed to a sufficient length to give the media an appropriate residence time for sterilization. For viral inactivation of the protein A product, the same principles apply, except that the heat exchangers would be replaced with pH adjustments. The continuous pH inactivation may be accomplished using a simple silicone tubing coil to provide for a single-use solution. A starting estimation for the length of tubing required can be found using the incoming flow rate Q_{PAP} according to Equation 11.10.

$$L_{\mathrm{VI}} = 2\frac{(Q_{\mathrm{PAP}} + Q_{\mathrm{VIA}}) \cdot \tau_{\mathrm{VI}}}{a_{\mathrm{VI}}} \tag{11.10}$$

where L_{VI} is the length of tubing, Q_{VIA} is the flow rate of acid required to adjust the pH down for viral inactivation, and a_{VI} is the inner cross-sectional area of the desired tubing.

Care must be taken to design the tubing coil to provide the desired inactivation time on the microscopic scale and as such, Equation 11.9 is only a starting point for design calculations. The actual tube length needs to take into account any nonidealities associated with the flow in the tube, which may result in protein exiting the coil prior to τ_{VI}. As a result, coils used for viral inactivation should be well characterized by classical residence time distribution (RTD) analysis. RTD analysis refers to the amount of time each individual molecule of a trace solution spends inside the tubing coil and relies on the assumptions of constant flow rate and a Dirac input function of tracer solution to the tube. A thorough treatment of residence time distribution analysis is given by Fogler [28] as well as Froment and Bischoff [29]. An analytical solution to the tracer material balance given by Fogler [28] was used to generate the curves shown in Figure 11.16. It can be seen that as dispersion decreases in the tube, decreases, the tracer peak in the effluent becomes sharper and leaves the column later. It should be noted that tracer solution is detected in the column effluent prior to calculated residence time in the tube calculated based on flow rate and coil volume alone ($\Theta = 1$). This difference from the ideal tube residence time must be taken into account to ensure that all of the protein A product flowing through the coil is appropriately inactivated.

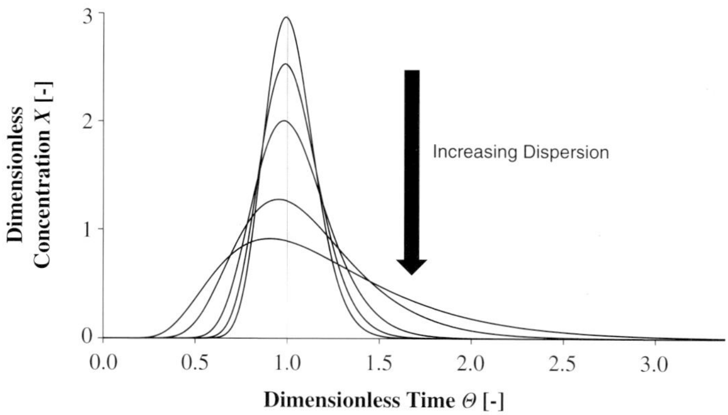

Figure 11.16 Simulated effluent curves from pulse tracer injections using the equation with increasing dispersion in the tube where Θ is dimensionless time ($\Theta = t/\tau_{VI} = t\upsilon/L_{VI}$), υ is the superficial fluid velocity, X is the dimensionless concentration ($X = C/C_0$), and c_0 is the concentration of the tracer solution. For RTD analysis, c_0 is defined as the mass of acetone in the pulse injection divided by the entire system volume between the injection point and the UV detector.

The target pH of the viral inactivation is set based on inactivation kinetics to provide several logs of clearance of virus – typically >6LRV. As such this pH set point is a critical process parameter that must be met to ensure product safety. A challenge to conducting a continuous pH adjustment is the typical pH gradient observed during the pH shift elution from the protein A columns as shown in Figure 11.17a. Here, the elution pH spans from pH6.5 to <pH = 4. By pooling several column elutions from the CMCC step in the previral inactivation surge bag, transients in the observed pH in that vessel can be minimized, but not eliminated. Figure 11.17b shows the pH profile in the previral inactivation hold bag over a period of 20 h and represents >210 individual column elutions. Here the transients are limited to +/− 0.1 pH units over time. Due to these transients, a rigorous control strategy must be put in place to ensure that only fluid with the proper pH will be sent forward into the holding loop for viral inactivation. This would include automated pH control and an automated valve system to direct flows. By using silicon tubing for the holding loop, it is possible to insert pH probes at different residence times to ensure a stable pH profile throughout the entire hold time.

The effluent of the viral inactivation coil must be properly conditioned for the next unit operation – in this instance, anion exchange chromatography. As such, the pH of the stream needs to be adjusted with a basic solution and in some instances a diluent must be added to reduce conductivity. The flow rates of the modifying solutions are accounted for in outlet flow rate of the viral inactivation step calculated as

$$Q_{VIOut} = Q_{PAP} + Q_{VIA} + Q_{VIB+}Q_{VID} \tag{11.11}$$

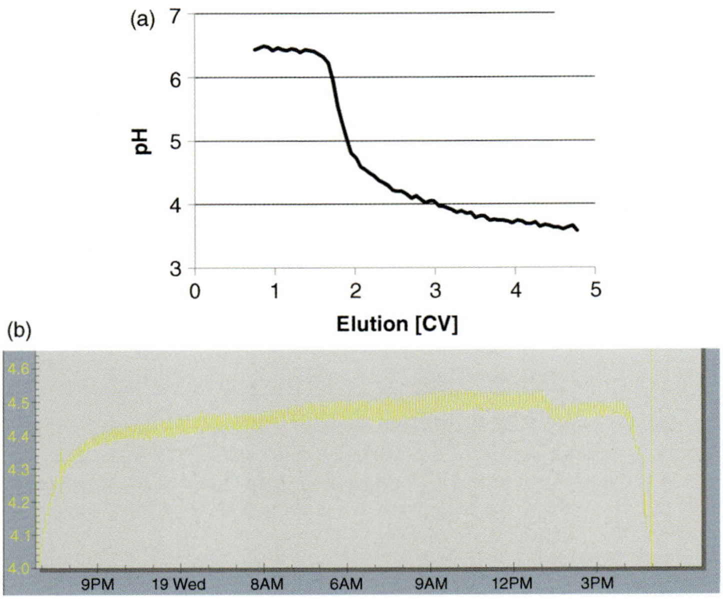

Figure 11.17 Typical pH profiles for (a) a single protein A column elution from CMCC and (b) in the previral inactivation surge bag with no pH control operated over 20 h.

where Q_{VIB} is the flow rate of base solution needed to reach the proper pH and Q_{VID} is the flow rate of diluent needed to reach the desired conductivity for the subsequent unit operation.

11.2.4 Fine Purification: Flow-Through Anion Exchange Chromatography (AEX)

Membrane chromatography is an alternative to the traditional packed-bed chromatography [24]. The advantages of using membrane adsorptive chromatography, for removal of high MW contaminants, such as DNA and viruses host cell protein (HCP), aggregates, protein A ligand, viruses, have been well established and include reduced processing time and buffer usage, higher flow rates, and ease of scale up [30–32]. Zhou showed scalability from 00.8 ml to 5 l for example. For conventional bead-based chromatography, adsorptive transport of solutes, particularly high molecular weight contaminants, such as DNA and viruses, to the binding sites relies on diffusion and is relatively slow. This mass transfer resistance leads to low efficiency with long column bed heights and slow linear flow rates on the order of 100–150 cm h^{-1} with dramatically oversized columns [33]. Whereas membrane adsorption relies primarily on convective mass transport with minimal pore diffusion, resulting in increased overall throughput.

Another advantage of membrane adsorption is its lower bed height to diameter ratio, which results in smaller pressure drops compared to column chromatography, which allows for flow rates on the order of 1–10 membrane volumne (MV) per minute. The synthetic porous multilayered membranes are generally available in single-use formats of various configurations – discs, capsules, or cartridges – which simplifies operations (column packing eliminated) and scale-up (modular formats), and minimizes validation requirements [31]. For these modules, linear scale-up of frontal surface area, bed volume, and flow rate is possible while the dynamic binding capacity remains constant.

A variety of functionalized membranes (e.g., affinity, ion exchange, hydrophobic interaction ligands) are available on the market, but the most popular application involves the use of anion-exchange (AEX) membranes as a polishing step in the mAb purification platform. These membranes have been shown to be effective for scavenging trace amounts of impurities in flow-through mode [24]. The properties of typical AEX resin (Poros HQ50) and scale-down membrane units from Pall (Mustang Q), Millipore (ChromaSorb), and Sartorius (Sartobind Q) are shown in Table 11.5.

11.2.4.1 Effects of Sample Flow Rate on AEX Membrane Chromatography

One of the main differences between traditional and continuous processing for membrane chromatography steps is the flux through the membrane. Because the rate limiting step in continuous process is not AEX, the flow rate for the step is much lower than typical for batch-based processes. The flow rate for the continuous anion exchange (Q_{AEX}) step is equivalent to the flow rate of the effluent from the VI step such that $Q_{AEX} = Q_{VIOut}$.

The experimental results at different flow rates are summarized in Figure 11.18. At flow rates from 1 to 10 MV min^{-1}, typical for batch-based processing, there were no significant differences for both HCP level and yield. When the flow rate was reduced to 0.3 MV min^{-1} for the continuous processing scenario, the HCP level was reduced compared to the higher flow rates (>75 ppm) while still maintaining a high recovery yield (>95%). It is suggested that operation in continuous process mode at reduced flux values could significantly enhance the impurity removal. It should be noted however that the increased residence time in the membrane adsorber may decrease the yield of the step with some molecules as a result of the timescale of binding kinetics. To date, this phenomenon has not been observed experimentally by the author.

11.2.4.2 Effect of Sample Loading Amount on AEX Membrane Chromatography

Sample loading is another significant factor for the process optimization of AEX membrane chromatography. In order to determine the sample loading quantity, a dynamic binding capacity study was carried out at the optimal pH, conductivity, and flow rate conditions. Figure 11.19 shows the breakthrough curves for both HCP and DNA concentrations at low flow (0.3 MV min^{-1}). The typical loading for membrane adsorbers depends on the quality of the feed material, but

Table 11.5 Summary of properties for anion exchange bead based resin and membrane adsorber units.

Name	Resin	Membrane		
	POROS HQ50	**Pall Mustang Q Coin**	**Millipore ChromaSorb**	**Sartobind SingleSep Q**
Sorbent/ device				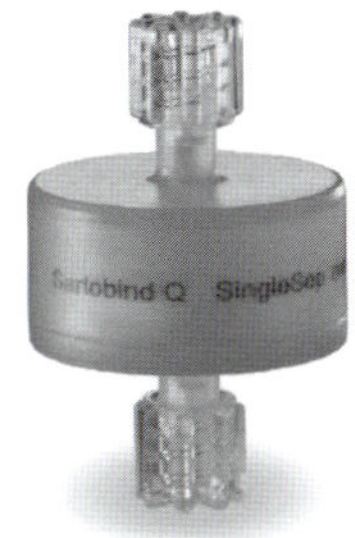
Unit size	2.0 ml	0.35 ml	0.08 ml	1.0 ml
Pore size	0.36 μm	0.8 μm	0.65 μm	>3 μm
Chemistry	Quaternized polyethyleneimine	Quaternary ammonium	Polyallylamine	Quaternary amine
Support matrix	Cross-linked poly (styrenedivinyl-benzene)	Polyethersulfone (PES)	Ultrahigh molecular weight polyethylene (UPE) membrane	Stabilized reinforced cellulose

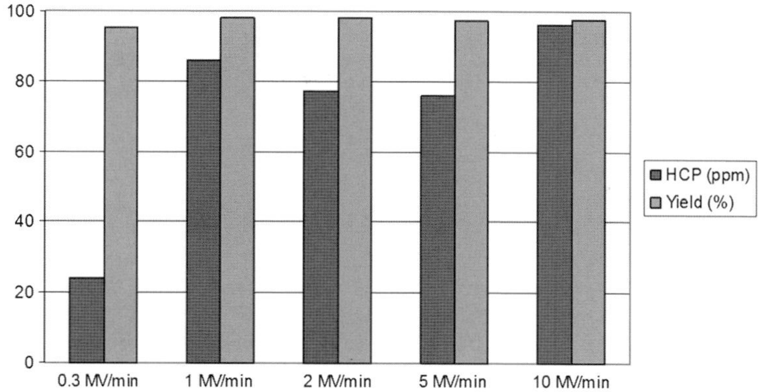

Figure 11.18 Comparison of Pall Mustang Q membrane adsorber performance for host cell protein concentration (ppm) and yield (%) in the flow through pool as a function of flow rate.

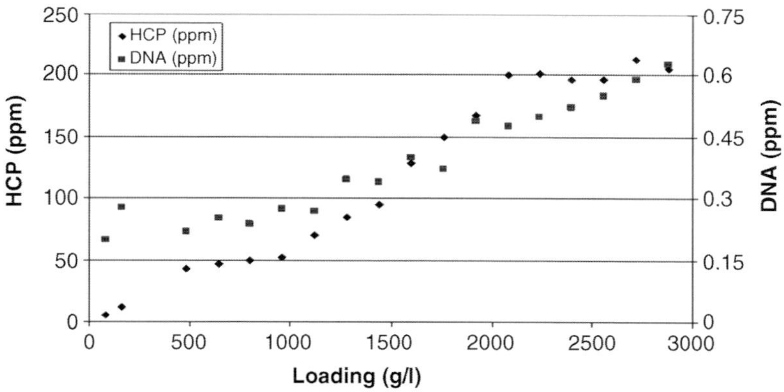

Figure 11.19 HCP (ppm) and DNA (ppm) concentration as a function of Pall Mustang Q membrane adsorber loading at optimal pH and conductivity values.

is typically in the range of 1000~3000 g l^{-1}, which is approximately 10 times greater than traditional AEX column loadings for the same separation (~100 g l^{-1}).

11.2.4.3 Scaling-Up Membrane Chromatography for Continuous Processing

In traditional AEX column, the loading linear velocity and column bed height are conserved upon scale-up, but for membrane chromatography, flux is held constant because the number of membrane layers (analogous to bed height) remains the same regardless of the total membrane volume in the module. In a case study, three scales of membrane processes were performed with Pall Mustang Q adsorbers. The experimental conditions and analytical results for all three scales are summarized in Table 11.6. A 3× buffer reduction was demonstrated in this case study using a much smaller device (260 ml membrane vs. 2.5 l resin) as

Table 11.6 Summary of results of Mustang Q membrane at different scales.

Scale	Small (MV = 0.35 ml)	Medium (MV = 60 ml)	Large (MV = 260 ml)
Flow rate	0.3 MV min^{-1}	0.1 MV min^{-1}	0.1 MV min^{-1}
Feed HCP	343.5 ppm	92.7 ppm	818.6 ppm
Feed DNA	2.2 ppm	0.7 ppm	7.9 ppm
Yield	95.1%	95.6%	>95%
HCP	24.0 ppm LRV: 1.16	9.8 ppm LRV: 0.98	57.8 ppm LRV: 1.15
DNA	1.3 ppm LRV: 0.28	0.2 ppm LRV: 0.54	1.6 ppm LRV: 0.70
Monomer	n/a	n/a	98.85%

compared to the AEX column. The scale-up study also shows more than 95% step yield with HCP <60 ppm and DNA <2 ppm in the flow-through pool at all scales using Mustang Q adsorbers with membrane volumes of 0.35, 60, and 260 ml. (Note: the designed flow rate was 0.1 MV, but it was not feasible to test in the small scale Mustang Q coin (0.35 ml) due to flow rate limitations). In the continuous process, the flow rate for the AEX step ($Q_{AEX} \equiv Q_{AEXIn} \equiv Q_{AEXOut}$) is equal to Q_{VIOut}.

11.2.5
Fine Purification: Continuous Multicolumn Chromatography – BioSMB Cation Exchange Chromatography

Continuous multicolumn chromatography can be used for other bind and elute modalities, such as cation exchange chromatography. Cation exchange is traditionally used in antibody processes to separate closely related species to the product, such as aggregates and charged variants. Product may be eluted from cation exchange columns by using either pH or conductivity gradients or steps. A pH adjustment of the cation exchange feed stream to acidic conditions is necessary to protonate proteins in solution, which promotes binding to the negatively charged adsorbent. The CMCC step development performed on the BioSMB was similar to the approach presented in Sections 11.2.3.1–11.2.3.2 for protein A chromatography.

11.2.5.1 Cation Exchange Loading Zone Optimization

The loading zone for cation exchange chromatography was designed in either of the two configurations presented in Figure 11.20. In Figure 11.20a, feed is uninterrupted as it was presented for protein A chromatography. In Figure 11.20b, the feed is periodically suspended during the time Wash 1 is sent to the second stage for product recovery. Both load zones were tested for capture efficiency using (8) or (6) columns (1.2 cm diameter × 3.4 cm, Poros HS50) for the two different load zones accordingly. A design model was created for CEX following a similar approach to that defined for protein A capture using Equations 11.6–11.8. The

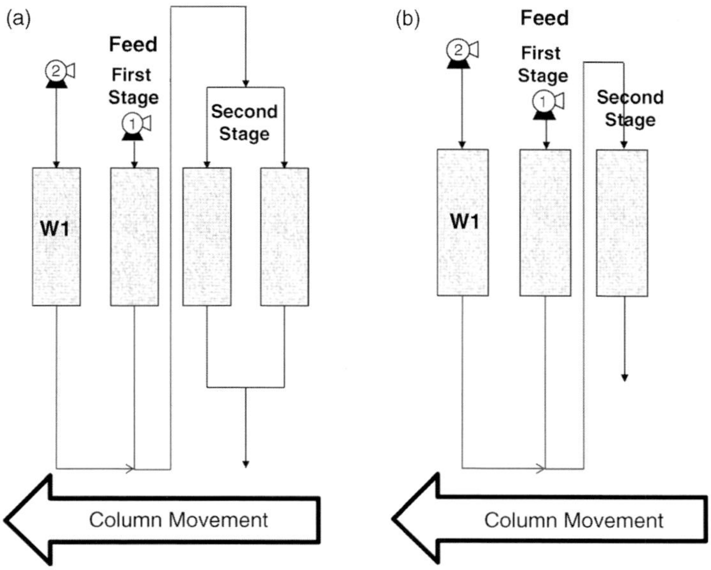

Figure 11.20 BioSMB Load zone configurations for cation exchange monoclonal antibody capture: (a) (1) column stage 1 and (2) column stage 2 with (3) total columns, and (b) (1) column stage 1 and (1) column in stage 2 with (2) total columns. In configuration (a), Wash 1 is combined with the effluent from the first stage and sent to the second stage for protein recovery. In configuration (b), feed is suspended as Wash 1 is sent to the second stage for recovery.

capture efficiency model predictions are shown in Figure 11.21. As with protein A chromatography, the models provide a good fit to the experimentally derived data (within 1%) regardless of load zone configuration. Due to the reduced number of columns and the possibility to match cycle times with the protein A step, the configuration presented in Figure 11.20.b was selected as the preferred loading zone configuration.

11.2.5.2 Cation Exchange Elution Zone Considerations

After binding conditions were finalized, the elution zone of the cation exchange process was optimized to achieve a similar separation compared to the batch-based processes. Since cation exchange chromatography is providing fine separations of product-related proteins (aggregates, fragments, variants, etc.) it requires tight control with high reproducibility. However, the requirement to use smaller chromatography columns with reduced bed heights in continuous multicolumn chromatography to gain efficiency in the loading zone may lead to detrimental effects in the elution zone due to reduced total plate counts and residence times. As a result, the resolution of critical components must be verified upon transition to a CMCC process. The cation exchange step is primarily responsible for separating mAb aggregate from monomer; as such, aggregate clearance was utilized to demonstrate comparability of CMCC to the reference batch process.

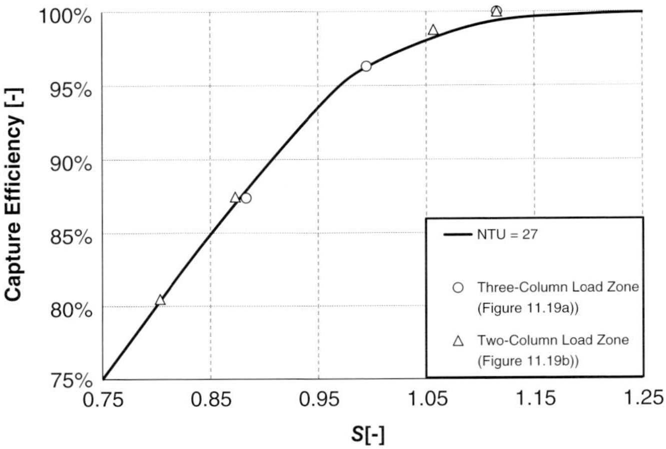

Figure 11.21 Theoretical capture efficiency curves (lines) for a monoclonal antibody on a cation exchange adsorbent (Poros HS50) plotted as lines with corresponding experimental data for (a) 10 g l^{-1} mAb feed stream using a six-column (1.2 cm × 3.4 cm) method. The predictive design models for BioSMB show a good fit to the BioSMB experimental data within 1% as well as operational ranges where >99% capture efficiency can be achieved.

The aggregate clearance profiles presented in Figure 11.22 were generated on standard batch columns (0.5 cm diameter × 20 cm), reduced bed height batch columns (1.2 cm diameter × 6.8 cm), and with the continuous chromatography configuration using (6) 1.2 cm diameter × 3.4 cm columns all packed with Poros

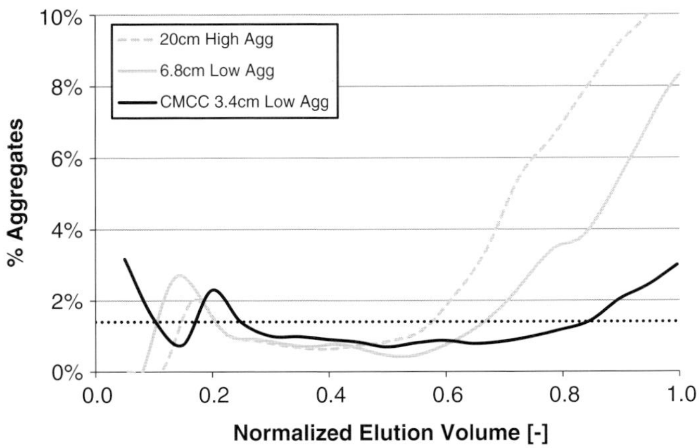

Figure 11.22 Aggregate elution profiles from cation exchange chromatography using Poros HS50 media. The continuous chromatography results are compared with batch chromatography results using two different column configurations; 0.5 cm diameter × 20 cm and 1.2 cm diameter × 6.8 cm. The CMCC separation is comparable to the batch-based separation. The dotted horizontal line represents the aggregate percentage in the feed.

HS50 adsorbent. It can be seen that aggregate clearance profiles of all three scenarios are similar with a small aggregate peak eluting near the beginning of the profile as well as an increasing aggregate percentage as elution proceeds. The aggregates are held to a lower final percentage in the CMCC CEX pool compared to the batch alternative. The position of the leading aggregate peak in the profiles is shifted for the different curves as a result of varying system voidages and fraction sizes for each experiment. In addition, the falling aggregate percentage seen at the onset of the CMCC elution is carried over from the preceding cycle in the eluate line and is not included in the product pool. The separation achieved with the CMCC system was determined to be comparable or better than the reference batch-based process. The similar aggregate trends observed at different bed heights in this work is in part due to the nature of the Poros media, which allows for convective flow throughout the bead and relies less on diffusive mass transport. Similar performance may not be observed on more traditional agarose-based media.

In multicolumn chromatography, peak collection can be accomplished by traditional means, that is, UV, pH, conductivity peak characteristics or time/volume based. In the case of the cation exchange chromatography step described earlier, time-based collected was chosen as the preferred method. Using those cut points, the CMCC process was scaled up to 2.5 × 5 cm columns for 16 cycles. The UV traces from those cycles (overlaid) are shown in Figure 11.23. Over the course of the 16 cycles, the standard deviation of peak area for each column was <0.5% and the standard deviation among all six columns was 1% demonstrating the robustness of the process.

11.2.6 Formulation: Continuous Ultrafiltration

In recent years, single-pass tangential-flow filtration (SPTFF) has been suggested as an alternative traditional multipass tangential-flow filtration (MPTFF) for protein concentration. In SPTFF, stacks of ultrafiltration membranes are arranged in such a manner as to create stepwise changes in the flowpath, which results in a consistent channel velocity throughout a single membrane cassette [34,35]. Constant retentate flow rate in the membrane channel is considered a key scaling rule in conventional multipass tangential-flow filtration because it determines the effectiveness of the sweeping action of the fluid flow at the membrane surface. This sweeping action is responsible for minimizing the deleterious effects of the concentration polarization layer, a build-up of solute compounds including ions, macromolecules, colloids, and the protein product at the membrane surface, on flux [34].

Traditional tangential-flow filtration is a low conversion process and as a result, the retentate must be passed through the membrane cassette many times before the final concentration factor (CF) can be achieved. As a result, a recirculation tank and pump are considered mandatory in these systems. Alternatively, single-pass tangential-flow filtration is a high conversion process requiring only

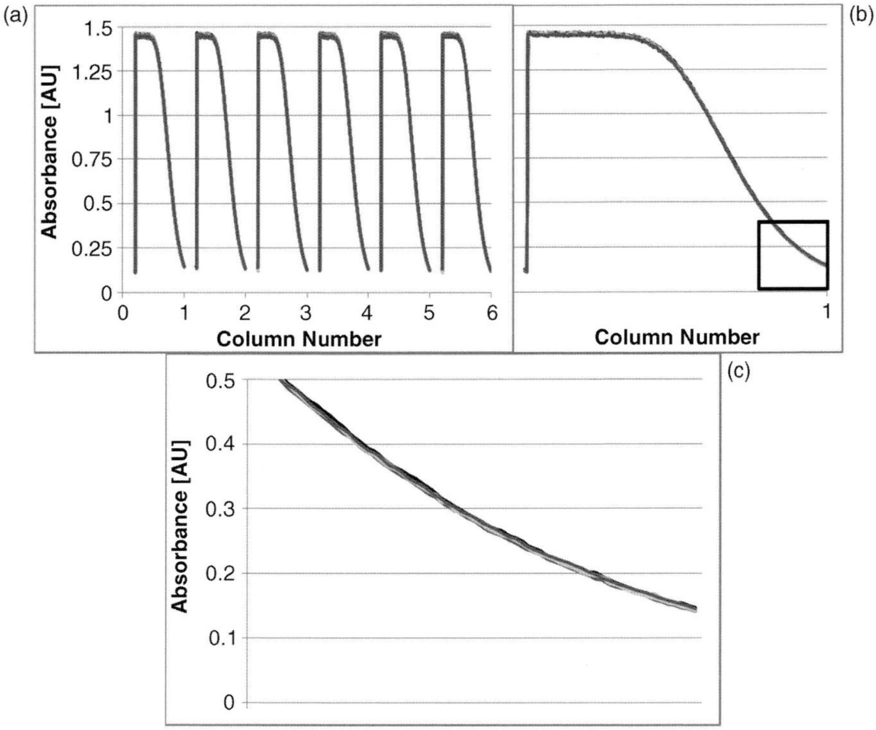

Figure 11.23 UV (280 nm) elution profiles from 16 cation exchange cycles overlaid for (a) all six columns used in the CMCC method, (b) a close-up of just column 1 elutions, and (c) a zoomed-in region of column 1 elutions at the tail edge of the peak. All elution peak areas were within 1% standard deviation.

one pass through the membrane cassette. Process flow diagrams for MPTFF and SPTFF are presented in Figure 11.24a and b, respectively. Initial applications for SPTFF have been focused on three main areas: (i) high titer concentrations where the reduced system hold-up and efficient product recovery are advantageous, (ii) systems with sheer sensitive proteins or foamy streams where the lack

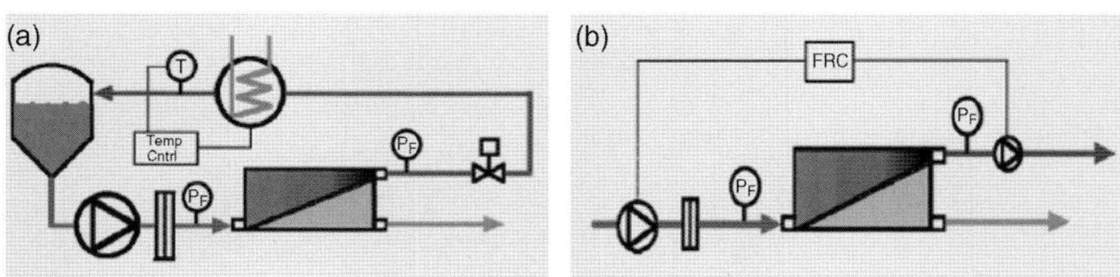

Figure 11.24 Block flow diagram for (a) traditional MPTFF showing the large recirculation tank and pump required for the concentration and (b) SPTFF showing the flow ratio control logic (FRC) required to meet the desired concentration in a single pass [36].

of recirculation can minimize the deleterious effects on product quality or flux decay, and (iii) as a flow-through concentration device used to de-bottleneck processes due to tankage limitations. Similar to the third application, the nature of the SPTFF mode of action is also amenable to continuous operation where the incoming stream is relatively dilute, and the outgoing retentate is at the target concentration.

The final ultrafiltration step may also be responsible for formulating the product into drug substance by the addition of a diafiltration stage of the filtration either in the middle or at the end of the concentration phase of the process. In MPTFF, diafiltration is a simple operation of either: (i) feeding and bleeding the diafiltration buffer into the recirculation tank at a rate matching the permeate flow rate, or (ii) by a series of 5–8 successive whole volume additions of the buffer to the recirculation tank followed by a concentration back to the original volume. In addition, due to the low efficiency per pass, the final concentration can be finely tuned by extending the filtration time. To date single-pass tangential-flow filtration suffers from the inability to accomplish the diafiltration in the same single-pass through the membrane cassette and also relies on the RFC control loop to finely tune in the final protein concentration. By placing a conventional MPTFF, solely responsible for diafiltration and concentration following the SPTFF step, both of these issues are eliminated. The continuous process can run with some variation in the concentration factor (within bounds) and final formulation can be done offline of the continuous equipment train using a relatively small filtration skid with low hold-up volumes.

The concentration factors that can be achieved in single-pass tangential-flow filtration are a factor of four principal parameters. First is the length of the channel and as such SPTFF membranes are sold in cassettes of varying configurations (4-in-series, 7-in-series, 9-in-series) to extend the flow path while maintaining the linear velocity in the channel. Second is the flow rate; longer residence times leads to higher concentration factors. The third parameter is the inlet and outlet pressures, which are a function of flow rate and manually applied retentate backpressure. The final parameter is the feed concentration, which has implications on the concentration polarization layer formation. To understand the interdependence of the first three key operating parameters listed, an experiment was performed on a partially purified monoclonal antibody solution with an incoming concentration of $9.3\,g\,l^{-1}$. The solution was passed through the SPTFF apparatus at different inlet pressures (i.e., transmembrane pressures as the retentate pressure = 0 psi) and flow rates (i.e., residence times) with two different membrane configurations. The results of this experiment are presented in Figure 11.25a and b for a 4-in-series ($0.065\,m^2$) and 7-in-series ($0.12\,m^2$) cassette configurations. Because the inlet pressure, outlet pressure, and flow rate are intrinsically linked, the operating space becomes complex in that a desired concentration factor can be achieved by multiple combinations of flow rate and pressures. For this experiment, a 5 l of feed solution was placed in a bottle along with the retentate and permeate

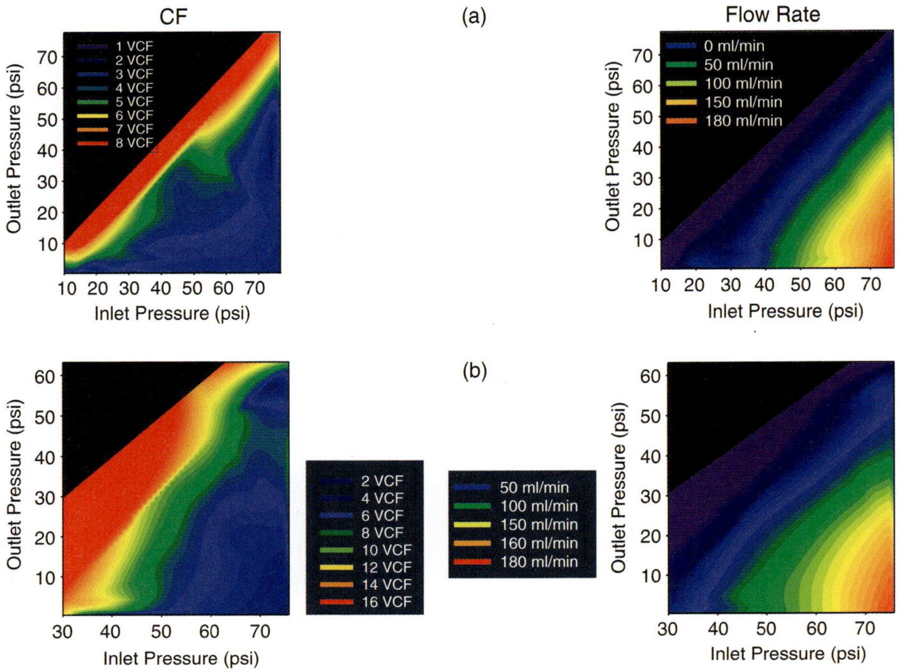

Figure 11.25 Single-pass tangential-flow filtration data (a) 4-in-series cassette with 0.65 m^2 membrane area and (b) 7-in-series cassette with 0.12 m^2 membrane area. The left panes are surface plots of the concentration factor as a result of the inlet and outlet pressures. The right panes are surface plots of the flow rate as a result of the inlet and outlet pressures. Data generated by Taylor Chartier at Merck Research Labs, Rahway, NJ.

resulting in total recycle of the process streams. After conditions were set, the SPTFF system was run for 15 min to establish equilibrium before recording the concentration factor and pressure information. In the data presented in Figure 11.25, the concentration factor for each cassette can be selected in the left-hand pane thus setting inlet and outlet pressures. Those pressures can be translated to the right-hand pane to determine the operating flow rate (or the reverse).

The incoming flow rate to the SPTFF is set by the preceding anion exchange chromatography step such that $Q_{\mathrm{SPTFFIn}} \equiv Q_{\mathrm{AEX}}$. The SPTFF is then set to concentrate to a specific volumetric concentration factor (VCF) such that

$$Q_{\mathrm{SPTFFIn}} = Q_{\mathrm{SPTFFR}} + Q_{\mathrm{SPTFFP}} \tag{11.12}$$

Where Q_{SPTFFR} is the retentate flow rate and Q_{SPTFFP} is the permeate flow rate, and $VCR \equiv Q_{\mathrm{SPTFFIn}}/Q_{\mathrm{SPTFFR}}$.

The SPTFF was not originally designed for use on continuous processes where incoming flow rates are at the laboratory scale (<200 l bioreactors) where typical incoming flow rates are often <50 ml min^{-1}, hence the relatively large cited membrane areas. As a result, the permeate flow is often restricted in the continuous processing scenarios to prevent overconcentration of the stream in the cassette and the formation of a gel layer at the membrane surface. This issue would be eliminated if appropriate scale-down membranes were available on the market. At larger scales, current membrane offerings become more appropriate for continuous processing purposes.

11.3 Pilot-Scale Demonstration of the Integrated Continuous Process

The demonstration of the continuous process at the pilot scale was conducted with 100 l of cell culture fluid produced in a single-use bioreactor with a product titer of ~2 g l^{-1}. The crude cell broth was processed through the following unit operations continuously: kSep Single-Use Centrifugation → Depth Filtration → Protein A Capture Chromatography (CMCC BioSMB) → Low pH Viral Inactivation → Anion Exchange Chromatography (Membrane Adsorber) → Cation Exchange Chromatography → Continuous Ultrafiltration. To achieve this, each of the individually optimized unit operations described in Section 11.2 was scaled-up individually and connected through the use of surge bags at the appropriate flow rates. This setup is shown in Figure 11.26a while the time each step in the continuous DSP was in active operation is shown in Figure 11.26b. The unit operations were started up sequentially starting with the centrifugation step and ending with the continuous ultrafiltration. The unit operation then ran for a

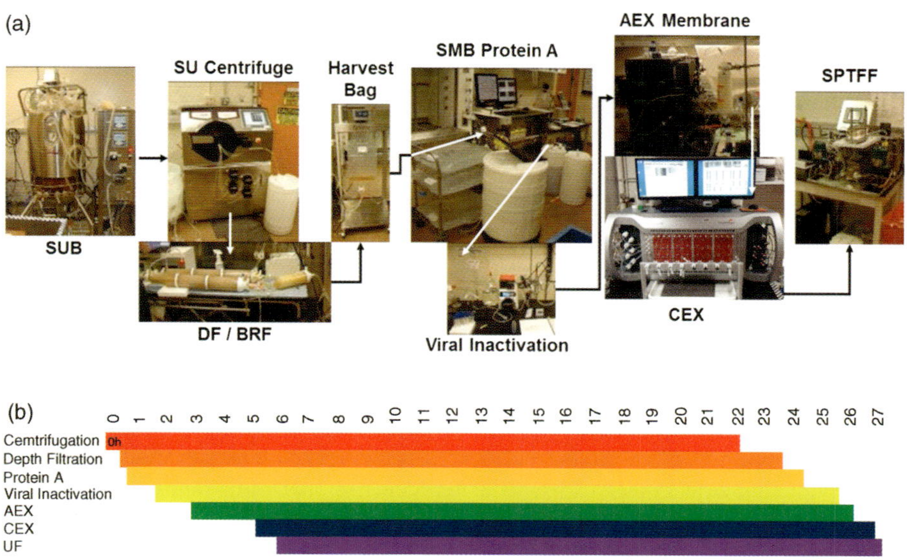

Figure 11.26 (a) Pilot setup of the first-generation 100 l continuous purification demonstration and (b) unit operation usage schedule.

Table 11.7 Summary of performance for the proof of concept pilot scale continuous processing of CHO expressed mAb with the single use enabled platform.

	Average yield [%]	DNA* [ppm]	HCP [ppm]	Res. ProA [ppm]	% Monomer
Centrifugation	97.3	N/S	N/S	N/S	N/S
DF/BRF	98.6	30 515	383 300	N/S	N/S
Protein A SMB	98.1	N/S	N/S	N/S	N/S
Viral inactivation	100	2	1063	2.1	89.8%
Anion exchange membrane	98.8	<LOQ	82	1.5	99.0%
Cation exchange chromatography	84.2	<LOQ	605	<LOQ	99.2%
SPTFF	99.5	0.001	35	<LOQ	99.0%
Overall	77.9	0.001	8.7	<LOQ	99.0%

period of ~18 h of continuous, uninterrupted operation before the unit operations were turned off sequentially as feed became depleted. The timescale of the process was set to harvest the batch through protein A chromatography over 24 h thus setting the timescale for the rest of the DSP. Future scale-up work will reduce the protein A harvest time such that the entire purification could be completed within a 24 h time period; requiring slightly different column dimensions in the protein A and cation exchange chromatography steps.

Each of the surge bags servicing the unit operations was sampled three times throughout the continuous downstream process demonstration. Titer analysis as well as HCP and DNA assays were performed on each of the samples. Table 11.7 summarizes the performance of each of the unit operations averaged over the course of the demonstration.

Surge vessels provide the analogous point in batch processing where intermediates are assayed for critical product attributes and purification progression. At a minimum, such analytic capabilities are currently required in the bag to measure any critical process parameters associated with the succeeding unit operation, such as pH and/or conductivity. However, a longer-term process analytic technology (PAT) objective for a continuous process will be to use online and rapid at-line analytical techniques to sample each bag at periodic intervals for process residuals, titer, and other quality-related methods Figure 11.27. Feedback into a multivariate data analysis (MVDA) system can then be incorporated to let operators know when a process starts going out of control so that corrective action may be taken. Furthermore, a detailed Failure Mode Analysis must be conducted to engineer in sophisticated controls that mitigate against loss of a batch from an individual out of control event. Out-of-spec material as measured by the PAT approach must be prevented from moving downstream in the continuous process and eliminate the possibility for contaminating all of the material processed prior to loss of control.

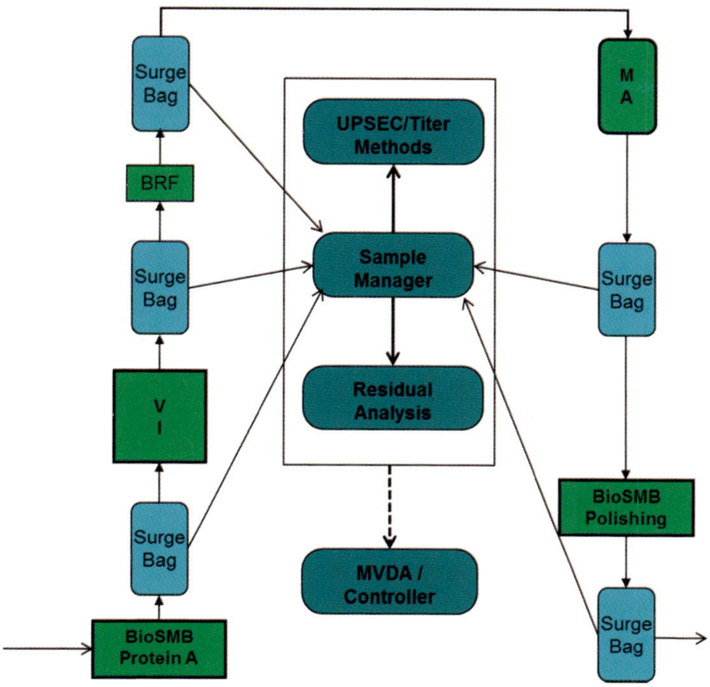

Figure 11.27 Future state of process monitoring and control. Each surge bag is sampled frequently for quality and process residuals. MVDA can then be applied to the continuous downstream process to alert operators if the process starts going out of control.

11.4 Summary

This work has provided the proof of concept for a single-use enabled continuous downstream processing for the next-generation CHO mAb manufacturing. The economic analysis shows that this approach can provide a significant economic favorable advantage over conventional stainless steel approaches. Combining this 2000 l single-use closed processing modular "ball room" type modular facility of the future will enable flexible processing solutions that can handle the fluctuations of capacity demand from blockbuster needs to smaller personal medicine type demands. The continuous processing provides rapid processing options that will accelerate not only commercial manufacturing but clinical manufacturing as well where speed to clinical studies is key. Continuous processing provides significant capital savings from the elimination of hold vessels as outlined in Figure 11.28. The move toward commercial implementation still requires significant development investment. This needs the development of automation approaches that integrate process models with PAT. In addition the robustness of single-use technology needs to be improved especially the reduction of leak issues by the

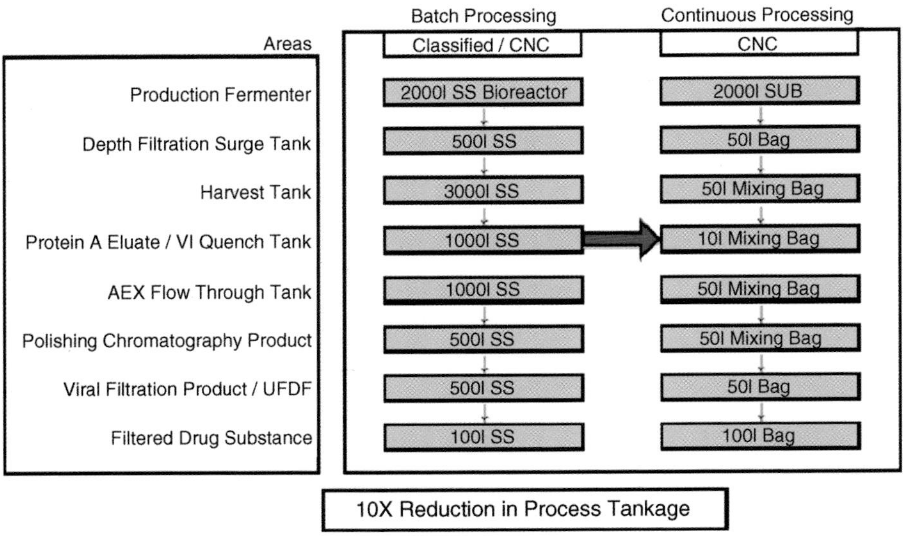

Figure 11.28 The impact of continuous processing to reducing tank volumes and providing a potential fivefold reduction in capital avoidance.

introduction of molded tubing/bag manifolds and supply chain transparency. These issues including improvements to commercial implementation, such as defining guidance for regulatory and GMP approaches for leachables and particulates, are being tackled by the end-user consortium of the BPOG disposables working group (biophorum.com). In addition, appropriate continuous processing scale-down tools need to be enhanced and integrated to enable rapid process development of continuous processing. It is predicted that this approach will provide a significant impact to the next-generation processing in the next 5 to 10 years.

References

1 Reichert, J.M. (2012) Which are the antibodies to watch in 2012? *mAbs*, **4** (1), 1–3.

2 Datamonitor (2010) Monoclonal antibodies: 2010.

3 BCC Research (2012) Antibody drugs: technologies and global market.

4 Kaitin, K.I. (2010) Deconstructing the drug development process: the new face of innovation. *Clin. Pharmacol. Ther.*, **87** (3), 356–361.

5 Alvin, K., Ly, J., Condon, R., Keil, G., Mou, X., Ye, J., and Pollard, D. (2013) Technology improvements to accelerate process development of biologics. *Am. Pharm. Rev.*, **20**, 1–9.

6 Bareither, R., Bargh, N., Oakeshott, R., Watts, K., and Pollard, D. (2013) Automated disposable small scale reactor for high throughput bioprocess development. *Biotechnol. Bioeng.*, **110** (12), 3126–3138.

7 Welsh, J.P., Petroff, M.G., Rowicki, P., Bao, H., Linden, T., Roush, D.J., and Pollard, J.M. (2014) A practical strategy for using miniature chromatography columns

in a standardized high-throughput workflow for purification development of monoclonal antibodies. *Biotechnol. Prog.*, **30** (3), 626–635.

8 Warikoo, V., Godawat, R., Brower, K., Jain, S., Cummings, D., Simons, E., Johnson, T., Walther, J., Yu, M., Wright, B., McLarty, K., Karey, K., Hwang, C., Zhou, W., Riske, F., and Konstantinov, K. (2012) Integrated continuous production of recombinant therapeutic proteins. *Biotechnol. Bioeng.*, **109** (12), 3018–3029.

9 Lim, J. and Sinclair, A. (2007) Process economy of disposable manufacturing process models to minimize upfront investment. *Am. Pharm. Rev.*, **10**, 114–121.

10 Foulon, A., Trach, F., Pralong, A., Proctor, M., and Lim, J. (2008) Using disposables in an antibody production process. *BioProcess Int.*, **6**, 12–16.

11 Bonham Carter, J., Weegar, J., NIeminen, A., Shevitx, J., and Eliezer, E. (2011) The use of the ATF system to culture Chinese hamster ovary cells in a concentrated fed-batch system cell concentrations and resulting protein concentrations are higher in a concentrated fed-batch process than in a standard system. *BioPharm Int.*, **24** (6), 42–48.

12 Bisschops, M., Frick, L., Fulton, S., and Ransohoff, T. (2009) Single use continuous countercurrent multicolumn chromatography. *BioProcess Int.*, **7**, 18–23.

13 Sen, M., Chaudhury, A., Ravendra, S., Joyce, J., and Rohit, R. (2013) Multiscale flowsheet simulation of an integrated continuous purification–downstream pharmaceutical manufacturing process. *Int. J. Pharm.*, **445**, 29–38.

14 Morrow, K.J. (2012) Inventive Approaches Redefine Downstream Ops.

15 Wu, D.J., Xie, Y., Ma, Z., and Wang, N.H. (1998) Design of simulated moving bed chromatography for amino acid separations. *Ind. Eng. Chem. Res.*, **37** (10), 4023–4035.

16 Beste, Y.A., Lisso, M., Wozny, G., and Arlt, W. (2000) Optimization of simulated moving bed plants with low efficient stationary phases: separation of fructose and glucose. *J. Chromatogr. A*, **868** (2), 169–188.

17 Rajendran, A., Paredes, G., and Mazzotti, M. (2009) Simulated moving bed chromatography for the separation of enantiomers. *J. Chromatogr. A*, **1216** (4), 709–738.

18 Miller, L., Grill, C., Yan, T., Dapremont, O., Huthmann, E., and Juza, M. (2003) Batch and simulated moving bed chromatographic resolution of a pharmaceutical racemate. *J. Chromatogr. A*, **1006** (1), 267–280.

19 Gottschlich, N. and Kasch, V. (1997) Purification of monoclonal antibodies by simulated moving-bed chromatography. *J. Chromatogr. A*, **765**, 201.

20 Bisschops, M. and Brower, M. (2013) The impact of continuous multicolumn chromatography on biomanufacturing efficiency. *Pharm. Bioprocess.*, **1** (4), 361–372.

21 Heeter, G.A. and Liapis, A.I. (1995) Perfusion chromatography: performance of periodic countercurrent column operation and its comparison with fixed-bed operation. *J. Chromatogr. A*, **711** (1), 3–21.

22 Pegel, A., Reiser, S., Steurenthaler, M., and Klein, S. (2011) Evaluating disposable depth filtration platforms for mAb harvest clarification. *BioProcess Int.*, **9**, 9.

23 Miyauchi, T. and Vermeulen, T. (1963) Longitudinal dispersion in two phase continuous flow operations. *Ind. Eng. Chem. Fundam.*, **2** (2), 113–126.

24 Shukla, A.A., Hubbard, B., Tressel, T., Guhan, S., and Low, D. (2007) Downstream processing of monoclonal antibodies—application of platform approaches. *J. Chromatogr. B*, **848** (1), 28–39.

25 Verhaar, R., Dekkers, D.W., De Cuyper, I.M., Ginsberg, M.H., de Korte, D., and Verhoeven, A.J. (2008) UV-C irradiation disrupts platelet surface disulfide bonds and activates the platelet integrin αIIbβ3. *Blood*, **112** (13), 4935–4939.

26 Liu, H.F., Ma, J., Winter, C., and Bayer, R. (2010) Recovery and purification process development for monoclonal antibody production. *mAbs*, **2** (5), 480–499.

27 Junker, B., Lester, M., Brix, T., Wong, D., and Nuechterlein, J. (2006) A next generation, pilot-scale continuous

sterilization system for fermentation media. *Bioprocess Biosyst. Eng.*, **28** (6), 351–378.

28 Fogler, H.S. (1999) *Elements of Chemical Reaction Engineering*, 3rd edn, Prentice-Hall, Englewood Cliffs, NJ.

29 Froment, G.F. and Bischoff, K.B. (1979) *Chemical Reactor Analysis and Design*, John Wiley & Sons, Inc., New York.

30 Marichal-Gallardo, P.A. and Alvarez, M.M. (2012) State-of-the-art in downstream processing of monoclonal antibodies: process trends in design and validation. *Biotechnol. Prog.*, **28** (4), 899–916.

31 Thommes, J. and Kula, M.R. (1995) Membrane chromatography. *Biotechnol. Prog.*, **11**, 357–367.

32 Zhou, J.X. and Tressel, T. (2006) Basic concepts in Q membrane chromatography for large-scale antibody production. *Biotechnol. Prog.*, **22**, 341–349.

33 Gottschalk, U. (2009) Disposables in downstream processing. *Adv. Biochem. Eng. Biotechnol.*, **115**, 171–183.

34 Casey, C., Gallos, T., Alekseev, Y., Ayturk, E., and Pearl, S. (2011) Protein concentration with single-pass tangential-flow filtration (SPTFF). *J. Membr. Sci.*, **384** (1), 82–88.

35 Dizon-Maspat, J., Bourret, J., D'Agostini, A., and Li, F. (2012) Single-pass tangential-flow filtration to debottleneck downstream processing for therapeutic antibody production. *Biotechnol. Bioeng.*, **109** (4), 962–970.

36 de los Reyes, G. and Mir, L. (2014) Method and apparatus for the filtration of biological solutions. US Patent 8,728,315.

12
Continuous Production of Bacteriophages

Aleš Podgornik, Nika Janež, Franc Smrekar, and Matjaž Peterka

12.1
Bacteriophages

Bacteriophages are viruses that specifically target bacteria, usually only one bacterial species and can operate by lytic or lysogenic life cycle. Lysogenic bacteriophages have the capability to integrate their genome into bacterial genomic DNA and do not kill bacteria immediately. Many of the lysogenic bacteriophages carry undesired genes that enhance virulence or stress tolerance of bacteria and once their lytic cycle is triggered these traits spread around bacterial population, for example, Shiga toxin in *Escherichia coli* [1]. Only lytic phages are acceptable as therapeutic bacteriophages because after infection they multiply rapidly within the bacterial cell and cause its lysis. The identity of bacteriophage can be comprehensively described by morphology, analysis of their genome content, host range, infection parameters, and so on [2] (Table 12.1).

Bacteriophages are a diverse group of viruses and are traditionally grouped by differences in morphology and type of nucleic acid. Among many morphological groups most relevant are tailed bacteriophages from the order *Caudovirales* (T4, lambda, T7), family *Inoviridae* (M13), and family *Cystoviridae* (phi6).

Majority of bacteriophages are tailed and consist of a capsid and a tail. The capsid is composed of many copies of main capsid protein and several minor proteins that assemble into a polyhedral shape, usually icosahedra. This structure is very stable, rigid, and varies in size. Genomic material is tightly packed into capsid and its release is controlled by protein connector between capsid and the tail. The latter is composed of several different proteins arranged with helical symmetry into a tube ending with a base plate and tail fibers. Tails are necessary to recognize bacteriophage hosts and to attach and deliver DNA to bacterial cytoplasm.

Bacteriophages are a valuable tool in biotechnology and applications, such as phage display [3,4], vaccine delivery vectors [5,6], targeted gene-delivery [7], and bacterial typing [8]. Due to their ability to kill target bacteria they were used as antimicrobial agents for the treatment of various bacterial infections like dysentery or staphylococcal skin disease in the past [9]. Soon after their

Continuous Processing in Pharmaceutical Manufacturing, First Edition. Edited by Ganapathy Subramanian.

Table 12.1 Basic traits of most common bacteriophages.

Order	Family	Example	Morphology	Genome type
Caudovirales	*Myoviridae*	T4	nonenveloped, long contractile tail	double-stranded (ds) DNA
	siphoviridae	T5, lambda	nonenveloped, long non contractile tail	dsDNA
	Podoviridae	T7	nonenveloped, short tail	dsDNA
/	*Inoviridae*	M13	nonenveloped, filamentous	single-stranded (ss) DNA
/	*Cystoviridae*	Phi6	enveloped, icosahedral	segmented dsRNA

discovery at the beginning of the twentieth century, bacteriophage-based products were commercialized by Elli Lilly or L'Oreal. Often uncharacterized mixture of bacteriophages of questionable efficiency and safety resulted in variable treatment outcomes [10]. Once antibiotics were introduced into healthcare practice, the usage of bacteriophages became limited to countries of the former Soviet Union. Eliava Institute in Tbilisi, Georgia and the Polish Academy of Sciences stayed centers of bacteriophage research and production [9]. They continued to develop bacteriophage therapy and conducted large human trials to treat *Pseudomonas, Klebsiella, E. coli,* and *Staphylococcus* infections [11]. Since bacterial resistance became important in recent years, bacteriophages have regained interest from the academia and industry in Western countries. Control of bacterial contamination is of major importance in clinical, food production, and agricultural environments. Among the first bacteriophage-based products was AgriPhage™ (Omnilytics, USA) [12] to treat tomato plants. More products are now marketed for use in foods or food-processing facilities. These are against pathogenic *E. coli* (EcoShield™) [13], *Listeria monocytogenes* (ListShield™) [14] and (Listex™ P100) [15], and *Salmonella* (Salmonelex™) [16]. Listex™ P100 (Micreos, The Netherlands) and SalmoFresh™ (Intralytics, USA) [17] have received status as "generally recognized as safe" (GRAS). Additionally, Listex P100 was approved as an additive to organic foods in the European Union (EU), and in 2013 as a processing aid in Australia and New Zealand [18]. In Georgia (Europe) several bacteriophage-based therapeutics are available on the market, for example, ENKO Bacteriophage and INTESTI Bacteriophagum. Bacteriophages can be successfully used also as diagnostic tools in biosensors due to their specific recognition of host bacteria, for example, VIDAS® (BioMérieux) [19].

Potency is, besides identity and safety, one of the most important traits of therapeutic phage. It can be determined by screening a large set of bacterial strains and/or species for susceptibility to a chosen bacteriophage. A therapeutic bacteriophage should be able to kill many different strains of one bacterial species. Therefore, they are often formulated as a cocktail of different bacteriophages in order to boost the efficiency of killing and avoid selection of resistant bacteria. Each of them has to be throughly characterized, produced individually and only at formulation step mixed to give a coctail.

Besides bacteriophage, bacterial strain also has to be characterized. Preferably, production of bacteriophages specific for pathogenic bacteria is done on a non-pathogenic species as in the case of Listex^{TM} P100 where bacteriophages against highly pathogenic *L. monocytogenes* are produced on *L. innocua*, a non-pathogenic and safe strain [20]. When this is not possible, recombinant strains of parental pathogenic strains without functional virulence genes may be used. The presence of any potentially immunogenic compounds, for example, endotoxins that can be released from bacterial host during production, has to be additionally addressed by downstream processing as discussed later in this chapter. In addition, production strains should not carry any functional lysogenic bacteriophage sequences within their genome, since the presence of another virus or other environmental stress during production may induce propagation of a lysogenic bacteriophage.

Therapeutic use of bacteriophages is regulated according to existing frameworks for biological agents in the EU (European Medicines Agency) or vaccines in the United States (Food and Drug Administration) [10]. Bacteriophage treatments done in Poland were all these years regulated within the Declaration of Helsinki that allows usage of bacteriophages where other therapeutics are not available or are ineffective [21]. In Australia bacteriophage therapy was allowed within compassionate use to treat *Pseudomonas aeruginosa* infection of cancer patients [22].

Traditionally, bacteriophages were prepared on a lab scale in shake flasks. These protocols are adjusted to low-volume batches, low cell densities, loosely regulated conditions, and consequently yield moderate phage titers. Among new production technologies, the continuous production system is efficient and convenient, especially for the production of bacteriophages aimed for biosanatization in food and agricultural environments. The aim of this chapter is to explain the process of bacteriophage multiplication and implement it to their continuous production in bioreactors. Furthermore, since bacteriophages intended for use in humans have to be highly purified, a special section is dedicated to continuous purification.

12.1.1 Life Cycle

Bacteriophage life cycle can be divided into different phases as shown in Figure 12.1. Lysis of cells infected by bacteriophages can be considered as their "birth" since they are released from the bacterial cells to freely diffuse into the media. The length of the period during which they exist as free bacteriophages depends on environmental factors, such as bacterial density and bacteriophage diffusion rate, as well as adsorption rate, at which bacteriophage adsorbs to the bacterial cell. Adsorption itself has two steps: reversible and irreversible [2]. Reversible binding is actually a physical adsorption of the

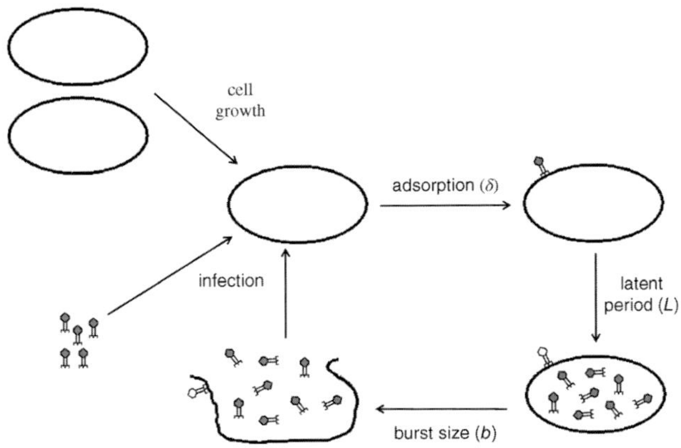

Figure 12.1 The life cycle of a lytic bacteriophage.

bacteriophage to the cell surface and is mediated by different interaction types, for example, electrostatic. The latter depends on the bacterial surface charge and bacteriophage, but also on media ionic strength and nature of ions [23]. This step facilitates the bacteriophage to find a target receptor for irreversible binding [24] through the receptor binding structures (RBS) located on the tip of the bacteriophage tail fibers. Typically, receptors of gram-negative bacteria are lipopolysaccharide or capsule components, outer membrane proteins (porins, transporters, enzymes), flagella, or pilli, while receptors of gram-positive bacteria can be peptidoglycan components, teichoic acids, and proteins associated with cell wall [25].

The time between DNA penetration into bacterial cytoplasm till bacteriophage assembly is called the eclipse period. Once bacteriophage is properly positioned on the receptor, DNA transfer from capsid through tail into bacterial cell starts. In general this procedure is as fast as 3000–4000 base pairs (bp) per second, but mechanisms that enable it differ between bacteriophages [26]. Lytic phages start to transcribe "early genes" that encode components for redirecting bacterial metabolism to synthesize bacteriophage components immediately after infection. Infection proceeds with replication of bacteriophage DNA and synthesis of structural proteins. Formation of bacteriophage particle starts with initiation of procapsid assembly and proceeds with DNA packaging into the head. The tail is assembled separately and is later attached to the full bacteriophage capsid. At this point the eclipse period is at the end. The number of assembled phage particles increases over time and although they are viable, they are still trapped inside the cell. Cell lysis and release of bacteriophages is regulated by the activity of holine and endolysine that digest membrane and peptidoglycane, respectively. After lysis, free phages are available for a new infection cycle. The time between bacteriophage adsorption and their release is called latent period, and the number of newly synthesized bacteriophages per single cell is assigned as burst size.

Each consecutive infection cycle results in an increase of bacteriophages in the media commonly referred to as bacteriophage fitness (λ), which is correlated to three bacteriophage life cycle related parameters:

1) Burst size (b), defining the average number of bacteriophages released from a single bacterial cell during lysis;
2) Latent period (L), the time from bacteriophage adsorption to its release from bacteria;
3) Adsorption rate (δ), a constant defining the rate at which bacteriophages adsorbs to bacterial cell.

It was shown [27] that for constant bacterial concentration bacteriophage fitness can be described by the following equation:

$$\lambda = \delta C\left(be^{-L\lambda} - 1\right) \tag{12.1}$$

where C is concentration of bacterial cells.

This equation is valid for ideal systems where one cell is infected by one virus and does not take into account inactivation due to multiple infection resulting in superinfection or lysis from without. Nevertheless, it still gives a reliable estimation in many cases [27]. Very importantly, it connects the effect of parameters b, L, and δ that depend on the bacteriophage–bacteria system as well as on environmental conditions.

Adsorption rate δ describes the affinity of the bacteriophage when it encounters a bacterial cell and also the encounter rate. It was demonstrated that adsorption kinetics obeys a steric mass model [28], and that the upper limit of δ is around 10^{-8} ml min^{-1} as estimated from bacteriophage diffusivity and bacterial cell size [29]. This value is approached when nearly all encounters result in infection. Since adsorption rate depends on the affinity of interaction between bacteriophage and bacteria, one can anticipate that it depends on the bacteriophage type, bacterial physiological state [30], and also on environmental conditions, especially concentration of various salts as discussed in detail elsewhere [2]. Even when the environment stimulates bacteriophage infection, adsorption rate values still vary from 9.90×10^{-9} ml min^{-1} [31] to 2 orders of magnitude lower [32]. As obvious from Equation 12.1 such a difference has a substantial effect on bacteriophage fitness.

Similarly to adsorption rate (δ), burst size (b) also depends on the bacteriophage–host system and the environmental conditions [2]. Different bacteriophages growing on the same bacterial host usually have different burst sizes [33] and vice versa [34]. In addition, the physiological state of bacteria can affect burst size for almost 2 orders of magnitude [35,36]. The burst size ranges from around 10 and up to over 1000 bacteriophages/cell [37–40] and influences bacteriophage fitness significantly.

The time between adsorption and cell lysis is called latent period (L) and it is affected by similar parameters as adsorption rate and burst size. Different bacteriophages growing on the same bacterial strain may have widely different latent periods [33,41] strongly dependent also on the bacterial physiological state [35,42]. Furthermore, there might be a twofold difference between the latent period of individual cells [43] and therefore it would be strictly speaking more properly described by a latent period distribution rather than a specific value [44]. Common average values of latent period were found to be between 10 and 70 min [31,39,40,44–46].

Latent period can be subdivided into two phases. During the first phase – eclipse period – essential components of the bacteriophage particle are synthesized and no infective bacteriophage particles can be found within the bacterial cell. The eclipse period of extremely fast growing bacteriophages like T7 [44] is 7 min long, but usually its length is 1/2 to 3/4 of the minimum latent period [2]. At one point bacteriophage components start to assemble and form infective particles. The number of bacteriophages formed within the cell depends on latent period length – the longer it is, the more bacteriophages will be formed and the burst size will be larger [47,48]. It was shown that bacteriophage number within the cell increases linearly over time before the lysis [40,49,50] (Figure 12.2) and estimated maturation rate for bacteriophage lambda is 7.7 bacteriophages per minute [40]. There are indications that accumulation of T7 bacteriophage particles might be a nonlinear process [44]. Since resources for the bacterial cells are limited, there is an upper limit of the burst size for a particular bacteriophage–bacteria system.

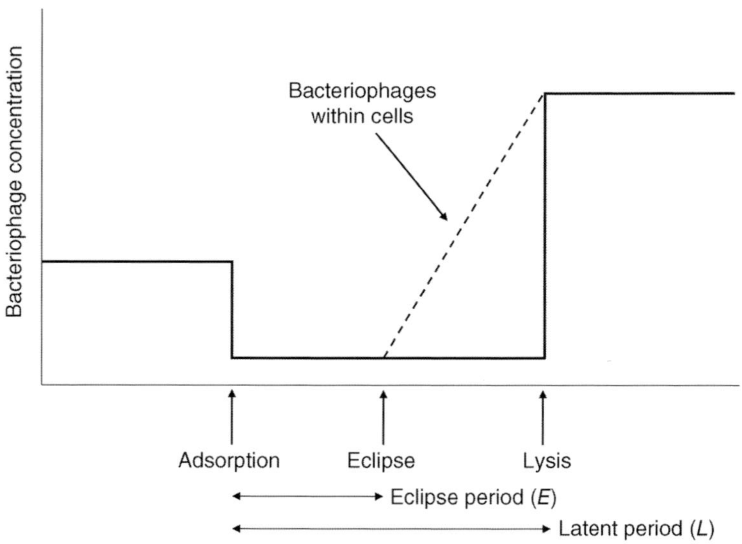

Figure 12.2 Bacteriophage concentration during the life cycle. Adsorption causes decrease of free bacteriophages concentration. During eclipse phase (E) no assembled bacteriophages are found within bacterial cell. After eclipse phase bacteriophages are accumulated inside bacterial cells and their number increases till cell lyses when they are released increasing concentration of free bacteriophages.

Due to interdependency of burst size and latent period, these two parameters might change when bacteriophage is adapting to a particular system. It was shown that latent period is highly dependent on bacterial cell concentration, which also sets a lower limit on generation time [39,40,46,51], and there exists a correlation between optimal latent period and bacteriophage fitness, which is described by the equation [52]

$$\hat{L} = E + \frac{1}{\hat{\lambda}} \tag{12.2}$$

where E is duration of eclipse period and ^ indicates optimal values in equilibrium. This equation suggests that latent period is changing due to changes in posteclipse period as a consequence to adaptation to environmental conditions. Based on this equation it is possible to predict, for a particular system, the maximal possible productivity in case of bacteriophage adaptation. The latter applies only for systems where bacteria are in excess with regard to bacteriophages. If this is not the case, a phenomenon known as superinfection might occur [53,54], which refers to multiple infection of a single bacterial cell. Infection can be caused by up to 10 bacteriophages simultaneously [55], whereas the maximum number of bacteriophages that can bind to a single *E. coli* cell is even 250 [42]. This might also lead to a phenomenon called "lysis from without" [36]. This occurs if a single bacteria cell is attacked by a very large number of bacteriophages causing lysis to occur without formation of bacteriophages. Cell death is in this case caused by damage in the bacterial membrane as a consequence of enzymatic activity of bacteriophages bound simultaneously on one cell. For such situations none of the mentioned equations is valid, but due to high selection pressure high mutation rate can be expected. It is therefore clear that each system has to be specifically characterized to predict its dynamics during continuous production, and to achieve this, all parameters have to be accurately determined.

12.1.2
Determination of Bacteriophage Properties

Bacteriophage infection parameters are key features of a bacteria–bacteriophage system and many methods were developed to determine adsorption rate, length of eclipse and latent period and burst size. They were recently summarized in detail by Hyman and Abedon [56] and here we will present only guidelines for experimental design.

As already discussed, bacteriophage adsorption follows first-order kinetics and its rate constant is linearly proportional to the concentration of bacteriophages and bacterial cells. Because of that, the number of bacterial cells during experiment should be constant and consequently the experiment should be short enough to avoid cell growth. If this is not the case, cell growth should be taken into account during data evaluation [31]. Since the adsorption constant depends on many factors discussed previously, experimental conditions should be as close as possible to the conditions encountered during bacteriophage production, for example, bacteria physiological state, media composition, and mixing. Experiment is usually performed by mixing bacteriophages and bacteria at a ratio of 0,1 or lower. In this way superinfection is mostly avoided. To calculate the adsorption constant, the number of free bacteriophages or bacteriophage-infected bacteria should be monitored over time. One or both can be assayed only when separated and this is achieved by physical separation of bacterial cells and bacteriophages using filtration or centrifugation [57]. When low-speed centrifugation [58] is used, dilution of the sample prior to centrifugation is required to slow down the adsorption process during sedimentation [59]. In this way we can assay free bacteriophages (supernatant) and bacteriophage-infected bacteria (pellet) simultaneously. This is recommended especially for the unknown systems or when only a small proportion of bacteriophages is bound during experimental time. Prior to analysis of free bacteriophages bacterial cells have to be inactivated using, for example, chloroform [60], and to determine the number of bacteriophage-infected bacteria free bacteriophages have to be inactivated by adding bacteriophage antibodies or dead bacteria. The adsorption constant can be determined by fitting data with the equation

$$P = P_0 e^{-\delta C t} \tag{12.3}$$

where P is concentration of bacteriophages, P_0 is initial bacteriophage concentration, and t is time.

Latent period is the time between adsorption of bacteriophage to bacterial cell and release of new bacteriophage particles. It can be determined by measurement of bacterial cell concentration with a turbidimeter or by monitoring free bacteriophage concentration [44]. While the former technique gives only an estimation of latent period length, the latter is more precise and laborious. Briefly, bacteriophages and bacterial cells are mixed to achieve low MOI (multiplicity of infection). After bacteriophages adsorb to bacteria, the mixture is diluted to stop adsorption and incubated under conditions that allow bacterial growth. Samples are taken in a reasonable period of time and free bacteriophages are enumerated by plaque assay. The end of the latent period is indicated by increase of free bacteriophages. The same protocol design can be used to determine the eclipse period, except that sampling should be more frequent and samples have to be treated with chloroform in order to kill noninfected cells and open bacteriophage-infected cells to release any bacteriophages within the cells. The eclipse period ends when the first bacteriophages appear inside the cell. The number of bacteriophages formed per bacterial cells (burst size) can be determined by the single burst technique [2]. Briefly, bacterial suspension is infected by bacteriophage at low MOI as described previously followed by serial dilution that yields only one cell per sample. They are allowed to grow and lyse and then the number of released phages is determined by plaque assay.

Both values, burst size and latent period, can be determined simultaneously by a so-called one(single)-step growth experiment introduced by Ellis and Delbrück [61] described in detail elsewhere [2,56]. One-step growth curve describes the infection of a single cell infected by one bacteriophage. This method can be designed also to study the influence of different environmental components, for example, ions on infection parameters. The experiment begins by mixing bacteriophage and bacteria at proper MOI. The time allowed for adsorption depends on specific bacteriophage, but it should be short. From the Poisson formula one can derive for each MOI the proportion of bacteria that is not infected, infected by a single bacteriophage, or by multiple bacteriophages. MOI should be high enough to shorten adsorption time, but low enough that majority of the infected cells is infected by a single bacteriophage. This can be calculated for each experiment, if cell and plaque count are carefully determined before addition of the bacteriophage. Once bacteriophages are adsorbed to bacteria, nonadsorbed (free) bacteriophages are inactivated by an antiphage serum. Infected cells are further diluted to contain approximately 100 infected bacteria in a sample in order to prevent interactions between the first released bacteriophages and non-infected bacteria. Samples are taken over time until infection is completed and then analyzed by plaque assay method. It is expected that plaque count will remain the same from the beginning until the end of the latent period. Once bacteria start to lyse, free infective bacteriophages can be detected and the number will rise until all bacteria are lysed completely. Burst size is determined by dividing the final number of bacteriophages by the initial number of infected bacterial cells.

12.2 Bacteriophage Cultivation

Bacteriophages are traditionally produced in batch mode cultivation [62]. Since bacteriophage multiplication is very fast, these bioprocesses are short and can be completed within one working day. High bacteriophage concentrations are commonly achieved without sophisticated regulation. On the other hand batch mode bioprocesses inherently require larger footprints and this becomes more important especially when operated under good manufacturing practice (GMP) required for bacteriophages intended for human use. Batch operation mode requires also a lot of manpower, for example, to sterilize and clean the bioreactor. Additionally, these procedures have to be validated. When several bacteriophages are consecutively cultivated in the same bioreactor, production costs increase substantially. Alternatively, disposable bioreactors could be used, but currently available designs are suitable for cultivation of mammalian cell cultures and do not provide enough aeration for bacterial cultures. Batch mode could be substituted also by continuous cultivation mode under which a substrate is continuously provided, and the final product, in our case bacteriophages, is continuously withdrawn from the bioreactor. The most common continuous cultivation mode is chemostat where there is constant inlet and outlet flow resulting in the establishment of a steady state due to substrate limitation.

12.2.1
Chemostat

Chemostat has been used in biotechnology for many decades [63] for the preparation of target products and also various other studies, because it enables a constant physiological state of cultivated microorganism. However, already the initial experiments indicate that microorganisms in such systems are prone to mutations [64]. That is why chemostat is not suitable for production systems, but is an invaluable tool to study bacteria–bacteriophage interactions and dynamics. This knowledge is necessary to understand the behavior of bacteriophage-based therapeutics especially with regard to resistance development. Bacteriophage resistance development studies were performed by cocultivation of bacteria and bacteriophages together in the same vessel and could reach long-term stable steady state [65]. Chemostat studies with temperate lysogenic *E. coli* 159T$^-$ lambda bacteriophage demonstrated that after a temperature shock causing instability, the system returned to steady state conditions, and that for a given steady state of cell population there can exist more than one steady state of free bacteriophages [66]. The coevolutionary dynamic of the bacteriophage–host system was demonstrated on *E. coli* and bacteriophage T7 [67]. A simultaneous cultivation in the chemostat caused initially sensitive bacteria (B_0) to develop resistance (B_1) toward the original T7 ($T7_0$). Change in sensitivity was probably due to mutation affecting the receptor on the bacteria, but soon the bacteriophage evolved ($T7_1$) to attack resistant bacteria B_1. Response to changes in host bacteria was probably caused by mutations in the T7 tail fibers expanding its host range to bacteria B_0 and B_1. It was shown that bacteria resistant to $T7_0$ and $T7_1$ can emerge and can eventually invade the community. The authors demonstrated that under certain conditions three populations of bacteria (B_0, B_1, and B_2) and two populations of bacteriophage phage ($T7_0$ and $T7_1$) can coexist. Various hypotheses to explain the coexistence have been proposed, such as the numerical refuge hypothesis [67], the arms-race hypothesis [68], the spatial refuge hypothesis [69], and the physiological refuge hypothesis [70,71] demonstrating versatility and complexity of this system.

Chemostat experiments also enabled to elucidate the resistance development mechanisms. For the *E. coli* to T2 bacteriophage system it was found that mutations on agar plates occurred at a slower rate than in continuous culture [72]. It was found that the resistance mechanism can evolve either from a single rare mutation or as a consequence of two common mutations. In chemostat, the partially resistant intermediates become rapidly fixed and consequently the rate at which T2 resistance evolves is accelerated [73]. Resistance development was extensively studied also for the system *E. coli* O157:H7 and bacteriophage PP01 [74,75]. This study was further extended to multiple bacteriophages, a cocktail of bacteriophages EP16, PP17, and SP22, introduced simultaneously into the bacterial culture [76]. Differences arose within the bacterial and bacteriophage population and were due to genetic

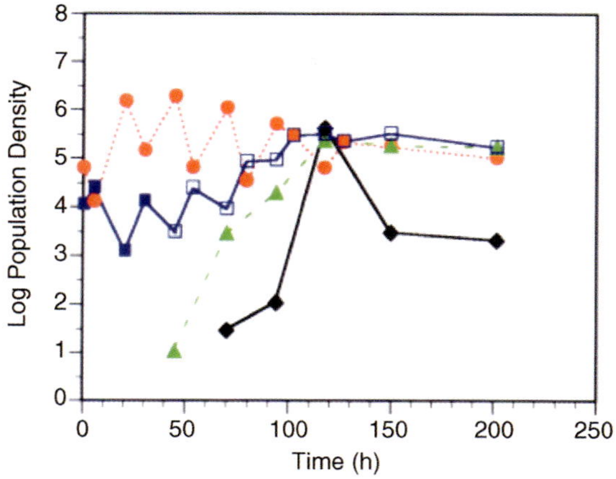

Figure 12.3 Population dynamics study in chemostat. Equilibrium state of bacteriophage T2 and sensitive *E. coli* was disrupted by invasion of partially resistant and completely resistant *E. coli* bacterial mutants. The population concentrations of bacteriophage T2 (red circles), sensitive *E. coli* (blue squares), partially resistant *E. coli* mutant (green triangles), and completely resistant *E. coli* mutants (black diamonds) are log-transformed. After the mutants invaded only total *E. coli* population (open squares) could be quantified (Reprinted with permission from Ref. [78]).

exchange between two bacteriophages during superinfection of the host cells. A highly complex *E. coli* population was found to evolve also in continuous culture of *E. coli* and lambda bacteriophage [77]. Equilibrium steady state was reported, but substantial dynamic differences in identically performed experiments indicate further complexity and sensitivity of such systems, as also demonstrated in Figure 12.3.

These experiments indicate continuous arms race between bacteria and bacteriophages. However, this cannot proceed indefinitely as demonstrated by Lenski and Levin [79]. Based on the mathematical model taking into account also mutations, they were able to predict mutation rate of both bacteria and bacteriophage when cultivated together. While bacterial resistance evolved in accordance to the model, much fewer were found for bacteriophages. Further tests with different bacteriophages demonstrated that there is a general asymmetry in the coevolutionary potential of bacteria and bacteriophages. The reason is that mutations providing bacterial resistance to bacteriophages may arise by either the loss or alteration of bacteriophage receptor gene function, while bacteriophage host range mutations depend only on specific alterations of receptor binding gene function. This asymmetry in coevolutionary potential indicates that natural communities of bacteria and bacteriophage are dominated by bacterial clones resistant to all co-occurring virulent phage. If a virulent bacteriophage encounters a bacterial population of predominantly susceptible strains these will either rapidly evolve resistance and/or be replaced by clones resistant to the bacteriophages. This explains the observation of many studies, where heterogeneity of bacterial

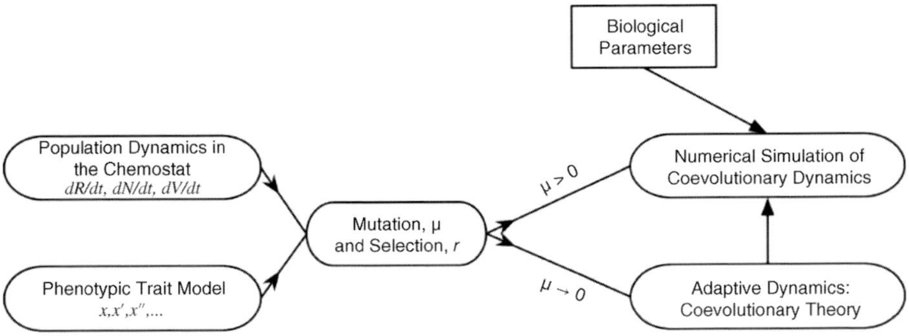

Figure 12.4 Mathematical model structure of population dynamics. The model considers resource uptake and adsorption of bacteriophages together with theoretical and numerical approaches for analyzing the evolutionary ecology. Adaptive dynamics is the limit of the evolutionary ecology in the small-mutation limit results from which are combined with biological parameters to guide stochastic simulations of coevolutionary dynamics of bacteriophage and bacteria in the chemostat (Reprinted with permission from Ref. [80]).

population was much higher than the one of bacteriophages. These conclusions were theoretically addressed by a mathematical model [80] taking into account various aspects of evolution as shown in Figure 12.4.

For various sets of parameter values, authors demonstrated the existence of conditions for coevolutionary branching leading to distinct quasi-species (clusters of different but related strains) mutants of both bacteria and bacteriophages that can coexist in a homogeneous medium with a single nutrient [Figure 12.5]. Interestingly, when diversification occurs, mutants of bacteriophage adsorb effectively to only a limited subset of the total number of bacteria mutants.

Many other mathematical models have been derived to describe different aspects of bacteria–bacteriophage dynamics in chemostat [70,72,79–90], but it is beyond the scope of this chapter to describe them in detail. In general, depending on model structure and its parameter values, they predict the existence of different equilibrium states either as constant values or oscillations, the latter not commonly observed in empirical studies [90], together with development and coexistence of multiples of bacteria and bacteriophage mutants.

Due to the almost endless possibility of various combinations occurring in chemostat, such experiments involving bacteria and bacteriophages were used to test several models and model applications of much broader scopes demonstrated by a few following examples.

Bohannan and Lenski used in chemostat a cultivated community of *E. coli* bacteria and T4 bacteriophage to compare predictions of prey-dependent and ratio-dependent food chain models [91]. By changing concentrations of bacterial substrate and comparing the concentration of bacteria, bacteriophages, population stability, dynamics, and mutation rate they found that experimental data were better described and predicted by a prey-dependent model.

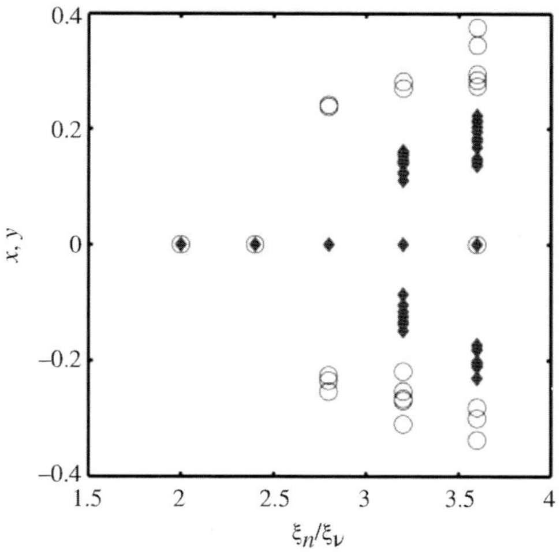

Figure 12.5 Simulation results of mathematical model from Figure 12.4. The parameter ξ_n is the stable uptake range of bacterial hosts defined as the range of possible bacterial host phenotypes whose maximal growth rate is within $e^{-1/2}$ of the maximum for all phenotypes. The parameter ξ_v is the host range of bacteriophage defined as the range of possible host phenotypes for which any given bacteriophage has an adsorption rate within $e^{-1/2}$ of its maximal adsorption rate. The *y* axis depicts the calculated steady-state values for bacteria (circles) and bacteriophage (diamonds). The depicted strains are those with at least 1% of the total bacteria or phage population, respectively. A succession of bifurcations leading to appearance multiple strain coexistence is shown. The strains group naturally into distinct clusters of quasispecies (Reprinted with permission from Ref. [80]).

Chemostat experiments also enabled the empirical test of geographic mosaic theory [92]. The theory proposes that the spatial variation in natural selection and gene flow across a landscape can shape local coevolutionary dynamics. These effects may be particularly strong when populations differ across productivity gradients, where gene flow will often be asymmetric among populations. This was tested by a series of chemostats in which bacterial *E. coli* and bacteriophage T7 were cultivated. Chemostats were operating at different productivity determined by the input concentration of glucose as the growth limiting resource each representing a community with a specific level of productivity. Communities were closed or opened by manual dispersal between the communities. In this way they demonstrated that gene flow across a spatially structured landscape alters coevolution of bacteriophage and bacteria and that the resulting patterns of adaptation fluctuate in both space and time.

Several recent experiments were directed toward long-term evolution studies of bacteria without the presence of bacteriophages [93,94]. Evolution was followed by genome sequencing over the course of 40 000 generations from a population of *E. coli*. They found that although adaptation decelerated sharply, genomic evolution was nearly constant for 20 000 generations. Such clock-like regularity is usually viewed as the signature of neutral evolution, but several lines of evidence indicate that almost all of these mutations were beneficial. The same population later evolved an elevated mutation rate and accumulated hundreds of additional mutations dominated by a neutral signature. While beneficial substitutions were surprisingly uniform over time, neutral ones were highly variable. Estimation of number and diversity of beneficial mutations was recently investigated by evolving 115 populations of *E. coli* for 2000 generations and sequenced one genome from each population [95]. A total of 1331 mutations were identified, affecting more than 600 different sites. Few mutations were shared among replicates, but a strong pattern of convergence emerged at the level of genes, operons, and functional complexes.

Due to the inherent development of resistant bacterial strains in chemostat this seems to be also an efficient model to study synergetic effects of applying bacteriophage in combination with antibiotics for bacterial infection treatment. Efficiency was tested on the treatment of *S. aureus* with bacteriophage SA5 and the antibiotic gentamicin [96]. The motivation of this experiment was the theoretical prediction that dual therapy can be more efficacious than single therapies ali therapy. In the presented experimental setup, treatment with gentamicin induced a population of cells with a strong aggregation phenotype. These aggregators also have an increased ability to form a biofilm, which is a well-known, nongenetic mechanism of drug resistance. However, the aggregators are also more susceptible than the parental strain to the action of the bacteriophage. Thus, dual treatment with gentamicin and bacteriophage resulted in lower final cell densities than either treatment alone. Unlike in the bacteriophage-only treatment, phage-resistant isolates were not detected in the dual treatment.

As can be concluded from the described experiments, results obtained in chemostat are very important for studies of evolution in population dynamics, but not suitable for a continuous production of bacteriophages, where long-term genetically stable bacteriophage and bacteria strains are required. To avoid as much as possible coevolution of either bacteriophage or bacteria, a different experimental setup was proposed.

12.2.2
Cellstat

A solution to overcome the problem of bacterial mutations was developed by Husimi *et al.* [97] by introducing a system consisting of two bioreactors connected in series (Figure 12.6).

In the first bioreactor bacteria are cultivated without the presence of bacteriophages. In this way a constant physiological state of bacterial culture is guaranteed and, more importantly, there is no selection pressure for bacterial mutation since no bacteriophages are in contact with bacterial culture. In the second bioreactor there is a mixed culture of bacterial cells and bacteriophages. Since specific growth rate of bacteriophages is significantly higher than that of bacteria, the second bioreactor, called by authors as "cellstat," operates at a higher dilution rate than the first one. More importantly, dilution rate is also higher than

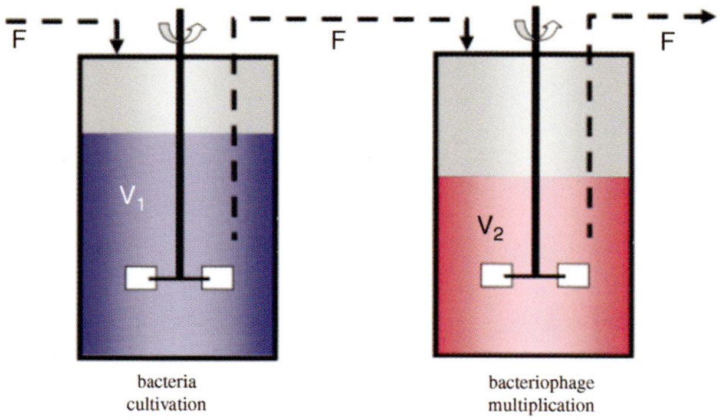

Figure 12.6 Schematic drawing of continuous system consisting of two bioreactors connected in series. While flow rate through the system is constant, volume in the second bioreactor is lower resulting in dilution rate higher than maximal specific growth rate of bacteria. Second bioreactor is called cellstat.

maximal specific bacterial growth rate. In this way, any potential mutant bacteria have no impact, since they are immediately washed out of cellstat and no accumulation of mutants is therefore possible. The authors demonstrated that steady state in both reactors was achieved already after 3 h of operation [97]. A mathematical model based on mass balances was able to predict the concentration of bacteriophage as a function of input cell density as well as to predict selectivity and demonstrate robust performance of the system. How fluctuations of operating conditions affect cellstat performance was theoretically studied on a system of two bacteriophages whose multiplication depended on the environment temperature [98]. Steady states obtained for various temperature oscillation and dilution rates were structured in a phase diagram. It was shown that stable steady-state operation is achieved for all evaluated parameter values and that three different outcomes are possible: steady state with the presence of a single bacteriophage as well as steady state where there was a coexistence of both bacteriophages. The robustness of cellstat performance was demonstrated theoretically and experimentally also by Schwienhorst *et al.* [99]. After infection of bacterial culture with bacteriophage, initial oscillations of the system were stabilized and results were in perfect agreement with the proposed mathematical model (Figure 12.7).

Robustness of continuous cellstat performance together with the absence of bacterial mutations were the reasons to conduct further studies also involving bacteriophages. One of the very first implementations was the continuous production of proteins. Cellstat was used to increase stability of recombinant *E. coli* during continuous cultivation. Protein β-galactosidase expression was obtained by use of temperature-sensitive lambda bacteriophage mutant [100]. By temperature change bacteriophage switched from a lysogenic state in the first bioreactor to a lytic state in the second bioreactor allowing protein expression. By

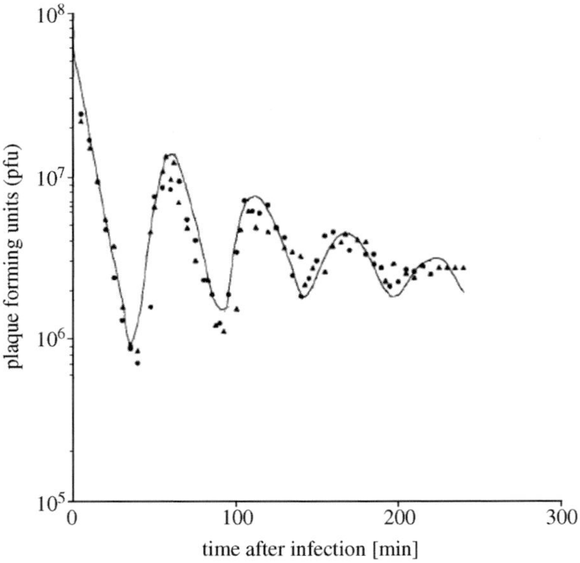

Figure 12.7 Stabilization of bacteriophage population in cellstat. The population density of the host bacterial cells in inlet flow was kept constant. The dilution rate of 7.48 h^{-1} was chosen to approximately compensate bacteriophage growth rate. Points are experimental data while solid line is mathematical simulation (Reprinted with permission from Ref. [99]).

optimization of operating conditions it was demonstrated that such a system provides high productivity of protein production [101]. Further improvement in operating performance was achieved by the addition of a third bioreactor between the two original ones [102].

Cellstat was implemented also to study the efficiency of antiviral drug applications in terms of emergence of viral escape mutants. For this purpose Qβ RNA bacteriophage as a model system mimicking the effect of an antiviral gene therapy was studied [103]. An experiment was performed over the course of more than 100 generations, simultaneously running 13 cultures. Results demonstrated that 12 out of 13 bacteriophage populations became resistant and only one became extinct. However, sequence analysis revealed that only two distinct bacteriophage mutants emerged in the 12 surviving phage populations. The results demonstrated the feasibility of the proposed strategy for the evaluation of antiviral approaches in terms of their potential to allow resistant bacteriophage mutants to appear.

Another interesting application based on the cellstat principle is a system for continuous directed evolution of biomolecules [104]. The authors constructed a bacterial strain containing two plasmids, namely, mutagenesis plasmid to enhance mutagenesis rate by up to 100-fold, and accessory plasmid encoding protein (pIII), which enables bacteriophage binding and infection of bacteria. On

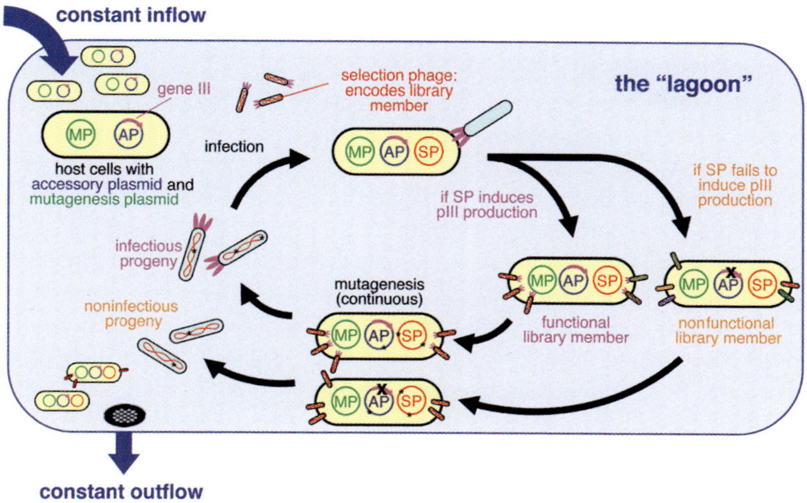

Figure 12.8 Schematic presentation of the system for continuous directed evolution of biomolecules. Bacterial cells continuously flow into bioreactor where they are infected with selection phage (SP) encoding library members. Functional library members induce production of pIII from the accessory plasmid (AP) and release bacteriophages capable of infecting new bacterial cells, while nonfunctional library members do not. Increased mutagenesis is triggered through induction of the mutagenesis plasmid (MP) (Reprinted with permission from Ref. [104]).

the other hand, bacteriophage with a deleted gene for the same protein was constructed. Selection of bacteriophages was based on their binding efficiency, which depended on the level of pIII protein. By inserting a gene for pIII protein into the accessory plasmid linking between bacteriophage selection and desired activity of interest was achieved as shown in Figure 12.8. In this way it was possible to stimulate dozens of rounds of evolution in a single day without human intervention and demonstrated successfully 200 rounds of protein evolution over the course of 8 days. One of the outcomes was the evolvement of T7 RNA polymerase that recognized a distinct promoter, initiate transcripts with A instead of G, and initiate transcripts with C. By greatly accelerating laboratory evolution, this system provides an excellent tool to study otherwise intractable directed evolution problems. In fact, in a further study this approach was used to investigate how changes in evolutionary conditions affect the outcomes of protein evolution [105].

A specific application of cellstat hardware setup was the addition of a self-cycling process used for the production of bacteriophages [106]. Similar to cellstat, in the first bioreactor, uninfected *E. coli* bacteria were cultivated, but under self-cycling fermentation conditions providing cell synchronization. The same operation type was executed in the second bioreactor also containing bacteriophage T4 besides *E. coli*. When each infection cycle (batch) was terminated, phages were harvested and a new infection cycle was initiated by adding cells from the first bioreactor together with a fresh medium and the small amount of bacteriophages left from the previous cycle to initiate the next infection cycle. Both bioreactors operated independently, except for bacteria transfer. Obtained bacteriophage titers were reproducible among cycles showing no significant difference in infectivity. Unfortunately, no direct comparison with continuous cellstat was performed.

One can anticipate that most of the studies involving cellstat were related to the bacteriophage evolution and selection. In an early example cellstat experiments were performed to simulate molecular evolution and providing realistic parameter values to Eigen's theory of quasi-species [107]. This was achieved by continuous cultivation of *E. coli* and various bacteriophages in combination with computer simulations. However, since bacteriophage evolution in cellstat is closely related to continuous bacteriophage production, both topics will be discussed simultaneously.

12.2.3
Cellstat Productivity

One of the key issues related to continuous production of bacteriophages is the determination of operating conditions under which high process productivity can be achieved. Taking into account bacteriophage life cycle including adsorption kinetics, latent period, and burst size, Bull *et al.* [90] developed a mathematical model based on mass balances for cellstat:

$$\frac{dU}{dt} = -UD + CD - \delta PU \tag{12.4}$$

$$\frac{dP}{dt} = -PD - \delta PU - \delta PI + be^{-DL}\delta P_L U_L \tag{12.5}$$

$$\frac{dI}{dt} = -ID + \delta PU - be^{-DL}\delta P_L U_L \tag{12.6}$$

where U is concentration of uninfected cells, I concentration of infected cells, C inlet cell concentration, P concentration of free bacteriophages, D dilution rate, b burst size, L latent period (time from infection to lysis), δ adsorption rate of bacteriophage to cells, and subscript L indicating value of the variable L time units in the past.

In Equations 12.4–12.6 the terms UD, PD, and ID represent washout from cellstat, CD represents inlet of fresh bacterial cells, δPU is infection kinetics, $be^{-DL}\delta P_L U_L$ is generation of bacteriophages during cell lyses, and δPI stands for superinfection (infection of already infected cells).

Steady-state values for these equations are described by the following set of equations [90]:

$$\hat{U} = \frac{C \cdot \left(1 - e^{-DL}\right) + \left(\frac{D}{\delta}\right)}{e^{-DL} \cdot (b - 1)} \tag{12.7}$$

$$\hat{P} = \frac{D}{\delta} \cdot \frac{C \cdot \left(b \cdot e^{-DL} - 1\right) - \left(\frac{D}{\delta}\right)}{C \cdot (1 - e^{-DL}) + \left(\frac{D}{\delta}\right)} \tag{12.8}$$

$$\hat{I} = \frac{e^{-DL} - 1}{b - 1} \cdot \left[C \cdot \left(b \cdot e^{-DL} - 1\right) - \left(\frac{D}{\delta}\right)\right] \tag{12.9}$$

where $\hat{U}$, $\hat{P}$, and $\hat{I}$ are steady-state values.

From the mass balances (Equations 12.4–12.6) several model assumptions can be deduced. One is that bacterial cells do not replicate, which is justified to some extent by very high dilution rate and, according to authors, omitting this term has no significant impact [90]. Furthermore, it was not taken into account that there is a limited number of receptors on a single cell, thus the model allows an unlimited number of infection per cell. Also, the phenomena that under very high bacteriophage concentrations lysis without bacteriophage release can occur [53] was not considered. Because of that, extreme values calculated by the model have to be interpreted with caution and verified experimentally. Nevertheless, Equations 12.7–12.9 represent a solid base to estimate bacteriophage productivity in cellstat [108]. For continuous bioprocess, productivity can be defined as

$$\mathrm{Pr} = P \cdot D \tag{12.10}$$

which, using Equation 12.10, gives

$$\mathrm{Pr} = \frac{D^2}{\delta} \cdot \frac{C \cdot \left(b \cdot e^{-DL} - 1\right) - \left(\frac{D}{\delta}\right)}{C \cdot (1 - e^{-DL}) + \left(\frac{D}{\delta}\right)} \tag{12.11}$$

Based on this equation it is possible to determine productivity of the cellstat for a specific set of variables (b, L, δ) and parameters (C, D). Estimation of inlet cell concentration (C) and dilution rate (D) on productivity of bacteriophage production is shown in Figure 12.9 for typical values of b, L, and δ commonly encountered for various bacteriophages.

We can see that both parameters have a substantial impact on bacteriophage productivity. Increasing inlet cell concentration increases monotonically productivity until the maximal value is achieved, determined by

$$\mathrm{Pr}_{\max} = \lim_{C \to \infty} \left(\frac{D^2}{\delta} \cdot \frac{C \cdot \left(b \cdot e^{-DL} - 1\right) - \left(\frac{D}{\delta}\right)}{C \cdot (1 - e^{-DL}) + \left(\frac{D}{\delta}\right)}\right) = \frac{D^2}{\delta} \cdot \frac{\left(b \cdot e^{-DL} - 1\right)}{(1 - e^{-DL})} \tag{12.12}$$

In terms of model assumptions, working at high cell concentrations seems to be meaningful since there is a lower probability of superinfection, and also mathematical model limitations related to limited number of receptors as well as lysis without production of bacteriophages are minimized. On the other hand, beyond certain cell concentrations, productivity is constant since bacteriophage physiological parameters become a limiting step. This is also confirmed by bacteriophage concentration in the cellstat, which follows precisely the curve of

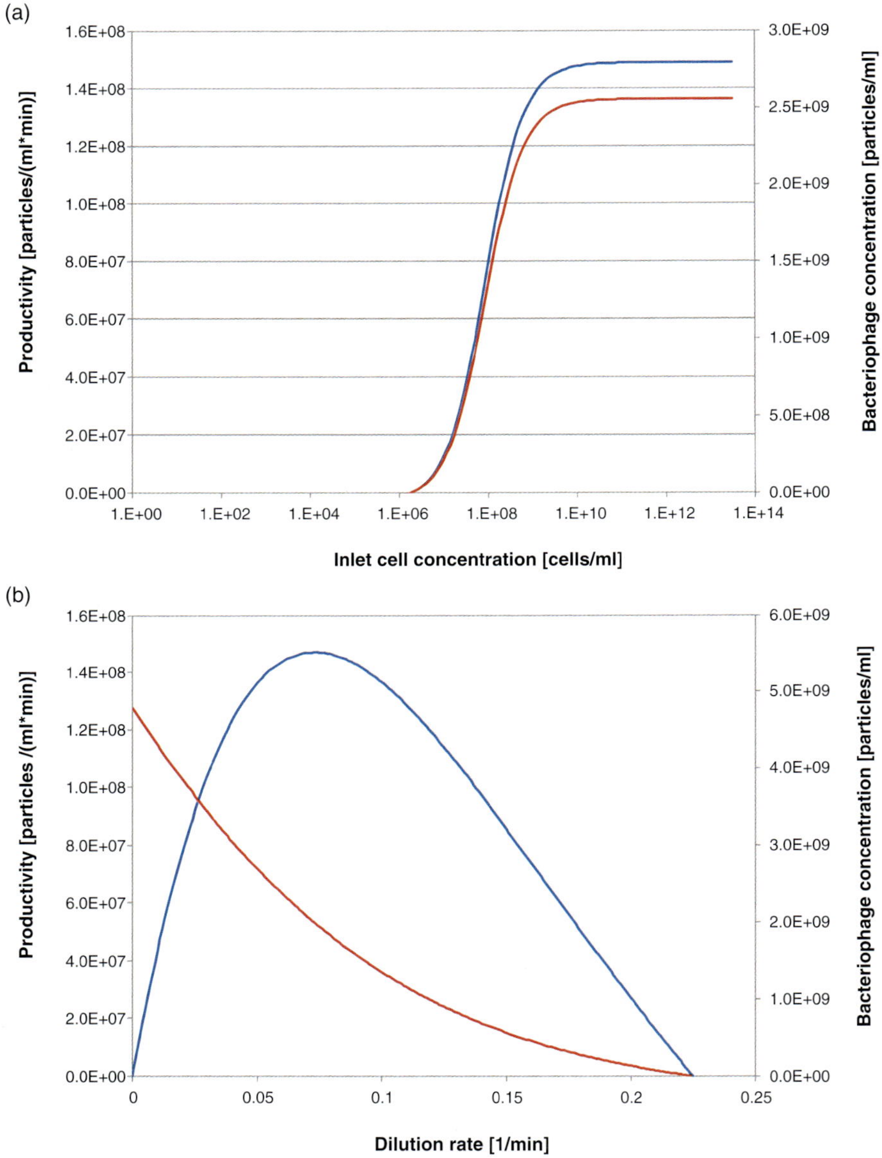

Figure 12.9 Simulation of cellstat productivity as a function of inlet cell concentration and dilution rate. Burst size was 100, latent period 20 min, and adsorption constant 1×10^{-9} ml min^{-1}. (a) Dilution rate is 0.0583 min^{-1}; (b) inlet cell concentration is 2×10^9 cells ml^{-1}.

productivity. We are therefore flexible to select any inlet cells concentration providing maximal productivity and our choice can be entirely based on the process economics. Of course, any cell concentration inhibition in the first bioreactor was not taken into account and has to be estimated case by case.

In contrast to the effect of inlet cell concentration (C) there is a single value for dilution rate for which maximal productivity can be achieved. This optimum can be understood, similar to a regular chemostat, as a trade-off between increased supply of substrate (bacterial cells in our case) and wash out from the cellstat. Once dilution rate is higher than bacteriophage specific growth rate, the latter is washed from the bioreactor and productivity drops to 0. In contrast to the effect of inlet cell concentration, however, bacteriophage concentration follows a different trend than productivity. We can see that maximal bacteriophage concentration is achieved at the lowest dilution rate due to the longest residence time in cellstat, while at maximal productivity it is substantially lower. This might represent a challenge in the downstream processing; therefore, operation at maximal productivity might not always be the best choice. If this is not an issue one can derive the equation to calculate values of parameter D at which maximal productivity is achieved, assuming that inlet cell concentration is kept high to provide maximal productivity (Figure 12.9A). The first derivative of Equation 12.12 gives

$$\frac{2D\left(-1+be^{-DL}\right)}{(1-e^{-DL})\delta}-\frac{bD^{2}e^{-DL}L}{(1-e^{-DL})\delta}-\frac{D^{2}e^{-DL}\left(-1+be^{-DL}\right)L}{(1-e^{-DL})^{2}\delta} \tag{12.13}$$

Since maximal productivity represents an optimum, the value of derivative (Equation 12.13) should be 0 and we get after some simplification the following correlation:

$$2\left(be^{-D_{\text{opt}}L}-1\right)-bD_{\text{opt}}Le^{-D_{\text{opt}}L}-\frac{D_{\text{opt}}Le^{-D_{\text{opt}}L}\left(be^{-D_{\text{opt}}L}-1\right)}{\left(1-e^{-D_{\text{opt}}L}\right)}=0 \tag{12.14}$$

Due to the mathematical structure of Equation 12.14, parameter D_{opt} cannot be explicitly expressed; therefore, a numerical solution is needed for a particular set of values. Interestingly, Equation 12.14 contains no adsorption rate (δ) term. Dilution rate at maximal productivity is therefore only a function of burst size (b) and latent period (L), which can easily be determined for specific bacteriophage–bacteria systems as discussed in Section 12.1.2. Values for different b and L values are shown in Figure 12.10.

Several interesting conclusions can be drawn from Figure 12.10. Latent period L and burst size b have a significant effect on optimal dilution rate. This is reasonable since they both define bacteriophage multiplication rate and therefore range of dilution rate where bacteriophages are not washed from the second bioreactor. This is especially true for low values of burst size, while for values above 100 optimal dilution rate becomes almost independent of the burst size approaching its limit value. In fact, this value can be calculated as a limit value of Equation 12.14 for burst size being infinite. The following simple expression is obtained:

$$2e^{-D_{\text{opt}}L}+D_{\text{opt}}L-2=0 \tag{12.15}$$

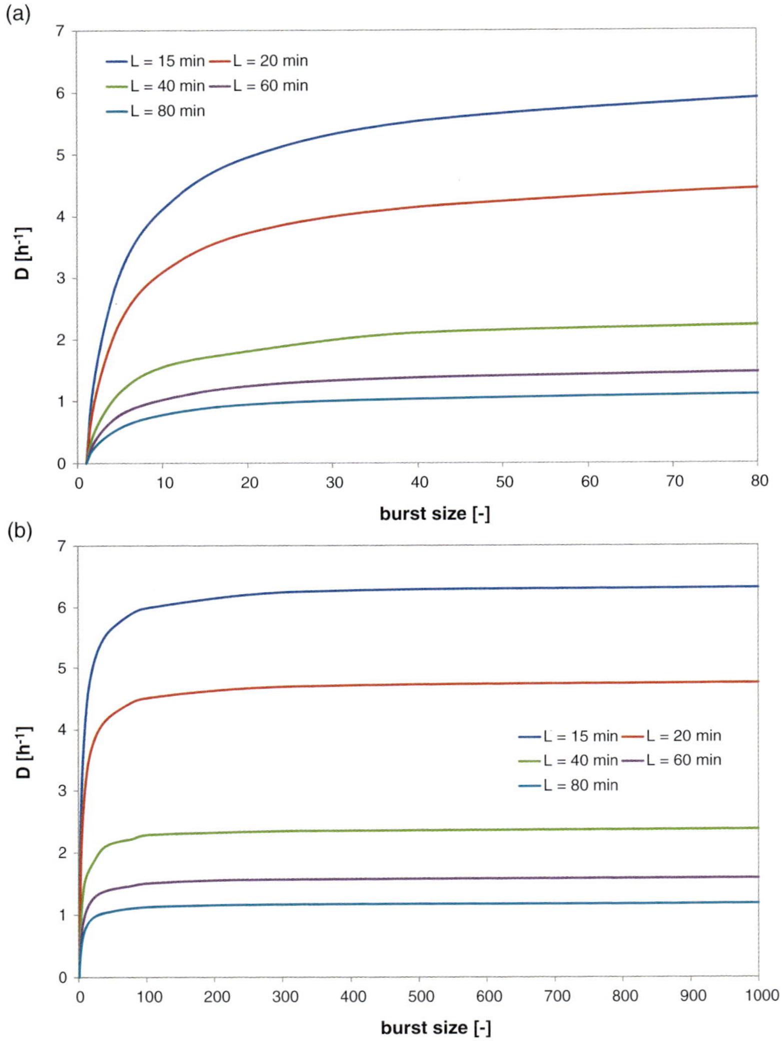

Figure 12.10 Effect of burst size (b) and latent period (L) on optimal dilution rate (D_{opt}). Burst size (a) 0 to 80 and (b) 0 to 1000.

which can be solved for $D_{opt}L$ product giving a value of 1.59362, therefore

$$D_{opt} = 1.59362/L \tag{12.16}$$

This gives a very simple estimation of optimal dilution rate in cellstat when burst size is high. On the other hand, the shape of curves in Figure 12.10 seems to be very similar to the Monod equation describing microorganism-specific growth rate under substrate-limiting conditions, and taking into account the value for optimal dilution rate at high burst size a similar empirical equation can be constructed. By fitting, the following equation is obtained:

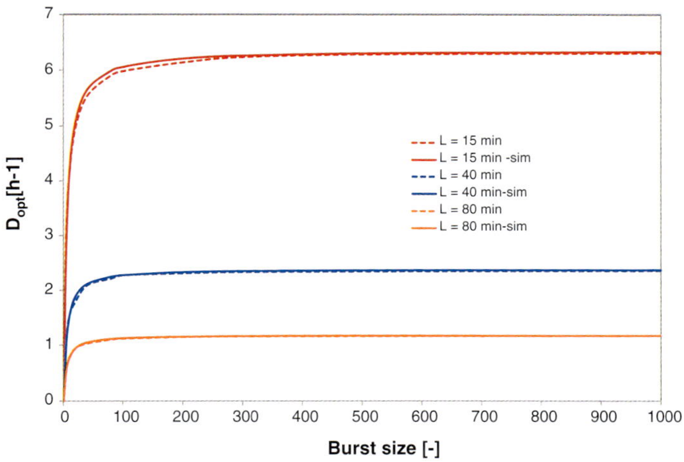

Figure 12.11 Effect of burst size (*b*) and latent period (*L*) on optimal dilution rate (D_{opt}). Comparison of results calculated from Equations 12.14 and 12.17.

$$D_{opt} = \frac{1.59362}{L}\frac{(b-1)}{4.931844 + (b-1)} \quad (12.17)$$

How accurately Equation 12.17 describes estimation of optimal dilution rate is examined in Figure 12.11.

We can see that there is good agreement between precisely calculated values (Equation 12.14) and one from Equation 12.17, and therefore we can use a simplified equation for estimation of optimal dilution rate. We can also see that values for D are for all but the smallest b values beyond maximal specific growth rate of bacteria, therefore, fulfilling the condition required to avoid mutation of bacteria.

The presented equations were derived from a mathematical model that does not assume any bacteriophage mutations, which do not occur even in the cellstat. Therefore, we have to determine the operating conditions under which selection pressure for bacteriophage mutations is low and stable bacteriophage production can be expected. Although this is extremely difficult, if possible at all, to predict quantitatively, one can intuitively conclude that mutation rate would be low when selection pressure is also low and target bacteriophage is close to optimally adapted to specific operating conditions.

Estimation of such cultivating conditions was theoretically derived for a system in which besides target bacteriophage there is also a competitor bacteriophage [90]. This is not necessarily present from the beginning of the process, but it might evolve due to selection pressure during operation and a mutant may even overgrow the initial bacteriophage. To evaluate competitiveness between two bacteriophages quantitatively, the authors defined as a criterion rate of infection (ROI), which represents the rate per minute at which a cell in a culture is infected by bacteriophage, and it is mathematically equal to $\delta{\cdot}P$. In case of the same δ value for both bacteriophages ROI ratio is equal to the concentration ratio of two bacteriophages. Since under equilibrium conditions cell division is balanced by cell death caused by bacteriophage and washout, ROI < 1 indicates that the average cell is infected by less than one bacteriophage during its life, therefore, most of the bacterial cells are single infected. It can be concluded that the larger the burst size, the higher the adsorption rate, and/or shorter the latent period (changing only a single variable at once); they all lead toward higher equilibrium ROI. As higher ROI can be considered a competitive advantage, this result might suggest in which direction evolution is expected to evolve. Let us assume that a new bacteriophage type occurred by mutation process, which was in a steady state. Mass balance for mutant bacteriophage can be written as follows (see Equation 12.5):

$$\frac{dP_{\mathrm{nb}}}{dt} = -P_{\mathrm{nb}}D - \delta^* P_{\mathrm{nb}}\hat{U} - \delta^* P_{\mathrm{nb}}\hat{I} + b^* e^{-DL^*}\delta^* P_{\mathrm{nb},L}U_{L^*} \tag{12.18}$$

where b^*, L^*, and δ^* are the values of mutant bacteriophage.

Since it is a linear differential equation its general solution has the form

$$P_{\mathrm{nb}}(t) = P_{\mathrm{nb}}(0)e^{\lambda t} \tag{12.19}$$

As the system was also in equilibrium at the moment mutant bacteriophage was starting to evolve (L time units before its appearance), U_{L^*} can be substituted by $\hat{U}$ to get

$$\lambda e^{\lambda t} = \left(-D - \delta^*\hat{U} - \delta^*\hat{I}\right)e^{\lambda t} + b^*\delta^*\hat{U}e^{-DL^*}e^{\lambda(t-L^*)} \tag{12.20}$$

or by division with $e^{\lambda t}$

$$\lambda = \left(-D - \delta^*\hat{U} - \delta^*\hat{I}\right) + b^*\delta^*\hat{U}e^{-L^*(D+\lambda)} \tag{12.21}$$

Since parameter λ defines bacteriophage-specific growth rate (bacteriophage fitness), we can see from Equation 12.21 how its number changes over time. If $\lambda > 1$ it means that the number of bacteriophages will increase, and vice versa, it will decrease and probably disappear. Furthermore, from the sign of partial derivatives $\partial\lambda/\partial b$, $\partial\lambda/\partial L$, and $\partial\lambda/\partial\delta$, selection direction can be estimated. It can be shown that for low ROI values, where no superinfection occurs, selection is directed toward higher ROI values by increasing burst size, adsorption rate, or decreasing latent period [90]. Once higher ROI values are reached, a different scenario under which superinfection is common, occurs. To estimate evolution direction for high ROI, we have to define competitiveness or, as named by authors, competitive ability (γ) defined later. The selection model assumes "fight" for a single cell through superinfection in the following manner: if a single cell is coinfected by i genomes of the original bacteriophage and j genomes of the competitor bacteriophage then the fraction of bacteriophages released from cells containing competitor genome is defined as $[j/(I+j)]^{1/\gamma}$. We assign competitor competitive advantage >1. Simulation was carried out assuming that both

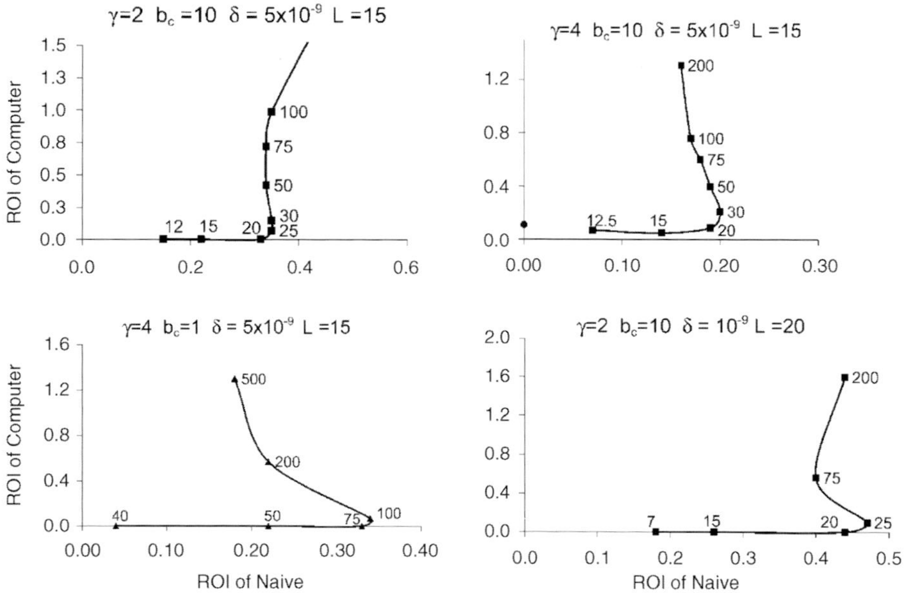

Figure 12.12 Equilibrium ROI in cellstat populations with both authentic and competitor bacteriophages. Vertical axes are the ROI for the competitor phage, and horizontal axes are ROI for the authentic bacteriophage in the same population. In all but the upper right figure, the competitor virus is not maintained until the ROI of the authentic bacteriophage reaches a threshold. Parameter values are given in each figure; γ is competitive parameter, b burst size of the competitor, δ adsorption rate, L lysis time. The numbers along each curve give the burst size of the authentic bacteriophage at that point (Reprinted with permission from Ref. [90]).

bacteriophages have the same latent period and adsorption rate while other model details can be found in the original article [90]. Results of this model demonstrated that there are many values of parameters when only one type of bacteriophage is maintained. Conditions under which our target bacteriophage is the "winner" are therefore operating parameters to establish long-term robust operation needed for cultivation of target bacteriophage. However, there are also many values of parameters for which both bacteriophages do coexist as shown in Figure 12.12.

These theoretical predictions were extensively tested experimentally providing important insight in the evolution processes. Small microvirid phage ΦX174 was commonly used as a model due to its small and simple genome structure and well-characterized molecular and structural biology [109]. Since the main motivation of these experiments was to study the adaptation process to two bacterial hosts, namely, *E. coli* and *S. typhimurium*, bacteria and bacteriophages were exposed to a very strongly selective environment provided by large population size and environmental changes through, for example, changes of the temperature resulting in very high mutation rate [90,110–114].

An excellent overview about the experimental evolution of *Microviridae* viruses can be found elsewhere [115].

However, as predicted by evolutionary trajectories [106] discussed before, the evolutionary succession is not inevitable. If the original bacteriophage starts at low concentration and is not capable of evolving sufficiently to achieve very high concentrations, then the competition phase will not occur. This is also the operating window for robust continuous production of target bacteriophages and can be affected by dilution rate (*D*) as seen in Figure 12.9.

Taking into account these conclusions we can re-estimate the operating parameters for continuous production of bacteriophages. As see from Figure 12.12, ROI values below 0.3 show that only target bacteriophage is present in the cellstat. Since ROI is defined as the product of adsorption kinetics and bacteriophage concentration this means that the slower adsorption kinetics is, the higher bacteriophage concentration can be allowed to minimize bacteriophage mutations. However, as discussed several times, these values depend on specific systems and assumptions of this derivation have to be taken with caution and must be experimentally tested.

12.2.4 Bacteriophage Selection

One of the important challenges is the fast and efficient selection of target bacteriophages. Although bacteriophages are present almost everywhere and their isolates might be screened in an efficient manner [116], there is a possibility to improve bacteriophage specificty towards particular bacterial strain. For this purpose, evolution occurring in chemostat and cellstat is advantageous. While in chemostat the evolution of bacteria and bacteriophages results in different bacterial strains, cellstat is limited to evolution of bacteriophages preserving original bacterial strain. This idea was tested using wild type phage T7 and recombinant *E. coli* host that constitutively expressed T7 RNA polymerase – an essential enzyme of the early viral metabolism [117]. Over the course of 180 generations a diversity of bacteriophage variants emerged and outgrew the wild type. The latter was replaced by fitter variants, in terms of host-range, restriction patterns, and one-step growth responses of isolated clones. The fittest variant, which required complementation by the recombinant host in order to grow, lacked at least 12% of its genome and replicated twice as fast as the wild type. Moreover, this variant was serologically indistinguishable from the wild type, based on cross-reactivities of antisera raised against both variants. These results demonstrate the feasibility of the proposed strategy for the development of bacteriophages with superior efficiency toward specific bacterial strain. In general, operating conditions in cellstat should be selected in a way to stimulate high mutation rate that depends on the infection properties of a particular bacteriophage. As seen from Figure 12.12 bacteriophage mutants occur for ROI values above 0.3, which can be a guideline for experimental design. Once conditions stimulating high mutation rate for particular bacteriophage–bacteria are defined, they can be obtained by adjusting cellstat inlet cell concentration (*C*) and dilution rate (*D*) as discussed in Section 12.2.3. Once bacteriophage with the desired properties evolves, operational conditions are changed in a way to decrease selectivity pressure and guarantee long-term robust production of target bacteriophage.

12.2.5 Technical Challenges

There are several technical issues that have to be addressed for a long-term, robust operation of continuous production of bacteriophages. They were realized already during initial experiments and are related to foaming, growth on the walls, and monitoring of bacteriophage concentration [97]. Foaming is associated with high aeration rate required by many bacterial cultivations. This is commonly avoided by adding various antifoaming agents like polyalkylene glycols, silicone emulsions, and others in the cultivation media. Details about different types, their action mechanism, and application can be found elsewhere [118].

Another issue related to long-term operations is growth of bacteria on the walls of bioreactors or tubings, substantially affecting the robustness of the operation [97,99,119]. Consequently, certain parts of the experimental setup have to be changed during operation [112]. In the case of *E. coli*, growth on the walls is mostly associated with bacterial pilli type I [99]. Several approaches were suggested to solve this problem. One technical solution is vibration of tubings during transfer of the cells between two bioreactors [97], but this was not very effective in the nodes, especially in the pump [119]. Husimi and Keweloh [119] described constant removal of adhered cells by gas bubbles and obtained better results than with the vibration method. Alternatively, two bioreactors instead of a single one switching in-between during long-term operation can be used, because washing cycles to achieve surface sterilization by regular flushing with NaOH are not necessary [120,121]. Another approach was recently proposed for cultivation on a small scale for preventing cell growth inside tubings, enabling operation in chemostat or turbidostat modes by tube moving and splitting it in different sections [122]. The optimal way to control growth on the walls depends on the type of cultivation and each system has to be tested in advance since failure might result in inappropriate functioning.

Finally, to provide robust operation of the cellstat, an appropriate regulation is required. Husimi *et al.* [97] discussed that it can be provided only when operated as a turbidostat, keeping cell density constant. While this is rather easy for bacterial cells using optical density as a measure of cell concentration, it is a much more challenging task for cellstat in which the concentration of bacteriophages has to be kept constant. Optical density cannot be used since bacteriophages are too small, and in addition, there are bacterial cells together with cell debris present, representing difficulty for the application of various spectroscopic methods, such as static or dynamic lights scattering or Nanosight [123]. Needless to say, conventional plaque assay has response time on orders of several hours or even days; therefore, no regulation on its base is possible. Because of this an alternative approach was recently developed, based on high throughput chromatography using monolithic stationary phases [124–126]. In contrast to conventional particulate chromatographic supports, monoliths consist of a single piece of porous material. This particular structure provides several advantageous properties, such as very high open porosity [127] providing low pressure drop, mass transport based on convection [128,129], and high dynamic binding capacity for extremely large molecules [130]. The latter two properties become very important when large biologic molecules, like proteins, polynucleotides, or viruses, have to be processed. Due to convective transport, molecules are transported by mobile phase and no diffusion resistance is present. Consequently, resolution and dynamic binding capacity are flow unaffected [131] enabling chromatographic analysis to be completed within a few seconds [132,133] and purification with very high productivity. This is further enhanced by high binding capacity related to the open monolith structure resulting in high accessibility of available surface area [130,134]. Suitability of monoliths for analysis and isolation of large biomolecules, like DNA or viruses, was reviewed in several recent articles [135–138].

Due to different surface properties of various viruses, including different bacteriophages [125], the chromatographic method has to be adjusted for every bacteriophage system. The reason is that the structure of bacteriophage capsid and tail consist of different proteins resulting in different isoelectric points; therefore, binding and elution on ion-exchange chromatographic matrix varies substantially. This results in bacteriophage-specific residence time on chromatographic column making identification of bacteriophage present in low concentrations difficult. Also, other compounds present in the medium like cell debris and host cell proteins (HCP), can elute at similar retention time making discrimination between contaminants and bacteriophages difficult, further limiting flexibility of the method. Bacteriophages detected by this method may not be infective, providing wrong information about bacteriophage titer. Therefore, genomic DNA released from lysed bacterial cells could be monitored instead of bacteriophage concentration in the bioreactor. Since charge of genomic DNA is constant, retention time is constant on ion-exchange monoliths and is eluted at a concentration of around 0.8 M regardless of the type of bacteriophage cultivated (Figure 12.13). It was shown that DNA concentration is directly proportional to the concentration of bacteriophages for a particular system (Figure 12.14). Of course, due to different burst sizes of particular bacteria–bacteriophage systems, one cannot predict the total concentration of infective bacteriophages in the second bioreactor; however, any changes in genomic DNA concentration indicate instability of operation. Since this information is obtained in a few minutes, it can be used for process control and consequently for regulation of the second bioreactor providing long-term robust performance.

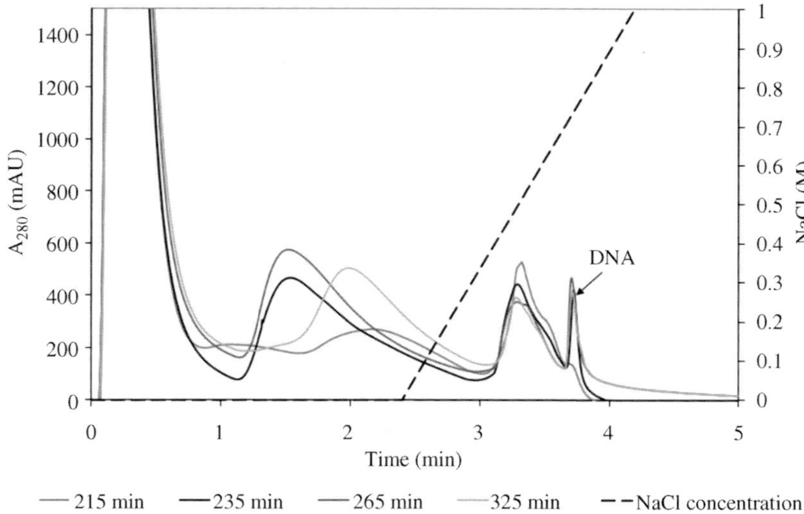

Figure 12.13 Typical chromatograms of batch process cultivation media containing bacteriophages and bacterial DNA released from cells during lysis. Note short analysis time (Reprinted with permission from Ref. [125]).

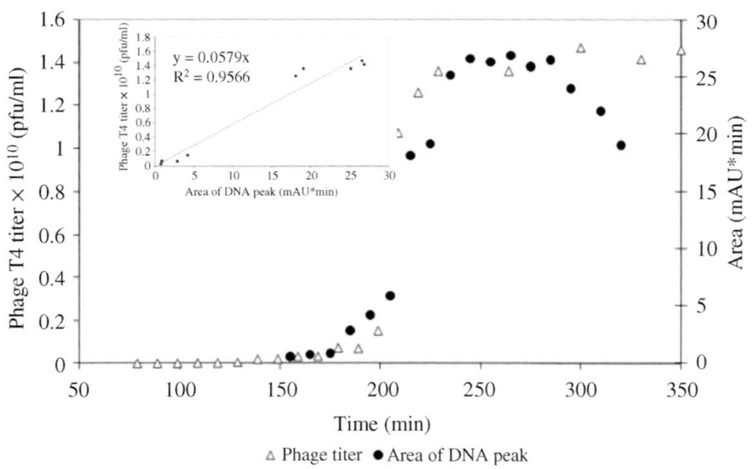

Figure 12.14 Bacteriophage T4 titer from plaque assay (Δ) and bacterial genomic DNA peak area from chromatographic analysis (•) profiles. Inset shows correlation between both variables (Reprinted with permission from Ref. [125]).

12.3
Continuous Purification of Bacteriophages

Downstream processing encompasses all process steps from cell harvest to the final purified product; therefore, different techniques are also applied for bacteriophage purification [139]. Selection of purification technique depends on a number of factors: quantity, quality, productivity, scalability, and finally cost efficiency. For pharmaceutical-grade purity harvest is followed by at least three unit operations comprising capture, purification, and polishing [140], and for each unit operation various techniques can be implemented. This is also commonly the case for bacteriophages intended for human treatment [141]. While most of the purification steps are commonly performed in batch mode, operating in continuous mode can substantially increase productivity [142]. Usually, batch and continuous mode require the same number of processing steps, providing the same quality of the product, but for sensible products, production in continuous mode results in higher yield, leading to better product : impurity ratio [143]. Due to the versatility of different purification protocols, only a short overview of different purification techniques used for bacteriophage purification is given with guidelines on how it can be operated in continuous mode.

12.3.1 Centrifugation

Centrifugation is present in almost all purification processes of bacteriophages and it can lead to a different degree of purity depending on centrifugation type. Low-speed centrifugation (3000–9000 *g*) is usually implemented as a first step, because it enables removal of cell debris [144]. While obtained purity is not sufficient for bacteriophage application for human treatment, it can already be acceptable for application in the agriculture and food industries [139]. Additionally, it can be efficiently applied in continuous mode [145,146]. Further purification of bacteriophages can be achieved by ultracentrifugation at speeds of around 30 000 *g*. On laboratory scale, CsCl gradient is commonly used and the process is rather time consuming since it takes several hours [144]. Because of this, a continuous flow ultracentrifuge is introduced for purification of large volumes of viruses even under GMP conditions [147], and instead of CsCl the sucrose gradient is used. Despite wide application of such ultracentrifuge types for virus isolation, no application in bacteriophage purification was reported.

12.3.2 Precipitation and Flocculation

Another frequently used isolation procedure, applicable to small and large volumes, is precipitation with polyethylene glycol (PEG). Although there are many precipitation agents available, PEG is the first choice because it is the most cost-effective and can be easily removed by dialysis [148]. Shear forces are minimal during precipitation and damage of the bacteriophage particle is very little compared to centrifugation [149]. However, it can also rather slow down the process.

Alternatively, precipitation can be induced also by change in pH value; for example, T2 bacteriophage precipitated when pH was decreased to pH 4 in the presence of alcohol [150]. In general protocol details depend on bacteriophage and its isoelectric point.

Continuous precipitation could be done also in a tubular reactor. The bacteriophage lysate and the precipitating agent are mixed by a static mixer or a small stirred tank reactor (STR) and precipitation occurs while the mixture flows through a tube. The reactor size is determined based on a time required to reach equilibrium and aging of the precipitate. A tubular reactor is often long because a certain shear is required to generate stable flocks and consequently the volume increases when high flow rates are used [140].

Flocculation is different from precipitation by the nature of chemical agents added. While PEG reduces solubility, flocculation agents cause aggregation forming floccules that can be further collected by filtration, sedimentation, or centrifugation at low speed. While no reports to implement flocculation for bacteriophage isolation can be found in the literature, this method is extensively used for purification of particular viruses. Farrah *et al.* performed flocculation of poliovirus from 1900 l of water containing aluminum chloride ($AlCl_3$) [151], while Katzenelson *et al.* isolated poliovirus from 500 l of test solution using organic flocculants [152].

12.3.3
Filtration

Filtration is present in almost all bioprocesses at several different purification stages. The start and end of the downstream process usually include microfiltration to remove bacterial debris at the beginning of the purification or as a sterile filtration through a 0.22 μm filter at the end. Additionally, in many processes ultrafiltration is included for concentration of a target product or in the form of diafiltration for buffer exchange. Implementation of filtration step depends mostly on final application determining purity requirements [153].

Purification of bacteriophage lambda was a combination of microfiltration and ultrafiltration [154]. The sample was first passed through a filter to retain cells and cell wall debris, while allowing passage of bacteriophages and smaller contaminants. In the second step, using a 100 kDa membrane, bacteriophages were retained, leaving through the membrane other components of the medium and cellular proteins. This approach can be performed in continuous mode and it is commonly referred as cascade filtration in the pharmaceutical industry. The operation consists of connecting several filtration units in a way that the permeate from one filtration unit is fed onto a subsequent unit [155]. Since size of filtration units is flexible, particular units can be adjusted to maximize productivity of a specific process.

The advantage of filtration is its ease of being representatively scaled down to laboratory level, enabling extensive testing and optimization on a small scale facilitating successful scaling to industry level. Continuous filtration can be performed in several ways: "batch topped off," single-pass tangential-flow filtration (SPTFF), diafiltration, and membrane cascades [140].

12.3.4 Chromatographic and Other Adsorption Methods

Chromatography is used to purify small and large volumes of bacteriophages when high purity is required. It can be used as a single- or a two-step purification process where both steps are chromatographic or chromatography is combined with other operations.

The combination of chromatography and centrifugation was used for partial removal of DNA and proteins from bacteriophage lambda lysate [156], and recently a similar approach was used for the purification of filamentous phage M13 [157]. As an alternative to column chromatography, Ling *et al.* reported the implementation of fluidized-bed adsorption based on an anion exchanger for cleaning of bacteriophage M13 [158]. The process was compared with centrifugation and found to be superior in terms of purification time and efficiency.

While chromatography is commonly considered as a rather slow process, especially for large molecules, this is not the case with monolithic stationary phases. A single-step purification of bacteriophages T4 [126] and VDX-10 (*S. aureus*) [159] on a monolithic anion exchanger was completed within minutes while retaining high dynamic capacity.

More frequently, the two-step chromatographic purification is applied. For example, bacteriophage T4 was efficiently purified using anion exchange polylysine agarose as a first step followed by size exclusion chromatography (SEC) for removal of smaller molecules [160]. The opposite order of chromatographic steps was reported by several groups. Boratynski *et al.* used celufine sulphate chromatographic column for removal of most endotoxins [141]. By using a hydroxyapatite column as a second chromatographic step, M13 bacteriophages with purity similar to one obtained with ultracentrifugation in CsCl gradient was achieved [161]. Such degree of purity was reported also when the second chromatographic step was substituted by PEG precipitation [162].

Chromatography can be used also to separate different variants of bacteriophages. This was achieved by monolithic chromatographic column bearing anion-exchange groups [125]. In a gradient elution the authors were able to separate T7, lambda, and M13 bacteriophage from a mixture. The same can also be achieved by chromatofocusing [163].

Continuous operation of chromatography was achieved in different ways. The easiest is to operate with several chromatographic columns being in different stages of purification. While one column is in the process of calibration, the second is loaded, on the third elution is performed, and so on [164]. Optimization of such process means that steps that take the most time are being done simultaneously. This approach was successfully implemented for separation of biomolecules [165], and on an industrial-scale continuous purification processes are reported based on rapid cycling of membrane chromatography units, which allow operating at really high velocities allowing over 1 000 000 l of cell culture supernatant to be processed [166]. The multicolumn approach can further be extended to allow step solvent gradients in each column [167] while its efficiency is further improved if countercurrent movement is introduced. As physical movement of stationary phase represents a serious challenge, it can be simulated by proper switching of mobile phase among chromatographic columns. This technique, named simulated moving bed (SMB) [168], is most efficiently used when two components are to be separated in isocratic mode, such as chiral separations [169]. Recently, this technique was also implemented for purification of viruses by introduction of the size exclusion separation principle [170]. To be generally applicable for adsorption-based chromatography of large biomolecules and viruses, a gradient elution from chromatographic support has to be introduced to SMB, as recently described [171–173]. The concept is called continuous multicolumn countercurrent solvent gradient purification (MCSGP), and although no application of bacteriophage or even virus purification has been reported so far, it can be easily adopted when required.

12.4 Conclusions

Currently, continuous production of bacteriophages is not yet an established technology. Technical challenges discussed extensively during this chapter can be nowadays solved; however, implementation of such processes is also market driven. Despite some large-volume commercially available bacteriophage products, for example, in the area of agriculture, and many more trials, they are still not accepted worldwide as a drug for human treatment. Nevertheless, due to many clinical trials and successful treatment cases, and considering the increased acceptance of continuous processing by the pharmaceutical industry, one can envision such processes in the near future. Furthermore, due to the unique extremely fast mutation rate of bacteriophages when exposed to high selection pressure, continuous systems can provide a powerful tool for the development of novel bacteriophage based drugs.

References

1 Canchaya, C., Fournous, G., and Brüssow, H. (2004) The impact of prophages on bacterial chromosomes. *Mol. Microbiol.*, **53**, 9–18.

2 Adams, M.H. (1959) *Bacteriophages*, Interscience Publishers, New York.

3 Smith, G.P. (1985) Filamentous fusion phage: novel expression vectors that display cloned antigens on the virion surface. *Science*, **228**, 1315–1317.

4 Benhar, I. (2001) Biotechnological applications of phage and cell display. *Biotechnol. Adv.*, **19**, 1–33.

5 Clark, J.R. and March, J.B. (2004) Bacteriophage-mediated nucleic acid immunisation. *FEMS Immunol. Med. Microbiol.*, **40**, 21–26.

6 March, J.B., Clark, J.R., and Jepson, C.D. (2004) Genetic immunisation against hepatitis B using whole

bacteriophage particles. *Vaccine*, **22**, 1666–1671.
7 Dunn, I.S. (1996) Mammalian cell binding and transfection mediated by surface-modified bacteriophage lambda. *Biochimie*, **78**, 856.
8 Goodridge, L., Chen, J., and Grifiths, M. (1999) Development and characterization of a fluorescent-bacteriophage assay for detection of *Escherichia coli* O157:H7. *Appl. Environ. Microbiol.*, **65**, 1397–1404.
9 Sulakvelidze, A., Alavidze, Z., and Morris, J.G., Jr. (2001) Bacteriophage therapy. *Antimicrob. Agents Chemother.*, **45**, 649–659.
10 Parracho, H.M., Burrowes, B.H., Enright, M.C., McConville, M.L., and Harper, D.R. (2012) The role of regulated clinical trials in the development of bacteriophage therapeutics. *J. Mol. Genet. Med.*, **6**, 279–286.
11 Alisky, J., Iczkowski, K., Rapoport, A., and Troitsky, N. (1998) Bacteriophages show promise as antimicrobial agents. *J. Infect.*, **36**, 5–15.
12 United States Environmental Protection Agency (2011) AgriPhage US Label. www.epa.gov/pesticides/chem_search/ppls/067986-00001-20111017.pdf.
13 Intralytix (2011) Intralytix completes regulatory clearance for phage-based *E. coli* food safety technology (press release), June 14, 2011. www.intralytix.com/Intral_News.htm.
14 Intralytix (2012) ListShield certificate and MSDS. www.intralytix.com/Certificates_and_MSDSs/ListShield%20-%20product%20description%20-%202012.pdf.
15 Micreos Food Safety (2012) Regulatory position Listex. www.micreosfoodsafety.com/en/listex-regulatory.aspx.
16 Micreos Food Safety (2013) FDA approves SALMONELEX™ against *Salmonella* as new food processing aid, December 30, 2013. www.micreosfoodsafety.com/images/docs/Press%20release%20Micreos_FDA%20approves%20SALMONELEX_v%20Dec%2030%202013-3.pdf.
17 Intralytix (2013) SalmoFresh certificate and MSDS. www.intralytix.com/Intral_Products_SalmoFresh.htm.
18 Food Standards Australia New Zealand. Approval Report – Application A1045 Bacteriophage Preparation P100 as Processing Aid, August 3, 2012. www.foodstandards.gov.au/code/applications/documents/A1045%20Bacteriophage%20as%20a%20PA%20AR%20FINAL.pdf.
19 BioMerieux. VIDAS UP. //microsite.biomerieux-usa.com/phage/.
20 US Food and Drug Administration (2006) Submission of GRAS Notification of Bacteriophage P100 for Use in Foods, December 21, 2006. www.fda.gov/ucm/groups/fdagov-public/@fdagov-foods-gen/documents/document/ucm263921.pdf.
21 Verbeken, G., De Vos, D., Vaneechoutte, M., Merabishvili, M., Zizi, M., and Pirnay, J.-P. (2007) European regulatory conundrum of phage therapy. *Future Microbiol.*, **2**, 485–491.
22 Khawaldeh, A., Morales, S., Dillon, B., Alavidze, Z., Ginn, A.N., Thomas, L., Chapman, S.J., Dublanchet, A., Smithyman, A., and Iredell, J.R. (2011) Bacteriophage therapy for refractory *Pseudomonas aeruginosa* urinary tract infection. *J. Med. Microbiol.*, **60**, 1697–1700.
23 Puck, T.T., Garen, A., and Cline, J. (1951) The mechanism of virus attachment to host cells. I. The role of ions in the primary reaction. *J. Exp. Med.*, **93**, 65.
24 Baptista, C., Santos, M.A., and Sao-Jose, C. (2008) Phage SPP1 reversible adsorption to *Bacillus subtilis* cell wall teichoic acids accelerates virus recognition of membrane receptor YueB. *J. Bacteriol.*, **190**, 4989–4996.
25 Guttman, B., Raya, R., and Kutter, E. (2005) Basic phage biology, in *Bacteriophages, Biology and Applications* (eds E. Kutter and A. Sulakvelidze), CRC Press, Boca Raton, FL, pp. 29–66.
26 Letellier, L., Boulanger, P., Plancon, L., Jacquot, P., and Santamaria, M. (2004) Main features on tailed phage, host recognition and DNA uptake. *Front. Biosci.*, **9**, 1228–1339.
27 Bull, J.J. (2006) Optimality models of phage life history and parallels in disease evolution. *J. Theor. Biol.*, **241**, 928–938.

28 Schlesinger, M. (1932) Über die Bindung des Bakteriophagen an homologe Bakterien. I. Die Unterscheidung von Gruppen von verschiedener Bindungsaffinitaet innerhalb der Bakterien des selben Lysats. Die Frage der Reversibilitaet oder Irreversibilitaet der Bindung. *Z. Hyg. Infektionskrankh.*, **114**, 136.

29 Schlesinger, M. (1932) Über die Bindung des Bakteriophagen an homologe Bakterien. II. Quantitative Untersuchungen ueber die Bindungsgeschwindigkeit und die Saettigung. Berechnung der Teilchengroesse des Bakteriophagen aus deren Ergebnissen. *Z. Hyg. Infektionskrankh.*, **114**, 149.

30 Hadas, H., Einav, M., Fishov, L., and Zaritsky, A. (1997) Bacteriophage T4 development depends on the physiology of its host *Escherichia coli*. *Microbiology*, **143**, 179–185.

31 Shao, Y. and Wang, I.N. (2008) Bacteriophage adsorption rate and optimal lysis time. *Genetics*, **180**, 471–482.

32 Heller, K. and Braun, V. (1979) Accelerated adsorption of bacteriophage T5 to *Escherichia coli* F, resulting from reversible tail fiber-lipopolysaccharide binding. *J. Bacteriol.*, **139**, 32–38.

33 Delbrück, M. (1946) Bacterial viruses or bacteriophages. *Biol. Rev. Camb. Philos. Soc.*, **21**, 30.

34 Barry, G.T. and Goebel, W.F. (1951) The effect of chemical and physical agents on the phage receptor of pliase II *Shigella sonnei*. *J. Exp. Med.*, **94**, 387–400.

35 Heden, C. (1951) Studies of the infection of *E. coli* B with the bacteriophage T2. *Acta Pathol. Microbiol. Scand. Suppl.*, **88**, 1–121.

36 Delbrück, M. (1940) The growth of bacteriophage and lysis of the host. *J. Gen. Physiol.*, **23**, 643.

37 Delbrück, M. (1945) The burst size distribution in the growth of bacterial viruses. *J. Bacteriol.*, **50**, 131.

38 Reader, R.W. and Siminovitch, L. (1971) Lysis defective mutants of bacteriophage lambda: genetics and physiology of S cistron mutants. *Virology*, **43**, 607–622.

39 Abedon, S.T., Herschler, T.D., and Stopar, D. (2001) Bacteriophage latent-period evolution as a response to resource availability. *Appl. Environ. Microbiol.*, **67**, 4233–4241.

40 Wang, I.N. (2006) Lysis timing and bacteriophage fitness. *Genetics*, **172**, 17–26.

41 Adams, M.H. (1951) The hybridization of coliphage T5 and salmonella phage PB. *J. Immunol.*, **67**, 313.

42 Delbrück, M. (1940) Adsorption of bacteriophage under various physiological conditions of the host. *J. Gen. Physiol.*, **23**, 631.

43 Adams, M.H. and Wassermann, F. (1956) Frequency distribution of phage release in the one-step growth experiment. *Virology*, **2**, 96.

44 Heineman, R.H. and Bull, J.J. (2007) Testing optimality with experimental evolution: lysis time in a bacteriophage. *Evolution*, **61**, 1695–1709.

45 Adams, M.H. (1949) The calcium requirement of coliphage T5. *J. Immunol.*, **62**, 505.

46 Abedon, S.T., Hyman, P., and Thomas, C. (2003) Experimental examination of bacteriophage latent-period evolution as a response to bacterial availability. *Appl. Environ. Microbiol.*, **69**, 7499–7506.

47 Dörmann, A.H. (1948) Lysis and lysis inhibition with *Escherichia coli* bacteriophage. *J. Bacteriol.*, **55**, 257–275.

48 Dörmann, A.H. (1952) The intracellular growth of bacteriophages. I. Liberation of intracellular bacteriophage T4 by premature lysis with another phage or with cyanide. *J. Gen. Physiol.*, **35**, 645–656.

49 Hutchinson, C.A. and Sinsheimer, R.L. (1966) The process of infection with bacteriophage Φ X174. *J. Mol. Biol.*, **18**, 429–447.

50 Josslin, R. (1970) The lysis mechanism of phage T4: mutants affecting lysis. *Virology*, **40**, 719–726.

51 Wang, I.N., Dykhuizen, D.E., and Slobodkin, L.B. (1996) The evolution of phage lysis timing. *Evol. Ecol.*, **10**, 545–558.

52 Bull, J.J. and Wang, I.-N. (2010) Optimality models in the age of

experimental evolution and genomics. *J. Evol. Biol.*, **23**, 1820–1838.
53 Abedon, S.T. (1994) Lysis and the interaction between free phages and infected cells, in *The Molecular Biology of Bacteriophage T4* (eds J.D. Karam, J.W. Drake, K.N. Kreuzer, G. Mosig, D. Hall, F.A. Eiserling, L.W. Black, E. Kutter, K. Carlson, E.S. Miller, and E. Spicer), ASM Press, Washington, DC, pp. 397–405.
54 Karam, J.D., Drake, J.W., Kreuzer, K.N., Mosig, G., Hall, D., Eiserling, F.A., Black, L.W., Kutter, E., Carlson, K., Miller, E.S., and Spicer, E. (eds) (1994) *The Molecular Biology of Bacteriophage T4*, ASM Press, Washington, DC.
55 Dulbecco, R. (1949) The number of particles of bacteriophage T2 that can participate in intracellular growth. *Genetics*, **34**, 126.
56 Hyman, P. and Abedon, S.T. (2009) Practical methods for determining phage growth parameters, in *Bacteriophages: Methods and Protocols, Volume 1: Isolation, Characterization, and Interactions* (eds M.R.J. Clokie and A.M. Kropinski), Humana Press, a part of Springer Science+Business Media, pp. 175–202.
57 Sarimo, S.S., Hartiala, M., and Aaltonen, L. (1976) Preparation and partial characterization of a *Lactobacillus lactis* bacteriophage. *Arch. Microbiol.*, **107**, 193–197.
58 Delbrück, M. (1942) Bacterial viruses (bacteriophages). *Adv. Enzymol.*, **2**, 1–32.
59 Heller, K. and Braun, V. (1979) Accelerated adsorption of bacteriophage T5 to *Escherichia coli* F, resulting from reversible tail fiber-lipopolysaccharide binding. *J. Bacteriol.*, **139**, 32–38.
60 Brown, A. (1956) A study of lysis in bacteriophage-infected *Escherichia coli*. *J. Bacteriol.*, **71**, 482–490.
61 Ellis, E.L. and Delbrück, M. (1939) The growth of bacteriophage. *J. Gen. Physiol.*, **22**, 365–384.
62 Sargeant, K., Yeo, K.G., Lethbridge, J.H., and Shooter, K.V. (1968) Production of bacteriophage T7. *Appl. Microbiol.*, **16**, 1483–1488.
63 Novick, A. and Szilard, L. (1950) Experiments with the chemostat on spontaneous mutations of bacteria. *Proc. Natl. Acad. Sci. USA*, **36**, 708–719.
64 Northrop, J.H. (1966) Increased mutation rate of *E. coli* K12 lambda cultures maintained in continuous logarithmic growth. *J. Gen. Physiol.*, **50**, 369–377.
65 Horne, M. (1970) Coevolution of *Escherichia coli* and bacteriophages in chemostat culture. *Science*, **168**, 992–993.
66 Paynter, M.J.B. and Bungay, H.R., 3rd (1970) Response in continuous cultures of lysogenic *Escherichia coli* following induction. *Biotechnol. Bioeng.*, **7**, 347–351.
67 Chao, L., Levin, B.R., and Stewart, F.M. (1977) A complex community in a simple habitat: an experimental study with bacteria and phage. *Ecology*, **58**, 369–378.
68 Kutter, E., Gachechiladze, K., and Poglazov, A. (1996) Evolution of T4-related phages. *Virus Genes*, **11**, 285–297.
69 Schrag, S.J. and Mittler, J.E. (1996) Host–parasite coexistence: the role of spatial refuge in stabilizing bacteria–phage interactions. *Am. Nat.*, **148**, 348–377.
70 Chapman-McQuiston, E. and Wu, X.L. (2008) Stochastic receptor expression allows sensitive bacteria to evade phage attack. Part I. Experiments. *Biophys. J.*, **94**, 4525–4536.
71 Kunisaki, H. and Tanji, Y. (2010) Intercrossing of phage genomes in a phage cocktail and stable coexistence with *Escherichia coli* O157:H7 in anaerobic continuous culture. *Appl. Microbiol. Biotechnol.*, **85**, 1533–1540.
72 Levin, B.R., Stewart, F.M., and Chao, N.L. (1977) Resource-limited growth, competition, and predation: a model and experimental studies with bacteria and bacteriophage. *Am. Nat.*, **111**, 3–24.
73 Lenski, R.E. (1984) Two-step resistance by *Escherichia coli* B to bacteriophage T2. *Genetics*, **107**, 1–7.
74 Mizoguchi, K., Morita, M., Fischer, C.R., Yoichi, M., Tanji, Y., and Unno, H. (2003) Coevolution of bacteriophage PP01 and *Escherichia coli* O157:H7 in continuous culture. *Appl. Environ. Microbiol.*, **69**, 170–176.

75 Fischer, C.R., Yoichi, M., Unno, H., and Tanji, Y. (2004) The coexistence of *Escherichia coli* serotype O157:H7 and its specific bacteriophage in continuous culture. *FEMS Microbiol. Lett.*, **241**, 171–177.

76 Kunisaki, H. and Tanji, Y. (2010) Intercrossing of phage genomes in a phage cocktail and stable coexistence with *Escherichia coli* O157:H7 in anaerobic continuous culture. *Appl. Microbiol. Biotechnol.*, **85**, 1533–1540.

77 Spanakis, E. and Horne, M.T. (1987) Coadaptation of *Escherichia coli* and coliphage lambda vir in continuous culture. *J. Gen. Microbiol.*, **133**, 353–360.

78 Bohannan, B.J.M. and Lenski., R.E. (2000) The relative importance of competition and predation varies with productivity in a model community. *Am. Nat.*, **156**, 329–340.

79 Lenski, R.E. and Levin, B.R. (1985) Constraints on the coevolution of bacteria and virulent phage: a model, some experiments, and predictions for natural communities. *Am. Nat.*, **125**, 585–602.

80 Weitz, J., Hartman, H., and Levin, S. (2005) Coevolutionary arms race between bacteria and bacteriophage. *Proc. Natl. Acad. Sci. USA*, **102**, 9535–9540.

81 Campbell, A. (1961) Conditions for existence of bacteriophages. *Evolution*, **15**, 153–165.

82 Smouse, P.E. (1980) Mathematical models for continuous culture growth dynamics of mixed populations subsisting on a heterogeneous resource base. I. Simple competition. *Theor. Popul. Biol.*, **17**, 16–36.

83 Crowley, P.H., Straley, S.C., Craig, R.J., Culin, J.D., Fu, Y.T., Hayden, T.L., Robinson, T.A., and Straley, J.P. (1980) A model of prey bacteria, predator bacteria, and bacteriophage in continuous culture. *J. Theor. Biol.*, **86**, 377–400.

84 Smouse, P.E. (1981) Mathematical models for continuous culture growth dynamics of mixed populations subsisting on a heterogeneous resource base. II. Predation and trophic structure. *Theor. Popul. Biol.*, **20**, 127–149.

85 Levin, B.R. and Lenski, R.E. (1983) Coevolution of bacteria and their viruses and plasmids, in *Coevolution* (eds D.J. Futyama and M. Slatkin), Sinauer, Sunderland, MA, pp. 99–127.

86 Bohannan, B.J.M. and Lenski, R.E. (2000) Linking genetic change to community evolution: insights from studies of bacteria and bacteriophages. *Ecol. Lett.*, **3**, 362–377.

87 Rabinovitch, A., Aviram, I., and Zaritsky, A. (2003) Bacterial debris—an ecological mechanism for coexistence of bacteria and their viruses. *J. Theor. Biol.*, **224**, 377–383.

88 Smith, H.L. and Thieme, H.R. (2012) Persistence of bacteria and phages in a chemostat. *J. Math. Biol.*, **64**, 951–979.

89 Jones, D.A. and Smith, H.L. (2011) Bacteriophage and bacteria in a flow reactor. *Bull. Math. Biol.*, **73**, 2357–2383.

90 Bull, J.J., Millstein, J., Orcutt, J., and Wichman, H.A. (2006) Evolutionary feedback mediated through population density, illustrated with viruses in chemostats. *Am. Nat.*, **167**, E39–E41.

91 Bohannan, B.J.M. and Lenski, R.E. (1997) Effect of resource enrichment on a chemostat community of bacteria and bacteriophage. *Ecology*, **78**, 2303–2315.

92 Forde, S.E., Thompson, J.N., and Bohannan, B.J.M. (2004) Adaptation varies through space and time in a coevolving host–parasitoid interaction. *Nature*, **431**, 841–844.

93 Travisano, M. and Lenski, R.E. (1996) Long-term experimental evolution in *Escherichia coli*. IV. Targets of selection and the specificity of adaptation. *Genetics*, **143**, 15–26.

94 Barrick, J.E., Yu, D.S., Yoon, S.H., Jeong, H., Oh, T.K., Schneider, D., Lenski, R.E., and Kim, J.F. (2009) Genome evolution and adaptation in a long-term experiment with *Escherichia coli*. *Nature*, **461**, 1243–1247.

95 Tenaillon, O., Rodríguez-Verdugo, A., Gaut, R.L., McDonald, P., Bennett, A.F., Long, A.D., and Gaut, B.S. (2012) The molecular diversity of adaptive convergence. *Science*, **335**, 457–461.

96 Kirby, A.E. (2011) Synergistic action of gentamicin and bacteriophage in a continuous culture population of *Staphylococcus aureus*. *PLoS ONE*, **7**, e51017-1–e51017-9.

97 Husimi, Y., Nishigaki, K., Kinoshita, Y., and Tanaka, T. (1982) Cellstat – a continuous culture system of a bacteriophage for the study of the mutation rate and the selection process at the DNA level. *Rev. Sci. Instrum.*, **53**, 517–522.

98 Aita, T. and Husimi, Y. (1994) Period dependent selection in continuous culture of viruses in a periodic environment. *J. Theor. Biol.*, **168**, 281–289.

99 Schwienhorst, A., Lindermann, B.F., and Eigen, M. (1996) Growth kinetics of a bacteriophage in continuous culture. *Biotechnol. Bioeng.*, **50**, 217–221.

100 Park, T.H., Seo, J.-H., and Lim, H.C. (1991) Two-stage fermentation with bacteriophage λ as an expression vector in *Escherichia coli*. *Biotechnol. Bioeng.*, **37**, 297–302.

101 Oh, J.S., Cho, D., and Park, T.H. (2005) Two-stage continuous operation of recombinant *Escherichia coli* using the bacteriophage lambda Q^- vector. *Bioprocess Biosyst. Eng.*, **28**, 1–7.

102 Oh, J.S., Choi, S.S., and Park, T.H. (2010) Enhancement of bacteriophage λ stability using a λQ^-S^- mutant in the continuous culture of *Escherichia coli*. *Bioprocess Biosyst. Eng.*, **33**, 1103–1107.

103 Lindemann, B.F., Klug, C., and Schwienhorstm, A. (2002) Evolution of bacteriophage in continuous culture: a model system to test antiviral gene therapies for the emergence of phage escape mutants. *J. Virol.*, **76**, 5784–5792.

104 Esvelt, K.M., Carlson, J.C., and Liu, D.R. (2011) A system for the continuous directed evolution of biomolecules. *Nature*, **472**, 499–503.

105 Leconte, A.M., Dickinson, B.C., Yang, D.D., Chen, I.A., Allen, B., and Liu, D.R. (2013) A population-based experimental model for protein evolution: effects of mutation rate and selection stringency on evolutionary outcomes. *Biochemistry*, **52**, 1490–1499.

106 Sauvageau, D. and Cooper, D.G. (2010) Two-stage, self-cycling process for the production of bacteriophages. *Microb. Cell Fact.*, **9**, 81–90.

107 Husimi, Y. (1989) Selection and evolution of bacteriophages in cellstat. *Adv. Biophys.*, **25**, 1–43.

108 Podgornik, A., Janež, N., Smrekar, F., Alegro, A., and Peterka, M. Modelling of continuous bacteriophage production in cellstat, ESBES, Lille, 7.-10.9.2014, France, L-D14.

109 Fane, B.A., Brentlinger, K.L., Burch, A.D., Chen, M., Hafenstein, S. *et al.* (2006) The microvirid, in *The Bacteriophages* (ed. R. Calendar), Oxford Press, Oxford, pp. 129–145.

110 Brown, C.J., Millstein, J., Williams, C.J., and Wichman, H.A. (2013) Selection affects genes involved in replication during long-term evolution in experimental populations of the bacteriophage øX174. *PLoS ONE*, **8**, e60401.

111 Wichman, H.A., Badgett, M.R., Scott, L. A., Boulianne, C.M., and Bull, J.J. (1999) Different trajectories of parallel evolution during viral adaptation. *Science*, **285**, 422–424.

112 Bull, J.J., Badgett, M.R., Wichman, H.A., Huelsenbeck, J.P., Hillis, D.M. *et al.* (1997) Exceptional convergent evolution in a virus. *Genetics*, **147**, 1497–1507.

113 Crill, W.D., Wichman, H.A., and Bull, J.J. (2000) Evolutionary reversals during viral adaptation to alternating hosts. *Genetics*, **154**, 27–37.

114 Wichman, H.A., Scott, L.A., Yarber, C.D., and Bull, J.J. (2000) Experimental evolution recapitulates natural evolution. *Philos. Trans. R. Soc. Lond. B*, **355**, 1677–1684.

115 Wichman, H.A. and Brown, C.J. (2010) Experimental evolution of viruses: Microviridae as a model system. *Philos. Trans. R. Soc. Lond. B*, **365**, 2495–2501.

116 Clokie, M.R.J., Millard, A.D., Letarov, A.V., and Heaphy, S. (2011) Phages in nature. *Bacteriophage*, **1**, 31–45.

117 Kong, D. and Yin, J. (1995) Whole-virus vaccine development by continuous culture on a complementing host. *Bio/Technology*, **13**, 583–586.

118 Junker, B. (2007) Foam and its mitigation in fermentation systems. *Biotechnol. Prog.*, **23**, 767–784.

119 Husimi, Y. and Keweloh, H.-C. (1987) Continuous culture of bacteriophage QP using a cellstat with a bubble wall-growth scraper. *Rev. Sci. Instrum.*, **58**, 1109–1113.

120 de Crécy-Lagard, V.A., Bellalou, J., Mutzel, R., and Marlière, P. (2001) Long term adaptation of a microbial population to a permanent metabolic constraint: overcoming thymineless death by experimental evolution of *Escherichia coli*. *BMC Biotechnol.*, **1**, 10.

121 Mutzel, R., Mazel, D., and Marlière, P. (2003) Method for obtaining cells with new properties. WO 03/004656.

122 de Crécy, E., Metzgar, D., Allen, C., Pénicaud, M., Lyons, B., Hansen, C.J., and de Crécy-Lagard, V. (2007) Development of a novel continuous culture device for experimental evolution of bacterial populations. *Appl. Microbiol. Biotechnol.*, 77, 489–496.

123 Kramberger, P., Ciringer, M., Štrancar, A., and Peterka, M. (2012) Evaluation of nanoparticle tracking analysis for total virus particle determination. *J. Virol.*, **9**, 1–10.

124 Smrekar, F., Ciringer, M., Štrancar, A., and Podgornik, A. (2011) Characterisation of methacrylate monoliths for bacteriophage purification. *J. Chromatogr. A*, **1218**, 2438–2444.

125 Smrekar, F., Ciringer, M., Jančar, J., Raspor, P., Štrancar, A., and Podgornik, A. (2011) Optimization of lytic phage manufacturing in bioreactor using monolithic supports. *J. Sep. Sci.*, **34**, 2152–2158.

126 Smrekar, F., Ciringer, M., Peterka, M., Podgornik, A., and Štrancar, A. (2008) Purification and concentration of bacteriophage T4 using monolithic chromatographic supports. *J. Chromatogr. B*, **861**, 177–180.

127 Krajnc, P., Leber, N., Štefanec, D., Kontrec, S., and Podgornik, A. (2005) Preparation and characterization of poly(high internal phase emulsion) methacrylate monoliths and their application as separation media. *J. Chromatogr. A*, **1065**, 69–73.

128 Tennikova, T.B. and Švec, F. (1993) High-performance membrane chromatography: highly efficient separation method for proteins in ion-exchange, hydrophobic interaction and reversed-phase modes. *J. Chromatogr.*, **646**, 279–288.

129 Štrancar, A., Barut, M., Podgornik, A., Koselj, P., Josić, D., and Buchacher, A. (1998) Convective interaction media: polymer-based supports for fast separation of biomolecules. *LC-GC*, **11**, 660–669.

130 Endres, H.N., Johnson, J.A.C., Ross, C.A., Welp, J.K., and Etzel, M.R. (2003) Evaluation of an ion-exchange membrane for purification of plasmid DNA. *Biotechnol. Appl. Biochem.*, **37**, 259–266.

131 Mihelič, I., Koloini, T., Podgornik, A., and Štrancar, A. (2000) Dynamic capacity studies of CIM (Convective Interaction Media) monolithic columns. *J. High Resolut. Chromatogr.*, **23**, 39–43.

132 Štrancar, A., Koselj, P., Schwinn, H., and Josić, D. (1996) Application of compact porous disks for fast separations of biopolymers and in-process control in biotechnology. *Anal. Chem.*, **68**, 3483–3488.

133 Švec., F. and Fréchet., J.M. (1996) New designs of macroporous polymers and supports: from separation to biocatalysis. *Science*, **273**, 205–211.

134 Yamamoto, S. and Kita, A. (2006) Effect of the molecule size on dynamic binding capacity. *Trans. IChemE Part C Food Bioprod. Process.*, **84**, 72–77.

135 Barut, M., Podgornik, A., Urbas, L., Gabor, B., Brne, P., Vidič, J., Plevčak, S., and Štrancar, A. (2008) Methacrylate-based short monolithic columns: enabling tools for rapid and efficient analyses of biomolecules and nanoparticles. *J. Sep. Sci.*, **31**, 1867–1880.

136 Jungbauer, A. and Hahn, R. (2008) Polymethacrylate monoliths for preparative and industrial separation of biomolecular assemblies. *J. Chromatogr. A*, **1184**, 62–79.

137 Podgornik, A. and Lendero Krajnc, N. (2012) Application of monoliths for

bioparticle isolation. *J. Sep. Sci.*, **35**, 3059–3072.

138 Podgornik, A., Yamamoto, S., Peterka, M., and Lendero Krajnc, N. (2013) Fast separation of large biomolecules using short monolithic columns. *J. Chromatogr. B*, **927**, 80–89.

139 Gill, J.J. and Hyman, P. (2002) Phage choice, isolation, and preparation for phage therapy. *Curr. Pharm. Biotechnol.*, **11**, 2–14.

140 Jungbauer, A. (2013) Continuous downstream processing of biopharmaceuticals. *Trends Biotechnol.*, **31**, 479–492.

141 Boratynski, J., Syper, D., Weber-Dabrowska, B., Lusiak-Szelachowska, M., Pozniak, G., and Gorski, A. (2004) Preparation of endotoxin-free bacteriophages. *Cell. Mol. Biol. Lett.*, **2**, 253–259.

142 Sen, M., Rogers, A., Singh, R., Chaudhury, A., John, J., Jerapetritou, M.G., and Ramachandran, R. (2013) Flowsheet optimization of an integrated continuous purification–processing pharmaceutical manufacturing operation. *Chem. Eng. Sci.*, **102**, 56–66.

143 Warikoo, V., Godawat, R., Brower, K., Jain, S., Cummings, D., Simons, E., Johnson, T., Walther, J., Yu, M., Wright, B., Mclarty, J., Karey, K.P., Hwang, C., Zhou, W., Riske, F., and Konstantinov, K. (2012) Integrated continuous production of recombinant therapeutic proteins. *Biotechnol. Bioeng.*, **109**, 3018–3029.

144 Bachrach, U. and Friedmann, A. (1971) Practical procedures for the purification of bacterial viruses. *Appl. Microbiol.*, **22**, 706–715.

145 Patrick, C.W. and Freeman, R.R. (1960) Continuous centrifugation in virus processing. *J. Biochem. Microbiol. Technol. Eng.*, **2**, 71–80.

146 Tebbe, J., Gudermann, F., Luthemeyer, D., and Lehmann, J. (1997) Removal of animal cells and cell debris by continuous two-stage centrifugation, in *Animal Cell Technology* (eds M.J.T. Carrondo, B. Griffiths, and J.L.P. Moreira), Kluwer Academic Publishers, pp. 391–397.

147 Alfa Wasserman (2014) Promatix 1000 laboratory ultracentrifuge (product description). http://www.awst.com/_codev/application/contents/content/pdf/Alfa_Promatix%201000%20System%20Brochure.pdf.

148 De Czekala, A., Luk, D., and Bartl, P. (1972) Large-scale production of lambda bacteriophage and purified lambda deoxyribonucleic acid. *Appl. Microbiol.*, **23**, 791–795.

149 Branston, S., Stanley, E., Ward, J., and Keshavarz-Moore, E. (2011) Study of robustness of filamentous bacteriophages for industrial applications. *Biotechnol. Bioeng.*, **108**, 1468–1472.

150 Stent, G.S. (1963) *Molecular Biology of Bacterial Viruses*, W.H. Freeman & Co., San Francisco, CA.

151 Farrah, S.R., Gerba, C.P., Wallis, C., and Melnick, J.L. (1976) Concentration of viruses from large volumes of tap water using pleated membrane filters. *Appl. Environ. Microbiol.*, **31**, 221–226.

152 Katzenelson, E., Fattal, B., and Hostovesky, T. (1976) Organic flocculation: an efficient second-step concentration method for the detection of viruses in tap water. *Appl. Environ. Microbiol.*, **32**, 638–639.

153 Grzenia, D.L., Carlson, J.O., and Wickramasinghe, S.R. (2008) Tangential flow filtration for virus purification. *J. Membr. Sci.*, **321**, 373–380.

154 Rembhotkar, G.W. and Khatri, G.S. (1989) Large scale preparation of bacteriophage lambda by tangential flow ultrafiltration for isolation of lambda DNA. *Anal. Biochem.*, **176**, 373–374.

155 Siew, W.E., Livingstone, A.G., Atesa, C., and Merschaer, A. (2013) Continuous solute fractionation with membrane cascades – a high productivity alternative to diafiltration. *Sep. Purif. Technol.*, **102**, 1–14.

156 Creaser, E.H. and Taussig, A. (1957) The purification and chromatography of bacteriophages on anion-exchange cellulose. *Virology*, **4**, 200–208.

157 Mojezi, R., Tey, B.T., Sieo, C.C., and Tan, W.S. (2010) Purification of bacteriophage M13 by anion exchange chromatography. *J. Chromatogr. B*, **878**, 1855–1859.

158 Ling, T.FC., Loong, C.K., Tan, W.S., Tey, B.T., Abdullah, W.M.W., and Ariff, A. (2004) Purification of filamentous bacteriophage M13 by expanded bed anion exchange chromatography. *J. Microbiol.*, **42**, 228–232.

159 Kramberger, P., Honour, R.C., Herman, R.E., Smrekar, F., and Peterka, M. (2010) Purification of the *Staphylococcus aureus* bacteriophages VDX-10 on methacrylate monoliths. *J. Virol. Methods*, **166**, 60–64.

160 Sundberg, L. and Hoglund, S. (1973) Purification of T4 phage by adsorption on polylysine agarose. *FEBS Lett.*, **15**, 70–73.

161 Smith, G.P. and Gingrich, T.R. (2005) Hydroxyapatite chromatography of phage-display virons. *Biotechniques*, **39**, 879–884.

162 Sain, B. and Erdei, S. (1981) Bacteriophage purification by gel chromatography. *Anal. Biochem.*, **110**, 128–130.

163 Brorson, K., Shen, H., Lute, S., Perez, J.S., and Frey, D.D. (2008) Characterization and purification of bacteriophages using chromatofocusing. *J. Chromatogr. A*, **1207**, 110–121.

164 Jungbauer, A. (1993) Preparative chromatography of biomolecules. *J. Chromatogr.*, **639**, 3–16.

165 Tish, T.L., Frost, R., Liao, J.L., Lam, W.K., Remy, A., Scheinpflug, E., Siebert, C., Song, H., and Stapleton, A. (1998) Biochemical separations by continuous-bed chromatography. *J. Chromatogr. A*, **816**, 3–9.

166 Vogel, J.H., Nguyen, H., Giovannini, R., Ignowski, J., Garger, S., Salgotra, S., and Tom, J. (2012) A new large-scale manufacturing platform for complex biopharmaceuticals. *Biotechnol. Bioeng.*, **109**, 3049–3058.

167 Antos, D. and Seidel-Morgenstern, A. (2002) Continuous step gradient elution for preparative separations. *Sep. Sci. Technol.*, **37**, 1469–1487.

168 Imamoglu, S. (2002) Simulated moving bed chromatography (SMB) for application in bioseparation. *Adv. Biochem. Eng. Biotechnol.*, **76**, 211–231.

169 Rajendran, A., Paredes, G., and Mazzotti, M. (2009) Simulated moving bed chromatography for the separation of enantiomers. *J. Chromatogr. A*, **1216**, 709–738.

170 Kröber, T., Wolff, M.W., Hundt, B., Seidel-Morgenstern, A., and Reichl, U. (2013) Continuous purification of influenza virus using simulated moving bed chromatography. *J. Chromatogr. A*, **1307**, 99–110.

171 Stroehlein, G., Aumann, L., Mazzotti, M., and Morbidelli, M. (2006) A continuous, counter-current multi-column chromatographic process incorporating modifier gradients for ternary separations. *J. Chromatogr. A*, **1126**, 338–346.

172 Aumann, L., Stroehlein, G., and Morbidelli, M. (2007) Parametric study of a 6-column countercurrent solvent gradient purification (MCSGP) unit. *Biotechnol. Bioeng.*, **98**, 1029–1042.

173 Aumann, L. and Morbidelli, M. (2007) A continuous multicolumn countercurrent solvent gradient purification (MCSGP) process. *Biotechnol. Bioeng.*, **98**, 1043–1055.

13
Very High Cell Density in Perfusion of CHO Cells by ATF, TFF, Wave Bioreactor, and/or CellTank Technologies – Impact of Cell Density and Applications

Véronique Chotteau, Ye Zhang, and Marie-Francoise Clincke

13.1
Introduction

High cell density in perfusion processes opens the way toward intensified processes with high total production of the product of interest in (relatively) small-size bioreactors. In the past decade, the use of disposable equipment has been increasing dramatically. The success of disposable equipment, however limited by the size of the bioreactor combined with the venue of more robust perfusion devices allowing high cell densities, has generated a new interest in the biopharmaceutical industry for perfusion processes. A better knowledge of these processes, for instance understanding the impact of high and very high cell densities on the process, is important since this will help us for the development and the economic predictions of these future intensified processes.

Wave-induced bioreactors were introduced by Singh in 1999 [1] and have become important players supporting, for example, cell seeding train, production of the product of interest, and cell banking. Tangential-flow filtration (TFF) was introduced several decades ago and has the advantage of reduced filter fouling compared to conventional filtration, thanks to a movement animating the cell suspension tangentially to the filter surface [2,3]. The alternating tangential flow (ATF) is based on the same tangential-flow filtration but the cell suspension is moved by an alternating diaphragm pump instead of using a peristaltic pump. The advantages of ATF compared to TFF are that the fouling tendency can be reduced by the alternating motion creating a back-flow flush in the filter and that no peristaltic pump, known to damage the cells, is required [4,5].

An alternative approach to perfusion bioreactors for cell suspension are systems in which the cells are adhering on or entrapped in a matrix. Well-known examples are the packed-bed bioreactors where the cells are adhering on the external surface or inside cavities of microcarriers [6]. The CellTank bioreactor (CT) is a new bioreactor, which has been developed to perfuse adherent or non adherent mammalian cells at high density. In this compact disposable system, the cells are entrapped in a non woven matrix caged in a cassette, which is

Continuous Processing in Pharmaceutical Manufacturing, First Edition. Edited by Ganapathy Subramanian.

immersed in a larger tank or reservoir. The reservoir contains the cultivation medium, free from cells, which circulates continuously through the cassette thanks to an integrated impeller pump. The bioreactor has been designed to ensure a homogeneous distribution of the fluid in the matrix. The CT has some common features with existing systems: the depth filter perfusion bioreactor in which the cells are trapped in a depth filter through which the medium is circulated by a peristaltic pump to a second tank equipped with monitoring and control systems [7]; the fibrous bioreactor in which the cells are anchored in a fibrous matrix immersed in a tank homogenized by magnetic stirring unfortunately with insufficient circulation through the matrix [8].

In the present study, the following continuous disposable systems were studied:

- W-ATF: wave-induced disposable bioreactor equipped with alternating tangential-flow filtration.
- W-TFF: wave-induced disposable bioreactor equipped with tangential-flow filtration.
- CT: CellTank, nonwoven fiber matrix-based bioreactor with integrated perfusion.

The goals of the study were to develop high-cell density perfusion processes with these systems and then carry out performance evaluations of the systems and understand the limits of the technologies. Two Chinese hamster ovary (CHO) cell lines producing different monoclonal antibody were used: CHO#1 used with the W-ATF and the W-TFF, and CHO#2 used with the CT.

Our strategy to develop the W-ATF and the W-TFF processes included the following steps: at first a learning phase including the development of the perfusion process and a study of the equipment, and then an evaluation of the limits of the system in terms of cell density. Following these phases, different applications of these technologies were performed: evaluation of IgG production, evaluation of cryopreservation, and cell banking. A comparison with fed-batch processing and a study of ultrafiltration (UF) in TFF and ATF instead of microfiltration were also performed and are presented in Ref. [5].

Concerning the CT, a study using a bioreactor prototype was performed. We developed first the perfusion process including a learning phase and some troubleshooting. Then we carried out an evaluation of the system at very high cell density and studied the cell growth arrest by lowering the temperature in a high cell density culture.

13.2
Equipment

A 10 l wave-induced bioreactor (Cellbag™, mounted on WAVE Bioreactor™, GE Healthcare), operated at 4 l working volume, was used for perfusion either

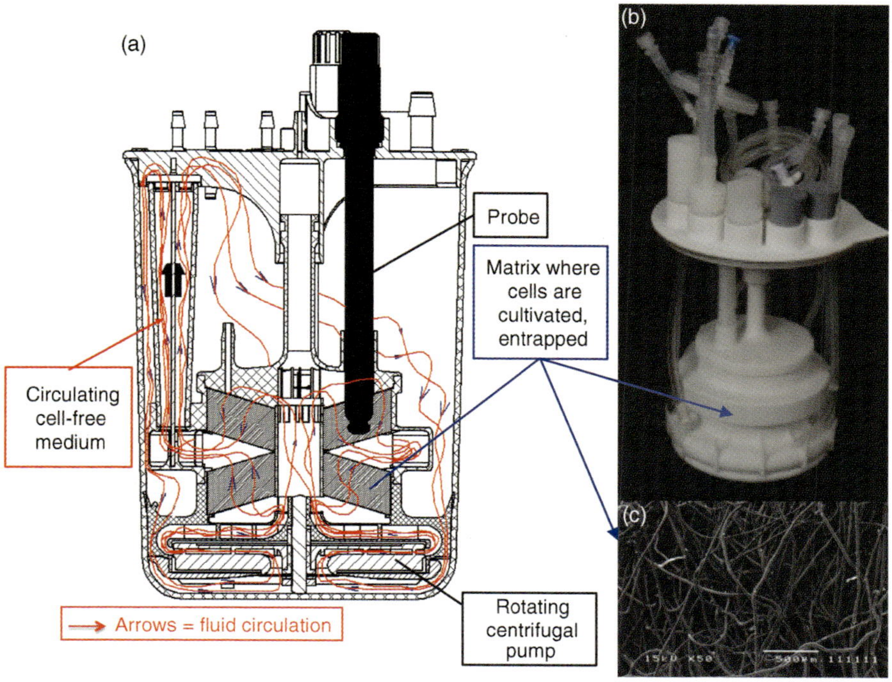

Figure 13.1 CellTank: (a) schematic representation, (b) setup, and (c) nonwoven matrix. *Courtesy* www.perfusecell.com.

connected to an ATF-2 or to a TFF system connected via a Watson Marlow 620S pump. In both cases, the filtration was operated using a hollow fiber filter RTPCFP-2-E-4X2MS with 850 cm^2 filter area (GE Healthcare). To operate the perfusion, the wave-induced bioreactor was connected to the hollow fiber filter (HF) via two dip tubes. A cell bleed line was mounted to pump out cell broth from the bioreactor. A complete description of the W-ATF and W-TFF systems can be found in Ref. [4].

A prototype of the CellTank 34 (PerfuseCell, Denmark), which contains a matrix of 150 ml, was used (see Figure 13.1). The cell density was measured by a biomass sensor EVO200 (Fogale). In the CT, the medium is recirculated through the matrix thanks to an impeller pump. The liquid is pushed upward from the reservoir bottom, entering at the matrix bottom, passing through the matrix, and exiting at the top of a rotameter, from where it pours back into the reservoir. The CT had been tested previously for adherent cells. The present study was a pioneer trial to test this bioreactor for suspension cells. The polymer matrix had been treated to favor cell adhesion of suspension cells despite the natural tendency of these cells to not anchor on support.

Apart from the bioreactors, the applied perfusion process and media/additives for all the runs were comparable. For a description see Refs [4] and [5].

13.3
Results and Discussion

13.3.1
Perfusion Using ATF or TFF in Wave-Induced Bioreactor

13.3.1.1 Cell Growth

A preliminary study to acquire information about the physical environment of the W-ATF, like the impact of the agitation and the working volume on the foam formation, was performed. This study gave us critical information about the optimal working volume, 4 l, and which agitation parameters were allowed without occurrence of air bubbles in the tube connecting the wave-induced bioreactor to the ATF. Air bubbles in this tube would jeopardize the ATF function and provoke cell death.

Several perfusion runs using the W-ATF and W-TFF systems with CHO#1 cells were then performed in cultures stabilized at 20 to 30×10^6 cells ml^{-1} by daily cell bleeding, maintaining the cells constantly in growing stage. An example of this is given in Figure 13.2 at days 7 to 20 of a W-TFF run. The purpose of this part of the study was to acquire a good knowledge of these systems and understand the impact of several factors: the perfusion rate, the rates of glucose and glutamine feeding and the associated cell metabolism, the medium, and the agitation. We opted for a cell-specific perfusion rate (CSPR) [9], that is, the perfusion rate was linearly correlated to the cell density. A CSPR value of ≈0.05 nl cell^{-1} day^{-1} selected in a previous study [10] was confirmed in our present experimental conditions and was then applied for all the W-ATF and W-TFF runs even at very high cell density. As a matter of fact, since the selected CSPR provided a cell environment satisfying the needs of nutrient and by-product

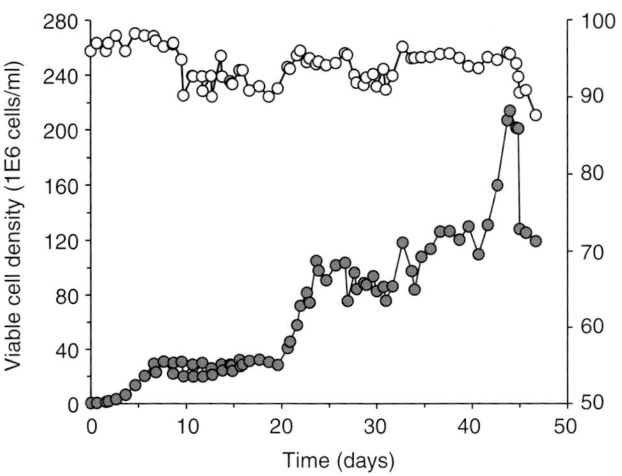

Figure 13.2 Perfusion run using wave-induced bioreactor connected to a TFF cell separation device: cell density (plain symbol) and viability (open symbol).

removal at moderate cell density, the same CSPR could then been applied for very high cell densities ensuring the same satisfying environment.

Thanks to the knowledge gathered at 20 to 30×10^6 cells ml^{-1}, the cell density could then be increased to 10^8 cells ml^{-1} in the W-TFF and even beyond as shown in Figure 13.2. The cells grew exponentially from 20 to 100×10^6 cells ml^{-1} by interrupting the cell bleeds and increasing the perfusion rate. Then, between day 24 and day 41, a healthy growing culture was maintained at $1–1.3 \times 10^8$ cells ml^{-1} by cell bleeds, demonstrating a consistent process. Finally, the cell density was increased again and reached a maximum of 2.14×10^8 cells ml^{-1} on day 44 followed by the interruption of the cell growth. The partial pressure of CO_2 then reached 31 kPa (or 232 mm Hg), a value known to hinder the cell growth [11]. Furthermore, the pressure in the recirculation loop of the TFF system reached 1 bar, a pressure actually too high for plastic disposable equipment. The cell broth viscosity provoked this high pressure at the inlet of the hollow fiber filter. It was also noticed that the aeration became limiting at this stage.

We observed a comparable pattern of exponential cell growth using the W-ATF (see Figure 13.3). In this run, the cells were growing exponentially while the perfusion rate was increased accordingly. At day 10, the cell density reached 1.32×10^8 cells ml^{-1}, but unfortunately the alternate flow of the ATF was interrupted due to the high viscosity of the cell suspension. The culture was reinitiated and the perfusion process was resumed at day 20. An exponential growth similar to the first one took place again up to a cell density of 1.23×10^8 cells ml^{-1} at day 28, interrupted again by failing ATF alternated flow due to the high viscosity. This confirmed the first observed maximal cell density. Notice that a normal ATF function could be restarted after bleeding the cells down to 10^8 cells ml^{-1} and the culture could be resumed at this density the following two days.

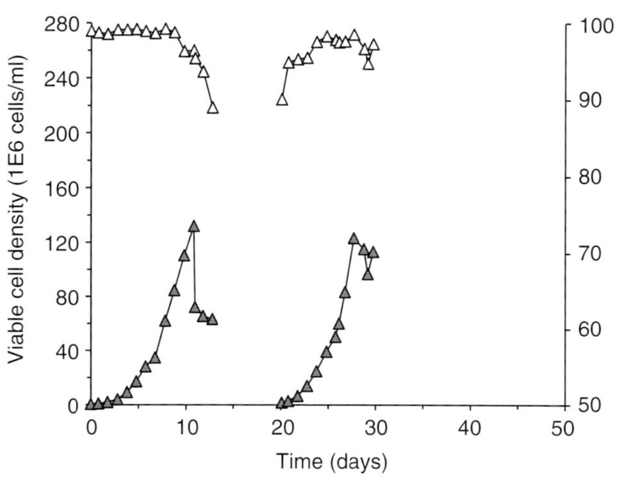

Figure 13.3 Perfusion run using wave-induced bioreactor connected to an ATF cell separation device: cell density (plain symbol) and viability (open symbol).

During both runs, high cell viability was maintained, higher than 90% and most often higher than 95%, probably thanks to the fact that the cells were constantly growing.

We were the first group to report a cell density of 2×10^8 cells ml^{-1} in a wave-induced bioreactor, to report data of consistent cell densities maintained at 0.9–1.3×10^8 cells ml^{-1} during 18 days, and to disclose an ATF process where the CHO cell density became larger than 10^8 cells ml^{-1}, in [4,5]. Before our study, other groups had reported high cell density studies at lower cell densities and never maintained during long periods, for example, 10^8 HEK293 cells ml^{-1} using an internal hollow fiber module [12]; 50×10^6 CHO cells ml^{-1} using hollow fiber cell separation [13]; 1.5×10^8 Per C6 cells ml^{-1} in a wave-induced bioreactor with an internal perfusion membrane unfortunately experiencing membrane blockage after 8 days of cultivation [14]; and using the same system 1.04×10^8 *Drosophila* Schneider 2 cells ml^{-1} maintained during 6 days [15].

13.3.1.2 **IgG Production**

The total antibody production obtained during a run is given by the accumulated sum of the daily productions. During a culture maintained at a stable cell density, the cell bleeds are usually discarded and consequently the product in these bleeds is lost. It is of course possible to harvest and further process this material. However, this requires supplementary equipment to eliminate the cells from the supernatant. Hence, it is usually not performed since it adds to the complexity of the system. The accumulated antibody productions obtained in the harvest, in the cell bleeds, and totally produced by the cells during the W-TFF run are given in Figure 13.4. At higher cell density, that is, $\geq 10^8$ cells ml^{-1}

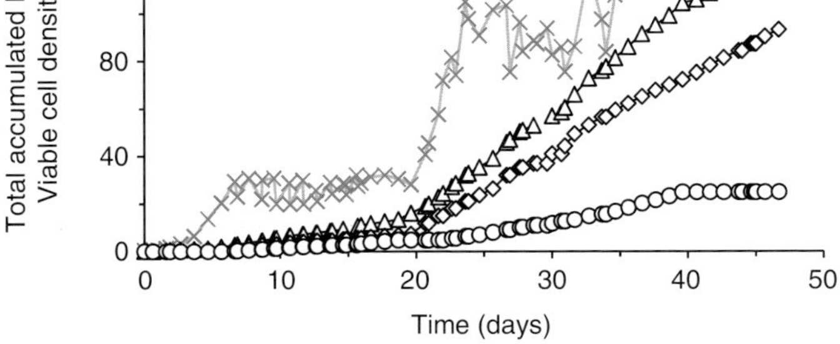

Figure 13.4 Total accumulated antibody production in the harvest (diamond), lost in the cell bleed (circle), and totally produced by the cells (triangle), and viable cell density (x) using wave-induced bioreactor connected to a TFF cell separation device.

after day 21, the accumulated IgG production was increasing at a much faster rate than at 20–30 × 10^6 cells ml^{-1} density. The W-TFF was performed as a demonstration exercise and was not representative of a real run for production. It was however interesting to observe that 93 g IgG had been harvested after 47 days in a working volume of 4 l. Notice that the actual amount of IgG totally produced by the cells was 125 g. The difference between this cellular production and the harvest was due to the loss in the cell bleeds and the residual material in the bioreactor at the run completion. In this setup, based on our cell density and production data, we calculated that a run of 17 days with a cell density stabilized at 10^8 cells ml^{-1} after an exponential growth would produce 34 g and continue to produce 22 g $week^{-1}$. This illustrates the potential of using high cell density. The cell line used here had a moderate cell-specific productivity of ≈9 pg $cell^{-1}$ day^{-1}, resulting in a production of ≈0.5 g l^{-1} IgG in a standard fed-batch process of 17 days [5]. Despite this low specific productivity, a large amount of IgG was produced in a small bioreactor of 4 l working volume.

Unfortunately, the IgG concentration in the bioreactor was larger than the one in the harvest line, indicating that the IgG molecules were partially retained by the hollow fiber filter. We observed that the IgG retention was systematically higher in the W-TFF compared to the W-ATF. This affected the harvest yield; since the IgG present in the cell bleeds was systematically discarded, the IgG loss in the bleeds was more severe using the W-TFF than the W-ATF. A direct comparison of the IgG production harvested during a W-ATF and a W-TFF run is shown in Figure 13.5, where the total accumulated antibody productions from two runs performed with a cell density maintained at ≈25 × 10^6 cells ml^{-1} for 17

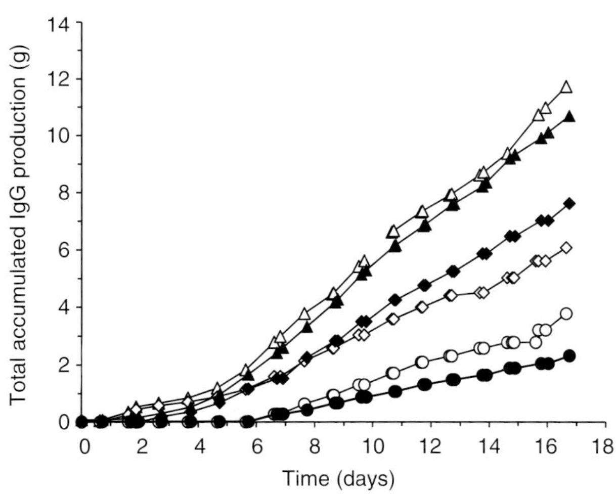

Figure 13.5 Total accumulated antibody production in the harvest (diamond), lost in the cell bleed (circle), and totally produced by the cells (triangle), using wave-induced bioreactor connected to a TFF (plain symbols) or to an ATF (open symbols) under 17 days at a cell density maintained ≈25 × 10^6 cells ml^{-1} by cell bleeds.

days are shown. The cells produced the same total IgG amount, 12 g, in both systems, but the IgG lost in the bleeds was higher in the W-TFF compared to the W-ATF and, consequently, the harvested antibody production was higher using the W-ATF in comparison to the W-TFF. The retention of the product of interest by the filter is a well-known drawback of membrane-based cell separation devices. It affects not only the yield as described here, but also increases the residence time of the protein inside the bioreactor. Most antibodies will probably not be affected, but this can become an issue for labile glycoproteins [16]. It has been reported [17] that (partial or total) spin-filter fouling is due to cell debris and nucleic acid. Unfortunately, in filter-based separation devices these clogging particles accumulate during the culture since they are not eliminated except in the cell bleeds, which is insufficient.

13.3.2 Perfusion Using CellTank

13.3.2.1 Cell Growth

Two runs were performed with the CHO#2 cell line, one aiming at reaching a cell density as high as possible and the other one to study the cell growth arrest at high cell density.

In the first run, after two weeks of troubleshooting and adjustments (this was the first trial with this equipment), the system became satisfying and an exponential cell growth took place. The cell density reached a maximum of 2×10^8 cells ml^{-1} at day 25 (see Figure 13.6). In the second run, the cell growth was exponential from day 1. The temperature was lowered to 32 °C when the cell

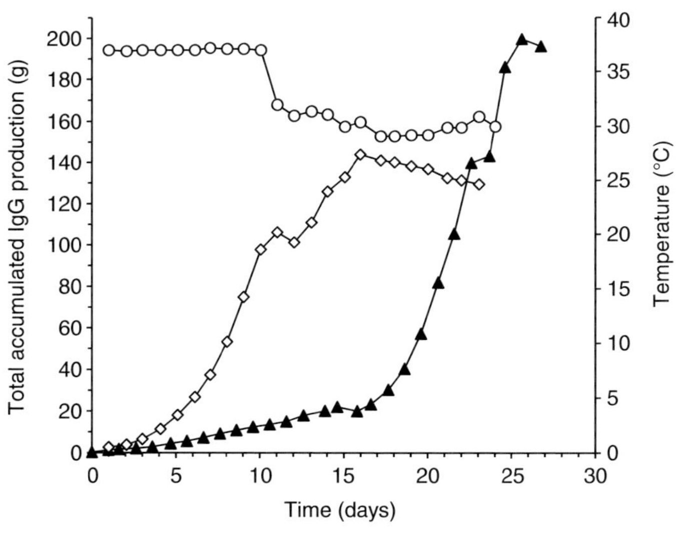

Figure 13.6 Perfusion runs using a CellTank: cell density in first run (triangle), cell density in second run (diamond), temperature in second run (circle).

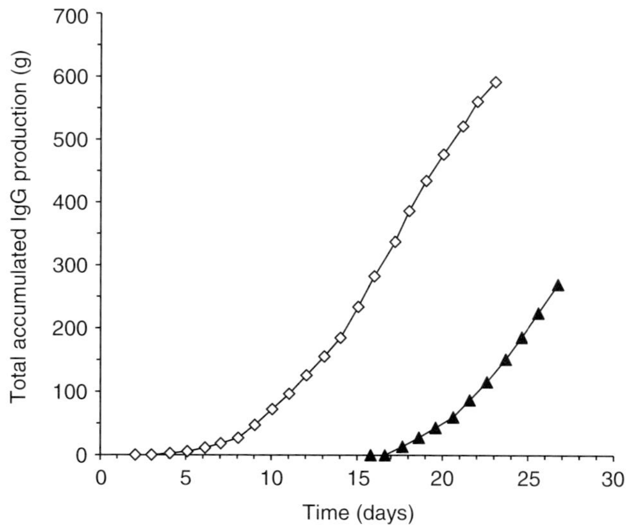

Figure 13.7 Total accumulated antibody production in the harvest in first run (triangle) and in second run (diamond) in perfusion runs using a CellTank.

density reached 10^8 cells ml^{-1} at day 10. This notably decreased the cell growth, but not completely. Further temperature reductions were then performed on day 11, to 31 °C, and on day 14, to 30 °C. At day 16, the temperature was even decreased to 29 °C resulting in total growth arrest. The temperature reduction resulted in a viable cell density around 1.3×10^8 cells ml^{-1} maintained for 14 days, from day 10 to day 24.

13.3.2.2 IgG Production

The accumulated antibody productions for both runs are given in Figure 13.7. These productions increased smoothly with time to 0.59 g at the end of the second run, that is, day 23, and to 0.27 g in the first run, accumulated between days 17 and 27. The cell-specific productivity of the CHO#2 cell line was unfortunately very low; on average 1.5 pg cell^{-1} day^{-1} in a batch shake flask. In the perfusion runs, the average cell-specific productivity was comparable; 1.7 pg cell^{-1} day^{-1}. It increased to 2.5 pg cell^{-1} day^{-1} when the temperature was decreased under 37 °C due to response to hypothermia. Despite the small working volume of 150 ml and the low cell-specific productivity, 0.27 g and 0.59 IgG were harvested using the CT.

13.3.3 Very High Cell Density

As described earlier, reaching high and very high cell densities provoked several unexpected scenarios, which led us to study factors that have no impact on the processes at usually encountered cell densities, that is, lower than 50×10^6 cells ml^{-1}.

At these cell densities, the cell suspension has rheological properties close to the ones of the medium without cells. As mentioned earlier, at high cell density the cell broth became more viscous. It is interesting to understand how dense the cells are in the medium at a microscopic level. The theoretical distances between the cells or intercellular distances (d_i) can be calculated for perfectly uncompressible spherical cells [4]. Several intercellular distances are represented in Figure 13.8a for different cell diameters. In the W-ATF and W-TFF cultures, the diameter of the CHO cells was ≈17 μm. As can be observed in Figure 13.8, at

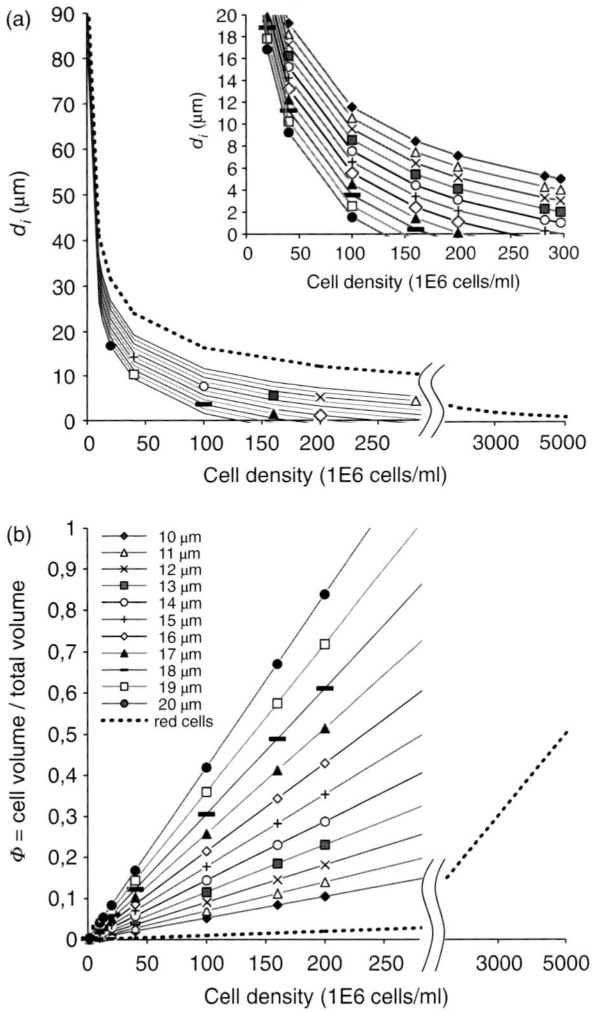

Figure 13.8 (a) Theoretical intercellular distances, d_i, in cell suspension for different cell diameters with zoom of x-axis in upper right corner (legend according to Figure 13.8b); (b) calculated fraction of the volume occupied by the cells for different cell diameters.

2×10^8 cells ml^{-1}, d_i was $\approx 0\,\mu m$; in other words the cells were theoretically against each other and against the filter wall as well. In these conditions, the fluid properties were drastically changed. It is interesting to put these numbers in relation to blood, a well-known physiological system of circulating cells. It is known that cells occupy $\approx 50\%$ of the blood volume and have a volume ≈ 100 fl (i.e., $100 \times$ 1E-15 l) – notice that the volume of a spherical CHO cell of 17 μm diameter is 2570 fl. In blood, the density of red cells is $\approx 5000 \times 10^6$ cells ml^{-1} (in human male). We calculated the intercellular distance between the red cells by approximating their shape by incompressible cylinders of the same size as red cells (7 μm diameter and 2 μm height). At 5000×10^6 cells ml^{-1} density, d_i was calculated to be 1.1 μm. This gave us an indication that in a well-known system of circulating cells, such as the blood, the cells are very dense. Consequently one can extrapolate that comparable d_i should be well tolerated by CHO cells, which are robust cancer cells. As a mater of fact in the W-TFF, W-ATF, and CT cultures, the cells were growing (unless when cell arrest was provoked) and had a very high viability. An important aspect in this parallel with blood is the size of the cell; the smaller the cell size, the larger the cell density for a given d_i with a power 3 relationship. Figure 13.8a exemplifies as well a drawback of the cell density as measurement unit while the cell biovolume could probably be a better unit.

Figure 13.8b shows the theoretical fraction of the volume occupied by the cells. One can see that CHO cells at densities $1.5–2 \times 10^8$ cells ml^{-1} occupied 40 to 50% of the cell broth. This is a number similar to the fraction occupied by the red cells in the blood, reinforcing the argument that these cell densities have been invented by nature well before man put cells in a bioreactor.

When 2.14×10^8 cells ml^{-1} was reached in the W-TFF, the pressure at the inlet of the HF, P_1, was about 1 bar. This very high pressure was too high for disposable equipment, so this cannot be recommended for normal operation. However, interestingly, it was indicative of a potential limitation of the settings. An analysis of P_1 as a function of the cell density revealed a quadratic correlation as shown in Figure 13.9.

Relative viscosities of different cell suspensions have been reported in the literature (rat aortic muscle CRL-1444 cells, [18] yeast, [19,20] plant cells [21], oil [22]). Their pattern as a function of the cell density is always similar to the one shown in Figure 13.9 and corresponds to the theoretical model of spherical particles in a liquid [23]. This model gave an excellent fit to our experimental data. The model is

$$\eta_{rel} = (1 + 2.5\varphi + 10.05\varphi^2)\eta_m/\eta_L \qquad (13.1)$$

where η_m is viscosity of the mixture of liquid and spheres, η_L is viscosity of the pure liquid, η_{rel} is relative viscosity, and φ is volume fraction of spheres or solid in the mixture = sphere volume * cell density.

An excellent fit of P_1 with the cell density and with the relative viscosity was observed as shown in Figure 13.9. The model of the relative viscosity was also confirmed by measuring the relative viscosity of exponentially growing cells in a shake flask concentrated at several densities. One can see that the quadratic

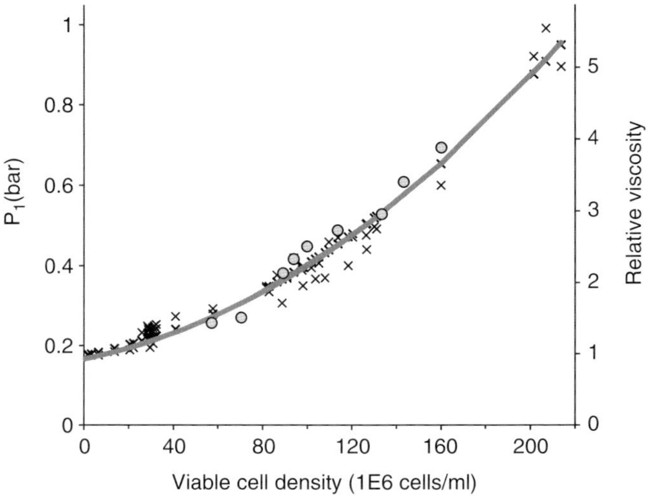

Figure 13.9 Correlation between the inlet pressure (x), P_1, and the viable cell density measured during the W-TFF run; correlation of P_1 and the viable cell density with the relative viscosity of the cell broth calculated by Equation 13.1 model (continuous line) showing an excellent fitting of this model; experimental data of relative viscosity of cells cultured in a shake flask and concentrated at different densities by centrifugation (circle).

increase of the viscosity as a function of the cell density began to be predominant above 80 or 10^8 cells ml^{-1}, while below this density the viscosity was still quite close to the medium viscosity. At this cell density and above, the equipment selection, like for instance the filter design, should take into account the cell broth viscosity, the intercellular distance, and include an understanding of the filtration process at a microscopic level.

13.3.4 Cryopreservation from Very High Cell Density Perfusion

An application of high cell density culture in a bioreactor is cell banking manufacturing. We performed trials of cell cryopreservation in 1 ml vials with cells taken at day 30 from the W-ATF at 10^8 cells ml^{-1} (case-1) and taken at day 44 from the W-TFF at 2.07×10^8 cells ml^{-1} (case-2). Two conditions were tested: cryopreservation using the cell broth after addition of 10% dimethylsulfoxide (DMSO) or after dilution with fresh medium 50/50 before adding 10% DMSO as described in Ref. [5], hence 1 ml vials of 0.5×10^8 or 10^8 cells in case-1 and of 10^8 or 2×10^8 cells in case-2 were manufactured. All the media were free of serum.

The results of cell growth after cell thaw are shown in Figure 13.10 as well as the data of IgG production tests. In case-1, the cells had a satisfying growth and a high viability, ≥90%, after the cell thaw for both 0.5 and 1×10^8 cells ml^{-1} vials, see Figure 13.10a. In case-2, the viability was low at thaw day, 80%, and decreased significantly the day after to values between 46 and 69% (see Figure 13.10b). The

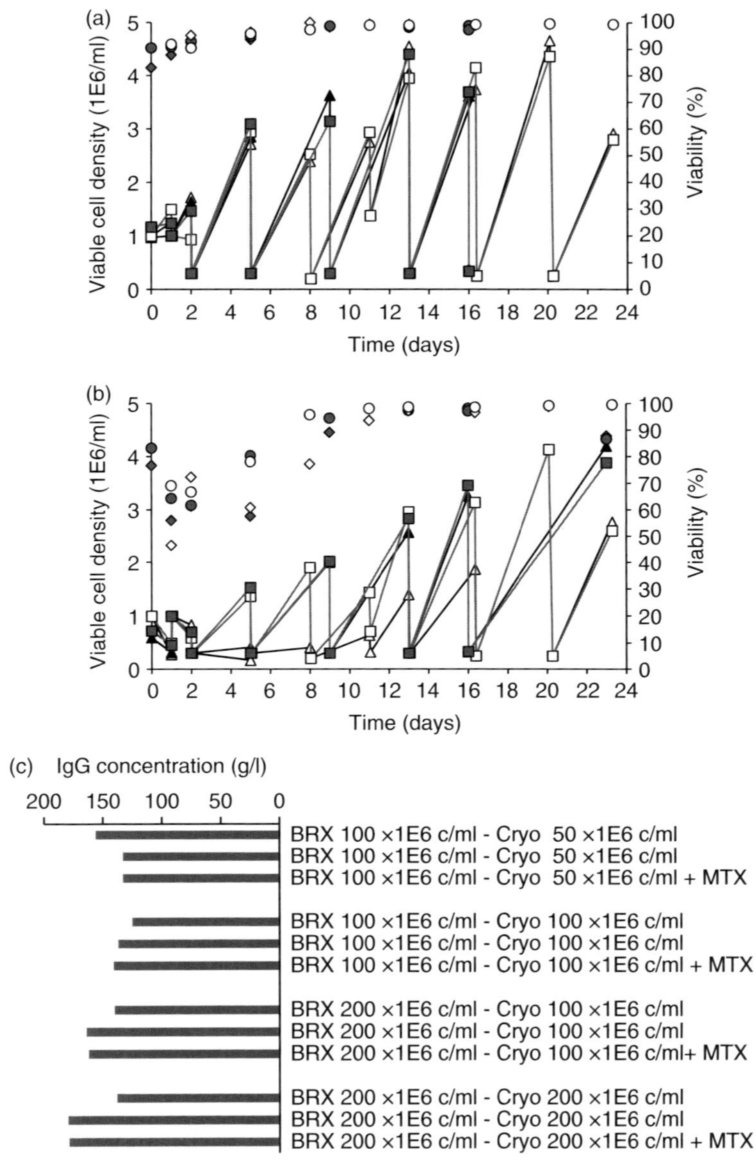

Figure 13.10 Cryopreservation study. (a) Revival after cell thaw of cells cultured at 10^8 cells ml^{-1} in W-ATF (duplicates represented by plain and open symbols): 1 ml cryovials containing 0.5×10^8 cells ml^{-1}: cell density (square), viability (circle), and 1 ml cryovials containing 10^8 cells ml^{-1}: cell density (triangle) and viability (diamond). (b) Revival after cell thaw of cells cultured at 2×10^8 cells ml^{-1} in W-TFF (duplicates represented by plain and open symbols): 1 ml cryovials containing 1×10^8 cells ml^{-1}: cell density (square), viability (circle), and 1 ml cryovials containing 2×10^8 cells ml^{-1}: cell density (triangle) and viability (diamond). (c) IgG production tests from cell thaw experiments shown in Figure 13.10a and b: IgG concentrations after seven days culture in batch shake flasks inoculated at 0.3×10^6 cells ml^{-1} where "BRX" indicates the cell concentration in the bioreactor at cell freezing, "Bank" indicates the cell concentration in the 1 ml vials, and "MTX" indicates supplementation of 200 nM MTX.

data gave no indication that the cells frozen at 10^8 or 2×10^8 cells had a different pattern in their resuscitation. After one week all the cells recovered to satisfying profiles of growth and viability. As described earlier, when the culture reached 2×10^8 cells ml^{-1} the cell growth stopped, coinciding with a pCO_2 of 31 kPa (or 232 mm Hg), a level known to inhibit cell growth. It is likely that this pCO_2 level was detrimental to the cell cryopreservation so at this stage we cannot conclude if cryopreservation from a 2×10^8 cells ml^{-1} culture is recommendable, but nevertheless the cells could recover within one week. Furthermore, similar to case-1, this experiment confirmed that no difference could be discerned between the cells cryopreserved as such with the addition of DMSO or after dilution to half their concentration.

Seven-day production tests were performed seven to nine passages after the cell thaws from case-1 and case-2 cells as described in Ref. [5]. Several of the duplicates were performed with supplementary addition of 200 nM methotrexate (MTX). As can be seen from Figure 13.10c, the IgG concentrations measured in the production tests were comparable; they were also comparable to the standard performance of this cell line (data not shown). During the production tests the cell growth was comparable in all the conditions (data not shown). This indicated that from the point of view of the IgG production, bioreactor cultivation at 1 or 2×10^8 cells ml^{-1} and cryopreservation from 0.5 to 2×10^8 cells ml^{-1} had no detrimental effect. The MTX addition did not have any effect on the IgG production or the cell growth. This showed that the cells were stable and that no subpopulation insensitive to MTX had emerged during the culture up to 2×10^8 cells ml^{-1} density.

We clearly demonstrated here that CHO cell cryopreservation from a 10^8 cells ml^{-1} perfusion culture is feasible and that 1 ml vials could contain up to 10^8 cells ml^{-1}. For the cryopreservation, we applied a simple operation on the cell broth directly taken from the bioreactor. Using the cell broth as such, or after dilution with fresh medium, had not impact on our conclusions. We observed highly satisfying cell growth and viability pattern after thaw, followed by a normal IgG production. We demonstrated as well that no subpopulation insensitive to MTX had emerged up to 2×10^8 cells ml^{-1}. Previous studies reported high cell number cryopreservation, 1.5×10^8 cells^{-1}ml^{-1}, however, in the presence of 20% serum [24]. Bioreactor operation for CHO cell bank manufacturing process has been reported previously [25]. However, in this study the cell density reached only 27×10^6 cells ml^{-1} and the cells were concentrated to 0.9–1×10^8 cells ml^{-1} by centrifugation. Cell banking manufacturing is traditionally carried out by expanding the cells in shake flasks in batch mode and centrifuging them before conditioning them in freezing medium. Contrary to shake flask cultivation, using a bioreactor offers the advantage of a controlled environment and omission of the centrifugation step. Furthermore, the perfusion mode ensures that the nutrients are not depleted and that the accumulation of toxic by-products is limited. In Ref. [25] as well as here, it is likely that replacing the batch shake flask culture by an expansion in the bioreactor operated in perfusion was highly favorable for the cryopreservation process not only ensuring the cell health but importantly increasing the reproducibility and reliability of the process.

13.4 Conclusions

We successfully developed perfusion processes of W-ATF and W-TFF. The systems were compared using identical filter cartridges and identical processes apart for the cell separation device. After consistency had been demonstrated in several runs at 20 and 30×10^6 cells ml^{-1} density, higher cell densities were studied. During 18 days, a very high cell density of 0.9 to 1.3×10^8 cells ml^{-1} was consistently maintained in growing phase at high viability by cell bleeds in the W-TFF. The cell density could then be further increased to a limit of 2.14×10^8 cells ml^{-1} with the present settings. Using TFF, the cell density was limited by the membrane capacity for the encountered high viscosity and the pCO_2 level. In order to achieve a higher cell density a larger total lumen section area of the HF and an increased CO_2 removal would have been necessary. This is however hypothetical since we calculated that at 2×10^8 cells ml^{-1}, the cell broth would be theoretically so dense that the cells would be against each other, that is, the theoretical distance between the cells became zero for this cell line, which would lead to critical modification of the fluid rheology.

The cell density reached a maximal value of 1.3×10^8 cells ml^{-1} in the W-ATF. It was observed that a limitation came from the vacuum capacity failing to pull the highly viscous fluid for the present settings. Pulling liquid by vacuum is not an operation as efficient as pressing the liquid, which is why the TFF could provide the necessary effect where the ATF failed. Hence, this failure was inherent to the used setup in combination with the ATF and not to the use of ATF technology as such. We have recently achieved a cell density of 2×10^8 cells ml^{-1} using the ATF as cell separation device [26].

Using the present settings a higher cell density was obtained with the W-TFF in comparison with the W-ATF; however, the product yield in the harvest was lower. The cells produced comparable amounts of IgG in the W-ATF and W-TFF. Unfortunately, the IgG molecules were partially retained by the HF and more heavily in the W-TFF. To maintain the cells at a stable cell density cell bleeds were daily performed, discarding the IgG present in the bleeds. A consequence of this partial retention was a higher residual IgG concentration in the bioreactor and consequently a higher loss of IgG in the bleeds.

A very high cell density of 2×10^8 cells ml^{-1} was again obtained using a second antibody producing CHO cell line in another perfusion system based on a different principle, the CellTank. In this new system, the cells were entrapped in a non-woven fiber matrix. Using the CellTank, a cell density stabilization was obtained by reducing the temperature causing cell growth arrest. The cell density was maintained around 1.3×10^8 cells ml^{-1} during 14 days with a temperature of $\leq 32\,°C$.

A direct cryopreservation of the cells from the 10^8 cells ml^{-1} W-ATF culture in vials up to 10^8 cells ml^{-1} was very successful. This system, benefitting from the controlled and stable environment of the perfused bioreactor had the advantage of being more reliable and robust for cell bank manufacturing than the established shake flask-based expansion. This application not only showed an elegant application of high cell density culture but it confirmed also that the cells were very healthy at this density.

The cell broth viscosity increased with the cell density and affected the filter operation. A model of the relative viscosity as a function of the cell density was established, from which it could be concluded that in cell broth at cell densities higher than 0.8 to 1×10^8 cells ml^{-1} the viscosity became significantly different from the medium viscosity. Hence, the viscosity became then an important parameter for the process design, in particular for the filtration. It was also showed that the cell diameter had a major impact on the cell density limit.

We reviewed here three different systems successfully operated at very high cell densities up to at least 2×10^8 cells ml^{-1} for two of them. This cell density seemed to be close to the limit for CHO cell cultures from our observations. At this density, the cells occupied $\approx$50% of the liquid, a fraction similar to the red cells in the blood, which could probably be viewed as a maximized suspension cell system. We do not think that such a high cell density should be the target for tomorrow's processes but it gives the reinsuring knowledge that operating at cell densities such as 1 to 1.5×10^8 cells ml^{-1}, lower than 2×10^8 cells ml^{-1} by a comfortable margin, should not be an issue for the cells. We presented also in Refs [4,5] that up to 1.5×10^8 cells ml^{-1}, the cell metabolism and IgG productivity were unchanged.

Acknowledgments

GE Healthcare (Sweden) partially financed this work. The Swedish Governmental Agency for Innovation Systems (VINNOVA) partially financed this work and supported the lab activities.

References

1 Singh, V. (1999) Disposable bioreactor for cell culture using wave-induced agitation. *Cytotechnology*, **30**, 149–158.
2 de la Broise, D., Noiseux, M., Lemieux, R., and Massie, B. (1991) Long-term perfusion culture of hybridoma: a "grow or die" cell cycle system. *Biotechnol. Bioeng.*, **38**, 781–787.
3 Velez, D., Miller, L., and Macmillan, J.D. (1989) Use of tangential flow filtration in perfusion propagation of hybridoma cells for production of monoclonal antibodies. *Biotechnol. Bioeng.*, **33**, 938–940.
4 Clincke, M.F., Molleryd, C., Zhang, Y., Lindskog, E., Walsh, K., and Chotteau, V. (2013) Very high density of CHO cells in perfusion by ATF or TFF in WAVE bioreactor. Part I. Effect of the cell density on the process. *Biotechnol. Prog.*, **29**, 754–767.

5 Clincke, M.F., Molleryd, C., Samani, P.K., Lindskog, E., Faldt, E., Walsh, K., and Chotteau, V. (2013) Very high density of Chinese hamster ovary cells in perfusion by alternating tangential flow or tangential flow filtration in WAVE Bioreactor. Part II. Applications for antibody production and cryopreservation. *Biotechnol. Prog.*, **29**, 768–777.

6 Meuwly, F., Ruffieux, P.A., Kadouri, A., and von Stockar, U. (2007) Packed-bed bioreactors for mammalian cell culture: bioprocess and biomedical applications. *Biotechnol. Adv.*, **25**, 45–56.

7 Lee, J.C., Chang, H.N., and Oh, D.J. (2005) Recombinant antibody production by perfusion cultures of rCHO cells in a depth filter perfusion system. *Biotechnol. Prog.*, **21**, 134–139.

8 Chen, C., Huang, Y.L., and Yang, S.T. (2002) A fibrous-bed bioreactor for continuous production of developmental endothelial locus-1 by osteosarcoma cells. *J. Biotechnol.*, **97**, 23–39.

9 Ozturk, S.S. (1996) Engineering challenges in high density cell culture systems. *Cytotechnology*, **22**, 3–16.

10 Chotteau, V., Tördal, K., and Perroud, P. (2009) Study of a perfusion process of Chinese hamster ovary cells by ATF filtration in bioreactor. Paper presented at the 21th ESACT Meeting, Dublin, Ireland.

11 Kimura, R. and Miller, W. (1996) Effects of elevated pCO_2 and/or osmolality on the growth and recombinant tPA production of CHO cells. *Biotechnol. Bioeng.*, **52**, 152–160.

12 Kyung, Y.S., Peshwa, M.V., Gryte, D.M., and Hu, W.S. (1994) High density culture of mammalian cells with dynamic perfusion based on on-line oxygen uptake rate measurements. *Cytotechnology*, **14**, 183–190.

13 Voisard, D., Meuwly, F., Ruffieux, P.A., Baer, G., and Kadouri, A. (2003) Potential of cell retention techniques for large-scale high-density perfusion culture of suspended mammalian cells. *Biotechnol. Bioeng.*, **82**, 751–765.

14 Adams, T., Noack, U., Frick, T., Greller, G., and Fenge, C. (2011) Increasing efficiency in protein and cell production by combining single-use bioreactor technology and perfusion. *BioPharm. Int. Suppl.*, **24**, 4–11.

15 Wang, L., Hu, H., Yang, J., Wang, F., Kaisermayer, C., and Zhou, P. (2012) High yield of human monoclonal antibody produced by stably transfected *Drosophila* Schneider 2 cells in perfusion culture using Wave bioreactor. *Mol. Biotechnol.*, **52**, 170–179.

16 Konstantinov, K., Goudar, C., Ng, M., Meneses, R., Thrift, J., Chuppa, S., Matanguihan, C., Michaels, J., and Naveh, D. (2006) The "push-to-low" approach for optimization of high-density perfusion cultures of animal cells. *Adv. Biochem. Eng. Biotechnol.*, **101**, 75–98.

17 Esclade, L.R.J., Carrel, S., and Peringer, P. (1991) Influence of the screen material on the fouling of spin filters. *Biotechnol. Bioeng.*, **38**, 159–168.

18 Zoro, B.J., Owen, S., Drake, R.A., Mason, C., and Hoare, M. (2009) Regenerative medicine bioprocessing: concentration and behavior of adherent cell suspensions and pastes. *Biotechnol. Bioeng.*, **103**, 1236–1247.

19 Malinowski, J.J., Lafforgue, C., and Goma, G. (1987) Rheological behavior of high-density continuous cultures of *Saccharomyces cerevisiae*. *J. Ferment. Technol.*, **65**, 319–323.

20 Reuss, M., Josic, D., Popovic, M., and Bronn, W.K. (1979) Viscosity of yeast suspensions. *Eur. J. Appl. Microbiol.*, **8**, 167–175.

21 Curtis, W.R. and Emery, A.H. (1993) Plant cell suspension culture rheology. *Biotechnol. Bioeng.*, **42**, 520–526.

22 Wu, L., Ek, M., Song, M., and Sichen, D. (2011) The effect of solid particles on liquid viscosity. *Steel Res. Int.*, **82**, 388–397.

23 Yuk, I.H., Olsen, M.M., Geyer, S., and Forestell, S.P. (2004) Perfusion cultures of human tumor cells: a scalable production platform for oncolytic adenoviral vectors. *Biotechnol. Bioeng.*, **86**, 637–642.

24 Ninomiya, N., Shirahata, S., Murakami, H., and Sugahara, T. (1991) Large-scale, high-density freezing of hybridomas and

its application to high-density culture. *Biotechnol. Bioeng.*, **38**, 1110–1113.

25 Tao, Y., Shih, J., Sinacore, M., Ryll, T., and Yusuf-Makagiansar, H. (2011) Development and implementation of a perfusion-based high cell density cell banking process. *Biotechnol. Prog.*, **27**, 824–829.

26 Chotteau, V., Clincke, M.F., Zhang, Y., and Thoring, L. (2013) Achievement of extreme cell densities in different perfusion systems and impact of the cell density. Integrated Continuous Biomanufacturing, ECI Conference, October 20–24, Castelldefels, Spain.

14
Implementation of CQA (Critical Quality Attribute) Based Approach for Development of Biosimilars

Sanjeev K. Gupta

14.1
Background

With the evolution of various mammalian-based novel expression platform technologies, achieving the desired productivity has become more feasible. However, for biosimilar development, establishing a proper product quality as well as expression yields of the final clone is critical. The right approach for selecting stable and high-producing clone and developing processes producing the desired product quality is a key factor for a successful biosimilar development program.

Critical quality attributes (CQAs) of the product is one of the major factors that needs to be considered while developing and selecting the potential biosimilar candidates (clones/cell lines). The CQA-based approach enables selecting the best of the better clones and optimizing clones and upstream and downstream processes for developing a commercially viable biosimilar product. The CQA-based approach is implemented for selection of the clones and processes by incorporating high-end analytical testing of the expressed recombinant products from clone development to commercialization as well as post-commercialization. The advanced analytical tools allow determining primary, secondary, and tertiary structures and associated CQAs of the recombinant products.

In order to develop potential biosimilar molecules, we should implement CQA approach from transfection to final clone selection, process optimization to formulation development, and commercialization.

The CQA-based product development approach allows the biopharmaceutical industries to develop the recombinant biosimilars with the highest quality and efficacy standards and a cost advantage that can be transferred back to the large population. This chapter does not attempt to provide information on analytical tools and techniques; it does, however, attempt to provide a brief overview on a CQA-based approach for a successful recombinant biosimilar development [1,2].

In this chapter, we summarize the critical quality attributes of the recombinant products at each stage of the product development cycle and the advantages of identification and implementation of the CQA approach from clone to clinic in developing a high-quality and efficacious biosimilar product.

Continuous Processing in Pharmaceutical Manufacturing, First Edition. Edited by Ganapathy Subramanian.

14.2 Biosimilar Product Development

Biopharmaceuticals are produced in living cells by recombinant technology. They consist of human proteins, such as monoclonal antibodies (mAbs), hormones, cytokines, and other therapeutic products. The huge majority of the biologicals are produced in genetically modified and well-characterized specific host cells [2].

"Biologics" represent one of the fastest growing segments of the pharmaceutical industry. Biologics are the substances produced by living cells using biotechnology (i.e., recombinant DNA technology, controlled gene expression, or antibody technologies), which have introduced many new treatments to life-threatening and rare illnesses such as cancer, diabetes, anemia, rheumatoid arthritis, and multiple sclerosis. They involve a wide range of substances, including recombinant hormones, growth factors, blood products, monoclonal antibody-based products, recombinant vaccines, and advanced technology products (gene and cell therapy biological products). The global biologic industry has come a long way since its first drug Humulin earned US Food and Drug Administration (FDA) approval in 1982. The ever-increasing pressure on healthcare budgets globally requires cost savings analogous to those arising from the generic versions of the original innovator product [3]. The pharma market is now open for generic versions of biologics, referred to as "biosimilars" in Europe, "follow-on pharmaceuticals" in the US and Japan, "subsequent entry biologics" in Canada, "biocomparables" in Mexico and, in this manuscript, "biosimilars." These terms arise from the loss of patent protection by many first-generation innovator products in the last few years, and the expectation that a few more will suffer the same fate in the next few years. However, unlike the relatively uncomplicated process of introducing a generic equivalent of an original chemical-based drug, the process of introducing a biosimilar to an innovator product is far more complex. This is apparent as (i) biologics generally exhibit high molecular complexity, (ii) biologics are produced by cells in culture or whole organisms, and (iii) major changes in the product can occur due to very minor changes in the process. Various complexities associated with approval of a biosimilar include: (i) evidence of integrity and consistency of the manufacturing process; (ii) conformance of manufacturing standards to applicable regulations; (iii) demonstration of product consistency with appropriate innovator product or comparators using assays that should be relevant and most of all standardized, so that several biosimilars of the same biologic can be comparable, including comparative pharmacokinetic and pharmacodynamic data and the extent of clinical data; and (iv) experience with the approved product. Furthermore, issues like post-translation modification and immunogenicity are the key concern related to approval of biosimilar products. The use of biosimilars is an opportunity for biopharma industries to use cutting-edge technology to solve health problems and guide clinical processes [4].

14.3
Attributes/Parameters in Biopharmaceuticals

- *Critical Quality Attribute (CQA)*: "A physical, chemical, biological, or microbiological property or characteristic that should be within an appropriate limit, range, or distribution to ensure the desired product quality." [5–7]
- *Critical Process Parameter (CPP)*: "A process parameter whose variability has an impact on a critical quality attribute and therefore should be monitored or controlled to ensure the process produces the desired quality." [5–7]
- *Material Attributes*: Raw material or component factors that impact CQAs.

14.3.1
Critical Quality Attributes

Critical quality attribute is defined as a physical, chemical, biological, or microbiological property of characteristics that should be within an appropriate limit, range, or distribution to ensure the desired product quality. More precisely the CQAs of a biopharmaceutical product are those molecular and biological characteristics found in ensuring the "safety and efficacy" of the products [5,6,8].

14.3.2
Critical Process Parameters (CPP)

"The critical process parameters are operating parameters that influence the quality attributes of the products being produced. For example, temperature and pH in a fermenter are considered critical parameters as they have a direct influence on the viability of the organisms and the chemical or biological activity of the product being produced." [9]

14.3.3
The ICH Q8 "Minimal Approach" to Pharmaceutical Development

The aim of pharmaceutical development is to design a quality product and its manufacturing process to consistently deliver the intended performance of the product. The information and knowledge gained from pharmaceutical development studies and manufacturing experience provide scientific understanding to support the establishment of the design space, specifications, and manufacturing controls.

At a minimum, those aspects of drug substances, excipients, container closure systems, and manufacturing processes that are critical to product quality should be determined and control strategies justified. Critical formulation attributes and process parameters are generally identified through an assessment of the extent to which their variation can have an impact on the quality of the drug product.

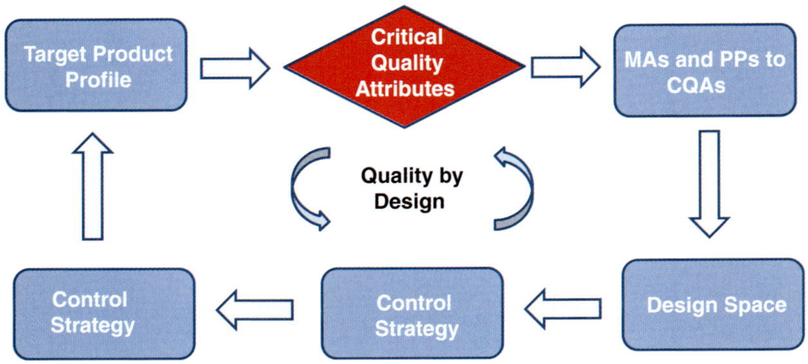

Figure 14.1 Steps in a quality-by-design approach.

14.3.4 Quality-by-Design

Quality-by-design (QbD) is centered on the patient. Understanding the patient's needs for managing his or her disease state helps define the QTPP (Quality Target Product Profile). Safety, efficacy, convenience, compliance, and cost-effectiveness of the product must be considered. The QbD is the quality of the pharmaceutical product that should be based upon the understanding of the biology or the mechanism of action and the safety of molecules [7]. The key steps involved in a QbD is depicted in Figure 14.1.

For QbD, the product and process knowledge base must include an understanding of variability in raw materials, the relationship between a process and product's CQAs, and the association between CQAs and a product's clinical properties (Figure 14.2). Successful implementation of QbD concepts requires cooperation across a multitude of company teams, from R&D to manufacturing, to quality control and regulatory affairs. This is necessary to ensure that QbD concepts are incorporated not only when the first activities are initiated around a product's design but also during the design of the process [10]. Analysis of QbD has identified many potential benefits. In terms of quantifiable benefits, value comes from the main areas: a reduction of cost of goods sold and capital expense, increased technical development productivity, improved quality, lower risk, and increased sales.

The two key components of quality-by-design are [10]

1) Understanding of the critical quality attributes of a molecule.
2) The design space of the process defined as the range of process inputs that helps ensure the output of desired product quality.

Over the last few years, several quality-by-design studies demonstrated the benefit of systematic approaches for biopharmaceutical development, and only

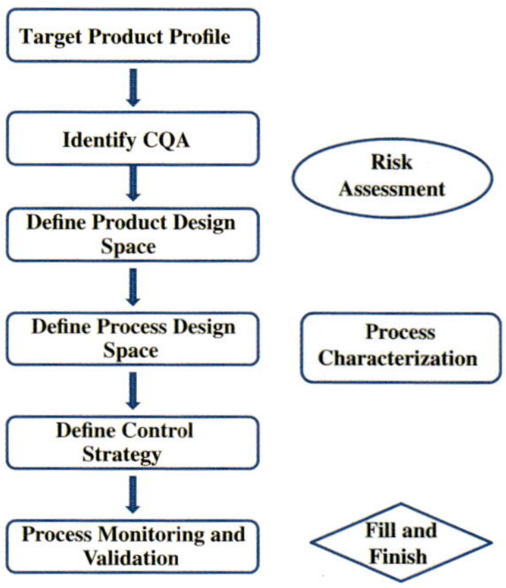

Figure 14.2 The key steps for implementation of QbD [10].

very few of them identified biosimilars as special for biosimilars development. The targeted quality profile of biosimilars is strictly defined by the originator and processing this information in biosimilar development has a major effect on risk management and process development strategies [11]. The International Conference on Harmonization (ICH Q9) was reviewed and three elements were identified to play a key role in targeted risk assessment approaches: proper understanding of target linkage, risk assessment tool compliance, and criticality threshold value. Adjusting these steps to biosimilar applications helped to address some unique challenges of these products, such as a strictly defined quality profile or a lack of process knowledge.

14.4
Quality Attributes and Biosimilars Development

A “biosimilar” is a medicine that is modeled on the original. In other words, biosimilar medicine is a biological medicine that is similar to other biological medicine that has already been authorized for use. They consist of small molecules (i.e., human insulin or erythropoietin) or complex molecules (i.e., monoclonal antibodies). Development of biosimilar products includes many challenges on the complex nature of biopharmaceutical entities and the highly protected manufacturing process of these entities. Like other medicines, biosimilars can only be marketed after registration [2,12].

Biomolecules are quite complex and heterogenous due to the various post-translational modifications that can occur and have been commonly observed. These modifications arise from the glycosylation, oxidation, deamidation, cleavage of the labile sites, aggregation, and phosphorylation, to name a few. As many of these modifications could impact the safety and efficacy of the molecules, defining the appropriate critical quality attributes of the molecule is an important starting point in the development cycle of a biopharmaceutical [2,12].

Understanding the CQAs at an early stage of the biosimilar development is very critical and clearly desirable. *Product quality studies conducted during mini-pool, clone, and process development stages* of a potential biopharmaceutical may entail evaluating various forms of a particular biomolecule in *in vitro* and *in vivo* animal studies. The outcome of such studies helps in developing a molecule with the desired quality attributes so as to be safe and highly efficacious.

On 9 February 2012, the US FDA issued the Agency's first set of three *draft* guidance documents outlining the framework for how it will evaluate applications for regulatory approval of biosimilar products. The long-awaited guidance provides the first detailed comments from the FDA on the topic. Although a great deal of interest has surrounded the release of information pertaining to the nature and amount of clinical testing required to demonstrate biosimilarity, one of the guidance documents deals with *Quality Considerations in Demonstrating Biosimilarity to a Reference Product.* The FDA identifies these quality considerations as the foundation of a biosimilar development program. The Quality Guidance "focuses on therapeutic protein products and provides an overview of analytical factors to consider in demonstrating biosimilarity between a proposed protein product and the reference product." [2,12]

The Quality Guidance identifies nine factors that should be addressed in assessing whether the proposed biosimilar and reference products are biosimilar, namely: (1) expression system, (2) manufacturing process, (3) assessment of physiochemical properties, (4) functional activities, (5) receptor binding and immunochemical properties, (6) impurities, (7) reference product and reference standards, (8) finished drug product, and (9) stability. The Quality Guidance also lists a number of known, relevant guidances for potential consideration during biosimilar product development, notably the guidances governing the International Conference on Harmonisation of Technical Requirements for Registration of Pharmaceuticals for Human Use (ICH) [5–7].

14.5
Quality, Safety, and Efficacy of Biosimilars

The quality, safety, and efficacy of a biosimilar product must be approved by the relevant regulatory body before marketing approval can be gained, which requires an appropriate comparability exercise. The EMEA requires comparison of the biosimilar product with the innovator product to determine the absence of any detectable differences. The quality comparison between the biosimilar and the innovator product is crucial, because the quality of a protein product affects its safety and efficacy.

It is known that biopharmaceutical manufacturing is a multistep process, involving cloning of the appropriate genetic sequence into a carefully selected expression vector, selection of a suitable cell expression system and scale-up and purification, up to formulation of the end product. Toward the particular manufacturing process used, biopharmaceuticals exhibited great sensitivity, and variation in product quality is commonly observed, even when the exact same process of manufacturing is used. The challenge then remains to assess and quantify these differences, and determine whether the new product is as safe and efficacious as the innovator product. *Furthermore, variability of source material has also been known to affect product quality* [12].

Thus, the product is affected both by the host cell and the processing steps that follow. In addition, protein molecules can be degraded during processing steps and impurities created in these steps can contribute to decreased potency and/or increased immunogenicity [7]. With the large number of quality attributes (Table 14.1), acquiring a complete knowledge of the impact of each of the attributes on clinical safety and efficacy is not feasible. However, the recent guidelines of the International Conference on Harmonization Q8 on pharmaceutical development, and the roll-out of the quality-by-design and process analytical technology initiatives from the FDA have improved the understanding of the impact of manufacturing processes and their starting materials on product quality.

Table 14.1 Method of quality, safety, and efficacy assessment of biosimilars [12].

Attributes	Analytical methods
Primary sequence (amino acid sequence analysis)	IE, HPLC, and gel electrophoresis
Potency	Cell-based bioassay, ADCC and CDC
Conformation	Near/far UV circular dichroism spectroscopy, X-ray crystallography, and differential scanning calorimetry
Glycosylation composition	Monosaccharide composition, oligosaccharide profile, CE, LC-MS, MS/MS, ESI, MALDI-TOF
Phosphorylation	Peptide mapping with MS
Truncation	SE-HPLC, analytical ultracentrifugation, gel electrophoresis, peptide mapping with MS, RP-HPLC
Glycation	Peptide mapping with MS, HPLC, methylation, isomerization (RP-HPLC)
Pegylation	HPLC, CE
Aggregation	SE-HPLC, gel electrophoresis, light scattering and AUC
Oxidation	Peptide mapping with MS
Deamidation	Capillary IEF, peptide mapping with MS, and CEX-HPLC, C terminal Lysine (capillary IEF, peptide mapping with MS and CEX-HPLC), misfolds (RP-HPLC)
Host cell protein	ELISA, DNA, endotoxin
Binding	Cell assays, spectroscopy, ELISA
Biological activity	Cell assays, animal models

Biochemical characterization of the protein product requires sophisticated analytical tools to detect the possibilities of changes to the product. Furthermore, the characterization of the product requires a variety of methods for different attributes or, alternatively, with orthogonal methods for the characterization of a given attribute, thus developing a comprehensive finger-printing of a protein product. However, key challenges remain that continue to require attention, primarily because of the high complexity of the products, processes, and raw materials that are part of the manufacturing of biotechnology products.

14.6 Implementing CQA Approach for Biosimilar Development

14.6.1 Identification of the CQA

The first step in biosimilar development is to identify the critical quality attributes of the molecule. CQAs are those attributes that are important to the quality of the drug product and that remain consistent with those used in clinical studies. Generally, industry associates them with ICH parameters such as identity, purity, potency, stability, safety, and so forth. CQA identification is the starting point for a biosimilar product development, which is identified based on either information available in the published data or knowledge and understanding available about the structure and function of a biosimilar product; for example, critical quality attributes for the biosimilar monoclonal antibody Rituximab is given in Table 14.2, which is identified at the start of the product development. Needless to say that identification of CQA helps in creating a desired clone and processes without compromising the product quality.

Prior to initiation of the biosimilar product development, it is advisable to identify the CQAs of the recombinant molecules to be able to develop an efficacious and desired product quality (Table 14.2). CQAs identification and analytical method development for the product quality assessment should be a parallel approach and implemented from the starting point of the product development, *preferably host selection and clone development*. The product quality should be assessed while developing the recombinant cell line/clone to ensure the authenticity of the cloning design, cell line selection, and successful transfection strategies.

The best approach for the biopharmaceutical development is to implement the CQA-based approach all the way from clone to manufacturing and clinical development (Figure 14.3). In most of the cases, the product quality is assessed after selecting the final clone and upstream process development, which may lead to poor-quality product created during clone and process development. The bioanalytical and bioassay methods are to be developed in parallel to the cell line and process selection, which allows evaluation of transfected and amplified cell pools as well as process parameters way before clone screening, selection, and process optimization. The quality measures of selected pools gives

Table 14.2 CQA identification and function of monoclonal antibody.

CQA for biosimilar Rituximab-Anti CD-20 mAb	
Quality attributes	**Impact on function of the molecule**
Afucosylation	Afucosylated Fc glycans enhances ADCC response
Gagalactose	Degalactosylation leads to threefold reduced CDC
High mannose	High mannose leads to faster clearance due to their interaction with mannose receptors
Sialic acid	Sialylated glycans may lead to higher immunogenicity
Methionine oxidation	Methionine 252 falls in FcRn binding region and its oxidation impacts serum half-life
Clips/truncations	Hinge region fragmentation releasing one Fab + Fc and one Fab and CDR clips lead to conformational changes (Increasing immunogenicity and reduced potency)
Aggregation	Covalent and noncovalent aggregation may lead to drop in potency
C-term Lysine variants	Has no biological or functional significance
N-terminus pE	Spontaneous physicochemical conversion and has no biological or functional significance
HCP, residual DNA and residual protein A	Robust consistent process restricts these attributes to permissible limits, has no biological or functional significance

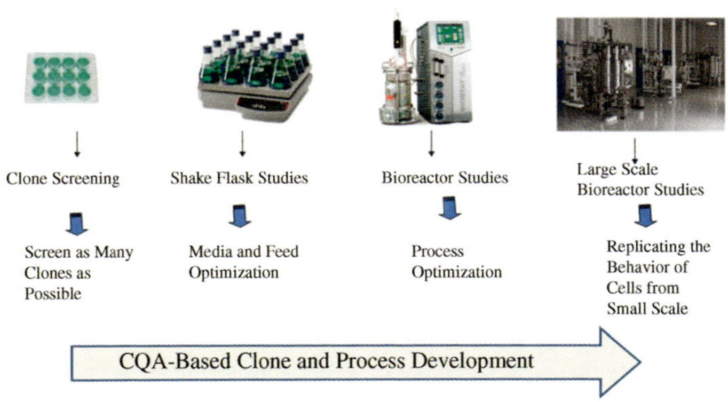

Figure 14.3 Implementing CQA from clone to manufacturing.

enough idea on the product quality as well as fate of the cell line and processes to move forward in product developmental path.

14.6.2 CQA-Based Clone Selection and Upstream Process Development

As stated in the previous paragraph the product qualities should be assessed in the following steps of biosimilar development.

Generation of a high-producing cell line remains a major bottleneck in therapeutic protein or antibody engineering. An ideal production cell line should be highly productive, stable, and deliver an antibody or protein having optimal product quality attributes including

- Minimal protein sequence heterogeneity
- Maximized functional activities
- Reproducible glycosylation profile
- Minimal charge variants
- Low potential for aggregation.

Cell line development typically involves screening of hundreds to thousands of clones in 96-well plates after stable transfection and gene amplification using DHFR or GS systems. This conventional process is time consuming and often leads to downstream development complexity. In most cases, productivity is the major criteria for clonal selection until a very late stage when only a handful of clones are assessed for the other quality attributes resulting in "increased complications and risk." This problem is particularly challenging for cell line development of biosimilar therapeutics because they are required to have the similar biophysical profiles of the innovator's products (Reference Medicinal Product). To overcome such issues, the CQA-based clone and process selection is implemented, which enables early assessment of the product quality without spending much time in clone and process development, the CQA-based approach facilitates rapid assessment of the product quality and deciding fate of the cell lines and processes, which are ultimately used for commercial production of biotherapeutic proteins or monoclonal antibodies.

14.6.3 Factors Affecting CQAs of the Biologics

Various factors are involved in recombinant product development life cycles that may affect the product quality attributes. Some of the major factors are listed here that need to be considered critical while developing the cell line or recombinant biologics as the product quality can be influenced at all stages of cell line and process development (Figure 14.4). These factors are as follows:

14.6.3.1 Expression Host and Recombinant Cell Line

- Inappropriate cloning design
- Change in the expression host
- Transfection/pool amplification
- Site of gene integration in the transfected host
- Genetic mutaion during clone development

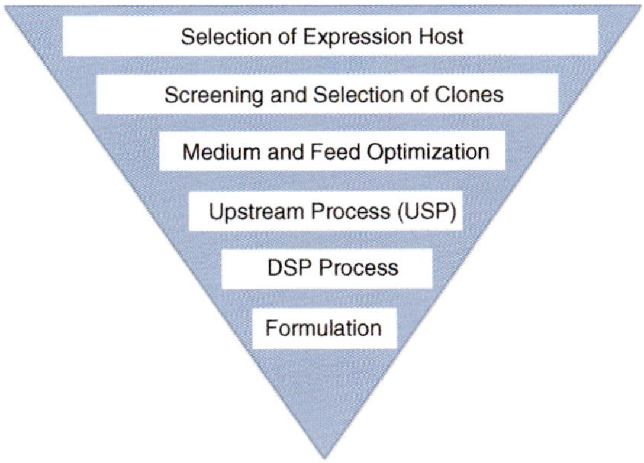

Figure 14.4 Variability of the product quality attributes at different stages [13].

- Incomplete processing of signal sequences
- Epigenetic changes during clone development
- Clone stability.

14.6.3.2 **Process Related**

- Upstream process type (batch, fed-batch, perfusion, etc.)
- Cell culture process parameters (dissolved oxygen (DO), pH, agitation, aeration, etc.)
- Cell culture supplements (medium, feed, and feeding regime)
- Spent medium/secondary metabolites (lactate, ammonium, glutamate, etc.)
- Downstream processing (each step)
- Scale-up of the upstream and downstream processes
- Hold time
- Formulation development
- Storage (buffer, container, conditions, etc.)
- Stability of the drug substance and drug product

These components might affect the CQA of the biosimilar molecules. The identified product's CQA needs to be verified at each and every step of a biosimilar product development. This approach allows the development of high-quality and potent biologics without compromising the targeted time lines. If the product quality does not match the reference molecules at any stage of the product development cycle, an immediate action can be taken at any of the mentioned steps to check and correct the product quality. This strategy enables us in saving the time and cost involved in biosimilar development significantly.

Maximum variability of the product quality attributes is seen at project start [13].

Table 14.3 Industrial relevant cell lines suitable for production of recombinant therapeutic proteins [14,15].

Cell line	Origin	Source	Product
CHO-K1	Chinese hamster ovary	ATCC	Eprex, Rituxan, Enbrel, Humira, FSH, Herceptin, and so on
CHO-DG44		Gibco/Invitrogen	
DUXB11		Chasin (Columbia Univ.)	
CHO-S		Gibco/Invitrogen	
PER.C6	Human retinal	Crucell	None
Sp2/0	Mouse myeloma	ATCC	Remicade and Erbitux
NS0	Mouse myeloma	ECACC	Synagis and Zenapex
BHK	Hamster kidney	ATCC	Factor-VIII
EB66	DUCK	Vivalis	None
HEK-293	Human	ATCC and Gibco/Invitrogen	None
CAP & CAP-T	Human aminocytes	Cevec	None

14.6.4 Protein Production Host and CQA

Currently, the European Union legislation on biosimilars does not exclude the use of a different expression system than the one used by the innovator for the reference product (Table 14.3). The development of alternative host gene cloning expression systems using different species can make the development of a biosimilar much more feasible from a financial perspective. Transfer of a gene encoding the same protein as the innovator's product to a different expression system can lead to a product with similar biologic activity despite some inherent differences that may be acceptable where there is no relevant impact on the function and/or safety profile of the molecule. Whatever the changes introduced, the new drug substance derived must be evaluated accordingly to *ensure quality, efficacy, and safety characteristics prior to market authorization approval.* The use of alternative expression systems may improve productivity and make biosimilars more affordable at reasonable prices.

Optimal glycosylation is critical for therapeutic glycoproteins, as glycans can influence their yield, immunogenicity, and efficacy, which impact the costs and success of such treatments. While several mammalian cell expression systems currently used can produce therapeutic glycoproteins that are mostly decorated with human-like glycans, they can differ from human glycans by presenting two structures at the terminal and therefore most exposed position. First, natural human N-glycans are lacking the terminal Galα1–3 Gal (alpha-Gal) modification. Glycosylation is a very critical modification of therapeutic proteins, known to significantly modulate yield, bioactivity, solubility, stability against proteolysis, immunogenicity, and clearance rate from

Table 14.4 Glycosylation patterns in different hosts and their implication.

Glycosylation	Chinese hamster ovary cells (CHO)	Mouse myeloma cells (Sp2/0 or NS0)	Implication
Terminal NANA	Very less	Absent	Undesired
Third GlcNac bisecting arm	Present (~10%)	Absent	Increases ADCC
Additional Gal α-1, 3-gal	Absent (~2–4%)	Present	Immunogenic and low half-life glycoforms
Terminal NGNA (different sialic acids)	Traces	Present (~1–2%)	
Oligomannose	Present	Present	

NANA, *N*-acetylneuraminic acid; GlcNac, *N*-acetylglucosamine; NGNA, *N*-glycolylneuraminic acid.

circulation. Depending on the source, the glycosylation pattern of the recombinant protein product varies greatly: starting with bacterial systems that do not glycosylate, followed by yeast, plants and insect cell systems generating immunogenic glycan types that are absent in humans, to mammalian systems with human-like complex glycans (Table 14.4).

Among all conceivable expression platforms, only mammalian systems are currently established in the pharmaceutical industry to produce biotherapeutic glycoproteins with homogenous human-like complex-type N-glycosylation. As bacteria, yeast, and plant-based expression systems represent the preferred industrial production platforms for nonglycosylated proteins today, they could be additional interesting alternatives for the future, once successful glycoengineering approaches establish systems capable of expressing nonimmunogenic human-like glycosylation patterns. Currently approved therapeutic glycoproteins are based on already optimized production platforms and could at first be tested for potential Neu5Gc contamination. If contamination is indeed present, addition of the precursor moleculeNeu5Ac to the feeding media may contribute to reduce and/or eliminate Neu5Gc contamination by metabolic competition [8,14].

The Quality Guidance states that it is expected that the expression construct for a proposed biosimilar product will encode the same primary amino acid sequence as its reference product. However, and very importantly, the guidance states that minor modifications, including N- or C-terminal truncations may be acceptable so long as they do not have an effect on safety, purity, or potency. Differences between the chosen expression system of the proposed biosimilar product and that of the reference product will need to be carefully considered because the type of expression system and host cell will significantly affect the types of process- and product-related substances and impurities. The characterization of the expression construct, including its genetic stability, should be demonstrated in accordance with principles recommended in ICH Q5B.

14.6.4.1 Cell Line Changes and CQA

Change in cell line is considered as the biggest risk among process changes. Therefore, to avoid host-related challenges in biomolecule development, the change in the host cell line has been practiced very conservatively in the biopharma industry.

Mainly three types of cell lines are changed during therapeutic product development: (1) Selecting different host cell line/expression platform. (2) Different clone from the same cell line. (3) Additional round of cloning. These components may lead to change in the glycosylation or quality profile of the final product. The CQA approach should be implemented to assess the change in the product quality and compared with the innovator's product (reference product) to ensure the biosimilarity and safety of the products as the changes lead to increase in the risk of CQAs of the molecules.

14.6.4.2 Host Cell Line and Clone Selection Criteria

In evaluating the risk of cell line changes and clone selection we must consider the following three criteria:

1) Post-translation capabilities of potential new host cell line
2) Clonal variability of the chosen host cell line in product quality attributes
3) Capability of mitigating comparability risks through process optimization and process development.

Selection of the final production clone is generally considered to be one of the most critical decisions in both early- and late-stage cell culture process development. Since changes in production cell lines during clinical development are considered major process changes, product comparability must be demonstrated if the cell line is changed during late stage development. Changing the cell line after Phase 3 clinical study typically requires additional human clinical studies. It is thus important to select the right clone prior to Phase 3 production of drug substance, and preferably at the Phase 1 stage. After being transfected, cells are diluted and cultivated in 96-well plates with a basal growth medium and screened for robust cell growth and high productivity. At this stage, in order to predict clone performance in large-scale production bioreactors, an enriched medium that is similar to the final production medium formulation and a similar feeding regime can be tested in shake flasks or in small-scale bioreactors [14,16].

As described in the previous paragraph, several clone attributes should be considered and evaluated for features such as product quality, manufacturability, and volumetric productivity. Maintaining consistent and comparable product quality is a challenge if changes to cell line, media, or other process changes are made as product candidates move forward from small-scale development lab to pilot plant scale, and eventually to commercial-scale cGMP manufacturing. Among these variables, the cell line has the most significant impact on many quality attributes because these attributes are clone

Table 14.5 Product quality assessment during clone selection [16].

Quality attribute	Analytical assay	Quality assessment criteria
Molecule integrity	cDNA sequence, peptide mapping, CE-SDS or SDS-PAGE	Avoid amino acid sequence mutation or truncated antibodies
Aggregation	Size exclusion chromatography (SEC)	Avoid high level of aggregation, which could be immunogenic.
Glycosylation	HPLC or CE-based glycan assay	Avoid high levels of unusually glycosylation forms
Charge heterogeneity	IEF or iCIEF, ion-exchange chromatography HPLC	Avoid usually high levels of acidic or basic variant, or extra acidic or basic peaks

CE, capillary electrophoresis; IEF, isoelectric focusing; iCIEF, imaged capillary isoelectric focusing.

dependent. *Some common analytical assays and quality assessment criteria employed during clone selection to test mAb molecular properties are summarized in* Table 14.5.

Cell line stability is another factor that should be considered since volumetric and specific productivity decline as cell age increases for some cell lines. Such unstable clones are not suitable for large-scale production since cell age increases with scale as the cell culture process is scaled-up through serial culture passages of the seed train and inoculum train. In addition to cell line stability, growth and metabolite characteristics that can affect process robustness and scalability also need to be assessed. Robust cell growth with high viability and low lactate synthesis is usually desirable. High-lactate-producing clones are not preferred in order to avoid the dramatic osmolality increase that accompanies the addition of base needed to maintain pH.

Screening and selection of highly productive and scalable clones among the transfectant population in a limited time frame is still a major challenge because the product quality, productivity, and even cell metabolic profiles are often dependent on cell culture conditions. Using miniaturized high-throughput bioreactors with full process parameter controllability to mimic the large-scale bioreactor environment could help to identify the best production clone at a very early stage [16].

14.6.5
Sequence Variants Identification by CQA

Sequence variants, defined as protein variants with unintended amino acid incorporation, are potential critical quality attributes for mAbs produced for therapeutic use.

Clone screening to select cell lines free of sequence variants is a general practice to support cell culture development. The process used to detect sequence variants is based on multiple peptide mappings with complementary enzymes, which generates peptides suitable for MS/MS analysis and generally covers 100%

of the protein sequence. The peptides are then separated by reversed phase (RP) high-performance liquid chromatography (HPLC) coupled with an accurate, high-resolution mass spectrometer.

This technique is very sensitive, as sequence variants with serine to asparagine changes due to codon specific mistranslation have been detected at levels as low as 0.1–0.2%.

Sequence variants can be generated by DNA/RNA mutation or amino acid misincorporation, and pinpointing the exact mechanism will enable the design of strategies to avoid sequence variants [17].

The mutation occurring in the final product can also be verified at mini-pool stage using various molecular biology and analytical tools. The implementation of CQA-based clone and upstream process selection approach can avoid any unwanted surprises that may occur after spending significant time and efforts in the clone selection and upstream process development.

Sequence variants can occur at different amino acids at random locations. The stop codons (UAA, UGA, and UAG) are important in protein translation because they are recognized by the release factors and signal the termination of the translation. With read-through, a process in which a stop codon is not recognized, the protein synthesis will stop at the next in frame stop codon in the expression vector and generate a protein with an extension. A stop codon-related mutation will generate a C-terminal extension in the protein and needs to be well characterized for biopharmaceutical development because it can affect the function of the expressed proteins [17]. Therefore, to avoid any protein extension, it is recommended to design the gene construct with two stop codons at least.

The observation of IgG1 variants with light chain extensions has been reported, in addition to the expected 220 amino-acid light chain. The variants were only expressed in one (clone B) of the four clones evaluated during clone screening (Figure 14.5). With a combination of different enzymatic peptide maps

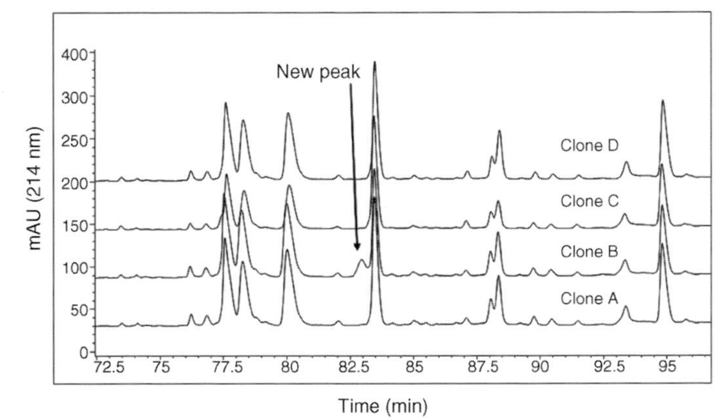

Figure 14.5 Overlay of tryptic peptides maps of IgG1 derived from four clones. The new peak at 83 min in clone B is absent from other clones.

and LC-MS and LC-MS/MS techniques, N-terminal sequencing, RP-HPLC, and nucleic acid based technologies, it is confirmed that such variants were generated because of a single base-pair mutation of TAA (stop codon) to GAA (Glu), enabling the selection appropriate clones for clinical therapeutic process development [17].

14.6.6 Incomplete Processing of Signal Sequences and CQA

The CQA-based early product quality analysis enables us to verify the processing of the signal/leader sequences cloned along with the mature protein sequences. During the cloning design we should be very cautious about selecting the signal sequences. Signal sequence is one of the key genetic elements in cloning design for optimal protein expression and secretion. Various tools nowadays available are used for signal sequence optimization and also to predict the fate of its processing in a particular host. However, often the signal sequences become limiting factors as far as product expression and quality is concerned. *Incomplete processing of the signal sequences results in erroneous product.* The cloning strategy needs to be changed if final product is incompletely processed or have additional amino acid/truncation in the N-terminus.

The signal sequence is the sequence that drives the trafficking of the mature protein from endoplasmic reticulum to Golgi and latter out from the expression host. The incomplete processing of the signal sequences may occur during protein trafficking that happens through various compartments of the hosts, the incomplete processing of signal sequence may hampers the product quality at any stage of the protein trafficking, which may or may not affect the potency of the molecules. *The addition or deletion of the terminal amino acid sequences to the mature proteins can be immunogenic too to the human body (depending on the sequence compositions).* Therefore, it becomes very critical to analyze the product quality (signal sequence processing) during clone and process development. The product quality of the biosimilar should be as close as possible to the innovator's product prior to the final clone and product development. The analytical tools such as HPLC-based cation exchange chromatography and mass analysis is usually used to verify the incomplete processed sequences if present at the N or C terminus of the mature protein.

The N-terminus amino acid composition of a protein completely affects the signal sequence processing and secretion efficiency; the incomplete processing may result in truncation of the protein. Hence, during the cloning design two or more signal sequences can be considered for successful cloning and protein expression. In case of mammalian platform the signal sequence processing and secretion efficiency can be checked at mini-pool stage before proceeding for the single cell cloning and clone screening. For signal sequence evaluation, cell culture harvest can be generated just after transfection and first phase of the antibiotic selection; the harvest can be generated in a shake flask for early assessment of the product quality. The cell culture harvest can be concentrated if enough quantity of protein is not expressed from the cells and further purified using a one- or two-step process that is able to generate sufficient materials to assess the product quality.

Various analytical tools, such as SDS-PAGE, western blot, RP-HPLC, amino acid sequencing, and CEX can be used to check the incomplete signal sequence processing, if any. The mass analysis of the expressed protein is the ultimate analytical tool to analyze the authenticity of processing of the various signal sequences incorporated during cloning design. In case of monoclonal antibody expression, we may get additional acidic or basic peaks in CEX profile if there is an addition or deletion of amino acids occurring in the mature protein. The material generated from mini-pool also tells the product quality and gives enough idea on the fate of the final clone selected after extensive screening exercises. The expression of truncated protein may result in a low-potent and high-immunogenic product.

Therefore, we should carry out the quality assessment of the expressed proteins starting from mini-pool to clone selection to assess the performance of the selected signal sequences.

14.6.7
Upstream Process Impact on Product Quality Attributes

14.6.7.1 Bioreactor Optimization and Scale Up

Culture operating parameter optimization is required to achieve *high expression of the product with acceptable product quality profiles.* The upstream cell culture process is a complex process, the flow of scale-up and bioreactor run is depicted in Figure 14.6. Various bioreactor parameters are optimized during a cell culture process development for recombinant products. These parameters are physical, chemical, and biological in nature. Physical parameters include temperature, gas flow rate, and agitation speed, while chemical parameters include dissolved oxygen and carbon dioxide, pH, osmolality, redox potential, and metabolite levels, including substrate, amino acid, and waste by-products (Figure 14.7).

Biological parameters are used for determining the physiological state of the culture and include viable cell concentration, viability, and a variety of intracellular and extracellular measurements, such as NADH, lactate dehydrogenase (LDH) levels, mitochondrial activity, and cell cycle analysis. Variations in the microenvironment parameters from optimal levels can have a dramatic impact on culture performance, productivity, and product quality. A typical stirred tank bioreactor is equipped with temperature, pressure, agitation, pH, and dissolved oxygen controls. Figure 14.7 illustrates the effects of cell culture operating strategies and parameters on culture environmental conditions, such as dissolved oxygen, pH, osmolality, dissolved CO_2, mixing, and hydrodynamic shear, and how the environment consequently influences measures of process

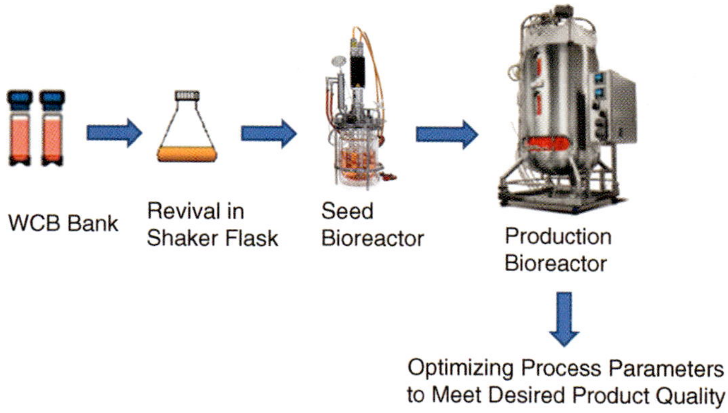

Figure 14.6 A typical cell culture process comprises vial thaw, seed expansion, and production stages.

performances, such as cell growth, metabolite concentrations, product titer, and product quality [10,16].

Due to the complexity of protein products that include isoforms and microheterogeneities, the performance of the cell culture process can have significant effects on product quality attributes and potency, especially with respect to glycosylation, posttranscriptional modifications, and impurity profiles. Therefore, the bioreactor operating parameters have to be optimized and characterized thoroughly to improve process performance and understanding of how the process affects product quality. Significant progress has been made in the last two decades in understanding the impact of the cellular environment on culture physiology and its subsequent impact on productivity, product quality, and downstream processes.

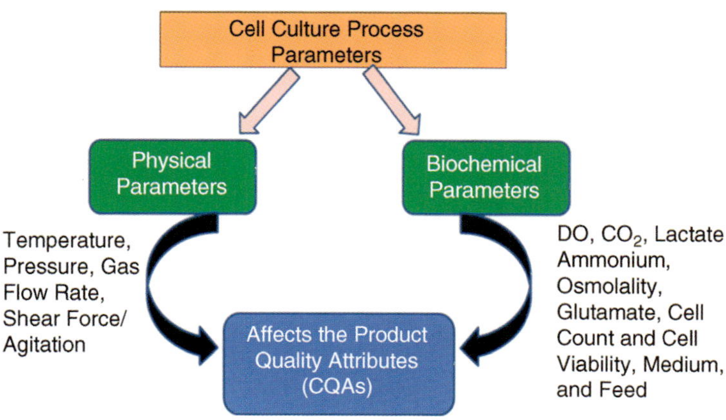

Figure 14.7 Cell culture process operating parameters affect process performance and product quality.

Another reason for the resurgence of research activity and innovation in this area can be attributed to the US FDA's process analytical technology (PAT) initiative. The PAT directive is a "system for designing, analyzing, and controlling manufacturing through timely measurements (i.e., during processing) *of critical quality and performance attributes of raw and in-process materials and processes, with the goal of ensuring final product quality*." It also encourages a better understanding of the manufacturing process by identifying relationships between process parameters and reproducibility, culture performance, and product quality attributes. Although originally conceptualized for small-molecule manufacturing processes, it is increasingly being extended to biological processes, which are inherently more complex [8,10].

Process parameters can be measured either online (or at-line by direct connection to calibrated analyzers) or offline via operator intervention. Typical examples of offline measurements include pH (usually for verification of online pH readings), cell counting, and viability measurements using a hemocytometer or automated cell counters, packed cell volume, osmolality, and certain metabolite concentrations. The temperature shift of the culture is often from 37 °C to 30–35 °C at 48 h postinoculation, which can retain cells in G1 phase longer, and therefore delay the onset of apoptosis.

Dissolved oxygen is typically controlled at a specific set point, usually between 20 and 50% of air saturation in order to prevent dissolved oxygen limitation, which might lead to excessive lactate synthesis, and excessively high dissolved oxygen concentrations that could lead to cytotoxicity. Although cell growth is relatively insensitive to dissolved oxygen in the range 20–100% air saturation, *the dissolved oxygen level can significantly affect product quality. Kunkel et al. reported that reduction in dissolved oxygen caused decreased glycosylation of antibody N-glycan chains.*

Dissolved CO_2 is also an important process variable because it can accumulate to inhibitory levels at values greater than 120–150 mm Hg and affects product quality [10,14]. Monoclonal antibodies are complicated glycoproteins subject to glycosylation heterogeneity and other modifications, such as N-terminal pyroglutamate and C-terminal lysine variants, methionine oxidation, asparagine deamidation, disulfide bond scrambling, aggregation, and fragmentation. Multiple process factors have the potential to change these product quality attributes, potentially resulting in clinical implications including efficacy and safety. While optimizing processes to achieve high yield, it is critical to monitor product quality changes at every stage of development.

Glycosylation variation, which can impact *in vivo* IgG functions and product stability, is one of the most sensitive quality-related attributes that is dependent on cell lines and cell culture conditions. Most mouse-derived cell lines are known to add Gal-α1,3-Gal onto antibody heavy chain N-glycan. High Gal-α1,3-Gal content, which is not found in human antibodies, *raises immunogenicity concerns.* It has been reported that this glycoform is varied in different NS0 clones. A high-throughput screening approach is used to select low Gal-α1,3-

Gal clones in early process development stages to match the product quality with the innovator's molecules.

The effects of cell culture media and conditions on antibody glycosylation have been extensively studied. Factors such as medium serum, glucose, ammonia, DO, dissolved CO_2, and culture osmolality have been reported to cause glycosylation changes in different cell lines.

These factors may affect the activity of monosaccharide transferases and/or sugar transport to the Golgi apparatus, which is the major glycosylation site in mammalian cells. Although the integrity of a protein's backbone is usually unchanged across different cell lines and culture conditions, some modifications can occur during cell culture processes. The IgG heavy-chain C-terminal is conserved as lysine, which is normally cut off through post-transcriptional modification.The presence or absence of C-lysine can result in product charge variants.

Carboxypeptidase B specifically cleaves C-terminal lysine residues. The activity of such metal enzymes can be affected by some medium trace element concentrations [8,14,16].

The majority of upstream critical process parameters are monitored online and offline. Online instruments, such as CO_2 probes, are verified against offline instruments to ensure that the conditions within the bioreactor have not caused the probes to "drift." Adjustments are made to the online instruments if drift is detected. Other outputs, such as cell count and viability, are measured strictly offline on a routine basis. PAT tools can be effective, though not necessary, to monitor parameters, such as temperature and pH, but are not necessarily value-added for culture health outputs, such as viable cell density, viability, or doubling time [16,18].

For upstream process, the following tools are being used by researchers:

- Surface plasmon resonance (to assess product concentration and affinity)
- High-performance liquid chromatography (to assess product concentration and structure)
- Capillary electrophoresis (to assess product concentration and structure)
- Dielectric spectroscopy (to determine biomass)
- *In situ* microscopy (to characterize cell population)
- Flow cytometry (to characterize cell population)
- Metal oxide field effect transistor (to sense biological contaminants)
- Infrared spectroscopy (to detect media components)
- *In situ* 2D fluorometry (to detect media components and metabolic end products)
- Raman spectroscopy (to detect media components and metabolic end products)
- UV spectroscopy (to measure homogenate components)
- Mass spectroscopy (to detect metabolic end products)
- HPLC (to detect media components and metabolic end products).

Protein glycosylation, for example, is generally determined during cell culture and minimally altered in downstream unit operations (at least for uncharged glycosylation species). Using this definition of CQAs, those CQAs observed to be potentially impacted during cell-culture steps include product attributes contained within the protein glycan distribution (e.g., afucosylated glycan), charge-variant distribution (e.g., glycated, deamidated forms), and to a lesser extent, molecular-size distribution (e.g., dimer or aggregate forms).

As a result of major advancements in analytical science, direct measurements of CQAs are performed in bioprocessing today. These would be product-quality related parameters, including host-cell impurities (e.g., host-cell proteins, DNA), process related (e.g., protein A leachate), and product related (e.g., aggregate, basic variants, acidic variants, and glycosylation pattern). Some of these CQAs, such as glycosylation pattern for mAb products, are primarily impacted by the upstream process and are particularly important to monitor during process development [10,16,18].

The variability and complexities associated with the upstream biological process make QbD a complex process, one that relies on defining operation-specific critical process parameters. CPPs are those likely to impact on the quality of a product or intermediate. For biological products, process control can be difficult to define and implement. O_2 pressure, catalyst concentration, and pH are examples of critical parameters. It is important to note that mAbs are currently the leading area of biopharmaceutical research. One of the key parameters to monitor in the implementation of QbD in mAb production is the glycosylation process during formulation. Glycosylation is one of the overriding contributors to mAb heterogeneity and has significant implications for the function of the antibody *in vivo* and immunogenicity. This means that glycosylation has been isolated as a critical parameter to follow during mAb manufacture. QbD for mAb development with specific glycosylation patterns enables researchers to optimize manufacturing and clinical efficiency [10,18].

Another set of challenges comes from raw materials that are complex and not well characterized (such as hydrolysates) as these can result in significant variation in the CQAs from lot to lot. For mAbs, besides the afore-mentioned factors, concentration of critical nutrients has been known to affect the glycoxylation pattern of the product, thereby impacting product efficacy.

Critical process parameters for the production bioreactor may include seed density, temperature, and process duration. Initial seed density can impact the overall growth profile and viability. Temperature is critical in maintaining viability and may impact the quality of the product being produced by the cells. Process duration will impact the viability of the culture at harvest, which can be tied to product quality.

Among the most difficult parameters to control in an upstream process is CO_2 concentration. The difficulty of controlling this parameter depends on the complexity of the aeration control strategy and availability of dissolved CO_2 probes.

Though there can be typically broad ranges of acceptable CO_2 during production, very high CO_2 concentrations can impact the product quality.

14.6.8 CQA in Purification and Formulation

14.6.8.1 Downstream Processing of Biosimilars

Once the recombinant is produced in cells, the product must be recovered and purified. Recovery and purification processes vary widely depending on the manufacturing process and specific product characteristics, but generally, the isolation and purification of mAbs and other proteins involve a centrifugation step to separate the cells from the cell culture fluid containing the recombinant product, one or more chromatography steps, which can include affinity chromatography, cation or anion exchange chromatography, hydrophobic interaction chromatography (HIC), and displacement chromatography, and innovations in biotechnology filtration or precipitation steps. Many of the purification steps are designed to remove contaminants and adventitious agents (e.g., bacteria, fungi, viruses, and mycoplasma) [8,16].

The predominant technology that has been used in the industry for buffer exchange and concentration is ultrafiltration/diafiltration using tangential-flow filtration. After this step, the drug substance is filtered and typically frozen as bulk for storage until filling occurs to produce the final drug product.

As enhancement of the final product titer and cell density of a cell culture process continues, the subsequent purification stage can become a bottleneck that impedes achieving a cost-effective and robust manufacturing process. A cell culture process with high product titer generates a heavy burden on the downstream process not only due to increased nonproduct impurities, but also because of a high amount of undesirable product-related isomers. Major challenges to developing an efficient downstream process for monoclonal antibody manufacturing with highly productive cell culture materials include the following three areas:

1) *Process capacity*: The equipment and manufacturing facility need to have an adequate capacity to handle the high-titer cell culture broth. This includes resin-binding capacity, process time, number of process cycles, overall facility size, schedule and facility flexibility, buffer and water consumption, and compliance with cGMP regulations.
2) *Removal of product-related impurities*: Heterogeneity is common in antibodies expressed by recombinant mammalian cell culture processes. These impurities include dimers, aggregates, and various isoforms resulting from amidation, deamidation, oxidation, and shuffling of disulfide bonds. Removal of these species cannot be achieved by protein A affinity chromatography alone, and requires additional polishing steps.
3) *Removal of process impurities*: Process impurities include host cell protein (HCP), nucleic acids (DNA, RNA), leached protein A, and potential viral contamination, all of which need to be cleared according to FDA

guidelines. Currently accepted levels of impurities for therapeutic antibodies reported in the literature are: <5 ppm for HCP, <10 ng dose^{-1} for rDNA, <0.5% for dimers or aggregates, and <5 ppm for leached protein A [8].

14.6.8.2 Downstream Processing and CQA

The CQAs for downstream are very product dependent. Glycosylation and sialylation are definitely two outputs that require product and product quality understanding and are the most common across different cell-culture processes. After that, variation in the product profile begins to manifest itself too much, preventing universal CQAs to be established. Some CQAs are generated in, or substantially changed by, certain downstream unit operations. Size variants or charge variants, for example, may be generated during hold times, and product quality attributes, such as host-cell proteins and size variants, are typically reduced through the purification process and controlled to an acceptable level by consistent purification process performance.

The downstream process attributes are similar to those mentioned earlier for upstream processing. These include process-related impurities (e.g., antifoam, additives added during the processing, protein A leachate), host-cell impurities (e.g., host-cell proteins), and product-related impurities (e.g., aggregate, basic variants, acidic variants, glycoxylation pattern). Chromatography unit operations are typically most sensitive to the pH and ionic strength of wash and elution conditions. Control of these critical buffers is managed through batch preparation and release prior to use based on acceptable pH and conductivity ranges. Process capability is sufficient to reproducibly prepare buffers within narrow pH and conductivity ranges, such that only a subset of the most sensitive buffers are typically determined to be CPPs.

Typical CPPs in downstream processing would include parameters, such as pH, conductivity, temperature, and gradient for chromatography steps; temperature, agitation rate, and sparge rate for refolding steps; and pH and hold time for the viral inactivation step. The challenge in downstream processing mainly comes from the fact that the steps are relatively short in duration [10,16].

Originator and biosimilar products have similar downstream CPPs. For chromatography steps, these may include protein load, pH (load or elution depending on step), temperature, flow rate, and conductivity for ion-exchange steps. Viral inactivation steps may have temperature, pH, or detergent concentration as a CPP depending on the modality of inactivation. Pressure and filter volume represent CPPs for viral filtration steps. Again, if engineering controls permit tight control of these parameters, some may be downgraded to a lower parameter designation.

Using a QbD approach, downstream CPPs would be proposed only through using risk assessments of the possible impact to preidentified CQAs. Downstream CPPs will vary greatly depending on the nature of the molecule, the purification strategy, and the order and timing of unit operations. The following list of operations/parameters is potentially responsible for affecting product quality/CQAs, particularly toward the end of a purification process. Not all of these would necessarily end up as CPPs:

- *Viral inactivation*: pH of inactivation, time of inactivation, and concentration of inactivation solution
- *Viral filtration*: filter load density (mg ml^{-1} membrane) and filtration pressure
- *Chromatography operations*: load density, pH and/or conductivity of buffers, residence time, volumes, and eluent concentration
- *Filtration operations*: load density, transmembrane pressure, crossflow rate, and diafiltration diavolumes.

The Quality Guidance states that applicants should characterize, identify, and quantify impurities (both product- and process-related as defined in ICH Q6B) in both the proposed biosimilar and reference products. If the manufacturing process used to produce the proposed biosimilar product introduces different or higher levels of impurities than those in the reference product, additional pharmacological/toxicological or other studies may be necessary.

Process-related impurities arising from cell-substrates (e.g., host cell DNA, host cell proteins), cell culture components (e.g., antibiotics, media components), and downstream processing steps (e.g., reagents, residual solvents, leachables, endotoxin, bioburden) should be evaluated. These assays should be validated using the product cell substrate and orthogonal methodologies to ensure accuracy and sensitivity of biologically significant impurities. The safety of the proposed biosimilar product with regard to adventitious agents or vial contamination should be ensured by screening raw materials and confirmation of robust virus removal and inactivation achieved during the manufacturing process [10,18].

14.6.9
CQAs in Formulation and Stability

14.6.9.1 Formulation and Quality Attributes

The formulation of the mAb therapeutic is chosen in part to ensure product quality during shelf life. Formulations are designed to minimize protein aggregation, decrease viscosity, and increase shelf life through preventing degradation. High protein concentration formulations are being developed to allow for subcutaneous or intramuscular delivery of mAb products. Historically, the most conventional route of delivery for protein drugs has been intravenous administration because of poor bioavailability by most other routes, greater control during clinical administration, and faster pharmaceutical development. Subcutaneous delivery allows for home administration and improved patient compliance. However, development of high protein concentration formulations involves unique manufacturing challenges compared to low-concentration formulations, such as higher viscosities and necessary changes to unit operation steps.

The Quality Guidance states that product characterization should be performed on the most downstream intermediate best suited for the analytical procedures used. Many times, the best suited product is the finished drug product. Though the guidances note that changes in the final formulation may occur, acceptability of the type, nature, and extent of any differences between the proposed finished biosimilar product and the finished reference product should be evaluated. Additionally, different excipients in the proposed product should be supported by existing toxicology data for the excipient or by additional toxicity studies with the formulation of the proposed biosimilar product. Since differences in excipients or primary packaging may affect product degradation and/or clinical performance, the guidance notes that differences in the formulation between the proposed biosimilar product and the reference product are among the factors that may affect the nature of subsequent clinical studies [10].

14.6.9.2 Stability and Quality Attributes

Accelerated and stress stability studies, or forced degradation studies, should be used to establish degradation profiles and provide direct comparisons of the proposed biosimilar product with the reference product. These studies should be conducted under multiple stress conditions that can cause incremental product degradation over a defined period of time [10].

14.7 Summary

To summarize, the identification and implementation of CQA-based approach allows developing a very potent and quality product comparable with the innovator's biosimilar product. The product quality measurement approach implemented from the start point to the commercialization of the biosimilar development program minimizes the risks involved at every stage of the product development path. CQA will provide immediate and critical measures of the control or variability of the processes and product. The strong knowledge on analytical techniques allows assessing the product quality in an efficient manner that ultimately results in developing the highest-quality recombinant biosimilar. Analytical characterization of the product also allows better understanding of cells, clones, and processes behavior, which directly or indirectly affect the CQA of a recombinant biomolecule. The CQA-based product development approach allows the biopharmaceutical industries to develop recombinant biosimilars with the highest quality and efficacy standards and a cost advantage that can be transferred back to the masses.

The chapter has attempted to present points to consider when developing high-potent biosimilar molecules. It also emphasizes how change in expression host, clone, and upstream and downstream processes affects the critical quality attributes of the recombinant biomolecules. Therefore, we highly recommend to implement the CQA-based approach for the development of an efficacious, safe, and affordable biosimilar molecule.

References

1 Rita Costa, A. (2010) Guidelines to cell engineering for monoclonal antibody production. *Eur. J. Pharm. Biopharm.*, **74**, 127–138.

2 Tsiftsoglou, A.S., Ruiz, S., and Schneider, C.K. (2013) Development and regulation of biosimilars: current status and future challenges. *BioDrugs*, **27** (3), 203–211.

3 Tsiftsoglou, A.S., Ruiz, S., and Schneider, C.K. (2013) Development and regulation of biosimilars: current status and future challenges. *BioDrugs*, **27**, 203–211.

4 Plitnick, L. and Herzyk, D.J. (2013) *Nonclinical Development of Novel Biologics, Biosimilars, Vaccines and Specialty Biologics*, 1st edn, Elsevier, Philadelphia, PA.

5 ICH (2009) Guidance for the Industry, Q8 (R2) Pharmaceutical Development. U.S. Department of Health and Human Services, Food and Drug Administration, Center for Drug Evaluation and Research (CDER), Center for Biologics Evaluation and Research (CBER), Revision 2, pp. 1–25.

6 van Beers, M.M.C. and Bardor, M. (2012) Minimizing immunogenicity of biopharmaceuticals by controlling critical quality attributes of proteins. *Biotechnol. J*, **7** (12), 1473–1484.

7 FDA (2004) PAT Guidance for Industry: A Framework for Innovative Pharmaceutical Development, Manufacturing and Quality Assurance. U.S. Department of Health and Human Services, Food and drug Administrative (FDA), Center for Drug Evaluation and Research (CDER), Center for Veterinary Medicine (CVM), Office of Regulatory Affairs (ORA).

8 Li, F., Zhou, J.X., Yang, X., Tressel, T., and Lee, B. (2005) Current therapeutic antibody production and process optimization. *Bioprocess. J.*, **5** (4), 16–25.

9 Dwivedi, C.M. (2006) Validation of cell culture-based process and qualification of associated equipment and facility, in *Cell Culture Technology for Pharmaceutical and Cell-Based Therapies* (eds S.S. Ozturk and W.-S. Hu), CRC Press, Taylor & Francis Group.

10 Haigney, S. (2013) QbD and PAT in upstream and downstream processing. *BioPharm Int.*, **26** (7), 28–37.

11 Zalai, D., Dietzsch, C., and Herwig, C. (2013) Risk-based process development of biosimilars as part of the quality by design paradigm. *PDA J. Pharm. Sci. Technol.*, **67**, 569–580.

12 Sekhon, B.S. and Saluja, V. (2011) Biosimilars: an overview. *Biosimilars*, **1**, 1–11.

13 Harmon, B.J. (2013) Establishment of a comparability strategy to support a cell line change during clinical development of a monoclonal antibody. Presentation by Drug Information Association (DIA), February 7, 2013.

14 Ghaderi, D. *et al.* (2012) Production platforms for biotherapeutic glycoproteins. Occurrence, impact, and challenges of non-human sialylation. *Biotechnol. Genet. Eng. Rev.*, **28**, 147–176.

15 Agrawal, V. and Bal, M. (2012) Strategies for rapid production of therapeutic proteins in mammalian cells. *BioProcess Int.*, **10** (4), 32–48.

16 Li, F., Vijayasankaran, N., Shen, A., Kiss, R., and Amanullah, A. (2010) Cell culture processes for monoclonal antibody production. *mAbs*, **2** (5), 466–477.

17 Zhang, T. *et al.* (2012) Identification of a single base-pair mutation of TAA (Stop codon) → GAA (Glu) that causes light chain extension in a CHO cell derived IgG1. *mAbs*, **4** (6), 694–700.

18 Rathore, A. and Winkle, H. (2009) Quality by design for biopharmaceuticals. *Nat. Biotechnol.*, **27**, 26–34.

15
Automated Single-Use Centrifugation Solution for Diverse Biomanufacturing Process

Sunil Mehta

15.1
Introduction

Separation of solids from liquids is a requirement for most biologics manufacturing processes. Although almost all microbial processes require this type of separation, the focus in this chapter will be on mammalian cell-based processes. Depending on a process, supernatant or solids may be the product or intermediate product. For example, antibody manufacturing requires separation of antibody containing supernatant from cells and cell debris. In cell therapy manufacturing, cells are the product and they need to be concentrated and washed prior to freezing. Independent of the location of the virus (intracellular, extracellular, or cell associates), almost all vaccine processes require separation between cells and liquid. Large-scale blood processing applications may require separating plasma proteins or platelets from red blood cells and white blood cells.

Separation can be achieved by several technologies. Most widely used technologies are centrifugation and filtration [1]. Centrifugal separation is mainly governed by the weight of solids whereas separation by filtration is mostly based on the size of particles. Many other factors including specific density and viscosity of fluids and shape and charge of particles can impact both centrifugal and filtration separations. Many processes utilize both centrifugation and filtration technologies in tandem to achieve the desired separation.

15.2
Separation by Centrifugation

Generally, centrifuges used in the bioprocessing are either tubular bowl or disk-stack based. Tubular-bowl centrifuges pack the cells tightly but require stopping of the spinning bowl between discharges. On the other hand, disk-stack centrifuges do not pack the cells tightly and do not require stopping of the rotor between discharges. Disk-stack centrifuges are not available in single-use format

Continuous Processing in Pharmaceutical Manufacturing, First Edition. Edited by Ganapathy Subramanian.

and require significant infrastructure for cleaning-in-place (CIP) and sterilization-in-place (SIP). In addition, CIP and SIP validations could also be challenging. Both types of centrifuges typically exert large amount of shear on cells and can easily lyse them [2]. Although cells are waste for harvest clarification processes, lysis of cells can release proteases and other detrimental enzymes and can change the quality attributes of the product [3]. In addition, large amount of host cell proteins in the centrate can pose huge downstream challenges [4]. Traditionally, disk-stack centrifuges have been employed by numerous antibody manufacturing processes [2]. In a typical antibody manufacturing process, depth filters are used postcentrifugation to provide the clarification needed prior to 0.2 μm filtration.

15.3 Separation by Filtration

Filters have the advantage of not having any moving parts and of low infrastructure requirements. Additionally, single-use formats are readily available from multiple manufacturers. However, depth filter based processes are known to consume large amounts of buffers and have large dead-volumes that can negatively impact recovery. For example, a manufacturer's recommended volumes for 1000 l harvest clarification process may exceed 20 000 l [5]. Filters are not generally suitable for processes requiring low shear. These are typically cell therapy manufacturing and some vaccine processes where cells are either the product or intermediate product. Large-scale cell banking also falls under the same category. Tangential-flow filtration (TFF) and alternating tangential flow (ATF) exert high shear on cells as the cells constantly rub against the membrane during processing. In addition, depending on the cutoff of the membrane, many particulate contaminants, dead cells, and cell debris may be retained in the concentrate during processing. The washing process is also inefficient as it is not plug-flow but a simultaneous dilution and concentration process (diafiltration).

15.4 Downstream Process Challenges of High Cell Density Cultures

As upstream processes are improving, the cell density of cultures as well as productivity is also increasing dramatically. Now, many processes have peak viable cell density of higher than 25 million cells ml^{-1} and antibody titers of greater than 5 $g\,l^{-1}$ [6]. Vaccine processes are also being developed with very high cell densities (>50 million cells ml^{-1}). High cell densities pose a challenge to traditional centrifugation technologies since the number of discharges in a process is directly proportional to the cell density. The losses could be as high as 50% as a fixed amount of product is lost with each discharge. Since high cell densities generally produce high titers, a very large amount of product could be lost using these processes. Therefore, overall product losses in this step could be significant. This is one of the reasons that rarely a biopharmaceutical process uses traditional centrifugation for high cell density cultures. One way to recover the lost product from the interstitial space between the cells is by displacing it with wash buffer, but both traditional centrifugation or filtration technologies are not capable of washing cells efficiently to recover the product.

15.5 Single-Use Centrifugation

Single-use technologies have several advantages over traditional reusable technologies including elimination of CIP/SIP (clean-in-place/sterilization-in-place) and risk of cross-contamination between batches and reduced cycle times and capital investment. Single-use centrifuges are not abundant due to engineering challenges in their development. Low- to medium-speed single-use centrifuges are now available and some high-speed centrifuges (based on automated piston discharge or APD technology) are under development.

15.6 kSep Technology

kSep technology is a low-shear technology that was developed to address the challenges of innovative biopharmaceutical manufacturing processes. Unlike traditional centrifuges where the rotor rotates in the horizontal plane, a kSep system contains a rotor that rotates in the vertical plane (Figure 15.1). Rotation in the vertical plane cancels the gravity effect (Figure 15.2) that is typically seen in traditional centrifuges that rotate in the horizontal plane.

Due to this gravity effect, solids form a slanted pallet after traditional centrifugation. Rotation in the vertical plain eliminates slant formation so that usable centrifugation volume in a chamber is maximized.

The rotor contains multiple conical chambers (one chamber is shown in Figure 15.1).

Fluid (containing particles) is continuously pumped by a bidirectional pump into the system from the tip of chamber and the clarified fluid exits from the base of chamber (Figure 15.1). As the rotor spins, centrifugal force is exerted on particles such that they move from the base toward the tip of chamber. At the same time, fluid entering from the tip of chamber creates fluid-flow force (due to flow velocity) that moves these particles from the tip to the base of chamber. The shape of the chamber is designed so that both centrifugal force and fluid-flow force balance out each other and the particles remain suspended. Both centrifugal force and fluid-flow force are highest at the tip and lowest at the base (Figure 15.3).

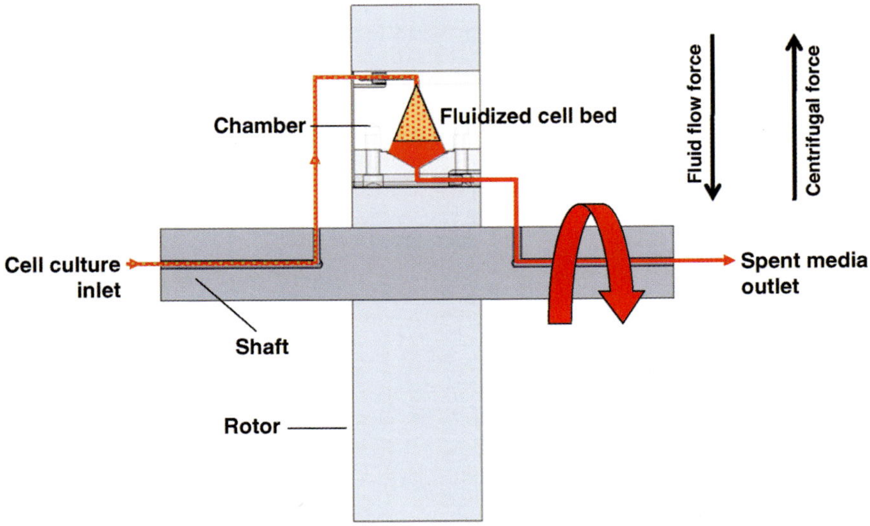

Figure 15.1 Mechanism of kSep technology.

Therefore, the two forces balance out each other and the net force on particles (independent of their position) is zero. As a result, a fluidized bed of particles is formed with a continuous flow of media through the fluidized bed. Interstitial space formed between the particles prevents aggregation and depending on process requirements this gap allows flow of nutrients, oxygen, coating fluids,

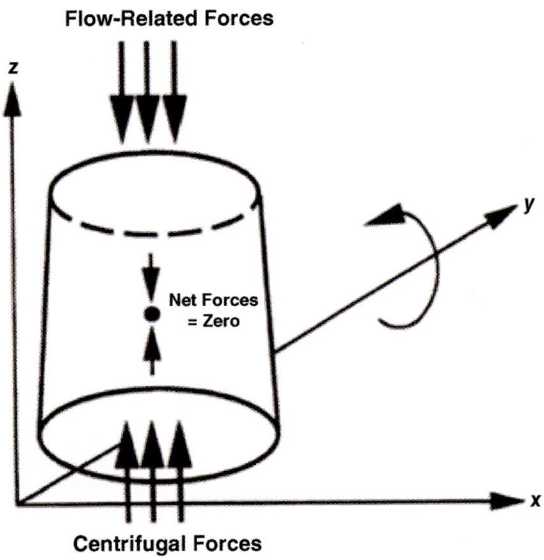

Figure 15.2 Rotation in the verticle plane cancels the gravity effect.

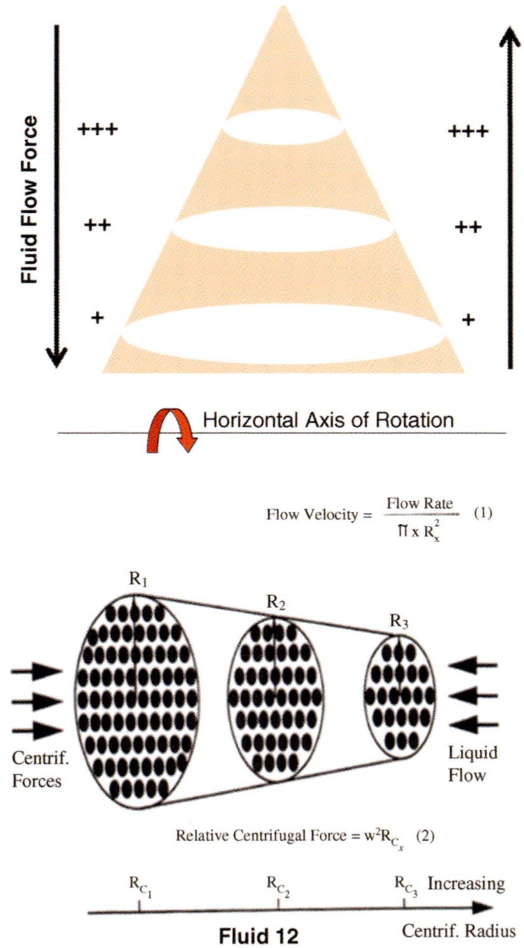

Figure 15.3 Complete balance of centrifugal force and fluid-flow force. Centrifugal flow and flow velocity are both highest at the tip and lowest at the base.

transfection complexes, or viruses so that they come in full contact with particles. In addition, due to plug-flow, a new fluid can completely displace the existing fluid resulting in efficient exchange of fluids or washing. This property is exploited to displace secreted product without dilution in high cell density cell culture processes. Cell therapy and vaccine processes also utilize washing to remove bovine serum albumin (BSA), Trypsin, and other contaminating molecules. The whole system poses minimal shear on particles as the particles never pack against each other and rather remain gently suspended.

Once the chamber is full of particles or when required, particles can be washed in a plug-flow to displace the product or contaminants from the interstitial space between the cells. The discharge is achieved by reversing the bidirectional pump so that the fluid-flow force and the centrifugal force act in the same direction and empty the chamber. Unlike traditional bowl centrifuges, the kSep system does not require stopping of the rotor. This results in short discharge time and less wear on the machinery. The whole process is automatically repeated until the bioreactor is empty. At that stage, the bubble sensor senses the end of process and the system completes the last cycle and empties the disposable. At this point the old disposable can be discarded and a new disposable set can be installed to start a new batch.

15.7
kSep System Configuration

kSep systems are equipped with a programmable logic controller (PLC), a human–machine interface (HMI), various sensors, pumps, and valves to be safe, fully automated, and prevent human errors. As rotary seals are not completely sealed, most kSep systems do not use rotary seals. These single-use systems utilize a unique completely closed high-speed rotary mechanism instead of rotary seals. All product contact surfaces are Class VI and all tubing connections to process are made via sterile tube welding. The kSep system is typically connected to a process via four connections: bioreactor or cell source, priming and wash buffer bag, product bag, and waste bag. There are two different systems (kSep400 and kSep6000) (Figure 15.4) and two different configurations of disposable sets and software.

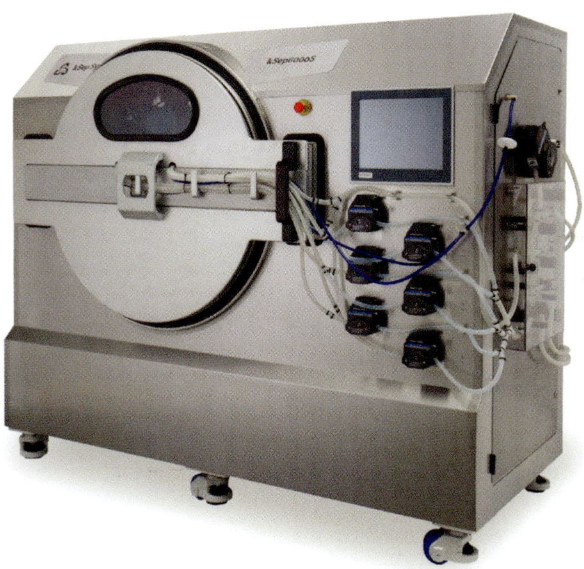

Figure 15.4 kSep6000 system loaded with a disposable set. One set is optimized to recover solids while the other to recover supernatant.

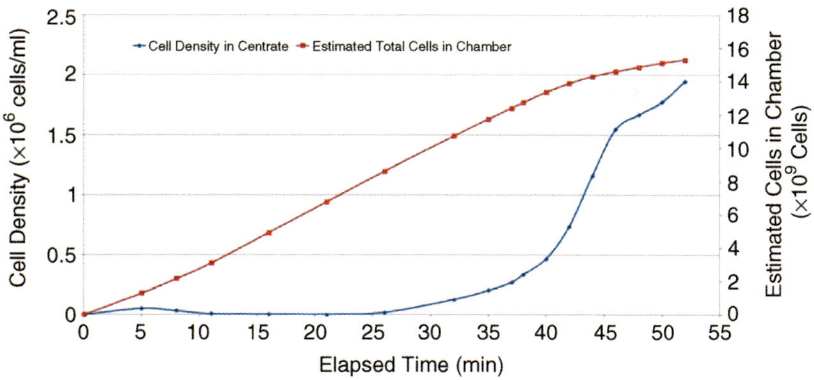

Figure 15.5 Chamber capacity determination [8]. Courtesy of Ravi Bhatia, Johnson & Johnson.

The kSep400 system has a total chamber volume of 400 ml (four chambers of 100 ml each) and kSep6000 has a total chamber volume of 6 l (six chambers of 1 l each). Total cell capacity per cycle is 40–80 billion cells for kSep400 and 600–1200 billion cells for kSep6000. The variation in cell capacity is mainly due to flow rate, size of cells, and density and viscosity of the media. A recent publication has reported about 10 billion CHO cells/chamber for kSep400 (Figure 15.5).

Each system has multiple chambers that can be used independently or in any combination as all chambers are filled (with prime liquid) during priming but selected chambers can be used for a process. Since the specific gravity of cells is very similar to the buffer, it does not create any imbalance. This built-in scalability has successfully been used to develop a process using one chamber and later scaled-up to all chambers (Figure 15.6). Images of each chamber are displayed on the HMI by a vision system composed of a camera, strobe light, and processing unit. The real-time video is useful for process development to assess the capacity of the system.

Although the system is designed for cGMP operations, users have ample flexibility for process development. For process development, recipe parameters can be modified during a cycle so that the next cycle uses new modified parameters. Therefore, users can generate a series of data from a single run. Also, depending on the volume of process, the user can easily choose to run any number of chambers (e.g., 1–4 for kSep400 and 1–6 for kSep6000).

Once the connections are made, the system can be automatically run by a user as per selected process recipe (Figure 15.7). After the process is completed, the system automatically empties the disposable kit so that it can be easily removed and discarded. Thereafter, a new disposable kit can be installed for a new batch.

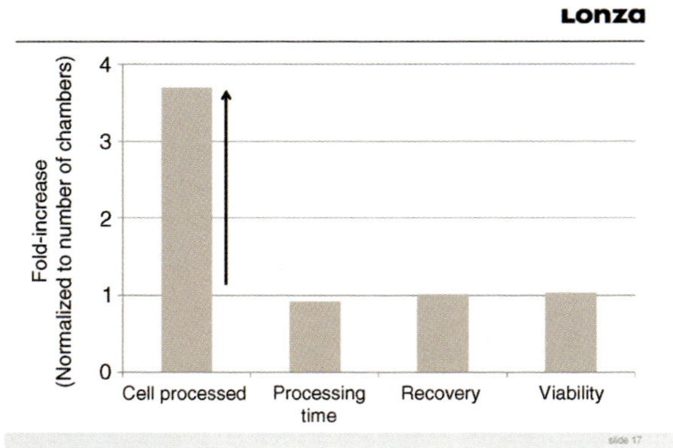

Figure 15.6 Comparable processing time, cell recovery, and viability when scaling from 1 to 4 chambers. Courtesy of Jon Rowley, Lonza.

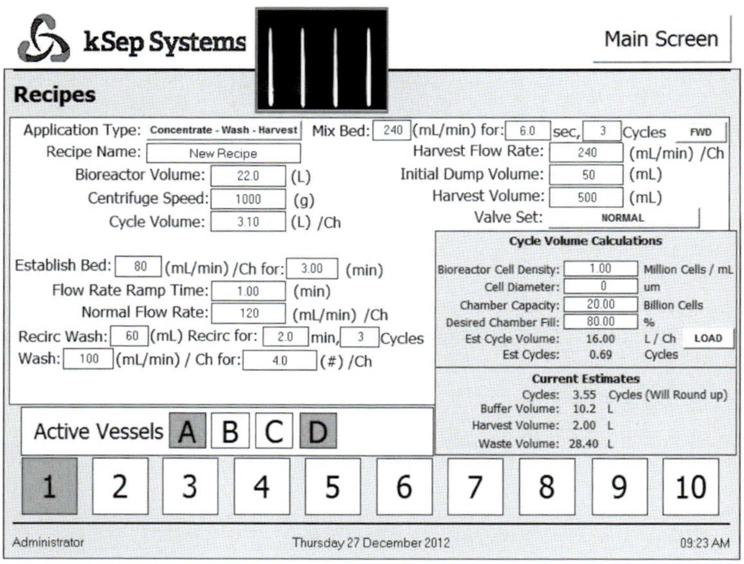

Figure 15.7 Automated recipe screen for concentrate – wash – harvest process.

15.8
Low-Shear Process

Low shear is strongly desired not only for cell therapy, cell banking, or blood processing but also for many continuous processes including perfusion and harvest clarification. It promotes viability of cells in a perfusion process and reduces

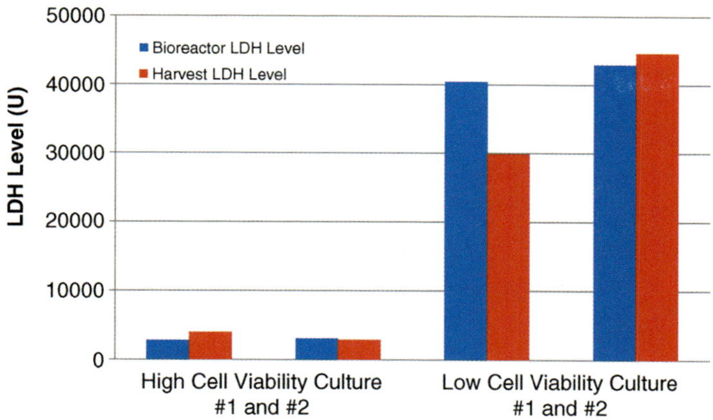

Figure 15.8 No change in LDH release after kSep centrifugation [8]. Courtesy of Ravi Bhatia, Johnson and Johnson.

downstream contamination for harvest clarification process. Measurement of shear force on cells is not trivial [7]. Trypan blue exclusion test is insensitive in determining minor cell wall damage [7]. Lactate dehydrogenase (LDH) has been used as a surrogate marker to detect any damage or shear exerted on the cell wall [7,8]. LDH is an intracellular enzyme present in mammalian cells. If shear is exerted on cells, LDH oozes out of the cell membrane and can be readily detected by a quick enzymatic assay [7,8]. Several independent reports have shown that there is no change in the LDH levels between pre- and post-kSep process samples. One such example from Johnson & Johnson is shown in Figure 15.8 [8] and another from Lonza in Figure 15.9.

In addition, measurement of cellular ATP by Vialight assay as well as plating of kSep-processed cells, exhibited similar vitality as unprocessed cells (Figure 15.9). These results indicate that kSep is indeed a low-shear technology.

15.9 Perfusion

A study was performed by KBI Biopharma, Inc. to assess the suitability of the kSep system for a short Chinese hamster ovary (CHO) perfusion process. Two bioreactors were set-up at the same time with a seed cell density of 0.3 million cells ml^{-1}. After 3 days, kSep was used as a cell retention system for one of the bioreactors and the perfusion process was initiated. After 6 days, the cell density reached around 15 million cells ml^{-1} in the perfusion bioreactor as compared to only 4 million cells ml^{-1} in the batch bioreactor (Figure 15.10).

The cells almost doubled each day after the kSep perfusion process was started. In addition, unlike traditional perfusion systems, there was no viability drop after the kSep perfusion process was started (Figure 15.11).

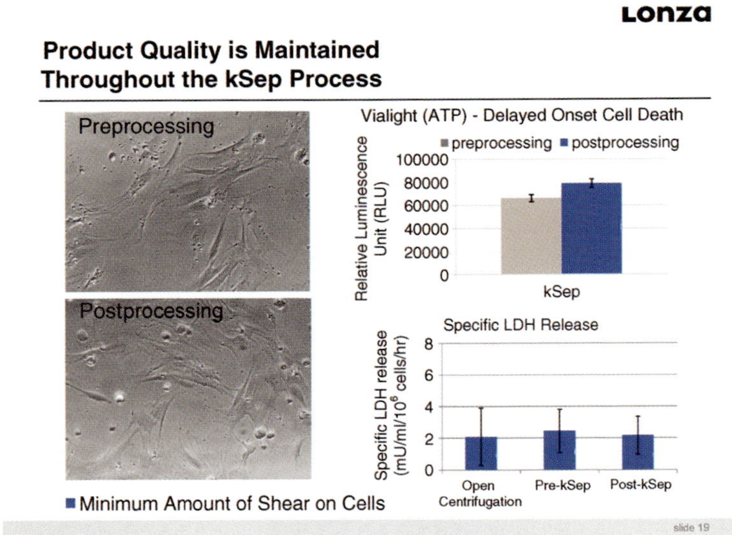

Figure 15.9 kSep maintains vitality of cells. Courtesy of Jon Rowley, Lonza.

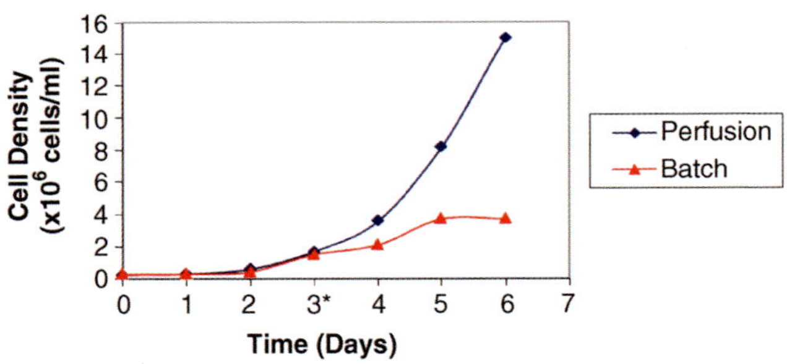

Figure 15.10 Comparison of cell density between kSep perfusion process and batch process. Courtesy of KBI Biopharma Inc.

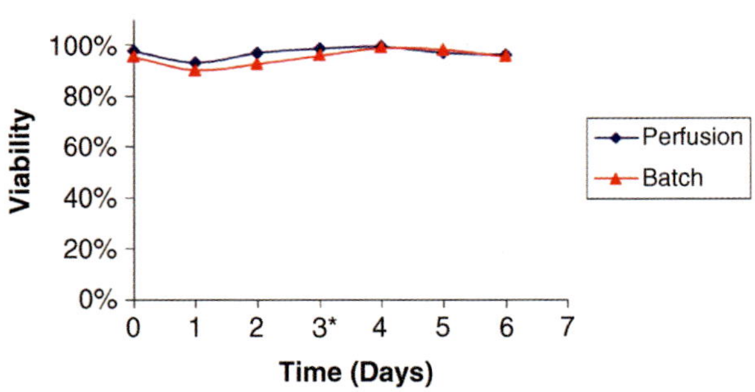

Figure 15.11 Comparison of cell viability between kSep perfusion process and batch process. Courtesy of KBI Biopharma Inc.

15.10
Concentration, Media Replacement, and Harvest of Cells

In another study, kSep was used in a vaccine process to concentrate and wash cells prior to transfection (Figure 15.12).

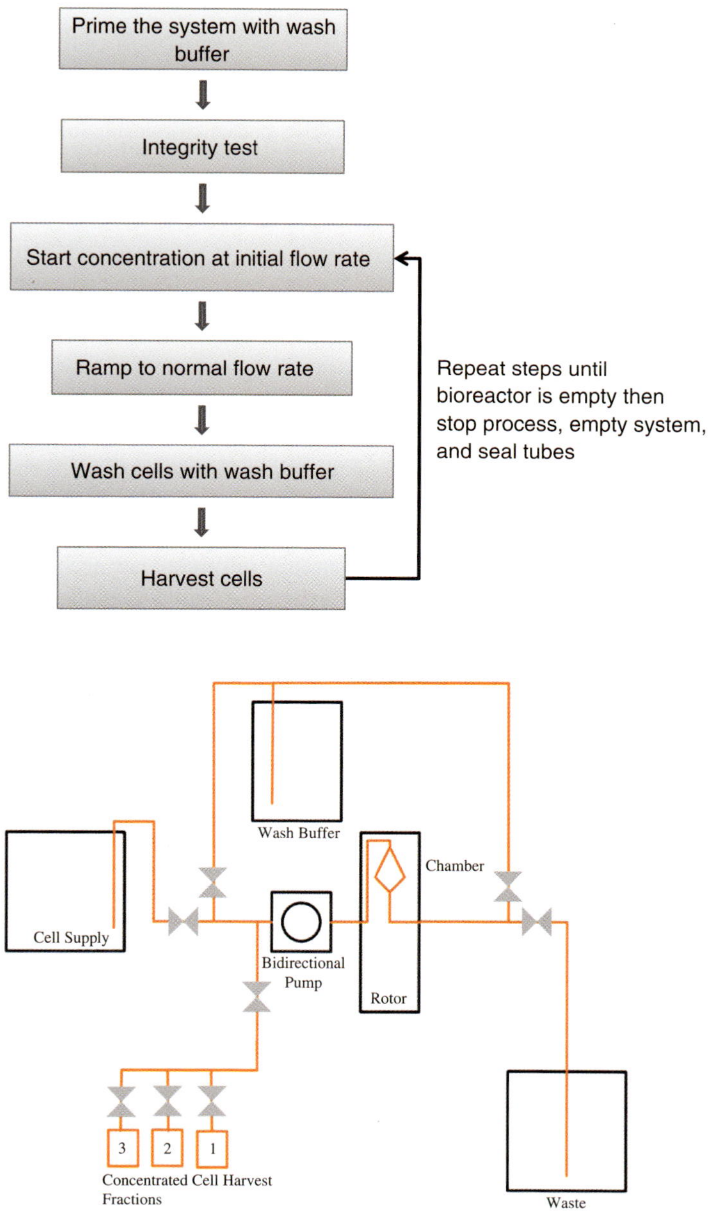

Figure 15.12 Automated concentration, media replacement, and harvest process.

	Volume (ml)	Viable Count/ml	Total Viable Cells	% Recovery	Viability	Size (uM)	Total Cells	% Recovery
Original Cells, Preprocessing	160	1.60E+07	2.50E+09		98.8	17	2.50E+09	
Control Cells	3.5	9.80E+07	3.40E+08		97.2	17	3.50E+08	
kSep® Concentrate 1	22	9.60E+07	2.10E+09	84.60%	96.4	16	2.20E+09	86.70%
kSep® Concentrate 2	25	1.60E+07	4.00E+08	16.00%	97.8	16	4.10E+08	16.20%
kSep® Total			**2.50E+09**	**100.00%**	**97.1**	**16**	**2.57E+09**	**102.99%**

Figure 15.13 Viability and recovery of cells after concentration, media replacement, and harvest process.

This process was successful with open centrifugation but not with TFF. The process required >90 million cells ml^{-1} at the end of the run with no change in viability. A kSep system was set-up as shown in Figure 15.12.

The system was primed with prime buffer and trypsinized Vero cells were pumped into the system and then washed with wash buffer. At the end of the wash, the flow was reversed to recover the cells at high density. Two fractions were recovered. The first was used for further processing and the second was used for mass balance and was discarded. Transfections were performed on the cells processed through kSep and control cells that were processed using a research process with manual open centrifugation and multiple washings. The results show that highly concentrated cells were recovered without any loss in recovery or viability (Figure 15.13).

Additionally, the viral titer was similar to the research process after transfection (Figure 15.14).

Another study by Lonza required concentration and thorough washing of cells for a cell therapy process. Figure 15.15 shows that high concentration of process contaminating residues (BSA) can be removed to very low levels (limited by assay detection sensitivity) by a couple of minutes of wash cycle.

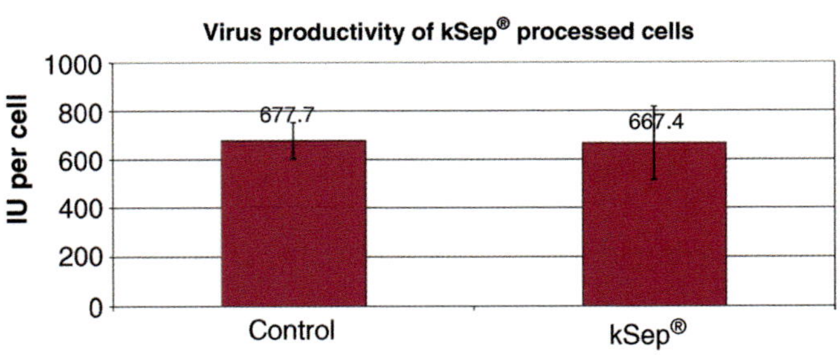

Figure 15.14 Virus productivity comparison of research process with scalable kSep process.

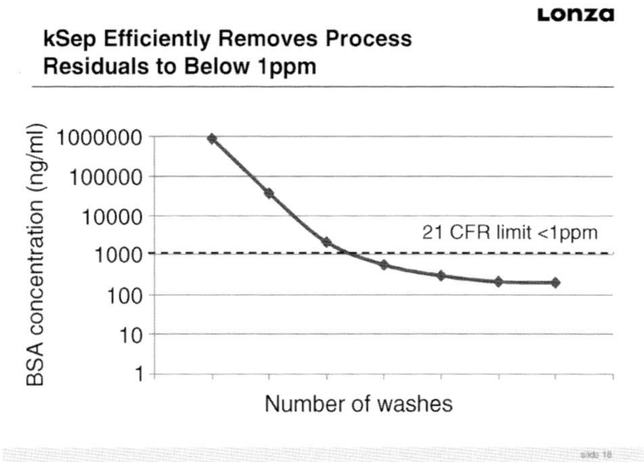

Figure 15.15 Efficient washing by kSep. Courtesy of Jon Rowley, Lonza.

15.11 Continuous Harvest Clarification

Several harvest clarification (Figure 15.16) studies using kSep systems have been performed for antibody production.

In some of these studies users performed continuous harvest clarification using kSep400 over a prolonged period (around 24 h) to process large amounts of material. Continuous clarification allows small equipment footprint and enhanced depth filtration capacity. Typical results show that independent of the

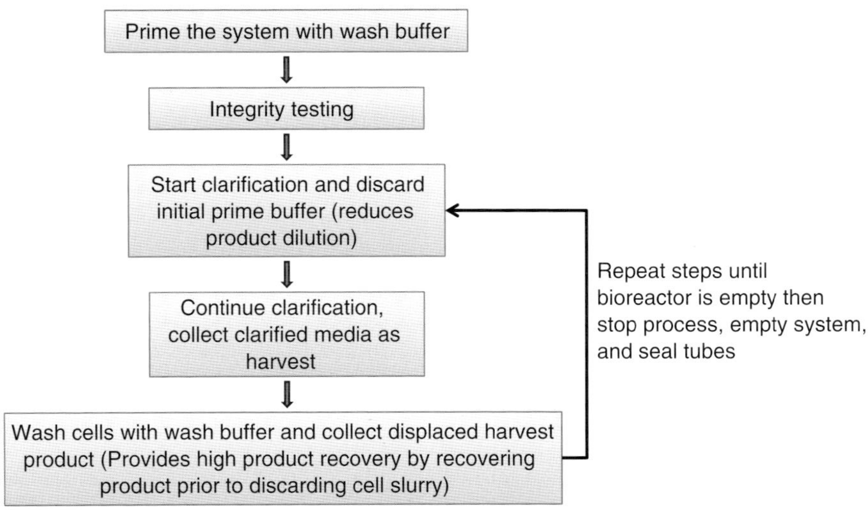

Figure 15.16 Automated harvest clarification process.

kSep Development Experiments

➢ Reliable cycling, consistent clarification (8 cycles shown)

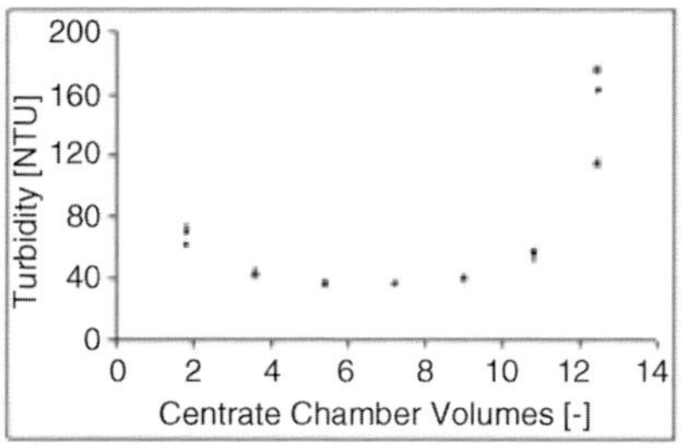

Parameter	kSep Performance	Disc-Stack Historical Performance
Clarification Efficiency	> 90%	> 95%
mAb Yield	> 99%	93–95%
DF Performance Post-CE	400l/m², 220 LMH < 20 psi	500l/m², 150 LMH, < 20 psi
Decrease in Viability	< 3% over processing time	No data available

➢ Ability Acceptable clarification shown with batch variations

- 3 CHO programs:
- Cell densities: 8–14e6 cells/ml
- Fermentation: fed-batch, SUB, Wave
- Harvest + up to 3 days (75–95%)

MERCK

Courtesy of Mark Brower, Merck, Rahway, NJ: Presented at BMD Summit in San Diego, September, 2011

Figure 15.17 Harvest clarification reliability and recovery. Courtesy of Mark Brower, Merck.

cell density (1–30 million cells ml^{-1}), >95% product can be recovered using the kSep systems [5,8]. Although at high cell densities the postclarification turbidity maybe high (300–500NTU) with kSep, the depth filter capacity is still excellent (>400 l/m^2) [5]. The results are consistent with particle sizing studies showing that kSep is efficient in removing large particles but not smaller particles that create higher turbidity but do not clog the depth filters easily.

In one specific example (Figure 15.17), Merck showed that the continuous harvest clarification process was robust with deliberate batch variations (different cell lines, cell densities, bioreactor type, and harvest days). In addition, within a batch, the cycling was reliable and clarification was consistent. The results were comparable to traditional disc-stack data with low cell densities. One of the key differentiating data is 100% product recovery with kSep centrifugation due to its ability to recover trapped product from the interstitial space between cells.

15.12 Separation of Cells from Microcarriers

Many cell therapy and vaccine processes use anchorage-dependent cells (e.g., MSCs, Vero) grown on microcarriers. Seed train propagation, harvest, and other processes require trypsinization of cells followed by separation of cells from the microcarriers. We have established proof-of-concept by mixing CHO cells with Cytodex microcarriers and then separating them using a kSep system. Our results show fast separation without any loss in viability or number of cells.

15.13 Summary

kSep is an innovative low-shear and single-use centrifugation technology that addresses challenging process requirements of continuous processing, high cell density cultures, cell therapy and vaccine manufacturing, and blood processing.

References

1 Abraham, S., Bingham, N., Green, K., and Kenworthy, J. (2003) Strategies for improving mammalian cell clarification. *Abstr. Pap. Am. Chem. Soc.*, **225**, 119-BIOT.

2 Liu, H.F., Ma, J., Winter, C., and Bayer, R. (2010) Recovery and purification process development for monoclonal antibody production. *mAbs*, **2** (5), 480–499.

3 Dick, L.W., Qiu, D., Mahon, D., Adamo, M., and Cheng, K.-C. (2008) C-terminal lysine variants in fully human monoclonal antibodies: investigation of test methods and possible causes. *Biotechnol. Bioeng.*, **100**, 1132–1143.

4 Yigzaw, Y., Piper, R., Tran, M., and Shukla, A.A. (2006) Exploitation of the adsorptive properties of depth filters for host cell protein removal during monoclonal antibody purification. *Biotechnol. Prog.*, **22**, 288–296.

5 Westoby, M. and Elouafiq, S. (2013) Evaluation of a single use fluidized bed centrifuge for cell culture clarification. Presented at ACS 2013, Pub#169.

6 Li, F., Vijayasankaran, N., Shen, A.Y., Kiss, R., and Amanullah, A. (2010) Cell culture processes for monoclonal antibody production. *mAbs.*, **2** (5), 466–479.

7 Legrand, C., Bour, J.M., Jacob, C., Capiaumont, J., Martial, A., Marc, A., Wudtke, M., Kretzmer, G., Demangel, C., Duval, D., and Hache, J. (1992) Lactate dehydrogenase (LDH) activity of the number of dead cells in the medium of cultured eukaryotic cells as marker. *J. Biotechnol.*, **25**, 231–243.

8 Ko, H. and Bhatia, R. (2012) Evaluation of single-use fluidized bed centrifuge system for mammalian cell harvesting. *BioPharm Int.*, **25** (11), 34–40.

16
The Review of Flexible Production Platforms for the Future

Maik W. Jornitz

16.1
Introduction

Presently, the need for a paradigm shift in the facility design and utilization of biopharmaceutical production sites has been stated in multiple papers and at conferences [1–4]. The reasons for such facility layout changes and use efficiencies are manifold; for example, newly evolving drug developments, changes in process technologies, transformation of the treatment or patient base, or purely for economical reason, which focus on capacity utilization and process flexibilities. Another motivation is the shift to continuous processing. Ultimately, there is a change process happening, a shift from large area and product-dedicated brick and mortar facilities to more agile and smaller facilities. The trend also shows that multiple facilities in different regions will be required in the future. Through that new mandate by the industry comes the promise of delivery of the expected, in the form of "flexible facilities," "modular facilities," "manufacturing on demand," or "continuous manufacturing."

Parts of the new facilities or the need of such is also a shift in the process equipment and unit operations. Single-use technology pushed rapidly into the industry over the last 10 years, though not too long ago single-use equipment components within the pharmaceutical and biopharmaceutical industry were considered novel, pioneering, and viewed with skepticism. Nowadays, single-use equipment utilization is widespread and is an integral part in upstream and downstream processing. The focus of single-use technology utilization is furthermore shifting from very much biopharmaceutical reformed to an acceptance also within the small-molecule industry. Anywhere where the need for containment is prevalent, protection of the product handled inside a process, but also guarding the outside environment, single-use technology seems to be the technology of choice. This rapidly surfacing, inventive power between end users and vendors has probably also been unique. The urge to gain flexibility, reduce processing costs, elevate the ease-of-use, and moreover create containment options opened the dialog between the industry and its suppliers [5]. Although, the containment reliance in single-use technology has been so extensive that some want

Continuous Processing in Pharmaceutical Manufacturing, First Edition. Edited by Ganapathy Subramanian.

to change the cleanroom segregation layout and call for ballroom cleanroom designs in which the entire process is running. This over-reliance on the containment reliability of single-use technology is probably haphazardous and does not fit all purposes. The criticality of segregation should not be dismissed, as single-use technology still shows material weakness and the human factor also poses a risk of failure.

16.2 Today's Processing Technology Advances

Today's single-use technology product portfolio is immense, in instances still immature with requirements of improvement. Figure 16.1 shows the current status and the industry penetration trend describing the implementation speed and experience level. It is obvious that the need to enable an entire single-use process caused a gap analysis of what is available and what is missing [6]. This gap analysis instigated the development of the absent parts.

16.2.1 Single-Use Liquid Hold and Mixing Bags

Besides filter Capsules, single-use bags were the pioneer in converting drug manufacturers from glass carboys and stainless steel tanks to polymeric flexible, disposable storage systems. The replacement of glass carboys and stainless steel vessels enabled the processes to utilize less water-for-injection and eliminated a large amount of heat sterilization time and energy. Set-up times for single-use systems can be minutes instead of an entire shift for a stainless steel hold vessel. Due to volume requirements, single-use bags are available in two- and three-

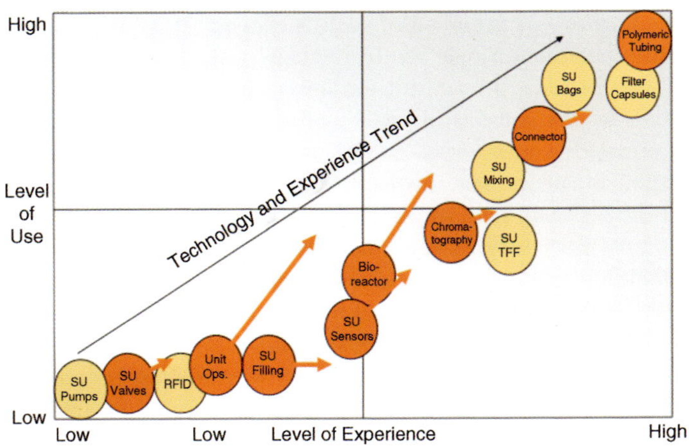

Figure 16.1 Single-use components existent, immature, and trends (dark orange circles represent trend technologies).

dimensional designs, whereby the trend goes to a larger three-dimensional volume portfolio. Bags are used in a multitude of applications, from low criticality applications like buffer and media mixing and storage to very critical applications for instance bulk drug substances storage or shipping containment. Other applications are bulk harvest, product pooling, fraction collection, bulk intermediate hold, virus inactivation, and controlled freeze/thaw. Low-volume bags start from 5 ml and scale up to 5 l. Medium volume bags range from 5 l to 50 l, and the largest volumes can end up at 1000 l. Medium- and large-volume hold and mixing bags are supported by either a stainless steel or polymeric outer shells, called totes, to create mechanical stability and mobility. Smaller volumes are usually stored in trays.

Single-use bags can be utilized as a single-bag system connected to the filtrate side of a membrane filter [7], which would represent the most simplistic unit operation. However, a larger share of single-use bags usage happens to be assemblies of several equipment components, that is, multiple small volume bags are interconnected to portion larger volumes on the upstream side. This permits end users to split larger volumes into smaller volumes, for example, to feed cell culture media into bioreactor systems or to be used for buffer wash and elute. A very common system configuration would be a larger-volume single-use mixing system, which is connected to a filter and small-volume bag manifold, which stores the filtrate. These systems already represent a unit operation within a biopharmaceutical process. The individual filled bags of the manifold are then disconnected from the tubing set by tube sealers or disconnectors.

The closed system configuration, from large bag through the filter to the smaller bag assembly, helps to avert potential contamination (Figure 16.2). Additionally, the fluid hold volume equipment does not need to be cleaned, as it is used once and discarded. Cleaning validation has been a prevalent citing in regulatory filings. Improper cleaning can cause cross-contamination or additives to the product due to cleaning agent residues. These possibilities of failure are averted due to single-use bag systems.

Another advantage of single-use bag systems is the small footprint need and inventory space savings. Carboys, glass or polymeric, and stainless steel tanks

Figure 16.2 Large volume to small volume transfer (courtesy Sartorius Stedim, Inc.).

use up a well-needed amount of valuable floor space. Bags are folded, stored flat, and stackable. Once needed the bags are unpacked, connected, and unfold, then filled. Large-volume three-dimensional bags, above 50 l volumes, are placed in totes or movable, stackable pallet tank systems. The pallet tank systems design avoids friction, pressure points, or bag crimping, which could damage the bag or weaken the polymeric layer. It also keeps the single-use bag in a fixed position, especially during transport. Movable pallet tanks also enable the end user to measure the volume within the bag, the withdraw or fill rate, by positioning the pallet tank with bag onto a platform scale or have load cells incorporated in the pallet tank system. Similar volume measurements can also be used for single-use bioreactors.

The critical key performance parameter of single-use bags is the polymeric film, besides the welds. The polymeric film has multiple key criteria to fulfill. The contact layer requires being compliant with the usual pharmacopeial standards in regard to particulate shedding and leachable levels [8,9]. Single-use technology suppliers can attest for the quality of their contact layers by submitting qualification reports, which show the particulate and leachable levels, as well as the leachable identities. Most vendors use similar contact layer polymers, mainly ethylene-vinyl acetate (EVA) or polyester (PE). Another important quality factor is the need for gamma irradiation stability of the film. Single-use bags are preassembled and sterilized by the supplier and afterward gamma-irradiated at a dose of up to 50 kiloGray (kGy). It has to be determined how the polymeric film reacts, whether there might be an elevated particulate or leachable release or the mechanical stability is compromised [10]. Short-and long-term (accelerated) stability studies with the irradiated devices have to be performed to establish the shelf-life duration of an irradiated device. Irradiation can lower the mechanical stability and chemical compatibility, and once irradiated the degradation effects do not stop. To determine the effects of gamma irradiation and the stability of the polymer used, manufacturers subject irradiated devices through a significant regime of qualification tests before the device is introduced to the industry. The qualification tests performed by the vendor can be utilized as guidance by the end user, but shall not diminish the need for process validation.

Qualification tests are performed under standard laboratory settings with solutions like water, water/solvent, or other pH-corrected fluids. The data of these tests are available from the manufacturer and can be used as assistance. Since the tests listed are qualification tests, the data are commonly name qualification data and should not be confused with process validation data. Process validation is performed under the process conditions of the end user and not standard settings experienced at the vendor level. Process validation studies can be supported by the services of the vendor, but are run under the process and operating conditions of the end user. Process validation studies would, for example, utilize a model solvent and simulate the process operating parameters within the particular application. Leachable testing with product cannot always be achieved since the product chromatographic profile would cover any potential leachable profile. For this reason, model solvents are often used, which are comparable to the base solvent used within the product stream. End users and suppliers work together at specifying the expected product performance for a given application and agree on the level of validation work to be performed and expected results. This joined validation work, though, can only be done when the supplier has an in-depth understanding of current regulatory and good manufacturing practice (GMP) requirements. End users expect appropriate quality systems being in place at the supplier's side to assure consistent product quality and raw material oversight. Vendors require controlling the raw material supplies to them and defining specification for such material, as well as in-process controls. The end user has to be able to rely on the vendor's quality specification and determinations.

The process validation requests are even more critical when bulk drug substances are stored in single-use bags, as the product stored is extremely valuable. The mechanical stability, cleanliness, sterility, and purity of the bag require meeting industry standards. Not only are the films and final assemblies scrutinized, but also the resulting quality documentation and batch records. To achieve required standards, like mechanical stability, oxygen barrier, and low leachable levels, bag manufacturers utilize multiple layers of different polymers to provide a robust film structure with low gas permeability and high chemical resistance. The polymeric layer, which comes in contact with the fluid, has to comply with usual pharmacopoeias [8,9] and requires providing a clean and inert contact layer. The contact layer alone may not have the mechanical resistance or air barrier properties. Therefore, a mix of other polymeric layers are utilized and laminated, which manifest the so-called backbone of the entire bag film. The backbone polymers can change depending on the application and specific needs of the application.

Mixing processes are one of the most commonly performed activities within biopharmaceutical processes to solute and mix solid/liquid, liquid/liquid, and solid/liquid/gas systems. Mixing or agitation process activities are also the most critical part of a bioreactor and fermentation system. A broad variety of mixing technologies are available, such as recirculation of liquids by peristaltic pumps, agitation via vibro-, wave-, or rocking mixing, magnetic impellers, stirrer bars, paddle or levitation mixer. An agitation plate with different orifices moves rapidly up and down performing vibro-mixing. It oscillates rapidly within the fluid and causes vortexes around the agitation plate and the orifices. The wave or rocking motion mixing utilizes a rocking device, which creates a wave motion within the fluid container. This wave motion again creates swirls and vortexes, which mix the fluid and agitate gas into the fluid. Levitating mixing is an advancement of magnetic mixing and uses the superconductivity to drive the mixer without touching the inner or outer side of the mixing bag and allows smooth mixing operations without any friction or shear stress. The benefit of noncontact stirring is the lack of friction and therefore particle release or potential weakening of the bag film.

Mixing systems require being scalable from smaller volumes to process volumes. Common working volumes found for mixing bags ranges from 20 to 3,000 l. Moreover, speed of mixing is essential to avoid process downtimes. The mixing speed though should never jeopardize the uniformity of the mixing. It is essential that the mixing process be validated to gain evidence of the total uniformity of the solution. This also means that sensor technology for single-use bag systems are of importance. There are single-use sensors available, mainly optical or potentiometric, which help determine the blend or mixing uniformity. If the mixing process is not efficient, the risk of performance problems of the next processing step is elevated. For example, in bioreactor applications, these sensors require to control dissolved oxygen and the pH level to gain an optimal expression rate. Single-use mixing systems can be found in the preparation of buffers and media, agitating of cell cultures in bioreactors, pH adjustment, virus inactivation, protein folding, and product compounding for final formulation purposes. The benefits of single-use mixing are the minimized set-up time, multiproduct mixing, and avoidance of cleaning and the inherent risk of cross-contamination due to insufficient cleaning. However, single-use mixing systems consist of a single-use bag, mixing device, and the associated tubing, sensors, filters, and connectors. All these components require to be checked for leachables, chemical compatibility, mechanical stability, and particulates. It has to be evaluated whether the mixing system withstands the process conditions. As for disposable bags, single-use mixing systems are commonly installed in stainless steel or polymeric protective shells or containers, some of these can be double-walled heat exchangers to maintain constant temperature profiles. Drive units actuating the agitation system are commonly placed below or above the mixing unit and are controlled in regard to revolutions per minute (rpm) or torque. The mixing hardware (drive unit, instruments, and probes) all are subject to installation qualification (IQ), operating qualification (OQ), and performance qualification (PQ) procedures to verify that the system is properly installed and operates according to user requirement specification (URS). In addition to typical equipment qualification steps, a major part of mixer qualification is the PQ carried out with the actual solution to be mixed or homogenized under process conditions. The PQ is performed under specified production conditions and will establish the mixing process parameters, such as mixing time, temperature, and rpm required, depending on the mixing application. Liquid/liquid or liquid/solid mixing require different process parameters and need to be properly established to make sure a uniform mix is achieved. When in-line monitoring is applied, the PQ will set limits for pH or conductivity to obtain reproducibility of the mixing process. Generally, three consecutive successful PQ runs must be achieved.

16.2.2
Filtration and Purification Technologies

As mentioned in Section 16.1, disposable encapsulated filters were the first single-use technology items used. These filter devices have been used for the last

30 years and are available in different sizes with different connectors and designs. A few years ago, filter Capsules were available within a narrow range of surface areas; they now range from laboratory-scale test filters with a filtration area of 150 cm^2 to process-scale filter devices of 3 m^2. The filtration area range creates the opportunity of filter optimization with pleated devices and appropriate scalability. The polymeric housing design reflects the traditional stainless steel housing formats and includes in-line or T-style designs. Both styles have their use, depending on the application. In some instances, these Capsule filters are interconnected to a serial filtration setup or, if larger filtration areas are needed, to a parallel assembly with a multitude of Capsules. However, the polymeric adapters are not as robust as the stainless steel counterparts, and larger encapsulated filter types require to be supported appropriately to avoid connector damage. The connector types available for encapsulated filters are manifold and range from sanitary flange to hose barb, to a variety of threaded connection categories. These connections can also be varied, meaning one can gain access to a Capsule filter with a sanitary flange inlet and hose barb outlet. The filter types are again various as the applications and requirements on the filters are. Most commonly, one finds encapsulated filters as membrane liquid filters, though the membrane requires being gamma irradiation stable, since these filters are connected to single-use bag systems and gamma irradiated. In a few instances the gamma irradiation is also used to deliver a sterilized filter Capsule. Some filter membranes or prefilter materials cannot be sterilized by gamma irradiation; these encapsulated filters are sterilized by others means, like autoclaving. In any case, the sterilization cycle and the compatibility with it require being qualified. First of all, most filter manufacturers analyze the extractable release of their filters after sterilization and flush the filters within their production processes, which result in the use of filters without or limited rinse requirement. Limited rinse volume needs, the connectivity of filter capsules, and the lack of filter assembly reduces the set-up time within the production process greatly. The production process turnaround is very much shortened and capacity utilization increased. The filter does not need to be installed into a stainless steel housing, with the potential risk of flawed installation or damage to the sealing O-ring or adapter system. Also, the filter units are often connected to tubing and aseptic connections, which reduce the possibility of filtrate contamination. The filter, tubing, and connection represent a containment solution, which can be connected to a mixing bag on the upstream side and a hold bag manifold on the filtrate side. When the Capsule filters are connected to a long tubing and are not gamma irradiated, but autoclaved, the sterilization efficiency within the tubing and Capsule filter has to be verified. Long tubing connections can entrap air, which would result in possible sterilization inefficiencies. Stainless steel housings with sterilizing grade filter are sterilized by autoclaving and aseptically connected. However, this connection type is less secure than the available single-use connection systems. Stainless steel filter housing systems have also a multitude of risk factors, more than encapsulated filters, beginning with the connection being often a sanitary flange connection with gaskets keeping the connection

sealed. When the system is subjected to temperature variations, for example, during steam sterilization, the polymeric materials and stainless steel will expand with different rates, which can cause the risk of leaks. Encapsulated filters with sanitary flange are polymeric, that is, the materials behave similarly. The only item that requires careful review when polymeric sanitary flanges are used is the stainless clamp. If it is tightened too much it can also warp the polymeric sanitary flange. The clamp should not be tightened too much to avoid such damage. Most single-use, gamma-irradiated Capsule assemblies utilize aseptic connectors, which elevate the connection safety. Stainless steel filter housings are clamped together with an O-ring or gasket between the housing base and the housing bell. This O-ring or gasket is another weakness and potential for failure, as is the filter cartridge adapter/housing recess connection. Here again, the O-ring or gasket seals are used, which once again can be a risk due to mishandling or temperature influences. Stainless steel filter housing systems have been used for many years successfully. Nevertheless, encapsulated filter elements avoid the O-ring seal between the base and cartridge adapter, and the housing bell and baseplate, as these two connections are welded together. Risk mitigation is improved with encapsulated filters. In addition, since the filter devices are encapsulated in a polymeric housing, the end user will not come in contact with the spent filter. When a filter is exchanged from a stainless steel filter housing, the end user needs to touch the upstream side of the filter, the side with the contaminants on it. Potentially, opening a filter housing may create a burst of aerosol of contaminants, which can be harmful to the person handling the filtration system. With an encapsulated filter device, the end user does not come in contact with neither the filtered product, which could be cytotoxic or of elevated potency, or the separated contaminants on the upstream side of the filter. The filter end user protection is greatly enhanced.

Disposable filter capsules are often regarded as operating cost intensive devices, as the filter is exchanged after each use. However, sterilizing grade filters require to be exchanged after every use, in most applications. From a consumable cost perspective, there would be no, or very limited, disadvantage to switching to encapsulated filters. Moreover, a filter element/stainless steel housing combination requires the inclusion of the necessary cleaning and sterilization costs into the total cost. The cleaning cost and the filter system downtime are more costly than the slightly higher price of a capsule filter. Capital expenses necessary for the purchase of stainless steel housings and depreciation costs are avoided. Cleaning validation, which needs to be performed with fixed equipment like filter housings, would be greatly reduced or eliminated. On top of costs for stainless steel filter housing use comes the energy costs for the sterilization process, spare parts, inventory space, and cleaning chemicals. Overall when one compares the total costs, one realizes that single-use encapsulated filters are actually very economic in comparison to filter housings, most of all with a lower risk probability.

As with all components within a biopharmaceutical process, the use of capsule filters depends on the requirements of the end user, often driven by the application. The end user needs to have a detailed understanding of all process parameters to be able to predefine the needs of particular single-use assembly designs or robustness. Since there is no one-fits-all solution, but rather an optimal solution to every application, in-depth knowledge will support to determine the appropriate filter equipment or system. Parameters that are critical for a filter choice are flow rate, pressure/temperature conditions, filter pore size or retention requirements, fluid volumes, filter size, which is determined by filterability trials, fluid properties to judge chemical compatibility and unspecific adsorption importance, filter and/or bag integrity test methods, and the fluid bioburden. All these factors are evaluated during the process validation of the filter or the filter/bag/tube assembly.

Sterilizing-grade filters are specified by the bacteria challenge tests with *Brevundimonas diminuta*, in qualification tests performed at standard conditions and with defined solutions [11]. Additional qualification tests are performed, for example, the compatibility with gamma irradiation or thermal and mechanical stability. The qualification tests though are performed under standard conditions in the manufacturer's labs and shall not be confused with process validation. Filter process validation requirement, requested by regulatory authorities, differ from the qualification tests as evidence has to be produced that the sterilizing-grade filter is working with the actual product under process conditions [12]. This means that bacteria challenge tests have to be performed under or as close to the process operating parameters with the actual drug product or a placebo, if the actual drug product cannot be used. In instances, challenge tests might be performed with the native bioburden, if different or known to be smaller than *B. diminuta*, which is the ASTM 838-05 standard challenge organism. When the drug product or process parameters would induce a mortality rate of the organism, the fluid or process parameters can be modified, though the reason has to be given why. These reasons are determined by viability tests, which show the challenge organism behavior within the fluid under the conditions defined. Any product bacteria challenge test has to be preceded by viability tests. If not done so the product bacteria challenge test result is ineffectual. In the viability test, the organism is inoculated in the product to be filtered at a certain bioburden level. At specified times the log value of the bioburden level is checked to determine whether the bioburden is reduced due to the fluid properties. If so, different bacteria challenge test modes become applicable. For example, one method would be to utilize a high-volume bioburden challenge test, done when the mortality rate is subtle or low, bearing in mind that the end challenge level should reach $10^7/cm^2$. If the mortality rate is too high, due to specific product components, the toxic substance is either removed or product properties are changed, for example the pH. This type of challenge fluid is called a placebo. Another methodology utilized circulates the fluid product through the filter at the defined process conditions as long as the actual processing time set by the filter user. Afterward the filter is flushed extensively with water or buffer and the challenge test is performed.

The base for the requirement of a product bacteria challenge test is threefold. First of all, the influence of the product and process parameters on the microorganism has to be determined. There may be cases of either shrinkage of organisms due to a higher ionic strength of the product or prolonged filtration times. In other cases the fluid or processing time could result in organism proliferation. It has to be determined whether this proliferation causes microorganism penetration or fouling of the filter. Second, the filter's chemical and mechanical compatibility with the product and the process parameters has to be tested. The filter should not show any sign of degradation due to the product contact. Chemical degradation would elevate leachable and particulate levels, if not destroy the filter. Mechanical and thermal stability requires to be evaluated to see that the filter withstands, for instance, pressure pulses, temperature spikes, or elevated viscosity settings. Third, there are two separation mechanisms prevalent in liquid filtration: (i) sieve retention and (ii) retention by adsorption or adsorptive sequestration. In sieve retention the biggest pore within the membrane structure retains the smallest particle or organism. The contaminant will be retained no matter what the process parameters are. This represents the ideal retention scenario. However, retention by adsorptive sequestration is a mechanism that is very customary with adsorptive membrane polymers and should not be underestimated. Adsorptive capture depends on the membrane polymer, surface charges, filtration process, and fluid conditions. Contaminants smaller than the actual pore size penetrate the membrane matrix and may be retained by adsorptive attachment to membrane or prefilter matrix. This effect is enhanced using highly adsorptive filter materials, for example, glass fiber as a prefilter or polyamide as a membrane material [13,14]. Yet certain fluid properties and process settings can minimize the adsorptive effect, which could mean penetration of organisms. Surfactants lower the adsorptive properties of a membrane and the retentivity of these filters goes down. Whether the fluid has such properties or process parameters that cause a retention influence has to be evaluated in specific product bacteria challenge tests.

Bacteria challenge testing is only one process validation activity item. Other tests, for example, the determination of the release of leachable substances or particulates have to be performed. Extractable measurements and the resulting data, established during the qualification process, are available from filter manufacturers for specific filters. These qualification tests though represent the worst-case conditions and are limited to standard fluids, mainly water or ethanol. For process validation purposes, explicit leachable tests have to be performed. These tests are commonly done only with the solvent or diluent used, but not with the actual drug product, as the drug product usually covers any leachable profile. Generally, the validation services of the filter manufacturers can support these efforts. Nowadays, sophisticated separation and detection methodologies, such as gas chromatography-mass spectrometry (GC-MS), Fourier transform infrared (FTIR), and reversed-phase high-performance liquid chromatography (RP-HPLC), are used. These methodologies are required due to the fact that the individual components possibly released from the filter have to be identified and quantified. Elaborated studies, performed by filter manufacturers showed that there is neither a release of high quantities of extractables (the range is ppb to max. ppm per 10 in. element) nor have toxic substances been found [15]. Particulates are critical in sterile filtration, specifically of injectables and the USP (United States Pharmacopeia) [8] and BP (British Pharmacopeia) [16] define limits of particulate level contaminations for defined particle sizes. These limits have to be met by sterilizing-grade filters. Filters are frequently tested as release control within the manufacturer's processes, evaluating the filtrate with laser particle counters. Furthermore, within specific applications the loss of yield or product components due to unspecific adsorption requires to be determined. Since encapsulated filters have a higher amount of polymeric material, unspecific adsorption could be of eminent interest. For example preservatives, like benzalkoniumchloride or chlorhexadine, can be adsorbed by filter membrane polymers like polyamide [17], and the adsorptive sites need to be saturated before the fluid can be processed. Preservative loss, for example in ophthalmics, can be detrimental due to long-term use of such solutions. Equally problematic would be the adsorption of targeted proteins within a biological solution. The value loss due to target protein adsorption on membrane filters can be substantial and requires being determined [18]. To optimize the yield within an application, adsorption trials have to be performed to find the optimal membrane material and filter construction. In some vaccine applications the yield can also be lost due to blockage of the membrane, even a 50% blockage of a filter results in lower filtrate yields. Filterability trials need to be performed to determine at what blockage level does the yield drop, which will become the set-point of scaling the effective filtration area needs. The process validation steps vary as the single-use devices have different purposes. Sterilizing-grade filters have to undergo a product bacteria challenge test under end user's process conditions. Product hold bags or mixing bags do not have to undergo bacteria challenge tests, but possibly bacteria ingress tests. Both filter and bags systems require to be tested for leachability. As mentioned, the end user should take advantage of the vendor's services, which is supported by the qualification documentation and process validation. Once process validation has been completed, the most important next activity is training. The process is only as good as the end user training and any process validation activity can be detrimentally influenced when the end user is not properly trained.

Besides microfiltration steps in various stages of the drug manufacturing process, there are highly important separation and purification steps in the downstream or purification process. Still, most purification steps, like cross-flow or tangential flow filtration, as well as chromatographic process steps are reusable and require intricate cleaning. Such cleaning steps require appropriate validation to ensure contaminants and cleaning agents are removed. It has ben experienced that insufficient cleaning can lead to biofilm formation or at least a potential threat of elevated endotoxin levels downstream of the processing step. These threats caused the design of single-use process steps within the purification processes, for example for tangential-flow ultra/diafiltration (UF/DF) steps, and,

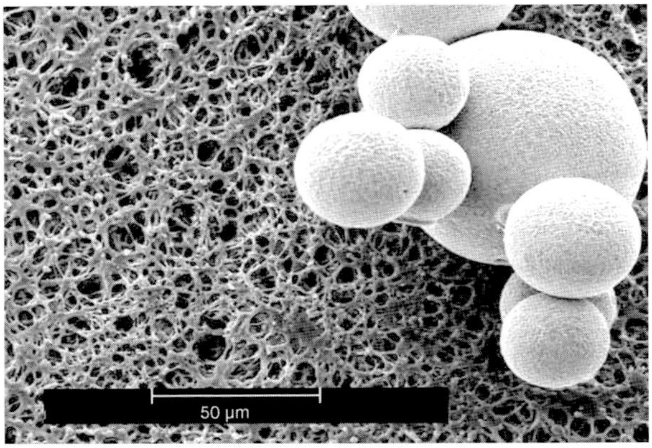

Figure 16.3 Membrane adsorber membrane matrix versus the classical chromatography bead (courtesy of Sartorius Stedim).

although limited, capturing and polishing chromatography operations. The most promising single-use chromatographic technologies are membrane chromatography devices, which prove to be an economical alternative to accustomed column/bead-based operations [19,20]. Surface-modified, microporous membrane structures with pore sizes ranging from 0.8 to 3 μm drastically reduce diffusion-related mass transfer effects (Figure 16.3). The open pore structure enables purification of large biomolecules (capturing) or the adsorptive removal of contaminants, such as host cell protein (HCP), DNA, endotoxin, and viruses in flow-through mode (polishing).

Another advantage of the membrane structure is the high flow rate at which the membrane chromatographic device can work at. This will reduce the size needed to accomplish the same task a classical column device performs. The smaller size of the membrane chromatography device does not only reduce buffer volume needs, but also high capital investment costs. The benefits of single-use versus the classical chromatography systems can be best viewed in cost models, which show the investment and running costs needed for the different technologies [21]. Membrane adsorbers should not only be viewed from the cost perspective but also from the containment and safety benefit. These chromatographic devices are available as encapsulate device, similar to the membrane filter devices described. Once again the benefits are obvious, the end user will be protected, but most of all any potential contamination due to improper cleaning or installation is avoided. The development of membrane chromatography devices has not stopped nor slowed down. New formats of membrane chromatography include disposable direct-capture devices allowing for processing of an unclarified (without depth filtration step) fermentor offload. Other disposable chromatography systems are classical, prepacked, presanitized columns. These units contain classical chromatography resins, but the end user benefit is that the columns just need to be connected to the fluid stream, without packing or testing the column. The sanitization agents used for such columns are either sodium hydroxide or solvents. It is of significance to determine whether all microorganisms have been removed to avoid biofilm formation. Often one experiences a column protecting microfilters in front of the chromatography step to assure a low or no bioburden.

Another step within the purification process is viral clearance. Combined single-use mixing bag, filter, and bag assemblies are used for pH titration and low-pH hold viral inactivation. The chromatography column eluate is titrated down to a low pH by adding acid through a filter to the eluate bag. The solution is then transferred via peristaltic pump to a second bag for low pH hold for viral inactivation and pH readjustment after the hold period, commonly 1 h. This viral inactivation process is nowadays available as single-use unit operation, which includes mixing, hold and feed stream bags, and filtration and tubing sets, all preconfigured and gamma sterilized. Another single-use viral inactivation technology is UV-C ray inactivation. The process fluid is swirled within the single-use fluid path by Dean vortices to ensure that the entire fluid volume is subjected to 254 nm irradiation. The benefit of the UV-C system is the precise control of the irradiation dose per fluid volume, since UV-C has a potential effect on the target protein; therefore, appropriate process validation has to evaluate these potentially detrimental effects. Single-use virus filtration capsules with retention ratings of 50 and 20 nm, have been developed and used for many years to remove viruses. Similar to sterilizing grade filters, virus filters are available in a variety of capsule sizes. To protect the viral filter from premature fouling, a multitude of different prefilter combinations are available, though most often 0.1 μm membrane filters are used. These viral filtration single-use systems include the viral prefilter, viral filter, collection bag, and all tubing.

Single-use concepts in tangential-flow filtration (TFF) or cross-flow applications have recently become very popular in vaccine manufacturing and are currently being evaluated in monoclonal antibody production. Ultra/diafiltration steps for buffer exchange and concentration of process intermediates are essential. Cleaning of such membrane structures is tedious and requires detailed cleaning validation. It has to be ensured that product and cleaning agent residues are removed from the ultrafilter membrane matrix. That structure is intricate and it is quite a task to clean the membrane matrix (Figure 16.4). Therefore, single-use TFF cassettes and devices have been deployed. These TFF systems with entirely disposable fluid paths are standard or customizable depending on batch size, concentration factor, and required processing time.

16.2.3 Product and Component Transfer

Aseptic transfer systems have been developed for the nuclear industry in the 1960s to introduce or extract components from rigid-walled isolators. Pharmaceutical use isolator technology was introduced in the mid-1990s and

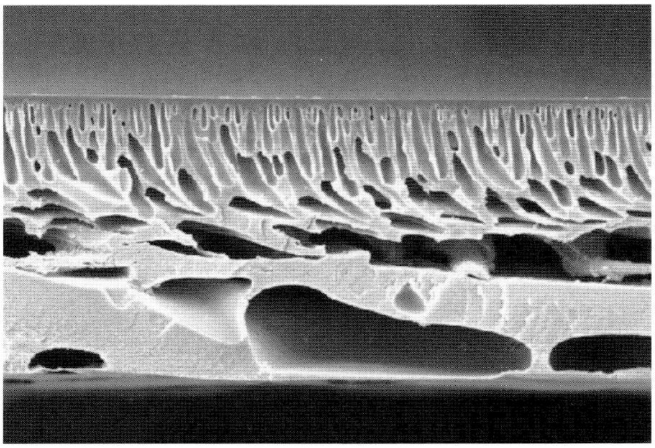

Figure 16.4 Ultrafiltration membrane structure (courtesy of Sartorius Stedim).

adopted the transfer port experiences from the nuclear industry. The transfer from an isolator into other isolators or containment systems required unique transfer ports to create an aseptic transfer. These transfer ports allow the introduction of sterilized components, like rubber stoppers, into the isolator. Earlier systems worked with a revolving mechanical bayonet lock system with reusable latch and single-use bags, but evolved to the magnetic system port, which is easier and safer to use. The single-use bags can be autoclave or gamma sterilized together with the components, for example, stoppers. The advantage of the current aseptic transfer principle is a safe and easy docking of the aseptic transfer bag port to the transfer port of a production isolator. The connection triggers the release of the latch and transfer of the components. The nonaseptic surface of the transfer port is covered by the counter connection on the port of the isolator. This prevents a contact of the inside of the isolator or transfer bag with the environment.

In some biopharmaceutical processes, product intermediates need to be stored because another required process step is still not ready or the bulk drug substance transferred since the process step is in another location. The storage of biological product often results in yield loses, especially due to enzymatic degradation and temperature or pH shift. Transportation of the liquid product can also cause yield losses due to friction and shear due to the movement of the liquid. To avoid such degradation problems, some product can be blast frozen, which is a process mainly used for lower volumes. Blast freezing requires to be qualified to determine any product degradation due to ice crystal formation, concentration gradients, or bag damage. Bags require to be stored in protective shells to avoid any damage respectively leak when the fluid is thawed (Figure 16.5).

Larger volumes and critical protein solutions should be control frozen and thawed. Controlled freeze/thaw avoids the typical build-up of concentration gradients, shifting pH/conductivity, and ice crystallization, which can damage the

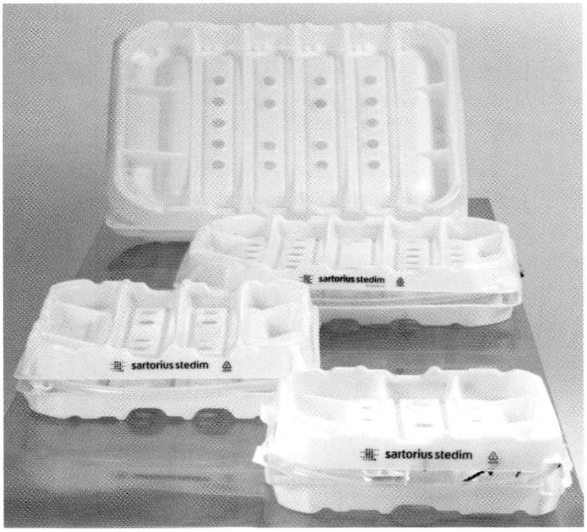

Figure 16.5 Clamshell around a blast freeze bag (courtesy of Sartorius Stedim).

target molecule and the hold bag. These systems consist either of a reusable vessel, but more commonly of a single-use hold bag within a reusable frame. A freeze and thaw module, which uses heat exchanger plates, ensures a homogeneous controlled freeze and thaw process. Volumes between 15 ml and 100 l can be processed from the development stage to process scale. It is also safer to transport such frozen bulk from the intermediate to the form/fill facility.

16.2.4 Aseptic Fluid Connections and Disconnections

Key elements of single-use technology are connections, disconnections, and transfer possibilities. These connections and disconnections require to be performed without the risk of microbial ingress. Manifolds of filter capsules and bags are most commonly connected via tubing and afterward gamma irradiated. These assemblies are then connected to a multitude of different processing steps, for example, to a feed stream either from a disposable mixing system or a single-use cell harvest filter. Another example would be when sterile filtered cell culture media within a hold bag needs to be transferred into a bioreactor. In most single-use process steps, the desire is to connect the equipment or process units aseptically to achieve a high level of sterility assurance and exclude the risk of contaminations. Classical connector designs, whether hose barb or sanitary flange, may be used, but often do not address the criticality and risk involved when aseptic connections are applied. Single-use aseptic connectors are presterilized by gamma irradiation and design so that the fluid path does not come in contact with the environment. The protection from the environment of those devices is assured using sterilizing-grade membranes or solid film layers. Aseptic connector devices are generally integrity tested by the manufacturers as a production release criteria. Aseptic connectors allow performing a connection between two single-use devices or unit operations without the necessary use of an isolator or laminar flow hood. The systems can be interconnected as contained units or unit operation.

Connectors are available in various different sizes and types. The optimal connector type for a particular application requires to be determent and validated. To assure that the aseptic connector design works as specified, especially the containment of the fluid contact surfaces, manufacturers run rigorous tests on these devices. The tests belong to typical qualification procedures, including particulate testing, bacterial ingress, and extractable testing. Qualification test procedures have to verify that the connector works as specified, but once again these tests run under standard conditions. Within the end user's environment the connectors are evaluated in process validation exercises.

Often the emphasis is put on connection of components with each other, but nowadays disconnections are as important. Connecting a filtrate bag to the downstream side of a sterilizing-grade filter requires to be done aseptically, safely to avoid any contamination ingress to the filtered fluid. However, the bag needs to be disconnected from the filter safely; therefore, disconnection designs require being as critical as connection. In recent years these disconnection devices were introduced successfully, again in a variety of designs and sizes. A very popular disconnection set-up, especially for sampling bags, is a crimping device, which is a metal sleeve around the tubing that can be pressed together to avoid any opening. These multiport sampling bags are easy to handle and have proven to be a very robust technology. Other devices are polymeric clamping systems for different tube sizes or heat sealing. The disconnection, as with connection, needs to be validated, most importantly to show that there is no leakage or ingress possible.

Welding thermoplastic tubing together performs alternative aseptic connections. This process has been successfully used for years. However, the welded tube is required to be dry, as wet tubing cannot be welded or only with difficulty. The weld process cuts the tubing and welds both cut ends together. Tubes of different diameters from 1/4 in. to 3/4 in. can be welded, each diameter requiring individual weld parameters commonly programmed into the welder unit. The blade used to weld the tubing heats up to 400 °C and therefore is sterilized during this process. The welding process requires being qualified within the end user process to ensure that the weld strength is according to specifications. Similarly, thermoplastic tubing can also be sealed using heat welding. These sealing devices are used for disconnection purposes. The problem with thermoplastic tubing is the mechanical stability when the tubing is used in peristaltic pumps. Over time the tubing starts weakening and bursts, if not stopped beforehand. Therefore, a mix of silicone tubing, peristaltic pumps, shear resistant, but not weldable, and thermoplastic weldable tubing, but not shear resistant, had to be used. Today, thermoplastic tubing has developed into having the benefits of both properties: weldable and fit for use in peristaltic pumps.

16.2.5
Single-Use Final Filling Systems

Fluid filling utilizing single-use equipment used to be restricted to manual filling, mainly for buffers and cell culture media from stainless steel hold tank into bottles. This manual filling process is not only tedious, but also has risks attached, since human errors can happen. The fluid transfer happens via peristaltic pump, actuated by a person in a manual fill. The fill volumes for manual filling commonly range from 100 ml to a few hundred liters. Manual filling does not have the precision that automated filling has and often happens in clean benches filling into open flasks or bottles. The single-use components are hold bags outfitted with tubing toward either a fill needle or to multiple small-volume bags. Single-use bag filling makes it possible to portion a large volume of fluid into smaller volumes with all downstream bags being connected to the large volume bag. This type of filling assembly has the benefit of being a closed system. Still the fluid volume filled into the smaller bags can be imprecise since the weight of the filled bags may not be measured. The fill volume is determined visually or by checking the stretch of the bag. Higher precision is reached when the fluid is portioned via automated systems, which measures the weight of each filtrate bag with load cell platforms (Figure 16.6).

Figure 16.6 Automated fill system, portion large volumes (courtesy of Sartorius Stedim).

End product filling, with the need of high precision and speed, has been an area of development needs. For years end product filling was restricted to small-volume fills. The desire has to be that future fill lines be designed with all drug product contact areas being single-use, as costly filling machinery could be used for multipurpose filling. Cleaning requirements would be greatly reduced, potential hazardous material filling would be eased, and the fill line utilization would be optimized. Most recently, single-use filling publications by established filling machine manufacturers held the promise that also larger-volume, high-speed fill lines could be established with fill precision required. New designs are forthcoming; readily configured assemblies, presterilized, which create a single-use fluid path, surrounded by the typical periphery. The pump action happens at every fill head and shows the precision necessary in critical product filling. The benefit of single-use filling is the fact that fill needles and all the typical pipework is not reused, cleaned, and autoclaved, but discarded after fill. The critical assembly of reusable fill needles is avoided. The single-use fill system assembly contains a hopper or buffer bag from which multiple tubing sets direct toward the single-use fill needle. The design of the buffer bag is critical to compensate for any pulsation, flexing, and potential drip.

16.3 Todays Facility Designs

16.3.1 Construction and Design Types

Besides the traditional brick and mortar facilities, there are other facility designs, for example container-based, stick-built, isolator or containment-based, and autonomous cleanroom POD designs (Table 16.1). Traditionally, pharmaceutical and biopharmaceutical facilities are large scale, product dedicated, and very cost intensive designs. Examples have been published that such facilities cost close to $400 million and have a time-to-run of over 4 years. The capital expenditure may be even acceptable, as it amortizes once the facility is up and running. However, the lengthy time-to-run is the major cost factor, as every day of output counts, especially under the short timeframe of patent protection. In addition, one cannot scale such facility, if the demand is higher or lower than expected. Once the product demand is lowered it will be difficult to run down certain cleanroom sections as all are interconnected, and a shutdown would influence the air balance and qualification. When the product reaches its lifecycle, the facility commonly cannot be repurposed, but is mothballed. Repurposing would mean that the facility needs to be gutted and rebuilt with new cleanroom spaces, including the convoluted air handling super structure.

To overcome the lengthy build of a traditional facility, so-called modular facility designs were introduced. These modular designs include container and stick-build based systems. The container-based design utilizes a multitude of

Table 16.1 Description of the different facility designs available.

Facility design	Description
Bricks and mortar	The traditional type facility, build often for one product and large scale. Lifespan of the facility is commonly one product lifecycle. Very dedicated and purpose-built facility design. HVAC systems in the mezzanine level supply large areas.
Modular container	Off-site build container systems, which are interconnected at the final location to a complete facility. The container modules can be outfitted and designed to purpose. Centralized HVAC system.
Modular Stick-built	The facility is framed out and finished with modular wall panels. The wall panels can be of different surface finish or designs to accommodate for example room-to-room pass through or windows. HVAC systems in the mezzanine level supplying multiple rooms.
Isolator or controlled environment module	Build off-site and most commonly introduced into either a cleanroom or at least CNC area. Depending on the system, it creates an excellent containment option and can be repurposed and effortlessly sanitized. Some systems are connected to a centralized HVAC system, others might have their own.
Autonomous POD	Off-site build autonomous cleanroom module. Available in various standard dimension, but can be modified into project designs. Effortlessly sanitized and decontaminated. The PODs are mobile and contain their own HVAC system.

dimensionally specified containers, each having its purpose. These individual containers are stacked and interlinked to each other to create a production facility. A well known example are the Pharmadule systems, which link together to assemble a production facility. Another modular system is the stick-built design, which comprises of a frame and wall panel interconnected and fast built. The frame and panel construction is done fast and the designs can be very flexible when built. However, the flexibility of scaling-up and -down, as well as the use of multiproduct purposes is lost with these two modular solutions, as the modularity become one inflexible facility once the designs are interconnected to one facility. The container-based as well as the modular stick-built designs fuse once again to a one-product facility and are very similar in their use to traditional brick and mortar facilities. If one wants to be more flexible and be able to repurpose cleanrooms, scale these containment options and be able to sanitize the cleanroom systems individually, one has to opt for either an isolator or POD-based autonomous cleanroom system.

All of these designs have their purpose, benefits, and disadvantages (Table 16.2). It is not that any one of the designs is the ultimate best. Often these designs are utilized in a hybrid mode and not necessarily totally independent. Once again any of these facility designs are a tool in the toolbox of choices for the drug manufacturer or the engineering firms supporting such. The very

Table 16.2 Strength and weakness analysis of the different facility designs available.

Facility design	Strength	Weakness
Bricks and mortar	• Extensive experience level with such facilities • Dedicated product segregation • Large areas • Time-to-run 24–48 mo	• Difficult to repurpose • One product lifecycle • High CAPEX • Up to 4 yr time-to-run • Inflexible • Large HVAC superstructure • Difficult to decontaminate if necessary
Modular container	• CAPEX 70–90% of traditional built • Time-to-run 18–24 mo • Off-site build-up	• Interconnected to one large facility losing its flexibility at that point • Large HVAC superstructure • Shipping costs • Not scalable
Stick-built modular	• CAPEX 50% lower than traditional built • Time-to-run 6–24 mo • Build into a shell building • Potentially scalable	• Interconnected to one large facility losing its flexibility at that point • Large HVAC superstructure • On-site build-up
Isolator or controlled environment module	• CAPEX 50% lower than traditional built • Time-to-run 12–18 mo • Modules are repurposable • Possible to decontaminate • Scalable	• Size limitations make the use of larger equipment difficult • BSL containment limitations • Centralized HVAC
Autonomous POD	• CAPEX 40–50% of traditional built • Time-to-run 6–18 mo • Moved into a shell building • PODs are repurposable • Easy to decontaminate • Redundant HVAC system in each POD • Scalable • 2–3 product life cycle life time	• Shipping costs • Equipment size excursions require project POD

specific choices, which need to be made, are requirement based. What is the purpose of the facility, what are the requirements to fulfill the purpose? Ultimately it boils down to the particular need of the application and end user.

A decision matrix will determine which of the tools shall be utilized for the project and/or for a section of the project or process flow. As mentioned, a facility does not necessarily be only designed with one of the facility options, but often resolves into a hybrid solution of two or three of the options listed. For example, cell therapeutic or antibody conjugate processing happens often in production isolators or other containment options, which are surrounded by a class B or C environment, which can be any type of cleanroom. Autonomous cleanroom POD solutions are most commonly connected to a stick-built corridor system. It is not that there is a one-fits-all approach, which makes a modern facility more viable; the approach is to pick and choose the right design solutions for an optimal fulfillment of the specified purposes. This approach has been utilized for many years in the design of the production processes and the implementation of single-use technology. The end user has moved away from the legacy models to evaluation of the best process equipment choice for a particular unit operation, even if it means multiple vendor use.

Facility designs as experienced in the past will change due to lower volume requirements; price pressures with the need to reduce the cost of goods sold and flexibility needed to be able to have a better facility utilization. Large-scale facilities, meaning bioreactor volumes of 10,000–20,000 l, will also turn to more flexible downstream processing steps. The large bioreactor volume will be reduced to a tenth of its volume after the initial harvesting step. Once this volume is reached the downstream process can be accommodated in more modular or podular designs, gaining appropriate segregation and sanitization opportunities. Currently, the facility designs are large not only due to the belief that the bioreactors require to be in a classified area or at least controlled but nonclassified, but also due to the space needs for all the equipment hold within the areas. Stainless steel hold and prep tanks of various sizes are held within the production steps, which mean not only a material flow inconvenience, but also large inventory areas that use costly cleanroom space. Single-use technology voided the need for equipment being held at ready within the cleanroom area or at least did not need the space required for a dedicated hard shell equipment room. Single-use technology made it possible to reduce the cleanroom space required, which is desired as every squaremeter of classified area is very costly. This though has also been pushed to the extreme, some making the suggestion to either use ballroom design concepts, which encompass the entire process stream in one large cleanroom or even use the single-use technology process in a controlled but nonclassified area. These types of suggestions not only lower the cost of goods sold, but also the safety and quality of the drug product processed. The ignorance of the human factor and the potential mistakes made thereby is argued by the lowering of the operating costs. However, all savings achieved by such insecure designs can be extinct with one leak or cross-contamination of a ballroom area. It is well known that single-use systems, as also stainless steel, are not fail-safe. The possibility of mishandling, human errors in connections, or a damaged bag, can happen and have happened. This would mean that the entire ballroom designed cleanroom area will require to be sanitized in addition to the large air handling super structure. Proof has to be given that shows the entire area and ductwork has been sanitized. Furthermore, any contamination excursions, as it happened in the past with mycoplasma or minute mouse virus cannot be contained in a confined area, but may become a rampant root cause for future excursions. As much as cost of goods sold and operating costs are of focus and require reduction, such reduction shall not be conveyed to safety and quality. Besides, one incident is sufficient to overcome all savings and cost reductions, as the products manufactured within these processes are low volume, highly valuable products. It should be up to the end user to determine via an appropriate risk assessment whether a nonchalant approach of cleanroom segregation and containment is justifiable or not. Any suggestions made by cleanroom designers, engineering, and architect firms can only be recommendations, as they do not have the ultimate responsibility over the product produced and quality required.

16.3.2 Process Location and Flow

Depending on the drug produced and process equipment used, the process location and flow can vary. Processes can run from being very simplistic to highly complex and unit operation intensive. Process simplicity though does not mean that the safety and quality of these processes is abridged; that is not the case, as any injectable from any process has to meet stringent specifications. In addition, process location and flow also depends on volumes handled, the development or commercialization phase the product is in, the type of product, large or small molecules, the modus of the cell culture process, if applicable, and the intensity of personnel flow needed, to name a few.

Small-molecule processes, whether small or large volumes, commonly have a lesser complexity than large-molecule biologics. Depending on the product, either large- or small-volume parenteral, the process can be a multiproduct or dedicated stream. In large-volume parenteral one finds that the compounding and filling activities often use the same equipment, which is rigorously cleaned and steam sterilized in between batches. In small-volume parenteral, the process stream including the filling line is often dedicated to one product. In a multiproduct processing system, the same or similar process flow and equipment is utilized within the same process building surroundings. On the other hand, dedicated product processing streams have their dedicated areas and personnel. These facility layouts show the dedicated personnel, material, and waste flow throughout the dedicated product processing stages. A facility can have multiples of these dedicated process streams and locations; it has to be ensured though that the air feeding these process streams is not mixed with air from another process. The air handling has to be separated from dedicated process stream to another. Most small-molecule processes still use an array of stainless steel equipment; therefore, the mentioned ballroom design for the cleanroom space is often only discussed in conjunction with single-use technology within biologics processing. If single-use equipment would be used within a small molecule process, one still would try to mitigate risks and probably would also not adhere to the ballroom concept. What may have worked for decades in the semiconductor industry may not work in an environment where the contaminant is a living organism. Besides, even the semiconductor industry is looking into more confined and segregated cleanroom environments.

In biologics, the process stream becomes more complex due to a multitude of process steps or unit operations. Within that complexity though natural breakpoints are present, which makes a facility and/or cleanroom layout straightforwardly applicable and clonable. The process flows vary from vaccine application to monoclonal antibody to recombinant proteins, but within the applications, the processes have a certain similarity. This means one can base new requirements on past experiences, from a process design to the facility layout. The major problem with new facilities is the fact that every facility and/or facility layout are different. The invention of a new wheel is no longer applied, but rather past process knowledge is conveyed to new production needs. The single-use equipment and unit operation introductions also define new facility layouts. In the past biologics were produced in large quantities in a dedicated production site. The trend is now to smaller volumes and utilization of either a small-scale production site or single-use equipment to process multiple products in that same site. Single-use systems are the first barrier and containment, which reduces the risk of any cross-contamination greatly, though the air handling system still requires to be sanitizable and such sanitization process needs to be validated. Any breach of the single-use equipment means a potential contamination of the air handling system. That contamination needs to be eliminated, which is not an easy undertaking with a centralized air handling system and a large ductwork superstructure. However, the designs require to be thorough at the beginning of a facility and process design to be able to achieve the optimal process utilization.

The process layout within a biologics process also depends on the modus of the cell culture process and the expression system. If a process is run in batch mode, the process will run in a staggered approach and will be of larger scale. A perfusion process would run more continuously and can be of smaller size. Both processes run the product through multistep unit operations and the potential bottlenecks of the unit operations are cleaning and set-up time. In instances it takes 8 h to get the process step ready. With single-use technologies and the newly introduced fully disposable unit operations, cleaning is voided and the set-up time reduces to minutes. Processing flows become faster and more efficient with single-use systems. It is easier and more rapidly deployable. The hope is that smaller volume process streams can be fully single-use, making the processes and cleanroom needs more compact and faster, lowering the inventory level needs and raising the capacity utilization.

16.4 Future Processing and Facility Requirements

The pharmaceutical and biopharmaceutical industry's needs are shifting from large volume, one product processes, and facilities to smaller volume, multiproduct facilities. These needs are nowadays not just restricted to small-scale, development process stages, but funnel right down to process scale. The flexibility is needed to be able to gain optimal capacity and facility utilization to stay competitive [22]. Smaller volumes enable single-use technologies, as the maximum volume range applicable to single-use technologies is around 2000 l. Higher expression rates in cell culture processes allow to move to the lower volumes, instead of the utilization of 10,000 to 20,000 l bioreactor sizes. The inherent risk with such large systems are possible set-up problems, insufficient cleaning, and facility dedication to only one product. If a contamination occurs, large bioreactor volumes are lost. Multiple small-volume systems would reduce the contaminated volume and therefore financial losses. Processing smaller volumes is simpler, but most of all can be done with single-use components or unit operations. The trend of using single-use components must be considered already during the design phase of the manufacturing facility. On the other hand, customized engineering efforts have to be reduced as much as possible in order to lessen cost and timelines. To support minimizing such efforts, generic platform concepts for the overall process enable a faster execution time as well as more efficient qualification procedures.

16.4.1 Upstream Technologies

Typical processes for the manufacturing of a biopharmaceutical drug products are commonly divided into upstream, downstream, and form/fill. In upstream processing, cell culture media are prepared, mixed, and sterilized by filtration through 0.2 or 0.1 μm filter and stored in hold bags. In some instances, mainly basal media, the media are introduced directly into the bioreactor after filtration. Single-use equipment helps to avoid contamination of prepared cell culture media, as the systems are closed systems, interconnected via aseptic connectors. Possible mycoplasma contamination of the cell culture media via human transfer is greatly reduced. A recently published new contaminant source, *Leptospira*, forced some upstream process to utilize high-temperature short-time pasteurization (HTST), as 0.1 μm filters could not remove the contaminant. It is, to find the root cause of such contamination, as with others, to reduce such ingress into the process. Single-use technology as a barrier technology and future autonomous containment options will help to prevent such contamination carry-over.

Single-use bioreactors up to 2000 l are available with different agitation technologies (wave-induced, stirred, orbital, or oscillating shakers). The sensor technology within the gamma irradiatable is also often single-use, lowering the risk of contamination points as ports are avoided. Once again the cleaning efforts, usually utilized for reusable reactors, are not necessary. Cleaning of bioreactors is onerous, which is amplified by the complex set-up and sterilization of the reactor. To set a stainless steel system up, it may take 8–10 h, whereby single-use bioreactors are installed into the supportive shell within minutes. Another advantage of single-use technologies is that even more complex process strategies, like fed-batch or perfusion, become easier to design, implement, and use. Considering the increasing productivity on the upstream side, this may result in a bottleneck in downstream processing. The cell harvest step still needs to gain a single-use development focus, as the only well established single-use cell harvest step is encapsulated lenticular filters. Other harvest technologies, like centrifugation or decanting options, would be beneficial in single-use designs. Fluid handling in bioprocess containers is well established, but designs and equipment placement can be improved. For example, reducing cleanroom demands by applying through-the-wall supply of media/buffer can drastically reduce cost; capital expense and operating expense for heat, venting, and air-conditioning. Alternatively, sanitizable cleanroom pods could be utilized (Figure 16.7). These containment options are autonomous and have their own air-handling system. Each pod can be dedicated to a specific use, for example media prep, buffer prep, cell culture process, and so on, and also repurposed for other options, since the pods are compact, have their own air handling system, and can be sanitized through vaporized hydrogen peroxide. The systems can be designed as a cleanroom area with typical cleanroom classes of ISO 5–8 or containment system classes BSL 1 – 2+. The benefits are dedication of the cleanroom, instead of a wide-open, easily cross-contaminated ballroom or classical area.

Cleanroom pod systems, which are similar to isolators but larger and walkable, find their use in a multitude of applications, even as a harvest pod for a

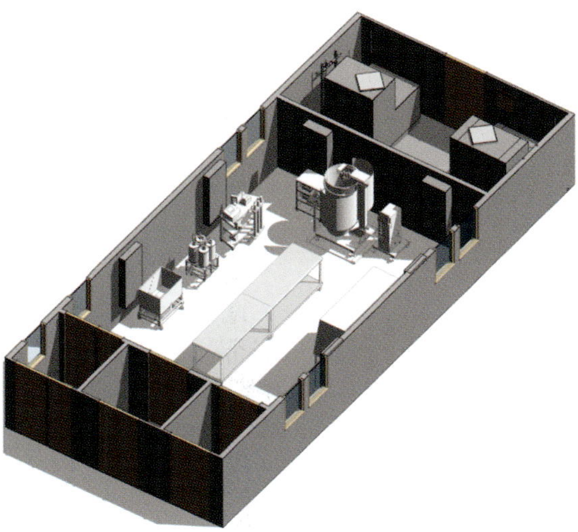

Figure 16.7 Cleanroom pod design for dedicated process purposes (courtesy G-CON Manufacturing Inc.).

large-scale fermentation system, since the fluid stream is concentrated down to a tenth of the original volume. The typical concerns with centrifugation and possible aerosol dispersion would be reduced as the area can be contained and sanitized efficiently.

16.4.2
Downstream Technologies

The subsequent downstream step, after the cell harvest step, is commonly an ultra/diafiltration (UF/DF) step with a cross-flow or tangential-flow (TFF) unit. The cell harvest volume is concentrated down via ultrafiltration and a buffer exchange performed using diafiltration. The product and design range of single-use ultrafiltration devices were very limited till recently. Now systems are available with multiple different filtration areas, membrane materials, and flow arrangements. Sensors, for example, for pressure, pH, and conductivity, are often single-use and connected to the control system of the ultrafiltration unit. To determine the volume conversions and right exchanged, the bags volumes can be measured with load cells. The single-use UF/DF systems are available as components to be connected together or as an entire unit operation. The bonus of these single-use systems is the ease of use and assembly, the multifunctionality of the system with different devices, and most of all the lack of cleaning needs. UF/DF filter membrane matrixes are complex. Aggressive cleaning regimes are necessary to gain the original flow back to remove all contaminants. These aggressive cleaning actions can potentially damage the membrane structure or elevate the leachable level. Such risks would be avoided by the use of single-use devices. Since UF/DF is utilized right after the harvest step, even larger bioreactor volumes are reduced to a lower volume, which can be accommodated by single-use technologies within the downstream process. So even when the upstream side is still a large bioreactor system, with volumes up to 20,000 l, the concentration step will bring the volume rapidly down and single-use technology finds its optimized application again.

Downstream steps that follow, guarantee the reduction of product impurities, for example, protein A leaching from the protein A column, host cell proteins, DNA, endotoxins, or any aggregates. Commonly ion-exchanger steps are used to remove such impurities (anion-exchange chromatography (AEX), cation-exchange chromatography (CEX)). However, these ion-exchanger columns customarily need to be cleaned rigorously after use. The cleaning is required to gain the original charge back, but moreover to eliminate any microbial contamination. If such contamination is not taken care of, possible biofilm formation may occur. Once a biofilm is introduced it is very difficult to remove and it can slough off or create endotoxin spikes. Packing, cleaning, setting up, and using traditional columns is tedious and prone to blunders. Single-use devices are now becoming available in different sizes, but also different designs, either classical beads or membranes, both with ligands attached. These devices can be scaled from small volumes to large process scales.

Virus removal with membrane filtration systems is nothing new, except better performance devices are constantly developed to the satisfaction of the industry. Problems of premature blocking are reduced due to protective prefiltration, either as a separate filter device or incorporated in the virus filter. Also, hold-up volumes are greatly reduced to avoid yield losses. Virus inactivation steps are upgraded as an entire single-use unit operation. The feed stream is connected to a pH or solvent introduction step, to a filter followed by a filtrate hold bag. Multiple ports and connectors are attached to the system to add adjustments, take samples or add probes. These systems can be easily installed and are presterilized to assure containment. A large, formerly, complex processing step is now easier to handle.

16.4.3
Single-Use Engineering and Design

The introduction and use of single-use technologies should start at the earliest stage to optimize the process from the beginning. Consequently, single-use components need to be available in a small scale to evaluate the performance and usefulness during the early stages of development, not just in the clinical, but also preclinical phase. Once chosen as appropriate for the application, the small-scale devices require being scalable to process scale. Small-scale devices are useless if these cannot be linear scaled, are not available in the same design, or have deviating performance patterns. Single-use suppliers have introduced several small-scale devices with the contemplation of performance pattern consistency. What is important is to accept that there are certain physical limitations of single-use technologies and one is required to evaluate when single-use technologies would be of benefit and when not. How much single-use and where to use these technologies has to be evaluated from various aspects and needs to be carefully analyzed with respect to application and end user specific situations. For example, some applications are extremely sensitive to unspecific adsorption, since single-use systems are polymeric materials; the adsorption to these materials requires to be evaluated. Such evaluation helps to create the optimal process design, which not necessarily needs to be total single-use nor reusable. There is the logical possibility of a combination of reusable and single-use technologies, being considered as a hybrid technology.

Currently, single-use technologies are mainly used during scale-up and clinical production. In instances the large volumes in commercial manufacturing does not allow single-use technology implementation. The use is most of the time still limited to feed bags, tubing, and filter cartridges. However, the development of large-volume single-use technologies opens the area for commercial production and the need for integrated single-use process designs become obvious. While in the past single-use products were recognized as useful component additions in the production of biopharmaceuticals, nowadays there are more and more processes that are almost completely made of single-use equipment steps or unit operations. Even in midscale processes with batch volumes up to 2000 l, several single-use unit operations and in-process fluid handling systems are adapted. A biopharmaceutical manufacturing concept is more than just the sum of its processing operations, but the foundation of the need for a generic manufacturing platform solution. A manufacturing or process platform is a well-defined sequence of unit operations. It will depend on the volume within the different processing steps and protein concentrations. The resulting process platform will end in a tailored single-use containment stream, which helps to reduce processing risks, but increases process utilization. These process platforms may be available for monoclonal antibodies, recombinant proteins, and vaccines processes, and can vary in size depending on the volume. All process platforms consist of several unit operations, for example, media/buffer preparation, cell culture, cell removal/harvest, pooling/storage, sterile filtration, capturing/polishing, virus inactivation/virus removal, ultrafiltration/diafiltration, and freeze and thaw as primary steps in a process. Generally, processes may have many unit operations to obtain the desired product purity and quality. However, each unit operation is made of standardized technological modules, which enables the fast and efficient design and execution of a project. Once technological modules and process platforms are defined, they do not need to be changed or newly developed. Unit operations, processes, or entire facilities can be cloned, reducing timelines, qualification/validation work, and engineering resources. The process and facility become a known entity to the owner and the regulator.

The debate of single-use standardization is fueled by the vendors' belief in competitiveness due to uniqueness. However, there are efforts to standardize single-use components and process equipment in the same way like stainless steel bioprocess equipment. In general, there are a number of factors, which have to be determined before implementing single-use equipment. These range from process compatibility, batch volume, fill and discharge, degree of agitation and the energy input required, operating pressure and temperature, measurement of process parameters, materials handling, space requirements, and environmental aspects are of importance [23]. Other areas of design concerns are the correct connection and fluid transfer from one process step to the other. There should not be a mix-up with these connections, as manifold as these are in a biopharmaceutical process. Correct connectivity could be enhanced by color-coding, connector designs, and bar or dot matrix coding.

16.4.4
Facilities and Process Design

The times of the so called "blockbusters" in the pharmaceutical industry are very much declining, which means that capital-intensive, product-dedicated facilities are not the ones that are planned or designed for right now [24,25]. The industry is looking at facility designs that enhance the flexibility of the processes and sites. Flexibility can have a multiple meaning and is interpreted differently by every individual demand. It can mean the ability to process multiple products, to scale the volume processing up and down according to demands, or to be able to move the site. Single-use technologies are enablers to fulfill this need, but the flexibility need also requires being reflective in the facility design itself. Single-use technology's flexibility in multiproduct production possibilities, ease and speed of set-up, and mobility is only given when the single-use components are not restricted by its surroundings, meaning the facility. The recent patent expiries and competitive pressures by generics and biosimilars, made it obvious that speed, not just in drug development, but especially in capacity build-up are essential. Furthermore, facilities require being repurposable, meaning if a drug development fails, the facility can be either used for another product or resold. The lifespan of drug products becomes lower, volume needs vary due to advancements in expression rates or just patient demands; therefore, capacities require being ramped-up and down rapidly. All these factors need to be addressed by new flexible facility designs.

Current developments in the area of facility design show promise, though so called modular cleanroom systems still have to be scrutinized as a fixture and not as flexibility. Anything that is not autonomous, especially in the air handling system, would mean requalification when expanded, added onto, or reduced. Most traditional cleanroom designs, including modular and container-based systems, are supplied by a central air handling system with a convolution of ductwork. Any change in this convolution will require requalification or at least rebalancing the entire cleanroom structure. Time is of the essence and requalification efforts lock down the processing area so desperately needed. Therefore, one requires being critical to determine what is truly flexible and what is not. The different cleanroom and containment options available nowadays are encouraging, as the ideas move toward mobility, flexibility, and reusability. Whether it is isolators, cleanroom cabinets or totally contained cleanroom pods, all have in common to create an end user solution choice that may fit best to the process stream and the single-use systems used. Single-use components, equipment, or unit operations are the key for flexibility and risk aversion. These systems avoid potential cross-contaminations and end user mistakes, but these will only be as good and flexible as the surrounding environment is. Therefore, facility designs experience focus and modifications, which ultimately will result in truly flexible factories, potentially "mini-factories" at the point-of-need.

The vendors have gone so far as that they now start combining the mentioned process platform designs into flexible factory layouts (Figure 16.8). They have started to define a multitude of applications and processes, which could be deployed fast track. The work, together with end user experiences and vendor receptiveness, helped to develop such process platform designs and will enhance future drug manufacturing further. It will not only lead to a fast deployment of facilities, but also to a reduction in engineering and qualification timelines, as well as create a known environment for the auditing regulator. The key of the latter is familiarity, which always supports an amicable environment.

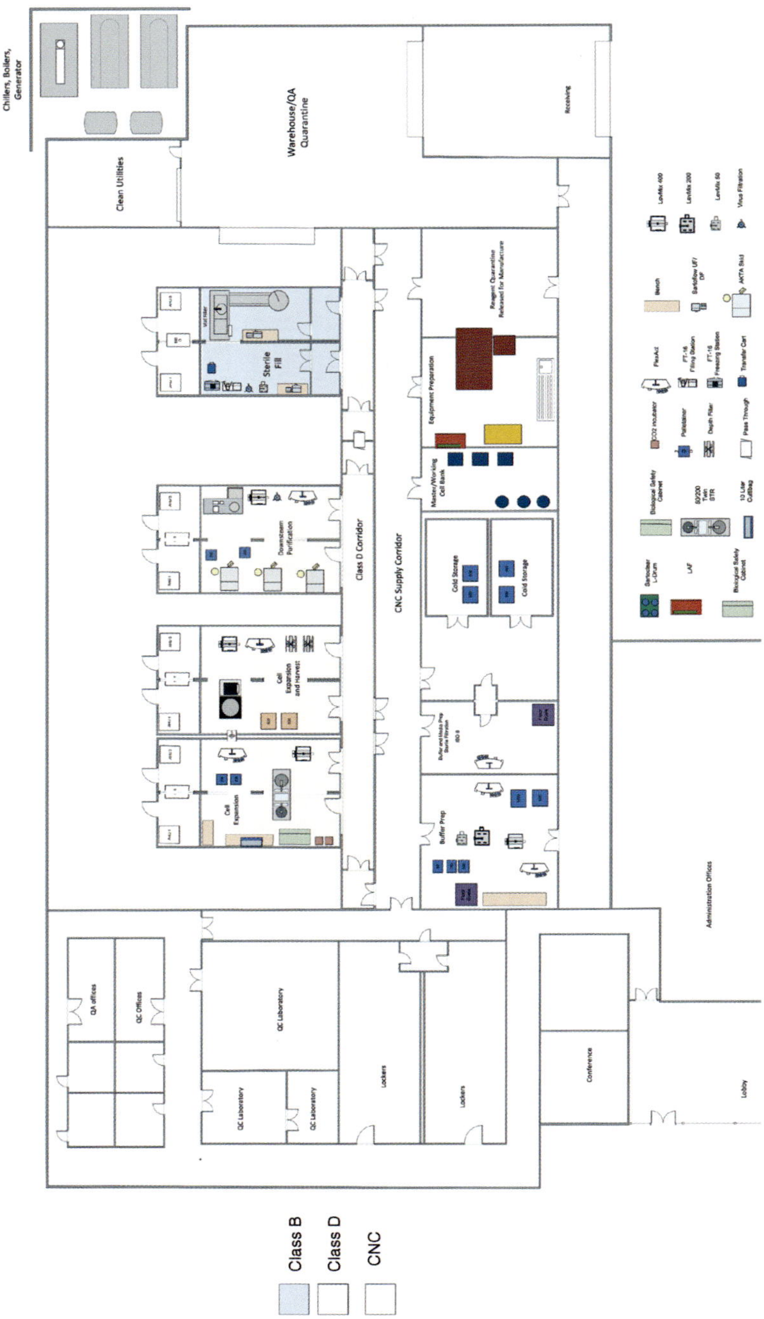

Figure 16.8 Process platform design for a 1000 l mAb facility (courtesy of G-CON LLC).

True flexibility comes with autonomy of the critical cleanroom space; as such autonomous, compact cleanroom systems can be painlessly decontaminated and sanitized, controlled, and reused. The cleaning and repurposing of autonomous cleanroom spaces make these prone for multiproduct processing. Furthermore, these systems can be deployed fast track and, if needed, moved.

Ultimately, the vision of flexible facilities has to be “mini-sites,” which can be utilized in any region of the world, as in-country/for country supply systems, built and run within months to fulfill the local healthcare requirements. Single-use process equipment created the first step to such sites, which now is completed by autonomous cleanroom modules.

References

1 Levine, H.L., Lilja, J.E., Stock, R., Hummel, H., and Jones, S.D. (2012) Efficient, flexible facilities for the 21st century. *BioProcess Int.*, **10** (11), 20–30.

2 Hodge, G. (2009) The economic and strategic value of flexible manufacturing capacity. ISPE Strasbourg Conference, September 28–29, Strasbourg, France.

3 Shanley, A. and Thomas, P. (2009) Flexible pharma: puzzling out the plant of the future. Available at PharmaManufacturing.com (accessed May 27, 2014).

4 Pralong, A. (2013) Single-use technologies and facility layout – a paradigm shift. *Biopharma Asia Mag.*, **2** (1).

5 Jornitz, M.W. and Paust, T. (2010) The evolution of single-use technologies in aseptic processing. *Pharm. Technol.*, **34** (4), 112–117.

6 Paust, T., Szarafinski, D., Manzke, C., Peuker, T., and Jornitz, M.W. (2010) A detail view of single-use equipment opportunities supporting new biomanufacturing paradigms. *PharmTech Suppl.*, **34** (3), s16–s20.

7 Jornitz, M.W., Cappia, J.M., and Meltzer, T.H. (2009) Disposable components in aseptic processing. *PharmTech Suppl. (Issue)*, S10–S15.

8 Plastic packaging systems and their materials of construction. (2013) United States Pharmacopeia, Rockville, MD.

9 E.P. 3.1.7.: EVA for containers and tubing. European Pharmacopoeia, (2010) EDQM, Strasbourg, France.

10 Goldstein, A. and Perrone, P. (2010) Method for implementing disposables into a bioprocess facility. ISPE Knowledge Brief.

11 ASTM F838-05 (2005) *Standard Test Method for Determining Bacterial Retention of Membrane Filters Utilized for Liquid Filtration*. ASTM, West Conshohocken, PA.

12 PDA (2008) Liquid Sterilizing Filtration. Technical Report 26, Parenteral Drug Association, Bethesda, MD.

13 Tanny, G.B., Strong, D.K., Presswood, W.G., and Meltzer, T.H. (1979) Adsorptive retention of *Pseudomonas diminuta* by membrane filters. *J. Parenter. Drug Assoc.*, **33**, 40–51.

14 Emory, S.F., Koga, Y., Azuma, N., and Matsumoto, K. (1993) The effects surfactant types and latex-particle feed concentration on membrane retention. *Ultrapure Water*, **10** (2), 41–44.

15 Reif, O.W., Sölkner, P., and Rupp, J. (1996) Analysis and evaluation of filter cartridge extractables for validation in pharmaceutical downstream processing. *PDA J. Pharm. Sci. Technol.*, **50**, 399–410.

16 British Pharmacopoeia, TSO, Norwich, UK.

17 Brose, D.J. and Henricksen, G. (1994) A quantitative analysis of preservative adsorption on microfiltration membranes. *Pharm. Technol. Eur.*, **18** (3), 42–49.

18 Jornitz, M.W., Meltzer, T.H., Bromm, H., and Priebe, P.M. (2005) Choosing the appropriate membrane filter – test requirements. *PDA J. Pharm. Sci. Technol.*, **59** (2), 96–101.

19 Gottschalk, U. (2008) Bioseparation in antibody manufacturing: the good, the bad and the ugly. *Biotechnol. Prog.*, 24 (3), 496–503.

20 Zhou, J.X. and Tressel, T. (2005) Membrane chromatography as a robust purification system for large scale antibody production. *BioProcess Int.*, **3**, 32–37.

21 Sinclair, A. and Monge, M. (2002) Quantitative economic evaluation of single use disposables in bioprocessing. *Pharm. Eng.*, **22** (3), 16–20.

22 Harrison, C. (2013) Dangling from the patent cliff. *Nat. Rev. Drug Discov.*, **12**, 14–15.

23 Ravisé, A., Cameau, E., De Abreu, G., and Pralong, A. (2009) Hybrid and disposable facilities for manufacturing of biopharmaceuticals: pros and cons. *Adv. Biochem. Eng. Biotechnol.*, **115**, 185–219.

24 Bioplan Associates Inc. (2012) 9th Annual Report and Survey of Biopharmaceutical Manufacturing Capacity and Production – A Study of Biotherapeutic Developers and Contract Manufacturing Organizations.

25 Holtz, B. and Powers, D. (2012) Integration of a single-use platform process within an innovative facility design. *BioPharm Int. Suppl.* **25** (11), s27–s32.

17
Evaluating the Economic and Operational Feasibility of Continuous Processes for Monoclonal Antibodies

Suzanne S. Farid, James Pollock, and Sa V. Ho

17.1
Introduction

Improving research and development (R&D) productivity while reducing R&D and manufacturing costs is a major challenge for the biopharmaceutical industry [1–5]. Biopharmaceutical manufacturers are looking to improve their manufacturing platform processes while maintaining flexibility and product quality. Given that the development and manufacture of biopharmaceutical drugs is a highly complex and heavily regulated endeavor, there has been debate within the industry on the best choice of biopharmaceutical production technologies [e.g., 6,7].

In recent years, there has been a resurgence of interest in continuous bioprocessing challenging the position of the established batch platform for the manufacture of biopharmaceuticals, such as monoclonal antibodies (mAbs). Companies are now asking whether they should choose conventional batch technologies or invest in novel continuous technologies, which may lead to lower production costs. This has led to several companies evaluating continuous technologies [e.g., 8–10] to see if they can leverage their benefits, such as potentially allowing smaller facility footprints and higher equipment utilization rates. Such investigations into continuous manufacture appear to be encouraged by recent Food and Drug Administration strategic plans [11] and quality-by-design (QbD) initiatives. Key questions to address when assessing continuous bioprocessing are as follows: How well do continuous bioprocess steps need to perform to compete with the traditional batch steps? Is there a business case for continuous bioprocessing for early phase manufacture? How does the business case change for commercial multiproduct manufacture? Will tomorrow's process be a hybrid of batch and continuous technologies?

This chapter aims to address these topical questions through the application of a prototype decisional tool developed at University College London (UCL), United Kingdom. The insights from the decisional tool will be illustrated through the use of three industrial case studies that provide economic and

Continuous Processing in Pharmaceutical Manufacturing, First Edition. Edited by Ganapathy Subramanian.

operational perspectives on the decision to select batch versus continuous processes for clinical and commercial mAb manufacture. The questions were explored in a stepwise fashion, first for upstream processing, then capture chromatography, and finally integrated continuous bioprocesses. On the upstream front, a comparison of fed-batch strategies to first-generation (spin-filter) and second-generation (alternating tangential flow filtration, ATF) perfusion systems for the commercial manufacture of mAbs is presented. The case study explores the impact of single-use bioreactors and scale of production on costs, of equipment failure rates on robustness, and qualitative concerns (e.g., ease of development) on the technology rankings. On the downstream front, a case study that explores the potential of continuous capture chromatography to reduce clinical and commercial mAb manufacturing costs is presented. The technology evaluation integrates small-scale experimentation with simulation assessment. Finally, a vision for a number of integrated continuous manufacturing processes is presented and their performance assessed with the decisional tool. The optimal combination of batch and continuous unit operations is determined for different combinations of development phase and company size. In all cases the whole bioprocess was modeled so as to capture the full impact of any upstream or downstream choice on the overall process economics.

17.2 Background on Continuous Processing

17.2.1 Perfusion Culture

Perfusion culture manufacturing strategies for cell-culture-derived biopharmaceuticals offer the potential of greater daily productivities and hence smaller facility footprints than fed-batch culture strategies [12–15]. However, their use has been hampered historically by perceived greater logistical and validation complexity as well as higher likelihoods of technical failures. More recent perfusion culture systems aim to overcome some of these obstacles with the promise of higher productivities and lower failure rates [16,17]. This combined with the introduction of single-use technologies for cell culture operations have triggered renewed interest in the potential of bioprocesses based on perfusion culture systems.

Table 17.1 highlights 10 commercial therapeutic biologics that utilize perfusion culture systems for their manufacture. These include recombinant blood factors, enzymes, and mAbs. The choice of perfusion culture has sometimes been a necessity in cases with labile products (e.g., Xigris® [Eli Lilly], Kogenate® [Bayer], Cerezyme® [Genzyme]). Historically for mAbs the choice has been due to company experience and low titers. For example, perfusion culture was the basis of Centocor's (now Janssen Biotech) platform process in the 1980–1990s for both low-dose products, such as Reopro® (30 mg), and

Table 17.1 Current perfusion cell culture manufacturing strategies.

Product	Protein or mAb	Indication	Company	First approved	Perfusion mode	Reactor size (l)	Reactor number
ReoPro®	abciximab	PCTA	Janssen Biotech**	1994	Spin-filter (internal)	500	5–20 (Leiden)
Cerezyme®	Beta-glucocerebrosidase	Gaucher disease	Genzyme	1994	Gravity settler*	2000	4 (Allston)
Gonal-f®	r.FSH	Anovulation	Merck-Serono	1997	Spin-filter*	ND	ND
Remicade®	infliximab	RA + other AI diseases	Janssen Biotech**	1998	Spin-filter (internal) and Spin-filter (external)	500 1000	5–20 (Leiden) 8 (Malvern)
Simulect®	basiliximab	Transplant rejection	Novartis	1998	Rotational Sieve Filtration	250	ND
Rebif®	Interferon beta-1a	Multiple sclerosis	Merck-Serono	1998	Fixed bed	75	22 (Corsier-sur-Vevey)
Kogenate-FS®	r.Factor VIII	Hemophilia A	Bayer	2000	Gravity settler	200	8 (Berkeley)
Xigris®	r. activated protein C	Sepsis	Eli Lilly	2001	Gravity settler	1500	2 (CMO)
Fabrazyme®	Agalsidase beta	Fabry disease	Genzyme	2003	Gravity settler*	2000	2 (Allston) 2 (Framingham)
Myozyme®	Alglucosidase alfa	Pompe disease	Genzyme	2006	Gravity settler*	4000	3 (Geel)
Simponi ®	golimumab	RA + other AI diseases	Janssen Biotech**	2009	ATF	1000 500	3 (Cork) 5–20 (Leiden)
Stelara ®	ustekinumab	Psoriasis	Janssen Biotech**	2009	ATF	500	5–20 (Leiden)

Sources: These data were derived through interviews with industrialists in each company.
ND = not disclosed. * = Microcarrier based process. ** formerly Centocor.

high-dose products, such as the blockbuster Remicade® (≤1050 mg). However, the increase in fed-batch titers combined with their ease of operation has established fed-batch cell culture as the platform of choice for most mAbs in recent years [6,9,18–20]. Table 17.1 also reveals that the most common perfusion systems adopted in commercial processes are spin-filters [21,22] and gravity settlers (often bespoke; [12]), with up to 4000 l bioreactors. However, examination of the postlaunch process changes for Remicade® revealed modifications to the perfusion systems used from 500 l internal spin-filter perfusion culture at the Leiden (Netherlands) site to 1000 l bioreactors with external spin-filters at the Malvern (Pennsylvania) site in an effort to minimize culture failure due to adverse filter fouling [23]. In its Ringaskiddy (Cork) site, Janssen Biotech has switched to a newer perfusion technology, alternating tangential flow (ATF) perfusion (Refine Technology, Edison, NJ) for the production of more recent mAbs, such as Simponi® [16]. The ATF system achieves media exchange by circulating the broth back and forth between the bioreactor and an external hollow-fiber filter via the action of a diaphragm pump [17,24]. The vendors report that the pulsating motion allows greater media perfusion rates, reduces the dead volume outside the reactor, and minimizes the shear stress the cells are exposed to. These multiple effects allow the ATF perfusion system to minimize filter fouling and achieve higher cell densities and therefore reach higher productivities compared to earlier perfusion systems.

17.2.2
Semicontinuous Chromatography

Over the last three decades mAb manufacturers have been looking to increase upstream productivity and yields. This has led to a dramatic increase in cell culture mAb titers from only mg l^{-1} values to the current norm of 2–3 g l^{-1}. This norm is likely to rise further with processes in development with reported titers of 5 g l^{-1} and higher [e.g., 7,25]. The notable success in upstream development has placed an increased burden on downstream operations and improvements are actively being pursued to tackle the growing downstream bottleneck [25–27]. The current and future mAb purification platforms are still dominated by chromatographic methods with Protein A as the preferred primary capture step [18–20]. Protein A resins are the leading material cost contributor in the current and future platforms [15,28]. During commercial manufacture Protein A contributes typically to 10% of the direct costs; however, in early development, it can account for 50% of the direct costs [28]. During clinical manufacture product-specific chromatographic resins are often used for just a few cycles, particularly if the drug candidate is unsuccessful, leading to the resin being discarded before reaching its full potential cycle lifetime. The impact of poor resin utilization is a particular concern in mAb development and improving utilization of these expensive resins can have a significant effect on the manufacturing and development costs by reducing the cost burden associated with failed drug candidates.

Typically, the Protein A column is loaded up to 90% of 1% breakthrough capacity, underutilizing the resin's capacity. This loading regime results in the entry (top) of the column being saturated and the exit (bottom) unsaturated upon completion of loading. This leads to excess buffer consumption caused by washing, elution, and cleaning of the unsaturated column portion. Various methods have been employed to increase the productivity and utilization of Protein A columns, including the use of dual flowrate loading strategies [29] and flow-through recycling in an effort to fully saturate the whole resin [8]. An alternative approach to increase utilization is to divide the column into multiple portions and wash and elute the saturated top portion of the column and continue loading the unsaturated portion of the column until saturated. This principle is applied in semicontinuous chromatography, which allows the columns to be loaded to a higher binding capacity, reducing the resin volume required and the overall buffer consumption. Semicontinuous chromatography has been shown by Mahajan *et al.* [8] to be an effective way to increase resin utilization. This concept is similar to the simulated moving bed (SMB) concept commonly used in the chemical and pharmaceutical industries [30–32], but to date this concept is not widely used in mAb purification. The expertise from these industries is now being applied to biopharmaceutical processes, with companies including Novasep (Pompey, France) offering BioSC (2–6 columns) and Tarpon (Leiden, Netherlands) with BioSMB (6–12 columns). This has also led companies already supplying the biopharmaceutical industry to develop their own systems based on the SMB concept, such as GE Healthcare (Uppsala, Sweden) with its periodic counter-current (PCC) system (3–4 columns). Recent papers have provided a proof-of-concept (PoC) for semicontinuous chromatography linked to a fed-batch process [8] and to an alternating tangential flow perfusion process [9,10] for mAbs. The disclosed activities and publications by a number of biopharmaceutical manufacturers on their assessment of semicontinuous chromatography is summarized in Table 17.2. Several large biopharmaceutical manufacturers and semicontinuous chromatography system manufacturers are included in Table 17.2.

Table 17.2 Current commercial use of semicontinuous chromatography.

Company	Systems evaluated/employed	References
Amgen	GE AKTA PCC	[33]
Bayer	Tarpon BioSMB	[34]
Biogen-Idec	Tarpon BioSMB	[25]
Centocor	GE AKTA PCC	[35]
Genentech	GE AKTA PCC	[8]
Genzyme	GE AKTA PCC	[9,10]
Lonza	Tarpon BioSMB	[36]
Merck	Tarpon BioSMB	[37]
Pfizer (formerly Wyeth)	Tarpon BioSMB, GE AKTA PCC	[28,38]

17.3 Tool Description

To successfully evaluate batch and semicontinuous biopharmaceutical unit operations, a decisional tool was created that captured the operational, economic, environmental, and risk features associated with each strategy. The decisional tool integrated models on mass balancing, equipment sizing, bioprocess economics, scheduling, uncertainty analysis, and multiattribute decision-making. The tool was built in a discrete-event simulation environment (Extend v6, Imagine That! Inc., San Jose, USA). This permitted the dynamic consequences of resource constraints, delays, uncertainties, and equipment failures to be modeled in a temporal fashion and their impact on the key metrics to be computed. The tool was database-driven (MySQL AB, Uppsala, Sweden) so as to facilitate the specification of processes and better manage the large input and output datasets required for multiple processes, uncertainty analysis, and optimization. The tool incorporated specific features to capture the dynamics of continuous manufacture. These included scheduling features of perfusion culture related to interactions between the generation of daily perfusion harvests and the subsequent pooling and purification operations as well as the scheduling consequences of failure events occurring at random times during the perfusion cultures. The models for the continuous chromatography operations captured the experimentally derived design logic to generate the optimal system scale and operating parameters (e.g., switch time between columns).

A precalculation and optimization module was created to run prior to the simulation of a particular scenario so as to assess all the possible equipment sizing strategies before selecting the optimum process configuration (e.g., $1 \times 6000\,l$ versus $3 \times 2000\,l$ bioreactors) for the given demand in terms of both production time and cost. Alongside equipment scaling the precalculation module also evaluated whether single-use technologies could be implemented in the form of single-use bioreactors and product holding bags, based on the process volumes generated and utilized by each unit operation.

Figure 17.1 summarizes the key inputs and outputs of the decisional tool. The key economic metrics calculated by the tool were the capital investment and the cost of goods per gram (COG/g) for the complete manufacturing process (fermentation to bulk drug substance). The capital investment was determined using the Lang factor method as a function of the total equipment purchase cost. The COG/g comprised the annual direct (materials and labor) and indirect (depreciation and facility-dependent overheads) operating costs divided by the annual product output as detailed by Farid [39]. The key environmental metric calculated by the tool was the E-factor [40], defined as the total mass of water or consumables used by the manufacturing strategy divided by the total mass of the product. The tool's quantitative outputs were combined with qualitative operational metrics, such as ease of validation using a multiattribute decision making (MADM) technique [41,42] as described by Pollock *et al.* [15].

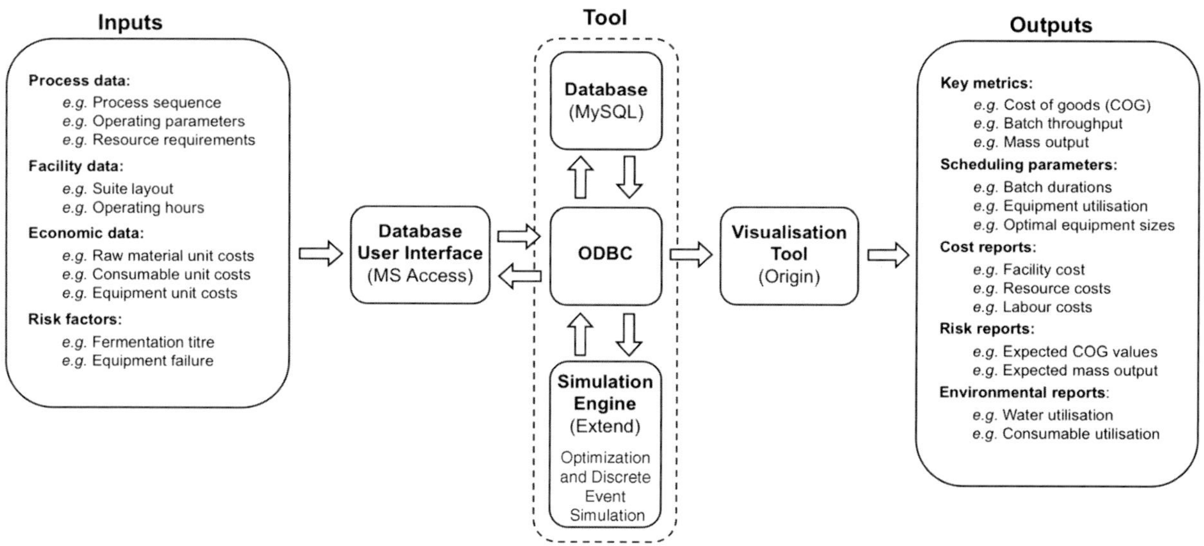

Figure 17.1 Overview of simulation tool structure highlighting key communication directionality and content with respect to key inputs and outputs. ODBC; open data base connectivity.

17.4
Case Study 1: Fed-batch Versus Perfusion Culture for Commercial mAb Production

The decisional tool was initially used to explore the current and future potential of continuous technologies in upstream processing for the commercial manufacture of mAbs [15]. Process economics comparisons of fed-batch and perfusion strategies can yield different rankings depending on several factors, such as the cell densities, media perfusion rates, pooling strategy, and probabilities of failure assumed as well as more qualitative concerns, such as the level of operational complexity and validation effort. For a fair economic comparison of fed-batch versus perfusion cell culture technologies it is important to capture the impact on downstream processing and the resulting equipment sizing changes. Furthermore, the ranking will vary across different production scales and titers as illustrated in the case study discussed later.

The case study explored when first-generation perfusion culture systems would cease to be cost-effective. The trade-offs between the lower productivities and higher upfront investments of fed-batch processes versus the higher chances of equipment failure with perfusion processes were analyzed. It also investigated whether newer emerging perfusion culture technologies that offer higher cell densities and lower failures rates than first-generation systems, as well as the ability to integrate with single-use bioreactors, would be able to compete with fed-batch processes at the large scale. The operational, economic and environmental feasibility of whole bioprocesses based on fed-batch (FB) culture, spin-filter perfusion (SPIN), and alternating tangential flow (ATF) perfusion systems was evaluated across a range of titers (equivalent fed-batch titers of 2–10 $g\,l^{-1}$) and commercial scales (100 $kg\ yr^{-1}$ to 1000 $kg\ yr^{-1}$) so as to visualize how their ranking changes in different industry scenarios.

Figure 17.2 illustrates the process flowsheets for the production of mAbs using the three culture technologies, FB, SPIN, and ATF. Figure 17.2 also highlights the differences between the primary recovery operations in each flowsheet where the FB process requires the most steps for cell removal and liquor concentration in contrast to the ATF process that does not require any given its external hollow fiber filter. The purification train was based on a generic mAb purification platform using three orthogonal chromatographic steps with intermediate filtration and viral clearance steps [6,18,43]. The perfusion culture purification train also includes a post-Protein A pooling stage of the daily harvests, with the advantage of operating a smaller highly utilized Protein A column [13,23].

Table 17.3 lists a number of key assumptions that differ between the processes. The FB culture step ran for 12 days in contrast to the SPIN and ATF cultures, which ran for 60 days. Typical maximum cell densities of 10 million cells ml^{-1} for FB culture, 15 million cells ml^{-1} for SPIN and 50 million cells ml^{-1} for ATF were assumed given the culture durations and perfusion rates. The cell culture technologies also differed in terms of scalability and the potential to use single-use bioreactors (SUBs). FB reactors can reach 20 000 l, whereas

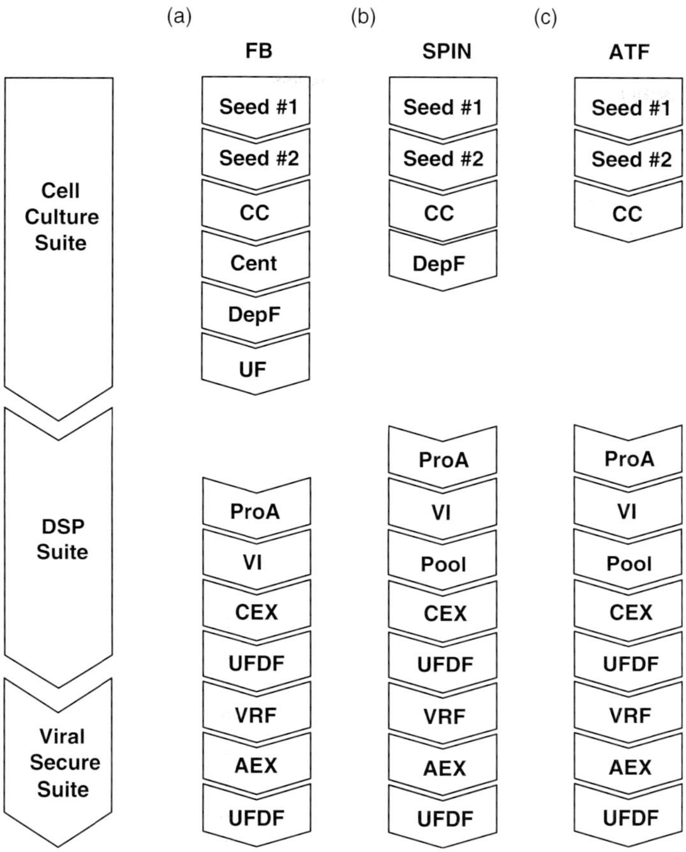

Figure 17.2 Case study process sequences and suite configuration for (a) the fed-batch (FB), (b) the spin-filter (SPIN), and (c) the alternating tangential flow (ATF) process. CC = cell culture, Cent = centrifugation, DepF = depth filtration, UF = ultrafiltration, ProA = Protein A chromatography, VI = virus inactivation, Pool = daily perfusate volume pooling, CEX = cation exchange chromatography, UFDF = ultrafiltration/diafiltration, AEX = anion exchange chromatography, VRF = virus retention filtration.

SPIN and ATF systems peak at 1500–2000 l. The ATF system can successfully employ SUBs in all scenarios due to its use of an external cell separation device. The fed-batch system is capable of employing SUBs for reactor volumes below 2000 l.

Figure 17.3 shows the COG/g for the FB, SPIN, and ATF strategies for the $5\,g\,l^{-1}$ scenario across a range of scales of production ($100\,kg\,yr^{-1}$, $500\,kg\,yr^{-1}$, $1000\,kg\,yr^{-1}$). Interestingly, these deterministic simulation results (without risks) illustrated that both the FB and SPIN processes have similar cost of goods per gram at low commercial production scales of $100\,kg\,yr^{-1}$. However, SPIN processes become less economically attractive at the higher production scales

Table 17.3 Key assumptions for the fed-batch, spin-filter, and ATF processes in Case Study 1.

Step-specific data

Variable	FB	SPIN	ATF
Input			
Cell culture time (days)	12	60	60
Max VCD (million cells ml^{-1})	10	15	50
Max bioreactor volume (l)	20 000	2000	1500
Max perfusion rate (vv day^{-1})	–	1	1.5
Calculated			
Process yield	65%	68%	69%
Annual # batches	22	5	5
Max product concentration (g l^{-1})	2–10	20% FB	45% FB
Annual bioreactor capacity required	1 × FB	1/9 × FB	1/29 × FB
Installed bioreactor capacity	1 × FB	1/2 × FB	1/6 × FB
Grams of product/liter of media	1.2–6.3	19% FB	44% FB

General cost data

Resource	Investment cost ($)	Consumable cost ($)
Single-use bioreactor [a)]		
200 l	88 000	4200
500 l	98 000	5460
1000 l	110 000	8260
2000 l	175 000	9800
Perfusion device [b)]		
Spin-filter	35 000	N/A
ATF 4 System	30 000	714
ATF 6 System	90 000	3570
ATF 8 System	130 000	7140
ATF 10 System	180 000	16 300
Other key materials		
Protein A resin cost ($/l)		8000
Cell culture media[c)] ($/l)		3.15
Fed-batch feed additions ($/l)		13.1

a) Investment cost includes: disposable bioreactor support vessel, agitator motor, gas and fluid pumps, Consumable cost includes: bioreactor bag.

b) Investment cost includes: filter unit, controller and auxiliary media pump, consumable cost includes: filter.

c) Cell culture media used for initial media fill in fed-batch cell culture and daily perfusion media exchanges.

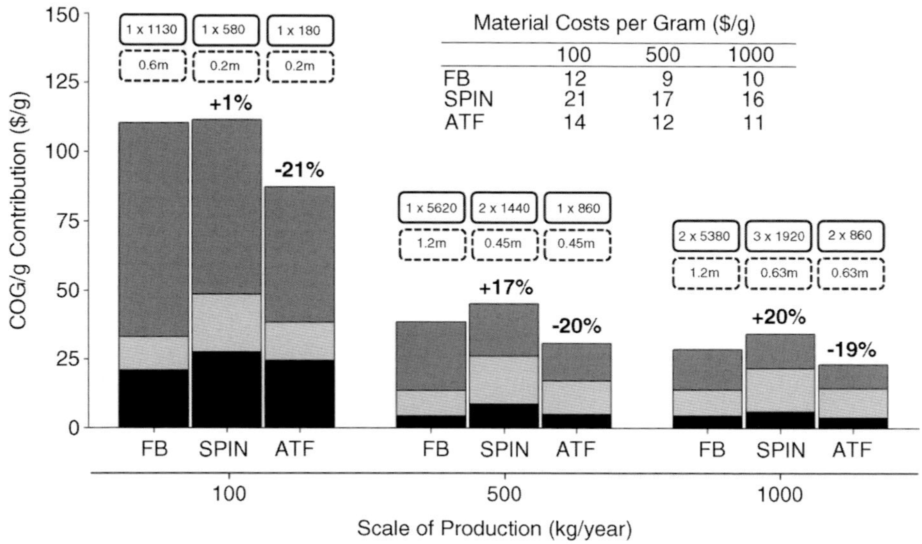

Figure 17.3 A comparison of the cost of goods per gram on a category basis for labor costs (black), direct material costs (light gray), and indirect costs (dark gray) between the fed-batch process (FB), the spin-filter process (SPIN) and the alternating tangential flow process (ATF) over a range of scales of production for an equivalent fed-batch titer of 5 g l^{-1}, where the percentage difference is relative to the fed-batch process. The embedded table highlights the materials cost per gram for the production strategies. The optimal sizing strategy for each process is indicated in the boxes above each bar highlighting the number and scale (l) of bioreactor(s) (solid box) and the column diameter for the Protein A chromatography step (dashed box) across a range of scales of production.

where the material costs dominate the COG/g; hence, the ~1.8-fold higher material costs exhibited by the SPIN strategy relative to the FB strategy due to the higher usage of culture media and product-holding bags become more significant. In contrast the ATF strategy is seen to offer cost advantages across all production scales of ~20% in the 5 g l^{-1} scenario since its superior cell density and hence volumetric productivity coupled with a smaller highly utilized purification train results in significantly larger savings in indirect costs (~40%) combined with only a ~1.2-fold increase in material costs. This translates into overall savings irrespective of the dominance of either indirect or material costs at either extremes of the production scales. Savings were also seen when the ATF peak cell density dropped from a fivefold to a threefold increase over the FB strategy for most combinations of titers and production scales. In contrast the fed-batch strategy performed better in terms of environmental sustainability with a lower water and consumable usage profile.

The study was extended to include the perceived risks associated with perfusion strategies due to contamination or filter fouling over the long culture durations (Table 17.4) using Monte Carlo simulation. Figure 17.4 shows the

Table 17.4 Assumptions for probabilities of equipment failure and consequences for fed-batch and perfusion processes.

Process event	***p*(Failure)**	**Consequence**
Fed-batch culture contamination	1%	Batch loss
Spin-filter culture contamination	6%	Batch loss and discard two pooled perfusate volumes
Spin-filter filter failure	4%	Batch loss and no pooled volumes are discarded
ATF culture contamination	6%	Batch loss and discard two pooled perfusate volumes
ATF filter failure	2%	Replace filter and discard next 24 h of perfusate
In process filtration failure; general	5%	4 h delay and 2% yield loss
In process filtration failure; postviral inactivation	20%	4 h delay and 2% yield loss

expected kg output and COG/g values for the FB, SPIN, and ATF strategies under uncertainty at a 500 kg yr^{-1} scale of production and a titer of 5 g l^{-1}. The risk analysis results demonstrated the enhanced robustness of the fed-batch process as indicated by the narrower frequency distributions for output and cost. The frequency of annual output values for the FB scenario has a distinct shape, which was found to relate directly to the number of batch failures in any given year of production. This is highlighted in Figure 17.4c where the biggest bar represents no batch failures and the subsequently smaller bars represent the occurrence of one and more batch failures per year. The SPIN strategy is seen to have the highest probability of failing to meet the output target given the long tail in its output frequency distribution. The analysis highlighted also that the ATF process was still the most cost-effective option even under uncertainty (Figure 17.4b).

However, when the analysis was extended with multiattribute decision-making to consider not only process economics but also operational feasibility (e.g., ease of operation and validation), the picture changed. The operational feasibility scores and weightings were obtained through a survey questionnaire sent to industrial experts with experience operating both fed-batch and perfusion culture. The participants were asked to rank the cell culture technologies against each of these qualitative attributes: ease of control/operation, ease of validation (time/effort), ease of development (time/effort), operational flexibility, and batch-to-batch variability. The resulting sensitivity plots (Figure 17.5) enabled identification of the critical ratio of weightings of economic and operational benefits that affect the choice between ATF perfusion and fed-batch strategies. Figure 17.5 illustrates that if the operational and economic benefits were considered equally important, then the fed-batch and ATF strategies were tied in ranking. It provided also an insight into the limited use of spin-filter perfusion strategies in the industry.

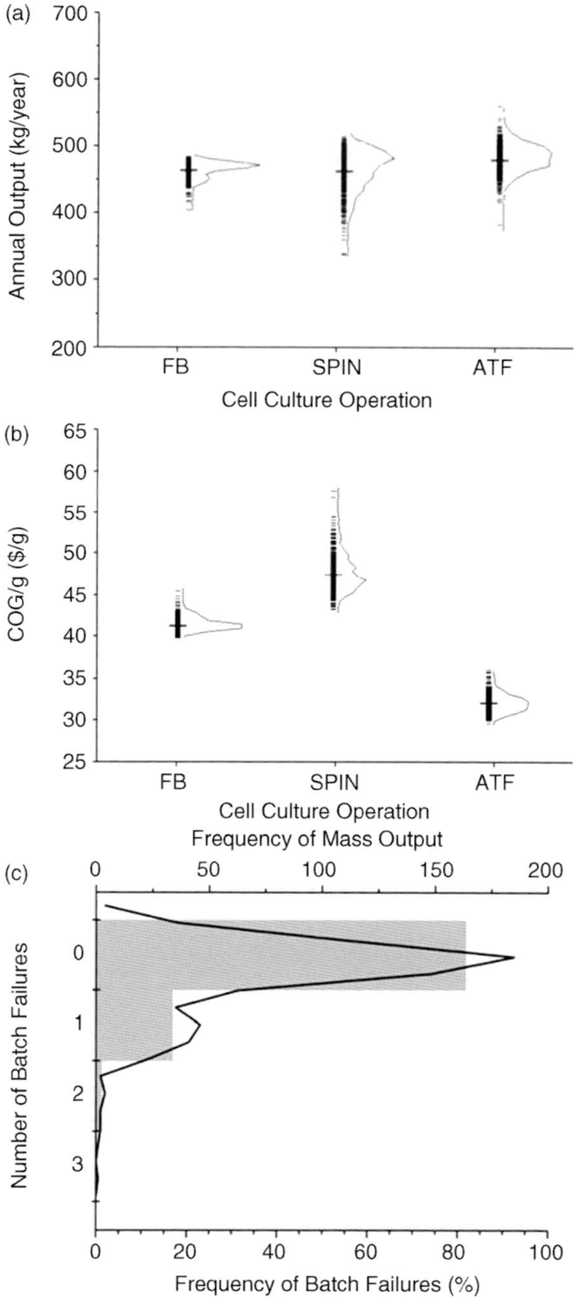

Figure 17.4 Frequency distribution plots depicting the expected process outputs under manufacturing uncertainty for (a) the expected annual kilogram output, (b) the expected cost of goods per gram, and (c) the number of fed-batch culture failures, for a 500 kg yr^{-1} scale of production and equivalent fed-batch titer of 5 g l^{-1}.

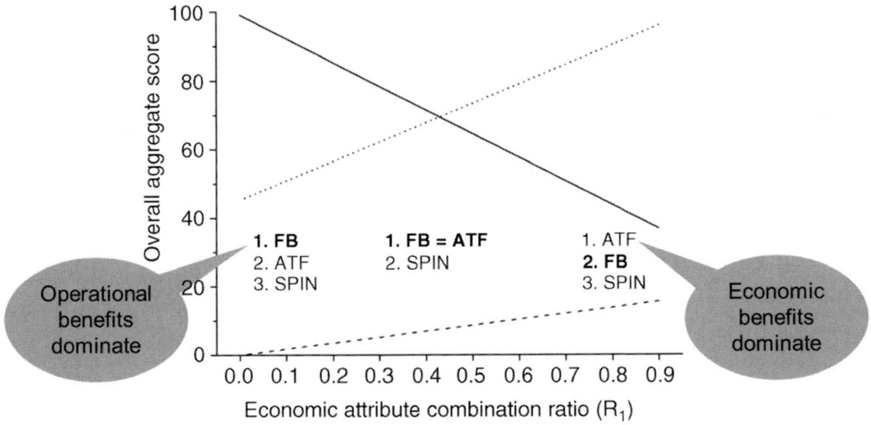

Figure 17.5 Sensitivity plots showing the effect of the economic attribute combination ratio (R_1) on the overall aggregate score for the fed-batch (solid line), spin-filter (dashed line), and ATF (dotted line) processes. The overall aggregate score comprises the weighted sum of the economic, operational and environmental benefits. The environmental attribute combination ratio is fixed at 0.1. For 500 kg yr^{-1} scale of production and equivalent titer of 5 g l^{-1}.

17.5 Case Study 2: Semicontinuous Affinity Chromatography for Clinical and Commercial Manufacture

The second case study focused on the potential of retrofitting existing batch facilities to use continuous affinity capture chromatography instead of standard batch chromatography [28]. Given that costly capture resins are often used for just a few cycles in clinical manufacture, the impact of development phase as well as scale on the cost-effectiveness of the technologies was investigated. An integrated experimental and modeling approach was adopted to evaluate the potential of semicontinuous chromatography for the capture of mAbs in clinical and commercial manufacture.

Small-scale single-column experimental breakthrough studies were used to derive design parameters and design equations for the semicontinuous affinity chromatography system. Verification runs with the semicontinuous three-column and four-column periodic counter-current chromatography system indicated the robustness of the design approach for determining the optimal switch times and flowrates so as to minimize potential losses of unbound material. The product quality profiles and step yields (after wash step optimization) achieved were comparable to the standard batch process (Table 17.5). The experimentally derived design equations were incorporated into a decisional tool comprising dynamic simulation, process economics, and sizing optimization. The decisional tool was used to evaluate the economic and operational feasibility of whole mAb bioprocesses employing PCC affinity capture chromatography versus standard batch

Table 17.5 Protein pool product quality for standard batch and continuous chromatography.

	% Species of protein pool		
CEX-HPLC	**Acidic**	**Designated**	**Basic**
Standard (3 cycles)	18.4 ± 2.5	74.8 ± 2.7	6.9 ± 0.3
3C-PCC (6 runs)	18.3 ± 0.6	75.8 ± 1.5	5.9 ± 1.0
Cycle (100 cycles)	19.3 ± 0.8	75.0 ± 1.2	5.7 ± 0.9
SEC-HPLC	**HMW**	**Designated**	**LMW**
Standard (3 cycles)	1.0 ± 0.1	96.9 ± 0.1	2.1 ± 0.0
3C-PCC (6 runs)	0.4 ± 0.1	98.0 ± 0.1	1.6 ± 0.2
Cycle (100 cycles)	0.7 ± 0.2	97.6 ± 0.3	1.7 ± 0.2

chromatography across a product's lifecycle from clinical to commercial manufacture. Table 17.6 illustrates the clinical trials estimates used throughout this case study to calculate the amount of mAb required for each phase of the clinical trials throughout the development pipeline. The case study uses the quick win, fail fast development paradigm [4], where the material required for Phase I and II is generated in a single PoC batch and the Phase III material in multiple batches at the

Table 17.6 Key assumptions for the batch and continuous capture chromatography processes in Case Study 2.

Variable		**Value**
Clinical trial estimates		
Dosage (mg kg^{-1} body weight)		7
Number of doses per patient per year		26
Individuals in Phase I clinical trials (single dose)		40
Individuals in Phase II clinical trials (6 month dose)		200
Individuals in Phase III clinical trials (year dose)		2000
Process parameters		
Maximum binding capacity (g l^{-1})		65
Bed height (m)	– Standard batch process	0.25
	– PCC process	0.1
Shift duration (h)	– Standard batch process	12
	– PCC process	24
Maximum media hold time (h)		72
Cost parameters		
Protein A resin cost ($/l)		8000
AEX resin cost ($/l)		1500
Virus removal filtration membrane ($/$m^2$)		3250
Labor cost ($/h)		58
Chromatography process skid (15–600 l h^{-1}) ($)		226 000
PCC process skid (15–600 l h^{-1}) ($)		1 080 000
Chromatography column (Dia = 0.2 m) ($)		132 000
Chromatography column (Dia = 2 m) ($)		218 000

commercial scale. The cell culture titer was assumed to increase twofold from the PoC batch ($2.5\,g\,l^{-1}$) to the Phase III and commercial batches ($5\,g\,l^{-1}$). The manufacturing process used in the case study was based on a generic two-column mAb process [6,44]. The key differences between the PCC-based process and standard batch process lie in the operation of the capture chromatography step (Protein A) and are highlighted in Table 17.6. The standard batch process employs a single column utilizing multiple cycles, which are loaded with harvested cell culture fluid (HCCF) up to 90% of 1% BT (safety factor accounting for capacity losses with resin reuse), resulting in a maximum protein challenge of $40\,g\,l^{-1}$. The PCC systems employ multiple columns (3 or 4) for multiple cycles, which are loaded to 100% BT resulting in a dynamic binding capacity of $65\,g\,l^{-1}$.

The integrated techno-economic evaluation predicted that semicontinuous capture chromatography would offer more significant savings in direct costs for early-stage clinical manufacture (PoC) (~30%) than for late-stage clinical (~10–15%) or commercial (~5%) manufacture. Early phase savings are important due to the high attrition rates. A detailed examination of the direct manufacturing costs highlighted in Figure 17.6 reveals how the decreased

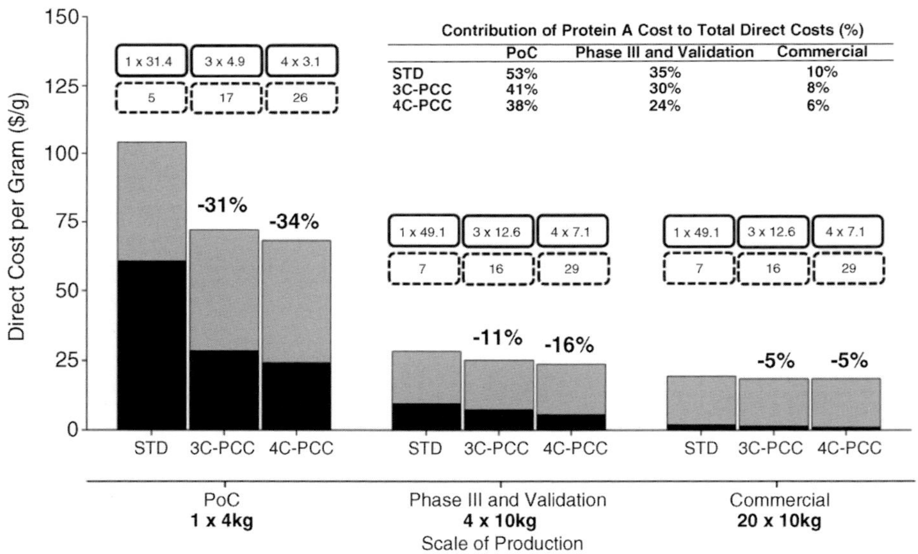

Figure 17.6 A comparison of direct cost per gram highlighting the Protein A cost (black) to the other direct costs (gray) between the standard batch process (STD) and the three-column (3C-PCC) and four-column periodic countercurrent chromatographic (4C-PCC) process over a range of scales of production for the low titer scenario, where the percentage difference is relative to the standard batch process. The embedded table highlights the percentage contribution of the Protein A resin towards the total direct costs. The optimal sizing strategy for each process is indicated in the boxes above each bar highlighting the number and scale (l) of columns (solid box) and the number of system cycles (dashed box) across a range of scales of production.

competitiveness of the PCC system with production scale can be attributed to the decreasing contribution of the Protein A resin cost to the total cost, as illustrated in the embedded table. The savings offered by the PCC system are reduced significantly as the scale of production increases from the generation of PoC material (1 × 4 kg batch) to the generation of Phase III clinical material (4 × 10 kg batches) and commercial material (20 × 10 kg batches per annum). This effect is due to the fact that the Protein A resin is only used for a few cycles in the PoC batch and Phase III batches. Due to the requirement to keep the resins product-specific, it cannot be reused for another drug candidate, resulting in a higher cost burden because the resin may be discarded before reaching its full potential cycle lifetime. For example, the Protein A cost ($250 k) accounts for over half the direct costs at the PoC scale for the standard batch process. However, for a 10 kg batch the resin costs $390 k (49.1 l column, 7 cycles) and this cost is split between the multiple batches and therefore reduces the overall cost contribution to 34 and 10% for the Phase III (4 batches) and commercial (20 batches) material, respectively. The PCC systems maintain the same level of column volume reduction with the increase in scale, but as shown by the embedded table in Figure 17.6 they fail to offer the same level of savings as the Protein A cost becomes less significant as other process costs dominate the manufacturing cost. For cases where it is possible to use the same lot of Protein A for both PoC and Phase III batches, the Protein A cost contributions for late-phase batches would be even lower.

A retrofitting analysis established that the direct cost savings obtained by eight PoC batches would be sufficient to pay back the investment cost of the pilot-scale semicontinuous chromatography system. The investment cost required for the PCC system designed for the PoC scale of production could be balanced with the savings realized in the direct costs (~$130–150 k per batch) after 8–9 PoC batches (8–9 drug candidates). With the increase in production scale to the Phase III and commercial manufacture (10 kg batch), the standard batch process employs a larger skid scale (45–1800 l h^{-1}) to support the larger column volume requirements, resulting in an increase in equipment cost (~$380 k). The equivalent PCC system can still utilize the same specification skid as in the PoC scale of production with larger columns, meaning it is only three times more expensive for the 10 kg batch scale of production. The reduced savings in direct costs per batch highlighted at the larger scale of production shown in Figure 17.6 mean the investment cost would take longer to be recouped, requiring 25–40 Phase III batches (6–10 drug candidates). However, in producing 6–10 Phase III drug candidates, a higher number of candidates must have entered the PoC scale of production given the attrition rates in clinical trials. Taking this lifecycle perspective highlighted that the direct cost savings obtained by 8–9 PoC batches (8–9 drug candidates) would be sufficient to pay back the cost of the larger-scale PCC system for late-stage manufacture.

17.6
Case Study 3: Integrated Continuous Processing Flowsheets

The analysis presented in the previous two sections was extended to assess the cost-effectiveness of integrated continuous bioprocesses that link continuous upstream and downstream technologies. In the integrated continuous process, the daily harvested cell culture fluid (HCCF) from the perfusion culture was loaded onto the continuous capture chromatography step. The discrete eluates from the capture step were individually passed onto the subsequent anion-exchange (AEX) column and its flow-through stream continuously passed through the virus retention filtration rig (VRF). The case study focused on comparing whole bioprocesses that used either batch, continuous, or a hybrid combination of batch and continuous technologies for cell culture, capture, and polishing steps (Figure 17.7). In all cases the sub-batches post-VRF were pooled into one stream prior to the final ultra/diafiltration step. This was to help solve the regulatory requirement for batch traceability and reduce the quality burden associated with batch release testing.

The COG/g of each strategy was established across combinations of different development phases and company sizes. Each development phase required different manufacturing scales, batch numbers, and material reuse strategies. Each company size resulted in different numbers of drug candidates at each development phase. For example a medium-sized company may aim to launch 1 new

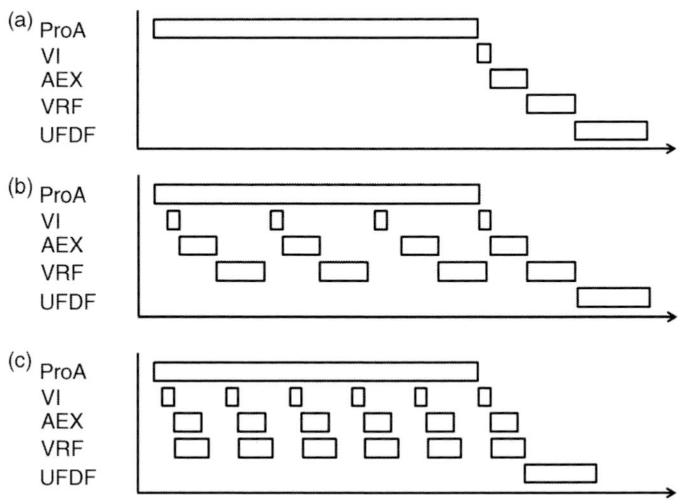

Figure 17.7 Downstream process scheduling for (a) the base case process sequence, (b) the continuous to batch process sequence, and (c) the continuous process sequence. ProA, Protein A chromatography; VI, viral inactivation; AEX, anion-exchange chromatography; VRF, viral retention filtration; UFDF, ultrafiltration/diafiltration.

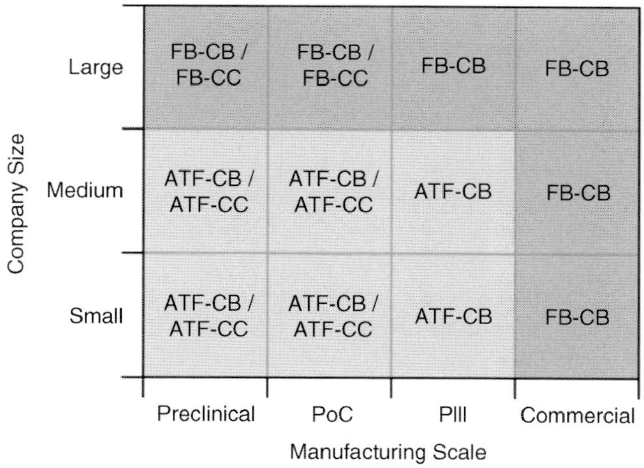

Figure 17.8 Contour plots showing the impact of manufacturing scale and manufacturing strategies on the most economically attractive manufacturing strategies for each scenario. FB = fed-batch, ATF – perfusion using alternating tangential flow filtration, CB = continuous capture followed by batch polishing, CC = continuous capture followed by continuous polishing. (Preclinical, 1 × 0.5 kg; PoC, 1 × 4 kg; Phase III, 4 × 10 kg; Commercial, 20 × 10 kg).

product per year, which required 10 new drug candidates to enter preclinical trials each year given the attrition rate assumptions.

Figure 17.8 summarizes the optimal manufacturing strategies for different combinations of manufacturing scale (Pre-clinical, PoC, Phase III, Commercial) and company size (small, medium, large). The tool outputs predict that the integrated continuous strategy (ATF-CC = ATF perfusion, continuous capture, continuous polishing) appears as the optimal strategy for early phase production and small/medium-sized companies. However, the ranking of strategies switches for commercial production and large companies to the hybrid strategy with fed-batch culture, continuous capture, and batch polishing (FB-CB).

Perfusion-based processes linked to continuous capture become less economically attractive for larger demands and product numbers when there is a requirement for multiple parallel perfusion reactors, each with dedicated purification trains, which becomes costly to install. Continuous chromatography appears to offer advantages in all scenarios explored given its ability to reduce the volume of expensive Protein A resin required and to generate a more concentrated elution pools that allow smaller virus filtration membrane areas to be adopted. The optimal polishing strategy switches from continuous to batch at larger scales since the cost of the single-use virus filters required for each sub-batch in the continuous process becomes more expensive than a single larger virus filter in the batch process. Further considerations outside the scope of this work include the impact of adopting continuous processing on process development efforts.

17.7 Conclusions

This chapter has presented an evaluation of the feasibility of continuous biopharmaceutical manufacturing strategies utilizing perfusion cell culture and semicontinuous chromatography throughout the product lifecycle from preclinical to commercial manufacture. A decisional tool was created to cope with the continuous nature of upstream and downstream process sequences, the consequences of failures as well as the use of single-use bioreactors and bags when the scale was appropriate. The case study comparing fed-batch versus perfusion culture for commercial production identified that the economic competitiveness of continuous perfusion processes depends on the cell density increase achievable and the failure rate; critical threshold values were identified for the scenarios explored in the case study. The tool predicted limited use of first-generation perfusion systems in industrial-scale processes since they would struggle to compete on economic, environmental, operational, and robustness fronts at most cell culture titers and production scales. In contrast, second-generation perfusion systems were predicted to be competitive under certain scenarios where process economics savings were considered more important than operational feasibility (e.g., ease of operation and validation). The integrated techno-economic evaluation of whole bioprocesses that utilize continuous chromatography for product capture predicted that such processes have the ability to offer significant direct cost savings in early clinical phase material generation; this can have a large impact considering the high clinical attrition rates. The insights from the final case study were that integrated continuous processes can offer savings for early-phase manufacture in companies with small portfolio sizes. However, for late-phase manufacture of large portfolios, hybrid processes with fed-batch culture, continuous capture chromatography, and batch polishing can be more economical. The decisional tool therefore acts as a valuable test bed for assessing the potential of novel continuous strategies to cope with different scales of operation, phases of development, and company sizes.

The analysis has demonstrated that continuous processing can offer COG benefits in different scenarios. Further considerations that will affect the uptake of such technologies include the technology readiness for large-scale manufacture (e.g., availability of GMP skids, online analytics and control, hardware reliability), protocols, and training to deal with the extra operational complexity, the development effort required, and regulatory concerns.

Acknowledgments

The authors would like to thank the following industrialists for sharing their experience with running continuous systems: Joseph McLaughlin, James Bouressa, Glen Bolton, Jon Coffman (ex-Pfizer); Richard Francis (Francis Biopharma Consulting); Morten Munk, Christoffer Bro and Jacob Jensen

(CMC). We are very grateful to the representatives from Centocor, Genzyme, Merck-Serono, Novartis, Bayer, and Eli Lilly for their contributions towards Table 17.1. Financial support from Pfizer and the Engineering and Physical Sciences Research Council (EPSRC), UK, is gratefully acknowledged. The Advanced Centre for Biochemical Engineering at UCL hosts the EPSRC Centre for Innovative Manufacturing in Emergent Macromolecular Therapies in collaboration with Imperial College and a consortium of industry and government users.

References

1 DiMasi, J.A. *et al.* (2010) Trends in risks associated with new drug development: success rates for investigational drugs. *Clin. Pharmacol. Ther.*, **87** (3), 272–277.

2 Farid, S.S. (2009) Process economics drivers in industrial monoclonal antibody manufacture, in *Process Scale Purification of Antibodies* (ed. U. Gottschalk), John Wiley & Sons, Inc., Hoboken, NJ, pp. 239–262.

3 Morgan, S. *et al.* (2011) The cost of drug development: a systematic review. *Health Policy*, **100** (1), 4–17.

4 Paul, S.M. *et al.* (2010) How to improve R&D productivity: the pharmaceutical industry's grand challenge. *Nat. Rev. Drug Discov.*, **9** (3), 203–214.

5 O'Hagan, P. and Farkas, C. (2009) Bringing pharma R&D back to health. Bain & Company.

6 Kelley, B.D. (2007) Very large scale monoclonal antibody purification: the case for conventional unit operations. *Biotechnol. Prog.*, **23** (5), 995–1008.

7 Kelley, B. (2009) Industrialization of mAb production technology – the bioprocessing industry at a crossroads. *mAbs*, **1** (5), 443–452.

8 Mahajan, E., George, A., and Wolk, B. (2012) Improving affinity chromatography resin efficiency using semi-continuous chromatography. *J. Chromatogr. A*, **1227**, 154–162.

9 Warikoo, V. *et al.* (2012) Integrated continuous production of recombinant therapeutic proteins. *Biotechnol. Bioeng.*, **109** (12), 3018–3029.

10 Godawat, R. *et al.* (2012) Periodic counter-current chromatography – design and operational considerations for integrated and continuous purification of proteins. *Biotechnol. J.*, **7** (12), 1496–1508.

11 FDA (2011) Advancing regulatory science at FDA – a strategic plan. Available at http://www.fda.gov/downloads/ScienceResearch/SpecialTopics/RegulatoryScience/UCM268225.pdf (accessed 2014).

12 Voisard, D. *et al.* (2003) Potential of cell retention techniques for large-scale high-density perfusion culture of suspended mammalian cells. *Biotechnol. Bioeng.*, **82** (7), 751–765.

13 Lim, A.C. *et al.* (2006) A computer-aided approach to compare the production economics of fed-batch and perfusion culture under uncertainty. *Biotechnol. Bioeng.*, **93** (4), 687–697.

14 Lim, A.C. *et al.* (2005) Application of a decision-support tool to assess pooling strategies in perfusion culture processes under uncertainty. *Biotechnol. Prog.*, **21** (4), 1231–1242.

15 Pollock, J., Ho, S.V., and Farid, S.S. (2013) Fed-batch and perfusion culture processes: economic, environmental, and operational feasibility under uncertainty. *Biotechnol. Bioeng.*, **110** (1), 206–219.

16 Centocor, I.L.A (2006) Centocor IPPC licence application. Available at http://www.epa.ie/licences/lic_eDMS/090151b2800c1411.pdf (accessed 2011).

17 Crowley, J., Wubben, M., and Coco Martin, J.M. (2012) Process for cell culturing by continuous perfusion and alternating tangential flow. US Patent 8,206,981.

18 Farid, S.S. (2006) Established bioprocesses for producing antibodies as a basis for

future planning. *Adv. Biochem. Eng. Biotechnol.*, **101**, 1–42.
19 Gagnon, P. (2012) Technology trends in antibody purification. *J. Chromatogr. A*, **1221**, 57–70.
20 Marichal-Gallardo, P.A. and Álvarez, M.M. (2012) State-of-the-art in downstream processing of monoclonal antibodies: process trends in design and validation. *Biotechnol. Prog.*, **28** (4), 899–916.
21 Deo, Y.M., Mahadevan, M.D., and Fuchs, R. (1996) Practical considerations in operation and scale-up of spin-filter based bioreactors for monoclonal antibody production. *Biotechnol. Prog.*, **12** (1), 57–64.
22 Yabannavar, V.M., Singh, V., and Connelly, N.V. (1992) Mammalian cell retention in a spin-filter perfusion bioreactor. *Biotechnol. Bioeng.*, **40** (8), 925–933.
23 Wojciechowski, P.W. *et al.* (2007) Making changes to a biopharmaceutical process during development and commercial manufacturing: the REMICADE story, in *Process Scale Bioseperations for the Biopharmaceutical Industry* (eds A.A. Shukla, M.R. Etzel, and S. Gadam), Taylor & Francis Group, London, pp. 507–523.
24 Shevitz, J. (2003) Fluid filtration system. US Patent 6,544,424.
25 Bisschops, M. *et al.* (2009) Single-use, continuous-countercurrent, mulitcolumn chromatography. *BioProcess Int.*, **7** (6), S18–S23.
26 Holzer, M., Osuna-Sanchez, H., and David, L. (2008) Multicolumn chromatography: a new approach to relieving capacity bottlenecks for downstream processing efficiency. *BioProcess Int.*, **6** (8), 74–84.
27 Langer, E. (2012) CMOs and biodevelopers taking different approaches to DSP problems: CMOs get serious about new technologies. Pharmaceutical Outsourcing, July 23.
28 Pollock, J. *et al.* (2013) Optimising the design and operation of semi-continuous affinity chromatography for clinical and commercial manufacture. *J. Chromatogr. A*, **1284**, 17–27.
29 Ghose, S. *et al.* (2004) Use and optimization of a dual-flowrate loading strategy to maximize throughput in protein-A affinity chromatography. *Biotechnol. Prog.*, **20** (3), 830–840.
30 Juza, M., Mazzotti, M., and Morbidelli, M. (2000) Simulated moving-bed chromatography and its application to chirotechnology. *Trends Biotechnol.*, **18** (3), 108–118.
31 Pellek, A. and Arnum, P.V. (2008) Continuous processing: moving with or against the manufacturing flow. *Pharm. Technol.*, **9** (32), 52–58.
32 Strohlein, G. *et al.* (2007) Continuous processing: the multicolumn countercurrent solvent gradient purification process. *BioPharm Int. (Suppl.).*
33 Materie, J. (2010) Advances in continuous chromatography: increasing the productivity of the MAb direct capture step using 3-column periodic counter current chromatography. 239th ACS National Meeting, March 21–25, San Francisco, CA.
34 Daszkowski, T. (2013) Continuous processing in biotech production as an alternative to a modern batch, single-use facility. ECI Integrated Continuous Biomanufacturing, October 20–24, Barcelona, Spain.
35 Lacki, K. *et al.* (2004) A feasibility study of periodic counter-current chromatography for the capture of monoclonal antibodies from crude harvest with MabSelect protein A resin. GAb, Nice, France.
36 Ransohoff, T. (2013) The potential for continuous chromatography in clinical manufacturing of biopharmaceuticals. IBC Antibodies, Huntingdon Beach, CA.
37 Bisschops, M. *et al.* (2012) The impact of variations in column packing on a multicolumn chromatography process. PREP Symposium, Boston, MA.
38 Lyle, S. (2010) Continuous protein A chromatography for the purification of monoclonal antibodies using a three-column system. IBC Antibodies, Carlsbad, CA.
39 Farid, S.S. (2007) Process economics of industrial monoclonal antibody manufacture. *J. Chromatogr. B*, **848** (1), 8–18.
40 Sheldon, R.A. (2007) The E factor: fifteen years on. *Green Chem.*, **9** (12), 1273–1283.

41 Hwang, C.L. and Yoon, K. (1981) *Multiple Attribute Decision Making – Methods and Applications. A State-of-the-Art Survey*, Lecture Notes in Economics and Mathematical Systems, Springer, Berlin.

42 Farid, S., Washbrook, J., and Titchener-Hooker, N.J. (2005) Combining multiple quantitative and qualitative goals when assessing biomanufacturing strategies under uncertainty. *Biotechnol. Prog.*, **21** (4), 1183–1191.

43 Liu, H.F. *et al.* (2010) Recovery and purification process development for monoclonal antibody production. *mAbs*, **2** (5), 480–499.

44 Kelley, B.D. *et al.* (2008) Weak partitioning chromatography for anion exchange purification of monoclonal antibodies. *Biotechnol. Bioeng.*, **101** (3), 553–566.

18
Opportunities and Challenges for the Implementation of Continuous Processing in Biomanufacturing

Sadettin S. Ozturk

18.1
Introduction

Biomanufacturing is an established industry used to generate valuable medicines for the treatment of life threatening diseases including cancer, autoimmune diseases, and metabolic and blood disorders [1,2]. Therapeutic proteins such as interferons, blood clotting factors, enzymes, vaccines, and monoclonal antibodies (mAbs) are produced from genetically engineered microbial, yeast, and mammalian cells using validated processes involving several unit operations and employing characterized and optimized process parameters [2,3].

The process used to manufacture therapeutic proteins depends on the specific requirements of the molecule, the available technology, the experience and the expertise of the development organization, the reliability and scalability of the process, and finally, on the manufacturing and regulatory constraints [1,4]. The manufacturing processes can be classified as batch and continuous operation, even though there are hybrid processes that can use some unit operations as batch, some as continuous.

The batch process has been adopted in the pharmaceutical industry mainly for historical reasons; it is easier to define a batch, it is easier to capture all the events in the batch history, and it is easier to operate and control [5–7]. Batch processes require frequent downtime between the batches to turnaround the equipment and they are not as efficient as a continuous process in terms of process yields [7,8]. Accordingly, there has been a great interest in implementing continuous processing in biomanufacturing [9–12]. Although it had been successfully used in other industries, such as food, automotive, and petrochemical industry, continuous processing had limited application in the past because of the challenges encountered during its implementation [13]. Continuous processing is more complicated to design and operate compared to batch; process scalability, reliability, and consistency can be problematic and process validation and regulatory acceptance are not straightforward [14]. These challenges will be discussed in detail in this chapter.

Continuous Processing in Pharmaceutical Manufacturing, First Edition. Edited by Ganapathy Subramanian.

18.2 A Brief History of Continuous Processing in Biomanufacturing

Although a true continuous process does not exist for biomanufacturing of proteins by recombinant DNA technology, there has been a great interest in developing such systems and there has been application of it to some of the unit operations [9–14]. In particular, continuous processing had been implemented to upstream cell culture processes to enhance process yields and to control the product quality [9,10].

Since the early days of biomanufacturing process development there has been a great interest in continuous processing [10,15]. Continuous culture with cell retention, or perfusion, was very popular in the 1980s as it allowed reaching high cell densities and thus higher volumetric productivities. The cell culture media used in those days were not very rich in nutrients and as a result cell densities achievable in batch mode were about 1–2 million cells ml^{-1}. Continuous perfusion operation allowed an order of magnitude increase in the cell density in the bioreactor by perfusing medium at an exchange rate of 2–10 bioreactor volumes a day. Continuous perfusion also offered the advantage of low residence time in the bioreactor for the products and offered better quality for unstable, liable proteins, such as enzymes and blood coagulation factors [10–12,15].

Although several products have been developed using continuous cell culture processing, the complexity of running a perfusion operation, its reliability, scalability, and manufacturability hampered its widespread acceptance by the pharmaceutical industry [1,4,9]. By the early 1990s, fed-batch operation emerged as the method of choice for biomanufacturing [5–7]. Three factors played a role in this move: (1) simplicity of batch operation, (2) focus on monoclonal antibodies by pharmaceutical companies, and (3) advancement in feed development and medium enrichment. Monoclonal antibodies are relatively robust proteins and their quality is not impacted by residence time. Using an optimized feed strategy in a fed-batch with specially formulated feed solution and medium, more than a 1 order of magnitude increase in cell density and in productivity was accomplished. All of these factors combined established the fed-batch operation as the platform of choice and continuous processing remained an option for special molecules only [3,7].

Continuous processing is an important part of biomanufacturing as evident from the number of products in the market (Table 18.1). There are about 15 biologic products ranging from replacement enzymes, blood coagulation factors, and monoclonal antibodies. Some of these products generate more than a billion dollars a year with Remicade from J&J reaching about US $6.8 billion in sales in 2012.

While platform technologies are commonly used and fed-batch is the platform of choice, enhancing productivity and reducing manufacturing cost prompted pharmaceutical companies to consider alternative manufacturing technologies. Continuous processing offers a number of advantages over batch and it had

Table 18.1 Approved biopharmaceutical products produced by continuous cell culture (adopted from Ref. [9] and revised to include the latest data).

Product	Company	Approved	2012 sales million USD
Cerezyme	Genzyme	1994	855
ReoPro	Centocor/J&J	1994	400
Gonal-F	Serono	1997	300
Remicade	Centocor/J&J	1998	6800
Simulect	Novartis	1998	100
Rebif	Merck-Serono	1998	640
ReFacto	Wyeth	2000	114
Kogenate-FS	Bayer	2000	1400
Xigris	Eli Lilly	2001	160
Advate	Baxter	2003	1000
Fabrazyme	Genzyme	2003	380
Naglazyme	Biomarin	2005	338
Myozyme	Genzyme	2006	624
Stelara	Centocor/J&J	2009	800
Simphoni	Centocor/J&J	2009	1200
VPRIV	Shire	2012	—

been successfully implemented in other industries. Use of continuous processing in biomanufacturing started with cell culture as discussed before and it is feasible to apply it to all manufacturing unit operations in the future. Many of the issues related to the implementation of continuous processing have been resolved due to recent advances in bioprocess engineering, automation, and process optimization.

18.3 Opportunities for Continuous Processing in Biomanufacturing

Continuous processing has several advantages over batch operation in terms of process yield, process efficiency, facility utilization, and production consistency. These advantages offer several opportunities for the next generation of biomanufacturing facilities with respect to their design, construction, and operation.

18.3.1 Higher Process Yields

One of the main advantages of continuous processing over batch processing is achieving a higher productivity per volume. This applies to both upstream and downstream processes. Continuous processes run at their maximum capacity

Table 18.2 Comparison of a batch (fed-batch) and continuous (perfusion) process for monoclonal antibody production [15].

	Fed-batch	Continuous perfusion
Viable cell density	17[a)]	60
Total cell density	34	90
Viability	50[b)]	70[b)]
Titer (g l^{-1})	6	1.1
Medium exchange rate (vol day^{-1})	0.05	2
Volumetric productivity (g l^{-1} d^{-1})	430	2200
Number of runs/year/reactor	20	7
Total amount, kg $year^{-1}$ for a single 500 l bioreactor	60	400
Total bioreactor volume to make 1000 kg $year^{-1}$ purified product	12 000 l or (6 × 2000 l)	2000 l or (4 × 500 l)

a) Maximum cell density.
b) Minimum viability.

and at a steady state while a batch process goes through a cycle where only a portion of the run is fully effective.

A comparison of a batch and continuous (perfusion) process is presented in Table 18.2 for monoclonal antibody production [15]. Both cell culture processes are operated under similar conditions, using the same starting medium, and seeded at the same cell density. The batch culture presented in Table 18.2 received feed supplements as part of the fed-batch operation and about 17 million cells ml^{-1} were obtained at the peak of the growth. The viability was high in the beginning but it dropped to 50% at the end of the culture, on Day 14. The product concentration at the end of the batch was about 6 g l^{-1} that translated into a volumetric production rate of 430 g l^{-1} day^{-1}. In the continuous perfusion case, the cell density reached 60 million viable cells ml^{-1} (or 90 million total cells ml^{-1}) using a two-volume/day medium exchange rate. The volumetric production rate for continuous perfusion was 2200 g l^{-1} day^{-1}, about fivefold higher than batch culture. With these enhanced volumetric productivities, a single 2000 l perfusion bioreactor or four 500 l bioreactors will produce the same amount of mAb (1000 kg yr^{-1}) made in a 12 000 l bioreactor or six 2000 l reactors operated in a fed-batch mode.

Continuous processing can also offer similar opportunities for other biomanufacturing steps including downstream operation. Compared to an upstream process step using continuous perfusion, the application of a continuous process to a downstream step is relatively new and is not as straightforward to implement. Downstream processing often utilizes chromatography resins and relies on batch operation for column equilibration, loading, elution, and washing. Although there are ways of operating a column continuously, using radial

Table 18.3 Comparison of a batch and continuous downstream process to purify 30 kg of monoclonal antibody [13].

	Batch	Continuous (SMB)
Resin volume (l)	460	100
Column size	140 × 30 cm	40 × 5 cm
Cycles/column	3 cycles	16 columns
Process time (h)	21	20
Productivity (g l^{-1} h^{-1})	2.9	10.4

flow chromatography, for instance, semicontinuous methods received wider acceptance by the pharmaceutical industry [13,16]. Simulated moving bed (SMB) chromatography provides the benefits of a continuous operation by operating and cycling multiple columns in tandem. The capacity of each column is significantly enhanced by this operation and higher volumetric yields were reported in the literature (see Table 18.3). Continuous processing requires smaller columns and provides faster processing times [13].

18.3.2
Higher Process Efficiencies

A batch process is run for a short time and a lot of time is spent between the batches for termination of the previous batch, cleaning, and reconditioning of the equipment (turnaround), and preparation and build-up of the process intermediates for the next batch. The time period between the batches, referred to as downtime, is not used to manufacture the product and it impacts the cycle time and plant utilization efficiency [15,18]. Continuous processes can be operated for a long time (in some cases, for months) minimizing the impact of downtime on the overall utilization rate [18]. Depending on the lengths of runtime and downtime, plant utilization rate for a batch process can be as low as 60% while a continuous process can achieve >90% plant utilization.

18.3.3
Compact and Flexible Facilities

Because of the high volumetric yields achieved, a continuous process requires smaller equipment for the same production capacity. Coupled with a high plant utilization rate, this advantage translates into building and operating more compact biomanufacturing facilities [15,17]. As a result, facility construction, capital expenses, and operating costs are more favorable for continuous processes. Smaller equipment also allows flexibility to the operation; more units can be easily added if more capacity is required [15].

18.3.4 Stable and Consistent Production

Continuous processes also offer an opportunity for establishing stable and consistent production as it operates at, or near, a steady state. This feature of continuous process is very valuable to maintain a uniform environment, to operate the system at optimal conditions, and to ensure high product quality. By comparison, the environment changes over time in a batch system, and only a portion of the run is fully effective, or optimal, for the production. In a cell culture process, for instance, depletion of nutrients, accumulation of metabolic by-products, growth, and death of cells create a constantly changing environment for the cells [9]. The changes in the environment influence the growth characteristics of the cell, cell physiology, metabolic activity, and production rates. The quality of the product secreted from the cells can also change because of variable intracellular and extracellular events. In addition, change in the growth rate may result in the production of less active product. Finally, product- and process-related impurities increase continually during the culture and the levels of these impurities are typically higher in a batch than a continuous process. A continuous process, on the other hand, results in stable and consistent production while minimizing the transient changes to the system and their impact on cell physiology and cellular productivity [9,10].

18.3.5 Better Product Quality

Finally, continuous processing offers opportunities in biomanufacturing by increasing the speed and reducing/eliminating the hold time, or residence time, during the process. Reducing the residence time during the cell culture process is highly beneficial to minimizing product degradation for labile protein products, such as therapeutic enzymes or blood coagulation factors [9,10,12]. In a batch cell culture process, product-degrading enzymes, such as proteases or sialidases, can act on the product altering, and in many cases, reducing its activity. While degradation can take place in all stages of the manufacturing process, it is most significant in cell culture bioreactors as they operate at 36–37 °C, where enzymes are more active than they are at lower temperatures. Product quality is therefore better for continuous processes for two reasons: (i) the levels of product-degrading enzymes are typically lower in the culture, and (ii) the product is constantly removed from the bioreactor so the residence time is minimal [9,12].

18.4 Challenges for Implementing Continuous Processing in Biomanufacturing

Compared to batch, continuous processes are more complicated and there are several challenges to overcome for their development and implementation [9].

Specialized equipment and control strategies are required to run a continuous process reliably, consistently, and efficiently. The design and operation of the equipment is complicated requiring expertise, skills, and highly qualified personnel to run the process. The continuous processes are highly dynamic and simple process excursions can have a long lasting impact. Scalability, consistency, and validation of the process are also more complicated when compared to batch processes [9,14]. We will focus on a continuous (perfusion) cell culture process and discuss these issues in detail in this section.

18.4.1 Process Complexity

Although batch[1] and continuous cell culture process use the same medium, utilize similar process equipment, and are operated under the same conditions, continuous processes are more complicated to design and operate. These complications are not insurmountable and will be discussed here for continuous perfusion culture by focusing on (a) cell retention, (b) higher cell density, and (c) longer run time.

18.4.1.1 Cell Retention

In a continuous cell culture system nutrients are constantly provided to the cells while the product is constantly removed from a bioreactor. The cells can be retained in the bioreactor (perfusion operation) or be removed constantly as part of the harvest stream (chemostat operation). By separating and maintaining the cells in the bioreactor, a perfusion bioreactor achieves much higher cell densities and higher productivities than a bioreactor in chemostat operation.

There are several methods of retaining the cells in the bioreactor for perfusion operation. Immobilization and/or entrapment of the cells in beads or in fibers are effective methods for retaining the cells in the bioreactor but introduce complexities in operation [9]. These systems are heterogeneous in nature, the delivery of nutrients to the cells and the removal of waste products can be problematic, gas exchange requires special devices, and sampling of cells is not straightforward. Another method for retaining the cells in the bioreactor is the use of cell retention devices [9–12]. These devices utilize several physical methods to separate the cells out from the harvest stream yet allow the bioreactor to operate as a homogeneous cell suspension. Continuous perfusion utilizing a cell retention device is easier to operate, to sample, control, and scale-up compared to cell immobilization and/or entrapment systems.

Many cell retention systems have been developed, scaled-up, and implemented for continuous cell culture processes for commercial production [9]. These systems use filtration, centrifugation, gravitational settling, and sound waves to

1) For the sake of simplicity, we will use the term "batch culture" to refer to both batch and fed-batch operations.

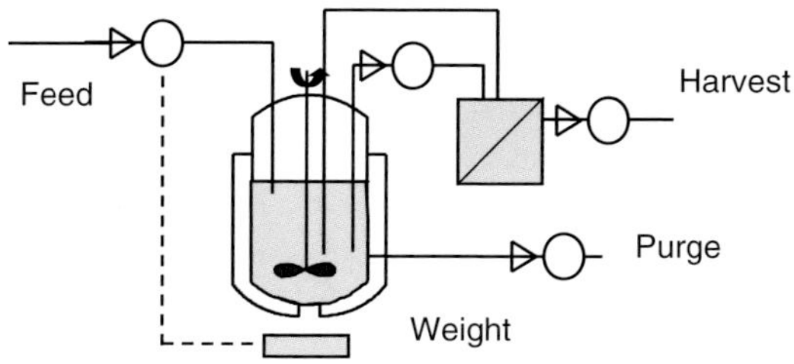

Figure 18.1 A typical configuration for a continuous perfusion bioreactor.

separate the cells from cell culture medium and to retain them in the bioreactor. Spin filters, inclined settlers, continuous centrifuges, hollow-fiber based filtration systems, and acoustic separators are incorporated to a basic bioreactor, either as an internal or an external device, enabling it to run in a continuous mode [9,10]. In addition to a cell retention device, several pumps (harvest, feed, purge) and a level (or weight) controller are required for a continuous perfusion operation to run (Figure 18.1). If the cell retention device is used as an external device, it often necessitates a circulation pump to receive the cells, separate them from the harvest stream, and return them back to the bioreactor.

Table 18.4 presents some of the cell retention devices and their use for the manufacturing of biotherapeutic products. Products like Reopro and Remicade use a spin-filter to retain the cells in the bioreactor. This technology was developed in 1990s and it utilizes a rapidly spinning screen. Even though the pore size is typically larger than the size of the cells, the spinning motion prevents cells from passing through the screen and retains them in the bioreactor. Cell settlers use gravity as separation mechanism and they have been used effectively for microcarrier-based cultures. For suspension cultures the performance of cell settler can be enhanced by cell aggregation and by providing more surface area to settle as in an inclined plate settler [9]. Cell settlers have been used for the production of biotherapeutics such as Cerezyme, Xygris, Kogenate-FS, Fabrazyme, Myozyme.

Table 18.4 Cell retention devices used in large-scale biomanufacturing [4].

Cell retention device	Mechanism for cell separation	Internal or external	Biomanufacturing application
Spin-filter	Filtration	both	Reopro, Remicade
Centrifuge	Centrifugation	external	VPRIV
ATF	Filtration	external	Stelera, Simphoni
Settler	Gravitation	External	Cerezyme, Xygris, Kogenate-FS, Fabrazyme, Myozyme
Acoustic Sep	Sound waves	external	none

Figure 18.2 Continuous centrifugation units used for a perfusion process (from Ref. [18]).

The use of continuous centrifugation and alternative tangential filtration (ATF) devices in a biomanufacturing facility is shown in Figures 18.2 and 18.3. Both systems are used as external devices. ATF is used for the manufacture of two monoclonal antibody products, Stelara and Simponi, while VPRIV, a therapeutic enzyme, uses continuous centrifugation in the manufacturing process. Both systems can be operated with large-scale bioreactors with a continuous operation at 1000–3000 l day^{-1} by the simultaneous use of a pair of either device.

When the cell retention device is used externally, cells are transferred from the bioreactor to the device periodically. During this transfer, cellular environment is

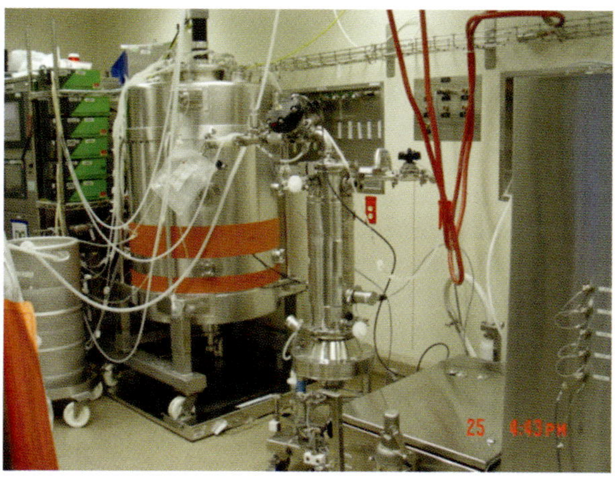

Figure 18.3 Alternating tangential filtration (ATF) unit connected to a 500 l bioreactor used for a perfusion process (from Ref. [15]).

not controlled and circulation through the cell retention device can impact the performance of the cells. A drop in temperature, oxygen limitations, and lower nutrient levels and/or pH can have a prolonged effect on the cells. Most of the external cell retention devices also require a circulation pump creating additional complexity and creating a potential for shear damage to the cells. Understanding the impact of these mechanical and biological issues is critical for the successful design and operation of a cell retention device.

The cell retention device must demonstrate reliability and robustness for a long-term operation. A continuous process has to run for months and the cell retention device should perform at optimal level during this period. Some retention systems, especially the filtration-based designs, require change-out due to decline in performance over time. If the change-over is not possible, or not desired, the run has to be limited to a period where stable operation is possible.

Cell retention devices are complicated units and they require special connection, sterilization, automation, validation (or qualification), and cleaning procedures. Aseptic integration of the cell retention device to the bioreactor requires modifications of the bioreactor. The cell retention devices may require additional utilities and ancillary equipment, such as pumps and pressure sensors, to support their operation. All of these elements should be taken into account in the overall design of the bioreactor and the biomanufacturing facility.

18.4.1.2 **High Cell Density**

Continuous cultures typically reach higher cell densities than a batch system as they provide more nutrients to the cells by medium exchange. The number of cells supported in the bioreactor depends on the composition of the medium, medium exchange rate, aeration capacity of the bioreactor, growth characteristics of the cells, efficiency of cell retention, and process control strategies [9,19]. Cell densities in the order of 30–80 million cells ml^{-1} are typical for a perfusion culture although some groups achieved even higher values [23]. Cells at these densities occupy about 10–30% of the volume in the bioreactor and they require a special bioreactor design and process control strategies to keep them healthy and productive.

High cell density can also impact the operation and performance of cell retention devices. For acoustic cell separation and for inclined settlers, the volume fraction occupied by the cells can impact the retention efficiency negatively [9]. For filtration-based systems, high cell densities can shorten the run time before the filter is clogged making them no longer operational for perfusion [9,16]. The high cell densities attained in continuous cultures means more attention must be paid to culture mixing, aeration, and process control. Each is discussed next.

Mixing

There are several reasons why mixing is more critical for high cell density cultures and why it needs to be optimized for better culture performance [19]. First of all, cells at high densities can impact the hydrodynamics and mixing characteristics in the bioreactor negatively. Second, due to high metabolic demand of the cells, local gradients for nutrient levels, pH, and dissolved oxygen can develop leading to poor mixing conditions. Third, the impact of localized cell death due to additions of base or alkaline/high osmolarity feeds is elevated at high cell concentrations. Mixing has to be optimized for homogenization and impeller design is critical. Axial flow impellers, such as pitched blade impellers, are preferred for high cell density cultures as they provide more homogenization and blending with minimal shear to the cells [19,20].

Aeration

Delivery of oxygen to the cells and the removal of CO_2 from the cultures are more critical for high cell density cultures [19,21]. A cell density of 80 million cells ml^{-1} will require an oxygen mass transfer rate of about 20–40 $mM\,h^{-1}$. This high oxygen transfer demand cannot easily be achieved by traditional macrospargers unless very high gas flow rates are used. The use of a microsparger is preferred for high cell density cultures because of its higher oxygenation capacity. However, CO_2 removal can be a problem when a microsparger system is used. This can result in an accumulation of CO_2 in the culture, which can negatively impact the cells [19]. For optimal performance, bioreactors can be equipped by two spargers; a microsparger for oxygen delivery and a macrosparger for CO_2 removal [22].

Process Control

Due to high cell densities and the associated elevated metabolic activity, continuous cultures are extremely dynamic and they are more difficult to manage. Nutrients and oxygen must be delivered rapidly to the cells to keep up with their high metabolic demands. A brief pump failure for a feed, the interruption of gas flow, pH, and dissolved oxygen (DO) control issues, and a malfunction in cell retention operation can have an irreversible impact on the culture. A high level of automation is required to control not only the culture in the bioreactor but also the cell retention device. The process control system has to be tightly tuned and all systems need to be in perfect working condition for a continuous perfusion operation [9,22].

18.4.1.3 Longer Run Times

Another consideration for the scale-up and technology transfer of continuous perfusion operation is the longer run time. Compared to a fed-batch culture, which runs about 2 weeks, a continuous cell culture is expected to continue for 2–6 months at steady state to fully utilize its benefits. The run time of a continuous operation is determined by consideration of several factors including cell line stability, culture productivity, product quality, process economics, and operational reliability and consistency. During the run both equipment and the process are expected to operate reliably and consistently but operational issues can arise resulting in a decline in performance or even in termination of the run.

Process Reliability and Stability

Although cell retention devices are specially designed for long-term culture and their operation can be perfected to prevent mechanical failures, changes in their performance due to changing culture conditions can happen. Filtration-based devices, for instance, can clog as cellular mass builds up on the filtration surface. If the cell density and the flow rates are not controlled in the bioreactor properly, a buildup or a decline in cell density can take place. If the perfusion rate is not controlled and/or adjusted, the cellular environment can change and the cell performance can be impacted.

Cell Line Stability

Cell line stability needs to be established for biomanufacturing to ensure no genetic or epigenic change in the cell takes place during the manufacturing process [24,25] whether the process is batch or continuous. Typically, the stability studies are incorporated into the clone selection process before a master cell bank (MCB) is manufactured; thus, unstable clone candidates are eliminated from the process in the beginning. However, there is still a risk of instability during the manufacturing process as cells go through multiple generations or doublings during the cell scale-up process. Regulatory agencies require demonstration of genetic stability by analyzing the end of production cells and comparing them to the master cell bank. Continuous processes run for a longer time than batch, and cell line stability may need to be evaluated for a longer period as cells will have more time to generate or double [25].

Both batch and continuous processes rely on stability studies that require passaging cells over a period of time and monitoring cell growth, productivity, gene copy number, and product RNA levels. More involved stability studies would include locating gene integration sites, characterization of the gene of interest, and other genetic markers. Product quality also needs to be evaluated as part of the stability studies. Based on the data, a limit of allowable number of generations (or cell doublings) is established.

Figure 18.4 shows data generated for a cell line producing a monoclonal antibody. Cells during the clone selection were expanded using multiple passages and specific productivity was calculated at each passage. A decline in specific productivity by the number of generations is clearly observed over time. Depending on the product and the manufacturing strategy, a 30% drop in productivity can be acceptable. Thus, for the process studied in Figure 18.4, the cell line is considered stable for 90 generations and it can be used for the generation of master cell bank, and later, in the manufacturing process.

A typical manufacturing process for cell culture requires expansion of cells at different stages before they are seeded to the production bioreactor: (a) expansion of cells to make an MCB, (b) expansion of an MCB vial to make a master working cell bank (WCB), and (c) expansion of a vial of WCB in seed train process so a sufficient number of cells are obtained to seed the production bioreactor. These expansion processes require about 30 cell doublings, or

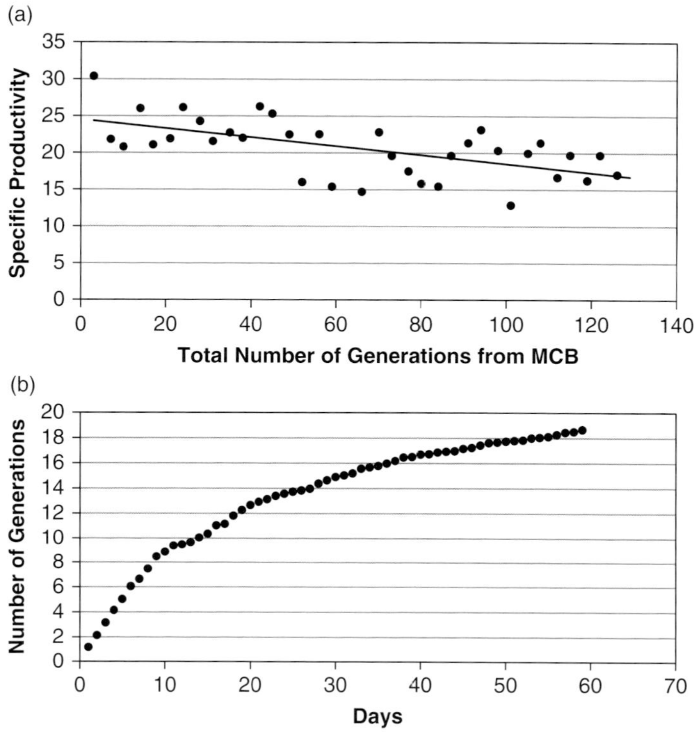

Figure 18.4 Cell line stability for a monoclonal antibody process. (a) Trend in specific productivity over generations and (b) the number of generations achieved in a continuous perfusion bioreactor.

generations. Since the cell line is stable for 90 generations in the example presented in Figure 18.4, a maximum cell generation of 60 is allowed in the bioreactor (90 minus 30).

In a biomanufacturing environment, the number of generations in the bioreactor is routinely monitored and the bioreactor needs to be terminated before the number of generations reaches the limit established from stability studies. While this issue remains important for long-term culture of the cells in a continuous perfusion, factors, such as slowing down the growth and retention of the cells in the bioreactor, need to be considered. The relationship between number of days in the culture and the number of generations is not always linear and the continuous perfusion may not lead to excessive cell doublings. Figure 18.4 presents the data obtained from a filtration-based cell retention system as an example. In the beginning, active growth results in a rapid increase in number of generations. This increase slows down as the culture progresses and over the subsequent 60 days of operation, only 19 generations are obtained. This feature of continuous perfusion, the slowing down of the growth rate, allows for longer run times in the bioreactor without worrying about the stability of the cells. In the example provided here, the bioreactor run can be as long as 60 days or even more.

Maintaining Sterility

The equipment used for continuous processes are more complicated than the ones used for batch. In addition, the number of manipulations, such as sampling, continuous feeding and harvesting, purging the cells, and changing the media and harvest bags is significantly higher. It is clear that maintaining sterility is a major challenge for continuous processes. Aseptic controls, operator training, and the use of sterile connection devices can minimize the chance of contamination. By establishing proper quality systems, several companies had successfully run continuous processes with no contamination.

18.4.2 Process Scalability in a Continuous Perfusion Process

Regarding process scalability, we will discuss two issues: (i) scale and capacity limitations for cell retention device, and (ii) scalability of the continuous process and scale-up strategies.

18.4.2.1 Scale and Capacity Limitations

Because of complexities in their design and operation, cell retention devices have a limited capacity in terms of volumetric output, maximum cell density, and the run length they can support. The performance of the cell retention device is dictated by these factors and how they interact with each other. The maximum volumetric output (or perfusion rate) and run length, for instance, can be impacted by the cell density. On the other hand, the maximum cell density in the bioreactor can be limited by the perfusion rate and the nutrient composition of the medium. Filtration-based cell retention devices eventually clog and the maximum run length becomes dependent on perfusion rate and cell density. The scale of operation can also be limited by the complexity of mechanical design and operation of the cell retention system.

Table 18.5 presents a guideline for some of the cell retention systems based on data presented in the literature [9]. Spin filters have been used in bioreactors up to 1000 l for biomanufacturing and their operation up to 60 days were

Table 18.5 Scale and capacity of cell retention systems [9,15].

Cell retention		MM ml^{-1}	l day^{-1}	Bioreactor size (l)[a]	Days
Spin-filter	ext, int	15	1000	1000	60
Continuous centrifuge	external	20	3000[b]	2000	60
ATF	external	50	1000[b]	1000	60
Settler[c]	external	20	2000	500	200
Acoustic separation	external	20	200	200	60

a) Size used/recommended for manufacturing.
b) With 2 units connected to the bioreactor.
c) Suspension cultures only, excludes the use of microcarrier cultures.

reported [14]. They are limited to maximal densities of 10–15 million cells ml^{-1} because of issues related to clogging of the screen, and continuous loss of cells through the openings on the screen. Continuous centrifugation was used for up to 60 days at 2000 l scale with 20 million cells ml^{-1} [18]. The ATF system, on the other hand, has a maximum capacity of 500 l day^{-1} even with the largest commercially available hollow-fiber cartridge and the diaphragm (ATF-10). Gravitational settlers do not suffer from clogging or fouling issues and they have been demonstrated to run over 6 months (200 days) at perfusion rates of 2000 l day^{-1} [12]. The performance of the settlers depends on the cell aggregation in the culture and they need to be operated at lower perfusion rates for nonaggregating cells. Finally, for an acoustic separator, the mechanical design of the cell retention system limits its scalability. This device relies on sound waves applied to a chamber where cells are concentrated in layers and returned to the bioreactor by gravity [9]. For this type of cell retention to be effective, the penetration distance of the sound needs to be a couple of centimeters. This limits the physical size of the separation chamber and the maximum flow rate that can be achieved. Even though these systems can be scaled up by using multiple units, this strategy becomes impractical as the scale goes up.

18.4.2.2 **Process Scale-up**

A continuous perfusion process typically uses a stirred tank type bioreactor coupled with an internal or external cell separation device. For scaling-up a continuous perfusion, both bioreactor and cell separation device need to considered. Bioreactor scalability in terms of vessel geometry, hydrodynamics, mixing, and aeration can be addressed using conventional scale-up methods. However, cell retention devices are not easily scalable as their mechanical design can be very complex. Furthermore, the interactions between the bioreactor and the cell retention device can complicate these efforts especially for the internal cell retention devices.

Scaling-up of a cell retention device is rather complex as there are multiple factors affecting its performance. Although some guidance is available for their scale-up, the presence of cells, changes in the culture properties due to cell and debris build up, and the changes in the operational effectiveness of the cell retention device add complexities. A successful scale-up effort should ensure the cell physiology is not impacted by the scale and by the operation. This is a challenging but achievable task for a continuous perfusion system as discussed here.

Some cell retention devices are easier than others for scalability and there are general guidelines to aid process scale-up [9]. For gravimetric cell separation devices, for instance, the guidance suggests scaling-up the volumetric throughput (l day^{-1}) based on settling area. Similarly, a filtration-based cell retention system can be scaled-up based on filtration area. Unfortunately though, scaling-up using a single parameter, like settling area or filter surface area, does not secure the success of scale-up. Other factors such as the hold-up volume, circulation rate, cycling frequency, cross-flow, and residence time need to be considered as well.

Table 18.6 Scalability of ATF cell retention devices.

System	Approx. filter surface area (m^2)	Approx. filtration capacity ($l\ day^{-1}$)
ATF 2	0.09	3
ATF 4	0.42	30
ATF 6	2.1	120
ATF 10	9.6	500
2× ATF 10	19.2	1000

The scalability of a cell retention device is discussed below for ATF (alternating tangential filtration) device. This system uses a hollow fiber filtration unit and a diaphragm pump to displace the culture volume in and out of the fibers while a constant flow of permeate is drawn from the shell side of the fibers. The diaphragm pump is actuated by alternating pressure and vacuum cycles and the frequency of cycles can be controlled at user-defined set points.

Several ATF units are available allowing the continuous perfusion operation from $3\ l\ day^{-1}$ (ATF-2) to $500\ l\ day^{-1}$ (ATF-10). The filtration capacity of ATF units is scaled up linearly with the filter surface area (Table 18.6). While this sounds simple and easy to implement using several available hollow fiber options, changing filtration surface area changes other physical variables, such as the hold-up volume, residence time, and the cross-flow rate through the fibers. Even for the same size of ATF, depending on how the unit is connected to the bioreactor and how it is operated, differences in the performance are observed. Table 18.7 shows data from three different sites with different bioreactor/ATF configuration. The difference in cell density (3×) was related to the differences in main residence time that originated from the hold-up volume in these systems.

It should also be pointed out that culture conditions in the bioreactor can also impact the performance of the cell retention device. For establishing scalability, factors, such as cell density and viability, cell size and degree of aggregation, dissolved oxygen, and pH, need to be considered and characterized for a successful scale-up activity.

Table 18.7 Importance of hold-up volume and residence time for ATF operation.

Parameters	Site #1	Site #2	Site #3
ATF pump head volume (l)	6.73	6.73	6.73
Diaphragm pump displacement volume (l)	5.7	5.7	5.7
Hold-up volume above pump head (l)	4.75	5.15	5.42
Pressure/vacuum cycle time (s)	15	15	15
Mean residence time (min)	1.8	3.1	6
Relative maximum sustainable viable cell density	3	2	1

18.4.3
Process Consistency and Control

Although a continuous process can run at a steady state, achieving and maintaining a consistent operation requires sophisticated process monitoring and control strategies. In addition to physical parameters, such as pH, temperature, and dissolved oxygen, the cellular environment in terms of nutrient and metabolic by-products needs to be maintained at optimal levels for process consistency.

There are typically two stages for the continuous perfusion process: (i) an initial cell build-up phase where the cells accumulate in the bioreactor to a level sufficient for production, and (ii) a production phase where the cell density is maintained typically at a constant level and the product is collected. The cell build-up phase can last for about a week and the production phase can extend up to 6 months. Different control strategies are applied for these phases as they serve two different purposes. For the build-up phase the cell concentration increases in the bioreactor and the perfusion rate needs to be adjusted accordingly. In the production phase the perfusion rate is typically fixed and the cell density is controlled by using a purge (or bleed) stream from the bioreactor (or from the retention device). If these controls are not in place, and the cellular environment is not maintained optimally, the performance of continuous perfusion bioreactor can vary from one run to another. Since these systems run continuously, any small differences in operational parameters in the early phase of the run can have a long-term impact. Process inconsistencies and process fluctuations have been observed in the literature for continuous perfusion [26].

Stable and consistent operation of perfusion cultures can be achieved by cell-specific perfusion rate (CSPR) control [19]. This control strategy is originated from mass balances for substrates and products:

$$D \cdot (S_o - S) = q_s \cdot X_v$$

$$D \cdot (P - P_o) = q_p \cdot X_v$$

where S, P, and X_v are the concentrations of substrate, product, and viable cells, D is the dilution rate, q_s, and q_p are the consumption rate of substrates and production rate of products. The symbols S_o and P_o are the concentrations in the feed for the substrate and product, respectively.

Defining CSPR as the combined process parameters

$$\mathrm{CSPR} = D/X_v$$

We obtain

$$S = S_o - q_s/\mathrm{CSPR}$$

$$P = P_o + q_p/\mathrm{CSPR}$$

By maintaining a constant CSPR, metabolite concentrations (substrate and product) should be maintained at constant levels.

Cell-specific perfusion rate control relies on cell density determination and although daily cell counts can provide some guidance, online cell density measurements or cell density estimates are required for continuous and precise control. Cell density probes, online oxygen consumption rate measurements, glucose consumption, and so on can be used for online monitoring and control [19].

For the control of perfusion rate in the build-up phase, the harvest rate is adjusted proportional to cell density. The proportionality constant is the CSPR, which is optimized for a given process and the cell line. A high CSPR allows delivery of more nutrients to the cells, allows cells to grow better, but it results in low product titers. A low CSPR, on the other hand, delivers fewer nutrients to the cells, results in slow cell growth, but allows reaching high titers.

For CSPR control to be successful in the production phase, the cell density needs to be controlled by purging the cells out of the system. The purge pump is started once the target cell density or the target perfusion rate is reached at the end of the cell build-up phase. The CSPR is maintained at the optimal level for production phase. During this period, the perfusion rate is fixed and the cell density is controlled at a level dictated by CSPR. A reliable and robust purge algorithm needs to be developed to control the cell density successfully. Online measurement or estimate of cell density is preferred as they allow a feedback control and result in incremental adjustments for the purge rate.

18.4.4
Process Characterization and Validation

Continuous processes must consider more factors than batch processes during process development, scale-up, process characterization, and product commercialization efforts. Three of these issues will be discussed here: (i) complexity of a scale-down model for a perfusion process, (ii) the complexity of generating data using design of experiments (DOE) and defining a design space, and (iii) issues related to process validation.

18.4.4.1 Complexity of a Scale-down Model for a Perfusion Process

Scale-down models are essential for process development, process characterization, and process characterization studies. When a cell retention device is coupled with the bioreactor, it impacts culture performance; and in a perfusion system, both the bioreactor and the cell retention device need to be scalable. A small-scale bioreactor with 0.5 to 2 l working volume can successfully be qualified as a scale-down model for a commercial-size bioreactor (10 000 l or larger) by utilizing established scale-up strategies. Cell retention devices are more difficult to scale-up and scale-down as multiple factors govern their performance as presented earlier for the ATF system. Some of the cell retention devices cannot be manufactured or operated at small scale. In some devices, the cell retention system occupies a large proportion of the total culture volume and it can no longer represent the large-scale operation.

Based on these limitations, a scale-up model of a perfusion system typically uses a larger-volume bioreactor, a 5–10 l bioreactor, with the appropriately sized cell retention device. This scale is an order of magnitude higher compared to a scale-down model for a batch culture. Running multiple systems together for DOE studies thus requires a lot of space, labor, and raw material cost for the development of a continuous perfusion culture process.

18.4.4.2 Process Optimization and Characterization for a Perfusion Process

Process optimization and characterization studies require a lot of experimentation where several parameters, such as pH, temperature, and dissolved oxygen, are evaluated for their impact on the culture performance [27]. A formal DOE study is often used to define design space as outlined by the quality-by-design (QbD) paradigm. For batch cultures this is an easy task as several systems (typically 16–32) can be run simultaneously and in a short time (typically 14 days). Batch cultures run reliably, consistently, and without complications, most of the time. Continuous cultures, on the other hand require a more complicated setup (with cell retention devices and automation), operate for longer times, and they may not operate reliably [28,29]. In a DOE design, a failed run due to mechanical glitches or contamination will eliminate the usefulness of all the data generated. Another consideration during development of a continuous culture process is that the parameters need to be evaluated for both cell build-up phase and for production phase, effectively doubling the work.

There are ways of dealing with the development of perfusion processes using DOE studies. One approach is to use segmentation by taking advantage of having a steady state for continuous culture. Once a bioreactor reaches a steady state, culture parameters can be altered from one set point to another. The response of the system can be monitored immediately. Under these conditions the impact of several parameters or several set points (3–4 conditions) can be studied in one bioreactor, by applying segments at every 3–4 days. Running simultaneous bioreactors allow screening a large number of conditions in relatively short time, minimizing the number of bioreactors and the total duration of the studies.

18.4.4.3 Process Validation

The last topic we will cover for continuous perfusion is related to process validation and product commercialization. Process consistency needs to be demonstrated by at least three separate runs and since each run can take 2–4 months, for perfusion cultures, the validation efforts are dramatically longer compared to a batch process. In addition, because of product consistency and long-term stability concerns, the product needs to be characterized at early, middle, and late phase of the run. There is no question that the process validation efforts are more complex compared to a batch process and require significant resources. However, the additional work during validation and the related costs can be justified by the long-term savings obtained from the efficiencies during commercial manufacturing.

18.5 Conclusions

Continuous processing for cell culture is a viable alternative to batch culture and it is used already for the production of several biotherapeutic products. There are clearly several advantages of using a continuous process as it provides higher volumetric yields, uniform environment to the cells, and results in consistent product quality. There are, however, complexities and challenges to overcome for the design, scale-up, and technology transfer of continuous processes as illustrated here. These issues can definitely be worked out by process understanding, by designing and implementing required control strategies, and by characterizing the process and the product. Cell retention devices are complicated to design and operate but there are several options to choose from; some of these devices are already used in the manufacture of commercial products. Operating a high cell density culture requires proper mixing, aeration, and control strategies in place. Continuous processes run longer compared to batch and they can have issues related to cell line stability, process validation, and process consistency. However, these issues can be managed by selecting stable cell lines and by demonstrating the product quality during a consistency run.

Acknowledgment

I would like to thank Dr. Roger Anderson for the review of the chapter and for his valuable comments.

Abbreviations

CHO	Chinese hamster ovary
GMP	Good manufacturing practices
ATF	Alternating tangential filtration
SMB	Simulated moving bed
MCB	Master cell bank
WCB	Working cell bank

References

1 Ozturk, S.S. and Hu, W.-S. (eds) (2006) *Cell Culture Technology for Pharmaceutical and Cell-Based Therapies,* CRC Press, Taylor & Francis Group, Boca Raton, FL.

2 Kelley, B. (2009) Industrialization of mAb production technology. The bioprocess industry at a crossroads. *mAbs,* **1**, 443–452.

3 Shukla, A.A. and Thömmes, J. (2012) Recent advances in large-scale production of monoclonal antibodies and related proteins. *Trends Biotechnol.,* **28** (5), 253–261.

4 Pollock, J., Ho, S.V., and Farid, S.S. (2013) Fed-batch and perfusion culture processes: economic, environmental, and operational feasibility under uncertainty. *Biotechnol. Bioeng.*, **110** (1), 206–219.
5 Jayapal, K.P., Wlaschin, K.F., Hu, W.-S., and Yap, M.G.S. (2007) Recombinant protein therapeutics from CHO cells—20 years and counting. *Chem. Eng. Prog.*, **103**, 40–47.
6 Li, F., Vijayasankaran, N., Shen, A., Kiss, R., and Amanullah, A. (2010) Cell culture processes for monoclonal antibody production. *mAbs*, **2** (5), 466–477.
7 Andersen, D.C. and Reilly, D.E. (2004) Production technologies for monoclonal antibodies and their fragments. *Curr. Opin. Biotechnol.*, **15**, 456–462.
8 Fenge, C. and Lüllau, E. (2006) Cell culture bioreactors, in *Cell Culture Technology for Pharmaceutical and Cell-Based Therapies* (eds S.S. Ozturk and W.-S. Hu), CRC Press, Taylor & Francis Group., Boca Raton, FL, pp. 155–224.
9 Ozturk, S.S. and Kompala, D. (2006) Optimization of high cell density perfusion cultures, in *Cell Culture Technology for Pharmaceutical and Cell-Based Therapies* (eds S.S. Ozturk and W.-S. Hu), CRC Press, Taylor & Francis Group, Boca Raton, FL, pp. 387–416.
10 Bonham-Carter, J. and Shevitz, J. (2011) A brief history of perfusion biomanufacturing: how high-concentration cultures will characterize the factory of the future. *BioProcess Int.*, **9** (9), 24–31.
11 Warikoo, V., Godawat, R., Brower, K., Jain, S., Cummings, D., Simons, E., Johnson, T., Walther, J., Yu, M., Wright, B., McLarty, J., Karey, K.P., Hwang, C., Zhou, W., Riske, F., and Konstantinov, K. (2012) Integrated continuous production of recombinant therapeutic proteins. *Biotechnol. Bioeng.*, **109** (12), 3018–3029.
12 Vogel, J.H., Nguyen, H., Giovannini, R., Ignowski, J., Garger, S., Salgotra, A., and Tom, J. (2012) A new large-scale manufacturing platform for complex biopharmaceuticals. *Biotechnol. Bioeng.*, **109** (12), 3049–3058.
13 Pennings, M. *et al.* (2011) A continuous multicolumn chromatography process for polishing of mAbs. Presented at 7th HIC RPC Conference, Estoril, Portugal.
14 Whitaker, S.C., Francis, R., and Siegel, R.C. (1998) Validation of continuously perfused cell culture processes for production of monoclonal antibodies, in *Validation of Biopharmaceutical Manufacturing Processes*, ACS Symposium Series (eds B.D. Kelley and R.A. Ramelmeier), American Chemical Society, Washington, DC, pp. 28–43.
15 Ozturk, S.S. (2013) Cell culture technology: a historical perspective with future directions. Keynote lecture. Annual Biomanufacturing Leaders Summit, Boston, MA, pp. 11–12.
16 Wolfgang, J. and Prior, A. (2002) Continuous annular chromatography. *Adv. Biochem. Eng. Biotechnol.*, **76**, 233–255.
17 Farid, S.S. (2007) Process economics of industrial monoclonal antibody manufacture. *J. Chromatogr. B*, **848** (1), 8–18.
18 Slaman, P. (2012) Single use and simplicity at Shire HGT – three years in. IBC Conference, Boston, MA.
19 Ozturk, S.S. (1996) Engineering challenges in high cell density cultures. *Cytotechnology*, **22** (1–3), 3–16.
20 Nienow, A.W. (2010) Impeller selection for animal cell culture, in *Encyclopedia of Industrial Biotechnology: Bioprocess, Bioseparation, and Cell Technology*, vol. 5 (ed. M.C. Flickinger), John Wiley & Sons, Inc., Hoboken, NJ, pp. 2959–2971.
21 Godoy-Silva, R., Berdugo, C., and Chalmers, J.J. (2010) Aeration, mixing, and hydrodynamics, animal cell bioreactors, in *Encyclopedia of Industrial Biotechnology: Bioprocess, Bioseparation, and Cell Technology* (ed. M.C. Flickinger), John Wiley & Sons, Inc., Hoboken, NJ, pp. 791–820.
22 Ozturk, S.S. (2014) Equipment for large scale mammalian cell culture, in *Advances in Biochemical Engineering/Biotechnology: Mammalian Cell Cultures for Biologics Manufacturing* (eds W. Zhou and A. Kantardjieff), Springer, New York.
23 Clincke, M.F., Mölleryd, C., Zhang, Y., Lindskog, E., Walsh, K., and Chotteau, V. (2013) Very high density of CHO cells in perfusion by ATF or TFF in WAVE

bioreactor™. Part I. Effect of the cell density on the process. *Biotechnol. Prog.*, **29** (3), 754–767.

24 Ozturk, S.S. and Palsson, B.O. (1990) Loss of antibody productivity during long-term cultivation of a hybridoma cell line in low serum and serum-free media. *Hybridoma*, **9** (2), 167–175.

25 Bailey, L.A., Hatton, D., Field, R., and Dickson, A.J. (2012) Determination of Chinese hamster ovary cell line stability and recombinant antibody expression during long-term culture. *Biotechnol. Bioeng.*, **109** (8), 2093–2103.

26 Vits, H. and Hu, W.-S. (1992) Fluctuations in continuous mammalian cell bioreactors with retention. *Biotechnol. Prog.*, **8** (5), 397–403.

27 Bhambure, R., Kumar, K., and Rathore, A.S. (2011) High-throughput process development for biopharmaceutical drug substances. *Trends Biotechnol.*, **29** (3), 127–135.

28 Fernandez, D., Femenia, J., Cheung, D., Nadeau, I., Tescione, L., Monroe, B., Michaels, J., and Gorfien, S. (2009) Scale-down perfusion process for recombinant protein expression, in animal cell technology. *Basic Appl. Aspects*, **15**, 59–65.

29 Rex, M.L., Magill, A., Goldberg, K., and Barnthouse, K. (2013) Development of a bioreactor scale-down model for a monoclonal antibody perfusion process. 245th ACS National Meeting and Exposition, April 7–11, New Orleans, LA.

19
The Potential Impact of Continuous Processing on the Practice and Economics of Biopharmaceutical Manufacturing

L. Richard Stock, Marc Bisschops, and Thomas C. Ransohoff

19.1
Introduction

Successful commercial-scale production of biopharmaceuticals derived from recombinant cell lines to treat a wide variety of diseases has been practiced for over 30 years, beginning with the approval of recombinant human insulin in 1982 [1]. The technologies for producing, characterizing, and testing these products have advanced significantly over the course of the past 30 years to enable evolution from a "process defines product" mentality to today's emerging "quality-by-design" (QbD) framework for process and product development [2].

Our ability to define and analytically characterize protein therapeutics is certainly not yet complete; however, it has advanced to the point where we can begin a discussion around the possibility of substitutable or interchangeable biosimilar products. This is a topic of significant controversy [3], but the recently approved US Biologics Price Competition and Innovation (BPCI) Act provides for this possibility, and the Food and Drug Administration has signaled that it may be possible in its initial draft guidance documents [4]. The concept of biopharmaceutical interchangeability was almost unthinkable 20 years ago. Similarly, while opportunities for improvement clearly remain in the processes we use to produce biopharmaceuticals, the efficiency of our processes has advanced – particularly for monoclonal antibodies (mAbs) – to a level of "industrialization" that is well described by Kelley [5].

Despite these advances, our industry operates manufacturing processes almost exclusively in batch mode, whereas many more mature process industries operate continuous or semicontinuous manufacturing processes to capture the inherent efficiencies embodied in this approach to manufacturing [6]. While there have been some examples of commercial implementation of unit operations operating in a semicontinuous fashion (i.e., perfusion cell culture), these examples have – to date – been the exception rather than the rule for biopharmaceutical manufacturing. And while the ability to effect continuous processing for biopharmaceuticals is now being demonstrated at bench-

Continuous Processing in Pharmaceutical Manufacturing, First Edition. Edited by Ganapathy Subramanian.

scale [7,8], its practical implementation in manufacturing has yet to be realized.

The current status quo is not a mistake – there are legitimate and compelling reasons for operating batch processes to manufacture biopharmaceuticals. First, the cost of manufacture for biopharmaceuticals is currently far less than the selling price, so the immediate pressure to drive costs down is limited. Additionally, although capacity is now tightening, the industry has had more than adequate capacity to produce its products over the past decade. Finally, continuous processing is more challenging to implement – particularly for complex, poorly understood processes.

However, there are equally compelling reasons to consider moving from batch to continuous/semicontinuous operation of biopharmaceutical and pharmaceutical manufacturing processes, and this transition is increasingly contemplated by industry [7,9], academics [10], and regulators [11]. As competitive forces and increasing product demand drive the need for improved development and manufacturing efficiencies, the driving forces for continuous manufacturing will be amplified in importance. Additional driving forces include products with the potential to require very large scale manufacturing (e.g., anti-PCSK9 MAbs [12]) and labile products requiring rapid processing. Furthermore, as our process understanding and analytical methods improve, the barriers to implementing continuous processes will be reduced, removing the risk associated with this transition. Nonetheless, the transition for the initial practitioners will almost certainly be challenging, risky, and time-consuming. As always, those who "go first" will pave the way to an eventual landscape where continuous processing is an accepted approach to biopharmaceutical manufacturing.

This chapter describes the major economic benefits that are anticipated from a transition to continuous manufacturing and speculates on the ways that this transition may eventually impact the practice of biopharmaceutical manufacturing. The latter objective is admittedly a "crystal ball" exercise; however, it is presented in the spirit of advancing concepts that may be helpful to consider in the course of implementing continuous or semicontinuous biopharmaceutical manufacturing.

19.2
Background (Review of Status Quo – How We Make Biopharmaceutical Products Today)

The current batch processes for production of biopharmaceutical products include an "upstream" section, comprising growth of the production organism, which produces the product of interest, in a cell culture bioreactor or fermenter; and a "downstream" section, comprising a series of unit operations to recover and purify the product of interest to a purity level that is suitable for its intended use. While each biopharmaceutical process is different, there are many similarities among unit operations used to manufacture monoclonal antibodies. For

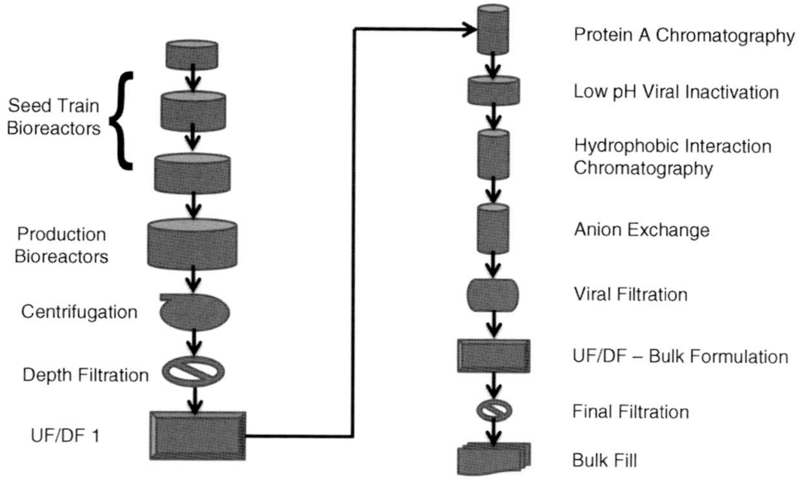

Figure 19.1 Typical monoclonal antibody batch production process (adapted from Ref. [13]).

purposes of illustration, a typical process for production of a monoclonal antibody product is shown in Figure 19.1.

Current monoclonal antibody processes typically use Chinese hamster ovary cell lines that have been engineered and selected to provide a product with the desired quality attributes at a high specific productivity. The "upstream" process, during which cells are expanded and the product is produced, involves a seed train and production bioreactor, which is typically used to operate a fed-batch process to produce the product of interest. With process and media optimization, cell culture titers in a well-developed fed-batch process range from 1 to $5\,g\,l^{-1}$ or even higher.

After the completion of the bioreactor run, the "downstream" process is initiated. This section of the process involves a series of unit operations to remove the cells and cell debris and then purify the product of interest from a wide range of impurities to arrive at a bulk drug substance meeting specifications required for the antibody's intended use. With process optimization, a well-behaved antibody downstream process can have an overall yield of 65–70% or even higher. Downstream process development groups typically use a platform approach for monoclonal antibodies [14,15] to enable rapid development of clinical-enabling and commercial processes based on information and data from other antibody products. The downstream process generally contains the following unit operations:

- Centrifugation and depth filtration for harvest and recovery of the product-containing clarified cell culture supernatant.
- Protein A affinity capture purification, coupled with a low pH hold after product elution for viral inactivation.

- Anion-exchange chromatography or membrane adsorber step, operated either in flow-through or "weak partitioning" [16] mode for removal of host cell proteins, DNA, endotoxin, and viruses.
- A third polishing chromatography step is generally required to remove specific product-related impurities, such as aggregates or charge variants. A cation exchange, hydrophobic interaction, or mixed mode chromatography step is often developed for this polishing step.
- Nanofiltration for viral clearance.
- Ultrafiltration and diafiltration of intermediates (where necessary) and of purified bulk for concentration, buffer exchange, and formulation.
- Bioburden reduction filtration using 0.2 μm filters for process intermediates and final purified bulk drug substance.

In a typical batch process, each process step proceeds only after completion of the previous step. So, for example, in the process shown in Figure 19.1, the viral filtration step would be initiated once the anion-exchange step has been completed and the product has been recovered and pooled from this process step. In some cases, cycling is used on chromatography columns (i.e., multiple cycles on a chromatography column are run and the eluates from each cycle are pooled before proceeding to the next step). This is often used to reduce resin requirements when the cost of the resin is high, such as with the Protein A capture step [17]. A representative process timeline is shown in Figure 19.2 for the downstream section of our typical mAb process (Figure 19.1).

The typical duration of the entire manufacturing process for a batch of monoclonal antibody product, from cell bank vial to bulk drug substance (BDS), is approximately 5–6 weeks. Depending on the scale of the production bioreactor, several weeks are required in the inoculum and seed train stage, to expand the cells up to the quantity required for inoculation of the production bioreactor. A fed-batch cell culture process, lasting approximately 2 weeks, is then conducted in the production bioreactor to grow the cells to a relatively high cell density and allow the expressed product to accumulate in the bioreactor. Finally, depending on the complexity of the downstream process and the operation staffing level and shift schedule, approximately

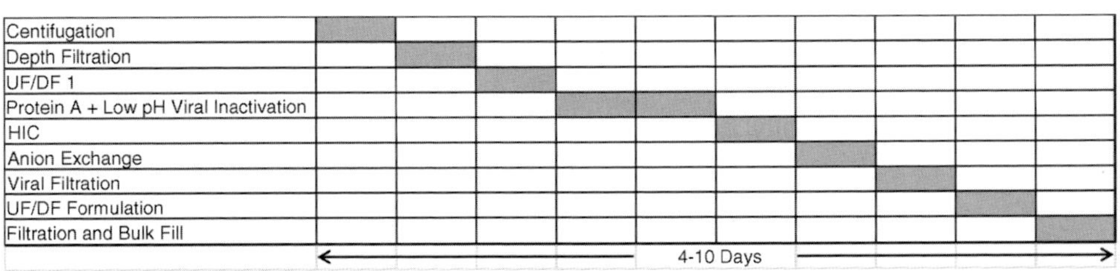

Figure 19.2 Representative DSP timeline for batch production process.

1–2 weeks are required to complete the downstream processing section and produce purified bulk drug substance. Prior to fill-finish manufacturing to make a drug product, the bulk drug substance is typically stored during QC testing and QA release, which can take an additional 4–6 weeks. One of the greatest potential benefits of continuous processing is the ability to significantly shorten the time from batch initiation to availability of purified bulk drug substance.

19.3
The Rationale for Continuous Processing

As described by Kelley [5], a modern monoclonal antibody batch process is a mature, efficient, well-engineered process that can be considered "industrialized." This type of industrialization, coupled with a high level of process understanding, should reduce the obstacles for those wishing to make the transition from batch to continuous processing. Research and development efforts to combine certain steps and run them in tandem [18] is further evidence of our ability to successfully implement more sophisticated manufacturing strategies based on ever-increasing process knowledge. Although different process decisions may be made for optimizing operation of a process in batch or continuous mode, the successful implementation of continuous processing relies on a strong understanding of the production process. As process understanding continues to improve and as process efficiency gains through improved productivities and yields begin to slow due to technological maturity, the ability to further improve manufacturing efficiency will be focused increasingly on process intensification approaches, such as continuous processing.

The rationale for considering continuous processing for the manufacture of a wide range of products is well described in other chapters in this book and in many other sources (cf. [7,10,19,20]), so our focus in this chapter will be on key benefits that will impact manufacturing practice and drive improved process economics for biopharmaceuticals. These benefits include

- *Process intensification/Improved facility utilization.* This is perhaps one of the most important benefits to continuous processing in biopharmaceutical manufacturing. The improved utilization of equipment – by minimizing nonproductive time – enables the use of significantly smaller equipment at all stages of the process. This reduction in equipment scale will lead to reduced manufacturing facility size, lowering capital costs and time of construction for new capacity.
- *Enables single-use equipment for larger processes/Improved manufacturing flexibility.* A highly related benefit to the process intensification just described is that facilities using single-use equipment at the maximum currently practicable scale (e.g., 2000 l bioreactors, ~45 cm single-use

chromatography columns) will be able to produce far more material if operating continuous or semicontinuous processes instead of batch processes. As a result, manufacturing flexibility (i.e., the ability to move processes between facilities, to "change over" quickly between production campaigns of different products) will be enhanced as well.

- *Reduced water and consumables usage.* For certain unit operations, such as chromatography, operation in continuous mode will reduce water and resin usage. This is due to the ability to run chromatography operations at higher loading capacities at equivalent yields when operating a continuous, countercurrent, multicolumn process as compared to a batch process [9]. In addition to economic benefits, this benefit may have added importance in applications where capacity is limited by buffer or product tank volume.
- *Improved process control and understanding.* For those of us who have spent our careers operating batch processes, it is somehow counterintuitive that continuous or semicontinuous operation of these unit operations would improve process control. In fact, continuous processes – by nature – are fully controlled. This should not only result in a reduction in labor demand, but should also enhance product quality control. In addition to this, one should expect that enhanced process control will result in fewer deviations. This is also reflected in the occurrence of incidents and accidents in continuous processes of more matured process industries. The vast majority of incidents and accidents happen during transient operations, such as startup and shut-down. During normal steady-state operation, incidents and accidents are far less common. Furthermore, we anticipate the ability to more rapidly extend process understanding through the increased ability to obtain data from continuously running unit operations.
- *More rapid availability of product.* As we improve our ability to operate processes continuously, the ability to rapidly startup a continuous processing line for a new product (or production campaign) will allow us to deliver product more quickly than is possible with batch processes. As described earlier (see Figure 19.2), the sequential nature of unit operations in batch processes leads to a 5–6 week lead time from vial thaw to purified product availability. The operation of a fully continuous processing line where unit operations are operated in parallel, with only brief lags between startup of sequential operations, should dramatically compress the time to the first availability of purified drug substance.
- *More efficient utilization of labor.* Particularly in conjunction with emerging facility concepts, such as flexible, modular facilities (e.g., GEs Flex Factory line) along with improvements in isolator technologies, it is possible to envision operation of multiple processes in the same hall being operated by the same labor team. While there are many obstacles (i.e., regulatory acceptability and ensuring adequate segregation) to implementing this mode of operation, it is reasonable to expect that this will be possible in the future. Of course, this is possible with both batch and continuous operations; however,

there are several reasons that continuous processes are better aligned to this operating mode:

- Smaller processes enable operation of multiple processing lines in a smaller footprint.
- While batch processes are characterized by periods of heavy intensity and long periods of downtime/low activity, continuous processing operations are active at a more consistent, predictable level.

With all of these potential benefits, a legitimate question for proponents of continuous manufacturing is: why aren't continuous processes already routinely used in biopharmaceutical manufacturing? As described in Section 19.4, there are some very good reasons for the industry's caution in adopting continuous processing of biopharmaceuticals.

19.4 The Obstacles for Implementation of Continuous Processing for Biopharmaceuticals

The biopharmaceutical industry has grown over the past decade into a major segment of the pharmaceutical industry, with sales of biopharmaceuticals topping \$100 bn in 2010, or approximately 12% of estimated total pharmaceutical revenues [21]. Importantly, this industry segment has continued to grow strongly with double-digit revenue growth forecast for the next few years at least, driven largely by the phenomenal growth of monoclonal antibodies and antibody-related products. As in any significant industry, most major biopharmaceutical manufacturing organizations are highly rational organizations, which are run by experienced, intelligent executives. These organizations are focused on meeting corporate objectives in a range of areas, including productivity, product quality, efficiency, speed of new product development, and profitability.

The industry's collective decision to manufacture products using batch processes and to cautiously evaluate alternative manufacturing technologies, such as continuous processing, is entirely rational. The gross margins for biopharmaceutical products are quite high (generally estimated in the >90% range). As a result, in comparison to most other industries, the benefit of increased profits gained by reducing cost of goods (COGS) for biopharmaceuticals is disproportionately small relative to the risk of decreased profits through lost sales due to technological or regulatory failures. As long as high profit-margins for biopharmaceuticals exist, implementation of new technologies *solely on the basis of COGS reduction*, will be a "tough sell." This is potentially less true for CMOs whose profit margins are lower. Nevertheless, there are many other potential benefits to implementing continuous processing technologies, and these are likely to be more important than the COGS advantage in the near-term.

In this environment, the obstacles and risks involved with implementing changes in manufacturing tend to get magnified. The perceived risks of implementation of continuous processing include

- *Regulatory uncertainty.* Most of the remaining concerns or potential objections are covered under the larger umbrella of regulatory uncertainty: "Will this delay approval of my product (or ability to start clinical trials)?" "Will there be some unknown regulatory requirement that will delay my program because I am using a new technology?" Even though regulators have publicly stated that they expect to see more continuous processing as the industry matures, the uncertainty that ensues from a lack of industry experience in getting approval for regulatory filings based on continuous biopharmaceutical processes creates a significant perceived risk.
- *Uncertainty with the definition of a batch.* Although regularly mentioned in discussions around continuous processing, this seems to be one of the easiest to address and has even been specifically called out by regulators as addressable [11].
- *Complexity of the equipment and process.* In many unit operations, the requirements of a continuously operating process require more complex equipment or processes than batch processes. For example, valving and pumping systems to simultaneously deliver multiple solutions (e.g., feed, equilibration buffer, wash buffer, etc.) to multiple columns requires more complex equipment for continuous chromatography systems than for conventional batch systems.
- *Process validation.* Specific concerns related to validation of continuously operated processes have been raised as a concern. In particular, for mammalian cell culture-derived processes, the ability to perform viral clearance and inactivation validation on steps that will be operated in a continuous rather than batch manner has been raised.
- *Equipment failure and management of process upsets.* The potential for process upsets and equipment malfunctions need to be taken into account for any practical solution to continuous processing. Surge capacity for storing solutions during down-time of a process section and strategies for orderly process line startup and shut-down need to be developed by groups who implement continuous processing for biopharmaceuticals.
- *Pooling of material from semicontinuous processes.* Pooling of harvests from perfusion cultures or of eluates from semicontinuous (i.e., simulated moving bed) chromatography operations carries risk that "good" material will be contaminated by "bad" fractions.
- *Uncertainty of cost benefits.* Despite many studies demonstrating the cost benefits of continuous manufacturing at bench scale or in other industries, there is little to no practical experience with continuous production of biopharmaceuticals at a production scale. Therefore, the anticipated cost benefits associated with adopting the technology have not yet been proven at scale.

Risk reduction will come from demonstrated successful operation of continuous processing for biopharmaceutical manufacturing by those who "go first," particularly as successful regulatory hurdles (i.e., first clinical material supply; first product approval) are overcome by early adopters. Initial applications are likely to focus on converting a single unit operation or process section to continuous processing as opposed to the entire process. These initial successful case studies will also undoubtedly provide some "lessons learned" that will – to the extent that these lessons are publicized – help subsequent adopters of the technology avoid costly or time-consuming aspects of implementing the technology and optimize the benefits from using continuous processing.

19.5 The Potential Impact of Continuous Manufacturing on Process Economics

The most significant process economic impacts anticipated for those who adopt continuous processing for biopharmaceuticals are based on process intensification, that is, the ability to produce more product with less capital and in a smaller footprint. This ability will result in lower capital costs for construction of the facility and purchase of equipment, lower energy and water usage, and less overhead related to facility footprint.

There are additional related benefits, including the ability to use single-use equipment to produce significantly larger quantities of material than could be achieved in single-use batch mode. Since others have already demonstrated the economic benefits of adopting single-use technology [13,22], this will provide a further economic benefit.

Finally, for virtually every unit operation, there will be operating cost savings due to the reduction in the percentage of processing time that is occupied by the "startup" and "shut-down" transitions. During these transitions, labor and materials (in addition to capital) are less efficiently utilized to manufacture product. By reducing the percentage of operating time in these transitions, the cost of manufacturing per unit should be reduced.

In addition to these generalized benefits for reducing operating costs, certain unit operations have specific economic benefits that will be derived from continuous operation. For example, operating chromatography in a multicolumn semicontinuous mode, using simulated moving bed technology (e.g., Tarpon's BioSMB® technology) or periodic countercurrent chromatography (e.g., GE Healthcare's 3C-PCC) will result in lower media and buffer requirements due to the higher column loadings that can be achieved with equivalent yields using these modes of operation [9,23].

To illustrate the potential economic benefits of converting a single unit operation to continuous processing, we conducted a study to evaluate the process economics for operation of a Protein A chromatography step in batch and in continuous mode. The continuous mode chosen for modeling was Tarpon's BioSMB system. This model was an integrated process design and process economic model, utilizing Tarpon's proprietary process design model [9] to generate batch and continuous operating parameters coupled with a proprietary process economic model developed by BPTC. The model is capable of evaluating a wide range of operating scenarios and parameters, including the ability to vary assumptions for resin, buffer, and other material costs, scale and type (e.g., clinical vs. commercial) of operation, labor rates, capital cost assumptions, and process parameters (e.g., binding capacity and wash column volumes).

For purposes of the comparison presented herein, a commercial operation case for purification of a monoclonal antibody using Protein A resin was modeled. In this particular case, resin lifetimes are assumed to be equal (200 cycles) between the batch process and continuous process operations model. Published studies [7,8] have indicated that large cycle numbers are feasible in continuous process operations. For the batch operation, it was assumed that the larger columns would be purchased and packed by the manufacturer. For continuous operation, it was assumed that the smaller columns would be purchased as prepacked columns. The major assumptions for the comparison evaluated are summarized in Figure 19.3.

Process Specifications		
Bioreactor volume:	2,000	l
IgG concentration:	3.00	g/l
Density	1050	kg/m^3
Viscosity	1.00E-03	Pa.s
Molecular weight IgG	150	kD

Process Cycle Analysis		
Step	**Volumes (Batch)**	
Equilibration	5.00	BV
Wash 1	3.00	BV
Wash 2	5.00	BV
Wash 3	3.00	BV
Elution	5.00	BV
Post-elution wash column	3.00	BV
Post-run column cleaning	5.00	BV

Resin Specifications		
Equilibrium capacity	65.00	g/l
Dynamic binding capacity	35.00	g/l
Particle diameter	85	μm
Void fraction (packed bed)	40%	
Moisture content (intraparticle)	90%	
Diffusion coefficient liquid:	4.0E-12	m^2/s
Matrix	Agarose	
Maximum linear velocity	800	cm/h
Calculated koL a	256	1/h
Media costs	$15,400	USD/l

Batch Process Design		
Cycles	4	
Batch linear velocity:	300	cm/h
Column Type	Stainless Steel	
Bed height:	24	cm
Bed diameter:	50	cm
Actual bed volume:	47.1	l
Total processing time:	13:00	h
Capture efficiency at 11.67 BV	99.73%	
Specific Productivity	234	g/l/day

BioSMB Process Design		
Separation factor	1.25	
Processing time equal to Batch	NO	
Specify processing time	13:00	h
PrA Processing time:	13:00	h
Loading zone:		
Columns in series	2.00	
Columns in parallel	2.00	
Safety factor:	0%	
Column diameter	14.00	cm
Bed height	15.15	cm
Bed volume/column	2.33	l
Numberof columns	8.00	
Total resin volume	18.66	l
Specific Productivity	591	g/l/day
Cycle time	02:06	
Number of cycles/batch	6.18	

Figure 19.3 Key assumptions for Protein A batch vs. continuous (BioSMB) process model.

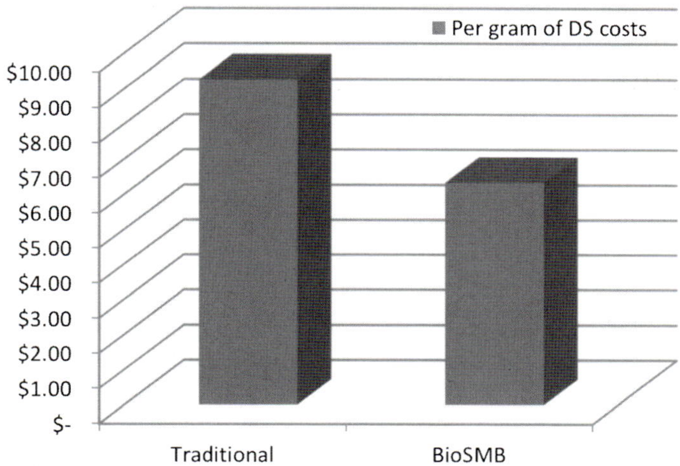

Figure 19.4 Process economic modeling results comparing traditional batch and BioSMB operation of a Protein A chromatography step.

The process economic model was constructed to account for differences in material, labor (direct and indirect), critical utilities, and allocated capital costs directly associated with the operation. We assumed that the facility was purpose-built for the operation (i.e., that the potentially smaller footprint associated with continuous processing could be realized). The cost savings for implementing the continuous process step within an existing batch-based facility would, therefore, be reduced. The results of the process economic analysis for this particular case are shown in Figure 19.4. As shown in the figure, the estimate for savings achieved by operating a single Protein A step using continuous (BioSMB) processing technology as compared to conventional batch operation in a commercial operation case is 32% ($6.33 per gram [BioSMB] vs. $9.25 per gram [Batch]).

As described earlier, these estimated savings result from savings in materials (both resin and buffer), labor, and capital. A breakdown of these costs for both operations is presented in Figure 19.5. The modeling results project some savings in every category in this case through the use of continuous processing, due

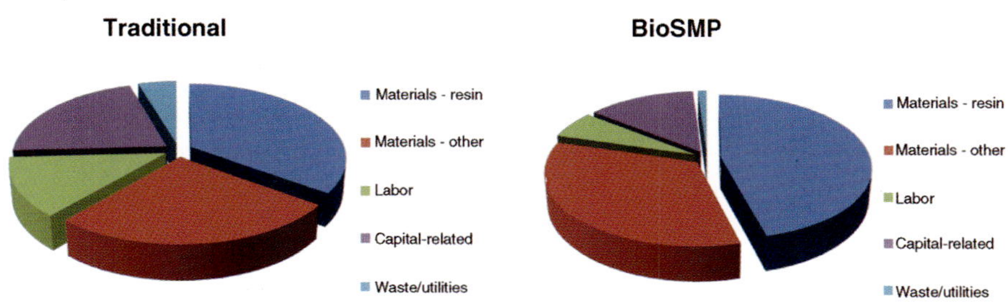

Figure 19.5 Distribution of costs by category for traditional and BioSMB cases.

both to more efficient utilization of the resin, and better overall utilization of capital and labor.

While the results shown in Figure 19.4 demonstrate significant savings for continuous operation in commercial manufacturing, the savings from continuous operation are dramatically greater for the case of clinical production, particularly for expensive chromatography resins such as Protein A. The reason for this is that the resin is often discarded after completion of a clinical campaign since long-term storage of chromatography resins is costly and raises complex questions. As a result, a common (and understandable) practice among many manufacturers is to utilize chromatography resins to a lifetime equal to the manufacturing campaign for clinical manufacturing operations.

For conventional batch manufacturing operations, Protein A chromatography columns are typically operated "cycled" to reduce the required column volume; 3–5 cycles per batch is common. For a continuous operation, columns can be cycled much more frequently. Depending on the selected operating conditions and processing constraints, it is reasonable to anticipate 12–20 cycles per batch. As a result, chromatography resin costs for a clinical campaign are estimated as being threefold to sixfold lower for continuous processing as compared to batch processing. This will result in significant savings for expensive chromatography resins, with projections of savings of $200,000–400,000 k per campaign estimated for the Protein A step alone [24].

19.6
The Potential Impact of Continuous Processing on Biopharmaceutical Manufacturing Practices

As significant as the impact of continuous processing on the process economics of biopharmaceuticals may be, the impact on other aspects of the practice of process development and manufacturing for biopharmaceutical products could be even greater. Some of the concepts presented in this section are not yet proven for biopharmaceutical manufacturing; however, in the authors' opinion, their implementation requires creative engineering and continued technical progress as opposed to major scientific breakthroughs.

For example, as we improve our ability to practice continuous processing, pilot-scale continuously operating production lines should be able to be started up in several days. Once a line is running, purified bulk drug substance will be collected at the outlet of the processing line. The impact of this on the speed of supply of materials for early nonclinical and clinical evaluation could be significant. Meaningful quantities of purified drug substance could be available for testing in days instead of weeks. And once a line is up and running, the ongoing production rate of drug substance should be far more predictable than in current operations, allowing for smoother planning of nonclinical and early clinical studies.

To operate a biopharmaceutical manufacturing process continuously will require a strong understanding of the impact of process parameters on product quality attributes and on process performance, rewarding firms with strong process and analytical development capabilities. Furthermore, translation of batch data from process development experiments to a robust continuous process design will be required for successful implementation. The industry's strong "pull" for powerful analytical methods that can be implemented online, at-line, or with rapid response will only be strengthened by adoption of continuous processing. This will also be critical in developing strategies to ensure that out-of-specification material resulting from process upsets is diverted from the product stream before it is able to impact product quality. These attributes will become core competencies of biopharmaceutical manufacturing firms who are successful in implementing continuous processing.

Relatedly, continuous processing lines will be a fertile source of data to allow for more rapid expansion of process understanding than is currently possible with today's batch approach to manufacturing. Today, many products reach Phase 3 clinical trials with only a few pilot-scale production batches. While significant bench-scale data exist, manufacturing experience with biopharmaceutical molecules is often limited until late in development. The adoption of continuous processing essentially provides the ability to obtain greater "n"s earlier in development. For groups that take advantage of this ability, there should be an opportunity for process development scientists, engineers, and manufacturing personnel to gain more experience with process operations early in development. By more rapidly advancing understanding of the impact of process control strategies and critical process parameters, these groups should be better prepared for process qualification at commercial production scale with little if any impact on development timelines. Looking way into the future, the ideal outcome of this approach to biopharmaceutical manufacturing would be processes that are so well understood and controlled that product quality attributes can be "dialed in" by adjusting process parameters.

Finally, a transition from batch to continuous operations for biopharmaceutical production will have a significant impact on the design and operation of our manufacturing facilities. There could be great synergies between some of the emerging facility and manufacturing technologies and continuous processing operations. In particular, modular construction, isolators and barrier systems, and single-use manufacturing equipment could enable the establishment of low capital, highly flexible production "halls" with continuous processing lines operating in parallel. If equipment is closed and segregated so that the product stream is sufficiently isolated from the surrounding environment and the operators, it is not inconceivable that multiple continuous processing lines could be operated and monitored by a single team of manufacturing and quality personnel. Significant advances in equipment and in quality assurance systems are needed before such an operation is practical; however, it is a state of operation worth pursuing – the opportunities for improving capital and labor utilization in our industry are significant.

Additionally, with this type of operation, strategies for rapid changeover of production lines between products could be developed to allow new processes to be implemented quickly and down-time to be minimized. This would further improve operational efficiencies and also increase the speed of material supply, which is often rate-limiting, particularly in early clinical development.

19.7 Summary

Continuous processing for biopharmaceuticals is not yet a commercial reality. There are many good reasons for this, including the risks associated with process changes and the relative complexity of continuous processing operations. However, the increased technological sophistication and improved process understanding of a maturing biopharmaceutical industry create an environment and set of capabilities that reduce the barriers to successfully implementing continuous manufacturing on a commercial scale. Given the inherent and well-known benefits of continuous manufacturing over batch processing, it is likely that continuous manufacturing operations will be implemented in biologics manufacturing within the coming decade. Once it has been successfully implemented by early adopters, the capital, material, and labor efficiencies and process economic improvements forecast here and elsewhere should be more widely recognized, as well as other potential benefits in the practice of biopharmaceutical development and manufacturing, such as improved process robustness and speed of material availability. The realization of these benefits coupled with the perceived and actual reduction of the risk of implementing continuous manufacturing should lead to more widespread adoption across the industry over time.

References

1 Genentech (1982) First recombinant DNA product approved by the Food and Drug Administration. Genentech Press Release.

2 Martin-Moe, S. *et al.* (2011) A new roadmap for biopharmaceutical drug product development: integrating development, validation, and quality by design. *J. Pharm. Sci.*, **100** (8), 3031–3043.

3 Berkowitz, S.A. *et al.* (2012) Analytical tools for characterizing biopharmaceuticals and the implications for biosimilars. *Nat. Rev. Drug Discov.*, **11** (7), 527–540.

4 FDA (2012) Biosimilars: questions and answers regarding implementation of the Biologics Price Competition and Innovation Act of 2009. US FDA Draft Guidance for Industry.

5 Kelley, B. (2009) Industrialization of mAb production technology – the bioprocessing industry at a crossroads. *mAbs*, **1** (5), 1–10.

6 King, C.J. (1980) *Separation Processes*, 2nd edn, McGraw-Hill, New York.

7 Warikoo, V. *et al.* (2012) Integrated continuous production of recombinant

therapeutic proteins. *Biotechnol. Bioeng.*, **109** (12), 3018–3029.
8 Brower, M. *et al.* (2013) What can continuous processing do for you? Presented at IBC Life Science's Biopharmaceutical Development & Production Conference, Huntington Beach, CA.
9 Bisschops, M. and Brower, M. (2013) The impact of continuous multicolumn chromatography on biomanufacturing efficiency. *Pharm. Bioprocess.*, **1** (4), 1–12.
10 Trout, B. and Bisson, W. (2009) Continuous manufacturing of small molecule pharmaceuticals: the ultra lean way of manufacturing. Presented at MIT Leaders for Global Operations Conference, Cambridge, MA.
11 Chatterjee, S. (2012) FDA perspective on continuous manufacturing. Presented at IFPAC Annual Meeting, Baltimore, MD.
12 Sullivan, D. *et al.* (2012) Effect of a monoclonal antibody to PCSK9 on low-density lipoprotein cholesterol levels in statin-intolerant patients. *JAMA*, **308** (23), 2497–2506.
13 Stock, R. (2012) Economic impact of single-use bioreactors. Presented at BIO International Convention, Boston MA.
14 Shukla, A.A. *et al.* (2007) Downstream processing of monoclonal antibodies – application of platform approaches. *J. Chromatogr. B*, **848** (1), 28–39.
15 Levine, H.L. and Jagschies, G. (eds) (2010) *The Development of Therapeutic Monoclonal Antibody Products*, BioProcess Technology Consultants and GE Healthcare, Woburn, MA.
16 Kelley, B.D. *et al.* (2008) Weak partitioning chromatography for anion exchange purification of monoclonal antibodies. *Biotechnol. Bioeng.*, **101** (3), 553–566.
17 Fahrner, R.L. *et al.* (1999) The optimal flow rate and column length for maximum production rate of protein A affinity chromatography. *Bioprocess Eng.*, **21**, 287–292.
18 Shamashkin, M. *et al.* (2013) A tandem laboratory scale protein purification process using Protein A affinity and anion exchange chromatography operated in a weak partitioning mode. *Biotechnol. Bioeng.*, **110** (10), 2655–2663.
19 Van Walsem, H.J. and Thompson, M.C. (1997) Simulated moving bed in the production of lysine. *J. Biotechnol.*, **59**, 127–132.
20 Miller, L. *et al.* (1999) Chromatographic resolution of the enantiomers of a pharmaceutical intermediate from the milligram to the kilogram scale. *J. Chromatogr. A*, **849**, 309–317.
21 Ecker, D.M. *et al.* (2011) The State of Mammalian Cell Culture Biomanufacturing, BioProcess Technology Consultants, Woburn, MA.
22 Novais, J.L. *et al.* (2001) Economic comparison between conventional and disposable-based technology for the production of biopharmaceuticals. *Biotechnol. Bioeng.*, **75** (2), 143–153.
23 Bisschops, M. *et al.* (2009) Single-use, continuous-countercurrent, multicolumn chromatography. *BioProcess Int.*, **7** (Suppl. 5), 18–23.
24 Noyes, A. *et al.* (2010) Development of a protein A SMB step for a mAb with up to 10 g/L titers. Presented at IBC Life Science's Biomanufacturing and Development Summit, Boston, MA.

Index

Continuous Processing in Pharmaceutical Manufacturing, First Edition. Edited by Ganapathy Subramanian.

c

l

m